# SCOTLAND
## The Making of the Kingdom

## THE EDINBURGH HISTORY OF SCOTLAND

### General Editor
#### GORDON DONALDSON, D.Litt.
*Fraser Professor of Scottish History and Palaeography
in the University of Edinburgh*

---

# SCOTLAND

## The Making of the Kingdom

### A. A. M. Duncan

**The Edinburgh History of Scotland**

**Volume 1**

**MERCAT PRESS**

**1989**

MERCAT PRESS
James Thin Ltd.
53–59 South Bridge
Edinburgh EH1 1YS

Hardback edition first published, 1975
First published in paperback edition, 1978
Reprinted in paperback, 1989

ISBN 0 901824 83 6 *paperback*

Printed and bound in Great Britain
by Billing & Sons Limited, Worcester

# PREFACE

The early history of Scotland attracted little study or writing between the Edwardian era and 1945; in the past thirty years, however, a great deal has been done and a new account is overdue. For the earliest periods, prehistoric and early historic, archaeology remains the most important single source, a discipline which increasingly turns away from a historical purpose to a scientific one. My limited understanding of archaeological techniques, and of the fluidity with which they are interpreted means that the first five chapters of this book can be only a sketch, and that insofar as they are based on archaeological discoveries they will be out-dated fairly rapidly.

I have tried to base the historic portion of the book, from chapter 6 onwards, upon the primary sources, but the reader will remark that my policy in giving references has varied. In the narrative chapters footnotes are sparse (as in volumes 3 and 4 of the series to which the book belongs) because the invaluable collections by A. O. Anderson provide a ready guide to both chronicles and documents. In chapters 12–19, which are an attempt at 'old' (descriptive) economic and social history, I have documented the discussion more fully.

Several colleagues have aided me without becoming in any way responsible for the sense I have taken from their helpful comments: Professors Leslie Alcock read chapters 1–2, Derick Thomson chapters 3–5, and Gordon Donaldson the whole manuscript. My greatest scholarly debt however is to the students of my University, Glasgow, who over a decade have helped me to evaluate the sources, to model a factual narrative and to discern some general trends in the twelfth and thirteenth centuries. The patience of the publisher in awaiting a belated manuscript has been outdone only by the care and sympathy of my wife and family during the writing of it. To all these I offer my thanks, and to Ann the dedication of this book.

ARCHIE DUNCAN

*Note on 1978 impression (paperback edition)*

In this impression I have been able to insert some addenda on pages 116, 215, 280, 308, 312, 462, 501, 529, 551. No general revision has been attempted, even on matters where my own views have changed somewhat. I am indebted to Dr M. O. Anderson, Professor G. W. S. Barrow, Dr G. G. Simpson and Professor D. E. R. Watt for their helpful criticisms. Some friendly critics find my judgments on the church unduly severe, and their weighty views should be borne in mind when reading what I have to say.

August, 1977.                                                            ARCHIE DUNCAN

# CONTENTS

# LIST OF ABBREVIATIONS USED
# IN FOOTNOTES

Bibliographical details are not given except for a few works which do not figure in the Sources and Bibliography (below pp. 635–53).

| | |
|---|---|
| *Aberdeen Burgh Recs* | = *Early Records of the Burgh of Aberdeen, 1317, 1398–1407*, ed. W. C. Dickinson. |
| *Aberdeen Registrum* | = *Registrum Episcopatus Aberdonensis.* |
| Adamnan, *Columba* | = *Adomnan's Life of Columba*, ed. A. O. and M. O. Anderson. |
| Anderson, *Early Sources* | = *Early Sources of Scottish History, 500 to 1286*, ed. A. O. Anderson. |
| Anderson, *Oliphants* | = J. Anderson, *The Oliphants in Scotland* (Edinburgh, 1879). |
| Anderson, *Scottish Annals* | = *Scottish Annals from English Chroniclers 500 to 1286*, ed. A. O. Anderson. |
| *APS* | = *The Acts of the Parliaments of Scotland*, ed. T. Thomson and C. Innes. |
| *Arbroath Liber* | = *Liber S. Thome de Aberbrothoc.* |
| *Balmerino Liber* | = *Liber Sancte Marie de Balmorinach.* |
| Barbour, *Bruce* | = J. Barbour, *The Bruce*, ed. W. M. Mackenzie. |
| Barrow, *Kingdom of the Scots* | = G. W. S. Barrow, *The Kingdom of the Scots.* |
| Bede, *Hist. Eccles.*, ed. Colgrave and Mynors | = Bede, *Historia Ecclesiastica . . . Gentis Anglorum*, ed. B. Colgrave and R. A. B. Mynors |
| *Cal. Docs. Scot.* | = *Calendar of Documents relating to Scotland*, ed. J. Bain. |
| *Cal. Papal Letters* | = *Calendar of Entries in the Papal Registers relating to Great Britain and Ireland: Papal Letters*, ed. W. H. Bliss. |
| *Cambuskenneth Registrum* | = *Registrum Monasterii s. Marie de Cambuskenneth.* |
| *Cawdor Bk.* | = *The Book of the Thanes of Cawdor* (Spalding Club, 1859). |

| | |
|---|---|
| *Chron. Bower* | = *Joannis de Fordun Scotichronicon cum Supplementis et Continuatione Walteri Boweri*, ed. W. Goodall. |
| *Chron. Fordun* | = *Johannis de Fordun, Chronica Gentis Scotorum*, ed. W. F. Skene. |
| *Chron. Guisborough* | = The Chronicle of Walter of Guisborough, ed. H. Rothwell (Camden Third Series, no. LXXIX, 1957). |
| *Chron. Holyrood* | = *A Scottish Chronicle known as the Chronicle of Holyrood*, ed. M. O. Anderson. |
| *Chron. Lanercost* | = *Chronicon de Lanercost*. |
| *Chron. Melrose* | = *The Chronicle of Melrose*, ed. A. O. Anderson and others. |
| *Chron. Picts-Scots* | = *Chronicles of the Picts; Chronicles of the Scots*, ed. W. F. Skene. |
| *Chron. Wyntoun* | = *The Original Chronicle of Andrew of Wyntoun* (S.T.S.). |
| *Coldingham Correspondence* | = *The Correspondence, Inventories, Account Rolls and Law Proceedings of the Priory of Coldingham*, ed. J. Raine (Surtees Society, London, 1841). |
| *Coldstream Chartulary* | = *Chartulary of the Cistercian Priory of Coldstream*. |
| *Coupar Charters* | = *Charters of the Abbey of Coupar Angus*, ed. D. E. Easson. |
| *Coupar Rental* | = *Rental Book of the Cistercian Abbey of Cupar Angus*, ed. C. Rogers (Grampian Club, 1879–80). |
| Dowden, *Bishops* | = J. Dowden, *The Bishops of Scotland*. |
| *Dryburgh Liber* | = *Liber S. Marie de Dryburgh*. |
| *Dunfermline Registrum* | = *Registrum de Dunfermelyn*. |
| *Eng. Hist. Rev.* | = *English Historical Review*. |
| *Exch. Rolls* | = *The Exchequer Rolls of Scotland*, ed. J. Stuart and others. |
| *Fife Court Bk.* | = *The Sheriff Court Book of Fife 1515–22*, ed. W. C. Dickinson. |
| *Foedera* | = *Foedera, Conventiones, Litterae et Cuiuscunque Generis Acta Publica*, ed. T. Rymer, Record Commission edition. |
| Fraser, *Annandale* | = W. Fraser, *The Annandale Family Book*. |
| Fraser, *Menteith* | = W. Fraser, *The Red Book of Menteith*. |
| *Glasgow Registrum* | = *Registrum Episcopatus Glasguensis*. |

| | |
|---|---|
| Haddan & Stubbs, *Councils* | = A. W. Haddan and W. Stubbs, *Councils and Ecclesiastical Documents relating to Great Britain and Ireland.* |
| *Highland Papers* | = *Highland Papers*, ed. J. R. N. Macphail. |
| *Holyrood Liber* | = *Liber Cartarum Sancte Crucis.* |
| *Inchaffray Chrs.* | = *Charters, Bulls and other Documents relating to the Abbey of Inchaffray.* |
| *Inchcolm Chrs.* | = *Charters of the Abbey of Inchcolm*, ed. D. E. Easson and A. Macdonald. |
| *Inventory of* [county] | = *Report and Inventory of the Royal Commission for the Ancient (and Historical) Monuments (Scotland)*, volumes by county. |
| *Kelso Liber* | = *Liber S. Marie de Calchou.* |
| *Laing Chrs.* | = *Calendar of the Laing Charters 854–1837*, ed. J. Anderson. |
| *Lamont Papers* | = *An Inventory of Lamont Papers* (Scottish Record Society, 1914). |
| *Lanark Recs.* | = *Extracts from the Records of the Royal Burgh of Lanark*, ed. R. Renwick. |
| Lawrie, *Annals* | = *Annals of the Reigns of Malcolm and William, Kings of Scotland*, ed. A. C. Lawrie. |
| Lawrie, *Charters* | = *Early Scottish Charters prior to 1153*, ed. A. C. Lawrie. |
| *Lennox Cartularium* | = *Cartularium Comitatus de Levenax.* |
| *Lindores Chartulary* | = *Chartulary of the Abbey of Lindores.* |
| Macphail, *Pluscardyn* | = S. R. Macphail, *History of the Religious House of Pluscardyn.* |
| *Melrose Liber* | = *Liber Sancte Marie de Melrose.* |
| *Moray Registrum* | = *Registrum Episcopatus Moraviensis.* |
| *Newbattle Registrum* | = *Registrum S. Marie de Neubotle.* |
| *North Berwick Carte* | = *Carte Monialium de Northberwic.* |
| *Paisley Registrum* | = *Registrum Monasterii de Passelet.* |
| Palgrave, *Docs. Hist. Scot.* | = *Documents and Records illustrating the History of Scotland*, ed. F. Palgrave. |
| *Proc. Soc. Antiq. Scot.* | = *Proceedings of the Society of Antiquaries of Scotland* (1851–). |
| Raine, *North Durham* | = Appendix to J. Raine, *The History and Antiquities of North Durham.* |
| *Recs. Sc. Church Hist. Soc.* | = *Records of the Scottish Church History Society.* |
| Ritchie, *Normans* | = R. L. G. Ritchie, *The Normans in Scotland.* |

R.M.S.                    = *Registrum Magni Sigilli Regum Scotorum*, ed.
                          J. M. Thomson and others.

Robertson, *Concilia*      = *Concilia Scotiae*, ed. J. Robertson.

Rot. *Chartarum*           = *Rotuli Chartarum in turri Londinensi asservati*,
                          i, ed. T. D. Hardy (Record Commission, 1837).

Rot. Litt. *Clausarum*     = *Rotuli Literarum clausarum in turri Londinensi
                          asservati*, ed. T. D. Hardy (2 vols, Record
                          Commission, 1833–4).

Rot. Litt. *Patentium*     = *Rotuli Literarum patentium in turri Londinensi
                          asservati*, i, ed. T. D. Hardy (Record
                          Commission, 1835).

Rotuli Scotiae           = *Rotuli Scotiae in Turri Londinensi et in Domo
                          Capitulari Westmonasteriensi asservati*, ed. D.
                          Macpherson and others (1814–19).

R.R.S.                    = *Regesta Regum Scottorum.*

St Andrews Liber         = *Liber Cartarum Prioratus Sancti Andree in
                          Scotia.*

Sc. Hist. Rev.           = *The Scottish Historical Review.*

Scone Liber              = *Liber Ecclesie de Scon.*

S.H.S.                    = Scottish History Society.

Spalding Misc.           = *Miscellany of the Spalding Club* (Spalding
                          Club, 1841–52).

Stevenson, Documents     = *Documents Illustrative of the History of
                          Scotland 1286–1306*, ed. J. Stevenson.

Stevenson & Wood, Seals  = J. H. Stevenson and M. Wood, *Scottish
                          Heraldic Seals.*

S.T.S.                    = Scottish Text Society.

Theiner, Vet. Mon.       = *Vetera Monumenta Hibernorum et Scotorum
                          Historiam Illustrantia*, ed. A. Theiner.

# 1

## PREHISTORIC PEOPLES

The theme of this book is the making of the kingdom of Scotland. The words were chosen advisedly for the kingdom did not 'emerge' but was made by man. On the other hand 'Scotland' is a land area in which natural forces have created a wide variety of geological and soil conditions on which climatic variation, ever since the last major retreat of the ice about 8000 B.C., has acted to produce an ecology which has changed greatly over the years; by comparison, the impact of man was trivial until the first millennium of the Christian era. For this reason, as well as the very different nature of earlier evidence, this volume attempts nothing more than a sketch (soon to be outdated by the rapidly advancing techniques of scientific archaeology) of the history of prehistory.

Yet the form of Scotland is worth a moment's consideration. Tilted between the slowly sinking basin of the North Sea and the rocks of the north recovering from the pressure of the last ice-cap, the land-mass is cut by geological faults—the Great Glen and the Highland lines. On the west the long sea inlets separated by mountain ridges encouraged water-borne human access and impeded land contacts; on the east the impediments were fewer. A description of the geology and natural resources of Scotland must be sought elsewhere. The physical map is itself an elementary lesson on the natural obstacles in the way of economic and political development, but that map should also show that, in addition to geological faults like the Great Glen, Britain is divided from east to west by the basin of the Forth, with its associated moss, impassable until the eighteenth century. This basin acted as a barrier between human societies from an uncertain prehistoric time until the end of the first millennium A.D., though a barrier of decreasing effectiveness. It was breached at one

place, Stirling, where a crossing of the Forth was controlled by a
natural rock fortress. Stirling was truly 'the brooch that holds
together the two parts of the country' in historical times,[1] but it
became that only after the fabric of society in each part, north and
south, was matched to the other through centuries of human traffic:
armies, traders, missionaries, all played their part, and the history
of that traffic is the central theme of this book.

We may begin at the farm of Morton in the north of Fife, four
kilometres from the sea and rather less from the Firth of Tay, where
a promontory projecting from the surrounding sands has yielded
traces of the earliest occupations of man in the northern part of
Britain. The coast line (which has maintained a relative stability since
4000 B.C.) was still fluctuating and peat, formed at the head of the
Firths of Tay and Forth about 6500 B.C., was buried under the heavy
clays of carseland deposited by marine transgression—the rising of
the sea level to something like 8.5 m above its present line—in the two
thousand years after that date. As the sands accumulated around the
Morton outcrop about 6000 B.C., when it was first occupied, they
were washed beyond it by the rising sea to form a spit to the westward, which at low tide joined the outcrop to the mainland; at high
tide it became a small island. To the north marshes were formed,
attracting fauna which supported the latest predator to venture thus
far north—man.

He came to hunt and he left behind the stone tools, scrapers, awls
and other flaked edges for cutting and working hide, whittling wood
for implements and stakes, and preparing carcases cooked on the
hearths, which succeeded one another on the site as evidence of many
occupations. Over some two thousand years men came and went in
groups of three or four, perhaps as many as a dozen staying a week
or two at a time, sometimes even as long as a season, when a shelter
was built, stakes driven into the ground and joined with hides to
form a windbreak, or pitched to meet like a roof and covered with
hide or reeds. He ate the flesh of deer, boar, wild cattle, even hedge-
hog and a wide range of land and sea birds, caught, perhaps, while
scavenging on the midden of bones and shells, or even at sea. Fish,
especially large cod, formed part of his diet, so that he was master of
a technique of fishing which brought in large fish rather than small
—fish traps on the shore or in inlets. He also ate large quantities of

[1] R. M. Mitchison, *A History of Scotland* (1970), 2.

molluscs, leaving behind a great weight of shell. That the occupants had boats is very likely, for a dugout, or hollowed out tree-trunk, was found long ago near Perth, buried in the peat below the clay washed in by the sea during the period of occupancy of Morton. Other places to which they could have moved on in search of food may be identified at Dundee and Broughty Ferry, where similar food and tool detritus has been found, though not so clearly datable.[2]

Morton is indeed, at the moment of writing, the earliest excavated, recorded, dated and published occupation site in Scotland; but its occupation was so discontinuous that we can be dealing only with nomadic hunters of mammals, birds and fishes and gatherers of molluscs who ranged widely in east-central Scotland in search of food: elsewhere, for example, they may have gathered and eaten the fruits and seeds of wild plants. In many parts of Scotland there are similar sites, well over a hundred in number but not so well dated and thought to be rather later than the earliest occupancy of Morton: shell heaps at Inveravon in West Lothian were deposited from about 5000 B.C. until as late as 2500 B.C., and other middens in the Forth valley have yielded antler implements (there are some bone implements in the late phases of Morton). Associated with these middens are the bones of whales, caught at a time when the shore line was higher, whose flesh the tools may have cut and scraped. Occupancy older than Morton will probably be discovered, perhaps among the collections of flint implements in the Tweed valley, for there is no disagreement that our early hunters and fishers came from the south of Britain into the north. Their numbers were small: a would-be census taken in 1962 suggested that 'the population at any one time can hardly have exceeded two people for each of the modern counties' or seventy in all.[3] The reader may guess at his own multiplier but should not over-react to this tiny figure.

After 4000 B.C. there came to Scotland people who still did not know the use of metal but who were nonetheless infinitely more sophisticated than the scanty hunters and fishers. That there was a migration, or several migrations, does not seem in doubt, for the 'revolution' (now an unfashionable term) which they wrought seems far too great to be explained by independent invention and

[2] J. M. Coles, 'The early settlement of Scotland: excavations at Morton, Fife', *Proceedings of the Prehistoric Society*, xxxvii (1971), 284–366. Perhaps I should note that I have tried to give C14 dates as calibrated in the light of knowledge in 1973.

[3] R. J. C. Atkinson in *The Prehistoric Peoples of Scotland*, ed. S. Piggott, 6–7.

adoption by hunter-fishers, and the animals and plants which they domesticated were probably brought with them. The literature on the origins of these Neolithic, or new stone-implement-using, people is large, and debate on their diffusion as evidenced by burial structures and artefacts is lively and continuous. That they came by sea both up the Atlantic approaches and by an east-coast route seems fairly clear, but the number of stages of such migrations and the place of Ireland in them must be left for study in archaeological literature.

The migration was perhaps made possible and attractive by a climatic improvement during the fourth millennium B.C. which took some cold-susceptible plants further north than they may now be found. In a warm wet climate forest flourished—it has been discovered below the sand of treeless Harris and was apparently widespread in the Outer Hebrides—and a palaeobotanist could argue that open grassland was almost unknown in fourth millennium Britain. The onslaught of Neolithic man, the tiller of soil and tamer of animals, upon this fertile environment would perhaps be first by 'slash-and-burn'—cutting down brushwood to make fires round trees—and turning over the ash-enriched soil between the charred roots and stumps with primitive implements of wood, the hoe or ard (a scratch plough). So far there have been no traces in Scotland of Neolithic ard cultivation, preparing a seed-bed by scratching or ploughing with the ard first in one direction and then at right angles thereto. But the existence of the stone shares of ards from Shetland suggests that all-wooden crook-ards existed on the Scottish mainland, just as the existence of Neolithic structures in Shetland near areas cleared of stones and surrounded by low dry-stone walls suggests that primitive fields, such as have been discovered under the peat blanket in western Ireland, existed also in mainland Scotland. It is certainly likely that early Neolithic cultivation of a particular clearing was sporadic, since fertility would fall by repeated cultivation. But the evidence for settlement is so firm that distinct fields are surely implied.

Neolithic man has left few recognised traces of his dwelling places. About 2200 B.C. or later in Orkney a village of stone houses was built as Skara Brae which blown sand preserved intact, save for the roofs, until the present century. Square, and measuring between fifteen and twenty feet (4.5–6 m) across, each was entered by a single doorway. The internal fittings in stone have brought dramatically to life the domestic environment of Neolithic man in a way not possible for his successors until the Roman period. The hearth, the elaborate tiered dresser or cupboard, the bed recesses and the carefully lined box sunk in the floor to hold sea-foods, these can only be the work of a settled community of some wealth and stability. Other Neolithic houses have been identified in Shetland which, though less prosperous, indicate the same conclusions. Now, of course, these are geographical outliers, the products of an environment poorly endowed with wood but with a stone which split easily and along straight lines so that symmetrical building was possible. Archaeologists must be given time to identify houses, presumably in timber, which were the parallel settlements of Neolithic man on the mainland. Some such settlements must have existed to use the flint axes from a factory on the side of Creag na Caillich, at Killin in Perthshire, in production some time after 2500 B.C. and exporting its wares to Aberdeenshire and doubtless elsewhere.[4]

On mainland Scotland Neolithic settlement is only inferred, for homes have not been identified. But it is inferred from the graves which are clustered in many parts of Scotland, works of engineering which could have been produced only by settled and wealthy communities. These tombs are the chambered cairns of which the most spectacular examples are found in Shetland and Orkney but which are widely diffused in Galloway, Arran and Argyll, in the Uists, and in the east of the northern counties. There are examples in Aberdeenshire and Perthshire, but they are undoubtedly thinner on the ground east and south of the Findhorn. Here, however, earthen long barrows, of which about 50 are known, derived from and suggesting migration from Yorkshire, may fill the gap. Burials within are sometimes by cremation, sometimes by inhumation, and in those with a gallery of graves the buried corpses are sometimes found with disarticulated limbs—moved, that is, to make way for another generation. A chambered tomb in Arran has yielded a date of about 3700 B.C., but some (obviously built later) were still in use about 2000 B.C. They yield fragments of pottery and traces of the bones of cattle or sheep as well as charred grain or impressions of grain upon pottery. They tell us of a society of farmers of wealth and even sophistication who disposed not merely of chattels but also of the labour of men. It is not too early to think of an hierarchical society, for wherever there is wealth (as distinct from a struggle for subsistence) man will pursue it and retain it by dominance over his fellow men.

[4] *Proceedings of Prehistoric Society*, xxxviii (1972), 415.

But these remains also surely tell us that the men who built them or for whom they were built lived with a sense that life was not only a struggle to match skills with animal cunning. Nature must have seemed a force which with wind, rain, frost or even occasionally burning sun challenged the endeavours of man to husband wealth. In nature there were forces to be placated, givers and takers away; in short Neolithic man got religion. The tombs themselves would otherwise be pointless; and the carved stone balls, most of which cannot be associated with a culture, but one of which was found at Skara Brae, are most convincingly explained as charms or prophylactics against supernatural forces.

At the end of the second millennium B.C. a new form of burial suggests at least a change in ritual attitudes; the body was disposed crouched within a stone cist too short to carry it elongated, and with it were placed a pot of a shape known as a Beaker and occasionally other simple grave goods such as an arrow, or stone battleaxe, and in one per cent of cases copper or bronze objects. The cist might then be covered by a mound of stones, without a passage or entry; many of these mounds may have been so small that they have been ploughed away. Sometimes the cist was introduced into the mound of a Neolithic chambered tomb, and at Kilmartin in Argyll a series of burials stretches from late Neolithic times into the age of Beaker burials. Archaeologists are sure because of change in the physical type of the people buried that these burials represent another migration, of Beaker Folk; they were taller by three inches (.08 m) and more heavily built than their Neolithic predecessors, with broader face and shorter skull. Also associated with Beaker people are stone circles and groups of standing stones, though archaeologists are clear that sometimes such complexes are not necessarily of one period. Aerial photography has also revealed at Huntingtower, near Perth, the traces of such circles and of a long avenue, but in timber posts, not stone, rivalling Stonehenge in significance, though not, of course, in scale of achievement. It may be accepted that stone circles are ritual or at least religious sites, but most recently a strong bid for respectability is being made on behalf of the evidence that standing stones were observatories to establish midsummer or the equinoxes. The matter is highly controversial since it requires a change in assumptions about non-literate prehistoric societies, and he who would understand it must have a stomach for mathematics.

Again, the origins of the Beaker folk who migrated to Scotland may be left to those with a feel for typology and a faith in archaeological cultures. On the evidence of Beaker forms, migration to Scotland was direct from continental Europe between the Elbe and the Rhine, but it is now doubtful whether they brought with them the technology of metalworking in bronze with which their arrival used to be associated. Rather, it would seem, smiths or other technicians brought their skills from central or northern European workshops, and perhaps, too, from Spain. Then in the middle of the second millennium burial customs changed, the older tradition of cremation reasserted itself, with burials either directly in the ground or in an urn in the ground. The urns themselves recall late Neolithic pottery, and strengthen the argument for a resurgence of a 'native' tradition and culture after the waning of the impact of the customs imported over the North Sea by the Beaker folk. But because burial was of a cremation we will not find much of the material culture of these people in their graves. Early Bronze Age metalwork exists sometimes in the context of burials, sometimes of hoards, but from the mid-second millennium we rely upon the latter. A remarkable series of studies during the 1960s has investigated the typology of objects produced and their significance; from this wealth of detail tentative conclusions have been drawn which it would be impossible to summarise in part of one chapter and the reader must be encouraged to approach these model studies through visits to some of the museums which house the material described.[5] Something, however jejune, must be said: bronze metalwork is suitable for weapons and adornments but not for efficient cultivation implements. The Early Bronze Age yields axes, halberds, daggers and knives. Axes are the most frequent finds and their importance is underlined by the illustrations of them cut into living rock and into parts of burial cists at Kilmartin in Argyll. Some were certainly locally made, for moulds have been found from Easter Ross to Donside and the products of these are identifiable, scattered from that north-eastern zone to Strathtay, Carrick and Dumfriesshire. Bronze metalwork, then, speaks also of trade, not only in the finished articles but also in the ingots of tin which must have come from Cornwall to be combined with local copper.

Yet, remarkably, it is in the Late Bronze Age, from about 1000 to 600 B.C., that bronze technology achieves its finest products in

[5] J. Coles in *Proc. Soc. Antiq. Sc.*, xciii (1959–60, late b.a.); xcvii (1963–4, middle b.a.); ci (1968–9, early b.a.).

Britain, for this was a period of worsening climate, hostile to seaborne long-range contacts. The socketed axe-head replaced earlier and less satisfactory means of attaching a stock. Swords suitable for slashing rather than stabbing, sickles, knives, chisels, cauldrons and buckets, personal ornaments (in gold) are found in Scotland. At Duddingston Loch there was discovered in the eighteenth century the stock of a bronze-founder, damaged or old swords and spearheads ready to be melted down; another hoard at Kilkerran in Ayrshire contained axes, but the total number of such finds is evidently small in comparison with the equivalent period in southern Britain. Nonetheless, native manufacture of these objects, however influenced by Irish and English archetypes, was very active.

Yet, what dwellings and peoples may be associated with this society, evidently having a weapon-conscious aristocracy, are unknown. For we are now in the millennium in which the origins of historic peoples may surely be sought; we look for the Picts who are 'indigenous' to the region north of the Forth by the time of Christ, and for the Celts who are similarly indigenous to Ireland and Britain south of Forth. In doing so we are looking for something which is defined not in material remains but in place-names, and particularly in river-names, which preserve the oldest linguistic layers. The marriage of archaeological cultures with language is fraught with even more perils than human wedlock and is certainly not to be performed by a layman, however anxious to learn from the priests of other mysteries. But the Late Bronze Age has left to us, among the native styles of metalwork, traces of an intrusive culture which takes its name from Covesea in Moray and which is associated not only with particular pottery forms but also with fittings for horse harness and wheeled vehicles. Its derivation from the lower Rhine seems fairly well accepted, as also its limited geographical spread, but its significance is by no means clear. It may represent a movement of Celtic people from Europe to north-eastern Scotland in the eighth century B.C., bringing that element of Celtic speech which is evident among the historical Picts, its material culture assimilated rapidly to that of Early Bronze Age peoples; for whatever the rules of linguistic change and assimilation, they are different from those for fashions and forms of weaponry, utensils and adornment.

Moreover, dwelling sites long known and once believed to date to a much later period, hill-forts of considerable size, their stone walls stabilised by internal timber lacing, have now been shown to have been constructed in a number of cases in the eighth or seventh century B.C. Many were subsequently set on fire and hence vitrified by accident or enemy intent, and these are the most readily identified of timber-laced forts; they are found mainly around the Firth of Clyde, near the Great Glen and in Strathmore, Gowrie and Fife, and one of the finest examples, Abernethy, gave a name to the culture supposed to have produced these forts. Two points may be ventured: the origins of the culture, or more probably cultures, which they represent lie in the Late Bronze Age, when the forts may suggest the growing authority of princelings of a partly Celtic, partly indigenous, people, the proto-Picts. Like the weaponry of the period, they represent an expansive, war-making and wealth-seeking society, a phase which may have been stimulated by the Covesea migrants. And secondly, the later date once imputed to them was based upon the finds within, which sometimes show their continued occupancy or intermittent occupancy down to the first century B.C. But it is a thesis worth airing that the art of fortification seems to have arrived in Britain early in the first millennium B.C., and to be associated with Bronze Age weaponry. Both may represent the arrival of Celtic peoples.

At Traprain Law in East Lothian, a hill-site occupied in the first millennia B.C. and A.D., the work of Late Bronze Age smiths has also been identified. But this coincidence of settlement and artefacts is all too rare and it would be wishful over-simplification to sketch an historical account from the intractable problems with which archaeologists wrestle in the first millennium B.C. Sometimes a sequence of structures helps to give an historical dimension to what might otherwise seem an endless game of prehistoric industrial espionage—the pursuit of typology among artefacts and bidding with alternative culture-models for lines of development. Parallel with the timber-laced forts north of Forth are the palisaded settlement sites found in Northumberland and the upper Tweed valley and now attributed, on the basis of absolute dates from two of their number, to the seventh century B.C. and later. Their construction, in some instances with two close-set palisades, had affinities with timber-lacing and demonstrates how, in environments differing relatively little, there may be produced obviously different structures which yet have something in common. And while timber-laced forts have affinities with the structures of continental Celtic peoples, palisaded settlements do not and seem to be of native rather than intrusive origin.

At Hayhope in Roxburghshire a palisaded settlement was

excavated to reveal at least twelve circular huts each about 40 feet (12 m) in diameter within the double palisade which, oval on plan, measured 285 feet (87 m) on the longer axis. Outside this palisade a second palisaded rampart was begun but not completed; its purpose is therefore obscure.[6] It has been calculated that this hill-village would have required 2,600 eight-inch (.20 m) posts for the palisades, and hurdling equivalent to the produce of 9 acres (3½ ha) of coppice, all presumably cleared from near-by groves which might then become available for cultivation. There is, in fact, terracing for cultivation on two sides of Hayhope which may represent the primitive fields of this village.[7] But there is nothing nearby which might represent the fortress of a lord for this village and it could be regarded as a settlement of stock-rearing peasants migrating for new opportunities to an upland (and unpromising) environment.

The subsequent history of this site (and its duration) are alike unknown. At Hownam Rings in the same county is another palisaded settlement whose history has been revealed by excavation; it must be stressed that this is only an example and by no means typical. The palisaded enclosure was subsequently recast as a stone fort with massive walls twelve feet (3.5 m) thick at base and once perhaps ten feet (3 m) high, and in a comparable site in Northumberland the same change took place when the palisade was not very old. How long that wall housed a settlement is unknown, but perhaps early in the Roman period, to cope with the weaponry of sling and chariot, an attempt was made to provide the settlement (continuing or re-established) with four concentric broad ramparts scraped up to form ditches only a few feet in depth. But the conditions of unsettlement or warfare which demanded such defences passed fairly soon and the houses spread over the abandoned defences which were presumably rendered superfluous by the 'Roman peace'.[8] Much of the history of this site must belong to the second half of the first millennium B.C., when smaller settlements, homesteads of one to three houses within an enclosure, perhaps palisaded, were being built widely in southern Scotland. They retain—as do most prehistoric house sites in Britain —the round shape which contrasts with continental rectilinear houses, and from the late second century B.C. onwards they yield evidence of agriculture in the form of rotary querns to grind meal (re-

---

[6] *Inventory of Roxburghshire*, no. 665.
[7] *Inventory of Roxburghshire*, nos. 665, 754; Piggott, *Ancient Europe*, 204.
[8] *Inventory of Roxburghshire*, no. 301.

placing the saddle querns of the Bronze Age) and produce the spindle-whorls and safety pins which show the uses of pastoralism. Indeed, all geographical considerations and the absence of grain-storage pits (also attributable to geological factors) suggest that in Scotland agriculture was of much less importance to the inhabitants than stock-rearing.

Such a site was excavated at West Plean in Stirlingshire on the crest of a hill where a bank and ditch enclosed a nearly circular enclosure of some 90 feet (27.5 m) diameter, in the centre of which was a house, originally a simple round hut of wattle or hide on timber posts and 23 feet (7 m) across. Subsequently replaced by a house almost twice as large with two concentric rings of posts, this can only have been the home of a farmer living in comparatively settled times, for even the ditch round his home had the function of a drain rather than a defence. A series of flimsy rectangular shacks on one spot by the dwelling probably housed stock but to tell of his living standards the site produced only a sandstone cup or lamp, whetstones (but not the iron tools on which they were used) and part of a rotary quern of an early (that is pre-Roman) type.[9] Did the occupier of this and similar sites farm only with his family, or did he have a slave or two? Was there a nearby lord to whom he paid tribute for protection and if so did the lord live in greater splendour with vassals and slaves in a palisaded or stone-walled hill-fort? The contemporaneity of various structures and types of structures is still uncertain, but it is perhaps allowable to say that variable local conditions may have been more important than was once allowed in producing different types: a fifty-year stretch of order imposed by a wilful chief in, say, Fife or Lothian, might encourage open homesteads as at West Plean, while the roistering kings of Irish literary tradition would drive men and their cattle into larger collective groups behind the security of broad and high stone walls. There is no fortress-, settlement- or hut-form which is general; rather the innovation of fortification might be ascribed to one migrant people, the Celts, an innovation which took various forms under the influence of indigenous building traditions and local circumstances.

With the increasing use of iron late in the first millennium B.C., we lack not only iron artefacts incidental to excavation of habitations; there is also little chance of survival for the votive offerings which Celtic peoples made to their gods by depositing valued objects

[9] *Inventory of Stirlingshire*, no. 104.

in sacred pools and lakes. If indeed such deposits are a mark of established Celtic chieftains (and this is hypothesis, not certainty), then we can point to their presence in the Late Bronze Age: six bronze shields set on edge in a bog at Beith (Ayrshire), shields found at Achmaleddie (Aberdeenshire) and Yetholm (Roxburghshire), as well as three swords found in Shuna (Argyll) thrust together, point downwards, into the peat. But of similarly offered ironwork which would complement the structures of Celtic Scotland down to the arrival of the Romans scarcely a trace remains. Certainly there is something to put into the scales from Scotland to match the panoply of La Tène art from Celtic Europe; but it is pathetically little, and the best piece, a ceremonial pony cap from Kirkcudbrightshire, is generally thought to be an import. Is it therefore just to the Celtic inhabitants of this period to point to the lack of metal artefacts and the undistinguished pottery, and to judge their culture as impoverished after the collapse of Bronze Age trade routes?

Probably not. For what we lack is 'the panoply and equipment of the battle-drunk, screaming tribal chieftain in his chariot hung with the decapitated heads of his foes, the air raucous with the sound of the *baritus* and the *carnyx*'.[10] That there were chieftains is put beyond doubt by the reception given to the Romans in the first century, and there is even the mouth of a *carnyx* from Deskford in Banffshire as well as bronze plaques, some of them richly ornamented, from a shield, and found at Balmaclellan, to show that they might have the accoutrements of war. But the tribal *oppidum* where it existed, as at Traprain (a major one) or Norman's Law in Fife (a minor one), was modest by Continental or English standards and betokens the very limited wealth of tribal chiefs. And this in its turn may be attributed not so much to poverty and isolation from the workshops of Europe as to the homesteaders' society from which the chieftains drew their tribute; homesteads were widely scattered, and difficult to assemble into a tribal war-band, nor perhaps could they be easily persuaded to yield substantial tributes in cattle (of which they perhaps had many) or grain (of which they certainly had little), which alone would have supported the cultural sophistication of a chief's hall in contemporary Gaul. Essentially settlement was too scattered and population too thin on the ground to support wealthy chieftains; but that does not mean that individual farmers were poor, for the lack of ornaments is less significant than the evident

[10] Piggott, *Ancient Europe*, 243.

availability of axes, knives, spades and no doubt many other tools to put up the homes of the various types already discussed.

When and whence, then, the Celts? The archaeologist would place the earlier migrations late in the times of that first cultural phase of the Continental Celts known as 'Halstatt' (from the site of important discoveries) before 600 or even 700 B.C. and influencing some of the Late Bronze Age metalwork found in Scotland; he would perhaps envisage the intermittent migration of Celtic bands from the Continent over the remainder of the first millennium; one such, a late example, was the movement of *Belgae* to Kent before 100 B.C. mentioned by Caesar, itself displacing earlier Celtic peoples. Both an Atlantic and a North Sea route would be used and the numbers of migrants were sufficient to establish Celtic languages generally south of Forth; north thereof proto-Pictish included a Celtic element possibly from the Covesea migrants. The model provided very tentatively by Professor K. H. Jackson in 1955[11] was rather different, for archaeological knowledge was not then affected by absolute dating. It teaches us how resolutely we must resist the temptation to any kind of dogmatism based upon either archaeological or linguistic evidence; but it teaches also the importance of linguistic and literary evidence in seeking a people or peoples who are defined by the language they speak.

In the fourth century A.D. the writer of the poem *Ora Maritima* incorporated in its text fragments of an account of a journey from Marseilles to Tartessos on the Iberian Atlantic coast, a city destroyed by the Carthaginians. This account, the *Massiliote Periplus*, was written before 530 B.C. and describes the Tartessians as trading as far north as the *Oestrymnides* (usually identified as Brittany), whose people traded with the inhabitants of two large islands, Ierne and Albion. Undoubtely these are Ireland and Britain as known to peoples speaking a Celtic language, ancestor of the group known as Q-Celtic (of which there are traces upon the Continent) and thought to preserve more archaic features than the other branch, P-Celtic. This latter branch is represented first by Gallo-Brythonic, a common ancestor of the Gaulish and Brythonic languages spoken in the first century B.C.; it may have been the language spoken by the migrants who brought a Celtic element to the proto-Picts, since some names in historical Pictland 'remind one of Gaulish rather than of British'.[12]

---

[11] Wainwright, *Problem of Picts*, 155–8; 'purely speculations' was his own introductory phrase.   [12] K. H. Jackson in Wainwright, *Problems of Picts*, 138.

In the fourth century B.C. another Massilian voyager referred to the 'Pretanic' islands and, although he evidently included Ireland therein, the name is P-Celtic and its primary meaning and origin was probably that which it still has—Britain.

This evidence puts in these islands Q-Celts by the sixth century presumably in Ireland, and P-Celts presumably in Britain by the fourth century;[13] this in no way conflicts with a Late Bronze Age (eighth or seventh century) arrival of P-Celts in Britain followed by further waves of settlers, but it does seem to push the settlement of Ireland back into an even more remote period, and to raise the possibility that the widespread Celtic presence in western Europe recorded by Herodotus in the fourth century was the consequence of a much earlier spread of settlement than the archaeological record of the diffusion of the Hallstatt culture. Perhaps, as Professor Dillon suggested, we might even look back to the Early Bronze Age (itself a receding date), to the Beaker folk as the earliest Celtic settlers in Britain.[14]

An argument against so early a date is the geographical description of Britain given in Ptolemy's geography, a second century A.D. source based on first century A.D. materials. The peoples described there as inhabiting Britain include names so closely related that a relationship by migration, even if only of warrior chiefs, has been argued. A non-Scottish example, the Parisi of Yorkshire, with an obvious link to northern Gaul, has also produced evidence of La Tène culture in chariot burials and rich horse-trappings. Ptolemy places in Caithness the Cornovii, people of the horn or promontory, and another people of the same name on the northern Welsh border, where the Wirral peninsula could explain the name; the Dumnonii, who give their name to Devon, are also placed in Clydesdale and may have migrated there (as they were later to migrate to Brittany) from southern England. But only the latter suggestion carries much probability and at best it is evidence for only one migration within the few centuries before Ptolemy's time.[15] Moreover there is little material evidence to evaluate such a migration.

[13] D. Greene, 'The making of Insular Celtic', *Proceedings of the Second International Congress of Celtic Studies, Cardiff, 1963* (Cardiff, 1966), 123–36, is a stimulating introduction. H. Wagner, *Studies in the Origins of the Celts and of Early Celtic Civilisation* (Belfast and Tübingen, 1971) (a reprint of two articles), is of great methodological interest though, it seems, not accepted in all academic circles.

[14] Dillon and Chadwick, *Celtic Realms*, 4.

[15] See Map 4 in Dillon and Chadwick, *Celtic Realms*; Tacitus, *Agricola*, ed. Ogilvie and Richmond, 39–40.

Ptolemy's geography includes a group of five islands, *Ebudae*, lying between Scotland and Ireland,[16] and in the far north the *Orcades*, a name already known to Pliny. In one or both of these two groups of islands the first century B.C. saw the gradual spread of a new and remarkable structural form which has always caught the imagination of visitors and engendered scholarly controversy: the broch, a round tower perhaps twenty feet (6 m) high with an internal diameter of between twenty-five and forty feet (7.6 and 12 m). Externally the broch has a broad base sloping gently inwards over the first ten or fifteen feet (3 or 4.5 m) of height and presenting the appearance of a stone cooling tower or a mighty funnel. Largely but not wholly confined to the Northern and Western Isles and to the mainland shores opposite them, some brochs can be dated by Roman finds to occupancy in the first century A.D. It is generally agreed that the fashion for them was comparatively short-lived—say 200 years from 100 B.C. The best preserved of them (and that most frequently used for illustration), on Mousa in Shetland, is aberrant in that its walls are very thick and hence it has survived almost intact, complete with staircase in the thickness of its wall. In many cases the building was raised or partly raised as two skins of stone bound together by transverse slabs and platforms which acted as an internal scaffolding during building, reduced the weight of the walls and provided at least at ground level an internal mural gallery. The entrance at ground floor level would have provision for a guard cell or two. The dramatic appearance of these towers, even though they may survive to a height of only six or ten feet (1.8 or 3 m), is enhanced, particularly in the west, by the way they are perched upon hills and headlands with good views of distant approach-waters.

They were built not by raiders but by resident lords with some labour to command. As refuges for man from a sea-borne enemy they would provide effective protection from slings, bolts and fire arrows, and their particular form may be a response, like multiple-ditch hillforts in the Southern Uplands, to these techniques of warfare. Those which have been excavated may reveal hearth and post-holes for an internal lean-to shelter, but the traces of pre-Roman habitation are few—as in many Iron Age sites elsewhere in Scotland; this lack of finds, therefore, is no argument against the brochs having been permanent dwellings rather than places of occasional refuge.

[16] Ebudae was correctly attached to the Western Isles as 'Hebrides', but at a much later date.

They are certainly too small to have held stock as well as humans, and this too suggests that they were permanent dwellings. The most recent work has produced a refined typology distinguishing three groups found respectively in Hebrides, Orkney and Shetland while those of the northern mainland fall into all three groups. It is unlikely that the broch evolved in Shetland and archaeologists are divided between a Hebridean and an Orkney-plus-mainland origin; a Hebridean development from forts with a simple wall with internal gallery (found mainly in Skye) seems the most persuasive argument currently offered.

The broch is certainly a unique native response in stone in a tree-less environment to a problem which need not be seen as unique; other zones would produce a different response in different materials. The problem is likely to have been the unsettlement produced in Celtic Britain as a whole by the arrival of the Belgae in Kent and their (first century A.D.) spread westwards, which may have driven some of the inhabitants of south-western England or of the region south of Chester to migrate by the Irish Sea. The cultural links of the Hebridean broch province with this 'Wessex' society are urged on grounds of distribution of spiral finger rings, bone dice, pottery and various other elements; but a direct migration to Tiree or Skye seems unlikely even when a class of professional fort designers and builders is hypothesised, presumably gambling glass beads, bronze rings, pins and fibulae on the roll of parallelopiped bone dice, as the native population toiled to raise the broch wall—to what purpose? In brief, the broch argues the sophisticated construction work of which a poorly endowed, remote and primitive people was capable in order to provide itself with protection in troubled times, troubles which may have been wholly local to northern and western Scotland, or which may have been caused by predatory slave-raiders from the Roman world. Even after a thorough combing of archaeological journals the historian may not feel inclined to go much further than that.[17]

[17] E. MacKie, 'English Migrants and Scottish Brochs', *Glasgow Archaeo-logical Journal*, ii (1971), 39–71. This paper seems to me to show a valuable new approach in classifying brochs by relative dimensions; and in arguing migration from Wessex it seems to show the weakness of the traditional approach by the analysis of types of pottery etc. But Dr MacKie has most generously discussed many features of the archaeology of Scotland with me.

# 2

# ROMAN ANTIQUITIES

In the century before the Roman conquest of A.D. 43 southern
Britain was racked by the wars of rival kingdoms, perhaps the
consequence of Belgic expansion and of the economic importance
of the region as a source of tin and corn for the continental Roman
Empire. Trade with Rome is reflected, for example by wine am-
phorae found on a number of native sites in the south, but this
sophistication does not extend to the territory of the Brigantes
between Humber and Tyne or Tees, described by Tacitus as the
most numerous people in Britain, and therefore of considerable
military power. To the north of the Brigantes and south of Forth lay
the territory of Ptolemy's *Otadinoi*, the Votadini, while to the west
were the Selgovae, in the central uplands, where Ptolemy identifies
their *oppidum* of Trimontium, undoubtedly the Eildon Hills. Galloway was the territory of the Novantae and Clydesdale that of the
Damnonii, whose lands may have extended beyond the Campsies
and Flanders Moss to include southern Perthshire, if modern conjectures be allowed. This would make them neighbours of the Caledonians to the north, a people who inhabited the Highlands as far
as the Great Glen according to Ptolemy, but who are to be identified
with the central Perthshire place-names of Dunkeld (the fort of the
Caledonians) and Schiehallion.[1] If Breadalbane and Atholl formed
the kingdom of the Caledonians, their hegemony may have extended
at various times beyond the Mounth—though the historian should
realise the formidable natural obstacles to such an hypothetical empire and be prepared to interpret Ptolemy's Caledonians as a temporary alliance against the Romans, for his information seems to be
derived from the surveys of Agricola's spies in the early 80s.

[1] K. Jackson, 'Two Early Scottish Names', *Sc. Hist. Rev.* xxxiii (1954),
14–18.

The pace and nature of Roman conquest in southern Britain must be studied elsewhere: by A.D. 69 the lowland zone, but not the Brigantes or Wales, was under Roman control, when a political crisis shook the empire and weakened the forces in Britain. The breakdown of a Roman alliance with the Brigantes led to the latter's defeat between 71 and 74 and the establishment of a legionary fortress at York. After several campaigns in Wales, the completion of the conquest of Brigantia was carried through in 79 by the new governor, Gnaeus Julius Agricola. Of his work we are fortunate in possessing a literary account by his nephew, Tacitus, eulogistic no doubt and partisan but invaluable for describing not merely a man known otherwise as governor from two inscriptions, but also campaigns whose success is recorded on the ground as well. The archaeological record for the whole Roman period is still far from complete, and presents many problems of chronology and interpretation. But discoveries through air photography are gradually falling into place in the narrative of Tacitus to reveal that his subject was indeed a general of consummate strategic skill. The roads which he later had built suggest that the Brigantes were conquered by a double advance from Chester and York with fierce strikes at native peoples followed by offers of favourable terms which enabled Agricola to establish forts in their territories. In 80 the advance continued from Carlisle and Corbridge to the Forth at Inveresk, and with a reconnaissance beyond to the Tay which established the advantages of the Forth-Clyde isthmus as a possible frontier. The Votadini and Selgovae had now been broken and conquest of them was completed in 81 by the establishment of forts and fortlets along the lines of Roman advance, and along the boundary with the northern barbarians now decided upon, perhaps as a result of limiting instructions from the Emperor Titus. A large fort was established below the Selgovan *oppidum* on the north-west hill of Eildons at Newstead which was the pivot of the system of roads: that to Inveresk separated the Selgovae from the Votadini, while the road from Carlisle by Birrens and Milton bifurcated to reach Inveresk and to descend the Clyde, patrolling the relations of the Selgovae with their western neighbours.

Somewhere between Forth and Clyde Agricola established a frontier of forts. Apart from Camelon near Falkirk these forts cannot be identified with certainty, and the general view that Agricolan forts must be under some of those on the Antonine wall is now less widely held than was once the case. There are small forts under later forts at Bar Hill and Croy Hill, but they may be construction camps for the Antonine forts rather than Agricolan forts.

In the following year, 82, Agricola turned west into Ayrshire and Galloway, crossing the Solway by sea and marching up a river valley, perhaps the Nith, where an Agricolan fort was built at Dalswinton. Others have been identified at Glenlochar, Gatehouse of Fleet and Loudoun, and it is generally agreed that the system of roads and forts must have extended to the Ayrshire coast and the Rhinns of Galloway, though evidence to back up this view is slow to appear on the ground. Agricola may now have looked upon Ireland and it is possible that he was tempted to consider an invasion, estimating that law and order might be taken there by a legion with some auxilary troops. Modern comparisons would be profitless; if Agricola's good sense did not warn him off, other opportunities deprived him of this one.

In 83 the policy of resting on the Forth-Clyde frontier was reversed, probably by permission of the new emperor, Domitian, and the advance northward was resumed, aided by the reports of merchants or naval spies who, having sailed about the Western Isles, revealed the impossibility of a continued advance in two strikes or columns. The dangers of the march of a single force along the eastern plain and straths north-eastward to Stonehaven and then north-westward were great, for the terrain was new, and the inhabitants achieved such co-operation to resist the Romans as to suggest that they were rightly regarded as a single ethnic group—the Caledonians—their country as Caledonia. On the way north Agricola did indeed rout a native force, which attacked the ninth legion at the camp of *Victoria* and fled to the wilds when reinforcements came up. The site of this camp is unknown but if Tacitus' remark that Agricola divided his forces before the battle is to be relied upon, then it should perhaps be placed in southern Scotland. The reason for this conjecture is the identification of marching camps of between 23 and 40 acres (9 and 16 ha), suitable for one legion, some of which have a distinctive form of gate (exemplified at Stracathro and usually so called), and others which do not; all may plausibly be assigned to this campaign, and may represent the operation of a number of battle groups splitting and joining up so as to demand camps of varying sizes.

The surveyors who laid out 'Stracathro' camps were with a large force at Dalswinton (40 acres, 16 ha) in Dumfriesshire, only part of which crossed Flanders Moss by Lake of Menteith (23.5 acres, 9 ha) and advanced by Dalginross (25 acres, 10 ha) up Strathearn and Strathmore, but joined by others, perhaps from Dalswinton, before making camp at Stracathro (39 acres, 16 ha). Most of that force advanced by the lower Don to Ythan Wells in Aberdeenshire and fifteen miles (24 km) further on to Auchenhove, at the gateway of Banffshire. The other camps show perhaps two battle groups, one marching from camps at Dunblane (34 acres, 14 ha) to Ardoch (30 acres, 12 ha) and Dornock in Perthshire (23.5 acres, 9 ha), the other from Bonnytown in East Fife (35 acres, 14 ha) across the Tay to Cardean in Angus and so to Finavon (37 acres, 15 ha). At Bellie in Moray there is a camp of some 25 acres (10 ha) which may represent the furthest penetration of one of the legions engaged in this campaign; but even if this camp belongs to some other occasion the great length and boldness of the strikes made by the Roman forces are remarkable and it must have greatly disappointed their commander that the Caledonians were not brought to that open encounter by which he hoped to reduce them to the status of clients of Rome. Only by effective and permanent garrisons, it seemed, could clientage be induced, and for this Agricola now began to plan. The lowland east-coast plain and straths were to be held by a legion with permanent headquarters at Meikleour near Dunkeld, plugging the exit from highland Strathtay into open carseland. This legionary fortress of Inchtuthil, begun probably in 83 with a 45 acre (18 ha) builders' camp, would like York and Chester in their time, be well behind the extreme of planned Roman control to the Don or the Moray Firth.

In 84 came the last and most successful campaign, associated with recently identified camps of large dimensions at Dunning (115 acres, 46 ha) Abernethy and Carpow where the Tay would be crossed. Four days' march to the north-east at Logie, another large camp may represent the crossing of the North Esk beyond which at Raedykes is the first of a series of camps, at Normandykes, Kintore, Ythan Wells and Muiryfold of between 90 and 110 acres (36 and 44 ha) which took Agricola's whole army, this time in one force, to the still unidentified site of Mons Graupius. The Caledonians under their numerous leaders, Calgacus among the chief of them, at last came to grips with Roman might there and were heavily defeated.

Agricola went on to the lands of the *Borestii* (a name perhaps related to Forres in Moray), where he took hostages, presumably from others besides the Borestii. The army then withdrew slowly but the fleet sailed on at Agricola's command, to subdue the Orkneys, catch sight of Fair Isle, and return, proving that Britain was an island.

Although it suited Tacitus to say otherwise, Agricola's recall from Britain was probably a matter of routine, if only so that he might be honoured for his undoubted victories. He had achieved much in extending the territory under Roman authority, subjecting it to control by brilliantly sited forts which stopped up the river valleys and separated the uncontrolled highland Caledonians from those in the lowland zones. He used naval power to extend the scope of campaigns and some of his forts are identifiable because of innovations in the design of their ditch systems and gateways. In southern Scotland he was responsible for the building of at least twenty forts, and north of Forth of a further nine or ten, together with Inchtuthil. Over 1300 miles (2080 km) of roads were surveyed and built north of the Tyne to connect the extended garrisons in the task of containing and dominating the native peoples in their upland kingdoms. The effect of his campaigns in cowing the northern peoples was certainly immediate and may well have been long-lasting. In fact, Agricola probably overextended the resources in manpower at his disposal by seeking to hold Strathmore and the whole eastern seaboard up to the Mounth; the Laigh of Moray was certainly beyond his capacity.

It was again imperial and not local decision which dramatically (or so Tacitus has made it) undid the most northerly part of Agricola's work; the withdrawal of a legion and auxiliary units from Britain to the Danube necessitated the withdrawal of a legion to Chester from Inchtuthil, still under construction when abandoned in A.D. 87. Equipped with sixty-four large barracks, four tribune's houses, six granaries, hospital, workshop and drill-hall as well as headquarters building, this military city was defended by a stone wall over 2000 yards (1.8 km) long. Ovens had not been fired, a bath-house awaited its hot-water system, and various buildings were incomplete when the sophisticated construction process went into reverse with the clawing out of nails, uprooting of structural timbers and burning of wattle walls. Pottery and glass from the stores were dumped in the gutter and pounded to fragments, flagstones were lifted and the stone wall round the fort systematically pulled apart. One million nails 'surplus to requirements' were deliberately buried in a pit to deny their iron to the Caledonians—and to be found again in the present century. 'The evident intention was to leave not an empty fortress but a *tabula rasa*.'[2]

By A.D. 92, it has been argued, only Ardoch was retained and rebuilt as an outpost, its six successive temporary camps (in addition to the fort) evidence of its strategic importance in Roman plans for Scotland in many different circumstances. The frontier was pulled back to the Forth-Clyde isthmus according to this view, which however cannot point to archaeological evidence of occupancy of forts there. Another view holds that the withdrawal was less drastic and that the line of the Earn was held by forts including Bertha and Strageath, linked by the enigmatic Gask ridge signal stations.[3] Whichever view is correct, both are agreed that great effort was also put into strengthening the forts behind this line, at Newstead, Dalswinton, Milton, Glenlochar and Birrens, evidently with the intention not only of discouraging trouble among the Novantae and Selgovae, but also of containing the other tribes up to the frontier at the Forth or Earn. Whatever the discomfort felt by the Romans about their hold on this cross-country stretch, it was evidently justified. Not long after 105 a disaster occurred in which the forts at Newstead, Dalswinton, Glenlochar and others down to Corbridge on the Tyne were burned to the ground. There has been special pleading for a planned withdrawal, but this can have happened only at Milton, where the fort was dismantled. Elsewhere we must surely admit of a native rising, though whether originating among the Caledonians or among the Selgovae (who must have been involved) only excavation of more northerly forts may reveal.

For the first time the Romans withdrew from Scotland to a frontier on the Tyne, the end of a period of imperial expansion in other provinces as well as Britain. Yet even at the time of the emperor Hadrian's accession in 117 there was more trouble in Britain, suppressed in 118, and his decision to build a *limes*, a fixed frontier, separating Brigantians from Selgovae and Novantae, strongly suggests that these three peoples were allied in mischief against Rome. The achievement of Hadrian's Wall in stone is as impressive as Agricola's conquests—though they epitomise the very different outlooks of the

---

[2] Tacitus, *Agricola*, ed. Ogilvie and Richmond, 71–3. This account of Agricola's campaigns was revised in the light of Dr St Joseph's article cited below p. 26 n.

[3] Frere, *Britannia*, 120; Tacitus, *Agricola*, ed. Ogilvie and Richmond, 76. The latest evidence is that the Gaskridge stations are Flavian.

two centuries—but attention may be directed particularly to the vallum which paralleled the wall to the south. This great ditch, twenty feet (6 m) wide and ten (3 m) deep, was the centre of a defensive strip eighty feet (24 m) wide which was crossed by causeways only at mile-castles and forts on the wall. It was a barrier to access to the wall from the Brigantian south except at fixed points of entry, and was designed to restrict and supervise contact between a subject people (the Brigantes) and (it was hoped) a client one, the Selgovae. But only in the west, where the wall had no commanding outlook, did the Romans maintain outposts beyond the wall, four in number including Birrens.

Yet within twenty years, under Hadrian's successor, Antoninus Pius, this very permanent-looking frontier was being 'moth-balled' and its garrisons advanced into southern Scotland to hold again the Forth-Clyde isthmus. The reasons for this change of policy are obscure but a rising by some Brigantes is mentioned by a contemporary, and this may have involved the more northerly peoples, convincing the emperor that Hadrian's Wall was wrongly placed. Campaigns were fought between 139 and 143, and in 145 drafts of Britons into the Roman army appear on the German frontier—men transported from the tribes, presumably of Selgovae and Novantae, which had surrendered to the Roman advance. If Hadrian's Wall was now rejected, the Hadrianic concept of a fortified *limes* was not; for, Antonine's governor, Lollius Urbicus, 'after driving back the barbarians, built another wall, of turf'. The Antonine Wall, 37 miles (60 km) long from the fort at Old Kilpatrick on the Clyde to Bridgeness on the Forth, a little west of the fort at Carriden, was indeed carried out to a specification unaltered during the progress of the work. The ditch to the north was forty feet (12 m) wide and twelve (3.66 m) deep, greater than that at Hadrian's Wall because the wall itself was less substantial. Built of turf upon a stone base fourteen feet (4.27 m) wide, the wall was probably some nine feet (2.75 m) high with a rampart walk and wooden breast-work. The eighteen forts were spaced at intervals of about two miles (3.2 km), and varied considerably in size, the largest being able to hold a cohort of 1000 men. Taken with the reconstruction of some earlier forts and the building of a number of new fortlets in the area between the walls, these eighteen forts do suggest a careful spreading of scarce manpower resources thinly over a large territory. Small contingents and quick reinforcement seemed more likely to be effective than fewer and larger garrisons. Moreover, the flanks of the wall were carefully kept under surveillance by forts to east and west, and outposts were again established in Strathearn. Inscriptions have revealed the division of the work of construction among the three legions of Britain, each of which had two working parties and all of which co-operated on the dangerous four-mile (6.5 km) stretch at the west end where a preliminary fort had been established at Duntocher.

It is common ground among modern scholars that the first Roman occupation of the Antonine Wall lasted until 154 or 155 and most would agree that it was ended by a major revolt of the Brigantes behind Hadrian's Wall. The evidence of coins found at the northern wall is again and again 'nothing later than 155'. Similarly there seems little disagreement that in 157-8 the southern wall was again brought into commission and the destroyed fort of Birrens was rebuilt as an outpost. From this point argument rages over a half century of discrepant evidence, coins, pottery and literary sources. There is no doubt that southern Scotland and the Antonine Wall were reoccupied once, and after long disagreement over a period placed variantly from the 160s to just after 180, a wholly new scheme was proposed in the late 1960s. According to this we should allow that, after the 155 withdrawal, the Antonine Wall was still unoccupied when in 180, as Dio Cassius describes it, the British tribes crossed 'the wall' which separated them from the Roman garrisons and slew a general at the head of his army. The emperor, Commodus, sent against them Ulpius Marcellus, who did them great harm; the Romans were celebrating victory in Britain in 184-5. From archaeological evidence it is suggested that although the tribes may have been Caledonian, the wall at which they inflicted great damage was Hadrian's Wall and that after 185 there was a period during which it was not the frontier.

In 185 Ulpius Marcellus (according to this reconstruction of events) reoccupied the Antonine Wall, partly because of extensive damage to the southern wall, partly no doubt in order to control more effectively the tribes which had been the source of trouble. It remained the frontier for sc•ne twenty years, despite the withdrawal of substantial forces from Britain in 196-7 in pursuit of the imperial ambitions of Clodius Albinus; the tribes were slow to stir at this weakening of defences, and the first governor appointed by the Emperor Severus was able to buy peace in 197-9 by the payment or renewal of subsidies to the Maeatae, whom the Caledonians were preparing to assist. By, or in, 207–8, this situation changed and the governor had to tell the emperor of a large barbarian invasion requiring either substantial reinforcements or an imperial expedition; to this incursion should be attributed the final abandonment of the Antonine Wall.[4]

But by 1974 a new formulation of the evidence—a redating of Samian ware—seems to have swept this scheme into the crowded archaeological charnel house which saves old theories from burial until it is time to re-examine their bones. We must now admit that the absence of pottery types datable to 165 or later seems to demand that the second Antonine phase be fitted within the short period 158–65. It would indeed be natural that once the Brigantes were pacified and Hadrian's Wall secured there should have been a return to Antonine policy and to the northern wall about 159–60, leaving the southern one with smaller or fewer 'maintenance' garrisons. About 162 Calpurnius Agricola was sent to Britain to meet a threatening situation; he may have decided that both walls could not function effectively without reinforcements, which were not to be forthcoming. Accordingly, in 163 the Antonine Wall was finally abandoned and Hadrian's Wall regarrisoned to be held together with outposts, the forts at Newstead and Birrens.

The events of 180–5 would be much as described in the alternative scheme, save that they ended not with occupation of the Antonine Wall but with the loss and abandonment of Newstead. In the 190s the Maeatae were again unsettled and there was destruction at Hadrian's Wall c. 197 or c. 205; the troubles of this latter period prompted the great Severan effort in the following years, conspicuously directed north of Forth, and perhaps at the re-establishment of the Antonine Wall as the frontier.[5]

The fact that Dio clearly understood both Maeatae and Caledonii to be amalgams of various separate peoples is, however, a noteworthy consequence of Roman policy and pressure, probably in the four decades before 207, when the governor sought to stabilise the northern frontier by alliances with and subsidies to native peoples. This policy would be to treat with the most powerful tribes and, through bribes and fear, to hold them responsible for the good

---

[4] This account of 150–207 is based on J. P. Gillam and J. C. Mann, 'The Northern British Frontier from Antoninus Pius to Caracalla', *Archaeologia Aeliana*[4], xlviii (1970), 1–44.

[5] This account attempts to summarise B. R. Hartley, 'The Roman Occupation of Scotland . . .' *Britannia*, iii (1972), 1–55 especially 36–42.

behaviour of their powerful neighbours. It is possible that the first steps were now taken towards the creation of a single Pictish kingdom uniting the peoples south of the Mounth under one war-lord. The name of Maeatae, a confederation of peoples unknown to Ptolemy and indeed unique to Dio Cassius in this Severan period, seems to occur in two Stirlingshire hill-names, suggesting that they were a people close to the Antonine Wall; but, perhaps as a confederation, the name applied to a much wider area, for instance, Fife or even Angus. It seems perverse therefore to refer to Hadrian's Wall the statement of Dio that they live 'close to the wall which divides the island into two parts, and the Caledonians next to them'[6] and the need to do so disappears if the wall meant here, the Antonine Wall, was being contrasted with the one 'separating them from the Roman garrisons', Hadrian's Wall.

This interpretation of Maeatae is to some extent confirmed by written accounts of Severan campaigns in Scotland between 208 and 211; the archaeological record, though scanty, is quite plain since it shows that the Lowlands and Southern Uplands were wholly ignored, neither Newstead nor any other fort being occupied, and that Severus established bases at Cramond and perhaps Inveresk on the Forth and at Carpow on the Tay, which must have been supplied by sea. The movements of the army are however plotted by two series of huge marching camps, one 63 acres (25 ha) in size, the other 165 acres (66 ha) south of Forth and 130 acres (52 ha) from Ardoch northwards, larger than any camps elsewhere in Britain and than most in the empire. The 63-acre series might be interpreted as an army marching by Kirkpatrick in Dumfriesshire possibly to Inveresk, then to Carpow on the south bank of the Tay. A small camp on the north bank establishes this as the site of the river crossing and must surely be connected with the imperial coins of Severus and Caracalla, showing, the former a permanent bridge, the latter a bridge of boats with the legend 'crossing' (*traiectus*). These coins, which have been dated to 208 or 209, certainly refer to the Scottish campaigns and one (or even both) of them to the crossing at Carpow. The route from Inveresk to Ardoch apparently went by the newly discovered camp at Craigarnhall on the Teith, and other camps suggest an army advancing from Ardoch to the Earn at Broomhill and thence down

---

[6] Watson, *Celtic Place Names*, 56. What follows was revised in the light of J. K. St Joseph, 'Air Reconnaissance in Roman Britain, 1969–72', *Journal of Roman Studies*, lxiii, 1973, 214–33, after this book had gone to the publisher.

that river to Carpow, across the Tay by bridge, down the Carse of Gowrie to Longforgan and north up the coastal plain by Kirkbuddo and Kinnell to Keithock in Angus. The return march to Ardoch is represented by camps at Marcus, Lunanhead, Eassie, Lintrose, Scone and Innerpeffray; only the camp at Auchtermuchty is not explained by this route of march. Since the 63-acre camps are earlier, but only slightly earlier than the 130-acre ones it is possible that in 209 the army was split into two commands under Severus and Caracalla and advanced, the former by a westerly route and fixed bridge over the Forth to Ardoch, the latter by an eastern route and ferry across the Forth to Fife, then by Auchtermuchty to Carpow. The two armies would then advance in parallel, Severus up Strathearn and Strathmore, Caracalla up the east-coast plain, returning by the same routes. Whichever view of the evidence is correct, this campaign involved a double penetration of Gowrie and Angus and must surely have been directed against the Maeatae and Caledonii.

The following year's campaign camps show a huge army advancing by Newstead, St Leonards, Channelkirk and Pathhead to the Forth (165 acre, 66 ha camps). Some forces were probably then deployed to control the Forth-Clyde gap but three-quarters of the army marched on, often in the footsteps of Agricola. From Ardoch 130-acre camps marking the stages of its march can be traced by Innerpeffray, Scone, Cardean, Oathlaw, Balmakewan in the south of the Mearns to Kair House. Although Dio Cassius writes of Severus advancing to the far north, where he made observations of the sun's height in summer and winter, the 110-acre camps from Kair House to Muiryfold are taken here to belong to Agricola's last campaign, and not to be Severan. Dio and Herodian tell of two campaigns: the first against the Caledonii, who yielded territory, the second, led by Caracalla owing to the illness of Severus, against the Maeatae, who had revolted. If, as seems likely, these belong to 209 and 210, then in 211 the Caledonii were again in arms when Severus died at York in February preparing to march against them. Since the 130-acre camps were constructed after the 63-acre camps, and since it is unlikely that the further enemy was attacked before the nearer one these narrative sources may be confused: it is suggested that the Maeatae were dealt with in 209 by Severus and his son, that in 210 Caracalla was unsuccessful against the northerly peoples, the Caledonii, and that a new expedition against them was planned for 211 which may have been carried through by Caracalla. There was now a permanent fort at Carpow which shows clear evidence of occupation by detachments from two legions at this time.

Unsatisfactory as our knowledge of these expeditions is, their results are not in doubt, for the third century, like the thirteenth, was predominantly peaceful on the northern frontier; the Romans withdrew again to Hadrian's Wall, as may always have been their intention, although the permanent forts at Cramond and Carpow built and abandoned in Severan times argue that it had once been hoped to hold at least some outposts to keep watch on the northern tribes. A system of defence in depth was created by putting garrisons in some forts (for example Birrens) immediately north of the Wall, beyond which *exploratores* or scouting parties maintained a careful watch over the Votadini (presumably Roman allies) and Selgovae (thought to have been reduced to client status). This peace was a vindication of the Severan invasion and indeed of the Hadrianic wall-line as instruments of Roman policy.

Early in the fourth century renewed troubles broke out in north Britain, leading to a repetition in 306 of the Severan campaign a century earlier. The emperor, Constantius and his son, Constantine, later emperor, advanced, according to the only account, to remote parts of Scotland, leaving traces, in pottery, only at Cramond and Carpow. It was a brief interlude, evidence that the Picts (for so they may now be called without challenge) were again anxious to plunder the riches of the province of Britain. From 360 the Picts and Scots from Ireland were actively ravaging the districts near the Wall and in 367 they swept over the Wall to plunder and bring disorder to much of the northern part of the province. Although there was some recovery by 369, the situation was not restored, since the forts beyond the Wall were abandoned and the character of occupation of the wall forts changed remarkably to become fortified villages held by militiamen (and their families). The Picts and Scots were again active in 382 and may be assumed to have continued so from this date until the final Roman withdrawal after rebellious commanders had stripped the province of its security in bids for the imperial purple—first Magnus Maximus between 383 and 388 then Constantine III in 407–11. As the empire struggled to restrain the barbarian incursions, it became less and less possible to attend to the problems of remote Britain, where, in these last decades of 'Roman' rule, the Picts are thought to have taken to seaborne attacks upon the richer southerly parts of the province, as the Scots were certainly making sea attacks on North Wales. About 400 the Wall was abandoned; in 410 the province was instructed to make shift for its own defence against the Saxons and northern barbarians and by 430 its 'civilisation' had so deteriorated that the use of coinage for trafficking was a thing of the past. Yet the local 'tyrants' who inherited Roman authority continued a form of Romanised life even in the towns and undertook the defence of that life by traditional Roman means. The most important of these, Vortigern, was responsible for the introduction and settlement of Saxons as *foederati* in vulnerable zones, to repel the Picts. Men of the Votadini under Cunedda were brought from Lothian to North Wales in order to contain the Irish settlers there. The most likely date for both these events is around 430 and by such measures the British were able to contain and repel the Picts.

The impact of Roman occupation, whether to Hadrian's or to Antonine's Wall, upon the native occupants of Scotland can be measured only in archaeological terms, for the comments of literary sources are too scarce and too Roman in bias to weigh heavily: what they assume may, however, be more trustworthy than what they say. Traces of one civilian settlement (*vicus*) attached to a Roman fort have been found in an inscription from the eastern end of the Antonine Wall, where there would be a port for landing sea-borne supplies. There is a scatter of material outside other forts which may represent nascent *vici*, but the long rectangular houses of stone or wood set end-on to a street, characteristics of civilian settlement beside a fort, have been found nowhere in Scotland—not even at Newstead which was for a period the nodal point of the Roman occupation. The only annexes to the Antonine Wall forts which have been discovered are those that contain a bath-house, at Old Kilpatrick, Balmuildy and now Bearsden.[7]

Undoubtedly in the regions which they occupied the Romans distrusted the independence which fortifications gave to the native peoples. Near to an Agricolan fort at Easter Happrew in Peeblesshire are a number of unfinished defences at existing or new hill-forts, while other such abandoned works lie close to Roman roads in the county. The coincidence is sufficiently marked to suggest that it was the arrival of Roman forces in the district which led to the beginning of these works and their intervention which caused the Selgovae to

---

[7] P. Salway, *Frontier People of Roman Britain* (1965), 155–64.

desist from them.[8] Other works in the Lowlands were slighted, notably the broch at Torwoodlee, which may represent an incursion of a war-band from the north or west in the first century and which was systematically dismantled by the Romans perhaps early in the second century. This site was in Selgovan territory, where hostility to Rome was harboured long: thus in the excavation of the hill-fort of Bonchester no Roman objects of any kind were discovered. In other hill-forts the ramparts were abandoned and encroached upon by the huts of (presumably) an increasing population. Finds of querns are relatively numerous and are to be linked with permanent fields which must be among the many undatable field systems numbered in surveys of the eastern border counties.

The evidence of trade is in random finds of Roman pottery, coins and other objects. A map of such finds from non-Roman sites in the first century shows a heavy concentration along the line of Dere Street in East Lothian and on or near the Upper Clyde, the territories of the Damnonii and Votadini, generally friendly to Rome. More northerly finds on the Teith, Earn, Tay and Don suggest that river valleys were then important native routes for trade from the coast. The second-century finds are much more numerous, and while their distribution is not dissimilar south of the Antonine Wall where the more valuable objects tend to be found, to the north the thickest cluster is in Strathmore and Strathtay and seems to imply overland trade, presumably under the protection of Roman arms. It has been suggested that the tribes for some distance north of the Antonine Wall were under a Roman protectorate even after the first abandonment of that wall, and it is possible that the Maeatae were a confederation first formed in clientage and not in opposition to Rome, coin-hoards in Fife, Kinross-shire and Angus the douceurs which retained their fidelity—for a time. With the third-century withdrawal trade certainly abated. This has been noted particularly in the south-west, where the evacuation of Roman garrisons 'deprived the Selgovae, the Novantae and the Damnonii of the opportunities which they had previously enjoyed for acquiring small quantities of Roman pottery'—a conclusion which might require to be revised in the light of further excavations.[9] Certainly in the east the large en-

[8] *Inventory of Peeblesshire*, 28.

[9] Richmond, *Roman and Native*, 101. See also the evidence and maps in A. Robertson, 'Roman Finds from Non-Roman Sites in Scotland', *Britannia*, i (1970), 198–226.

closed settlements, many overlying abandoned hill-forts, which were occupied in the second and third centuries, and latterly under the surveillance of the *exploratores*, represent communities of farmers and herdsmen living in society so peaceful and well-organised that political unity must have existed as well as treaty relationships with Rome.[10]

This was the territory of the Votadini with their tribal capital at Traprain, where successive fortifications are still in need of investigation but the importance of which was put beyond doubt by excavation early in this century; Traprain shows us how native life was affected by the coming of the Romans, whose civilisation, however remotely perceived, stimulated demands for manufactories. Examination of the finds there suggests, however, that there were phases of occupation one of which ran from the second half of the first century A.D. to the last quarter of the second, at which time (perhaps during the second occupation of the Antonine Wall) there seems to be a gap. Early in the third century, coincident with the Caracallan reorganisation of the Hadrian Wall frontier, the *oppidum* was again inhabited and so continued until the mid-fifth century, apart from a possible short break about 300. Despite a muddled excavation it has been possible to show that objects of characteristically Roman style, brooches, finger rings and swords, come from the lower (mainly second century) levels, along with harness-mountings, dress-fasteners, terrets (harness-rings) and clasps of native style sometimes under Roman influence. The upper (third to fifth century) levels yielded little that was Roman but much that was native or Romano-British in style. Imitation of Roman articles was limited to personal trinkets; tools and similar articles show only similarities to those of the Roman world. Swords and spears tell us that the Votadini were not disarmed by their Roman allies, sickles and ploughshares that they cultivated the ground in peaceful circumstances. Here, at the *oppidum* of a people who preserved a notable loyalty to Rome, was found a stone scratched with the first four letters of the alphabet—the earliest evidence of native literacy and a fragmentary indication that one important aspect of Roman civilisation was not utterly unknown to this people.

Perhaps the most interesting evidence of the impact of Roman civilisation is found in the remains of native metalwork discovered

[10] K. Steer, 'John Horsley and the Antonine Wall', *Archaeologia Aeliana*[4], xlii (1964), 1-21, especially valuable for maps.

in Kirkcudbrightshire, Roxburghshire and Berwickshire, two in cauldrons and all three probably votive offerings by Celtic peoples to the deity thought to dwell in the loch or pool in which each was deposited. Like other hoards, such as a first century collection deposited at Newstead, their character is peaceable, reflecting the farmers and craftsmen of the semi-Romanised province. Only one hoard, that from Carlingwark in Kirkcudbright, shows the presence of warriors (perhaps Novantian) in the tips of eight swords and fragments of chain mail. 'All else points to farmers, shepherds, peasants and the village blacksmith.'[11] Fragments of bridle and harness might come from a chariot-pony used in peaceful pursuits, iron tyres and a pole-tip could suit a farm cart, and the horse-bits look very utilitarian. These things belong to the native Celtic traditions as exemplified in hoards founds outside Scotland, as do the cauldrons in which they were found and which can be paralleled in Britain and Ireland and in Celtic metalwork on the continent. Among Roman elements is a scythe, an important innovation in British husbandry, a field anvil, sickles, and horseshoes. Improved heavy hammers, picks, axes and adzes can be attributed to the superior iron craftsmanship of the classical world, but smaller tools, chisels, gouges and saws are of forms common to the native (Celtic) and Roman worlds. Perhaps the most interesting items are two iron ploughshares from the eastern hoards comparable with others from Traprain and Oxnam, and to be contrasted with the (roughly contemporary) wooden stilt and head of a plough which would take a wooden share, discovered in the timber foundations of a crannog at Milton Loch in Kirkcudbrightshire.[12] The iron shares vary in shape but seem to represent native developments upon an innovation known to southern British Celts but brought north in the wake of the Romans. They may be associated with the groups of geometrical fields observed in upland parts of southern Scotland, fields whose length suggests the plough rather than the more primitive ard.[13] It would be dangerous to argue that iron-tipped ploughs were unknown in the south-west, but their absence from surviving evidence does suggest that they were less frequently used. We are entitled to conclude that

[11] S. Piggott, 'Three Metal-Work Hoards of the Roman Period', *Proc. Soc. Antiq. Sc.*, lxxxvii (1952-3), 1–50. The quotation is from p. 8.

[12] For an ard dated to *c.* 80 B.C. see *Tools and Tillage*, ii (1972), 64.

[13] A. Fenton, 'Early Cultivation Implements in Scotland', *Proc. Soc. Antiq. Sc.*, xcvi (1962-3), 269–76; C. M. Piggott, 'Milton Loch Crannog I', *Proc. Soc. Antiq. Sc.*, lxxxvii (1952-3), 134–51, esp. pp. 143-4.

the Romano-British peoples of south-east Scotland, the Votadini and some Selgovae, were under an incentive to innovate and to increase production in Roman times; while this stimulus may have been in part the presence (and market) of Roman troops, the Romans were not less active at least as far west as Annandale, yet do not seem to have stimulated much activity among the Novantae, whose crannogs (a form of lake-dwelling known also in Ireland) and ards suggest a scattered population of small farmers. It may be concluded that trade on the east, slight though it may have been by thirteenth-century standards, was sufficient to stimulate increased production and hence innovation both by coastal craft and up the length of Dere Street. A surviving list derived probably from the third and fourth century names eight *loca* in Britain—meeting-places, perhaps of tribes under Roman protection, but certainly also places for trafficking during the *pax Romana*. Three are unidentified, but *Maponi* is probably the Clochmabenstane near the Solway as well as the name of a tribal deity, *Taba* is related to the Tay, *Manavi* probably Clackmannan (another 'tribal' stone) and *Segloes* and *Dannoni* should be found among the Selgovae and Damnonii.[14] The others, *Mixa, Panovius, Minox*, may have lain among the Votadini; more probably the Romans placed no restrictions upon gatherings of, and commerce with, the latter, and hence designated no *loca*. From whichever source we take our evidence, the contrast between the pre-Roman Iron Age and the period of Roman occupation is marked; archaeology suggests advances in techniques especially of cultivation and transport, and if they are securely dated the multiplying settlement sites indicate increases in the population, and their fields and cattle-pounds show increases in production. With the Roman occupation we are already in presence of that demographic and economic expansion which continued unevenly and with at least one major setback until the explosion of the mid-eighteenth century.

Whereas in Ireland a later generation committed to parchment the 'laws' and the cycles of tales of the heroic age of Irish society (corresponding in part to the Roman occupation of Britain), there are almost no remains of the same period from Scotland, either Pictish or British. The stone heads which represent the head-hunting of Gaul and Ireland (the head was seat of the soul), the sacred groves and the priestly caste of druids, these can be shown to have existed in southern Britain, but there is scant trace of them in Scotland. That

14 Richmond, *Roman and Native*, 148, 155.

the gods of Celtic and of proto-Pictish tribes dwelt in Scotland as elsewhere in lochs and springs is attested by the recovery of votive offerings from these as well as the carrying-over of their cult into Christian times, at the many St Ninian's or Ringan's Wells in Scotland. The existence of sacred groves common to the Celtic world may be deduced from the name Medionemeton ('middle sanctuary'), to be placed near the Antonine Wall (Cairnpapple has been suggested), but there are no certain temples of Celtic deities from Scotland. Something much simpler has been identified in Glenlyon, a small stone shrine no more than three feet (1 m) high with a range of cult-objects like petrified bollards in front; until the present century this shrine was regularly thatched and unthatched, a ritual which can be paralleled in literature in ancient Gaul and Ireland. A small wooden female figure recovered from the peat at Ballachulish in Argyll was accompanied by wickerwork which may have been the shrine of this goddess carved in a sacred wood. A cult object common to the Celtic world was the severed head represented in different ways; the most sophisticated is as three faces carved on a stone ball, of which one example may possibly come from Sutherland, but archaeology has produced few examples of the human head in Scotland, even when examples on metalwork are taken into account. On the other hand folk-tales show its persistence among Gaelic-speaking peasantry until this century. Associated with the 'well of the head' or 'heads' (*Tobar a' Chinn, nan Ceann*) in the Gaidhealtachd—the area in which Gaelic speech persisted until, say, the seventeenth century—are tales which seek to explain the deeply rooted traditional association of severed heads with sacred waters. We are right to be sceptical of the form which these tales now take but wrong if we dismiss the survival of archaic cults under their guise, which is fully attested in the richer archaeology and early literature of Ireland.

The cult of a horned god (Cernunnos), representations of which show a human but antlered head, was fairly widespread in Britain. As a god of aggressiveness and fertility he has turned up in two representations at Cramond in Midlothian, in one, of uncertain origins, at nearby Blackness, and as a stone head mutilated of its horns, recently discovered near Perth. As late as the eighth century a Pictish stone at Meigle, on the borders of Angus, seems to carry a representation of this god even in a Christian context. The argument that Ptolemy's Cornavii in Caithness are 'people of the horn' rather than 'promontory dwellers' carries less conviction. The goddesses of the Celts who in various guises—Medb, Macha, Brigit—pervade Irish heroic literature, must also have been known in Scotland. A single representation of a conventional trio of goddesses may have come ultimately from the fort at Cramond. The crude wooden goddess-figure from Ballachulish is the ancestress of the old hag of many Gaelic folk-tales, Queen Mab, surviving into the nineteenth or twentieth century.

No doubt Celtic religion was a matter of propitiating gods and goddesses whose control of natural forces ensured or withheld fertility and good times. The names of these deities probably varied from one tribe to another: thus Ptolemy's Epidii in Kintyre are the 'horse-people'; it may be taken as a measure of the archaism of such a region that the name MacEachern, 'son of a horse-lord,' is still common in Kintyre today. And while we may not import holus-bolus to Scotland the ideas found in the literature of the Irish heroic age, we may surely accept that there were tribal gods and that their relationship to the people and the times was the responsibility of the tribal king, descended from the eponymous tribal god and bringing fertility and well-being to the tribe if correctly chosen.

What tribes and kings (or kingdoms) did the Romans leave behind to the north of Hadrian's Wall when it was finally abandoned about A.D. 400? The Votadini, certainly, in the east, still occupying Traprain Law until the mid-fifth century; during this final occupancy a hoard of silver objects cut and hammered to reduce their bulk and perhaps prepare them for the melting pot was buried within the hill-fort, a dramatic illustration of the wealth upon which a Roman client tribe might lay hands. It has been suggested[15] that this cannot be loot, but must be a payment from a Roman governor for continued clientage or to pay mercenaries, but there seems no more compelling reason to accept this than any other intrepretation. A buried hoard means troubled times and this one fits the early or middle fifth century, after the Roman withdrawal, in that as in most other respects. The Votadini must have abandoned Traprain, and concentrated upon Din Eidyn, Edinburgh, and perhaps upon Stirling also, during the fifth century. A Pictish symbol stone of the earliest category, with no Christian symbolism, was discovered at Edinburgh and suggests an occupation, perhaps as early as the period of Pictish pressure and Roman withdrawal about 400. (There is general reluctance to date the symbol stones as early as this—but dating

15 Alcock, *Arthur's Britain*, 254.

evidence for them is really non-existent and there is scarcely any opportunity for Pictish occupation later than the fifth century.) Probably we should envisage the north-west frontier of the Votadini as a fluctuating one in the fourth and fifth centuries. This is certainly implied by the only native literary source for this period, Gildas, who tells of two repulses of the Picts and Scots by the Britons before the introduction of Saxon mercenaries by a British 'tyrant'.

There was also a British kingdom, descending from the Novantae, in the south-west; the genealogy of its kings is thought to be one of those which stem from Magnus Maximus, who sought to become Emperor in 383 and who may have established a line of kings or 'tyrants' in Galloway, later the rulers of 'Rheged' whose name is preserved in Dunragit. There was almost certainly such a line in the lower reaches of the Clyde at Ail Cluaide, Dumbarton, ruling over Damnonii.

Beyond these British peoples lay the Picts, occupying for the most part the lowland zone and river valleys in the east, but presumably also peopling the Western and Northern Isles. The name Maeatae disappears, until mentioned by Adamnan in the seventh century, but at the end of the third century Eumenius refers to the 'Caledones and other Picts' while about 360 Ammianus Marcellinus informs us that the Picts were divided into two peoples (*gentes*), Dicalydones and Verturiones, in whom we may recognise northern and southern groups respectively. The name 'Picts' has not been satisfactorily explained though no one questions that it describes the Maeatae, the Caledonii and the peoples of Ptolemy's description. It may be quite simply the Latin word *picti*, painted people, with references to a practice of tattooing; but there was probably also a native word resembling 'Pict' which made the Latin form particularly appropriate. The evidence is slight and contentious and we had best leave it at an understanding that the people had been there for a millennium when, in 297, Eumenius first used the name 'Pict', and that by the departure of the Romans they were divided into two principal groups.

The evidence does not allow us to see the degree of political sophistication with which these peoples tackled the Roman departure. The use of 'tyrants' rather than 'kings' has been held to imply a response within the British area to the departure of imperial authority, whereby men of rank and ability to whom Rome had accorded recognition now took over or revived tribal kingships to which they were not entitled by descent. Certainly the southern Britons between *c.* 400 and *c.* 450 regarded themselves as Romans, and there is reason to think that the Christianising of the country-side proceeded more quickly after the Roman departure than before, because of the decay of town life, with which Christianity had been too closely identified.

Within one year of the complete toleration of Christianity in the empire, the bishops of three of the four provincial capitals in Britain attended a church council at Arles (314). Thus fourth-century Britain knew territorial bishops, overseers of the clergy, and it has been persuasively argued that with the new northern province of Valentia, at the end of that century, a bishop also had his seat in Carlisle. A map of non-portable Christian objects from Roman Britain shows a fair concentration around Carlisle to confirm this conjecture. How and when Christianity was taken beyond the Wall and into Scotland is another matter. Writing in the early eighth cen-tury at Jarrow, the Anglian Bede knew something of one part of the story, that part associated with the see which later became Anglian:

> The southern Picts who live on this side of the mountains had, it is said, long ago given up the error of idolatry and received the true faith through the preaching of the Word by that reverend and saintly man Bishop Nynia, a Briton by birth, who had received orthodox instruction at Rome in the faith and mystery of the truth. His episcopal see is distinguished by the name and church of St Martin the bishop, and there his body lies along with those of many saints; this see now belongs to the English race. This place, belonging to the province of the Berni-ceans, is commonly called 'at the white house' inasmuch as he built there a church of stone in a manner unusual among the Britons.[16]

What reliance may be placed upon this distant version of events which themselves bear no date has been intensively debated over the past half century. Our immediate concern is with Nynia's kirk at Whithorn, which by the eighth century was dedicated to St Martin; Bede does not make Nynia builder of the first kirk there nor call him the first bishop, and there is a measure of agreement that Nynia came to a church and see already in existence.[17] Material evidence for such a conclusion comes from the memorial stone to Latinus and his daughter erected near the kirk of Whithorn by the middle of the fifth century (on the epigraphic evidence) and from a stone of similar date from nearby Kirkmadrine to 'the holy and eminent priests (*or*

[16] Bede, *Hist. Eccles.,* ed. Colgrave and Mynors, 222.
[17] This is rejected by R. P. C. Hanson, *St Patrick*, 56–63.

*perhaps* bishops) Ides Viventius and Mavorius',[18] while archaeology has revealed the existence of burials which are likely to be Christian below those of the Middle Ages and under the site of the Anglian kirk at Whithorn. It is likely that a group of Christians among the Novantae in Galloway had asked for a bishop in the last century of Roman rule.

But Nynia himself is generally dated to the first half of the fifth century; that date may rest as the best we have. The fact that his mission was to the Picts and not to Galloway creates a presumption that the British peoples of southern Scotland were already Christian. The evidence is largely circumstantial but the case is quite strong. Thus if the Angles later took over the see of Whithorn there is a case for regarding their see of Abercorn on the Forth as formerly British, for the British name of the place was also preserved and nearby Kirkliston has yielded an early memorial stone (the 'Catstane') to Vetta son of Victus as well as an early cemetery of Christian type. Also there are many long-cist burial sites, oriented east-west, in the Lothians, which are probably evidence of early Christianity. Similarly Melrose, site of an Anglian monastery, preserved its British name, while a number of sixth- or seventh-century memorial stones are known in the Tweed valley, two at Peebles alone, of which one was a memorial to a bishop.[19] Finally, the bishop, Kentigern, to whom a later generation attributed the founding of the kirk of Glasgow, and much else that was fabulous besides, was probably the Kentigern who died in 612; he was certainly a bishop at Glasgow and may have been the first, but the Britons of Strathclyde were already Christian when St Patrick upbraided their king Ceretic for his evil ways in the mid-fifth century.[20] Of the many possible early homes for St Patrick with his decurion father, Strathclyde seems to fit the sources best; as its ruler, Ceretic had been responsible for a massacre and for selling Christians into captivity among the Scots and Picts, thereby making himself and his men *socii Scottorum atque Pictorum apostatorumque*. In another place Patrick repeats the same epithet: 'apostate Picts', which must surely be taken as evi-

---

[18] J. Wall, 'Christian evidences in the Roman Period', *Archaeologia Aeliana*[4], xliii (1965), 208–11.

[19] K. Steer, 'Two unrecorded early Christian Stones', *Proc. Soc. Antiq. Sc.*, ci (1968–9), 127-9.

[20] A. C. Thomas, 'The Evidence from North Britain', in *Christianity in Britain, 300–700*, ed. M. W. Barley and R. P. C. Hanson; A. C. Thomas, *Early Christian Archaeology of North Britain*, chapter 2.

dence confirmatory of Bede's account of Nynia—that he had converted the southern Picts, that is some of those south of the Mounth.[21]

The degree of continuity between Roman and sub-Roman (that is, fifth- and sixth-century) north Britain is a complex subject which can be assessed only as an incidental to the degree of continuity in south Britain. Some have argued for a very limited Christian influence and pointed to restored pagan places of worship in the fourth century as an indication of ineffective Christianity; but it is arguable that Christianity and Mithraism (whose enemies are secularism and indifference) would flourish and decline in the same circumstances, and therefore that Christians increased in numbers and multiplied their churches and bishops. A good case has been made for the spread of episcopal organisation into southern Scotland and not only to Whithorn in sub-Roman times; but Christian memorial stones do not turn up in Pictland and there must be great caution in the use of the dedications of kirks as evidence for a proselytising saint.

On the other hand the distribution of early long-cist cemeteries, thickly in the Lothians (the territory of the Votadini), scattered round the Fife coast, one at Perth and three near Dundee, is suggestive of the spread of early Christianity.[22] Moreover the vulgar Latin word for a church, *eclesia*, taken into Primitive Welsh and Cumbric as *egles* is thought to have the significance of a very early church when preserved as a modern 'Eccles' place-name.[23] The distribution of these names has recently been plotted and corresponds remarkably to that of long-cist cemeteries, though with an extension into northern Angus.[24] The kirk in whose parish Stirling lay before the establishment of the burgh kirk, appears early as Eccles and is therefore the one dedication to St Ninian most likely to be ancient; since the rock of Stirling was probably a sub-Roman tribal *oppidum* the placing of a kirk at a distance of one and a half miles (two km) from it is suggestive of the cautious acceptance of a new religion by a

[21] Hanson, *St Patrick*, 22–5, 107–8, 112–9.

[22] See map in *Christianity in Britain, 300–700*, ed. Barley and Hanson, 107, and discussion in A. C. Thomas, *Early Christian Archaeology of North Britain*, chapter 3.

[23] Another word for a cult centre, *annat*, requires further investigation as a place name as well as archaeologically. Such an investigation appeared in *Scottish Studies*, xvii (1973), when the present volume was in the press.

[24] Barrow, *Kingdom of the Scots*, 62.

tribal king, who in the fifth century could well have been Pictish. We may therefore accept a Christianising of the southern Picts in Fife and Angus by the mission of Nynia in the fifth century. We have no means of assessing the spiritual value of that Christianising, for it has left no recognised kirks or hermitages, and no saints' lives unless there be some grains of truth in the dross of late medieval lives of Saints Nynia, Kentigern and Serf (of Culross and Loch Leven). Of one thing we can be fairly certain: Christianity made scant difference to the wars among the rival tribes and peoples on whom the Scots and the Angles were already preying in the fifth and sixth centuries respectively.

# 3

# THE AGE OF MIGRATIONS, 500–800

The critical evaluation of sources for early Scottish history is nowhere more difficult than in the annals, genealogies and and lawbooks written in medieval Ireland, for the most part long after the period to which they purport to refer and in a vernacular the use of which marks off Insular culture as profoundly different from the rest of western learning. In this field much is speculative and must remain so because the sources are cryptically brief and allusive. Archaeological studies are sometimes unable to distinguish between earlier Iron Age sites and later (dark age) occupations; Gaelic place-name studies, much less systematic (in their published form) than English, are similarly limited. In consequence the historian of Dal Riata, like the historian of England fifty years ago, still relies essentially upon literary sources and must give an account circumscribed by those limitations.

Primitive annals whether from Wessex or Iona—and the earliest 'Irish' annals were written at Iona between c. 563 and c. 740—deal with the leaders of the peoples, *cenéla,* who made up Dal Riata, a name now for the kingdom but in early sources for the people themselves. The foundation of the small Irish kingdom of that name on the coast of Antrim took place possibly as a consequence of the expansion of another Irish family confederation, which indeed may also explain the migration of Dal Riata to Kintyre and Argyll during the fifth century. Bede calls their leader Reuda, and there is fragmentary Irish evidence to suggest an origin legend which made Cairpre Riata, ten generations or so earlier than c. 500, the leader under whom the Dal Riata came to Scotland. If that suggests an impossibly early date, the traditional date of c. 501 is, however, probably too late. It was believed later that a ruler of Dal Riata in

Ireland, Fergus son of Erc, descended from Nes (perhaps a river goddess), also established his authority over Riata (or a part thereof) in Scotland and that he died in 501.

But the tenth century version (*Senchus fer nAlban*) of a probably seventh century treatise which tells us of these *cenéla* tells also of the *Cenél Loairn* and *Cenél nOengusa*, whose territories are to be placed respectively in Lorn (by implication) and Islay (explicitly); the ancestors of these kins, Loarn and Oengus, are said also to be the sons of Erc, and Dal Riata is thus provided with a neat tripartite division. There are good reasons for rejecting this relationship as a late invention and for regarding these two *cenéla* as ruling kindreds from an earlier migration of Dal Riata to Scotland; the *Cenél nOengusa* at least seems to be found in Ireland before the time of Fergus, who, on this view, cannot have been the first of the Dal Riata to conquer Kintyre. However, it is not possible to show which kindred preceded him there, nor when the Scots first occupied that land. A contemporary of St Patrick (of whose dates no historian east of Dublin will claim certain knowledge; current fashion favours putting his death *c.* 485–500), Fergus perhaps came to Scotland only shortly before his death; his son died *c.* 507 and was succeeded by Fergus's two grandsons in succession, Comgall who died after a peaceable reign about 537–8, and Gabrán twenty years later. The kindred of these two men are known in the eighth century, when the *Cenél Comgaill*, giving their name to Cowal, where they were the ruling kindred, emerge probably as a result of the declining power of the *Cenél nGábrain*, who are placed in the seventh century in Cowal and Kintyre. The fact that Fergus's son is referred to as 'of Kintyre' is strong evidence that this was the region reduced to obedience by Fergus and that his son and grandsons rapidly extended into Cowal and Arran, bringing Dal Riata into contact not only with the Picts but also with the British kingdom of Dumbarton.

In the annals which represent the lost chronicle of Iona, no fewer than twenty-four sieges or other events connected with fortresses are mentioned between the years 638 and 740. Thus it is known that in this period the *Cenél nGábrain* had fortified duns at Dunaverty and Tarbert, the *Cenél Loairn* at Dunollie and Dunadd; these duns were clearly constructed by and for powerful warriors and represent the hold of aristocratic chieftains of Scottish Dal Riata over the surrounding territory, from which they drew tribute and beyond which they led raiding parties. Nonetheless the *Cenél nGábrain*, perhaps because they were kings of Irish Dal Riata, were also accepted as kings in Scottish Dal Riata during the sixth century. The effect of this relationship on the other *cenéla* can only be surmised, but Adamnan (seventh century author of a life of Columba) suggests that in Columba's time this kingship was not a transient war overlordship. Gabrán already had a link (now obscure) with a British principality when he died in the same year as a defeat of the Dal Riata by Picts under King Brudei, a defeat which may explain why his successor Conall, son of Comgall, gave Iona to Columba in 563. It is likely that Conall was acting as overlord or over-king of Dal Riata, since Iona surely lay in the territory of the *Cenél Loairn*.

The succession of Aedan, son of Gabran, in 574 was represented by Adamnan as the work of a reluctant Columba; Aedan may have been a refugee from Dal Riata, carving out for himself a principality on the Forth which included Aberfoyle. One of his sons, Gartnait, became a king of the Picts, implying a Pictish mother; another son or grandson was called Artur, a name drawn from the same eastern milieu. It looks, therefore, as if Aedan came back to Dal Riata from the east by strength of arms in 574, a possibility which would explain why in the following year Aedan with nobles and clergy, including Columba, met a neighbouring Irish king at Druim Cett (County Derry) to regulate the position of the Irish Dal Riata. Aedan yielded the right to their 'expedition and hosting' by land but kept their tribute and ship service, an agreement which may indicate both the new strength of Aedan in Ireland and a shift in the power of Dal Riata to Scotland.[1] Aedan's expeditions to Orkney in 580–1 and to Man (or possibly Manau on the Forth) in 582–3 show the aggressive purposes of his ship service, but on land Aedan was no less a war leader. That he fought for a considerable period against the Picts seems clear, for various sources record a victory over the Miathi (perhaps in the region of Stirling), and a defeat in Circinn (north of Tay).[2] In the light of these wide activities Aedan becomes an aggressive warrior-king, whose aims are more likely to have been booty and tribute than the conquest of territory; his wars against the Angles (in which historians have professed surprise that he was not allied

---

[1] J. Bannerman, 'The Convention of Druim Cett,' *Scottish Gaelic Studies*, xi (1966), 114–32; F. J. Byrne, *Irish Kings and High Kings* (1973), 110–11; Anderson, *Kings and Kingship*, 147–9.

[2] Dr M. O. Anderson discounts the last-named (*King and Kingship*, 36–7, 146).

with the British) were not part of a delicate balancing of power among the peoples of Scotland but similarly predatory. Two such expeditions are known, one about 598 in which two of Aedan's sons were killed, the other in 604 which ended in defeat at 'Degsastan' somewhere in Northumbria. Aedan suffered the fate of others who stumble in a freebooting career: he died in his seventies in 608 and there are good (though not conclusive) reasons for thinking that he was no longer king at the time. Behind Adamnan's pious Aedan consecrated by Columba's hand lies a tough opportunist, enemy of all his neighbours and master of most of them.[3]

This example of the reign of one of the kings (perhaps the best recorded) of Dal Riata may explain sufficiently the view taken here that they differed little from the barbarian Teutonic rulers of sub-Roman Europe in aims or conduct. As with the other kings they seemed much less aware of the racial origins of their opponents (and, occasionally, allies) than were later commentators; their restlessness represents a constant search for the movable wealth through which a truly 'heroic' king maintained his reputation as a generous giver and hence his authority among the warrior class of his own kingdom. Aedan's successors do not depart from this category. His grandson, Domnal Brecc (c. 629–c. 643), fought in five battles, the first two in Ireland and apparently leading to the eclipse of the Dal Riata there; of three defeats in Scotland, two were at unidentified places, it has been surmised in war against the Picts, the third in Strathcarron c. 643, when Domnall Brecc fought Owen, King of the Britons ('great sturdy men') of Dumbarton: 'I saw an array, they came from Kintyre, and splendidly they bore themselves around the conflagration . . . I saw great sturdy men, they came with dawn. And the head of Dyfnwal Frych (Domnall Brecc), ravens gnawed it.'

After this date the eclipse of the *Cenél nGabráin* and of Dal Riata as an aggressive power seems complete, even if temporary. For a century until 740 the annals seem to concern themselves with the internal wars of the *Cenél nGabráin* and *Loairn,* referring more frequently to the latter than to the former, who in their weakness were recognised as two cenéla: *nGabráin* and *Comgaill.* It is possible to rationalise some of the confusion of these years into individual

[3] For an early legend of Aedan and the kings of Dal Riata see P. MacCana, 'The Theme of King and Goddess in Irish Literature,' *Études Celtiques,* vii (1955–6), 382–412.

reigns in Dal Riata, and by the eleventh century this had been done.[4] Contemporary sources however show that, for example, in 678 the *Cenél Loairn* were heavily defeated by the Britons, and it therefore seems unlikely that their leader, Ferchar Fota, ruled Dal Riata until his death in 697. During these twenty years 'Dun Fother' was besieged twice, Dundurn and Dunadd once each, and Donollie was burned. Although the identification of 'Dun Fother' with Dunnottar has been generally accepted it seems geographically improbable that these sieges had anything to do with the internal turbulence of Dal Riata between 680 and 740, when Dunaverty was besieged also and Tarbert twice burned. During this period it must be doubted whether there was a line of recognised kings of Dal Riata: thus Selbach of the *Cenél Loairn* was defeated in 719 by the *Cenél nGabráin*, whose ruler, described as 'king of Kintyre', died in 721; Selbach, 'king of Dal Riata', himself entered a monastery in 723, a description which, if meaningful, implies that he had established authority over the other *tuatha*; this need not have lasted long in the hands of his successor, and indeed this is the period when Pictish kings seem to obtain an interest in Dal Riata.

Careful analysis of the relationships of these early kings has suggested that by *c.* 700 the three *cenéla* of the *Senchus* had dissolved into at least seven families, each lording it over a territory: Kintyre, Cowal, Mid-Argyll, Islay and three divisions of Lorn. Almost certainly the contemporary name for these territories would be that used for the smallest political unit in Ireland, *tuath*, and the ruler of each would be 'king'. The king was chosen from the eligible descendants in the male line of the preceding king, his *derbfine* or 'certain family', as wide as the first cousins in each generation back to the common great-grandfather, not by some dark-age Representation of the People Act but as the outcome of faction fights.[5] This would be even truer of an over-king (*ri tuath*), whether of Ulster or Dal Riata, than of a tribal king (*ri tuaithe*), for example of Kintyre, where the territorial unit was small enough for orderly succession by brother or cousin to take place. Yet even among the kings of Dal Riata there is only one exception to the rule that each in the list was son of an earlier king, not usually his immediate predecessor,

---

[4] I am here following Dr J. Bannerman in *Celtica*, ix, 256–7. For another and more detailed description see Anderson, *Kings and Kingship*, 155–7. She dates the rise of *Cenél Loairn* a little later.

[5] Byrne, *Irish Kings and High Kings*, 36–7, 122–3; Anderson, *Kings and Kingship*, 164.

until at the end of the seventh century the *Cenél Loairn* compete to become *ri tuath*.

The reaction of the Picts to Scottish settlement in Dal Riata must have been hostile, but Pictish 'narrative' history does not exist until the late sixth century, from which date, for over a century, valuable indications are given by Bede. Unfortunately, he contradicts the Scottish evidence that Columba received Iona from a king of Dal Riata by stating that he received it from Brudei, king of the Picts, at best an improbable statement even if Brudei was overlord of Dal Riata. Bede had seen a Pictish king accept the Roman Easter and expel Columban monks; it perhaps suited his critical attitude to Iona (on the Easter issue) to believe that the Picts had authority there. In other words, it is well to be sceptical about a Pictish Iona in '565'.

Adamnan, writing late in the seventh century, is quite clear that the 'spine of Britain', Drumalban, was the boundary between Pict and Scot, and this geographical feature, of varying width but general inhospitability, is a likelier boundary than any line which might now be drawn upon a map. It leaves us uncertain how far north the Scots settled, but Adamnan's tale of the aged chief of the 'cohort' of Geon who came to Columba on Skye and was converted through an interpreter seems to place that island in Pictish hands, a suggestion which accords with the presence of symbol stones there and in Benbecula.

Adamnan, too, knows King Brudei, describing his hill-fort near the river Ness, with wooden doors which could be barred, in which he held the hostages of a 'kinglet' of the Orkneys then visiting him. But Adamnan, who refers several times to the 'province' of the Picts and calls Brudei only 'king', describes in his first chapter a miracle performed by Columba on his return from staying *in regione Pictorum* and a second miracle (while staying in the same *regio*) before King Brudei and his familiars. The word *regio*, kingdom, is Adamnan's synonym, used only in this chapter, for *provincia*, and suggests that he saw Pictland as similar to the loose federations of petty tribes (*tuatha*), each with its client king, which made up the provinces of Ireland. Each province had an over-king as high king who was also the king of a *tuath*; this over-kingship tended to stay in the hands of the kingly family of one *tuath*.[6] Such a view is not

---

[6] The number of provinces, traditionally five (Ulster, Munster, Leinster, Connacht, Meath) in fact varied somewhat. There was no high king of Ireland till much later.

contradicted by Bede, for whom Brudei was 'a most powerful king, reigning over (? the) Picts'.[7] In stating that Columba came to the 'provinces' of the northern Picts, the Picts of southern 'regions' being already Christian, Bede uses 'province' and 'region' differently from Adamnan to mean a lesser unit, perhaps a *tuath*, as elsewhere he writes of the province of Bernicians and the province of Deirans among the people (*gens*) of Northumbrians.[8] It is likely that Brudei was over-king of northern Picts only, for a kingdom would follow the faith of its king; this view of the situation *c.* 600 is confirmed by a king-list and annal which tell of Galam Cennelath, king of Picts, who died in Brudei's time and was presumably over-king of southern Pictish provinces.[9] Bede describes the Mounth as dividing northern from southern Picts, and as late as 782 an annal refers to a 'King of the Picts on this side of the Mounth'.

Yet the king-list gives for the most part one king at a time, showing occasional 'joint' reigns. In 710, according to Bede, Nechtan mac Derile ruled 'all the provinces of the Picts', and the same author tells us how the Picts chose their king,[10] but the sieges of Dun Fother in annals for 681 and 694 are most likely to have occurred in the course of struggles between north and south for the over-kingship of the Picts. A northern and southern over-king may have been usual in the sixth century, but in Bede's lifetime there was only one over-king and exceptions to this were unusual but not unknown thereafter. Probably more important than the over-king or kings were the kings of provinces and tribes.

The list of Pictish kings, which in its surviving form is not earlier than the tenth century, gives the usual eponymous tale of a founder Cruithne[11] whose seven sons Fib (Fife), Fidach (? Moray), Fotlaig (Atholl), Fortriu (Strathearn), Caitt (Caithness), Ce (Mar and Buchan), Circinn (Angus and Mearns) undoubtedly represent provincial names, three of which, Fotlaig, Fortriu and Circinn, are mentioned in annals between 600 and 750. The identifications suggested are of varying certainty, but only the second name is placed by elimination, in Moray. The antiquity of these names cannot be doubted, though only Fortriu is identifiable with a name

[7] The preposition 'over' in English may mislead: *regnante Pictis... rege potentissimo.*
[8] Bede, *Hist. Eccles.*, eds. Colgrave and Mynors, 222, 188.
[9] M. O. Anderson, *Kings and Kingship*, 91, 116, 130.
[10] *regem sibi eligerint*, Bede, *Hist. Eccles.*, eds. Colgrave and Mynors, 552, 18.
[11] The Irish word for Pict.

among Ammianus Marcellinus' peoples, the Verturiones. But they are alliterative and therefore arouse the suspicion that other non-alliterating names such as *Orci (of the Orkneys) have been ignored; seven sons and seven provinces is later mythologising of the kind which gave Ireland five provinces. Behind the myth lies a larger number of peoples and provinces each at some stage with its own king, gradually brought into obedience by a neighbour and perhaps by 600 paying tribute to one of two over-kings, northern or southern, who would himself be king of a people and province.[12] From 692 kings of Fortriu occupied a dominant position among the Picts and usually held the over-kingship, though the years 724–34 were marked by a bloody conflict in which the kings of other provinces probably sought the over-kingship.[13] The victor was Oengus mac Fergus, who even as late at 739 destroyed the king of Atholl.

Bede's statement that *when in doubt* the Picts of his day chose their king 'rather from the female stock of kings than from the male' is another example of Bede's inadequate understanding of Pictish history, since matrilineal succession was not occasional but regular. The origins of this matrilineal kin group, which in the whole of Europe is peculiar to Pictland and thought to be non-Indo-European, must be very remote; it has been presumed that it gave a right to kingship to the sons of a mother, and in the next generation, to the sons of their sisters. Certainly the king-list shows a man succeeding his brother, as his mother's son, but never his father; and only late in Pictish history is there a possible case of father and son as kings and even then not in direct succession. But it has also been shown that there is a striking contast between the fathers' names, which are nearly all different, and the kings' names: thirty-four kings share only fourteen names. These fourteen names are certainly held by others than kings; thus Talorcan was the name of three contemporaries of Oengus mac Fergus in the 730s: his brother; Talorcan son of Drostan, king of Atholl, whom Oengus drowned; and Talorcan, son of Congus, probably a Dalriadan defeated by Oengus's son Brudei and drowned by Oengus. Talorcan and Oengus were the names of Pictish kings after but not before Oengus mac Fergus and must surely represent a new stock from whom kings were chosen, but linked to the older stock of kings, as the name Brudei (given to

---

[12] On this see Anderson, *Kings and Kingship*.
[13] Cf. M. O. Anderson, *King and Kingship*, 176–83, which prefers a genealogical explanation.

Oengus's brother and son) shows. These names are also evidence of a few lineages, or even a single lineage,[14] decending through females, but choosing names for sons from a small stock of 'royal' names; it is also evidence of marriage outside these kin-groups (or this kin-group). Pictish exogamy has been much debated and is not acceptable to all scholars, but there are enough instances of Pictish kings with non-Pictish fathers to show that the custom must have had some force. These customs, however, gave only a right to claim, and kingship must have passed from one to another by might in most instances. This is not the view presented by Bede, whose Pictish 'choice' in 'doubt' is a bold effort to rationalise his own puzzlement at the working of the system, but it is certainly the view suggested by the annals and, so far as reliable, the king list.

Moreover, it is in accord with material evidence, which in the case of the Picts is the only cultural relic left to us. The symbol stones of Pictland are the most striking of that evidence; they are not readily classified, much less easily understood. The earliest group consists of rough or simply-shaped stones upon which symbols have been incised in line; the stone does not bear a cross nor any other unequivocally Christian device. The second class is of slabs usually well shaped, bearing a cross on one face and, almost always on the other, the symbols; the representation is in relief not line. The symbols themselves are usually found in combinations of two, three (most common), or four, and while the beasts and birds found in many cases are obvious enough, and other symbols such as mirror and comb reasonably certain, there remain symbols the interpretation of which is more controversial. Two symbols, the V and Z rods, are frequently delineated over another symbol such as a crescent or a 'pair of spectacles'; these rods have been persuasively shown to be a broken arrow and spear respectively, representing a dead (because broken) warrior, perhaps from social groups conventionally associated with arrow and spear. Other symbols are by the same argument objects seen from above—a cauldron with handles through which is passed a carrying rod, a wheeled chariot with two ponies. Where the symbol can be so identified, the object which it represents seems to come from the armaments of an earlier, apparently first century, date. By this argument (and it is not accepted generally, though no better seems to be in the field) the symbol stones are monumental versions of designs which for some four or five hundred

[14] As Dr M. O. Anderson has assumed.

years must have been transmitted in perishable materials, or in tattooing, for the link between first and sixth century is not otherwise obvious.[15]

The stones are often associated with burial grounds and in one view marked the burials, or at least the cenotaphs, clearly of important persons. Class I stones were erected by the eighth century, but how much earlier and whether in pre-Christian times is in dispute. The sixth century seems too early a date for some students, but with the support of others it may be allowed to stand. The statements which the stones seek to make remain cryptic. The animal symbols do not fall into territorial groupings such as their use as tribal-totems would require. On the other hand, the bull is found carved on several small loose stones at Burghead fort in Moray, the boar on a rock at Dunadd in Dal Riata. Animal symbols may represent not a tribe nor a province, but an ancestry, the animal deity with whom the ancestor of the person commemorated is associated. Other symbols represent, it is suggested, the status or position of the commemorated; the double disc a king, the crescent an under-king, the snake and the cauldron a druid. The person responsible may also be indicated: the mirror and comb comes usually third in a group, perhaps to show that the widow of the man commemorated was responsible for the stone.

Other disciplines may take the study of the symbols further towards a solution. Anthropology suggests valid comparisons if it is assumed that the stones commemorate not the dead but alliances, including marriage, among the living. The mirror and comb symbol then shows, perhaps, the payment of a tocher, while the other symbols are paired to represent the two (matrilineal) kin-groups which were party to the bond.[16] Since dark age monoliths elsewhere generally commemorate the dead, this suggestion stands more in need of confirmatory evidence than the preceding one; but even if

---

[15] This follows A. C. Thomas, 'The Animal Art of the Scottish Iron Age and its Origins', *Archaeological Journal*, cxviii (1961), 14–64, and his article 'The Interpretation of the Pictish Symbols', *Archaeological Journal*, cxx (1963) 31–97; his views have been criticised by Dr I. Henderson, 'The Meaning of the Pictish Symbol Stones,' *The Dark Age in the Highlands*, (Inverness, ?1971), 53–67; and by R. B. K. Stevenson, 'Sculpture in Scotland in the 6th–9th Centuries A.D.', *Kolloquium über spätantike und frühmittelalterliche Skulptur*, ii (1971), 65–74. These writers regard Professor Thomas's work as too hypothetical and have pointed to specific errors which they see in it.

[16] A. Jackson, 'Pictish Social Structure and Symbol-Stones', *Scottish Studies*, xv (1971), 121–40.

its premises are wrong, the anthropological study itself has made significant points from which a better understanding may grow.

If these tentative interpretations be rejected (and some scholars seem to regard their speculative character as downright sinful), then the stones retain the secret of their symbols; but their sureness of line and the vigour of their design marks them out as masterpieces of barbarian art. They surely were erected by and probably commemorate the ruling aristocracy of a society in which local power was more important than the prestige of a distant 'king of the Picts'.

A word must be said on the Pictish languages. Apart from place and personal names, one language survives only in some twenty-five inscriptions, of which two or three are in Latin letters, some are in the ogham alphabet introduced from Ireland by the Dal Riata and about half are in scholastic oghams of the eighth or ninth centuries; they are fairly evenly distributed down the east from Shetland to Fife, and some are incised on symbol stones:

(1) besmeqqnanammovvez

(2) etocuhetts ahehhttanan hccvvevv nehhtons

(3) irataddoarens

It is possible to recognise in (1) and in a few other inscriptions the word *maqq* or *meqq*, common in Irish oghams of Gaelic origin and meaning 'son of' or possibly 'of the kin of' and hence supporting one interpretation of the symbols. In (2) the personal name Nechtan seems to occur, and elsewhere the names Ethernan, Drostan, Uovet (Pictish) and Forcus (Gaelic) have been identified. But otherwise these jumbles of letters have defied philologists and must belong, it is thought, to a long-surviving non-Celtic, non-Indo-European, language used for arcane and religious purposes and perhaps more generally in the far north, beyond the Ord of Caithness. In most of Pictland, as place names show, a Celtic language of the P-Celtic group was widespread.

Perhaps also we may trace the Celtic element in the ancestry of the Picts in the drowning of enemy leaders by Oengus mac Fergus in 734 and 739. This recalls the ritual drownings said to have been practised in Gaul and possibly depicted on Celtic metalwork elsewhere, and is surely a pagan survival, a propitiation of water-spirits.

The fragmented authority suggested by the symbol stones is also implied by the many hill-forts which are scattered across Pictland. These stone ramparts and other defensive works girding the tops of hills or of rocky spurs of land are often, without excavation, indistinguishable from much earlier forts, another link between the first century and the dark ages which stresses the continuity of Pictish society. That these are the 'castles' of territorial magnates is the inescapable conclusion from the resources in labour and building skill which their construction must have demanded.

The wealth of these chieftains survives, moreover, in striking splendour today in the form of silver work for the adornment of the male person, notably some ten massive chains, sometimes of double links, over half a metre long, which were apparently worn around the neck. These take us back to the world of heroic deeds, gluttony and chieftainly generosity depicted in Welsh, Irish and Anglo-Saxon literature. Although the chains are peculiarly Pictish in form, their purpose was surely no different from such splendid accoutrements as those found at Sutton Hoo in East Anglia and recently paralleled at St Ninian's Isle in Shetland—they were a mark of power and social distinction. The means by which this wealth and status was achieved and kept was doubtless a combination of the pursuits of war and peace: tribute from foe and subject, for the most part in produce, cattle and horses, but sometimes in coin and plate which could be turned into chain. Wealth was display, not commerce.

In sum, although their language and lore are alike unknown, the Picts of the dark ages had, we may think, a society more primitive than, but not in essentials distinct from, the British society to the south (whose hill-forts seem indistinguishable from Pictish ones), nor indeed, in its aristocratic character and values, from the society of Anglo-Saxon England or Merovingian Francia.

The argument from cultural flowering to political supremacy is always dangerous, and nowhere more so than in the uncharted desert of Pictish history. It is agreed that the distribution of Class I symbol stones is preponderantly northern, in the Don, Urie and Spey valleys and on the coast northward from Inverness; there is a scattering in north Fife, Gowrie and Angus as well as a very few in the west. By contrast the Class II stones are best represented in Gowrie and Angus; there are very few in the north or, interestingly, in Fife.[17] In interpreting this evidence it has been shown that the heavy incidence of Class I in Aberdeenshire includes examples of poor quality (and therefore late), which seem to be contemporaneous

[17] I. Henderson, 'The Origin Centre of the Pictish Symbol Stones', *Proc. Soc. Antiq. Sc.*, xci, (1957–8), 44–60.

with the superb Class II stones of Angus and Gowrie. Thus a preponderance of excellent Class I stones on the Moray Firth yields the
palm to Class II stones in Angus and Gowrie, while Mar and
Buchan adhered conservatively to Class I designs. Such a cultural
phenomenon might—and no stronger word is appropriate—represent the passing of Pictish hegemony and patronage from a northern
to a southern king, perhaps during the seventh century.[18]

Certainly during that century the Picts had to face a more
powerful enemy than the Dal Riata on the west. A marriage between
the exiled Eanfrith, son of Ethelfrith of Bernicia, to a Pictish woman,
involved in Northumbrian affairs their son Talorcan, who obtained a
Pictish kingdom between 653 and 657 and defeated the Dal Riata.
Bede states that Oswy of Northumbria 'subdued the greater part of
the Picts' and implies that this happened in 658; the event is therefore likely to be connected with the death of Talorcan. That southern
Pictish provinces were occupied is likely, and in 676 there was a rebellion against the Angles in which northerly tribes participated. It
was heavily defeated by Egfrith of Northumbria; the defeat of the
Angles did not take place until 685. Brudei, son of Bili (this latter
was probably king of the British of Dumbarton), who had subdued
Orkney in 682, lured the invading Egfrith of Northumbria into
Strathmore and killed him in a battle at Dunnichen ('Nechtansmere')
in Angus which was recorded in Irish annals as well as Anglian
hagiography and historiography. It was indeed a famous victory
but the purpose of Egfrith's invasion remains obscure. Bede describes
it as aggressive, but Bede's view of the Picts was coloured by their
rejection of the Columban church, so that he provided them with
early testimony of divine favour. Much would be understood if we
knew the extent of Anglian dominion. It seems to have extended to
Fife, which probably henceforth was slowly anglicised along its
southern shores, but not necessarily far beyond; it is certainly unwise
to assume that Dunnichen had been in Anglian hands for thirty
years.

The effects of the battle were perhaps unlooked for. The Angles
withdrew to the Forth but kept peace with the Picts. The centre of
power in Pictland moved south, perhaps to Scone, and this no doubt

[18] I. Henderson, 'Northern Pictland', *The Dark Ages in the Highlands*, 37–42,
argues against this kind of reasoning, adducing in particular the rarity of symbol
stones in Fortriu (Strathearn) which was a dominating Pictish province. But
'Fortriu' seems to be used in the Irish annals for all southern Pictland.

helped to consolidate the border. When Brudei died he was called by the Irish 'king of Fortriu'. And, despite king-struggles in the early eighth century, the Pictish kingdom reached its greatest strength in the mid-eighth century, under Oengus mac Fergus (729–761). Already aged about forty when he became over-king (for his son led an army for him in 731), Oengus fought and terrorised his domestic enemies ruthlessly. He turned on the Dal Riata, whose fortresses and divided kings were defeated in 741. In 740 he was fighting against Northumbria and in 744 against the Britons of Strathclyde. In succeeding years Oengus seems to have allied with the Angles against the kings of Dumbarton, and their joint armies took that fortress in 756 only to be wiped out a few days later. But he was still the dominating figure in the north when he died, probably aged more than seventy, in 761. If Oengus had a permanent achievement it was the subduing of Dal Riata as king of all Picts, and hence the reducing of all Scotia, Scotland north of the Forth, to his authority. As his contemporary Ethelbald of Mercia foreshadows the unity imposed on England by Wessex, so Oengus foreshadows the unity imposed on Scotia by the Scots.[19]

Yet after the death of Oengus it would almost seem that rationality departs from our sources. Thus the Dalriadic king Aed, who won a victory in Fortriu in 768 and died in 778 after a reign of 'thirty' years (the value of such reign-lengths is very doubtful), was presumably the king commemorated in the 'laws of Aed' which were reputedly taken to Pictland by the Scots in the ninth century. These laws were not of course legislation but rather 'the laudable customs of the time of a good and memorable king', one, perhaps, who asserted his independence of the Pictish king. From 789, when Conall son of Tadc was expelled, to 820, the Picts were ruled by a King Constantine and it has been thought that the contemporary king of Dal Riata 'Donald son of Constantine', was his son. Yet one group of sources knows this Donald and makes him king of Dal Riata about 781 before his 'father' became king of Picts: the Irish annals do not mention him but show Conall Tadc's son, expelled from Pictland in 789, being killed in Kintyre in 807 by another Conall who died perhaps in 811.

Indeed there seems little doubt that for a century from 741 the periods in which Dal Riata was free from Pictish overlordship were short. The annals are well enough informed about the affairs of Iona

19 Anderson, *Kings and Kingship.* 184–7.

(and presumably therefore of Dal Riata) and of Pictland. They tell us that in a battle among Picts in 789 or 790 Conall son of Tadc was defeated and Constantine was the victor, and the Pictish lists agree that these men were successively Pictish kings. On the other hand the annals have a group of entries relating to the deaths of kings of Dal Riata (778, 781), including the death of Donncorci ('brown oats') in 792. In him we may recognise the name which was misinterpreted by a scribe of the Dalriadic king-list as Donald, supposed son of the slightly later Pict Constantine.[20] If that link with Pictland is thus discarded, then the Dalriadic succession, according to the king-list, from Donncorci passed to two Conalls (said in one version to be brothers but this is improbable). It may be coincidence that the annals place in 807 'the killing of Conall son of Tadc by Conall son of Aedan in Kintyre'; the latter was surely a king in Dal Riata, but if coincidence is rejected then the first Conall (son of Tadc) in Dal Riata was the Pictish king ousted by Constantine in 789 or 790 who had then become (or remained) king of Dal Riata. In this interpretation the annal for 807 (like those for 778, 781 and 792) relates to Dalriadic kings, though unlike them it calls neither by such a title. Acceptance of the identification of the two king-list Conalls with the two annalistic Conalls involves rejection of their reign-lengths as given by the king-list, but, on the other hand, fits in well with the evidence that previously and subsequently Pictish kings were lords of Dal Riata. Expelled from Pictland, Conall son of Tadc may have preserved his power in Dal Riata after Donncorci, with Conall son of Aedan as under-king, possibly in Kintyre. After the elimination of the Pictish Conall son of Tadc, Conall son of Aedan was king of Dal Riata, whose independence was brief. Thus the aged Constantine, king of the Picts, is said (though again only on the evidence of the list of kings which placed his 'son' in Dal Riata) to have ruled in Dal Riata for the nine years before his death in 820, apparently after a brief interlude of independence under Conall son of Tadc and his slayer Conall. If the chronology were certain it might be argued that the former Conall, a dispossessed Pictish king, had set himself up in kingless Dal Riata on the death of Donald 'son of Constantine', that schism begat faction in the shape of a Dalriadic leader, the second Conall, and that in 811 Pictish rule was restored by Constantine.

[20] I am suggesting the misreading of *Donncorci*.

Such hypothesising could be continued, but only by doing violence to some feature of the sources, up to the resolution of the problems in the 840s when, it is agreed, Kenneth mac Alpin was ruler of Alba, of Picts and Scots. On the one hand there are the king-lists, one Dalriadic, the other Pictish. Each is in two versions and most versions are supplied with reign-lengths of which no con-cordance is really possible without such blatant improbabilities as Donald, son of Constantine, being made king in Dal Riata, before his (apparently young) father, Constantine, in Pictland. In the two lists, Dalriadic and Pictish, there are some names in common, and some unique not merely to Dalriadic or Pictish but to one or other version of each. On the other hand are the Irish annals, providing for some names not merely a designation but also a date.

Thus the Dalriadic list gives as successor to the Conalls a Con-stantine, certainly (since the name is so novel) the contemporary Pictish King; his brother Oengus II succeeded him in both Dalriadic and Pictish lists. Their deaths as kings of Fortriu are given in the annals under 820 and 834; by the latter date Dal Riata had known only a Pictish king for some twenty years.

The agreement of the sources seems to break down after 834. The Pictish list names two joint kings with Pictish names, Drest son of Constantine with Talorcan, followed by Eoganan son of Oengus; the Dalriadic list names Aed son of Boanta followed by Eoganan son of Angus. Now the annals show that in 839 the Norse defeated the men of Fortriu, killing Eoganan and Bran, sons of Angus, and Aed son of Boanta 'and numberless others'. Thus Eoganan and Aed were concurrently and not successively kings, the latter perhaps under-king in Dal Riata only, leading his host under Eoganan, king of Picts; is it misleading to see in Eoganan the first who might reasonably be called high king of all Scotia?[21] The Pictish list indeed continues for a further two or (in the other version) five reigns or joint reigns before acknowledging the succession of Kenneth mac Alpin. The Dalriadic list does not know the kings named between

[21] I have taken it that the *Book of Leinster* is wrong in making this a battle with a Norse fleet sailing north from Dublin in which the Dal Riata were led by Eoganan son of Angus 'king of Dal Riata'. Anderson, *Early Sources*, i, 277. But if there was a battle near the Dalriadan coast then either the *Book of Leinster* is correct or it had dropped the italicised words from its account: 'Eoganan son of Angus *king of Picts*, Aed son of Boanta king of Dal Riata'. In either case, it seems to me, the authority of one of the last Pictish kings over Dal Riata is indicated.

Eoganan and Kenneth mac Alpin in the Pictish lists; in one version however it makes the comment that Kenneth was the first of the Gaels to assume the kingdom of Scone, while the Irish annalist records his death in 858 as 'king of the Picts'.

It is doubtful if any interpretation of such limited evidence can pass tests of general acceptability, and the reader must understand a degree of tentativeness greater than usual even for dark-age studies. Nonetheless, it cannot be fortuitous that the problem of disentangling Dalriadic history from Pictish coincides with the sudden rise of Norse attacks down the western seaboard, attacks recorded when they touched Iona and Ireland in the 790s, but perhaps already affecting the Northern Isles in the 780s. The destruction and plundering which the Norse accomplished must have greatly weakened Dal Riata (as we know they were to weaken the Frankish kingdoms) and allowed Pictish influence to increase. In this interpretation Conall son of Aedan, victor in Kintyre in 807, is the last name of a Dalriadic ruler in the Dalriadic king-list, and, since none of his immediate predecessors was called Aedan, he seems not to be descended from the main royal line. From about 810 the Pictish Constantine had either taken over the kingship of Dal Riata or at least was the only possible king to whom the otherwise kingless Dal Riata might look. The situation after the death of his brother Oengus II in 834 is scarcely susceptible of any other explanation, for then we find most clearly evidence of a client king of Dal Riata.

Another view recently offered deserves study in its author's own argument and can be summarised here only briefly. Conall son of Tadc has a first name which suggests that he was part-Scot, while his rival in Pictland, Constantine, was son of a Fergus, probably the king of Dal Riata who died in 781, and a Pictish wife, as was his successor Oengus II mac Fergus (died 834). We should conclude that Constantine and Fergus ruled among Picts and Scots lawfully according to their different succession customs and that they represented not Pictish dominance in Dal Riata, but Scottish influence in Pictland over a whole generation. Thus after 834 for the first time we have Pictish kings who were the sons of previous Pictish kings, Drest son of Constantine and Eoganan son of Oengus, and the latter, though not the former, was also king of Dal Riata. Thus matrilineal succession among the Picts was breaking down even before the accession of Kenneth mac Alpin because of the growth of Scottish

influence, and perhaps even migration, among the Picts.[22] The fact
that Irish annals represent these early rulers of both peoples as kings
of Fortriu (and not 'of Picts') is to be taken as evidence of the province upon whose resources their power was based.

Whichever view is correct, the separation of the two peoples for
a short time after 839 is common ground. The versions of Dalriadic
history, all written much later, narrate in a puzzlingly tentative way
the rise of Alpin and his son Kenneth; not all are agreed in giving
Alpin a place in the king-list, and there is a suspicion that the
known rearrangement of the chronicle of Dal Riata so as to bring
four earlier kings (including an Alpin) into the ninth century was
done in order to provide Kenneth with a father who was king. Alpin
remains a wraith whose very descent from the royal line of Dal Riata
may be suspect, since his patronymic, son of Eochaid, is that of the
earlier King Alpin. This, however, is contrary to the general opinion
of scholars that, among many doubtful things about Kenneth mac
Alpin, his descent from Fergus mac Erc is firm.

Royal or not by birth, Kenneth mac Alpin won his way by his
abilities as a warrior. Again we must choose between conflicting
versions of reign-lengths, eighteen years (?841–858) or twenty-eight
(834–?861), and while the former derives from the often reliable
Scottish chronicle,[23] the latter is supported by an Irish annal narrating help brought to Dal Riata at the bidding of Kenneth mac Alpin
in 836. Scholarly opinion seems to regard that date as insecure and
to prefer a reign of two years, 841–3, in Dal Riata followed by sixteen, 843–58, in Pictland. It is perhaps more important that we
understand what these reigns mean: his authority in Dal Riata was
a challenge not merely to the Norse but to Pictish lordship; it represents the leader of a war band seeking territory and tribute by
traditional means of conquest. In the nature of the Norse attacks
Kenneth was even less likely to keep his hold on Dal Riata than, say,
the Northumbrian kings on their kingdom, and he must logically
pursue his acquisitive aims against the Picts, and other neighbours.
Thus he became by force king of Scone, that is, probably, of Fortriu,
and entered on a four or five years' struggle to master the other provinces of Picts whose kings are recorded in the last names of the
Pictish king-lists. By 850 he was king of the Picts, king of what the

---

[22] Anderson, *King and Kingship*, 192–7.
[23] Formerly called the 'Pictish chronicle'. It begins with the reign of
Kenneth mac Alpin.

Irish called Alba, and free to range with his bands to Dunbar and Melrose for booty.[24]

Between the abandonment of the *oppidum* of Traprain by the Votadini in the first half of the fifth century and the expedition of the war-band of the Gododdin from Din Eidyn to Catraeth late in the sixth, the history of south-eastern Scotland is almost wholly blank. Yet the period between the departure of the Romans and the arrival of the Angles must have seen the waning of *Romanitas*, and the assertion or reassertion of the language and modes of thought and conduct of 'barbarian' society. Thus the Votadini who abandoned a sub-Roman treasure on Traprain emerge again in literature as the Gododdin whose warrior chiefs went to do battle against the Angles and to win immortal fame for their ferocity and bravery in the elegies of the poet Aneirin. The society which he depicted was that of a militant aristocracy vaunting its achievements at the board in hall, vowing bolder and braver exploits; its men rode forth in the companionship and rivalry of the war-band to 'earn their mead' by fighting for their lords. Such ideas are the echo of the Germanic warband of Tacitus and are to be found in later Anglo-Saxon poetry; there is nothing uniquely Celtic about them, but they might flourish best in a society under pressure from superior or more successful forces, Roman, Anglian or Viking.[25]

The war-band of 300 or 360 men which went from Edinburgh to Catterick included men from other British kingdoms, but its enemies were the heathens of Bernicia and Deira, in Northumberland and Yorkshire respectively. Pagan burials and cemeteries show that the Angles of Deira had settled up the river valleys during the sixth century but were still prevented from crossing the Pennines by the British kingdom of Elmet, while the Bernicians were much less numerous and successful.[26] Thus the host of Deira appears much more frequently than the Bernicians in the Gododdin poem, and it may be that the Bernician Angles were of no consequence at the

[24] I have left this paragraph as written before the publication of Dr Anderson's *Kings and Kingship*. Although she accepts a ninth-century King Alpin, she seems prepared to allow the interpretation offered here as a possible one, and gives as an alternative the view that the Dalriadan kingship became centred in the east replacing what had been the kingship of the Picts; *ibid*, 196.

[25] K. H. Jackson, *The Gododdin*, Introduction, *passim*; L. Alcock, *Arthur's Britain*, ch. 11.

[26] Map in Alcock, *Arthur's Britain*, 288.

time of the expedition.[27] There is certainly something curious about the facts as revealed by British sources: that the Gododdin attacked Deira, not neighbouring Bernicia, and that the attack on Bernicia was led by Urien, king of Rheged (in Galloway and around Carlisle); this might suggest that Bernicia had grown quickly at the expense of the Gododdin, decimated at Catterick. The ruling house of Bernicia probably established itself on the coast about 558; between 579 and 586 the Bernician king was attacked by Urien of Rheged, Rhiderch, king of Strathclyde, and two other British leaders, and between 586 and 593 Urien was killed while besieging the Angles in Bamburgh. Thereafter, it seems, the barriers to Anglian advance crumbled one by one.

The Scots of Dal Riata, who about 583 had won a battle of 'Mano', perhaps over the Gododdin of Manau at the head of the Firth of Forth, came into conflict with the Angles early in the seventh century and in 604 were thoroughly defeated by Ethelfrith of Bernicia at 'a most famous place called Degsastan, that is Degsastone'. The place has never been satisfactorily identified, though one would expect it to survive as the site of a monolith and to have the name Daystone; the most favoured candidate is Dawston in Liddesdale. The battle was probably a foray for plunder by the Scots, who seem to have given refuge to and been led there by the son of a previous Bernician king; it was certainly a famous victory for it found its way into the Irish annals. And it was followed by the conquest of Deira by Ethelfrith and the expulsion of its king Edwin. Edwin returned in 617 as ruler of both Deira and Bernicia, after an exile in which he is reputed to have been baptised by Rhun, son of Urien, so that Rheged evidently still existed and denied the Angles access to the Solway.[28] The three sons of Ethelfrith took refuge in Dal Riata, where they too were baptised; one, Eanfrith, seems to have gone also to the Picts, married into the royal house and fathered Talorcan, a Pictish king. In 634 Edwin was killed and, after a year's rule by Eanfrith, his brothers Oswald (635–43) and Oswy (643–71) became

[27] The earlier version represented by the B text seems not to mention Bernicia: if the verses in A which do refer to it were accretions, the poem might have been written several decades earlier ,than is usually suggested. And a battle at Catterick would make considerably more sense.

[28] N. K. Chadwick, 'The conversion of Northumbria', *Celt and Saxon*, ed. N. K. Chadwick, 138–66. Stenton (*Anglo-Saxon England*, 78) thinks that Ethelfrith could have ridden to the Solway through Anglian settlements. This does not seem possible if the Welsh evidence is accepted.

in succession kings of Bernicia and for a time of Deira also.[29] In these struggles of the early seventh century the external enemies were the ruler of Gwynedd in Wales and Penda of Mercia, and even the British sources have nothing to say of resistance by the descendants of Urien, while the Gododdin have vanished. In 638 the Irish annals record the siege of Etin, Edinburgh, which suggests that the Anglian advance was firmly established on the coast to the Forth and that the Britons of Lothian were losing their strongholds one by one.[30] In the struggles between Oswy and Penda before the latter's death in 656, Oswy fled to *urbs Iudeu,* pretty certainly a fort on Stirling rock, and handed over his treasure there to Penda, who gave it to his British allies, an event famous to the Britons as *atbret Iudeu* —'the restitution of Stirling'. Clearly Manau and the other territory of the Gododdin had passed wholly under Anglian control, and the Bernician king was now neighbour to the Picts.[31] Yet it is questionable whether political conquest was the motive behind these wars or whether they can be directly and simply related to new settlements. The expeditions themselves are sometimes revealed—and nowhere more clearly than in 'the restitution of Stirling'—to be treasure hunts, the heroic exploits of an aristocratic and warrior caste counting wealth in cattle. The expedition of Gododdin to Catterick is probably to be seen in the same light, and not as a defence of territory.[32]

The adventures of the Northumbrian kings among the Picts have already been told; after their defeat at Nechtansmere in 685 the Angles were again defeated in 698 but were victors in 711, after which date they maintained good relations with the Picts. The frontier between them may have been the Pentland (that is, Pict-land) Hills, the Carron or the Forth—more probably the first since some

[29] For all these events I have accepted the revised chronology offered by D. P. Kirby, 'Bede and Northumbrian chronology', *Eng. Hist. Rev.* lxxviii (1963), 514–27.

[30] K. H. Jackson, 'Edinburgh and the Anglian Occupation of Lothian', *The Anglo-Saxons,* ed. P. Clemoes (1959), 35–42.

[31] K. H. Jackson, 'On the Northern British Section in Nennius', *Celt and Saxon* (ed. N. K. Chadwick), 21–62. This corrects in details, as Kirby in the article cited in a previous note corrects in dates, the best account of these events: P. Hunter Blair, 'The Bernicians and their Northern Frontier', *Studies in Early British History* (ed. N. K. Chadwick), 137–72.

[32] *The Gododdin* seems to say little about the motives of the expedition, but the verse B30 = A39 praising Eithinyn, beginning 'He attacked in battle-stress for the cattle herds of the east', could well refer to the battle at Catterick (ed. K. Jackson, 109, 132).

Anglian retreat is likely; but as we have seen there are traces of Anglian influence across the Firth in Fife. The reasons for the peace of the eighth century are to be found less in Christianity and advancing civilisation than in the internal weakness of Northumbrian kinship, which was subject to continual challenge by pretenders. The kingdom itself was governed by provincial ealdormen of whom one certainly had a stronghold at Dunbar (and there may have been others in Scotland); geographical circumstances would prevent the king from exercising much control over him but conversely this northern province could hold aloof from dynastic wars.

The progress of Anglian settlement is a rather different story from the struggles of contending kings. For it we must turn to other disciplines—archaeology and place-names. On Doon Hill above Dunbar archaeology has revealed the remains, within a palisaded and irregularly shaped enclosure, of two timber halls built successively upon the same ground. The first, some 75 feet (23 m) long with ⟨ and ⟩ shaped gables and a door in the centre of each long wall, was divided internally, with a large central room and a smaller one at each end. The second hall was more simply rectangular and in many respects is so similar to the hall of King Oswald at Yeavering in Northumberland that its date cannot be many decades removed from 640. The facts that the earlier hall stood for some fifty to a hundred years, was then burned down and replaced by the later hall at no great interval of time, suggest that on this site stood first the hall of a British chief, destroyed during the Anglian expansion into Lothian before the 'siege of Etin' in 638, and then the hall of a new Anglian lord. Such an account relies upon the typology of the later hall, which seems secure, for the earlier hall is without known parallel in its gables though in other features recalls the earlier (c. 600) hall at Yeavering. This relationship, albeit a distant one, with an Anglian hall, draws our attention to the British origins of a hybrid[33] style of building represented at Yeavering and Doon Hill (the later hall); and warns us to consider carefully the cataclysmic views of chroniclers and later historians on the age of migrations and settlement. For here, above Dunbar, whose name is probably British *din-bar*, 'summit fort', on a hill with the British name Doon, 'fort' (both names were received into Anglian toponomy), the violence of the Anglian settlement suggested by narrative sources is exemplified by the burned timbers of the first hall. But at least a century of previous

[33] I.e., British and Anglian.

cultural contact between Angle and Briton is implied by the style of that hall, while the re-use of the hall-site suggests that boundaries, dues, even cultivation practices may also have continued on the estate of the new Anglian lord.[34]

Unfortunately there are few material remains to complement those at Doon Hill; no pagan Anglian cemetery has been found north of Tweed and no village to cast light on the problems of dark age settlement. Recent aerial photography has revealed the existence at Sprouston near Kelso of something remarkably like the *villa regia* at Yeavering, a site of great potential interest which may complement the Doon Hill excavation in revealing the pattern and nature of Anglian control. There is no trace whatever in Scottish place-names of those words for temple, or funeral pyre, or of Teutonic pagan gods, which would arise from early and intensive Anglian settlement. Relatively early, however, are some names in -ham and -ingham, each of which must mean a settlement and most of which are found in the Tweed valley, with half a dozen outliers in East Lothian. It may not be coincidence that the three Scottish names in -*worth* ('enclosure') lie in the Tweed valley with most -*ham* ('homestead') names while a few names in -*ingtun* (in which -*tun* is most likely to be early and mean 'enclosure') share the distribution of -*botl* ('dwelling') from East Lothian across into Ayrshire. These -*ingtun* and -*botl* names probably represent a rather late phase of Anglian settlement, internal in the Tweed valley but diffused and external elsewhere. If this conclusion be sound, it can be conjectured that in the Tweed valley Anglian settlement was intensive and largely exclusive of British landowners, a suggestion confirmed by the distribution of names in British *tref-* ('homestead') and *caer-* ('fortified homestead') which are found in the three Lothian counties, but in the lower Tweed valley rarely and in compounds meaning 'hill settlement' (Trabrown, Carfrae)—that is, they are confined to remoter hill stations. The Tweed was, it seems, at one period a magnet attracting to itself Anglian settlers in sufficient numbers to displace the native landowners; but the coastal strip of East Lothian beyond the Dunglass Burn was, in terms of early settlement, a frontier zone behind and beyond which the British landowner maintained his hold and possibly fragments of his tribal kingdom.

At the same time the persistence of a native British stratum in the population of the whole area from Forth to Tweed is amply

[34] *Medieval Archaeology*, x (1966), 175–6.

testified by the place-names in British which Anglian settlers adopted. The persistence of river-names, including Tweed and Teviot, is to be expected, but settlement names are also found including some (for example, Melrose) in the Tweed valley. However, with the possible exception of Peebles (which has an English plural added to the British word for 'tents' or shielings), none of these British names implies a settlement and all could have been transferred from natural feature to village after Anglian settlement of the village, though this is unlikely in all cases. Studies of place-names have shown that of names recorded in the Middle Ages the incidence of British names in West Lothian (70%) is twice as heavy as in Mid Lothian (35%), so that after the fall of Din Eidyn and its resettlement as Edinburgh, the expansion of Anglian settlement clearly faltered. Perhaps from the mid-seventh century it was not expropriatory of the British, but rather sought unsettled land among British settlements. In this way we might explain the straggle of Anglian names across the Southern Uplands, including several on the Upper Clyde (for example, Crawford: 'crooked ford') which could have led to the Anglian settlement represented by Prestwick, Maybole and perhaps Cunningham in Ayrshire—which might, however, have been settled from the Solway.[35]

The boundary between Angle and Briton may have been defined quite carefully during periods of peace. This seems the most likely explanation of various fragmentary linear earthworks in southern Scotland and Northumberland, notably the Catrail in Roxburghshire. Over a distance of some twelve and a half miles (20 km) sections of linear earthworks of ditch and bank joining the courses of various small streams make a barrier which is too slight to serve any military purpose but which demarcates and impedes. The ditch may have been seven to ten feet (2 to 3 m) deep.[36] If we recall that dark-age wealth was often expressed in terms of cattle, it seems most likely that this border served to prevent stock from straying from one territory to the other, and from being stolen; the difficulties of preserving peace between petty kings were no less in the seventh or

---

[35] The many articles on place-names by W. F. H. Nicolaisen in *Scottish Studies* should be consulted. Particularly valuable is 'Celts and Anglo-Saxons in the Scottish Border Counties: the Place-Name Evidence', *Scottish Studies*, viii (1964), 141–71. For the small Ayrshire group see the article on *wic* in *Scottish Studies*, xi (1967), 80. See now his *Scottish Place-Names* (1976).

[36] *Inventory of Roxburghshire*, i, 33; ii, 479–83; *Inventory of Selkirkshire*, 126–7.

ninth century (and the Catrail cannot be attributed to any century with certainty) than in later times of reiving Border chiefs.

The history of settlement on the northern shores of the Solway is more complex than in any other district of Scotland. Assumed to be part of Rheged on the strength of one or two place names (for example, Dunragit), Galloway and Dumfriesshire do have a stratum of British place-names which is presumably the earliest, since the 'Picts' of Galloway are a fiction of the twelfth century. It is inherently likely that the Scots, who attacked North Wales in the fourth century and settled in Dal Riata from the fifth, would attempt to settle in the part of Britain closest to Ireland, Galloway, and traces of that settlement have been claimed in the place-name element *sliabh* with the meaning of 'hill' which is found most intensively in the Rhinns of Galloway and Islay. If this interpretation is correct then the first settlement was very limited and occurred rather later than the primary Scotic settlements in Kintyre. It would scarcely explain the strongly Gaelic character of medieval Galloway, which must be attributed to sustained migration.[37]

The faintest writing on this Gallovidian palimpsest is Anglian, probably not so much because it was later obliterated as because it was always slight. The disappearance of Rheged in the seventh century is unchronicled though the first wife of Oswy was a descendent of Urien, and this marriage may have sought to reconcile the British of Carlisle to Anglian lordship. It is significant that knowledge of northern events in Wales ceased by the mid-seventh century, evidently because the Northumbrians had reached the Solway and isolated Strathclyde from Wales. The later seventh century and the eighth saw a flowering of Northumbrian scholarship and art which may best be treated as part of the development of the church, but which is the best evidence of Anglian influence during the occupation of the shores of the Solway. Anglian place-names there are comparatively scarce. On the other hand an English source states that the Northumbrian king 'added the plain of Kyle to his kingdom' in 752, and this annexation may have encouraged the settlement already noted which gave us Anglian place-names in Ayrshire.

That the British of Strathclyde were under pressure from the south as well as the north is clear from the jejune annals of the

[37] W. F. H. Nicolaisen in *Scottish Studies*, ix (1965), 91–106; Thomas, *Britain and Ireland in early Christian Times*, 57. This question is discussed in the following chapter.

period. Battles with Dal Riata are recorded in 678, 711 and 717 and with the Picts in 744 and 750, the last being a defeat of the Picts at Mugdock, north of Glasgow. It bought only a temporary respite, for, after the loss of Kyle, Strathclyde was attacked by Angles and Picts and accepted terms on 1 August 756. Nine days later in unexplained circumstances the Anglian army suffered heavy losses and the pressures upon Strathclyde were released. Thereafter Northumbrian power declined; it is not known how long Kyle remained in Anglian hands, but the succession of bishops at Whithorn (the see was restored early in the eighth century) lasted until the end of the century and perhaps later.

We have seen that Whithorn was the best attested of the sub-Roman Christian centres of southern Scotland and that it was responsible for the conversion of at least some of the southern Picts. The Scotic settlers in Dal Riata must also have been Christian at least from the late fifth century; there is no evidence that the early organisation of Christianity in Ireland, a bishop for each *tuath* (tribe) or division of a tribe, crossed the Irish sea, but it is not beyond the bounds of possibility that archaeological evidence of early sixth-century Christian activity in Dal Riata will be found. At the moment there is no archaeology of this, the Patrician phase, of the church in Ireland.

The point is important since the British 'apostles', Nynia and Patrick, in each case went to existing Christian communities. When Columba crossed the Irish Sea in 563 Dal Riata was likewise in some sense Christian. What Columba brought was not a Gospel hitherto unheard, but a way of religious life in eremitical communities following the rule of the founder abbot and seeking spiritual maturity through work and meditation. The asceticism which marked the rule of Columbanus on the Continent was tempered in the houses of Columba at Derry, Durrow and Iona, but the ideal there was as truly monastic as among the cenobitic communities of the eastern Mediterranean which were the inspiration of early British monasticism. The change which Ireland brought about—and it seems to have been in progress in Columba's day—was to subordinate the episcopate to monasteries at first in esteem, but ultimately in organisation also. The reasons for this, by no means all certain, need not detain us.[38] Columba, unruly member of an Irish princely kin,

[38] For all this see the study of Dr Kathleen Hughes, *The Church in Early Irish Society.*

had already founded two houses in Ireland when with twelve companions he established the third in Iona. These three made up the first *paruchia* of Columba—houses with obligations both secular and spiritual to the founder and his kin, including the obligation of seeking or sending a new abbot from or to one another. The monks lived in individual cells of turf or stone within the defining vallum, roughly rectangular and in Iona[39] enclosing an area of about ten acres (4 ha)—which surely speaks of a community of not less than twenty men and perhaps many more.[40] The spirituality of their life is vouchsafed by the life of Columba written a century after his death in 597 by Adamnan, also Abbot of Iona. It is too much a catalogue of prophecies, miracles and visions for modern taste, yet scattered through it are hints of the round of toil in the fields or with the stock and of worship in the kirk which made Iona an example appealing to the imagination of Oswald of Bernicia. The *seniores* were largely responsible for the services in church, the 'working brothers' for manual labour and the *juniores* were novices under instruction. All were monks dressed in cowl, white tunic and sandals. Adamnan gives us glimpses of the brethren ploughing, sowing, reaping and winnowing, grinding the corn, milking and cooking, building with wood, and working in metal. But above all he shows us Columba as spiritual father and master of the whole community.[41]

Columba's *paruchia* certainly extended beyond Iona, and at least one other large monastery was founded by him on an unidentified island with a long beach called Hinba; Adamnan also mentions monasteries in Tiree and by Loch Awe. Columba's contemporary Moluoc established a community on Lismore and late in the seventh century Maelrubha extended the *paruchia* of Bangor to Applecross in Wester Ross, so that later a monk of Applecross could return to become abbot of Bangor. Lismore and Applecross survived until the Viking period.[42] Another site is recognisable at Kingarth, dedicated to the shadowy St Blane. There is nothing comparable with these as yet to be found on the east side of Drumalban; the nearest we can get to the early northern Pictish church is the remains of pre-Viking

[39] The name of the island is correctly I. From this came the Latin adjectival form found in Adamnan, *Ioua insula*, misread as Iona.

[40] Thomas, *Early Christian Archaeology of N. Britain*, 30–1. The number of monks is my suggestion. A late life of Columba gives 150.

[41] Adamnan, *Columba*.

[42] The name Maelrubha is preserved in Loch Maree.

kirks in the Northern Isles. The most famous of these in recent years is on 'St Ninian's Isle'!

The most important extension of the family of Iona was in Northumbria. In 635 or 636, little more than a year after the flight of Paulinus (of the Canterbury mission) from York, the monk Aidan, a man of true saintliness, came as bishop to the Northumbrians and, ignoring York in Deira, established his monastery on Lindisfarne not far from the king's fort of Bamburgh on the Bernician coast. The achievement of this mission was far greater than anything which can be claimed for Iona,[43] for out of the matching of Irish-Scottish monastic ideals with Anglian wealth and techniques came the greatest manuscript illuminations and sculptures of pre-twelfth century Europe, and a passion for learning which was an important source of the Carolingian 'renaissance'. There are also many traces of a cultural re- or retrofertilisation. The great 'Celtic' manuscripts like the *Book of Durrow*, the *Echternach* and the *Lindisfarne Gospels* (c. 700) were produced by the Northumbrian church, as was the high cross at Ruthwell, now generally dated c. 750, and the crosses at, for example, Closeburn, Hoddam and Wamphray.[44]

Much of the previous paragraph relates to the period after the synod of Whitby in 664, when a schism within the Columban church in Northumbria was ended by the withdrawal to Iona of the conservative element under Aidan's successor Colman. Sometimes presented as a clash between 'Roman' and 'Celtic', the issue in fact arose from the very strength of the Northumbrian church, its passionate pursuit of learning; and the leader of the innovating group, Wilfrid, was a monk of Lindisfarne. The immediate problem was the use by the Northumbrian church of the 84-year Easter cycle, which had remained current in Ireland when the rest of the church moved on to different calculations and a much longer cycle. The matter was not trivial, for Easter, the feast of the resurrection, is at the very heart of Christian teaching; without the death and promise of Our Lord there would be no significant difference between Mark's *Gospel* and Adamnan's *Life,* nor between one life of holiness and another of worldliness. Easter must therefore be observed in catholic unity or the church is false to the meaning of the resurrection. And this was

[43] But see the involved and stimulating review of the Andersons' edition of Adamnan, *Columba* by D. A. Bullough, 'Columba, Adomnan and the Achievement of Iona', *Sc. Hist. Rev.* xliii (1964), 111–30; xliv (1965), 17–33.

[44] E. Mercer 'The Ruthwell and Bewcastle Crosses', *Antiquity,* xxxviii (1964), 268-76.

surely the issue as Wilfrid (for he was clearly a man of passion) felt it and on which he won King Oswy's support. There was also dispute over the manner of the tonsure, of much less importance.

It will be noted that the subordination of bishop to abbot, a marked feature of the Irish church, was not brought to Britain (or at least not further than Iona) and was not an issue at Whitby. Aidan and the Irish monks who came to Lindisfarne evidently recognised that in a missionary situation the authority of the bishop must be untrammelled, and several additional sees were founded, as well as the monasteries of Melrose (where Cuthbert was a monk) and Coldingham. In 681 (according to Bede who may have been ignorant of earlier non-Anglian bishops) a see was established at Abercorn 'for the province of the Picts' and evidently to divide the responsibility of the bishop of York for the Northumbrians and the Picts under Northumbrian overlordship. When in 685 this political tutelage ended at the battle of Nechtansmere, bishop Trumwine fled and no more is heard of the bishopric; nonetheless it may have continued (as the monastery at Abercorn certainly did) or have been transferred into Pictish territory. It is probable that the southern Picts in Angus and Fife accepted Christianity generally and renewed their interest in Nynia during the seventh century. If, as seems likely, the burials in long cists, which are frequent in the Lothians, represent Christian influence and ultimately Christianity in that province in the seventh and eighth centuries, then the scatter of such burials round the Fife coast and in Gowrie and Angus fits well enough with Bede's bishop in Lothian for the Picts (to the north). St Cuthbert, when still a monk at Melrose (c. 664–c. 678) undertook a sea voyage in January to the Niuduera, apparently a Pictish tribe in Fife and already Christian.[44a] The fewness of class I (non-Christian) symbol stones in this zone would also fit well with the conclusion which this evidence suggests: that even if the Ninianic mission had introduced Christianity to southern Pictland, the Northumbrian church was also influential in Christianising the zones around the Forth and Tay estuaries.

What of the northern Picts? Adamnan tells us much of Columba the politician labouring among the tribal rivalries of Ireland and visiting Brudei, a Pictish king, at his hall near the Ness. There he had an encounter with a wizard and proved the superiority of Christian magic; it is clear from Adamnan that Columba visited both Ireland and Brudei several times and he was certainly much

44a See below, p. 78.

involved in the assembly which regulated the relationship between Irish and Scottish Dal Riata. Adamnan, however, has nothing to say on the one matter with which Bede deals: the conversion of Brudei and (what would presumably follow) the northern Picts. Bede gives a specific year, 565, the ninth of Brudei's reign, showing that he had annals or Easter Table which gave the death of Brudei's predecessor; as a consequence of the conversion, says Bede, Brudei gave Iona to Columba for a monastery. On the other hand Adamnan nowhere credits Columba with baptising Brudei or converting Picts in general, though he does describe the conversion of the dying Emchath of Urquhart (on Loch Ness) and of an unnamed man whose son was restored to life by Columba. He also speaks of wonders which led the 'barbarian gentiles' to glorify the God of Christians.[45] Such passages suggest that if Columba had baptised Brudei and his men, Adamnan would have made something of the fact. But he does not.

Although Bede's account was doubtless given in good faith, it is difficult to accept that Iona was given to Columba by the Picts and that it was given after a conversion; if this part of the account falls, the remainder must also be questionable. It remains true on the evidence of Adamnan that Columba went to northern parts to meet Brudei and that he baptised some Picts; from knowledge of this and of Nynia's conversion of southern Picts Bede may have conjured up a 'mission' for Columba to the northern Picts.[46] We should suspend judgement on their early conversion until there is archaeological evidence (so far lacking) of a monastic settlement or Christian cemetery of early character north of the Mounth.[47]

The total absence of any manuscript from a seventh-century Pictish scriptorium is powerful negative evidence that there were no such scriptoria at a time when monks in Ireland wrote assiduously. The Lists of Pictish kings have only a tenuous link with the reigns of Pictish kings as recorded in annals at Iona: no Pictish annalist was

[45] Adamnan Columba, 86–7.

[46] Bede, Hist. Eccles., ed. Colgrave and Mynors, 202–3, 562–3. It seems to me that the account of the northern Picts and of Nynia's stone church has been influenced by the episode of 710–11 (in which Bede was involved) when Nechtan, King of the Picts in the northern parts of Britain, asked Ceolfrith to send him men to build a stone church; ibid, 532–3.

[47] K. Hughes, Early Christianity in Pictland (Jarrow Lecture, 1970). I had reached some of the conclusions suggested here for the Pictish church in ignorance of Dr Hughes' lecture which powerfully reinforced the view I had taken. Most of the following paragraph summarises the argument of the lecture.

at work. The lively scenes on some symbol stones imply an oral tradition similar to that which in Ireland became a written heroic literature; the Pictish tradition appears nowhere in literature. There are no Christian (that is Latin) inscribed stones. Everything, in other words, indicates that in the seventh century any Columban settlements among the northern Picts were small and that their influence grew only gradually; it would receive a setback in 718 with the expulsion of the family of Iona. The king responsible, Nechtan, wrote (after the war of 711) to Ceolfrith, Abbot of Wearmouth,[48] for a refutation of the Irish paschal observance and of the Irish tonsure, and for architects to build a stone kirk dedicated to St Peter. In 697 Adamnan, Abbot of Iona, had secured acceptance of a law protecting the weak at a synod at Birr in the presence of an expatriate Angle, Egbert, and of Curitan, who, under the 'Roman' name Boniface, is associated with the see at Rosemarkie. The dedication of that kirk, and of a number of others, including Restennet (a pre-twelfth century kirk), to St Peter suggests that a Romanising group among Nechtan's clergy may have been led by Curitan about 714–17, when the conservative Irish were driven out of the Pictish church. Already Adamnan, Abbot of Iona, had visited Northumbria, accepted the Roman observance, and by 704 had brought the Irish church round to it. In 716 Egbert succeeded, where Adamnan had failed, in persuading Iona to follow suit, and it is therefore difficult to see why Nechtan should have expelled 'the community of Iona' across Drumalban in 717 unless this 'community' was a section of Irish clergy which refused to accept Roman observances.[49]

The king who took these steps was clearly committed to a rapid advance of Christianity within his realm, and there would follow a rapid expansion in the number of kirks together with the general imposition of nominal Christianity. By the middle of the eighth century there was an abbot at Kilrymond (St Andrews) and probably other religious communities in the southern Pictish zone. We enter upon a remarkable cultural flowering associated with the Pictish church in which the art of the sculptor, well established among the Picts, was given patronage in a specifically Christian context. We can explain in this way the Class II symbol stones (those with a cross) of which the best examples are found in southern Pictland. To the same tradition belongs the remarkable St Andrews sarcophagus

[48] He died in 714.
[49] D. P. Kirby, 'Bede and the Pictish Church', *Innes Review*, xxiv, 6–25.

or shrine possibly carved between 850 and 950. By 800 the monks of Iona probably had the gospel-book known as *The Book of Kells* which, while derived mainly from Northumbrian manuscript traditions, also shows the influence of the Pictish art of the Class II stones. It was written in Iona or in Pictland in the mid-eighth century. Much the same may be said of the styles influencing the (shattered) high cross of St John at Iona, which must share with the (maimed) Ruthwell cross the claim to be the finest work of art indigenous to Scotland.[50] Pictland and Dal Riata played an important part in the transmission back to Ireland of form and style in both manuscript illumination and sculptured crosses.

In sum, the conversion of the Picts was the work of many decades and was perhaps carried out most effectively among those of the south in the seventh century and in the north in the eighth. The apostles Ninian and Columba were important not only for what they achieved but also for what it later became politic to claim that they had achieved. And if we say that Scotland was Christian by *c.* 750, we should perhaps also distinguish the meanings of that statement to cleric and layman. To the former it meant observing the feasts and sacraments of the church, including the Latin mass, and maintaining the orders of the church, including the episcopal order. During the seventh and eighth century traces of bishops' sees are found at Iona, Abernethy and Kingarth in Bute, and it is likely that other sees existed among the Picts.

To the layman, however, the new religion meant a more powerful magic than any that had gone before. Adamnan describes the spring which was worshipped as a god and not drunk for fear of demons; when blessed, drunk and bathed in by Columba it became a healing fountain. The Pictish wizard Broichan, who refused to free an Irish captive, was near to death until, having promised to free the captive, he drank water containing a pebble blessed by Columba, and recovered. Holy wells, holy water, stones, these play the main rôle as agents of Columba's miracles in book II of Adamnan's life, and the many springs dedicated to saints in medieval Scotland and the continued use of stone charms bear out his emphasis

[50] R. B. K. Stevenson, 'The Chronology and relationships of some Irish and Scottish Crosses', *Journal of the Royal Society of Antiquaries of Ireland*, lxxxvi (1956), 84–96; most recently the same author, 'Sculpture in Scotland in the 6th–9th centuries A.D.', *Kolloquium über Spätantike und frühmittelalterliche Skulptur*, ii (1971), 65–74; T. J. Brown, 'Northumbria and the Book of Kells', *Anglo-Saxon England*, i (1972), 219–46.

upon them in popular religion. Yet they have obviously been adopted as miracle-workers and prophylactics from earlier poly-theistic nature-worship. The veneration of relics was an extension of the same need in a primitive but developing society; it attributed a special virtue to relics of a holy person, a virtue which would deflect evil or cure sickness and which would even transfer to articles which had touched the corporeal relics. In order to give access to the relics a special housing was necessary and this took the form of a house-shaped shrine, wooden at first, like churches and free-standing crosses, then from the eighth century (again like churches and crosses) in stone. Such shrines have been identified from Galloway to Shetland and the archaeologist responsible for recognising them has suggested that they illustrate 'the greatly intensified religious and technological intercourse (after 715) between the church in Northumbria and the church among the Picts—two areas of social vitality and advanced artistic experiment at this period'.[51]

The political and literary record reveals among Picts, Scots, Britons and Angles, in the sixth or seventh century a warrior society whose wealth was counted in cattle and whose heroic exploits would have been called, in another time and place, feuding and rustling. There is a temptation to look no further than these hill-fort chief-tains, to conceive of a tribal society in which lesser men were bound to their chief or king by kinship in protection of semi-nomadic pastoralism, and so perpetuate a distinction between the supposed free-peasant agrarian society of Anglo-Saxon England and the supposed aristocratic pastoral society of Celtic and upland Britain. Yet in England an increasing degree of continuity between Celtic and Anglo-Saxon economic institutions has won acceptance: the discrete Lowland estate, with a focus or *caput* and scattered depen-dent hamlets cultivating cereals in nearby fields on loamy soils once considered too heavy for dark-age ploughs, is now thought to have passed to the Anglo-Saxons from the Celtic society where it was already ancient. It was pre-eminently a means of exploitation of the land by peasants for the benefit of landowning chiefs whose dwelling often seems to represent a relocation from a nearby hill-fort. If rele-vant to early Scotland this pattern implies the existence of bondmen and perhaps slaves whose economy usually included some agriculture and was rarely if ever wholly pastoral. Agriculture, a labour-intensive

[51] Charles Thomas, *Early Christian Archaeology of N. Britain*, 149.

activity, is not carried on in scattered farms but by a hamlet community which is a unit of agrarian co-operation, and at the same
time part of a wider lordship.

It is necessary to stress that the literary and legal evidence in
England has little to say about such arrangements, whether continuous or discontinuous from Celtic into Anglo-Saxon society. This
evidence is concerned with assessment for tribute, and its unit is not
the hamlet, but the household and its land, the 'hide', *terra unius
familiae*, from which a hospitality rent is due. Bede tells us that Iona
was not large but was by English calculation land for five families,
and indeed hidages go in hundreds and fives. Thus in a document of
the eighth century the Mercian kings listed the peoples over whom
they had authority and the assessment of them in hundreds or
thousands of hides. The *Senchus fer nAlban*, a similar assessment of
the seventh century from Dal Riata, underlines the common vocabulary of dark age peoples for social structure:

> In Islay a hundred houses [*treb*], Oidech 20 houses [*tech*], Freg 120
> houses, Calad Rois 60 houses, Ros Deorand 30 houses, Ard hEs 30
> houses, Loch Rois 30 houses, Ath Cassil 30 houses. In this [? the] tribe
> of Angus [Cenél nOengusa] 30 houses . . .[52] but small are the lands of
> the houses of the tribe of Angus. . . .[53]

These districts cannot now be identified and hence it is not possible
to delimit the extent of the *Cenél nOengusa*. The same treatise
apportions the houses of the *Cenél Loairn* incompletely and not to
districts but to the kindred or descendants of Loarn, each with
between five and thirty houses; later the total for *Cenél Loairn* is
given as 420, and that for *Cenél nGabráin* (with no breakdown) as
560 in Kintyre and Cowal.

This document, with its many obscurities and difficulties, is not
a geographer's description but an account of the basis on which a
king, perhaps of Dal Riata, might exact tribute. Each group of
'houses' is a notional assessment, yet behind such notions must lie
the real thing; and it is clear that these 'houses' were tributary to a
nobleman who was at least assumed to be of the kindred of Angus,
Loarn or Gabran. In the treatise alternative words—*treb, tech,
teallach*—are used for 'house,' but the hundred houses (*ced treb*) of

[52] The sense seems to demand that the following word, *caillnae* or *cailline*,
qualifies these houses.

[53] Other translations are possible though this has the virtue of bringing the
total of 420 houses close to the total given later of 430 houses. I have left out the
final phrase 'namely 31 men', as quite obscure.

Islay recall the synonymous Welsh land division, the cantred, in origin a fiscal assessment at a hundred 'houses', and, of course, the Anglo-Saxon hundred, a fiscal assessment at a hundred hides.[54] It is indeed possible that Ireland and Dal Riata knew a similar hundred division, but if so it died early. Our treatise suggests rather that the parallel unit was of twenty 'houses' with sub-divisions of five, and multiples of between one-and-a-half (30) and six (120) times, for not only are the assessments for tribute so divided up, but for each *cenél* it is said that rowing service is owed in the form of two seven-bench boats from twenty 'houses'. Such service must have been of great importance in a land whose unity came from the links of sea-ways and sea lochs, and significantly the *Senchus* makes this, its most coherent, statement about the assessment for boat service, while its statement of military obligations seems to deal in round hundreds, unrelated to the 'houses', a difference which suggests the greater importance of boat-service.

The *Senchus* itself contains no clear definition of a 'house', save that it had associated land, but comparison with the use of *tref* in Welsh and *tech* in Irish evidence suggests strongly that 'settlement' is the meaning of all and that the fiscal 'house' on the ground was a hamlet of peasants paying *bes-tige*, house tribute, a food rent described in Irish texts but not Dalriadic. By dint of further borrowing from Ireland it would be possible to provide Dal Riata with an elaborate social structure of nobles and kings, for which unfortunately there is no comparable Scottish evidence. Undoubtedly the lords of the many duns of Argyll were 'nobles' supported by the food rents of tributary peasant settlements, and although we have no scale of honour-prices for them, they were surely also protected by wergelds of this kind. But it would be dangerous to venture beyond so obvious a generalisation and to import, for example, the elaborate detail of kingship according to the Irish law tracts.

The fiscal 'house' probably survived longest in Scotland in one province: Lennox. Here in the thirteenth century charters refer to the 'house from which smoke comes' (to distinguish dwelling from byre) and to the *villa* or *plenaria villa*, the settlement, as the basis for

[54] The *Senchus fer nAlban* is translated in Anderson, *Early Sources*, i, pp. cl–clii; there is an edition, translation and commentary by J. Bannerman in *Celtica*, vii–ix (1966–71), and now a commentary in Anderson, *Kings and Kingship*, 158–65. Dr Bannerman's full treatment of the *Senchus* in his *Studies in the History of Dalriada* (1974) appeared too late for this book.

tribute payments, sometimes in cheeses. The breakdown of such liabilities in proportion to holdings of arable land (ploughgate or davach) which was general elsewhere had probably not taken place in Lennox because the economy of the province, or at least of part of it, was almost wholly pastoral. Nonetheless, it remains a puzzle why the liability to service in the host was discharged by a payment in cheeses from each house in this zone.[55]

In the Anglian south-east the evidence for the discrete estate is to be found in its survival into the twelfth century as the Northumbrian shire. It was then in decay, but the glimpses we are permitted are of features plainly of great antiquity if only because they are found elsewhere in the Celtic world. For both Coldinghamshire and Berwickshire we have the names of the focal and the dependant *tuns* or hamlets. Other shires are attested in Lothian, held by thanes who paid rent for them; the thane is a *ministerialis* who is also noble by his association with the king. The shire is in many cases also an ecclesiastical parish, within which thane and priest collected the dues of secular lord and kirk from the peasantry in the dependent hamlets. These dues are known as *wayting,* hospitality, in Lothian, and recall the cornage of northern England and of the Welsh march, and the *commorth, gwestfa* and *treth Calan Mai* of Wales. They are not, it would seem, Anglian innovations, and must have existed at the time of the Anglian settlement; they are evidence, in other words, of the existence in the dark ages of a dependent, hospitality-rent-owing peasantry living in small nucleated settlements and of exploiting lords, for whose homes we should look first on Doon Hill, Arthur's Seat, Moncreiffe Hill, Norrie's Law and Mote of Mark.[56]

The last named was excavated in 1913 and 1973 and it has been shown that round an open settlement (of the fifth century) on this rocky outcrop was built a timber-laced rampart which was fired and so vitrified (perhaps early in the seventh century). After hurried repairs and a short occupation the site was probably given up, presumably by the British who had been under attack by the Angles of Northumbria. Within it were found not only traces of buildings but also the remains of the metalworker's art, including broken moulds from which were produced the penannular brooches found in hoards

[55] *Lennox Cartularium passim.*

[56] G. W. S. Barrow, 'Northern English Society in the Twelfth and Thirteenth Centuries', *Northern History,* iv (1969), 1–28. For Mote of Mark see *Current Archaeology* no. 39 (1973), 121–5.

and peculiar to dark-age Britain. The finest examples come from the Picts and from Ireland, but these moulds suggest that the British of Rheged may not have been far behind in the magnificence of their chiefly ostentation, even though British brooches are otherwise rare and poor.[57] We must imagine peripatetic craftsmen with the moulds and bellows of their trade visiting the dun or fort of a chieftain-land-lord to turn some of the gold, silver or other metal which he had accumulated from selling stock or produce to the occasional visiting merchant into items of personal adornment, which enhanced his status among the other lords of the province and which at the same time literally secured his wealth to his person.

With these dark-age hill-forts it would be pleasing to link assuredly the cultivation terraces which sometimes occur on hill slopes in conjunction, it seems, with the forts. They are found most thickly in Roxburghshire around the head streams of the Bowmont Water, and in the Upper Tweed and Upper Clyde valleys, with a similar concentration in northern England to the one side and out-liers in Perthshire to the other.[58] At Glenrath Hope in Peeblesshire a sequence of small square fields over one mile in length is the best of the examples of a 'Celtic' field system probably once general in southern England but rare north of the Humber; it may be attributed to the Roman period. This example has been partly wrecked by the sinuous line of cultivation terracing. On the grounds of such an example and of their distribution, cultivation terraces can generally be ascribed to Anglian settlers, though perhaps of the eighth and later centuries rather than of the sixth, and may be said to represent a discontinuity of economic practice between the 'Celtic' and 'Saxon' periods. However, the reasons for such changes may lie in advances in the technology of ploughing especially on slopes, rather than in ethnic distinctions, and in a reoccupation by Angles of uplands deserted, perhaps some time earlier, by Britons. Examples of disturbance and discontinuity—if that is what cultivation terraces in this zone represent—must not be allowed to outweigh the absence of such terracing in the earliest Anglian zone on the east coast, an absence which may support the continuity of settlement pattern argued for earlier in this chapter.

[57] There is a short account of penannular brooches in Alcock, *Arthur's Britain*, 236–7, 260–2, and a general discussion by E. Fowler 'The origins and develop-ment of the Penannular Brooch in Europe', *Proceedings of the Prehistoric Society*, xxvi (1960), 149–77.

[58] *Inventory of Peeblesshire*, i, 38, gives a distribution map.

*Note on the Niduarian Picts.* In his life of Cuthbert, Bede describes how the saint came by sea 'to the land of the Picts who are called Niduari'. Skene suggested that these were the Picts of Galloway on the Nith (*Celtic Scotland,* i, 132–4) and although this was rejected by, for example, W. J. Watson (*Celtic Place Names of Scotland,* 175–7) the identification of these people made no progress until in a paper of 1954, Mr Peter Hunter Blair made certain points clear (*Studies in Early British History,* 165–8): (1) Bede relied upon the earlier anonymous *Vita Cuthberti* wholly for this story; (2) The *Vita Cuthberti* puts the matter rather differently. Cuthbert travelling by land and sea in January reached the land of the Picts where it is called the *Niuduera regio.* There he was stormbound on a deserted part of the coast and lived on dolphin's or seal's flesh miraculously provided; (3) The second element of Niuduera is genitive plural of Old English *wer,* 'man', and *regio* in this source has the sense of district, province, shire. Niud could develop into a later Nith. So we might translate: where it is called the province of the Niud-folk. This name seems to have survived only in the parish and farm of Newburn on the southern Fife coast beside Largo. In the twelfth century and later this appears consistently as the name of a *villa* or *toun,* 'Nithbren', and the kirk there later had parochial status (*Dunfermline Registrum,* nos. 2, 3, etc.) The second element of this name was taken by Watson as Welsh, *pren,* a tree which is fairly widespread in eastern Scotland (W. F. H. Nicolaisen, 'Celts and Anglo-Saxons in the Scottish Border Counties', *Scottish Studies,* viii, 146–8). Sea-mammals, probably whales and seals, are well-attested denizens of the Firth of Forth in the twelfth century. For those landed on the Fife shore, see Lawrie, *E.S.C.,* no. LXXIV (p. 62), *R.R.S.,* i, 194, 221, 244, and on the Lothian shore, see Lawrie, *E.S.C.* no. CLIII (p. 118).

# 4

# LOCHLANNAICH, CUIMRICH, SASSUNAICH

From 792 for some eighty years the British Isles are known to have been subjected to attacks down the western seaways by Lochlannaich, men of Scandinavia; the attacks upon Orkney and Shetland would have begun a little earlier and have passed unrecorded. The motives for these voyages were recorded in the sagas in largely political terms as a desire by free men to escape from the tyranny of the kings of Norway, and notably of Harald Fairhair. But the sagas were composed only in the twelfth century, an age of kings, and this motive will scarcely serve for 800, though it may have more relevance a century later. Other evidence in Norway points rather to the pressure of increasing numbers upon scarce resources in a harsh climate as the strongest incentive to migrate; the earlier Vikings in Britain probably came to Orkney and Shetland from western Norway looking for land on which to establish homesteads, and they came in sufficient numbers over the following century to make these northern islands a part of the Scandinavian world in the sense in which Faeroe and Iceland, hitherto uninhabited, became and remain Scandinavian.

The inhabitants of the Northern Isles ceased to speak the non-Celtic Pictish which had probably been their language and spoke instead Norn. The survival of the names which they gave to settlements, mountains, fields, streams, seaways and even implements, and of their toponomy might suggest that native culture was submerged by that of the incomers. Our ideas of the level of that culture were somewhat modified when, in 1958, the more valuable possessions and accoutrements of some native chieftain of Shetland were discovered where they had been buried for safety beneath the floor of the little kirk on St Ninian's Isle, itself the site of an early Christian hermitage and near the more important early kirk, possibly a monastery, at Papil, West Burra. The hoard consisted of twenty-eight pieces of ornamented silver alloy including six bowls, a hanging bowl, a gilt pommel, two chapes, one of them inscribed with the name 'Resad son of Spusscio', and twelve penannular gilt brooches. Only the hanging bowl had certainly come from the non-Pictish world; the rest represents a family's treasures accumulated over three generations or more from native workshops, and the artistic motifs again represent that strong Northumbrian influence already remarked in Pictish art. The treasure was entrusted to the church no doubt because the sanctity and neutrality of the church had been observed in native quarrels; but the very fact that they were storehouses of treasure made churches the particular object of Viking raids. To this we may attribute the unvarying depiction of the Vikings as plunderers in western chronicles and annals, sources invariably compiled in churches.[1]

They were of course raiders but their greater significance was as settlers. The early Norse raids on the English coast in the 790s died away as the opportunities to settle in the Northern Isles attracted the raiders to a farming environment similar to that which they knew in Norway;[2] saga tradition was that Shetland, the first landfall (between one and two days' sail) from western Norway, was almost uninhabited and that settlement was peaceful. Doubtless this exaggerates the situation, for the St Ninian's Isle hoard indicates very disturbed times and there are several examples of promontories cut by ditch and bank, apparently hastily thrown up, defended sites which could well represent the early Viking landfalls among a hostile populace. It may be that the lull in attacks on Ireland between 813 and c. 820 marks the period when native resistance in Orkney was overcome.

Archaeology has revealed only two certain pagan graves in Shetland in contrast to the much more numerous finds in Orkney; but the only scientific excavation of a burial (on Rousay) is unfinished and unpublished and it would be a mistake to place too much emphasis on their archaeological balance. For archaeology has

---

[1] A. Small, C. Thomas and D. M. Wilson, *St Ninian's Isle and its Treasure* (London, 1973). The view of Mgr D. MacRoberts that the items of the hoard had ecclesiastical purposes has not found favour.

[2] Raids on England began seriously in 835 when the Danes found there an environment similar to that of Denmark.

revealed the way of life of Norse settlers at Underhoull and Jarlshof in Shetland and at Birsay in Orkney. The Shetland settlements are both beside brochs and, at Jarlshof, post-broch wheelhouses, while at Buckquoy in Orkney the replacement of native Pictish houses by a Viking homestead (though after a gap) can be demonstrated clearly. The Vikings built their long houses with curving windproof walls of stone and turf and a roof supported on a row or two rows of posts. Within, the length (as much as 20 m) was divided into three compartments: sleeping, living and byre, with external doors into the two last. The byre might be paved for cleaning but the floor of the living quarters was beaten earth to retain the heat of the fire. Later Viking houses would have straight walls, and in that form the type survived in the Outer Hebrides into the present century.

Agriculture was certainly practised, since the stone tips of ard ploughs have been found, and we may assume strips near to the houses which, as the sagas describe, would be manured and sown with oats and bere in the spring. In May lambing took place and from July hay was cut wherever it could be found, and dried for winter feed; the stone bases of hay-ricks were found at Underhoull. Some cattle were wintered indoors but sheep seem to have wintered on the grazings. The production of large quantities of wool is implied, for example, by spindle whorls found on many sites, and a heavy sheep population was probably supportable in the climatic conditions which applied in the ninth and tenth centuries, rather milder than in the better documented sixteenth to eighteenth centuries. The amount of land suitable for cultivation in Shetland was relatively small—much smaller than in Orkney—but possible grazings were extensive if poor. These surely account for the very heavy distribution of place names in *setr* in Shetland, a settlement with pastoral functions, though scarcely a shieling (but a Celtic Irish word for a shieling, *airig,* found its way back to Orkney and even to Norway).

Nearby, if the house is by salt water, the experienced eye will sometimes detect traces of a noost into which a small boat could be drawn up. The house-site at Underhoull produced sinkers for line fishing, while other sites suggest that the Norse settlers may have been familiar with the use of nets to catch herring. At Jarlshof, where the earliest houses probably ante-date Underhoull and are early ninth century, there was little trace of early fishing, for fishing seems to have been taken up by the Norse settlers gradually and presumably to eke out the limited resources in cultivable land. So first and foremost these settlers were farmers, and their language is recorded in the farm-names of the Northern Isles.[3]

Scandinavian toponymy accounts for 99% of place-names in the Northern Isles; archaeologists are now recognising the houses of the Viking and post-Viking periods there in increasing numbers. But only recently has there been excavation of a site (Buckquoy in Orkney) which is known to have been the home of native and Viking settlers in succession. The domestic objects recovered there are of particular interest, since they show that the Norse, at least in Orkney, adopted many everyday things in the form which they found already in use, and this too supports the view that settlement was not wholly violent.[4] They also brought their own house-forms, weapons, burial fashions and characteristic dress-ornaments. Many of the latter have been found with burials assumed to be female and suggest that perhaps wives migrated with or after their husbands. But the survival of *ordinary* native combs and similar gear supports the hypothesis that Christian worship by native peasants may have continued and been adopted by the Norse at an earlier date than the saga tale which attributed it to the behest of Olaf Tryggvason about 995. Viking artefacts in churchyards argue an acceptance of Christian burial sites, and place names in *kirkja* have an obvious significance. Since a number of these were formed with *bolstaðr* which is a name-element for 'farm' thought to be in use in the ninth century and not later, the acceptance of Christianity would seem to fall well before 900. On Papa Westray in Orkney, which was known to the Norse as Papa-ey, 'island of the priests', the many names of places and fields are all Scandinavian, yet one contains *byr* or *bolstaðr* which indicate early colonisation, negative evidence which hints that 'Scandinavians respected as well as recognised Christian sites and sanctuaries'.[5] The Vikings were not fiercely anti-Christian as Muslims were; the plundering of churches did not mean razing them nor slaying priests. On the contrary, Christ was assumed to be acceptable to the pantheon in Valhalla.

[3] In addition to Wainwright, *Northern Isles*, and Hamilton, *Jarlshof*, these paragraphs are based on S. Cruden, 'Excavations at Birsay, Orkney', *The Fourth Viking Congress*, ed. A. Small (Edinburgh, 1965), 22–31; A. Small, 'Excavations at Underhoull, Unst, Shetland', *Proc. Soc. Antiq. Sc.* xcviii (1964–6), 223–48; A. Small, 'The Distribution of Settlement in Shetland and Faroe in Viking Times' *Saga Book of the Viking Society*, xvii (1969), 145–55.

[4] I am indebted to Dr Anna Ritchie for permission to mention these conclusions from her lecture on this excavation.

[5] Wainwright, *Northern Isles*, 162.

Thus a Viking boat burial at Kiloran Bay, Colonsay (Kolbein's Island), contained sword, spear, axe, shield, arrows, knife, and a whetstone for them. Pins, buckles, fragments of iron and a cauldron and bronze set of scales completed the equipment of the Viking and his horse by whose skeletons they were found; the horse had evidently been sacrified by the striking off of a hind leg. All seemed pagan, yet the 'exploration' of this remarkable site in 1882–3 established that the man had been buried in a boat within a stone enclosure, the horse outside between two stone markers on each of which was clearly incised a cross. The significance of grave-goods for his sea-faring and land-faring activities is obvious; the acquaintance of the man's companions with Christianity was obviously slight but it was not hostile. The balance implies that he had engaged in trading, as perhaps do the three coins dating to 808–854 which placed the burial probably in the latter half of the ninth century. Three Viking balances have been found in Scotland, all in the zone between Gigha and Colonsay, indicating the function of Norse settlement there in transferring the wealth of Ireland back to the northern settlements.[6]

It is highly likely that Viking settlement in Lewis and western Skye began during the first half of the ninth century, when narrative sources record raids there. Place-name evidence suggests relatively heavy Norse settlement both there and in Caithness—it has been established that four-fifths of the 126 village names in Lewis are of purely Norse origin.[7] The proportion of Norse names from natural features has not been established in Lewis, but in Trotternish, Skye, while settlement-names are two-thirds Norse, for natural features the proportion is only one sixth.[8] Clearly the incidence of settlement in the Western Isles was much less heavy than in the Northern, a fact which is not to be attributed to unfavourable physical conditions only. The existence of Norse names for almost every island (-ay), promontory (nes, whence -nish) and many prominent mountains (fjall, whence -val), suggests that they were first named from the sea by navigators sailing to Ireland, and were settled subsequently. The

[6] Viking Antiquities in Great Britain and Ireland, ed. Haakon Shetelig, ii (1940), 48–61; Joseph Anderson 'Notes of Bronze Brooches', Proc. Soc. Antiq. Sc., xli (1906–7), 437–49.

[7] Magne Oftedal, 'The Village Names of Lewis', Norsk Tidsskrift for Sprog-videnskap, xvii (1954), 363–409.

[8] Bridget Gordon, 'Some Norse Place-Names in Trotternish', Scottish Gaelic Studies, x (1965), 82–112.

continuance of Viking raids by those who settled in the Northern Isles, Caithness, Lewis and Skye, in order to acquire movable wealth from Iona, Islay, Man and Ireland, explains the establishment of Norse settlements at Dublin and elsewhere on the Irish coast, for these were essentially camps from which plundering forays were conducted inland for silver but even more for cattle. They may also have been centres for trade, as they certainly were in the tenth century, and as the balances already mentioned suggest. The 'Olaf, son of the king of Lochlann', who came to Dublin in 853 was probably son of a Hebridean chief. Like his fellows he was attracted to Ireland to extort not to settle, for the environment of Ireland offered a way of life with which the Norse were not familiar.

The 'Scottish' Isles, then, were taken for settlement; we can only judge the phases and intensity of that process from the quaking ground of place-names. In studies of the distribution of settlement-names in *staðr*, its plural *staðir*, and *bolstaðr* the difficulties of using this kind of evidence are underlined. Not only is there some doubt whether *bolstaðr* had lost its particular meaning of *divided* farm, but it is also not agreed whether *staðir* names must be early because of their limited and thin distribution (Shetland: 37; Orkney: 25; Outer Isles, Skye: some 20; Coll, Tiree, Islay: 1 each) or late (after 870) because Iceland has almost 1200. In fact *staðir* names, though fewer, are not significantly different in distribution from the areas in which there is a heavy incidence of *bolstaðr*—except that *bolstaðr* was an important element in place-name formation in Caithness and Sutherland and is rare (17 occurrences) in Iceland.[9] The distribution has been calculated: Shetland, 50; Orkney, 50; Caithness, some 30; Sutherland, some 20; Hebrides, 102. But there are two distinct forms for *bolstaðr* names. (1) Those which preserve the *st* in the forms *-bister*, *-bster*, *-bost*; all the names in Shetland, Orkney and Caithness are of this kind, all but one in Skye, half the names in the Outer Hebrides, and two small groups (eight names) in Islay. The distribution is remarkably close to the distribution of *setr* (associated with pastoral activities), which, like *bolstaðr*, is absent from Iceland. (2) Those which lost the *st* and take the form *-bol, -pol;* half the names

---

[9] In addition to Wainwright, *The Northern Isles*, and Marwick, *Orkney Farm Names*, see J. Stewart, 'Shetland Farm Names', *The Fourth Viking Congress*, ed. A. Small (Edinburgh, 1965), 247–66; W. F. H. Nicolaisen, 'Norse Settlement in the Northern and Western Isles', *Sc. Hist. Rev.*, xlviii (1969), 6–17; Magne Oftedal, 'Norse place-names in Celtic Scotland', *Proceedings of the International Congress of Celtic Studies*, ed. Ó Cuiv (Dublin, 1962), 43–50.

in the Outer Hebrides take this form, all but one in Sutherland, almost all in the west mainland, Coll, Tiree and Mull names and six names in Islay.[10] Since Gaelic has a first-syllable stress and Norse does not it is difficult to resist the conclusion that (2) represent settlements in which there was much stronger Celtic influence than in (1).

The question of interaction of Norse and Irish or Gaelic is complex; it is possible that the changes in Gaelic spoken in Scotland at this period are attributable to Norse influence. But among these changes borrowing of vocabulary is infrequent—it has been calculated that Gaelic contains only fifty words of Norse origin.[11] On the other hand, there was also borrowing into island Norn of Celtic words, possibly not many but including the interesting Old Irish *airig* (Gaelic, *airigh*) a shieling, to which the Orkneyinga Saga gives the same meaning as *setr*, and which is found in Norse combination names as an -*ary* ending in the Western Isles, Sutherland and Caithness, and infrequently in the Northern Isles.[12] These and some other place-name forms were being taken to Dumfriesshire and Cumberland in the tenth century and should therefore be dated to the ninth century in the isles.

We have to place the Western Isles in a much wider setting than Scotland if we are to understand the key role which they played in the later ninth century. Language, place and personal names and blood groups combine to show that a very important element in the settlement of Faeroe and Iceland after 870 came from the Celtic west, while the sagas of Harald Fairhair suggest that Norway itself was subject to Viking attacks from the west in the late ninth century. In 873 began 'the forty years' rest' in Ireland which is best explained by the diversion of needy Orcadians and Hebridean Norse to Iceland. The internal colonisation in the Outer Hebrides and external colonisation in the Inner Hebrides and Sutherland, represented by *bol*, *pol*, and *ary* names, are likely to have come before the colonisation of Iceland and to be datable to *c.* 840–*c.* 870. Iona had been

[10] One could be in Kintyre at Glen Skibble near Skipness.
[11] K. Jackson, 'The Celtic Languages during the Viking Period', *Proceedings of International Congress of Celtic Studies*, ed. Ó Cuiv, (Dublin, 1962), 3–11; M. Oftedal, 'On the Frequency of Norse Loanwords in Scottish Gaelic'. *Scottish Gaelic Studies*, ix (1961), 116–27; M. Oftedal, 'Ardroil', *Indo-Celtica*, ed. H. Pilch and J. Thurow, (Munich, 1972), 111–25, and literature cited there.
[12] A. MacBain, *Place Names, Highlands and Islands of Scotland*, (Stirling, 1922) 289–92.

attacked time after time so that in 807 a new monastery was founded at Kells in Ireland to which the relics of Columba (or some of them) were removed in 831; when Kenneth mac Alpin became king of Picts a fringe of Norse settlements in Islay and regular Viking expeditions down the western sea-ways to Ireland must have ended the long commune between the peoples of Ulster and Argyll. How long Norse speech endured is not known, but the genealogies of leading medieval families on the western seaboard showing the continued use of Scandinavian personal names is not evidence of lingering Scandinavian speech, as the English Danelaw shows. They show that a Gaelic island aristocracy whose onomastic usages included Norse names emerged, probably during the tenth century, to rule lordships, no doubt warring with each other and of fluctuating size. One such family could trace its roots in early Irish history and emerged into documented history in the twelfth century in the person of Somerled (Norse, 'summer voyager'); another, the MacSweens (Gaelic *Suibhne* from Norse *Svein*) of Knapdale, has an authentic genealogy back to *c.* 1000. A third was probably the mainland family of Fergus, early twelfth-century lord of Galloway.[13] The significant legacy of the Viking age to the western seaboard was not an infusion of Norse blood and speech, but the design of ships and to a lesser degree of weaponry which had distinguished the Viking age. Ships with mast and rigging which could be sailed close to, as well as before, the wind, with hulls of astonishing flexibility to ride through rough waters, steered by a simple but effective rudder, of shallow draft and readily beached, with oars as an alternative to sail, these gave the Hebridean lord of the tenth century and later a mastery over his environment unknown to the tribe of Fergus in the sixth.[14] Now the Isles were no longer appendages of an essentially land-based Dalriadan kingdom, but home of a race of vigorous and independent chieftains who could choose the master they wished to serve—in Ireland, Man, Galloway or Scotia.

In the Northern Isles the communities at Jarlshof and Birsay, and like them doubtless hundreds of other Norse communities, grew and flourished from the ninth century till at least the twelfth. At some date probably after 900 Harald Fairhair of Norway came west to

[13] W. D. H. Sellar, 'The Origins and Ancestry of Somerled', *Sc. Hist. Rev.* xlv (1966), 123–42; the same, 'Family Origins in Cowal and Knapdale', *Scottish Studies*, xv (1971), 21–37.

[14] Sawyer, *Age of Vikings*, chapter 4, is the best recent short account in English of Viking ships.

end the Viking attacks from the northern isles. The saga states probably correctly, that he chose as earl (*jarl*) Sigurd, who earned his saga-name 'the Mighty' by his campaigns to bring Caithness and Sutherland to obedience. From his time the northern isles and Caithness had a history of their own, which comes to hectic life in the imaginative pages of the *Orkneyinga Saga*. It touches more than once upon the history of Scotland, but we must depart from it to assess the significance of the Viking age in the development of other provinces of the later Scotland, and first in the south-west, where the nature of earlier settlement is itself a matter of some debate.

The Gaelic character of Galloway (Carrick, Wigtownshire and Kirkcudbrightshire) is evident in the middle ages from names of persons and places, and it is from the latter that we must isolate evidence of the phase or phases of settlement.[15] Study of hill or mountain names is remarkably inconclusive. It was noted in the preceding chapter that *sliabh* names are heavily concentrated in Islay and the Rhinns of Galloway, indicating Irish settlement in the fifth or sixth centuries.[16] There is a slight scattering of *beinn* and *cnoc* names in Galloway and other hill-words, *maol*, *meall* and *torr*, occur, but not in a helpful way; they are either later or were in use for a long period.[17] Names in *barr* ('top' or 'height') are strikingly concentrated in Lorn and Mid-Argyll, and sprinkled through the counties of Renfrew and Ayr, thickly in Wigtown and Kirkcudbright. They are almost absent from Islay, Kintyre and Arran, where we should expect them if the word had been used by the early Dal Riata, but the distribution of this element could represent not the earliest, but sixth-century and later, Scotic migrations to Dal Riata and Galloway.[18] It must, however, be pointed out that *sliabh* is also virtually absent from Kintyre, perhaps because low small hills are lacking there. There is certainly a recognisable group of *Kil-* names which, when taken with some inversion compounds (that is, non-Gaelic names in Gaelic word-order) in *Kirk-* (representing an earlier *Kil-*), are identifiable with this period, since *Kil-* names are a feature of Gaelic toponomy not carried into Pictland in the ninth century

[15] All the articles cited in this paragraph are by Dr W. F. H. Nicolaisen unless otherwise noted.
[16] *Scottish Studies*, ix (1965), 91–106.
[17] *Transactions of the Gaelic Society of Inverness*, xlv (1967–8), 113–27.
[18] *Scottish Studies*, xiii (1969) 157–66.

and later. Study of the saints to whose names *Kil-* has been attached in Galloway leads to the same conclusion,[19] and the correspondence with the zone of greatest frequency of settlement-names in *Bal* (Gaelic *baile*) is striking. All these elements (*barr, Kil-, Bal-*) show a straggle of names northward through Ayrshire to the Clyde of greater or lesser intensity, and together with the more evenly spread *Auchen-* (Gaelic *achadh*, 'field', transferred to settlement sites) this could indicate the secondary phase of Gaelic influence, in the way in which *dalr* (-dale), widespread in Atlantic Scotland, represents a secondary phase of Norse influence and not settlement.[20] This secondary phase of Gaelic influence would belong to the five centuries after the seventh; as late as *c.* 1190 Maybole (an Anglian name) in Ayrshire was *Meibothel -beag* and *-mor*; an assart or new settlement had been made at a time of Gaelic speech in the district. In general we must conclude that Anglian control in the eighth century was probably not accompanied by significant Anglian migration but that Irish influence was sufficiently strong to change speech from British to Gaelic.

An impetus in this direction is thought to have been given by the Viking settlement in Dumfriesshire, Cumberland, Westmorland and Yorkshire. The settlement of a substantial Danish army in Yorkshire is recorded in the third quarter of the ninth century, and during the last quarter the route from this kingdom of York to the Irish and Hebridean Norse settlements was evidently freely open. In 919, the kingdom of York was seized by an Hiberno-Norse chieftain whose successors ruled intermittently until 954. Evidence of place-names and art forms as well as narrative sources reveal 'the presence of Norse settlers from Ireland everywhere in the coastal region from south Lancashire . . . to the estuary of the Solway . . . the central hills of Cumberland were theirs . . . they had occupied with the force of a migration Kentdale and the country for many miles on either side of the Cumbrian Derwent.'[21] There was an important extension of this settlement in Dumfriesshire, represented by names in *thveit*, *-beck*, and *-by*, but it was by no means intensive. The evidence of Norse penetration into Kirkcudbright and Wigtownshire is much

[19] J. MacQueen, 'The Gaelic Speakers of Galloway and Carrick', *Scottish Studies* xvii (1973), 17–33.

[20] *Studia Celtica,* v (1970), 15–35.

[21] Stenton, *Anglo-Saxon England,* 332; *Preparatory to Anglo-Saxon England,* ed. D. M. Stenton, 214–23.

weaker, for *Kirk-* and *-fell* names came there after adoption into English.[22]

The Scandinavian settlement in Cumbria was important; it may have included Hebridean Norse in some numbers, for the first Norse kings at York had sailed in Hebridean waters. But the evidence does not distinguish this element from the Irish; it does however distinguish in Ireland the 'foreign Gael', Gall-Ghàidhil, evidently Hebrideans, who came to Ireland to fight both for and against the Vikings there. It is usually accepted that these free-booters crossed to Britain with the Norse and settled, thus greatly reinforcing the Gaelic character of Gall-Ghàidhil, a name now Anglicised as Galloway. Eigg and Bute were also described by Irish sources as places of the Gall-Ghàidhil and of course the Hebrides were Innse Gall, that is, the Isles of the Foreigners. Yet there remains a clear distinction between Wigtown-Kirkcudbright (Galloway) where the only weighty evidence of a Norse element is the provincial name itself, and the much better evidence of Norse-Hebridean settlement in Dumfriesshire. It may be that the wider usage of 'Galloway' found in the twelfth century to include the counties of Renfrew, Ayr and Dumfries developed from a tenth century name for the Gaelic-Norse settlers in Dumfriesshire; or it may be (and this seems more likely) that the ruling family of Galloway (as usually understood) came as chiefs or kings of Gall-Ghàidhil and from that circumstance gave the name to the province. Hence in 1034 the annals record the death of Suibhne (Sweyn) mac Kenneth, *ri Gall Ghàidhil.* If these explanations do not meet the evidence, neither do those which have hitherto been on court.[23]

To the east of Norse-dominated Cumberland the rump of Anglian Northumbria lost its kingship by 900; a native earl, Eadwulf (died 913), and his son Ealdred maintained themselves at Bamburgh, ruling as 'Northumbria' the old Bernicia, for there was no significant Scandinavian settlement north of the Tees.[24] Plainly the eighth-century balance of powers had lost its fulcrum, a powerful

---

[22] *Scottish Studies*, viii, 96–103; G. F. Jensen, 'Place-Name Research and Northern History', *Northern History*, viii (1973), 1–23.

[23] Watson, *Celtic Place Names*, 172–3, gives the evidence. See also MacQueen, *Scottish Studies*, xvii, 26–7, where the attitude to a Norse element in Galloway seems ambiguous.

[24] Eadwulf's death in 913 is recorded by the Annals of Ulster which call him king, cf. Anderson, *Early Sources*, i, 403, n.3. Strictly he should be called ealdorman, not (Norse derived) earl.

Northumbria, and the striking of a new one could only be at the cost of the Norse of Yorkshire or at least of their kings. Their neighbours were the Northumbrian earls and the kings of Strathclyde. But no balance could ignore the kings of Scotia, as we shall call the kingdom north of Forth after the mid-ninth century (in preference to the Irish *Alba,* formerly meaning Britain, but by the tenth century, Scotland.)

The Viking impact upon this kingdom (like much else about it) is obscure. Kenneth mac Alpin was reputed to have taken some of the relics of Columba to a church built by him, presumably at Dunkeld, to have invaded Northumbria six times, burning Dunbar and Melrose, and to have suffered invasions by the Strathclyde British and by 'Danes' who devastated as far as Dunkeld. The invaders were probably Norse from the Northern Isles, and it is possible that there was more than one attack, since the Irish annals are unlikely to know the full tale. It is remarkable, on the other hand, that the sagas never describe ventures in these eastern waters and that after Kenneth mac Alpin's reign the fragmentary stories told by Scottish sources and Irish are pretty similar.

Thus Kenneth was succeeded by his brother Donald, for whose reign (858–862) no Viking attacks are reported. Constantine, Kenneth's son, ruled until *c.* 877; according to the annals put together by Duald mac Firbis a Viking attack on Fortriu in 864 or 866 adopted new tactics, taking hostages as pledge for a ransom, and this was probably the attack recorded in the Chronicle of the Kings by 'Olaf (of Dublin) with his gentiles', who stayed in Pictland for eleven weeks. Unfortunately the same source claims that Constantine killed Olaf in 869 or 871, whereas there seems to be good evidence that Olaf went back to Norway. Amid the conflicting computations of the different sources we can be sure only that Constantine's kingdom was invaded three or four times, probably from the west, that the 'gentile' armies exacted tribute during protracted stays, and that Constantine eventually gave battle and was killed. Dumbarton had been besieged and taken in 870, and it seems likely that for a time this was (like Dublin) a Viking headquarters while they mulcted the king of Strathclyde, whom Constantine caused to be killed in 872. 'Alcluyt', Dumbarton, is not heard of again until the thirteenth century.[25]

[25] J. Loth, 'Une généalogie des rois de Stratclut', *Révue Celtique*, xlvii (1930), 176–83.

Constantine's brother, Aed son of Kenneth, was killed in Strath-allan, after a year as king, by his cousin, Giric son of Donald, who then seems to have ruled concurrently during the period 878–889 with Eochaid, son of a daughter of Kenneth mac Alpin married to Rhun, king of Strathclyde. The stories told of these two men are irreconcilable, for while one source makes Giric foster-father and protector of Eochaid, another implies that they were rivals (which seems more probable). Most king lists ignore Eochaid, but he surely represents Pictish rights of succession, the reappearance of which is of some interest and may have clung for a time to part of Scotia north of Stirling (with which place his name is associated). Giric seems to have invaded Northumbria before his death at Dundurn in Perthshire, when the kingdom passed to Donald II (889–900), Constantine I's son.

Of Donald II it is known only that at one time the Vikings were defeated, at another Dunnottar was taken by them, and that Donald died at Forres. His cousin and successor, Constantine II, is slightly less shadowy, for he reigned for over forty years, critical years in the formation of the Scottish kingdom since Constantine had authority south of the Forth, the first king of Scotia to do so. The chronology of the reign is uncertain, and would become even more so if the dubious authority of the sagas were admitted.

The sources for the second decade of the tenth century may be juggled to yield a number of different accounts none of which can reconcile all the evidence. It seems clear that in 903–4 the Irish Norse raided Scotia to Dunkeld and it is likely that Strathclyde suffered in these attacks; Strathclyde seems to have been dependent upon Scotia, possibly ever since 870, and according to one Scottish annal the British King Donald was succeeded by Donald son of Aed and presumably Constantine's brother. Another version however makes Constantine give Cumbria to Owen, Donald's son, and an Owen certainly was king in 927.[26] These accounts may be reconciled in two ways: Donald died in 908, Donald son of Aed ruled 908–916, Owen, son of either Donald, from 916; or, assuming a mistake in the first version: Donald son of Aed died in 916, Owen, his son, ruled from 916. Either version illustrates Constantine's control of Strath-clyde between 910 and 920, the decade when Irish Norse attacks upon Yorkshire grew so heavy that in 918 the Danes of York sought the protection of Ethelfleda, lady of the Mercians. The English

[26] *Chron. Picts–Scots*, 9; *Chron. Fordun*, i, 163–4.

accounts show the Viking Rognvald landing in Northumbria by sea, driving out Ealdred of Bamburgh to take refuge with Constantine, and seizing estates of the bishop in county Durham.

If none of the sources is inaccurate, this invasion took place in 913–915. Believers in a single Rognvald have him withdraw to Ireland and return in 918; believers in two Rognvalds make the appropriate adjustments. Some have two battles at Corbridge in their creed, others invoke a trinity, the third battle on the East Lothian Tyne.[27] However many Rognvalds there were, only one battle is necessary: the Rognvald who left Ireland with companions in 918 devastated 'Dunbline' (Dunblane or Dublin) and attacked Scotland or, more probably, as Duald says, Strathclyde. He presumably then swung southwards and the Danes of York sought protection from Ethelfleda. Either now or in 914 she made the agreement with Scotia and Strathclyde (which Duald records) of mutual assistance against the Vikings and thus brought Constantine and Ealdred south against Rognvald to the battle at Corbridge in 918 in which both sides claimed success.[28] Constantine retired, Rognvald took York and in 920 Constantine, Rognvald, Ealdred and the king of Strathclyde and their peoples chose Edward, the successful Anglo-Saxon king, 'for father and for lord'. It was the first of several such commendations and its purpose is surely evident: to take assurances of peace beyond the Danelaw which Edward now largely controlled. No meeting of kings is hinted at, and Edward was not the only gainer from the treaties which were made,[29] but even when due allowance is made for the imperial outlook of the chronicler, Edward must surely have been the negotiator from strength.

By 927 two principal actors had changed; Rognvald was dead and Athelstan, King of England, had occupied York, one of whose rulers fled to Scotia. It seems that an Ealdwulf (possibly Ealdred of Bamburgh) was also expelled from Northumbria by him. Athelstan offered a show of force and on 12 July at Eamont on the Cumberland-Westmorland boundary Constantine, Owen and Ealdred made peace with him, promising to put down idolatry, presumably among the Irish Norse. This was probably a 'boundary-homage', a submis-

---

[27] A. Campbell, 'Two Notes on the Norse Kingdoms in Northumbria', *Eng. Hist. Rev.*, lvii (1942), 85–97; F. T. Wainwright, 'The battles of Corbridge', *Saga Book of the Viking Society*, xiii (1946–53), 156–73.

[28] The date of this battle is the one fixed point in the sources.

[29] As Stenton points out in his excellent assessment, *Anglo-Saxon England*, 334.

sion on Athelstan's frontier, by which the three undertook to keep
peace with him; but it did not reduce them to the status of vassals,
then lowly. Indeed, since Athelstan stood godfather to Constantine's
son, the gathering was of households not armies. Seven years later
Constantine gave Athelstan cause to mount a large-scale invasion on
land and sea by the east coast route. He probably reached Dunnottar
and not just Edinburgh, as an Irish annal maintains, and Constantine may have yielded his son as a hostage; yet the best account of the
reign makes no mention of this campaign, probably because Constantine refused battle. Three years later, in 937, Constantine and
perhaps the king of Strathclyde joined the Norse of Dublin in a
great invasion of England which was resoundingly defeated by
Athelstan at Brunanburh—a site which has not been identified. It
was a famous victory in chronicle and song and it cost Constantine
his son, and perhaps Owen of Strathclyde his own life, but it was not
followed by a submission or peace like those of 920 and 927; when
Athelstan died in 939, a Dublin Norse chief seized York and in 940
was ceded the Danelaw by King Edmund. In 941 he raided Northumbria as far as Tyninghame near Dunbar and Edmund did not
recover York until 944. He followed up in 945 by a harrying of
Cumbria; he blinded the sons of King Donald (possibly Owen's son)
and commended the province to the king of Scotia 'on condition
that he be his helper both on sea and on land'.[30]

However dense the Norse settlements in, for example, Cumberland, it is very probable that during Athelstan's reign Owen of
Strathclyde had established his authority over Dumfriesshire and
Cumberland, that is, as far as the Eamont. But after Brunanburh and
the harrying of 945 Strathclyde could well have abandoned to
England all beyond the Solway. Whether this conjecture be valid or
not, the kingdom raided and commended to the Scottish king in
945 was that known sometimes as Cumbria, sometimes Strathclyde;
the supposed existence of two kingdoms would depend only on the
two names and the assumption, disproved by ample twelfth century
evidence, that Cumbria must lie south of Solway. The evidence is
perfectly consistent with only one kingdom, and the commendation
of 'Cumbria' as south-of-Solway to the king of Scotia is geographical

---

[30] For this and subsequent events there is a particularly valuable essay in
*Preparatory to Anglo-Saxon England*, ed. D. M. Stenton, 214–23; D. Whitelock
'The Dealings of the Kings of England with Northumbria', *The Anglo-Saxons*,
ed. P. Clemoes (1959), 70–88, surveys the tenth and eleventh centuries.

nonsense if 'Strathclyde' intervenes on the map. After Brunanburh, Constantine's influence in Strathclyde must have been much reduced, while the renewed traffic between York and Dublin across Cumberland would offer the Strathclyde kings the alternatives of conniving or being harried. Whether this situation had anything to do with Constantine relinquishing the throne of Scotia in 943 to enter religion we cannot know; his action need not have been as voluntary as the annalists proclaim, and despite old age he lived for another nine years, demanding of his successor, Malcolm I, about 950, that England be invaded.[31]

Until 927 the English lord of Bamburgh was probably as much a client of Constantine as the king of Strathclyde, for the intervention of the Norse demanded that he find a patron and protector, and the West Saxon king could do nothing for him. In these years he turned to, and was treated along with, the king of Scotia; did he pay a territorial price?[32] It is arguable that in the later ninth century the Scots took over Lothian perhaps as far as Lammermuir (the Dunglass Burn) or even the Tweed, for Durham writers tell of the Scots crossing the Tweed to invade St Cuthbert's land c. 890, and show that St Cuthbert's possessions north of Tweed, for instance Melrose and Tyninghame, had been lost. The medieval bishopric of Dunkeld had detached parishes in Lothian, and that of St Andrews a south-pointing finger down the Gala-water, the parish of the ancient kirk of Stow.[33] These features certainly belong to the extension of Scottish rule but they do not help to date it, and we have to balance the indications of Scottish control before or just after 900 against the statement that Edinburgh passed to the Scots between 954 and 962. The difficulty would be solved if the Scottish kings controlled Lothian to Lammermuir or Tweed from c. 890 until 927 or 937 but then yielded it to the lord of Bamburgh and the English king; the commending of Cumbria to the Scottish king in 943 was then a division of spheres of interest or control, as well as an insurance against attacks from Dublin and a purchase of Scottish clientage.

It was of course a personal bond, renewed (under threat) to

[31] D. P. Kirby, 'Strathclyde and Cumbria', *Transactions of the Cumberland and Westmorland Antiquarian and Archaeological Society*, lxii (1962), 77–94, is a useful survey from whose interpretation I dissent. There is a criticism in the same Society's *Transactions*, lxvi (1966), 57–92, by P. A. Wilson.

[32] Barrow, *The Kingdom of the Scots*, 152–62 argues persuasively the case for a Scottish Lothian from c. 900.

[33] Stow means 'holy place'.

King Eadred in 946, but with the final establishment of a Norse kingdom of York (947–954) Malcolm (who may have connived at it) was free to exploit the weakness of his neighbours. About 950 he harried as far as the Tees, taking men and cattle, but was perhaps otherwise preoccupied with rebellions by the men of Moray, who finally killed him in the Mearns. His successor Indulf, Constantine II's son (possibly the one baptised in 927) was killed in 962 by Vikings perhaps driven from York and searching for a new settlement.[34] In 954 the fall of York finally brought Osulf, lord of Bamburgh, under the control of the English king; he was made earl of Northumbria including Yorkshire, and it cannot be coincidence that about the same time Edinburgh was abandoned to the Scots. A Northumbrian earl who must grasp York firmly and obey a royal master in Winchester or Bath had little time for a rock-fortress lying as far to the north as London is to the south. But if Edinburgh slipped away, could Dunbar or even Bamburgh be held?

From 962 until 1005 the throne continued to alternate between the two royal lines or segments.[35] Dubh ('the black') was challenged twice by his successor Culen ('the whelp'), first unsuccessfully in Atholl, when the abbot of Dunkeld and the mormaer of Atholl were killed, successfully in Moray (to which Dubh may have withdrawn) where he was killed at Forres (966). Culen and his brother were killed 'in Lothian' by Rhiderch, King of Strathclyde, after seizing Rhiderch's daughter (971), yet Kenneth II (971–995), brother of Dubh, immediately invaded Strathclyde and suffered a reverse. The only account of the rest of this campaign is more than usually garbled in its surviving fourteenth century text, yet it was undoubtedly written originally in or soon after Kenneth's reign.[36] English sources do not mention the campaign, but in 973, after Edgar had celebrated his long-deferred coronation, six or eight other rulers acknowledged him as lord at Chester. Kenneth II had been honourably escorted there by the bishop of St Cuthbert's see and the two earls of Northumbria to whom, probably in 966, Edgar had given the two parts of the earldom, the more northerly being from

[34] Indulf was killed at the mouth of a river, either the Cullen in Banffshire or the Cowie in Mearns.

[35] A royal line is a number of kings related to one another as father and son. A royal segment is all the descendants of a king whether they became king or not.

[36] *Chron. Picts-Scots*, 10 and facsimile facing p. 1; Anderson, *Early Sources*, i, 512. On this chronicle see M. O. Anderson, 'Scottish Materials in a Paris Manuscript', *Sc. Hist. Rev.*, xxviii (1949), 37–9.

Tees to 'Myreforth'—a name which has generally been identified with the Forth, but is, surely, the Solway.[37] Now Kenneth acknowledged Edgar as lord, promised (along with the other kings) to be his helper by land and sea, received Lothian and was sent home with every mark of honour, including perhaps a gift of English manors to sustain the Scottish kings on their visits to the English court. It seems clear that Edgar recognised a *fait accompli*, acknowledging a Scottish occupation for the sake of promises of peace and an end to the ravaging of Northumbria. The 'help by land and sea', which is a favoured phrase of the Old English chronicle, in the tenth century amounted to little, and is likely to be the chronicler's gloss on a bending of the knee rather than the promise of a vassal king.[38]

There are difficulties about the other kings present, who included Malcolm, King of Cumbrians, and five Welsh princes, one of them a Dufnal usually identified with Donald, King of Strathclyde, who died as a pilgrim to Rome in 975; but the other four Welsh princes were not all ruling in 973 and the list has suffered some accretions.[39] The superfluity of Cumbrian kings in the 970s can be explained: Rhiderch, Donald's son, king in 971, disappeared as a result of the Scottish attack in 972, Malcolm, 'King of Cumbrians' in 973, was his brother and died in 997, and their father Donald, who had been king of Strathclyde-Cumbria from *c.* 940, had entered religion, presumably before 971, and died at Rome in 975.

Kenneth seems to have held by his promise to keep the peace until towards the end of his reign. It is possible that in 994-5 took place the invasion of England to the borders of Cumberland and ravaging elsewhere, possibly in Northumbria, which is mentioned in a garbled form in the king-list already cited. A northern English source of later date tells that the earldom of Northumbria was given by Ethelred II to Uhtred after he defeated Malcolm II, and since Uhtred was made earl in 994-5, this may be a confusion of a defeat

[37] Professor Barrow, pointing out that it is not the Forth, suggests that it was a crossing of the Tweed (*Kingdom of the Scots*, 153). The name occurs also as Myreford. 'Mire', meaning 'mud' entered English from Old Norse; 'forth' is a northern form of 'ford'. Solway means 'muddy ford'.

[38] The homage of Kenneth and others is firmly dated 973. Kenneth's visit and the cession of Lothian must have occurred between 971 and 975; the sources do not give a year but to most historians it has seemed evident that the two occasions were one. The best discussion of the sources for the cession of Lothian is M. O. Anderson, 'Lothian and the Early Scottish Kings', *Sc. Hist. Rev.*, xxxix (1960), 98–112.

[39] J. E. Lloyd, *History of Wales* (1911), i, 349n.

of Kenneth II in 994 with the known defeat of Malcolm II in 1006.
The loss of Lothian by the Scots which must have taken place between 973 and 1018 may be attributed to 994–5, 1006 or even to
the year 1000 when Uhtred might possibly have invaded that province as King Ethelred was invading the 'land of the Cumbrians',
Strathclyde.[40] Kenneth II died in 995 in a blood feud at Fettercairn.
After his successor, Constantine III (995–7), Culen's son, the various
succession lists on which we depend fall into great confusion: some
tell of Constantine's death at the hands of Kenneth 'Malcolm's son',
who is unknown unless he be Kenneth (III) grandson of Malcolm I
and son of Dubh. These lists give Giric, son of Kenneth, son of Dubh,
as Constantine's successor (997–1005). There is a separate list-
tradition which does not know Giric; this makes his father, Kenneth
III, Dubh's son, king, and indeed the Annals of Ulster mention
Kenneth's death as king in 1005.[41] It seems more likely that Giric
would be omitted in one tradition than that he could be accidentally
inserted in the other, and the two were perhaps joint kings for
reasons discussed later.[42] (See page 116.)

This 'lost history of the north'[43] coincides with the renewal of
Scandinavian attacks upon England, this time aimed at extorting
movable wealth; the host which from 997 had plundered systematically from south Wales to Kent departed with its fleet to Normandy
in 1000, whereupon Ethelred II ravaged the land of the Cumbrians
and his fleet the Isle of Man. The act was more than that of an
erratic man; it may relate to assistance given from the northern
Viking settlers to the new raiders, but was more probably a punishment of the men of Strathclyde for a recent incursion (perhaps in
994) into England. By 1005, when Malcolm II killed his predecessor
at Monzievaird and took the throne, the English king was far too
preoccupied with Danes to react to Scottish raids. So in 1006
Malcolm ravaged widely in Northumberland, besieging Durham for
the treasures of St Cuthbert until soundly defeated by northern
levies under Uhtred of Bamburgh, whom Ethelred II had already

[40] I hope to discuss the evidence for these events and the reason for placing
the battle of Carham and acquisition of Lothian in 1018 in the *Sc. Hist. Rev.* for
1976.
[41] There is even one version which gives no king between Constantine III and
Malcolm II, but I take it that this is a scribal omission; *Chron. Picts-Scots*, 152.
[42] W. F. Skene resolutely averts his eyes from the problem, *Celtic Scotland*,
i, 382–3.
[43] Stenton, *Anglo-Saxon England*, 379.

made earl. Some or all of Lothian certainly passed from Scottish control in these decades.

It was recovered by the Scots in or just after 1018 when Malcolm II, hoping to take advantage of the uncertain position of Northumbria, launched an attack which met the levies of the land from Tees to Tweed under Earl Uhtred at Carham and thoroughly defeated them. The date and place of this battle are given by independent sources and we may not reject them,[44] but it has become usual to reject the name of Uhtred because his death is (erroneously) placed in 1016. Uhtred was killed not in 1016 but after he had lost the battle of Carham in 1018. He was then summoned to Cnut, who may have feared treason with Malcolm II, and was assassinated at court. His brother Eadulf was entrusted with the earldom, and gave Lothian to Malcolm II (who had doubtless recovered it) for a secure peace.[45]

Malcolm was supported at Carham by Owen the Bald, King of Strathclyde, who may be the Owen, Dumnagual's son, killed, according to Welsh annals whose date must be in error, in 1015. We do not know whether he was the last king of Strathclyde; all that can be said with reasonable confidence is that at some time Duncan I, grandson and successor (in 1034) of Malcolm II, was king of the Cumbrians (that is, Strathclyde) and that he is the last to be so called. It is likely that from the early tenth century Strathclyde had been a client of the king of Scotia, and that its independence was virtually ended when the king of Scotia acquired Lothian, between c. 960 and 1018. In addition to Duncan in Strathclyde, however, Duncan's brother, Maldred, was married to a daughter of Earl Uhtred and sister of Eadulf, Earl of Northumbria (1039–1041), a marriage supposed to have taken place during Uhtred's life when Maldred must have been very young. The possession by Maldred and his descendants of lands in Cumberland is suggestive of a division between the two brothers of Cumbrian possessions so that Maldred ruled under the Northumbrian earl and Duncan under the Scottish king. It is possible that after Carham, when the Scots obtained Lothian, Strathclyde also obtained Cumberland and that it was lost to Earl Eadulf, who is known to have 'ravaged the Britons'. But a writ of 1041–1055 by Gospatrick, probably Maldred's son,

---

[44] As Stenton does in his otherwise excellent account; *Anglo-Saxon England*, 390, 417–18.

[45] *Symeon of Durham*, ed. T. Arnold (Rolls Series), i, 218, 84; ii, 155–6.

referred to Cumberland in (Earl) Ealdred's time, that is, 1018–39, and it is therefore entirely possible that the kingdom of Strathclyde extended over Cumberland and Westmorland for only short periods.[46] These counties were certainly in English hands from the time of Earl Siward and King Macbeth.

Malcolm II was brought by Cnut to submission after an invasion in 1031 which may have reached the Tay, since a hoard of coins was buried at Lindores, a measure associated with troubled times, and a fragment of scaldic verse alludes to submission by 'the princes in the north from the midst of Fife'.[47] It is likely that Malcolm provoked the attack by alliance with (or offering refuge to) Scandinavian opponents of Cnut. Duncan I's attack on Durham in 1039 was however mere freebooting upon a centre of wealth, and was beaten off with heavy losses.

Malcolm II's reign was marked by internal feuds which are glimpsed fleetingly in the annals. The mormaer of Moray, Findlaech, was killed by his nephews Malcolm and Gillecomgain in 1020; Malcolm died in 1029 and Gillecomgain, now mormaer, was burned to death with his men in 1032. His widow, Gruoch, was a granddaughter of either Kenneth II or Kenneth III, and now married Macbeth, Findlaech's son, mormaer of Moray. How far Malcolm II was involved in this feud is unknown. One of his daughters Bethoc was married to Crinan, Abbot of Dunkeld, possibly a laicised office; in 1029 Dunkeld was burned, whether accidentally or in a war between king and mormaer of Moray is unknown. Certainly Crinan survived Malcolm II and ensured the succession of his own son Duncan, the first instance of succession in the direct line since the mid-ninth century. Duncan I was active enough to seek out the rebellious Macbeth in Moray, where in 1040 he was killed. Macbeth became king and Duncan's young sons fled, possibly to their uncle Maldred in Cumberland.

Macbeth's reign is one of remarkable contrasts. We know that he and his wife were generous givers to the Culdees of Lochleven and

---

[46] Gospatrick's writ has been many times printed and discussed. The best starting point is F. E. Harmer, *Anglo-Saxon Writs* (1952), 419–24, 531–6. For place-name evidence in north-western England see Kenneth Jackson, 'Angles and Britons in Northumbria and Cumbria', *Angles and Britons*, O'Donnell Lectures (Cardiff, 1963), 60–84. Professor Jackson concludes that the late Cumbrian village names are due to resettlement from Strathclyde; but the importance of internal colonisation should also be remembered.

[47] D. Whitelock, *English Historical Documents*, i (1955), 311.

that in 1050 he was in Rome 'scattering money like seed'. In 1052, when the English king was forced to expel his Norman retainers, two of them fled and were received by Macbeth. Pious in the way that Fulk Nerra was pious, more acquainted with the world beyond the Tweed than any of his predecessors, Macbeth was assailed from within by Crinan, who was killed in battle in 1045, and from without by Earl Siward of Northumbria, who is said to have expelled him (perhaps from Lothian) in 1046 'and appointed another, but Macbeth . . . recovered the kingdom'. In July 1054 a similar expedition had a hard struggle but expelled Macbeth (again possibly only from Lothian and Strathclyde, possibly beyond the Mounth) and set up Malcolm III, son of Duncan I, as king. Yet in 1057 Macbeth had still to be defeated and killed at Lumphanan and his stepson Lulach was then recognised by some as king until killed at Essie in Strathbogie (1058). The path of Malcolm III to the throne was long and bloody.

It is possible that these events should be set in a rather wider context. From 1020 until 1130 the Irish annals confer upon the rulers of Moray the title of 'king', and if we set aside the fourteenth-century phantasies of Fordun we might see Malcolm II as an unsuccessful ruler who lost control of northern Scotland to the rulers of Moray and sought to win it back by an alliance with the jarl of Orkney, Sigurd, who married a daughter of Malcolm II, presumably not Bethoc. Their son, Thorfinn, emerges from the pages of saga rather larger than life, but that he was a mighty ruler is perhaps confirmed by archaeological excavation at his chief seat, the Brough of Birsay in Orkney. A cousin of Duncan I, according to saga he fought long against Karl, Hundi's son, ('peasant, son of a dog') who might be Duncan I but is more probably Macbeth. Saga, however, is untrustworthy on detail; since Malcolm III's first wife was Ingibiorg daughter of Thorfinn, alliance between them against Macbeth seems likely. Thorfinn died between *c.* 1050 and 1066, but even the *Orkneyinga Saga* does not credit him with helping Malcolm III; if he did so, the details are not now recoverable.[48]

[48] The most recent discussions of this problem are Anderson, *Early Sources*, i, 577–8; A. B. Taylor, 'Karl Hundason "King of Scots"', *Proc. Soc. Antiq. Sc.*, lxxi (1936–7), 334–41.

Note: For corrections to this chapter see page 116.

# 5

## ALBANNAICH

The chronicle of these two centuries to 1058 cannot answer the general questions that must occur to any reader. Perhaps the most demanding is what happened to Pict and Scot, for if Pictland in 700 spoke a P-Celtic language influenced by an earlier non-Indo-European language, by 1100 Gaelic was in general use except in Lothian; even in Strathclyde Cumbrian was disappearing, and in Lothian a small number of place-names in *Baile* show that Gaelic landowners were making their way into this Anglian stronghold and bringing their speech with them.[1]

Since archaeology is unable to distinguish between the material cultures of Scot and Pict (except in the case of symbol stones), it is not possible to show in the ground migrations of the former into or among the homes of the latter. The legend which was already current by the twelfth century of a destruction of Picts is manifest nonsense, and it would be bold to argue for a migration even on the scale of the Anglo-Saxon conquest of England. Common sense would indicate that the Dal Riata could people the land of the Picts with only a scattering, at best a close scattering, of Gaelic-speaking landowners, and it is on this hypothesis that the matter should be examined. Essentially the problem is linguistic, and experts are examining the transition from the rare and almost unknown to the ubiquitous and well known. On that problem (taken alone) little progress is likely to be made. In the much better documented history of the Danelaw in England, a density of Danish place-names, far greater than that of Norse names in, for example, Cumberland, has

[1] W. F. H. Nicolaisen, 'Gaelic Place Names in Southern Scotland', *Studia Celtica*, v (1970), 18–19.

argued for a substantial folk-migration of women and peasants behind the Viking pathfinders, confirmed by the influence of Scandinavian upon English vocabulary, phonology, grammar and syntax. Yet this folk-migration passes unnoticed in the narrative sources and a powerful plea has been made for very modest Danish forces, thinly spread as lords of villages, a great deal of intermarriage and internal colonisation with consequent influences upon the English language.[2]

The feature of this debate which must strike the Scot is that both sides accept that the Danish settlement, light or heavy, merely *affected* and did not replace English, as perhaps Norse affected and did not replace Gaelic in the Western Isles. Yet in the Pict-Scot situation a comparatively small migration was accompanied by the replacement of Pictish by Gaelic, a process evidently complete by the twelfth century, when the Gaelic in the *Book of Deer* shows only slight divergences from Middle Irish. We shall need to know a great deal more about the historical conditions for major linguistic changes before a satisfactory explanation will be forthcoming.

One of the conditions which should bear investigation is that of social and economic change. England between the sixth century and the eleventh had a substantial (if unevenly paced) growth in population and a multiplication of villages by newly cleared or broken soil which can be documented in place-name studies. In Scotland similarly, while not every Scandinavian place-name in Dumfriesshire was a new Scandinavian settlement in the ninth century, many must have been formed then or before the eleventh century at the instigation of landlords who had taken Norse words into their vocabulary; in the eleventh century St Drostan of Deer was given 'the two Altries'; in 1095 St Cuthbert was given the two Aytons and the two Lambertons. That is the village of each name had earlier spilled over into subordinate settlements. In Fife there was already by 1124 a 'shire of Goatmilk', and both administrative term and district-name may be attributed to Anglian developers in a Celtic province. The best known Anglian developer in Lothian was Thor the Long, to whom *c.* 1100 King Edgar gave

---

[2] The main protagonists in this debate are K. Cameron and P. H. Sawyer; an introduction to it may be found in *Mediaeval Scandinavia*, ii (1969), 163–207. The literature is cited in Sawyer, *Age of the Vikings* (2nd edition, 1971), 250–6. There is also now a valuable general survey of place-name evidence in G. F. Jensen, 'Place-Name Research and Northern History: A Survey', *Northern History*, viii (1973), 1–23.

the part of Ednam which was unoccupied 'which I [Thor] inhabited with his help and my stock'.[3]

In the Carse of Gowrie the ancient settlement sites are to be found on the Braes of the Carse: Kinfauns, Kilspindie (earlier Kin-), Rait, Kinnaird, Benvie, with lower-lying settlements at either end; (Long-) forgan and Kingoodie to the east, and at the west end Inchyra and St Madoes, with archaeological evidence in the shape of symbol stones, though the form of the modern name 'St Madoes' is English. *Pit*-names are scattered along the western half of the Braes of Carse from Pitfour (which is probably a Pictish name in both its elements) near Inchyra to Pitmiddle; east of this to Dundee *Bal*-names seem to play the part of *Pit-* to the west. It is reasonable to explain both these as secondary and dependent settlements paying food-rents to the major centres, but *Bal-* may be later than *Pit-*. In the Carse itself, a series of Gaelic names stands out among the largely Scots and later toponomy: Inchyra, Clashbennie (eaglais[4] >clash), Errol (which may be a Pictish name), Inchcoonans, Inchmichael, Inchmartin, Inchture; at each of these places there is a higher contour line, an island of red sandstone among the estuarine clay, and loam suitable for early agriculture. Only Inchcoonans is not attested by the thirteenth century, and a date for all is suggested by -michael and -martin as between the eighth and twelfth centuries. These were perhaps settlements dependent on Errol. A study of *pit*-names in Fife has shown that they too show 'a distinct preference for loamy soils and for well-sheltered and well-drained positions'.[5]

Many more place-name studies by hands much more expert than the writer's are needed to lay bare the stages of internal colonisation between the fifth century and the twelfth. The logic of Dalriadic, Anglian and Norse settlement is not obliteration of earlier peoples, but exploitation and more intensive settlement, and this surely is what the successive elements of habitation names confirm even though their exact sequence and periods are still not fully explained.

In the history of the church we might expect to discern a clash of the cultures of the five peoples—treating Gall-ghàidhil and Dal

[3] Lawrie, *E.S.C.*, no. XXXIII; I take it that 'Edna*ham*' implies an existing, indeed early, settlement and that *Ednaham desertam* was only part of the village territory.

[4] Gaelic 'church'.

[5] G. Whittington and J. A. Soulsby, 'A Preliminary Report on an Investigation into *Pit* Place-Names', *Scottish Geographical Magazine*, lxxxiv (1968), 117–25.

Riata separately—who made up the kingdom of Scotland by 1058. But there is remarkably little sign of it. The abbey of Iona continued to exist during the Norse raids and settlements and retained its links with Ireland but not, apparently, with Dunkeld. Other monastic communities were established, but their origins are shrouded by conflicting legends. In the ninth century a movement towards reform, a stricter observance by clergy of celibacy, of a sabbatarian Sunday, and of canonical hours, spread from Ireland to Scotland. These 'vassals of God', céli De, whence Culdees, were established at Brechin, Abernethy, Loch Leven, Monifieth, Monymusk, Muthill and St Andrews, and indeed the only other monastic communities in Scotia are so shadowy that few are known to have existed. Dunkeld was dedicated to St Columba and Deer in Buchan to St Columba and St Drostan; the latter may just possibly go back to the seventh century as a Columban foundation, but is more likely to reflect the cult of (Pictish) Drostan in the eighth century or later, represented by dedications between Montrose and Beauly. The Monastery at Kilrymont, too, was founded before the 840s with relics of St Andrew, possibly from Hexham, possibly even from Byzantium,[6] and the community there had or adopted Culdee observances.

The foundation of bishop's sees, however, is also obscure. Some appear briefly and vanish, as at Iona and Abernethy; for St Andrews the evidence is rather better in the tenth century, but for the most part bishoprics are merely inferred. Thus St Andrews had a Culdee abbey and was a bishopric from the tenth century; Brechin had both in the twelfth century and is very likely to have existed in the tenth and eleventh. A sixteenth century source tells us of three bishops at Mortlach before the bishop found at Aberdeen *c.* 1140, and both here and at other medieval sees the succession of bishops must surely reach back to the effective acceptance of Christianity, in the seventh century, as at Glasgow and, even earlier, at Whithorn. But in the eleventh century several sees were probably vacant, their endowments passing into the hands of laymen; it is understandable that this should have happened under Macbeth or even Malcolm II, who needed to buy support, but it is remarkable that it seems also to have occurred under Malcolm III. Similarly, the abbacies of Culdee and other houses were laicised, probably because they became

[6] I am indebted to Mr R. G. Cant for an account of this interesting theory which would explain the appearance of Constantine as a royal name among the Picts *c.* 800.

heritable in a single family or fell into the patronage of aristocratic families who disponed them to younger sons. In the twelfth century there are abbots at Turriff, Kilspindie and Glendochart of whose abbeys no other trace is known, and this was the most extreme consequence of secularisation; the community at Deer probably disappeared by 1200. In other words the church in Scotland, apart perhaps from the east-central zone of the country, was characterised by secularisation and even decay in the eleventh century; how soon the process began is not known. It is noticeable, however, that no bishopric was founded or revived in Lothian after c. 960, and no religious community was formed in either Strathclyde or Lothian after they fell under Scottish control or influence in the tenth century; torpor already characterised the church.

It is likely that churches had been founded in the localities in considerable numbers, sustained by laymen and sometimes at the instigation of men of religion. The group of parishes in Lothian dedicated to St Baldred represents the activity of one such and others are less clearly indicated by more widespread dedications. Perhaps we should associate with the Culdee monastery St Regulus' tower within the conventual precinct at St Andrews. It is one of a group of early towers at Restennet in Angus, Dunblane, Muthill and Dunning in Strathearn, and Markinch in Fife. They belong to the broad family of Anglo-Saxon towers, though they may have been built at widely different periods, Restennet, perhaps, as early as the eighth century. Two were free-standing, Dunblane and Muthill, as were the round towers at Brechin and Abernethy, evidence of Irish influence in the tenth or eleventh centuries. Interesting as these buildings are, their fewness when compared with about 150 Anglo-Saxon towers surviving in England, is almost as striking as the restricted zone in which they are found.[7] When other evidence is taken into account—for example 'hog-back' and other commemorative stones —the number of kirks which can be inferred for eleventh-century Scotland is doubtless quite considerable. But only in the east-central zone does surviving building indicate a church which enjoyed substantial lay benefactions; it is probably not coincidence that this was also the only zone of complex diocesan boundaries. The detached fragments of the bishoprics of Brechin, Dunblane and Dunkeld scattered across the bishopric of St Andrews would arise from the

[7] G. Donaldson, 'Scotland's Earliest Church Buildings', *Recs. Sc. Ch. Hist. Soc.*, xviii (1972), 1–9.

diversion of episcopal conveth (hospitality rights) in a local kirk from one see to another and this diversion is likely to have been made by the lay patron of the kirk, the local landowner. Such kirks, it is clear, were often served by several clerics and had large parishes with dependent chapels to be served. These minsters survived into the twelfth century, most clearly in, for example, southern Scotland as at Kirkcudbright, Applegarth or Stow, but the non-Culdean monasteries of Scotia, such as Deer, were essentially of the same character, defined in the later Middle Ages as 'collegiate kirk'. Wherever we find in the twelfth century a large parish with kirk and dependent chapels over which the bishop was struggling to retain his rights, there we must suspect the earlier existence of a minster of clergy.[8] But the striking thing about this silent development is surely its silence; here was the literate class of contemporary Europe, and it has left us only one squalid gospel book to set beside the masterpieces of the Winchester scriptorium; the propagandists for emperor or king are paralleled by the genealogists of the king-lists. While we should be thankful for small mercies it is difficult to resist the conclusion that this was a church truly on the edge of Christendom.

Of course, secular society would have *filidh* and bards to retail a strong oral tradition and brehons who carried the lore of the law in their breasts. The existence of these in early days can be argued from the appearance of the *Gododdin* in Wales and the Dalriadan *Senchus* in Ireland, and from the existence of *sennachaidh* and *judex* in medieval Scotland.[9] It is an important feature of later historiography that it consistently underestimated and distorted the importance of Celtic Scotland in the Middle Ages, but the balance is not to be redressed by a wholesale importation of Irish institutions to fill out the exiguous evidence for the dark ages. Much that is commonplace in medieval Scotland has Scandinavian echoes: the land denominations in western Scotland, the ploughgate of the east, fencing the court to constitute it, the birlaw men who kept good neighbourhood, the long hundred of six score used for every commodity except money; of course, there is more that is Celtic or Anglian, but the eclectic nature of these institutions should warn against too heavy a borrowing from Ireland.

[8] I. B. Cowan, 'The Development of the Parochial System in Medieval Scotland', *Sc. Hist. Rev.*, xl (1961), 43–55.

[9] John Macinnes, 'The Oral Tradition in Scottish Gaelic Poetry', and Derick S. Thomson, 'Gaelic Learned Orders and Literati in Medieval Scotland', in *Scottish Studies*, xii (1968).

Social status was as important to a man in the tenth century as in the twentieth, but it depended upon fewer factors: the important ones were kindred and land. Perhaps early in the eleventh century or even in the tenth an attempt was made to put in writing the categories of men 'among the Bretts and Scots' according to the *cro* and *galnes* of each—the payment to his kindred for slaying him, in order to avoid a feud; the wergeld. Each grade had the same *cro* as the son of the grade above: king, earl, thane, son of a thane, and *nepos* (? grandson or nephew) of a thane or *ògthighearn* (literally 'young lord' but here in the diminutive sense, a lordling, laird, franklin). It seems likely that the thane's grandson was intruded by some later copyist or commentator who did not understand *ògthighearn,* but in any case the equivalence of thane and *tighearn* is implied; the thane was a lord, a landed man. The blood payments of the others were multiples or fractions of the thane's hundred cows, so that he was clearly the most numerous member of noble (that is, non-peasant) society.[10]

'All who are lower in kin (*bassiores in parentela*) are peasants' with a *cro* of sixteen cattle. The importance of kin is underlined by the bald statement that the *cro* and *galnes* are payable to the kindred while the *kelchyn* goes elsewhere.[11] Even more interesting is the equivalence of *cro* and *enach,* for this latter, though not discussed in the Scottish treatise, was well known in Ireland. It was a man's 'face' and hence (in the sense of 'lose face') his honour, and forms a part of the standard expressions for status—valuation or honour-price by which his oath and evidence and capacity in standing surety were measured. Although later in date, the early 'assizes' are often archaic and underline the importance of this valuation, for they have a deal to say about standing surety for the value of cattle alleged to have been stolen, evidently a common preoccupation. There is a list of prescribed 'steads', trysts as it were for rustled cattle, in Scotia, at

[10] The treatise is printed in parallel Latin, French and Scots texts in *A.P.S.*, i, 663–5. An important emendation is suggested by F. W. L. Thomas, *Proc. Soc. Antiq. Sc.* xix (1884–5), 73–4, which shows that the money equivalents are in the (Scandinavian) ora of 16 silver pennies (hence 10 ora = 1 merk), indicating an eleventh-century origin. Commentators have included the chapter on merchets in *Regiam Majestatem,* bk. IV, ch. liv (*A.P.S.,* i. 640), but I can see no strong reason for doing so. It does, however, give *filius thani = ògthighearn.* For a commentary of sorts see J. Loth in *Révue Celtique,* xlvii (1930), 383–400.

[11] It is not clear where. *Kelchyn* is apparently blood money also and a connection with *cylch,* hospitality payments, seems unlikely. The word in the French version is twice not *Kelchyn* but *Gelchach*; is this a clue to its derivation?

which ownership must be proven, and the core of this seems to go back at least to *c.* 1100.[12]

But the importance of the kin must have been even greater to the man who brought a successful appeal of theft against another, for the kindred of the judicially executed man might be expected to seek vengeance upon him. They would, of course, be punished by the king, who could not remit the penalty unless by agreement of the dead man's kin; if the king did so, 'without the knowledge of his kin, nonetheless his kin shall take vengeance of them that slew their kin.'[13] Behind such provisions must lie a society racked by blood feuds fostered by inadequate methods of proof; the dependence upon ordeal or oath helpers for guilt or innocence extended the range of feuds where public authority was remote and weak.

How extensive was the kin-group? No answer is forthcoming from treatises and assizes unless the '*cro* of a thane's grandson' be taken as evidence for the three-generation (descendents of a common grandfather) *gelfine*. Such lawyers' schemes seem untrue to reality and, it might be added, to other sources. But a three-fold categorisation, king: mormaer: toiseach[14] is found in the early (tenth-twelfth century) grants to the community of Deer in Buchan. Twice individuals are described as *toiseach cloinne A*, toiseach of the kindred of A, usually taken to mean 'chief of the descendants of a common ancestor' although again there is nothing to show how widely cast this *clann* would be. In the thirteenth century Neil, Earl of Carrick, (probably because his only children were daughters) made his brother's son, Lachlan, and his heirs, 'head of all his kin (*progenies*) both in *calumpnia* and other matters pertaining to kencynol', with the office of bailie and of leading the host in Carrick, under the earl and his heirs.[15] 'Kencynol', *ceann cineil*, meaning 'chief of kin' and synonym of *toiseach cloinne,* was recipient of tribute, *calp,* described much later in the Highlands as 'the best eighth' in cattle or other livestock paid to the chief at the succession of heirs 'for maintaining and defending of them against their enemies and evil willers'. In the

[12] *A.P.S.*, i, 372–3 especially c. IV; *ibid.*, 737, c. I. It is to be noted that in general the *Assise Regis Willelmi* are more archaic and authentic than the *Assise Regis David*. The attribution to a king should arise only from internal evidence.

[13] *A.P.S.*, i, 375, c. XV.

[14] The word 'toiseach' is pronounced *taw-shuch* with the emphasis on the first syllable.

[15] *Reg. Mag. Sig.* i, nos. 508–9, Appx. ii, no. 1953.

sixteenth century one clan could choose a neighbouring magnate to be its chief by the giving of *calp,* and it was remarked that, in token of the protection owed, the chief 'as use is' gave a sword in return at the making of the compact.[16]

The antiquity of this form of clientage is undoubted and we may discern the relics of an archaic kin-group, acknowledging a common ancestor, its members clinging together and recognising a leader for mutual protection of their lands, delimiting their numbers and the territorial scope of their chief's authority by the payment of *calp,* and their number perhaps fraying at the edges because 'as the propinquity removes they become less considered, till at last they degenerate to be of the common people'.[17] Commentators on the *duine uasal,* the petty aristocrat of the clan in the eighteenth century, remarked that he was often the chief's kinsman as well as his tenant; although it is not possible to demonstrate continuity of social organisation we cannot deny the intense conservatism or archaism of Gaelic Scotland, the Gaidhealtachd. The notion of a *clann,* of the 'noble' kin holding land, paying *calp* to the chief and following him with the sword in war, fits well enough to eleventh-century Buchan, thirteenth-century Carrick or sixteenth-century Argyll.

For the toiseach is not only head of a *clann;* the community of Deer was given lands sometimes 'free of mormaer and toiseach till doomsday'. From Malcolm II it received a king's dues in Biffie, a mormaer's dues in Altrie from (presumably) a mormaer, a toiseach's dues there from (presumably) a toiseach.[18] Complex though the texts are, we may perceive behind them the exploitation of land by a dependent peasantry, paying rent to the free landlord who may also be 'noble'—mormaer or toiseach. The descent of land within the *clann* is indicated by some of the Deer place names in the form *Pett Meic G,* 'the farm (or clearing) of the son of G' where *meic* may well have the sense of 'member of G's *clann*'. The lord of the *pett* could grant it to the church, but it might still be burdened by the render which he in turn had owed as a dependent to toiseach,

---

[16] Skene, *Celtic Scotland,* iii, 318–20, 368–9, quoting *A.P.S.,* iv, 548 (1617); Scottish and Irish Gaelic *calpa* (obsolete) = a full grown animal, cow or horse. See aslo *A.P.S.,* ii, 214b, 222a.

[17] Skene, *Celtic Scotland,* iii, 318.

[18] This paragraph benefits from the splendid new edition and commentary by Professor K. H. Jackson of *The Gaelic Notes in the Book of Deer* (1972). I have ventured to accept the hint on p. 43 that the latter part of no. II may relate to a single group, Domnall Cathal and Cainnech.

mormaer or king, and which only they could extinguish. But there remained other lay services which those in the *mund* ('protection'— the word is used in another early land grant)[19] of a greater man owed to him, notably following him with the sword. The struggles of tenth-century English monasteries to escape from the obligation to produce a military following in virtue of the lands which they held were perhaps sharpened by the tendency at the end of the century to demand money instead. There was a parallel struggle in Scotland, where about 880 the king gave 'liberty' to the church, hitherto held in Pictish servitude, but where his successors were less accommodating. Thus Deer claimed that their founder, a mormaer, had given 'freedom till Domesday from mormaer and toiseach', and, more credibly, recorded other examples of 'quenching' by laymen; evidently the term was not sufficiently specific, for the record was touched up in the twelfth century to specify 'freedom from mormaer and toiseach'. A mormaer and his wife and a toiseach 'quenched' the possessions of the community from secular exactions on four davachs, and David I expressed this as 'quit and immune from all lay office and secular exaction'.[20] Whether we take this as a total or partial exemption of Deer's lands, and whether the imposts were military or financial, they were taken upon the basis of a unit of land assessment, the davach, and not upon that of personal relationship of *tighearn* to *toiseach* or *mormaer*. Their root was the assumption (underlying the duty of hosting generally in Europe) that each house and its land will produce a warrior. The banding of those warriors in kindred groups and their service in provincial units may be just as archaic but we cannot trace its evolution in Scotia.

The mormaer appears first in the early tenth century; his title means 'great steward' and he can be traced between then and the twelfth century in a number of the provinces which may have arisen from the effect of geography upon the distribution of Pictish tribes. The mormaer is virtually absent from Ireland, and quite probably, therefore, existed in the Pictish kingdom. Whether he represents a demoted tribal kingship (*righ tuaithe*) is unknown, but the loss of some Pictish provincial names, Fidach, Fortriu, Ce, Circinn, and use of new names with the mormaers (for example, Moray, Strathearn,

---

[19] Lawrie, *E.S.C.*, no. **XIV**.
[20] Jackson, *Gaelic Notes in the Book of Deer*, 32. I have taken no. VI as 'quenched all the gifts to (the Deer community) from all imposts on the dues of four davachs'.

Mar, Buchan, Angus, Mearns), suggests new divisions; these are most likely to have arisen as a result of the Viking threat and the need for an efficient militia. It will already be plain that the mormaer was a territorial magnate, usually, if not always, toiseach, and, the *Book of Deer* apart, the narrative context in which he is found is as leader of a host, the 'army' of his province: in 918 in fighting the Norse 'neither the king nor any of the mormaers' of the Scots was killed; in 976 three named mormaers of Alba took part with two Irish kings in a foray. It is certain that the mormaer was leader of the army of his province, and the freedom of the church 'from mormaer' fits well into that context. Whether he held this office heritably is another question. Even among the mormaers of Moray it can only be said that the mormaership passed within a family sometimes as the result of family feud. There would certainly be a tendency to hereditary succession, strongest in the areas remotest from royal centres, as Moray in Scotland, Northumbria in England; in the heart of the kingdom, between Strathmore and Forth, a higher degree of responsibility, of success in maintaining order against external and internal foes, may have been expected by the king, with consequent changes of mormaer.[21]

The kings of Scotia and of Scotland stamped unity upon the four or five disparate peoples north of the Tweed and Solway; yet the precocity of a single kingdom of Scotia or Alba in the mid-ninth century (from which Scotland was made) seems to excite little comment. It is in marked contrast to the contemporary disunity of England south of Humber and to the progressive fragmentation of the Frankish realms. Most of all, the history of Scotland between the fifth century and the twelfth contrasts with that of Ireland from which the Scots of Dal Riata stemmed, lacking clear evidence of the petty tribal kingships and the provincial high kings of Ireland but producing a single kingship which, unlike the high kingship at Tara, ruled effectively, so effectively that the king was able to bring and keep under his sway peoples of different political traditions in Lothian and Strathclyde. The only Celtic realm with well-formed and independent political institutions at the beginning of the 'high middle ages' was that with, apparently, the smallest cultural heritage, Scotland.

[21] Skene, *Celtic Scotland*, iii, 49–60; Jackson, *Gaelic Notes in the Book of Deer*, 102–10.

It is unlikely that we shall ever know all the elements in this paradox, but something at least can be said of the kingship which is one element. The unique rule of succession among the Picts disappeared almost without trace in the 840s, and succession thereafter bears some resemblance to what can be discerned of succession in Dal Riata among the descendants of Fergus, but in more certain detail. Examination of the period 843–1005 reveals that while both brothers and sons of a king were eligible to reign, the succession of a brother was exceptional (in 858 and 877 only) and that son never succeeded father. Thus if the *derbfine* still existed, that is, if all descendants of a king to the fourth generation were eligible, even though the second and third generation had not reigned, it was never called into play and was unimportant. The only king whose father was not a king was Eochaid (878–889) who may represent a last fling of Pictish succession, a *leth-righ*, able to reign only in conjunction with Giric, Donald's son; or, conversely, Giric was able to make the title of his line effective only by allying with a member of the line of Kenneth mac Alpin. Most kings must have had a brother or brothers and each might be expected to prefer kingship to go to a brother rather than a cousin; yet except in 858, 877 and 971 no king's brother appeared as a ruling king.[22]

It is of course correct that succession took place within the royal house and within the *derbfine* of kings, but this is true of most or all European kingships and is scarcely remarkable. But the limitations already pointed out within the *derbfine* cannot be a matter of chance, and must reflect a balance of power between two segments of a dynasty. Each king descended from Constantine I and his close kin or *clann,* who made up Constantine's segment of the dynasty, and their clients, accepted that a particular descendant of Aed from Aed's segment of the dynasty should succeed him, to the exclusion of Constantine's own brothers, sons and other members of his segment; and contrariwise for each king descended from Aed. These two segments combined to alternate power in order to exclude all other lines and segments, such as the descendants of Donald I. Thus, the succession-history argues strongly for the existence of a *tanaise* (literally 'the expected one') or designated successor to each king; only this will explain the kingship of a second cousin, Malcolm I, at

---

[22] In 858 and 877 a king was succeeded by his brother; in 971 another king intervened between brothers.

the abdication of Constantine II.[23] The collusion of a king's brothers
in their own exclusion can only be explained by the power of the
alternate segment and the need to promise it the next bite of the
cherry in order to enjoy the current bite undisturbed.[24]

This delicate balance was upset when king Dubh was killed by
his (presumed) *tanaise* and successor Culen; for when he was killed
after a short reign, Dubh's brother Kenneth II became king and in
977 killed the brother and possible former *tanaise* of Culen. Two
sharing royal segments thus became three rival ones, a fact which
explains the turbulence and uncertain succession from 995 to 1005,
or indeed to 1058; the two versions of who ruled from 997 to 1005
may possibly be explained by an attempt on Kenneth III's part to
exclude other segments by associating his son Giric with himself not
just as *tanaise* but as joint king, *leth-righ*. If so the attempt was unsuccessful.

The segment or *clann* of Malcolm II successfully excluded that of
Aed-Constantine III and probably also that of Dubh, whose fate is
discussed later. Malcolm II, however, had a brother (or less probably
third cousin) Boite, whose son or grandson was killed by the king in
1033.[25] Since Lulach as king was called 'the nephew of Boite's son',
Boite may have had a special claim on the kingship, that is, have
been recognised as *tanaise* to Malcolm II, but, if so, after his death
Malcolm evidently took steps to secure the succession of his daughter's son, Duncan I, steps which gave his other grandson, Thorfinn,
the notion of a claim to the kingship. How far contemporaries were
disconcerted by the succession of a daughter's issue we do not know,
for Macbeth in his turn was even more distantly, if at all, connected
with the royal house. The accession of Lulach would be readily
explained if he had been acknowledged *tanaise* to his stepfather,
while the turmoil in 1093 would be explained if Edward, son of
Malcolm III, had similarly been *tanaise*. It proved impossible to re-
establish in the eleventh century the earlier tanistry among col-
laterals; the medieval chroniclers who invented a new succession law

---

[23] The abdication may have been forced because it was felt that a reign of
43 years had excluded the alternate line for too long.

[24] On the anthropological evidence see the introduction by Jack Goody to
*Succession to High Office*, ed. Jack Goody, (Cambridge, 1966).

[25] I suspect that in the manuscript transmission of the annals, this entry, *mac meic Boete
meic Cineadha* included an inadvertent duplication of *meic*, and that Boite's son, not his
grandson, was killed. I have not accepted the very late statement which makes
Macbeth's mother a sister of Malcolm II.

of Malcolm II had grasped the right stick if from the wrong end. Willingness to share with another segment had vanished in distrust, and kings looked instead for the succession of their own progeny at whatever cost.

Part of that cost was the support of other elements in the realm, particularly magnates, purchased by wars upon neighbours. The invasions of England in 972, 1006 and 1061, soon after a king's accession, and on many other occasions, (for example, in 937 and 1039) were not so much in pursuit of territorial gains as a necessary indulgence of the clients who had made him king, to fill their purses and his. The raids are a late relic of the cattle-raid on which a new Irish king embarked to show that success and wealth would characterise his rule; the 'good men' of Scotia went off to rustle Northumbrian cattle and plunder the treasuries of Northumbrian churches, and perhaps, too, to drive men north into slavery. This was not the turmoil of an 'heroic age' but the greed of men in an undeveloped economy selling their loyalty for the symbols of wealth and status—gold and silver. It is inadequate to characterise tenth-to eleventh-century society as barbarian or primitive, though it had something of both qualities; perhaps the most neutral description is 'archaic'.[26]

The discarding of the *clann* of Dubh as potential kings led to their becoming (as sometimes happened to discard segments in Ireland) enkinging and inaugural, possibly enrobement, officials. The inauguration ceremonies of the king of Scots scarcely appear in the light of day in 1292 and 1306 before they were drastically modified in 1329. But the enthroning of the king certainly had a continuous history from early times, and evidence shows that the earls of Fife played the leading part in placing the king upon his throne in the thirteenth and twelfth centuries. As early as 1095, the earls' family was known as Macduff and the members of it, called

[26] The literature on Celtic kingship is extensive, and Anderson, *Kings and Kingship*, does not deal with the period after 843. The most important contributions in periodicals are D. ÓCurráin, 'Irish Regnal Succession, a Reappraisal', *Studia Hibernica*, xi, 7–39 (which I found most helpful); G. MacNiocaill 'The "Heir Designate" in Medieval Ireland', *The Irish Jurist*, iii, (1968), 326–9. The best short account is D. A. Binchy, *Celtic and Anglo-Saxon Kingship* (O'Donnell Lectures for 1967–8, Oxford, 1970). Three general books of recent date have very different approaches; in order of appearance they were: W. A. Chaney, *The Cult of Kingship in Anglo-Saxon England* (Manchester 1970); J. M. Wallace-Hadrill, *Early Germanic Kingship in England and on the Continent* (Oxford, 1971), F. J. Byrne, *Irish Kings and High Kings* (1973).

Constantine, Duncan, Malcolm, were clearly close to the royal line in a special sense; to this may be attributed the unique position of the earl of Fife at a later date as 'chief of the law of clan Macduff', enjoying privileges of exemption from blood-feud and possibly of sanctuary.[27] This closeness, these functions, were given in compensation for exclusion from the kingship itself.

The king was made at Scone, near the meeting of Fortriu and Circinn, where the salt waters of the sea (and the powers of death who dwell in it) are finally turned back by the living waters of the river. Scone 'of the high shields', 'of melodious shields' as the eleventh-century prophecy of Berchan called it, referring surely to the clash of shields at the acclamation of a new king, was the scene of the promulgation c. 906 of freedom for the church at the 'hill of belief,'[28] and a battle in 728 at *Caislen Credi*, with the same meaning, makes Scone a place of significance in Pictish times. The Moot Hill there (as later centuries called it) was probably a barrow or chambered cairn associated with some eponymous ancestor of a royal line, and on it the new king was seated upon a stone and perhaps invested with rod and mantle. The enthronement links this ceremony with one of the most archaic in Ireland, a survival of the primitive Indo-European idea of kingship into historical times. The making of a king was his marriage (*banais righe*) to the land and people he ruled and to its earth-goddess, often in animal form. The Irish rites pilloried in the twelfth century describe the sacrifice of a mare, boiled in water in which the king bathed, while eating its flesh and drinking the broth; thereby he assured the fertility of land and people during his rule. Elsewhere in Ireland, and indeed in the periphery of the Indo-European world, the seating of the ruler upon a stone (Hindu, *rajāsūya*) is a surviving part of these fertility rites. The rite was performed in Westminster Abbey in 1953, in Carinthia and Ireland until the sixteenth century, and it stems from a very simple rite of Indo-European societies: man and woman sitting down together as token of marriage.[29] Lacking the equivalent of Middle

---

[27] Skene, *Celtic Scotland*, iii, 303–6. I am inclined not to dismiss completely the story which appears in Fordun of a Macduff fleeing Scotland and Macbeth to join Malcolm III. Behind the elaborate narratives of Fordun there is usually some brief annal, and although none can be identified for this tale, it does name, circumstantially, Macduff's landing at Ravenspur on the Yorkshire coast; *Chron. Fordun*, i, 197.

[28] Anderson, *Early Sources*, i, 273, 519, 445 *in colle credulitatis*.

[29] In addition to the literature on kingship cited above there is a valuable

Irish literature, we have in this ceremony at Scone an invaluable anthropological glimpse of the pagan sacral kingship which lingered on, increasingly archaic, until David I 'abhorred the *obsequia*' which the Scots offered to him at his inauguration. Whether this included sacrifice of an animal we have no means of knowing; but what lingered on until the 1290s was enthronement and possibly investment with rod or sceptre and sword, certainly enrobement, obeisance of leading men, and recital of the king's genealogy. The last named must have been carried over from Dal Riata and might have been impossible for a Pictish king; in general the enkinging at Scone was made up of ceremonies from the common stock of kingship in the Indo-European world, but much older than the Christian veneer with which they were covered in many realms.

The inheritance of Malcolm III was a Celtic realm, remote, moneyless, but with a tradition of submission to one king which, however slender, was two centuries old and no longer fragile. Its control of non-Celtic regions in the south was an historical consequence of the power vacuum created by the destruction of a sound and strong political unit between Humber and Forth; into this vacuum both Wessex (England) and Alba (Scotland) were drawn willy-nilly. The Tweed frontier was now so well established that only prolonged political upheaval in either realm could have led to its replacement by a Tyne or Forth border. For almost two centuries after 1058 the Scottish king hankered to increase the Anglian territory under his control; and meantime the drift of Celtic expansion was halted and reversed, and a long linguistic retreat began.

discussion in E. Goldman, *Die Einführung der deutschen Herzogsgeschlechter Kärntens in den slovenischen Stammesverband* (Breslau, 1903); see also P. MacCana, *Celtic Mythology* (1970); A. D. and B. Rees, *Celtic Heritage* (1961); M. L. Sjoested-Jonval, *Gods and Heroes of the Celts* (1949); A. D. Rees, 'Modern Evaluations of Celtic Narrative Tradition', *Proceedings of the Second International Congress of Celtic Studies, 1963* (Cardiff 1966), 31–61.

*Addendum to the 1978 impression.* On pages 92, 112 and 628 Giric (king 878–89) is called 'son of Donald'. Dr M. O. Anderson persuades me that he was 'son of Dungal' and not of the royal house. On pages 97, 113 and 628 'Giric son of' Kenneth may well be a copyist's slip, inserting a non-existent son for Kenneth III, as Dr Anderson (*Kings and Kingship*, 52) argues.

# 6

# CELT, SAXON AND NORMAN, 1058–1124

The kingdom to which Malcolm III succeeded on the death of his rival in 1058 was his, says the *Melrose Chronicle,* by hereditary right. As a king, Malcolm has enjoyed a substantial reputation, but one derived from the Shakespearean legend of Macbeth and the hagiography which extols Malcolm's wife, Margaret. That he was responsible for the death of his predecessor or predecessors calls for little remark in eleventh-century Scotland; it would be more remarkable if it were otherwise. That Queen Margaret achieved a reformation in manners and morals among the Scots may well be questioned in ecclesiastical affairs and is without supporting evidence in secular. Yet the reign of Malcolm is of great importance, for in it he tried to extend the frontier of his kingdom to include a more substantial Anglian territory. This aggressive intent is perhaps the outward manifestation of an attempted internal change of emphasis from the Gaelic inheritance of the monarchy to the English, and, perhaps, the Welsh.

The history of Malcolm III is closely interwoven with the turbulent history of the English earldom of Northumbria with which Scotland had a common frontier at the Tweed. Escorted by Earl Tostig Godwin's son (who had succeeded Siward in Northumbria in 1055), the archbishop of York and the bishop of Durham, Malcolm visited the court of King Edward in 1059; a visit at so short an interval after the recovery of the kingdom may suggest that Malcolm was renewing his predecessors' undertaking to be the helper of the English king, but it is more likely that he sought to recover English estates which had been set aside, perhaps in the tenth century, for the support of the Scottish king on his visits to the English king. One source, of indifferent value, suggests that he had already begun to make war on Northumbria and was brought to Edward to make peace. But we should be safer to accept that it was in 1061 that Malcolm, not yet married to a Saxon, not yet opposed to the Norman, ravaged Northumbria for the first time. He did this while Tostig was in Rome, and it seemed to the chronicler heinous that he should so attack his *conjuratus frater,* words which may support the suggestion that Malcolm was sworn to be the helper of the English; the attack earned King Malcolm nothing but a chronicle entry.

In 1065, when Tostig was expelled by the Northumbrians, he fled to Scotland, and Malcolm may have been privy to the expedition of King Harald Hardradi of Norway (1066) which, sailing by way of Orkney, was joined by Tostig from Flanders, attacked Northumbria and was overwhelmed by Harold II of England at Stamford Bridge. Malcolm was doubtless already (and perhaps long) married to Ingibiorg, probably daughter of Earl Thorfinn the mighty of Orkney and cousin of the first queen of King Harald Hardradi; but there was no certainty of loyalty through such alliances in such times. By this marriage Malcolm had two sons at least, Duncan and Donald, of whom the latter died about 1085. The fate of Ingibiorg is unknown but there is no reason to think that Malcolm put her away, and she probably died by 1069.

If Malcolm supported the Norse expedition of 1066 it was but another of his miscalculations, for it helped Harold II to lose the battle of Hastings and so to set William I upon the English throne. Yet for two years the north was left much to its own devices and disorders; in 1067 the earldom of Northumbria was sold by King William to Gospatrick, descended through his mother from Earl Uhtred, but son of Maldred (brother of Duncan I) and hence cousin of Malcolm III. In the following summer (1068) there fled to Scotland from William's court Edgar Atheling with his mother and sisters, Margaret and Christine, and, after William had occupied York, Gospatrick and other northern nobles took the same path. Malcolm had perhaps intended to support the disaffected English; if so, he was bought off by William.

In 1069–70, when the power of William was most seriously challenged, Malcolm played his part. A Danish fleet made junction in Northumbria with the disaffected English, including Edgar Atheling and Gospatrick and Waltheof, son of Earl Siward, representatives of the rival Northumbrian comital families. There is no evidence that Malcolm III gave assistance, and Symeon of Durham marks a second flight of Edgar Atheling and his sisters from England to Scotland in 1070, when the rebellion had collapsed. It failed because King William laid Yorkshire waste with unparalleled severity, because the Danes were bought off and because Gospatrick and Waltheof submitted to him. With a garrison in York, William again committed Northumbria to Earl Gospatrick, for he had pressing problems elsewhere. Gospatrick's first task was to deal with an invasion by King Malcolm by way of Cumberland into Teesdale; the barbarity of his expedition was redoubled when he heard that Gospatrick had attacked Cumberland, and the Scots were reputed to have killed all who could not be driven off to slavery in the north. It is possible that Malcolm's invasion was a belated attempt to help the English rising. But it bears few marks of that aim. Untimely and destructive, it has more in common with King William's campaign in Yorkshire, a deliberate attempt to subdue a province; it seems indeed to complement from the north the work of William, who with his army had reached the Tees from the south. Malcolm sought to benefit from the aftermath of war, but Gospatrick held the only great northern fortress—Bamburgh—against him, and the campaign had no known territorial result.

It was probably shortly afterwards that Malcolm married Margaret, sister of the Atheling. The date is uncertain though it was not later than 1071; the place was probably Dunfermline. The significance of this marriage should not be underrated, but it lies not so much in their own as in their children's relations with England. The disaffected English who fled to Malcolm's court would probably have done so without Margaret's presence, and the only one of them whom Malcolm greatly endowed, Gospatrick, was his cousin in the male line.

The marriage, however, was probably the immediate cause of King William's decision to come to grips with Malcolm, for it threatened a Scottish intervention in England more positively than hitherto. With naval support for his army, William followed the eastern route to the Forth, which he was able to cross. At Abernethy Malcolm 'came and made peace . . . and gave hostages and was his man'.[1] The terms of the peace are not known but it is likely that they forbade Malcolm to give refuge to English exiles; Edgar

---

[1] Anderson, *Scottish Annals*, 95, from the *Anglo-Saxon Chronicle*.

Atheling reappears two years later in Flanders, where, too, was Gospatrick, whom William had deprived of his earldom just after the submission of Abernethy, so that he fled to Scotland, which he shortly afterwards left again. Of the hostages, it is likely that Duncan, the king's eldest son, was one, and this mark of submission was completed by the formal homage which Malcolm evidently performed to William.

The peace did not hold, and once again it was Malcolm who broke it. In 1079 he ravaged Northumberland with, it would seem, the usual barbarities, and brought upon Scotland an invasion by Robert, eldest son of the Conqueror. This reached Falkirk and Malcolm again submitted and perhaps did homage to Robert, for the Norman chronicler Ordericus Vitalis, writing of 1092, states that William I had made Malcolm subject to Robert. To strengthen the royal hold upon Northumbria, a 'new castle' was erected upon the Tyne at the place which bears that name.

For a decade Malcolm stood by his word, but in 1091, when William II (Rufus) was in Normandy, Malcolm again invaded England, retreating before an English army with a great amount of booty. He was again joined by Edgar Atheling, perhaps before the expedition, but there is no indication that Edgar was the instigator of, or excuse for, this incursion. It brought the usual retaliation, this time by William II and Duke Robert, his brother, in person. Although their army lost its naval support by shipwreck in September 1091, Rufus advanced into Lothian, and there, by the mediation of Duke Robert, Malcolm III again made his peace, becoming the man of the English king (which implied homage) and swearing fealty as well. Rufus undertook to restore to him twelve vills in England and to pay twelve merks annually, rights which Malcolm had held under William I.

In the following year Rufus expelled from Cumberland Dolfin who had ruled it, built Carlisle Castle, restored the town and carried out a measure of peasant colonisation in the area. Malcolm III had not achieved any permanent occupation of this county and there is no evidence or likelihood that William I or II allowed him to keep it after his homages to them. During the reigns of Macbeth and Edward the Confessor it had been part of the Northumbrian earldom of Ealdred and Siward, and after 1066, therefore, of the various short-lived earls under William I, including Gospatrick, son of Maldred, the greatest landowner in the region, which Dolfin 'ruled' as grandson of Maldred, undisturbed because of its isolation. It has been suggested that the twelve vills restored to Malcolm in 1091 were Cumbrian, but the association with an annual fee suggests rather that the endowment was that to sustain the Scottish king on his visits to the English court. True, Malcolm does not appear as a landholder in Domesday Book (1086), but another survey showed him between 1068 and 1078 as tenant of three hides in Northamptonshire, which he had evidently lost by 1086. These may well be a part of those manors given to the Scots king in 973, for it is most likely these which Rufus promised to restore.[2] The point is of some importance, for in 1092–3 Malcolm's ambassadors were seeking fulfilment of his agreement with Rufus—only that of 1091 can be meant. The *Anglo-Saxon Chronicle* makes no attempt to link this with the expulsion of Dolfin from Cumbria, which comes in its narrative between the agreement of 1091 and the visit of 1093. The attempt to relate this visit to the Cumbrian situation is most unconvincing.[3]

The unfulfilled treaty brought Malcolm under safe conduct to Rufus at Gloucester late in August 1093. William refused to speak with him and is said to have sought to refer the issue to his own court while Malcolm wished a mixed commission upon the Borders; Malcolm returned to Scotland and rapidly gathered an army which was doubtless inadequate. In the ensuing invasion of Northumbria he was trapped by the earl thereof and was killed near the river Aln on 13 November 1093. Edward his eldest son by Queen Margaret was mortally wounded.

It is misleading to depict Malcolm in the tartan of a Lowland patriot. The narrative of his exploits suggests a brutality which the chroniclers may have overdrawn, but which surely made more remote the achievement of his supposed aim to push the frontier south to Tyne or Tees. He was an opportunist, ready to attack when the English king was abroad, refusing to fight and subservient when in turn his kingdom was invaded. He seems to have shown little regard for oaths and, by his attack in 1079, showed scant consideration for the safety of his son Duncan. The pointlessness of his incursions might be less marked if we could balance their cost against the booty driven off. Certainly, they show little thought for the native English, whether peasant or earl, and if made on behalf of Edgar Atheling

---

[2] E. W. M. Balfour-Melville, 'A Northamptonshire Estate of Malcolm Canmore', *Sc. Hist. Rev.*, xxvii (1948), 101–2.

[3] This is contrary to the view I took in *Sc. Hist Rev.* xxxvii (1958), 132.

(and those of 1079 and 1093 certainly were not) did nothing to forward his interest.

Yet the events which followed on his death, when the Scots chose as king, Donald, Malcolm's brother, and 'drove out all the English who were with King Malcolm before', must prompt enquiry whether this tale of enmity is adequate. The only 'Englishman' known to have been endowed by Malcolm was his cousin Gospatrick, to whom he gave Dunbar and other wide lands which in the twelfth century formed the earldom of Gospatrick II. It is likely that a few others, notably those associated with the events of 1068–71, were also endowed: Merleswain and Archill may have been ancestors of families known in David I's time. Two noble ladies of English name whose deaths were commemorated in the necrology of Canterbury Cathedral can be associated with Dunfermline Priory and were perhaps companions of Margaret; one was certainly endowed with lands in Fife. Yet the chronicle speaks rather of a courtly group than of an immigrant landed aristocracy, and we cannot envisage more than haphazard migration by a few of the dispossessed of northern England. It was in Normandy and not in Scotland that Edgar Atheling became a landed gentleman.

This conclusion, which may be only a reflection of poor evidence and is at best tentative, is mirrored by a similar conclusion on ecclesiastical affairs. A life of St Margaret by 'T'—probably Turgot, archdeacon and then prior at Durham, later bishop at St Andrews— is slender but positive evidence. Turgot speaks of her personal religious devotions and asceticism and her works of charity in maintaining twenty-four poor, in ministering daily during Lent and Advent to nine orphans, and, with King Malcolm, feeding three hundred poor in the royal hall, while fasting herself. His mention of the 'many councils' which she held to eradicate the malpractices of the Scots is reduced to an account of one three-day council in which she was helped by the king, who was able to interpret for both sides; Margaret, it seems, knew no Gaelic. The malpractices are significant. The church included Sundays in the computation of Lent; the people refrained from communion at Easter because of unworthiness; in certain districts of the Scots, mass was celebrated contrary to the custom of the church with 'I know not what barbarous rite'; work was done upon Sundays; marriage was permitted with a stepmother and a deceased brother's wife; there were 'many other matters which had arisen contrary to the rule of faith and statutes of ecclesiastical observances'. It is possible that Turgot's source for this account was a text of the council's statutes, the drawing up of which would imply a church busy with reforms of which there is no evidence. But the points listed come so close to those raised between 1112 and 1114 by Turgot himself, as bishop, with the pope that it is difficult to accept them as a true record of events twenty or more years earlier.

Most marked was Margaret's devotion to St Andrew, for she not only adorned the church of St Andrews, but also provided the Queen's Ferry over the Forth for pilgrims to that site. Land in Fife was given to the Culdees of Loch Leven by Malcolm and Margaret[4] and Turgot is emphatic about her support for men following an eremitic life. Her most striking act, however, was the introduction of three Benedictine monks, sent from Canterbury by Archbishop Lanfranc at her request, to found a priory at Dunfermline. This important initiative, an ingrafting to the monastic movement which was so fruitful and important in England, bore no further fruit in Scotland. The monastery of Iona, restored by her with monks according to Ordericus Vitalis, was perhaps a minster and not a Benedictine house. When part of the Benedictine mission to northern England settled in 1073 at Melrose (with Turgot among its number) it was persecuted for refusing fealty to King Malcolm, although Turgot seems to have joined Dunfermline Priory at a later date. Most striking of all, the Benedictine cathedral of St Cuthbert seems to have received no endowment at her hand, nor that of her husband. It is well to remark that Margaret supported and encouraged native devotion to native saints, and was little concerned with innovation in monastic life in Scotland.

On the vexed question of the state of episcopal sees there is little certainty. Malcolm is said to have founded one at Mortlach (Banffshire) but the story is late and dubious. It is more certain that the bishopric of Glasgow stood vacant, perhaps for many years. The see of St Andrew was occupied by Fothad, upon whom fell the first impact of a more regular ecclesiastical order in England.

In 1072 a dispute between the archbishops of York and Canterbury over canonical subjection was settled in an agreement which acknowledged that the archbishop of York had metropolitan status in northern England and the whole of Scotland. This was perhaps

[4] A King Malcolm (? III) granted land to Monymusk kirk and the cathedral church of St Andrew.

made effective shortly thereafter by reason of the political subjection of the same year, for Fothad is reported, in a York source of some two centuries later, to have performed subjection to York on the orders of Malcolm and Margaret. It is likely that this was intended by them to be similar to the subjection of York to Canterbury—that is, to leave the other Scottish bishops subject to York only through the subjection of the 'chief-bishop'. In practical terms the Scottish bishops would continue to consecrate one another, and doubtless Fothad, who died in 1093, forgot his subjection as readily as did Malcolm III.

If the sum of English influence is not impressive, the place and significance of Margaret is.[5] Her reiterated part in the ecclesiastical work of Malcolm cannot be greatly exaggerated in the sources, and suggests a pious character not without pride in its piety. But her influence over Malcolm is most strikingly exemplified in the names borne by her sons, of which four are those of her own ancestors of the royal house of Wessex: Edward, the eldest (after her father), Edgar (after her brother), Edmund (after her grandfather), Ethelred (after her great-grandfather); Alexander was named after Pope Alexander II or the Macedonian and David after the Welsh saint or the psalmist. Their daughters were called Edith (but later usually called Matilda) and Mary.[6] Entirely absent are the names of the house of Alpin, names which, by recalling predecessors and ancestors, were a proud assertion of belonging to the royal race. The fact that Margaret ignored a custom established in Malcolm's and doubtless many other families is indication enough that alien influences were strong at their court.

The death of Malcolm, Edward and Margaret within four days[7] was calamitous for these alien influences. One source states that Edward had been intended by Malcolm as his successor and he may

[5] Barrow, *Kingdom of the Scots*, 188-98.

[6] The order of sons given here is not the usual one but follows two early authorities: The *Durham Liber Vitae*, which gives all names, and *Dunfermline Registrum*, no. 1 in which David I names Edgar, Ethelred and Alexander in that order. The traditional view, which seems to be derived from a genealogy inserted into the Melrose chronicle late in the thirteenth century, would make Edgar the fourth son. But in that case Edmund would have been heir by primogeniture in 1094-97, when Edgar was certainly recognised as the oldest surviving son.

[7] 13-16 November 1093. Most sources imply that Edward died with his father on 13 November, but one states that he took until 15 November to die. Margaret died on 16 November, perhaps at Edinburgh—Fordun's gloss upon Turgot, who does not name the place.

even have been acknowledged tanist. Certainly Malcolm's eldest son, Duncan, who had been released from captivity by Rufus in 1087, had made no effort to return to Scotland and was scarcely a candidate for the throne had Edward lived. But he did not, and in the probable confusion of succeeding days the Scots, by which we may understand the leading magnates, chose Donald to be king, and expelled the English who had been 'with' his brother Malcolm, among them probably all the surviving sons of Margaret. Their refuge and their hope for the future was England.[8] Almost nothing is known of the reign of Donald III except his rivals. First to offer himself was Duncan, son of Malcolm, of whom it was perhaps already being said that he was bastard for his mother bore too close a relationship to his father. To Rufus he did homage and fealty and from Rufus he received a kingdom—Scotland. With an army of French and English he invaded Scotland, defeated Donald in May 1094 and was, we may presume, enthroned. But the Scots rose against him and after defeating him allowed him to retain his kingship but not the French nor the English nor the military service which they did for him. The rising is interesting for, unlike earlier revolts, it was not made in the interests of a rival; it seems to have arisen only from the strongest antipathy to the mail-clad knight and the foreign culture which he represented. It was followed by a revolt instigated by Donald III and his nephew and new ally, Edmund. On 12 November 1094 Duncan II was slain by the mormaer of Mearns in that province and Donald III reigned again. His relations with Edmund (who is said to have claimed half of the kingdom) are uncertain, but as Donald seems to have had no son, Edmund may have been his designated successor. By alliance with the rebel earl of Northumberland he renewed the hostility of Rufus, and it was perhaps in the summer of 1095, when dealing with the earl, that Rufus by investiture gave the kingdom of Scotland to Edgar as his vassal. Certainly, on 1 August 1095, in the cemetery at Norham, Edgar, calling himself king, and possessing the kingdom of Scotland and the land of Lothian by paternal inheritance and by gift of King William his lord,[9] made extensive grants of land in Berwickshire to St Cuthbert's church at Durham. With him were his

---

[8] A. A. M. Duncan, 'The Earliest Scottish Charters', *Sc. Hist. Rev.*, xxxvii (1958), 103–35. This article deals with Anglo-Scottish relations between 1094 and 1124.

[9] Lawrie, *E.S.C.*, no. XV: these words are an abbreviated translation.

brother Alexander, his uncle and namesake the Atheling, Constantine of the kin of Macduff, later Earl of Fife, and perhaps his nephew the young William son of Duncan II, with others who had no Scottish connection. The presence of Constantine is significant: not all the members of important native families adhered to Donald III. It was not until 1097 that Edgar Atheling was able to secure material help from Rufus to win the kingdom for Edgar, and Donald was defeated in a pitched battle. His fate is variously related but David seems to have played some part in it and Edgar owed his youngest brother a special debt.[10] Ethelred and Alexander were invested in the earldoms of Fife and Gowrie respectively.

The new king owed much to Rufus, who indeed found him a loyal vassal who carried the sword at the crown-wearing of 1099. But Edgar was still more closely allied with his lord when Henry I in 1100 married Matilda, the elder of Malcolm III's daughters. In 1102 Mary, the younger, was given in marriage by Henry I to the Count of Boulogne.[11] The community of outlook which these important marriages stimulated, though it was entered into in order to link the Norman kings with the house of Wessex, was soon apparent, though limited in its immediate effects. The two earliest documents of 'Scottish' provenances are exceptional in form, the product of exceptional circumstances. From about 1100, however, Edgar used the sealed writ, a Latin document of Anglo-Saxon origin, adapted and developed in Norman England and now transferred to Scotland, where the surviving examples of Edgar's reign, all at Durham, are notifications of grants made, with one letter of protection. Beneath them hangs, or hung, the royal seal, single faced, bearing the legend *Ymago Edgari Scottorum Basilei* and a crowned and enthroned king with sceptre and sword in his hands. The inspiration of this seal may have been that of Edward the Confessor; it was not that of the Norman kings. All the writs are addressed to his subjects 'Scots and English', and one, which alone has witnesses, bears these words out. The names in it are Anglian or Cumbrian; some may have been Northumbrian, but it is more likely that all were drawn from southern Scotland, where some are later found as land owners.[12] Robert, son of Godwin, alone is known to have come from England

---

[10] Edmund entered religion.

[11] Their daughter, another Matilda, was queen to King Stephen.

[12] Cnut, Carl's son, was perhaps a refugee from Norman Northumbria, now settled in Scotland.

with Edgar in 1097 as a knight; he received land in Lothian on which he began to build a castle and later died on crusade. But this is no indication that a wave of English refugees or colonists came to Scotland in the time of Edgar. We may be more positive that there was no Anglo-French settlement. The Scots who participated in the first Crusade were remarked for their simple faith and lack of knightly equipment.[13]

In the history of the church the reign of Edgar is equally unremarkable. The see of St Andrews, vacant since 1093, was not filled. Edgar founded no religious house and his great generosity to the bishop of Durham and St Cuthbert (whom one of Edgar's writs calls 'my lord') was tempered when, in 1099–1100, he deprived them of half of his previous endowments in Berwickshire. The remaining half, Coldinghamshire, a central manor with its ten dependent touns remained a fine patrimony for the saint, and Edgar was doubtless responsible for the building of a new church at Coldingham. Yet this was a minster or parish kirk, not a Benedictine monastery, and Edgar is otherwise known to have made only minor grants to existing religious houses. His brother Ethelred, Earl of Fife, held the laicised abbacy of Dunkeld.[14] The total impression is of a king with an outlook formed in the tradition of the late Old English state, concerned for Lothian (he died in Edinburgh) and for the saint who was the patron of Lothian—Cuthbert. Edgar seems to have cared little for Scotia, little for his Celtic inheritance in state and church. By his treaty with Magnus, King of Norway, who in an expedition in 1098 reduced the Isles to at least a temporary obedience, Edgar agreed that the Norwegian king should have all the islands to the west of Scotland. The Scottish king was left with the mainland areas, including Kintyre (for the story that King Magnus annexed Kintyre by being dragged in a boat from one Loch Tarbert to the other is probably legend).[15] Yet Edgar also abandoned the holy island of Iona in which (with two exceptions) the kings of the house of Alpin were said to have been buried until his own reign, when Donald III was carried there; and even if that, too, were a

[13] A. A. M. Duncan, 'The Dress of the Scots', Sc. Hist. Rev., xxix (1950), 210–2.

[14] Called 'a man of good (venerandae) memory, ... abbot of Dunkeld and also earl of Fife'. It must be said that this has been used as evidence that Ethelred entered religion.

[15] Kintyre belonged to Scotland under David I.

later legend invented by the monks of Iona, the place should surely have been uniquely holy to a king of Scots.

When Edgar died in 1107 he bequeathed, it was said, a part of his kingdom to his youngest brother. David seems to have played no part in Edgar's Scotland, and the new king, Alexander I, intended that he should continue at the court of Henry I as 'brother of the queen'. By 1113, and probably not long before that date, reluctantly and under threats Alexander gave his endowment to David: Lothian south of Lammermuir, Teviotdale and Strathclyde. Alexander's further concern with this region is represented by one letter to the prior of Durham confirming a gift by Edgar 'because I and my brother David will warrant the alms of our brother Edgar and ourselves'.

Alexander I is something of an enigma. Called 'the strong' even in the twelfth century, he was said by a contemporary to have held the kingdom *laboriosissime,* which surely means 'with a great deal of hard work'.[16] Like his brother Edgar he succeeded in dependence on the English king; unlike Edgar he married, being given an illegitimate daughter of Henry I who lacked both modesty and beauty; the match was childless. In 1114 he served as leader of a contingent, perhaps of Scots, in the Welsh campaign of King Henry. For the rest he is a man of Scotia. His Arab steed has been magnified by some historians into a cavalry cohort, but there is in fact no evidence that he introduced Frenchmen or Anglo-Normans to his court or his kingdom.[17]

On the other hand, his reign is marked by a serious effort to bring the ecclesiastical life of Scotland to a more regular order. Before becoming king, devotion had taken him to Durham to be present at the translation of the body of St Cuthbert to a new shrine. He filled the still-vacant bishopric of St Andrews as early as 1107 by the appointment of Prior Turgot of Durham. Turgot should have been consecrated either as a metropolitan or by his metropolitan, according to the status of his see as the law of the church, hitherto apparently ignored in Scotland, demanded. According to the judgement of 1072 his metropolitan would have been the archbishop of York, but the consecration of an archbishop of York had been delayed by refusal to promise obedience to Canterbury, and Arch-

[16] And not 'with difficulty': Ritchie, *Normans,* 164.
[17] King Edgar had a camel or an elephant.

bishop Anselm of Canterbury refused to permit the bishop of Durham and the bishops of Scotland to consecrate Turgot. Only on 1 August 1109 was he consecrated at York by the new archbishop, probably after a profession in which he reserved the authority of the church of St Andrew until the issues between it and York could be investigated. What these issues were is uncertain but the words of Symeon of Durham suggest that the king had forbidden Turgot to profess obedience to York and had further disputed his desire to refer the question elsewhere—probably Rome. Alexander was aware that the authority of an archbishop was necessary for an episcopal consecration, and it may have been this difficulty in relation to other sees which further exacerbated his relations with Turgot, who was forbidden to go to Rome in person. He withdrew to Wearmouth in 1114 or early in 1115 and died there on 31 August 1115.

Yet during his short episcopate he successfully raised a number of issues for reform of the church in Scotland, apparently with the co-operation of the king. Only the papal replies are known, but from them it is learned that King Alexander had directed Turgot to ask for guidance upon the four seasons of fasting and ordination (one of which was at the beginning of Lent), the giving of the eucharist to infants and the making of confession to priests, each an echo of a reform in Queen Margaret's supposed council. The Irish penitentials reveal a system, amateurish, even barbarous, of private confession, often to laymen, and a consequent infrequent recourse to communion; this system clearly had a hold in Scotland and lies behind both the 'infrequent communion' of the supposed council, and the 'confession to priests' of the pope's letter. The giving of the eucharist to infants could be the 'barbarous rite' at mass in the supposed council.

With this detailed letter came another of more general character, admonishing the Scots to abstain from vices, to preserve chastity and modesty especially in marriage, to do works of mercy, to go often to church, to confess sins frequently to priests, not to abstain from communion, and other generalities. Between them these two letters covered the same issues as Turgot's version of Queen Margaret's council, and the resemblances are most naturally explained as the result of a common derivation from the letter or letters sent by Turgot to the Pope. Thus, whereas misdirections of piety were answered by the Pope in detail, the breaking of divine law (Sunday work, marriage to a close relation, in Queen Margaret's council) was answered only by a general charge to abhor vices.[18]

Whether these issues relate to *c.* 1090 and *c.* 1113 or to the latter only, they cast considerable light upon the contemporary view of abuses: they are to be found in society at large and only marginally in the ecclesiastical order. They indicate an obsolete liturgy and calendar of feasts and ignorance of canon law. There was no concern with clerical immorality, simony, vagrancy or other abuses of clerical life which were the concern of reform movements elsewhere and which certainly existed in Scotland; the spirit of the reforms is not that of Lanfranc nor even of Dunstan, but is perhaps nearest to that of Theodore of Tarsus, the seventh-century archbishop of Canterbury. On the one hand 'close marriages' suggest the long survival in society of customs which survived from polygamy, and on the other the attitude to communion suggests enthusiasm in devotions; the two spirits are by no means inimical to one another, especially among recently converted peoples. But their survival from the sixth century into the twelfth is surprising.

Soon after Turgot's death King Alexander wrote to Canterbury, asking the archbishop to set aside the division of 1072 and re-establish the alleged custom whereby the bishops of St Andrews were consecrated by the pope or the archbishop of Canterbury. At the same time he ignored canonical order by procuring consecration of Scottish bishops by their own number. In 1120, when Alexander asked for a monk of Canterbury, Eadmer, to be bishop of St Andrews, the archbishop consulted Henry I, who tersely agreed, as if Eadmer were a chattel to be bundled off to Scotland. Thither he was sent, and one year later thence he went, unable to persuade Alexander that he should profess obedience to, and seek consecration at, Canterbury. The quarrel was a bitter one, but not perhaps of great importance, for the papacy and even Henry I supported the much more dangerous claims of York. The question of the investiture was raised and a compromise reached: by taking the ring from Alexander, the staff from the altar, Eadmer yielded much of his Hildebrandine principles. Thereafter we hear nothing of the issue in Scotland but royal control of this bishopric and of the church in

[18] D. Bethell, 'Two Letters of Pope Paschal II to Scotland', *Sc. Hist. Rev.*, xlix (1970), 33–45. In his discussion Mr Bethell dates the first letter '26 June', but his text reads *V. Kal. Iunii*, i.e. 28 May. This seems to rule out the year 1114. The relationship to Queen Margaret's council is my own suggestion.

general was clearly firm, and behind the special pleadings of York and Canterbury, which are our sources, we can discern a firm royal purpose to fill a key bishopric, too long vacant, with an able cleric who would help to bring to Scotland something of the monastic reform which was radically changing the face of the church in this half century. Unlike the Conqueror, Alexander I never found his Lanfranc, yet of his practical devotion to the church, the religious, and good works, there can be no doubt.

He had to turn to his ecclesiastical opponent of York for the means to further this devotion. From the community at Nostel in Yorkshire, which adopted the rule of St Augustine under Prior Athelwold (a royal cleric) and received vital material and ecclesiastical support from Archbishop Thurstan (a royal cleric), Alexander received six canons and a prior, Robert, as founding community of the priory of Scone. In view of the known concern of Henry I in Scottish ecclesiastical affairs and his later promotion of Athelwold to the bishopric of Carlisle, it was doubtless through Henry that Alexander negotiated this 'mission', perhaps as early as 1114. The canons came in 1115, and their church was perhaps dedicated by Bishop Turgot before he left Scotland in the same year.[19] Although associated with the reform which is comprehensively termed Gregorian, the Augustinians were concerned with leading a regular and spiritual life in communities and in no way rejected as inconsistent therewith the ecclesiastical claims and powers of Henry I and Alexander I. Early in 1124 Prior Robert was appointed (but not yet consecrated) to the see of St Andrew and probably at the same time the king projected a cathedral college of Augustinian canons there.

It was to the prime secular and ecclesiastical centres of Scotland that Alexander I sought to bring a regular common life and an example of spirituality. Why did this royal initiative make so little progress? We may compare the rapid and successful spread of the Augustinian or any other order elsewhere (or in Scotland at a later date) with the foundation of Scone priory and unfulfilled proposals by Alexander I for other foundations at Dunkeld or Inchcolm, Loch Tay, and St Andrews. Undoubtedly significant is absence of support from lay magnates, shown by the early charters to Scone Priory and Dunfermline Abbey, a marked contrast to the part played in

---

[19] There are difficulties about accepting a date so early, and Professor Barrow thinks the 'most probable date is nearer 1120' (*Kingdom of the Scots*, 171). There are also difficulties about accepting so late a date.

England by many if small donations from the baronage. Their enthusiasm eased new foundations not merely with gifts of rents, churches and lands but also with personnel. The indifference of the native aristocracy of Scotland was a barrier which could be broken only by a change in secular society.

The conventional view of these years 1058–1124 has stressed the innovations which mark them. Yet it may be doubted whether the innovations read into meagre evidence were important either in quantity or quality or, indeed, whether many of them took place in this period at all. For one characteristic of Norman and especially of Anglo-Norman penetration was a chronic scriptomania that left the records which have survived from the later twelfth century. Lacking the records, we may not argue that the men were nonetheless there, for the other works which are associated with them turn out, upon examination, to be rather the works of a queen, Margaret, and two kings, Edgar and Alexander. These three sought to influence, perhaps even to modify, but not to revolutionise. They were content with the framework of the Old Scottish state and, while Edgar may have permitted further English settlement in Lothian, under Alexander I the centre of the kingdom again moved north to Scone and Gowrie, the heart of Celtic Alba. They were less content with the Old Scottish Church and sought by way of Benedictine and Augustinian example to introduce the reformed monasticism which for centuries had failed to reach Scotland. That example had little immediate success.

# 7

## DAVID I AND MALCOLM IV

In this chapter three things concern us: the penetration of Anglo-French barons and knights into Scotland, the spread of the monastic order and the growth of the royal government. In much else that David I did or that happened in his reign we can discern the development of institutions and relationships not of his creation; we know little about them before this time save that they existed. In two of these three subjects, 'chaptourly gatherit', we are dealing with new influences in Scotland, the mailed knight and the grey-habited Cistercian monk, each following a way of life which grew up in Capetian France and which therefore shared common assumptions if not common ideals. The castle, the knight, the fief and homage arose from the endemic and often brutal warfare by which territorial principalities had been built up. They were still justified by the intermittent needs of defence. They had little relevance to the orderly development of government which nonetheless might protect or even encourage them, because they seemed part of a natural social order. Feudal order was undergoing radical transformation in the twelfth century as the castle became a home, knighthood became a brotherhood entered through a religious ceremony, the fief became a right, not a reward, and homage became a promise, not a way of thought. Society regarded government rather than war as its first resort because kings were stronger and because feudal warfare had produced a stalemate; but the formalities of feudal relationships remained.

Within the church the gross abuses of ecclesiastical office reflected the chaos of secular society. The demand for a purer order was insistent and could be achieved most simply by withdrawal from the world—that is, in the monastic life. The new monasticism was a reaction from lay disorder and interference in the church, but it flourished in a society progressively more orderly, more willing to accept the blessings and censures of the church. There were soon men to argue that the monastic ideal should not be pressed too literally if something was to be gained from compromise with the world. Monasticism too was changing, but the formalities of monastic life remained.

The Scotland in which David I was born about 1080–85 knew almost nothing of the feudal order or the monastic life. He was the youngest of the sons of Malcolm III and St Margaret;[1] some ten years at the Scottish court followed by exile and return were his upbringing, and he took this experience to the court of Henry I when in 1100 his sister married that king. Henceforth he was 'brother of the queen' (not brother of the king of Scots), growing into a place as one of Henry I's barons. He may have fought with Henry I in the conquest of Normandy, for he gave a confirmation of a church near Cherbourg granted by Robert de Brus to St Mary's, York. He was employed as a justice by Henry, which we may take as an indication of obvious, even outstanding, ability, for he was still landless or virtually so and, in terms of the early twelfth century, of little consequence. His succession to lands stretching from Glasgow to Berwick, bequeathed to him by his brother Edgar, was achieved by threatening King Alexander with a military following of Normans, a legitimate means of securing justice, and by 1113 he was in possession of at least the Tweed valley. Late in the same year or early in 1114 he received in marriage from Henry I Maud, daughter of Waltheof, Earl of Northumbria, and of his countess, Judith niece of William the Conqueror. Previously married to Simon de Senlis, to whom she had borne sons, Maud brought to David an earldom and the honour of Huntingdon with wide lands in Northamptonshire and other east Midland shires. The effect of this marriage upon Scotland's history was far-reaching, for it not only involved her kings in an attempt to acquire all the English possessions of Earl Waltheof and in an ambiguous dependence upon the English king for English lands, but also made a continuing relationship with Anglo-Norman knights and free-holders in midland England which brought them sometimes in a stream, sometimes in a trickle, to the kingdom of Scotland. A century later another Earl David, grandson of

[1] The date of the birth of David I is unknown, but as he was active in the campaign of 1097 it is likely to have been before 1083.

Maud and David I, was infefting Northamptonshire gentry in remote Aberdeenshire.

The span of these three generations, from the youth of one Earl David (1114) to the old age of another, his grandson,[2] is the period of Anglo-Norman penetration into Scotland. To take the story otherwise, to truncate it at 1153 or 1165, is to miss the sustained and transforming character of a movement which is one aspect of more general European trends. The land hunger or 'external colonisation' which took the Normans to England, Spain, Naples, the Holy Land, or for that matter the Frisians to the Elbe, is repeated in a more peaceful but nonetheless essentially similar colonisation of Scotland. David I did not transplant Normans to Scotland and feudalise the country in forty years; such a view needs qualification and modification at so many points that even as a rough generalisation it is seriously misleading.[3]

In the first place it is doubtful whether Normans were infeft in any significant number before 1124. Two substantial lists of witnesses to the inquest into the possessions of the see of Glasgow and to a confirmation of the possessions of Selkirk Abbey give the names of David's 'barons and knights'[4] along with native landowners. Many of these did not obtain lands in Scotland at any period,[5] while others[6] had insignificant holdings; they were present simply in the court of a powerful earl, and it is possible that their friends, also present, whom later we find as landholders, were not as yet endowed in Scotland. Robert de Brus was one of those in Scotland with Earl David; he was a Norman, from the Cotentin peninsula, who had thrown in his lot with Henry, brother of William II, and been rewarded with very extensive Yorkshire lands when Henry became Henry I. Soon after David became king, perhaps indeed at his inauguration, in 1124, Robert received from him the broad vale of Annan. That King David waited so long to grant land to his powerful older friend might suggest that during the reign of Alexander I he had hesitated to infeft his barons and knights in Scotland. Hugh de Moreville (a Norman family), with lands in the honour of Huntingdon, is a more consistent companion of David as earl and king; of lesser wealth in England, he was extensively endowed

[2] David, Earl of Huntingdon, died in 1219.
[3] Ritchie, *Normans*, deals with 1040–1165.
[4] Lawrie, *E.S.C.*, no. XLVI.
[5] E.g. Payen de Briouze, Osbert de Arden, Walter de Broy.
[6] E.g. Alan de Percy.

with an honour whose *caput* or chief place was, or was soon to be, at Lauder, an honour including Lauderdale and lands in the Tweed valley below Melrose at St Boswell's, Mertoun and Dryburgh. In the west he was given the lordship of Cunningham and he even held outlying lands in Galloway at Borgue. With Hugh we may mention the third of David's most favoured barons, Walter fitz Alan, a younger son of a Shropshire lord who had been born in Brittany. Walter seems to have entered the service of David I and visited Scotland in 1136, and later received another great western honour, Renfrew, Paisley, Pollock and other lands in Renfrewshire, with Innerwick in East Lothian. To these gifts by David I, Malcolm IV added in both west and east, and at the end of his reign may have granted Bute if it was indeed recovered from the kingdom of Man at this time. For his lands Walter owed to Malcolm IV the service of five knights.[7] David I gave him the honorific office of royal Steward which was confirmed heritably by Malcolm IV; to this office the family's later surname, Stewart, was owed. Perhaps a fourth man should be added to this especially favoured group, Robert Avenel (a Norman family), a young man from Northamptonshire, who came to Scotland *c.* 1141 and was granted Eskdale (beside the Bruce honour) by David I—perhaps because, like the king, he had lost his Northampton lands. He did not die till 1185 and by then was also in possession of lands at Innerwick.[8]

Most of the grants by David I were of far less extensive territories, and can be dated even less precisely. David Olifard (whence the Oliphants), who helped the king to escape from the rout at Winchester in 1141, was a tenant of the honour of Northampton; similarly Geoffrey de Melville (a family from the Pays de Caux) probably came to West Lothian; but the whereabouts of the first Scottish lands of both are uncertain. Later Malcolm IV, in recompense for Olifard's renunciation of his holding in Sawtry (Huntingdonshire) gave to him the lordship of Bothwell in Lanarkshire, evidence of a rare kind for it shows the king encouraging settlement of barons of his honour in his kingdom. One royal chancellor, William Comyn (a Norman family) had spent his youth in the household of Henry I's chancellor, who later became bishop of Durham; a see which David unsuccessfully sought for Comyn

[7] *R.R.S.*, i, no. 184.
[8] On all these families see Barrow, *Kingdom of the Scots*, ch. 11 and Ritchie, *Normans in Scotland, passim.*

1-4). His nephew, Richard Comyn, also came to Scotland and ved West Linton, marrying Hextilda, daughter of the lord of ndale and of Bethoc, only child of Donald III bàn. Another chancellor, Walter de Bidun (a Breton family), came from Northamptonshire. Randolph de Soules (a Norman family) came from Northamptonshire to be lord of Liddesdale; William de Somerville (a Norman family) came probably from Yorkshire to be lord of Libberton in Lanarkshire; Gervase Riddel (a family from Guienne) came from Northamptonshire to be lord of Cranston in Midlothian. A similar catalogue could be made of the arrival of Lindsay, Graham, Gifford, Herries—families which continued—or Engaine, Evermel, St Martin—families which did not. But it would only serve to illustrate further that this was a settlement by Anglo-French, mainly but not exclusively Norman by origin, and that the honour of Northampton sent more men to Scotland than the rest of England. They came because King David was their lord in both countries; many may have been younger sons like Walter fitz Alan with poor prospects at home, unwisely active perhaps on the side of the Empress in an area held for King Stephen. There can be little doubt that English events of the fifteen years 1138–53 were responsible for the decision by not a few to accept, or even to seek, fiefs in Scotland. Second to David's English honour (acquired by marriage) as an explanation of Anglo-Norman immigration to Scotland was the marriage of his son, Earl Henry, to Ada de Warenne, a connection which, especially perhaps in her widowhood, offered the attraction of fiefs to tenants of the great Warenne honour in England.

This account, which has taken in the reign of Malcolm IV, must be completed by the even more remarkable Flemish settlement in Scotland which took place in the same period. Disposing of estates in the Upper Ward of Lanarkshire which had anciently belonged to the see of Glasgow, David I and Malcolm IV settled in a distance of some ten miles a group of Flemings whose record is in village names: Crawfordjohn (John, stepson of Baldwin of Biggar); Roberton (Robert); Lamington (Lambin, brother of Robert); Wiston (Wice); Symington (Simon Loccard); Thankerton (Tancred). Baldwin, lord of Biggar, was the most important of this group, the king's sheriff of Lanark and perhaps the entrepreneur who brought the Flemings to the Clyde for the king.

As early as 1126 a Frenchman, Robert the Burgundian, held

land in Fife, which may have been given to him by Alexander I; probably equally early was the endowment of Merleswain, son of Colban (and perhaps grandson of the Anglian Merleswain who fled to Scotland 1068–70), in Kennoway. In the time of Malcolm IV, Ness, lord of Leuchars, son of a man with the French name of William, may have inherited his estate through a marriage between Celt and Norman. King Malcolm wrote to the magnates of Fife, naming the earl, Merleswain, Hugh son of (Earl) Gillemichael, G. mac Sluadach, Ness, and Alun;[9] only the last of these may have been French. Fife was a province in which there had been little foreign settlement. But its native aristocracy was already subject to the pervasive feudalisation found south of the Forth. The earldom had been held in turn by Constantine, Gillemichael, Duncan (I, died 1154) and Duncan (II). Their interrelationship is unknown, except that Duncan (II) was son of Duncan (I), whose predecessors were probably not father and son. This earldom, evidently now heritable, was granted by David I by charter to Duncan (I), as a fief in return for military service.[10] Thus, the most important earldom in Scotland was made akin to a French lordship, without dishonour to the earl and without an influx of land-hungry Anglo-French. When, early in the reign of King William, there was greater settlement in Fife by Anglo-French barons and knights, their pattern of tenures, their claim upon marriages, were already to be found among the native landowners there.

The colonisation of Moray is less well attested but must have taken place after an expropriation of some native landowners when the Moray rebellion of 1130 and the ancient earldom of Moray were alike suppressed. The distribution of forfeited lands in the Laigh of Moray, so far as our evidence goes, is strongly suggestive of a Flemish settlement in the area. Curiously, Freskin, to whom David I gave Duffus and an extensive northern territory, was lord of Strathbrock (West Lothian), while Berowald the Fleming, to whom Malcolm IV gave Innes and Nether Urquhart, has left his name in the truncated Bo' of Bo'ness (West Lothian).[11] Thus it would seem possible that the Flemish settlement of Moray was led by an entrepreneur from Lothian. Undoubtedly the king encouraged this

---

[9] *R.R.S.*, i, no. 181.

[10] *National Manuscripts of Scotland*, i, no. L.

[11] Berowalds-toun-ness. Houston near Broxburn may have belonged to another Fleming.

settlement as a means of providing himself with a contingent of adequately armed and mounted military retainers, for the service of a knight or half a knight's service is sometimes specified. Already it was necessary that, for the 'homage and service' of knight and baron, the king must grant fiefs heritably, and there is much to suggest that already the king was short of land for this purpose. The use of ecclesiastical property was an expedient of ancient but improper lineage to which the Scottish kings resorted, though perhaps only rarely. A grant of land with a supplementary money fee, payable until more land is granted, is found even under David I.[12] The diffuse character of several holdings can be demonstrated and was probably fairly general; at Crailing in Roxburghshire David Olifard had a tithe of the mill, Gospatrick the sheriff one and a half ploughgates and three acres with two house-plots, and Berengar Engaine had two bovates with one peasant and a toft, two other bovates and tofts, and a merk from the mill. This speaks of patches and fragments painfully assembled to make fiefs for vassals of the king; it contrasts markedly with 'the other Crailing' which belonged entire to a native Anglian landowner.

Perhaps we should distinguish baron from knight, putting among the former Bruce, de Moreville, Stewart and perhaps one or two others.[13] These richer men were lords of fairly compact honours and in order to fulfil their obligations they in turn had to grant fiefs on condition of military service. This is a process better attested for the later twelfth century than for the period before 1165, but without doubt it had already proceeded far by that date. So much we may conclude from the study of the early tenants of the Stewart honour of Renfrew: Ralph of Kent, Robert Croc (lord of Crookston), Henry of Nes, Peter and Robert fitz Fulbert, Robert of Montgomery, Ralph de L'isle, Henry of St Martin, Gilbert fitz Richer, Richard the Welshman (le Walleis), Nicholas of the Cotentin, all can with certainty or probability be assigned fiefs held of Walter fitz Alan, who died in 1177. All these names indicate French influence though not necessarily French descent; Kent, Ness, L'isle, are places in the Shropshire honour of the fitz Alans, while the honour of Montgomery in Shropshire and Wales gave their names to two more, and

---

[12] Lawrie, *E.S.C.*, no. CLXXXVI.
[13] David I would certainly have been more generous with the term baron, awarding it to men who personally served and advised him, but who held land offering the service of only one or two knights.

several of the 'surnames' (including 'of the Cotentin') can be found among tenants of the fitz Alan Shropshire honour. Unfortunately, the obligations of these men are not known and we must conjecture on other scanty, but nonetheless significant, evidence that sub-infeudation in return for military service was granted or imposed by the Stewart on at least some of his tenants. A similar account might be given for other honours of the early twelfth century. We must allow that in many cases the baron had limited resources of alienable demesne and that he may have had difficulty in infefting as many knights as he would wish. Nor was there a simple tenurial pyramid, with the king at its summit. Baldwin of Biggar, a royal tenant, was also tenant of fitz Alan but had granted his fief in turn to Hugh of Pettinain,[14] who also was a royal tenant elsewhere and who granted part of this Stewart fief to his brother. Complex relationships were characteristic of Scottish feudalism even by the mid-twelfth century.[15]

We hear very little of the personal relationship of vassal with lord; the ceremony of homage and oath of fealty we presume to have followed Anglo-Norman practice, but we are uninformed about the continuing loyalty owed by one to the other. Ailred of Rievaulx puts into the mouth of Robert Bruce a reproachful speech eloquent on the loyalty which the king owed to his faithful Normans, now his enemies; but the full account of the same episode, the battle of the Standard, suggests that many Scoto-Normans fought with King David. Bruce's second son and namesake had been infeft by his father with Annandale in clear anticipation of this clash of loyalties and in order to secure the whole Bruce honour for the family.[16] The revolt of the earls against Malcolm IV (1160) was suppressed undoubtedly with the help of his Norman vassals. It is also difficult to evaluate the relationship of incoming barons and knights with the native landowners of Lothian and Clydesdale. South of the Tay there is no evidence of expropriation, and it seems likely that these landowners would in some cases pass, or be placed, under the lordship of an incomer to whom obligations might be changed from money rent to knight service—and this can be shown to have happened in the later twelfth century in the de Moreville honour.

[14] Lord of Hugh's *toun*, Houston.

[15] Barrow, *Kingdom of the Scots*, chapters 10–12, are seminal studies.

[16] The source for this partition states that the son was taken prisoner by the father in a battle not explicitly said to be the battle of the Standard; below p. 370 n.

Society was doubtless aware of a distinction between incomers and natives. The address of royal charters to French and English, Scots and Galwegians shows that while we may grope today for the origin of a family, in the twelfth century the affinities of a free man were clear enough. The same formula stresses the descending social importance of the four groups named and too readily conjures up a picture of a kingdom oppressed by foreign rule. Such a view is partially true of England after the Norman conquest, but it would be a distortion if applied to twelfth-century Scotland. All four groups were the king's 'worthy men' (*probi homines*) and, however prominent the surviving charters (largely royal) suggest that the French were in David and Malcolm's court and household, the native aristocracy undoubtedly remained independent and influential in the countryside. In 1136 at Earlston the king endowed Melrose Abbey in the presence of men who are distinguished in his charter into two groups: the first, with eighteen names, is the king's court, largely Anglo-French but including Matad, Earl of Atholl; the second, with fourteen names, 'the men of that land' (Tweed-dale), names Earl Gospatrick, ten Anglo-Danish men of Lothian and finally three (including the younger Robert de Brus) of French origin. Often, though not invariably, where a grant of land is made the king's charter will tell the names of Anglo-Scottish laymen who were involved, perhaps as witness, perhaps as perambulator of bounds (related occupations), and who must have been the landowners of the neighbourhood concerned. In our preoccupation with the new men of David I and Malcolm IV we must not lose sight of the native landowners whom they left undisturbed, whose importance may have declined at court, but who were neither submerged nor depressed in their own or the king's eyes as a local gentry and even aristocracy.

In the course of this account we have hinted at the problem of explaining how the king found resources to graft the newcomers into Scottish society. There may have been as many solutions as there were incomers, but certain broad lines can be indicated. The Flemish settlement seems to be a systematic attempt to implant in upper Clydesdale and Moray, at the expense of the church and forfeited native landowners respectively, a new and foreign aristocracy and gentry which had no remaining ties with its land of origin. The endowment of Anglo-Norman barons and knights, on the other hand, seems the haphazard result of friendship and influence, drawn as it was from oddments of territory and revenue rather than from the main demesne of the king. For one thing, it was notably restricted to Lothian and other southern territories. Neither under David I, nor even under Malcolm IV, was there any alienation of the great royal estates north of Tay, a most telling indication that, while the king might replace native families who died out or were forfeited with newcomers, he would not replace himself as a landowner for the same purpose. The impact of Anglo-French penetration, then, was not general, but fell upon an important but nonetheless restricted part of the kingdom. The total number of incomers was never great and though already in 1165 they may have changed the landscape by erecting earthen mounds (or mottes) to carry their castles, the relations of free men by giving and demanding homage, the character of warfare, serfdom or even justice by new attitudes and techniques, nonetheless these things came gradually, were established in Lothian and Strathclyde, and only when accepted in these southern parts did they spread to Scotia. They were peacefully absorbed, and, as in any process of absorption, were themselves modified. In the making of feudal Scotland much was achieved by David I, but it is important to realise that his achievements were made without wholesale expropriation of native landowners, without intensive settlement by Anglo-French landholders throughout the whole kingdom, and without significant diminution of the resources of the king.

Relationships were by no means always smooth between the lay magnates and the religious patronised by the royal house. To the Culdee community of Lochleven, Sir Robert the Burgundian was the 'furnace and fire of all iniquity' who 'by the fervour of his rapacity and unbridled tyranny' took from them a quarter of Kirkness. There was clearly something contentious about Swinton in Berwickshire, which had been held by Liulf before being given to St Cuthbert by King Edgar, for when Alexander I confirmed it he added that the monks were not to answer to anyone for it unless he commanded, and in another brieve he made it clear that there was indeed a 'good-going plea' about it;[17] Earl David 'would not suffer any more that anyone should disturb you in it in any way, and that is for sure.'[18] By 1135 there was a monk at Coldingham to look after the rights of St Cuthbert, who was at law with Liulf over a wood,

[17] Lawrie, *E.S.C.*, nos. XX, XXVI, XXVII.
[18] Lawrie, *E.S.C.*, no. XXIX.

possibly at Swinton, for when the toun was later given by the king to his knight Arnulf we discover that Udard, son of Liulf, had held it; it is evident that the monks had been unable to get rid of him and had to settle for services from him which, when Arnulf succeeded, were commuted for 40s. yearly.[19]

A very similar tale can be told of Edrom and Nisbet. Edrom was given to St Cuthbert of Durham by King Edgar in 1095 as one of the dependent touns of the shire of Berwick, of which shire the saint was deprived by Edgar about 1100 because of his displeasure with Ranulf, Bishop of Durham. In fact, as the map shows, Edrom is something of an outlier to the rest of this shire[20] and the monks must somehow have retained a valid interest in this toun, as they certainly did in the other outlier of the shire of Berwick, Renton (by transferring it to the shire of Coldingham). But they faced stiff competition from Earl Gospatrick and not until the first decade of David I's reign did they obtain from the earl a charter of Edrom and its dependent toun, Nisbet, including a double threat of damnation upon anyone upsetting the gift; the cause of trouble had, of course, been Gospatrick himself. After his death in 1138 the king hurriedly ordered the Sheriff of Roxburgh to put the lands 'in respite' (that is, to exact no services from either the monks or Gospatrick's son, since giving the services would be a mark of ownership) until the king should come to Tweeddale himself, presumably to judge their dispute. In 1139 at Roxburgh he adjudged and confirmed the monks' title but as soon as he left in 1141 to support his niece in England the new Earl Gospatrick seized the lands and the monks' stock. He was sternly ordered by Earl Henry (as regent) to desist and return the cattle in return for the pledges which the monks offered. In 1147 a large royal court adjudged the issues again, and in consequence the monks were saddled with a liability for 30s. yearly and the performance of army service from the touns, in return for acknowledgement of a clear title.[21] At least in Lothian it is evident that whatever the king's will about lands which he thought were at his disposal, a sitting tenant could not be got rid of, and the best that might be obtained was a grudging payment of rent.

A later generation held that David I was 'ane sair sanct for the croun', a man more generous to the religious than his resources

[19] Lawrie, *E.S.C.*, nos. C, CI.
[20] Barrow, *Kingdom of the Scots*, 30.
[21] Lawrie, *E.S.C.*, nos. XV, XIX, CXVII, CXX, CXXI, CXXX, CLXXVIII.

warranted. There is something to be said for the view, especially as many of the economic benefits which the monastic orders brought were later developments arising in spite of, and not because of, the monastic rule. The late eleventh and early twelfth centuries were a period when the Rule of St Benedict, with its commitment to work and prayer for the welfare of all Christian souls, was subjected to several reinterpretations, all seeking a more spiritual life, a more thorough-going rejection of secular concerns within the monastic close. The Rule remained basic: poverty, chastity and above all obedience were the life of every monk. But from a few of the many monastic settlements or reformed monasteries which sought in France to practise a purer view of the Rule than did the older Benedictine houses, there spread daughter houses founded by laymen and faced with the old problems of reconciling needful endowments with poverty, and lay patronage with freedom from secular concerns. These problems were met in new ways, in new documents supplementary to the Rule. Hence there arose groups of houses sharing in the Benedictine rule but reinterpreting it, and usually adding constitutional links between houses such as were unknown to Benedictine monasteries.

The motives of secular lords in founding or endowing religious houses were doubtless mixed. The cost in material revenues alienated could scarcely be offset by hypothetical economic advantages. The patron, the founder and his heirs, especially where he was the king, might expect to nominate the abbot, and would expect a measure of hospitality. In his charters he will state that his gift is made for the welfare of the souls of his ancestors, himself and his descendents, and he may stipulate a service of prayers on their behalf. But such grants in Scotland are made 'in free alms', and substantially the grants were elemosinary, unburdened with quotas of knight service or other render. King David was doubtless better informed than most about the differing virtues of different orders, yet his patronage did not follow fashion and was given almost indiscriminately to the various new orders; in all of them he saw good. .The cost in land might be high, but the consequence, as the twelfth century saw it, of a spiritually affluent society, was worth the price. We may not doubt that the most compelling attraction of monasticism to lay society was the values proclaimed by the life of those who truly followed the Rule and gave themselves to God. 'The character which it impressed was one of order, of peace and of benignity, and it became a force of incalculable power not only for sanctification, but also for the lower but indispensable tasks of civilising and refining'.[22] A grant to the uses of regular clergy was made 'so that the place might be exalted in the service of God';[23] the whole kingdom shared in this spiritual leavening.

The earliest of David's foundations, made at Selkirk in 1113 before he became king, was a house of monks brought from Tiron (founded 1109), where liturgical uses had been pared down for a simpler and stricter life, and work, especially craft work within the cloister, received a new emphasis. It is in many ways the most interesting of David's foundations; the Tironensians seem already to have had a constitution whereby the discipline and rule of the order were discharged at annual chapters or meetings of abbots at Tiron. In 1120 abbots from overseas were excused attendance for two years out of three by William, Abbot of Tiron; his decision doubtless owed something to his having come to Selkirk from Tiron with twelve monks and with Earl David, who about 1116 visited Tiron in a vain effort to meet its recently deceased founder.

Abbot William had replaced the first abbot of Selkirk, who returned to the abbacy of the mother house; in 1118 William in turn went back to Tiron as Abbot. In 1128, in a move which is indicative if not typical of his rights as patron, King David transferred the abbey from Selkirk, which was 'unsuitable for an abbey', to a place as near as possible to his sheriff, castle and burgh of Roxburgh, across the Tweed at Kelso. From Kelso Abbey in 1144 a priory was founded at Lesmahagow, probably by the king and John, Bishop of Glasgow, together, and as a result of refuge given at Tiron to Bishop John.

In 1128 the Benedictine priory of Dunfermline was promoted at the instigation of the king to the rank of abbey. A unique light is thrown upon this process by the king's letter requesting the archbishop and convent of Christ Church, Canterbury, to send to him a person worthy of the abbatial dignity, with two or three monks, and carefully stipulating that the relationship of Dunfermline to Canterbury was to be fraternal and not filial; nonetheless, if in the future the monks of Dunfermline could find none in their midst suitable, they would accept an abbot from Canterbury.[24] In fact,

---

[22] Knowles, *Monastic Order in England*, 15.
[23] *in Dei obsequium*, Lawrie, *E.S.C.*, no. XLVII.
[24] *R.R.S.*, i, no. 8.

when the first abbot died in 1154 he was succeeded by his nephew, a Canterbury monk, who died only in 1178.

For twenty-five years David I showed his generosity to Dunfermline Abbey: lands in Fife at Dunfermline and Kinghorn and in Midlothian at Inveresk, with an eighth of judicial revenues in Fife, a teind of the king's produce-rents of all kinds (in considerable detail), a proportion of the seals taken at Kinghorn, tofts in five burghs, the church of Perth and a hundred shillings from royal revenues in England. These gifts were already made by 1128; by 1153 the list was much longer and showed some readjustments. There was added a teind of salt and iron brought to Dunfermline for the king's needs, a teind of the king's wild mares from Fife, half-ownership of the Queensferry passage, a teind of the king's *can* from Clackmannan, and a 'half of my teind of Argyll and Kintyre in that year, namely, when I receive *can* from there'. There were further lands, burghal tofts and revenues but, interestingly, the hundred shillings rent from England had gone; the king had helped to put the abbey on its feet by a temporary money revenue from England. His liberality in lands was striking, but he was less generous with lands in western Fife or with the patronage of churches and more generous in piecing together an income from his rights of lordship; and he gave nothing from north of Tay. Finally, we may note that there was already a royal burgh at Dunfermline itself, probably lying beside the royal hall or castle. The impression given by these endowments is of a calculated generosity based on a desire to consolidate a royal *Eigenkloster*, to complete the patronage begun by Malcolm and Margaret and to bring the monastery once more into communication with the Benedictine family.

A less favourable conclusion is suggested by the evidence of Coldingham, where King Edgar's church was still a non-monastic property of Durham Priory until *c.* 1135. About that year there was a monk, and by 1139 monks, at Coldingham; a decade later it was a priory. As we have seen, King David's charters show that he conferred Swinton, upon which Durham had a valid claim, on his knight Arnulf and thus caused prolonged trouble; his grant of Edrom and Nisbet was a confirmation of a prior gift by Earl Gospatrick, and he gave the church of Berwick in order to secure the surrender of Old Melrose kirk. For the rest he gave nothing new, merely confirming the alienation of an extensive royal demesne,

Coldinghamshire, already made by his brother Edgar; this was endowment enough.

The Cluniac order, with its emphasis on elaborate liturgical observances and its hierarchy of houses, seems to have had little attraction for the king. Between 1140 and 1150 William Gifford, prior or monk of Reading Abbey (Henry I's Cluniac foundation), was in Scotland and with the king walked the bounds of an estate, near Perth, the Rhynd, then granted to this house with the aim of establishing a cell there; about a decade later the cell was courageously established on King David's other gift, the isle of May in the Forth estuary, a holy place associated with a Celtic saint, Ethernan, but often storm-beaten or fog-bound. There are several connections which may explain the king's grant to Reading Abbey: with his sister Queen Matilda and her husband Henry I; with Brian fitz Count who dominated the Thames valley for the Empress; with the Gifford family who were his neighbours and his tenants. He was not unresponsive to the claims of family and party which Reading Abbey had upon his generosity; but his enthusiasm was discreet or even lukewarm, and it is tempting to believe that the reason for his failure to found a great Cluniac priory in Scotland lay in the strict dependence which a Cluniac mother house exacted from its daughter houses.[25]

It is in his support for the most remarkable of the new orders, the Cistercian, that King David's sympathy with monastic ideals can be seen most clearly. With the adherence of St Bernard to the Cistercian interpretation of the Benedictine rule and the foundation of Clairvaux, the popularity of this way of life grew, daughter houses were founded,[26] and the customs of what was now an order were committed to writing. Eschewing the elaborate ritual and liturgical accretions which were found in Benedictine and Cluniac houses, the Cistercians built their churches without adornment and their monastic buildings without concession to comfort—or sometimes even to the weather. They sought austerity and remoteness from the world in conformity with the Rule and to this end they rejected all revenues derived from rights; they would hold no proprietary churches, patronage, teinds, no profit from seigneurial courts, markets, bakehouses or servile labour. They looked for monastic sites remote

[25] A. A. M. Duncan, 'Documents relating to the Priory of the Isle of May', *Proc. Soc. Antiq. Scot.*, XC (1956–7), 52–80.
[26] There were 14 houses in 1119.

from village settlements and for land which could be tilled by the monks themselves and by lay brothers, who dwelt within the monastery or (where outlying properties required cultivation) in granges, and who were held to chastity and obedience as well as a minimum daily religious observance. In the annual chapters of abbots held at Cîteaux the order had a legislative instrument, while the regular visitation of each house by the head of its mother house ensured purity and regularity of discipline. This was a way of life which demanded fervour and spirituality in church and chapter-house, labour and patience in field and pasture, and above all a vocation.

If the four Cistercian houses which existed in Scotland in 1152 are less than one per cent of the number in Europe, they were nonetheless the largest and most significant contribution by David I to the religious life of his kingdom. The greatest was Melrose, founded in 1136, near the site of an ancient Anglian monastery, by monks brought from Rievaulx in Yorkshire, itself founded only in 1132.

Yet the foundation of Melrose Abbey may have been long in contemplation. Old Melrose kirk had been surrendered by Durham Priory, and the abbey of Selkirk or Kelso must have given up Eildon and the demesne of Melrose, for these now passed to the new abbey. King David may have had more than one connection with the Cistercian order, but the most probable link with which the foundation of Melrose Abbey may be associated was the activity of Walter Espec, a Yorkshire baron often found in David's train, in bringing the white monks to Rievaulx. About 1134 Ailred, a cleric of Hexham who had served the king at table and in diplomacy, suddenly became a novice at Rievaulx. The repute of the order in baronial circles in northern England was certainly great, and it is not surprising that King David earned the approval of St Bernard for his support. In November 1140, King David and his son founded a daughter house of Melrose at Newbattle, a few miles from Edinburgh, in 1142 a daughter of Rievaulx was founded at Dundrennan in Galloway—this perhaps not by the king—and in 1150 Cistercians from Melrose were brought to Kinloss in Moray and Holm Cultram in David's Cumbria. It seems possible that King David planned a Cistercian foundation in Angus; if so, he deserves some of the credit for Coupar Angus Abbey, founded by Malcolm IV with monks from Melrose. The endowments of Coupar are typical of all four houses save that they lie between Tay and Spey. A whole royal estate (Coupar)—one of four in Gowrie—was given, together with generous rights of fishing and pasturage in neighbouring rivers and forest. The church of Coupar was bestowed upon the abbey, in violation of the letter of Cistercian custom if not of its spirit. This is the first early sign that the falling away from the primitive purity of Cistercian observance which, already noticeable on the Continent, was appearing in Scotland too. The high repute of the order caused a rapid recruitment of monks and *conversi*, for whom sustenance and work were needed in the shape of wider lands. Should the order accept inhabited land with all that this entailed in secular revenues and secular concerns? Should it, could it afford to, refuse the generosity of laymen offering teinds or patronage? Whereas the Newbattle convent stipulated before 1150 that the *toun* of Pittendreich would not be moved nearer to the abbey, the convent of Melrose with episcopal approval before 1165 accepted the teinds of Eskdale from Robert Avenel.

In 1152 the general chapter forbade further Cistercian foundations because of the dangers of too-rapid expansion. Such dangers may not have seemed immediate in Scotland, where there were ample stretches of secluded valley and remote upland for further Cistercian colonisation. Broad as were the acres which David I and Malcolm IV conferred upon the order, they were for the most part under-settled territories close to 'forest' (that is, waste and scrub as well as wooded land) and hill-pasture. The development of a characteristic Cistercian economy based upon large-scale sheep farming cannot be documented at so early a period in Scotland. But not long after 1165 we read of boundary settlements and land exchanges which must be part of a drive for higher productivity and greater efficiency, and suggest that even in the last fifteen years of David I's reign his alienation of wide royal lands was repaid by a rapid development in exploitation of those lands.

That King David was influenced more by the small group of his intimate servants than by monastic fashion-mongering is most clearly brought out in the foundation of houses of regular canons during his reign. The priory of Scone already followed the rule of St Augustine with its accompanying observances, unwritten but elsewhere showing strong influence from the rule of St Benedict. Technically the regular canons were not monks; in practice their life was monastic. That they were allowed to undertake parochial cures seems a vital difference; but in twelfth- and thirteenth-century Scotland they were very rarely found serving parish churches (so far as we know).

In 1128 canons were brought from Merton in Surrey to found the abbey of the Holy Rood at Edinburgh. With them there came as abbot, Alwin, who had served as chaplain to David I when he was earl. About the same time a fellow chaplain, Osbert, became prior of Great Paxton (Huntingdonshire), also founded by David I. By 1150 this priory had vanished; its endowments and its prior had gone to Holyrood. Jedburgh Abbey owes its origin in all likelihood to the bringing of Augustinian canons from Beauvais in N. France by the king and John, Bishop of Glasgow, in 1138–9; John, as we have noticed, had been a chaplain of Earl David. A little later, the influence of the Cistercians and St Malachy, the Irish reformer, may have led to the adoption at David's cathedral of Carlisle of the stricter Augustinian observances of Arrouaise Abbey in Picardy. The king certainly gave revenues—hides and tallow from beasts slaughtered at Stirling—to Arrouaise, and by 1147 there was an Arrouaisian community beside Stirling, the beginnings of the abbey of Cambuskenneth.[27] At St Andrews an initiative towards an Augustinian foundation had been made by Alexander I. It took twenty years of exertion by king and bishop before a priory was founded there beside the Culdee community (1144), and the king's attempt to convey the Culdees' property to the Augustinians was a failure. In the island cell of Culdees in Lochleven the king threatened expulsion for those clerics who would not live *regulariter,* according to the rule; Lochleven became an Augustinian priory dependent upon St Andrews. The argument that canons replaced Culdees because both could serve parishes is of doubtful validity; but at Lochleven there is evidence that the Augustinian rule was used in Scotland, as it was so widely elsewhere, to bring a house of clergy to a more regular life. Malcolm IV was responsible for conveying the ancient church of Restennet in Angus to Jedburgh Abbey and so for the foundation of an Augustinian priory there. Thus, at the end of the period we are considering, two religious houses, Restennet and Coupar, were established in Strathmore, the heart of the old Pictish kingdom. Finally we should notice one private foundation: canons from Alnwick, following the Cistercian-inspired and strict version of canonical life practised at Prémontré, were brought by Hugh de Moreville to Dryburgh, the loveliest of all monastic sites in southern Scotland. The first settlement in 1150 became an abbey in 1152.

The scale of this effort whereby the tiny beginnings of Queen

27 It is often called the abbey of Stirling in twelfth-century sources.

Margaret and Alexander I were completed and then rapidly developed needs no emphasis. David I was not a northern king hearing of remote monastic movements which he sought to sample as by mail-order. Dunfermline Priory became an abbey and Coldingham kirk became a priory because of his family piety; his visit to Tiron was like a pilgrimage; he saw his clerical familiars become Augustinians and Cistercians, his friends at Henry I's court their patrons. He travelled among them and what he saw he thought good: they came to his court and what he could show them they thought good. It was the fortune of Scotland that when the greatest revival in the spiritual life of the undivided church was active, her king was one so much in sympathy with its aims. As yet his Anglo-French followers in the main lacked the resources, his Celtic earls the intuition or inspiration to emulate him. His brothers and grandsons, his English cousins did not share his outlook. As the ruler of a primitive and remote kingdom, David I is outstanding in the monastic movement of the twelfth century.

The authority of any government, the power of any state, depend in the last resort on the resources of which they dispose; the collection of revenue is administration stripped to its essential, while administration is for most governments no more than a means whereby political ends may be pursued. The twelfth century in Scotland has left us no ordinances of government, no survey of the kingdom or any of its regions and no unofficial treatise on administration, yet it is agreed that the agencies of medieval government were founded in that century.

The revenues of David I and Malcolm IV are known to us only from the teinds which they granted to religious houses; the terminology of the grants is not always clear and substantially it vanishes from the fuller record of William the Lion's reign, leaving us to grope for the outlines of an order which was already ancient when first documented.

The needs of the first monastic group at a new site were met by money secured on an English estate or by the surplus in kind from the king's residences. The canons of Arrouaise were attracted to Stirling by a half of the hides and a quarter of the fat of beasts butchered there; Alexander I made an elaborate assignment of woolfells, hides, fat and bread from his household north of Lammermuir to Scone Priory; with slight rearrangement a complementary grant was made, perhaps by David I, to Dunfermline Abbey, so that the by-products of the king's kitchen were wholly assigned to these two houses.[28] From his southern lands Earl David assigned to Selkirk Abbey half the hides and fat, all the woolfells and a tenth of the pigskins from beasts butchered for his kitchen, but no complementary grant is known.[29] The canons of Holyrood were assigned half the fat and hides of the Edinburgh killing, but they alone were given a money payment, £10 annually, from the king's purse (*camera*).[30]

These disbursements (which cannot always be reconciled one with another) suggest an income which was overwhelmingly in kind; diversions of part (usually a tenth) of renders due to the king are clearer evidence of the same thing. In 1128, Dunfermline Abbey enjoyed a portion of the following: the profits of justice from Fife and Fothrif, the king's cain brought to Dunfermline, the oats (*prebenda*) brought there from Fife and Fothrif, venison brought there, seals taken at Kinghorn, salt and iron brought to Dunfermline for the king's needs. Subsequently, a portion was granted of the king's cain of Fife, Fothrif and Clackmannan 'in flour, cheese, oats, bere, pigs and cows', but when this was included in the general confirmation of 1150 it appeared as the king's cain and bere of Fife and Fothrif and the cain of Clackmannan. The same abbey was given a portion of the king's wild horses and gold from Fife and Fothrif, of the king's *dominia* in Dunfermline and of the king's cain of the province of Stirling. The abbey of Cambuskenneth, however, enjoyed a portion of the judicial revenues of Stirling, Stirlingshire and Callendar and of the ferm of the king's *dominia* of Stirling.[31]

The most prominent of the resources mentioned in such endowments was *can* or cain. It is not found in Anglian Lothian or the Merse;[32] but it was due intermittently to the king from Kintyre and Argyll, whence a teind was divided equally between Dunfermline and Holyrood abbeys, due regularly from Argyll of Moray (the west coast of Inverness-shire), whence a teind was assigned to Urquhart Priory, and from the four 'cadrez' (Strathgryfe, Cunningham, Kyle and Carrick) of that part of Galloway which David held

[28] Lawrie, *E.S.C.*, nos. XXVI, LXXIV.
[29] Lawrie, *E.S.C.*, no. XXXV.
[30] Lawrie, *E.S.C.*, no. CLIII.
[31] Lawrie, *E.S.C.*, nos. LXXIV, CIII, CCIX, LXXVIII, CLXXIX.
[32] The bishop of St Andrews used the term in the Merse but by analogy with similar 'Scottish' rights.

as earl, whence a teind was assigned to Kelso Abbey.[33] We have seen that it was paid from Fife, Stirling and Clackmannan. North of Tay it is found in the grant to Scone Abbey of a portion 'of my oats and my bere and of the cain of my hides and cheeses' from the kings' manors of Gowrie 'as much from my earldᵣm as from my royalty'.[34] This phrase probably refers to the manors belonging to him in either capacity, for where the manors are named the phrase is dropped. In Angus the priory of Restennet enjoyed a teind of cain of cheese, bere, oats (apparently from Angus) and of hides and foals from the royal stud in Angus.[35] When, however, we turn to the records of the see of Aberdeen,[36] the word cain is not used in this context; we read instead of 'the teind of those things which are between Dee and Spey'[37] and this grant seems to have become the basis of the bishop's claim to a teind of the king's revenues from thanages, rents and the issues of justice, the second teind of the province. A very similar grant by King William to the cathedral of Moray seems analogous: 'my teind of my rents in Moray and of my pleas in the whole bishopric of Moray; of my rents, that is of my cain[38] of cows, pigs, wheat, bere, oats, cheese and butter which my predecessors did not give nor assign to other churches.'[39]

Geographically the king's cain is found throughout Celtic Scotland save only in the far north, where documentation is very scanty. The word seems to have the primary meaning of 'law', whence 'right' and ultimately 'tribute'. Cain is a payment due to a lord, in this case the king, but it is not *every* payment due to him. While it seems usual to include payment in grain, animals and cheese, even this is not consistent. In Gowrie oats and bere were not cain but hides and cheeses were; in Angus cheese, bere and oats were cain, hides were not. In Fife bere was usually cain but once was distinguished from it. Fish and seals, mills, burgh rents, the profits of justice, these are consistently mentioned as revenues which are not cain, and there are *dominia*, demesne rents, which are also distinct.

---

[33] A teind of cain in cheeses was given to Selkirk Abbey, of cain in animals and pigs to the church of Glasgow, but later transferred to Kelso Abbey—all from the four quarters of Galloway (Lawrie, *E.S.C.*, nos. CLIII, CCIX, CCLV, XXXV, CXCIV; *R.R.S.*, i, no. 131).

[34] 'tam de comitatu quam de regali meo,' *R.R.S.*, i, no. 245.

[35] *R.R.S.*, i, no. 195.

[36] I use only the bull of Adrian IV (*Aberdeen Registrum*, i, 5-7), which seems to be authentic.          [37] decimam eorum que sunt inter duas aquas.

[38] de redditibus meis scilicet de cano meo.

[39] *R.R.S.*, i, nos. 195, 243, 245, 248; ii, nos. 139, 273.

There is only one explanation which will meet these distinctions: that cain was a render in kind traditional not in amount but in the commodities paid. Cain had been the revenue due to the king in virtue of his lordship, and it had been paid in the produce of the area. This payment in kind was now understood to be the king's cain but other and newer sources of revenue were not.[40]

Probably the largest single source of cain, or renders in kind, was the king's right as landlord to the hospitality-rent called 'conveth' in Scotia and 'wayting' in Lothian, due from the lands which were or had anciently been estates of the king. Thus the twelve touns of Coldinghamshire, although alienated to a monastic house, paid wayting to the king, commuted by the time of King William for an annual 20 merks, while Earl Gospatrick owed 'corrody' (hospitality or conveth) to the king for Edrom and Nisbet, for which Coldingham Priory, holding these vills of the earl, paid 30s. to him. The incidence of conveth was heavy upon the 'men'—both free and unfree it seems—of the land, who paid it; thus David I permitted Scone Abbey to take annually as conveth from each ploughgate of its lands a cow, two pigs, four measures of flour, ten thraves of oats, ten hens, two hundred eggs, ten bundles of candles, four pennyworths of soap and twenty and a half *mela* of cheese, and we must allow that a similar burden lay upon the peasantry of the king's thanages. There are very few references to conveth in Scotia before 1165, but thirteenth century evidence makes it abundantly clear that it was owed in kind, in very substantial amounts, from the estates of the king in Fife, Angus and the north-east. By then it was called 'wayting' even in these areas, and it seems to be the only burden which those estates owed to the king at that time. There can be no doubt that in the time of David I it was owed under one name or another to the king from estates in Lothian, Fife and Gowrie also. It stands in the place of the right of a lord and his retinue to hospitality from men on his land, one of the most simple, even primitive, of the marks of lordship. When David I gave a tenth of his cain in livestock from Ayrshire and Renfrewshire to the church of Glasgow he excepted those years 'when I myself come there staying and consuming my cain there'; the cain which he would consume in this way was surely his conveth.

[40] Thus Malcolm IV took his ferme from Longforgan in wheat, of which Scone Abbey received a teind. But he envisaged that a ferme 'of another kind' (*aliusmodi*) might be taken in the future. *R.R.S.*, i, no. 243.

But there must have been other sources of cain, for the king is unlikely to have had estates in Kintyre or Argyll. Cain may have been paid by a great lord such as Somerled, ruler of Argyll, in amounts which were little more than a token of the king's lordship. Native landowners may have rendered such tribute to the king both north and south of Forth. But there seems little doubt that such ancient renders were obliterated when the king granted land as a fief, for we hear nothing of them in Clydesdale nor in other parts of southern Scotland granted to Anglo-French incomers. Their survival on the lands of Coldingham and of Earl Gospatrick is an indication that these new landholders of the time of King Edgar or his father were assimilated to the ancient pattern of society and its obligations in Lothian, but that the new landholders of King David's time had different obligations.

There were other important royal revenues in kind. The profits of the king's demesne mills were clearly substantial, and the *dominia* of Dunfermline and Stirling seem to have been cognate revenues, perhaps including fishings, the right to fuel, quarries and their stone and the produce of demesne land in its strictest sense of royal land whose produce belongs wholly to the lord. The profits of justice, variously described as pleas, fines or agreements, were listed along with cain and other dues in such a way as to imply that they, too, were usually paid in kind. In Cumbria (that is, Strathclyde) payment was made 'in money or in livestock' and in Gowrie and Angus 'in gold and silver and livestock'. Offences against the king's express will were already punished by a 'forfeiture of ten pounds', but failure to pay teinds to the church was punished by a forfeiture to the king of twelve cows. An older code of fines in kind was now accompanied by monetary penalties for at least some offences.

We have dwelt upon the complex evidence for the royal revenues in kind in order to stress three points. These were the only revenues the king disposed of from the various provinces of his kingdom, with the exception of money fines and, in rare cases, money fermes. Secondly, although we cannot show that they came from all provinces, nonetheless they came from royal estates and rights of lordship distributed from the Tweed to the Beauly in the east and from Glen App to Glenelg in the west. Thirdly, they were often of great antiquity.

It will be appropriate to deal with the history of urban development in Scotland at a later point. But if this survey of important revenues is to be complete, we must anticipate to point out the significance of the burghs as a source of money-income. The king's alienation of burgh revenues, almost always in terms of a precise sum of money, is in striking contrast to the rather vague tithing of revenues in kind from the landward. There were two main sources of burgh revenues. The first, the ferme of the burgh, was a payment by royal officers who were responsible for collecting the rents of burgh tofts. The amount of each rent was a few pence, but the aggregate might be a significant sum for we find that payments of 100 shillings and 40 (or in certain contingencies 80) shillings were assigned from the ferme of Edinburgh, and smaller amounts from other burghs. The second source was the king's cain or 'cain and custom' of ships. The origin of this due is unknown but probably lies in the right of the king to a portion of the cargo of any ship breaking bulk in a Scottish port.[41] In the time of David I it was probably paid as an import duty in money, though on what commodities is uncertain. A lawbook of thirteenth-century date lays down that a ship arriving with grain, peas, beans or salt must pay an anchorage due of twelve pence and two bolls of the commodity, and arriving with wine, honey, or oil must pay the same anchorage due and on each tun of commodity fourpence on entering and threepence on leaving the port.[42] This petty custom cannot be the whole story, for cain of ships seems to have yielded amounts no less significant than the burgh ferme.[43] Assignments were not infrequent; one of the most interesting is the grant of a hundred shillings from the cain of Perth and this from the first ships which came to do business at Perth: 'and if perchance they do not come' the king granted a like amount from the rents of three burghs. Cambuskenneth Abbey was given the right to a cain-free ship but exchanged it for 50s. from the cain of ships at Perth. From the same source a further 66s. was assigned first to Dunfermline Abbey, then to May Priory, and 40s. of silver in place of the cain of one ship to the abbey of Tiron. If trade at

[41] 'Cain of ships' and 'custom of ships' were certainly synonymous and therefore 'cain and custom' is an alliterative jingle for one due. The point is of importance when applied to the parallel 'cain and conveth' which are sometimes assumed to be two different revenues.

[42] *A.P.S.*, i, 671-2.

[43] Dunfermline Abbey received from David I the anchorage dues of ships calling at Inveresk but not the toll due to the king if the merchants broke bulk. This toll was presumably the main part of cain of ships, though not called cain in Anglian Lothian (Lawrie, *E.S.C.*, no. LXXXVII).

Perth alone could yield such revenues, and if 50s. was the approximate value of the cain of one ship, clearly the 'business' of these ships was an important source of royal revenue as well as a significant factor in the economic life of the country.[44]

The unit of royal demesne with which the king was concerned in Lothian was his 'portion' or shire. North of the Forth we have no clear evidence of a Gaelic equivalent name, and the same word was already in use in the twelfth century in Latin charters for royal estates as far as the Mounth or even in Aberdeenshire.[45] The king's agent in the shire was sometimes the thane and it would seem that northern shires were already named 'thanages' after his office. South of Forth we hear little of thanes in the twelfth century—the king's agent was, perhaps, in most cases a simple grieve—and we hear nothing of thanages. Such variations in nomenclature are not the end of a problem which has kept historians happily ruminant since John of Fordun wrote his account of thanages in the fourteenth century. Thus, of the four *maneria* of Malcolm IV in Gowrie, three (Scone, Longforgan and Strathardle) were thanages, and the fourth (Coupar) was alienated to the Cistercians. The 'manor' here may have its later sense (in Scotland) of a residence, but clearly the revenues which the king was tithing for Scone Abbey could equally well have been described as coming from the king's four thanages of Gowrie. Again, the king certainly had demesnes in Moray after the suppression of the earldom in 1130, for burghs and castles were established there by the king, especially on the coast, while fiefs were granted to Flemish incomers. The recorded thanages beyond the Spey are few and unrelated to the burghs, but later evidence shows that attached to burgh or castle was a *prepositura,* the 'griefschip landis', which looks remarkably like an area of royal demesne for which the king's grieve was responsible. If these grieve-ships were a late creation, perhaps of the reign of David I, the thanages and shires of Moray, Mar, Mearns, Angus, Gowrie, Stormont, Fife, Fothrif and Lothian are probably of considerable age for, as we have

[44] The abbey of Scone was given the cain of one ship, and King William, addressing the merchants of England, granted that all merchants dwelling *extra regionem Scotie* (probably outside the kingdom, not outside Scotia) who wished to come to Scone with their merchandise in that ship should be answerable for the cain only to the abbey. It does not seem likely that cain was payable only on foreign merchandise.

[45] The names and descriptions of lands in the otherwise bogus charters of Malcolm IV to the bishop of Aberdeen may be authentic.

seen, their burdens have an ancient look, and it seems that their very
names were long-established.[46]

In every case they take their name, as in Coldinghamshire or
Berwickshire, from a hall or village settlement, and not from a
district. They are groups of touns, each linked to a single centre
where the king's thane or other officer resided and to which the
king's tribute must be carried or driven. It seems likely that the thane
had always owed the king beasts and produce not to the full amount
of the shire but to a predetermined amount, sometimes already un-
varied from year to year—firm, whence ferme or 'a farm'. His
office was probably hereditary, and where we know it his name was
native and not Anglo-French. If he paid a varying render and not a
farm, he probably made little profit and there is a suggestion that in
the early twelfth century he was a freeman of low social standing. In
the first half of the twelfth century his farm or render was still consumed by the king at the royal residences around which he must
progress. Cain, provender, venison, salt, iron were brought to Dunfermline, the king had a killing for feasts at Stirling, a killing of
Edinburgh, a killing of Teviotdale (at Roxburgh almost certainly),
and all these phrases speak of a few greater royal centres where the
'provender of the palaces' came from the king's 'demesnes and
manors'.[47] The frequency with which the king dwelt at these very
places is shown by the relative frequency of their occurrence in
charter-dates. Under David I, Edinburgh, Stirling, Scone and Dunfermline occur most frequently, with Roxburgh not far behind,
thereafter Kinross, Perth and Berwick. Under Malcolm IV, Edinburgh is relatively more frequent; Stirling, Perth (perhaps including
Scone), and, not far behind, Roxburgh, are followed by Dunfermline, Jedburgh, Berwick, St Andrews and Clackmannan.[48] The cain
and other revenues of Scotland beyond Tay were doubtless brought

[46] On all this see 'Pre-feudal Scotland, Shires and Thanes', chapter I in
Barrow, *Kingdom of the Scots.*

[47] Myln, *Vitae Dunkeldensis Ecclesie Episcoporum*, 6, a grant to the bishop of
Dunkeld of *decimam de cana regis de prebenda de palaciis de regiis dominiis ac
maneriis pertinentibus ad abbaciam de Dunkeld*. Perhaps this is intended to mean
a tenth of (1) the king's cain, (2) the provender of the palaces, (3) the produce
of royal demesnes, (4) the produce of abbatial manors. cf. *R.R.S.*, i, no. 65.

[48] The figures for David I are Edinburgh 14; Stirling 13; Scone, Dunfermline
12; Roxburgh 9; Kinross 5; Perth, Berwick 4; Clackmannan, Eldbottle, Strathir-
vine, Haddington, Cadzow, Peebles 2; Traquair, Glasgow, Banff, Abernethy,
Cluny, Earlston, Coldingham, Kinghorn, Forfar, Aberdeen, St Andrews 1. The
larger figures for Malcolm IV are Edinburgh 20; Perth, Stirling 13; Roxburgh
10; Dunfermline 7; Jedburgh 6; Berwick, St Andrews 5. See *R.R.S.*, i, 80.

to royal centres there, and the infrequency of Forfar, Aberdeen and Banff in these lists is to be accounted for by the fewness of charters relating to that area and probably only partially by a relative infrequency in royal residence there. The king's *rannaire* or food-divider was a magnate of Anglian origin, Alfwin mac Archill[49] whose duties would certainly include supervision of the renders made to the king's 'palaces', their assignment to the king's kitchen and table, to other dignitaries, to charitable uses and to sale. His office was exercised, we think, not in the hall but in the store-room. There is no evidence that a clerk was employed or records kept though there must surely have been a tally of what had been demanded and what rendered.

The king's revenues in money came from his burghs. Of the administration which collected them at this period we know little, and where mercantile affairs (always liable to rapid change) are concerned it is dangerous to use later evidence. Rents and customs were probably collected by burgh grieves appointed by the king; this money was ultimately paid to the king's chamberlain, though whether through the sheriff or direct is uncertain. Sheriffdoms were few in number and burghs such as Renfrew, Aberdeen and Elgin were outwith any sheriffdom; burghs such as Perth and Berwick had a strong element of foreign settlement likely to assert financial independence of the sheriff from the first. A rural community such as Haddington would be in no position to do so. The authority which, at a much later date, the chamberlain exercised in the burghs in commercial and financial matters (and which he did not exercise over the sheriffs) suggests that they had always been his direct responsibility and that perhaps he appointed the king's grieve in most of them. In smaller burghs, however, the sheriff may have done so. The office of chamberlain was held by a layman, Herbert, from *c.* 1136 to *c.* 1159. His predecessors are mentioned once each and probably neither they nor their office were of much importance. Herbert was lord of Kinneil (West Lothian) and tenant of lands in Lincolnshire, a frequent witness of charters at King David's court and obviously an important functionary. As a layman he must have had a clerical aide, but as yet no records were kept of his work nor, it seems, was there an exchequer to view any accounts he might keep. His successor, Nicholas, was a cleric who at the time of his appointment was sent on embassy to Rome, a sign that there were subordinate chamberlains to carry on his duties. As yet the chamber

[49] Succeeded by his son Gillandres.

was doubtless itinerant, no more perhaps than a few boxes of
coins carted from one royal residence to another.

The introduction to Lothian and Clydesdale of Anglo-Fre
settlers may have disturbed but did not seriously dislocate the c
plex tenures of native landholders. In these areas the king
revenues in kind, some few perhaps in money from native lords.
was entitled to service in his army, to work upon his castles an
bridges from all landholders, and he had feudal rights to knig
service, castle-guard, and rights to temporary occupation of fiefs by
reason of wardship. How were these multifarious rights to be
exercised?

Even before he became king, David had his agents in Teviotdale
and Tweeddale, for he addressed instructions there to John, Bishop
of Glasgow, and to Gospatrick and Colban, and Gospatrick appears
in one charter as 'the earl's depute' (*vicecomes*). After 1124 he continued to hold that office and, although there is no direct statement
to that effect, we need not doubt that he exercised it from Roxburgh.
The sheriffdom of Roxburgh or Teviotdale was held by Gospatrick,
Gervase Ridel and Robert, son of Wido, before 1153. Berwick was a
sheriffdom before 1139, held by a 'Norman' who must have been
of French origin and who held land at Corstorphine near Edinburgh.[50] Edinburgh under David I was probably the chief castle of
a sheriff of Lothian whose territory we should call 'the Lothians' but
which contemporaries knew as 'Lothian' or 'between Avon and
Cockburnspath'. Not only was the Dunglass burn at Cocksburns-
path a natural feature, it was also the 'previous land division' of
Lammermuir, dividing the lands of Earl David and King Alexander
I and, earlier still, the southern boundary of the lands of Tyninghame monastery. Its earliest sheriff, Thor, son of Swain, was lord of
Tranent and doubtless a native Anglian laird, like Sheriff Gospatrick; but his name also appears in the Romance guise of
Durand.[51] If William, son of Thoraud, sheriff of Stirling in the
1190's, was his son, then we have some evidence for the ministerial
families whose existence we can otherwise only suspect. In the reign
of Malcolm IV the sheriffdom of Lothian seems to have been
broken down into two or three parts. Before 1162 there was a
sheriff of Linlithgow named Uhtred, acting along with Robert,

[50] It is not clear why the sheriff of Roxburgh should be dealing with litigation
over Edrom in Berwickshire in 1138; above p. 143.
[51] I.e. Thoraud.

sheriff of Edinburgh, and in 1170 a Hervey the sheriff (perhaps ancestor of the Keiths) may have held office in Haddington. T sheriffdoms of Selkirk and Traquair or Peebles are something of a problem, being attested only from the later twelfth century; there was a royal castle at Selkirk before 1124, at Peebles before 1152, and these were undoubtedly the chief places for large tracts of royal land. But the land itself was mainly forest (hunting land, not necessarily wooded) and may have been the responsibility of forest officials such as the Norman the Hunter to whom Malcolm IV gave land in the parish of Manor, a few miles from Peebles. We might even surmise further that the king's kitchens at Roxburgh and Edinburgh received some of their beasts from the forests of Selkirk and Traquair respectively, and that in this way the great forest between Borthwick Water and the Tweed was divided between the sheriffdoms of Roxburgh and Edinburgh, and so, later in the century, between those of Selkirk and Traquair–Peebles.

Beyond the Avon lay the lands of Callendar, a thanage lying within the 'castle-province', *castrensis provincia*, that is within the sheriffdom of Stirling. The early sheriffs, named Gilbert and William, were perhaps Anglo-French in origin. The westward extent of their bailiwick at this early date is unknown, but it may already have been as great as in later medieval times before a large part of the Lennox was attached to Stirling. The remaining southern sheriffdom was Lanark or Clydesdale, probably excluding the Steward's lordship of Renfrew, and held by the Flemish Baldwin of Biggar.

So far as we can tell the sheriffs of this southern region had acquired most of their later wide responsibility, and the shire had ceased by 1165 to be the responsibility of a thane except at Callendar. It was to the sheriff of Stirling that David I wrote to order delivery to Dunfermline Abbey of its teinds and rights—the teind of his cain of his whole 'castle-province', as the abbey's grant has it. We cannot doubt that the thane had given way to the sheriff, or in some cases had perhaps grown to the office of sheriff, who was now aided in the discharge of his demesne functions by subordinate ministers. For the sheriff must now have had those wider functions, extending beyond the king's demesne to a whole province, which are the later mark of his office; he probably commanded the 'common army' or 'hosting', military service to which the king was entitled from his free landholders; he doubtless commanded the drengs of Lothian, peasants who owed riding service to the king, and he probably collected and transmitted their rents to the king. These functions are implied by our sources and we may not be explicit on their character. What we may be explicit about is the sheriff's association with the king's demesne and the king's castle. The shires and castles of Edinburgh, Linlithgow and Stirling, the shire (by inference) of Berwick and the shire of Haddington are vouched for in our sources; there were demesnes and castles also at Lanark and Roxburgh. Haddington, even if not a sheriffdom till c. 1180, because it had no castle so far as is known is difficult to fit into the theory that the Scottish sheriffdom 'was the counterpart rather of the continental châtellany than of the Anglo-Saxon shire',[52] and reflection on the absence of natural defences at Linlithgow and Berwick castles (especially when compared with the rest) prompts the thought that castles were a consequence and not a cause of the choice of these centres to be sheriffs' seats. Their common feature was the existence of royal demesne; because of it the king built his castle there for his sheriff. The early royal castle in the south was a structure for security rather than warfare. Defensive in site as Edinburgh and Stirling were, it would be difficult to show that they were now defensive in function. These castles were storehouses and palaces, erected to keep out human and animal intruders, symbols of their master's status and prestige; in the case of Haddington there was perhaps a hall and outbuildings.

The association of a larger province with the demesne shire came about for reasons which may be called feudal only in the broadest sense. The new fiefs and, perhaps, some older holdings were linked to the king's castle by the obligation to provide a quota of castle-guard proportional or equal to the number of knights owed to the king's host. The sheriff held a court (which was a royal court) for this sheriffdom and the suitors to it were those who held land of the king within that area. But we must remember that the new military fiefs fitted into the interstices of pre-existing non-feudal tenures, and that therefore the sheriffdom cannot have been delineated by grouping only the new tenures. It was the sum of all free tenures which delineated the sheriffdom. In the king's army the mail-clad knight served not with the men of his sheriffdom but in the king's cavalry force; militarily the sheriffdom must have been represented by native landowners. In the sheriff's court the suitors included many free landholders whose tenure was not that of a military

[52] *Fife Ct. Bk.*, 370.

fief but who owed rent and service to the king. By analogy such landholders came (and were perhaps already coming) to be regarded as feudal tenants of the king, so that the sheriff court was a feudal court, and presence at it a feudal obligation. If the new sheriffdoms were truly 'artificial units coinciding with no previous land-division and ruled by no natural geographical bounds' then we could fairly regard them as entirely the creation of David I, laid out on the ground around his new castles and new sheriffs. But the bounds are usually natural and can sometimes be shown to be ancient, the obligations to rent and service were usually customary and only the obligations to castle-guard and suit of court were probably, though not certainly, new. If we had more information about the courts of southern Scotland before 1124 we could be more definite about the antecedents of the sheriffdom and its institutions. In the absence of that information we should not be too ready to attribute all its qualities to Anglo-Norman influence.

There were still wide areas of southern Scotland which lay in no sheriffdom. In the great feudal lordships of Renfrew, Lauderdale, Ewesdale, Eskdale, Liddesdale and Annandale the rights which the sheriff elsewhere exercised for the king were doubtless exercised by an agent for the lord. Of the three 'Galwegian' *cadrez* which made up modern Ayrshire little is known save that they had no sheriff and no known great lord. Galloway proper, the modern counties of Kirkcudbright and Wigtown, was under the lordship of Fergus, whose antecedents were probably Norse-Celtic and may have been West Highland. When and how he came to hold this lordship is not known; it is worth noticing that before 1124 we hear of Earl David as *princeps Cumbriae*, and after 1124 of Fergus as *rex Galwitensium, princeps Galwaie* and *comes*. In the eyes of contemporaries Fergus was no less than an earl, and King David seems to have recognised his right to an unwonted degree of independence. The Galwegians served the king in war as fierce soldiers and the lord of Galloway owed the king a cain or tribute of a thousand beasts annually under the sons of Fergus and doubtless under Fergus himself, but there were no royal agents in Fergus's lordship.[53] The same is probably true of neighbouring Nithsdale, held by a native lord, Dunegal.

In 1160 Fergus joined with five earls to besiege the king at Perth, 'being enraged against the king because he had gone to Toulouse', but the king put down this rebellion in three invasions of

[53] Henry II was offered a tribute of 500 cattle and 500 swine in 1174.

Galloway. Fergus retired to become a canon of Holyrood and his
territories were divided between his two sons. One point, however,
should not escape notice—that even as Hugh de Moreville was lord
of Borgue to the west of Kirkcudbright (probably Fergus's chief
residence) so the Cistercians were planted perhaps by David I at
Dundrennan just to the east of the same place. Both settlements
suggest that so long as the king ruled Cumberland his influence or
authority in Galloway was strong. That ceased to be the case in
1157, which may explain the events of 1160. During the reign of
Malcolm IV the more northerly lordships of Cunningham and
northern Kyle were granted to de Moreville and the Steward,
leaving the crown in possession of unknown rights in southern Kyle,
probably Carrick, and (from *c.* 1165) lower Nithsdale.

North of the Forth, and beyond Clydesdale as far as the Spey,
only Fife had been affected by the new influences which were to
transform the whole kingdom. The traditional provinces remained
intact: from Menteith to Buchan this was the land of earls. The
origin of the Scottish earldom is uncertain but not an insoluble
historical problem. The provinces were doubtless ancient land divisions: Menteith, Strathearn, Fife (including Fothrif), Atholl, Angus,
Mar and Buchan had earls; Stormont, Gowrie, Mearns and Garioch
had no earls in historical times, and in consequence contained much
royal land.[54] It is likely, and in the case of Mar and Buchan it is
known, that the man who bore the Latin designation of *comes* (earl)
was known in the vernacular as mormaer. Such continuity is likely
but cannot be proved for all provinces which had mormaers. Our
earliest list of earls, in Alexander I's 'foundation charter' for Scone
Priory, is of uncertain authenticity and best ignored as evidence in
this matter.[54a] In the case of Fife two of the names of the three early
earls suggest a relationship with the royal house, and their known
predecessor as earl was Ethelred, son of Malcolm III and Margaret.[55] The earldoms of Lennox and Menteith are not documented
before 1165. Strathearn occurs from the beginning of David I's reign,
and its second known earl, Ferteth, was one of those responsible
for the attempted constraint of King Malcolm in 1160. A connection

[54] See the case of the manors of Gowrie quoted above p. 153.

[54a] See below pp. 640–1.

[55] Earl Constantine was dead by 1130 (*Dunfermline Registrum*, no. 29,
witnessed by Earl Aed). Earl Gillemichael, who died by July 1136, had a son
Hugh (ancestor of the Abernethy family) who was not earl, and it is presumed
that the next earl, Duncan, was his elder brother.

between Matad, who is known to have been earl of Atholl before 1136, and the royal house is suggested by Norse sources which make his father Maelmuire, brother to Malcolm III. Their grandfather Crinan, Abbot of Dunkeld may have been ruler of the province of Atholl. The earldom of Angus does not occur until the very end of David I's reign and its earl, Gillebrigte, survived until 1187–89, when he was succeeded by his son Adam. The silence of our sources about an earl of Angus before 1150 is slender evidence on which to build an hypothesis, yet we must note that in this province the king had wide and rich demesnes held as thanages, as he did in neighbouring Gowrie and Mearns (a royal forest). When, later, we can discover something about this earldom we find it surprisingly poor and unimportant for so large a province, and we may therefore suspect that it had been in royal hands for some time before it was conferred, with only a partial endowment, upon Gillebrigte.

The northern group of earldoms is documented by marginal and other late entries in the *Book of Deer*. From them we learn that Colban (a Gaelicised Norse name?), mormaer of Buchan (elsewhere called earl), was married to Eve, daughter of Gartnait, who was probably the 'Earl Gartnait' of a royal charter of *c.* 1150 and the 'Gartnait son of Cainnech'[56] who gave land to the church in 1131–2. We learn that Gartnait and Colban could make grants of land free of secular burdens, to which they, therefore, must have enjoyed a right. For Mar, we have two occurrences at witness of Ruadri once as mormaer, once as *comes,* both before 1136, and from *c.* 1150 this earldom was held by Morgrund, whose right to succeed was challenged a century later. A charter of Morgrund from the years 1165–78 is more eloquent than the *Book of Deer* upon this earl's secular rights in Scotia; he granted a church and its land, but he also granted a teind of his rents from all his land in hides, grain and other produce, of his killing in the hunt, of his pleas and of his reliefs.[57]

Beyond the Spey lay the earldom of Moray, the province of Macbeth, his stepson Lulach and of Lulach's son Malsnechtai whom Malcolm III defeated in 1078 and who died, perhaps in clerical orders, in 1085. The subsequent history of Moray is a blank until early in the reign of David I, when an earl Aed or Heth occurs as a

---

[56] I.e. Gartnait, son of Kenneth, married to Ete, daughter of Gillemichael (? earl of Fife).

[57] Jackson, *Gaelic Notes in Book of Deer*, no. III; Lawrie, *E.S.C.*, no. **XXXVI** (if genuine); *St Andrews Liber*, 246–7.

witness to charters and would seem (because the other provinces are associated with other earls) to have held this earldom. In 1130 there was a rebellion by Angus, Earl of Moray (who is not found in charters),[58] son of Lulach's daughter, who invaded Scotia and was defeated and slain by a royal army under Edward, the king's constable, at Stracathro. Angus's ally was Malcolm, possibly illegitimate son of Alexander I, who yet is called Malcolm 'mac Heth' and whose descent is one of the important unsolved problems of early Scottish history. It is likely that he was related to the line of mormaers and earls of Moray represented by Angus and possible that he was regarded by David I as a contender for the throne as well as the earldom. There is no very sound evidence that his ambitions ran so high as this and his patronymic, macHeth, suggests a relationship with Earl Aed. Of his significance in the eyes of contemporaries there can be no doubt; before 1130 he had married a sister of Somerled, Lord of Argyll, a fact which proves his standing. In the following years King David failed to subdue him and called upon the help of English northern barons, who provided ships and men, so that in 1134 Malcolm was taken. He was not executed but imprisoned at Roxburgh, which suggests that he had not only royal blood but some justice on his side. After 1142 there was a further rebellion by a Wimund, consecrated Bishop of the Isles, who claimed to be a son of the earl of Moray (either Angus or Malcolm), was offered peace with lands in Furness and accepted and was then cruelly mutilated to ensure that his days were passed in religious seclusion. The problem of Moray is different from that of other earldoms. Here we know of too many earls and pretenders, too little of their interrelationships and aims.

Somerled, Lord of Argyll, was certainly of a Norse-Celtic family from the western isles. How he obtained control of Argyll, and, it seems, Kintyre, is unknown, but he was doubtless the leader of the West Highland contingent in King David's army in 1138. Until 1153 he remained loyal to the king, owing and probably paying a cain as a mark of royal lordship. In January 1154, along with his nephews, the sons of Malcolm macHeth, he rebelled against Malcolm IV and in 1156, when Donald, son of Malcolm macHeth, was taken and imprisoned in Roxburgh with his father, Somerled turned to the conquest of the Isles, ruled by the king of Man under Norwegian suzerainty. In two battles, in 1156 and 1158, Somerled

---

[58] Irish annals call him king like his eleventh century predecesssors.

triumphed, the Manx king fled to Norway, appearing at Malcolm IV's court at Roxburgh on his journeying, and a large central portion of the kingdom of the Isles, stretching from Mull to Islay and perhaps from North Uist to Arran, passed to Somerled to be divided between his sons. In 1160, Somerled made his peace with Malcolm IV, visited his Christmas court at Perth and there acquired the nickname of Sit-by-the-king; their reconciliation was doubtless eased by the release in 1157 of Malcolm macHeth, who was made Earl of Ross. David I had addressed his writ for the protection of a cell of Dunfermline monks at Dornoch in Caithness[59] to the Norse earl of Orkney and Caithness. Dornoch lay close to the boundaries of Ross and it was probably to this cell that Malcolm IV referred when he commanded Malcolm, Earl of Ross, to protect the lands of the monks of Dunfermline. The whole of the mainland beyond Moray was technically Scottish, in fact dominated by the earl of Orkney and Caithness. The province of Ross may well have been attached to that of Moray for the exercise of Scottish royal and comital authority and, if so, the appointment of Malcolm as earl was both a partial restoration of the heir to the house of Moray and an attempt to extend Scottish authority to a province which had perhaps fallen into anarchy. So far as is known, when Earl Malcolm died in 1168 King William appointed no successor, but undoubtedly the mac Heth descendants were determined on their claim to the earldom of Ross and unforgetful of their claim on Moray.

Only in Fife do we have evidence of the penetration of feudal relationships, and this is marked by the grant of the earldom itself by King David to Earl Duncan on feudal terms and recorded in a charter. The lord of Leuchars, early in the reign of King William, was Ness, son of William, of whom we may conjecture that his mother was a Celtic landowner married to a Frenchman. Robert the Burgundian was lord of Lochore in Fife before 1130, and his demands upon the property of the clergy of St Andrews led to the hearing of his claim before the men of the province of Fife and Fothrif. The gathering was composed of Earl Constantine and the army of Fife with the army of the bishop under its leaders, and a little later the king, in providing for the right of the abbot of Dunfermline to hold a court for his own lands, addressed his brieve to 'the bishop of St Andrews and the earl and all his good men of all

---

[59] Correctly not in the ness (or promontory) but in the southern land (Sutherland) of the province of Cat.

Fife'.[60] In Fife as in other provinces, the earl was responsible for leading the host or 'common army' of that province, of which an element, and perhaps an independent one, comprised the men from the lands of the bishop. We even find the earl of Fife confirming a royal grant of exemption from the host.[61] The significance of the case of Robert the Burgundian is that it shows us a court for the province presided over by the earl and composed of the army or armies of the province.

From the period under review there is evidence enough of the existence of a widespread obligation to 'hosting' or *exercitus,* and, particularly from the thirteenth century, further evidence as to its character. It was then called forinsec service, or, in Scotia, Scottish service. It could take the form of non-military aid but was usually military and sometimes said to be for defence. Its basis, however, is territorial throughout, falling upon the free occupiers of the soil, by virtue of the land which they held, and proportionate to its extent, whether measured in ploughgates or davachs. There was no distinction here between Lothian and Scotia, nor, for that matter, was there any substantial difference between the hosting and the Anglo-Saxon fyrd or other 'pre-feudal' military assemblies of Europe.[62]

Thus the assembled army represented those who occupied land in a province and thereby defined the province itself. It would seem that, at least in Fife, a court existed which was made up on the same basis, and before which a territorial dispute might be investigated. Nothing is known of such courts in other provinces save that 'pleas' and 'profits of justice'[63] were a widespread source of royal revenue and imply courts. Nor is there evidence sufficient to show the character of the business of such courts and we may not assume that they had the same importance as in the sixteenth century. Personal injuries were settled according to a tariff of payments in kind and probably did not come to court. In Scotia and Galloway disputes over property were settled according to the facts as remembered by witnesses and according to the law as expounded by the 'lawman' or *judex* of the province. Before the coming of sheriffs to Scotia it may be that the *judex* shared with the earl, and perhaps the bishop, the right to hold the court of the province.[64]

Late in the reign of David I and in that of Malcolm IV sheriffs

[60] Lawrie, *E.S.C.*, nos. LXXXX, CV.
[61] *R.R.S.*, i, no. 280.        [62] See below pp. 378–83.        [63] Placita, lucra.
[64] For the *judex* see Barrow, *Kingdom of the Scots*, chapter 2.

are first mentioned in Scotia, always at places known to be shires or at least demesne-centres, six in all, only three of which had castles: Clackmannan, Dunfermline, Crail, Scone, Perth and Forfar. These sheriffs seem to have been mainly though not exclusively native Celts and their original jurisdiction is uncertain. The sheriff of Perth secured the payment of teinds five miles away, sheriffs and other officers controlled the taking by Dunfermline Abbey of timber from the king's woods, and the collecting of aids in the lands of Scone Abbey was expressly forbidden to the earl of Angus and the sheriffs of Forfar and Scone. This last writ is of particular interest, for the lands of Scone can be identified as lying in three groups, one near Scone (Perthshire), another at Blairgowrie and Coupar Angus (Perthshire and Angus), and a third near Dundee (Angus), so that the sheriff of Forfar was clearly already for some purposes sheriff of Angus, sharing duties with the earl, while the sheriff of Scone was probably already sheriff of Gowrie. It seems not unlikely that wider duties with the title of sheriff were laid upon certain thanes where comital authority had fallen to the king as in Gowrie, or was weak as in Angus.

The situation in Fife is less readily explained, for the three sheriff-doms strung along the Forth shore balance the lands of the bishop and earl in the north. The sheriff of Crail was (until 1178) the officer of the king's mother—a clear indication that a sheriff in Scotia was in the first place a demesne officer. When Malcolm IV assigned half the blubber taken between Forth and Tay to Dun-fermline Abbey, he notified his justice of Fife and sheriffs of Dun-fermline and Clackmannan. These two sheriffs were more than demesne officers, though it is difficult to believe that their jurisdiction stretched to the Tay and we may suspect that the justice of Fife was none other than the earl, exercising royal authority over the whole province. In this way, just as his lands were feudalised so his ancient authority as an earl could have been wedded to the develop-ing ministerial functions of sheriffs. We also read of the justice of Scotia as superior to the sheriff of Perth[65] and by analogy, would expect him to have authority also over the sheriff of Scone in Gowrie and perhaps even over the sheriff of Forfar. As the king's sheriffs and sheriffdoms were planted in the provinces formerly ruled by earls they were overseen by the king's justices. If we would under-

---

[65] For Scotia as the area associated with Perth see Lawrie, *E.S.C.*, no. LXIX; *R.R.S.*, i, no. 223.

stand the justice, however, we must turn again to evidence from southern Scotland.

Alexander I forbade the monks of Durham to go to court over the lands of Swinton unless the king commanded it 'mouth to mouth or by letters', that is to say 'before the matter comes before me'.[66] Thus the king extended his protection to these lands to which there was, apparently, another claimant. That claim, or 'challenge', could have been heard by the kings or could have been remitted by him to one of such standing that his judgement would be unsuspect. Protection and justice go together, and justice is both the judgement and the man responsible for providing it. Under David I, it is apparent that the king would often protect his gifts from challenge by a personal perambulation of boundaries, and we can see him acting as justice when the rights of the parish church of St Ninian, Stirling, were adjudged before the king and his son on the 'record' or testimony of 'the king's barons'.[67] About the middle of the reign we begin to read of justices, both in the singular and the plural, in the king's writs and this delegation may be linked with more frequent royal residence at Carlisle, as well as with increased demand for the king's protection. Malcolm IV, in a writ of 1162 × 65 to the sheriff of Berwick, took all the possessions of Coldingham Priory under his protection so that the priory was not to go to court in pleas pertaining to the royal power 'unless in my presence or in the presence of my *supprema iusticia*'.[68] From the king's protection there has developed a category of pleas which may be heard only before the king or his justice and not before the sheriff; certainly, among these pleas were land-disputes where one title depended upon a royal grant. If we assume that a justice did not hold office as a sheriff did, but rather was the man to whom certain pleas were habitually referred, then we have an explanation as to why, before 1165, no justice is named. We find Geoffrey de Melville acting in land pleas then, and shortly after 1165 he becomes our first named justice, probably of Lothian; the task is now becoming an office. The 'supreme' justice is mentioned only once and is perhaps to be explained as the man who would act judicially in the king's place during a possible royal absence.[69]

---

[66] Lawrie, *E.S.C.*, nos. XXVI, XXVII.

[67] Lawrie, *E.S.C.*, no. CLXXXII.        [68] *R.R.S.*, i, no. 220.

[69] In England the king's absence in France had much to do with the development of the office of chief justiciar. In Scotland the king was occasionally absent but seldom for long; the office of supreme justice did not develop.

Government was the king's will and what we know of its exercise is the result of one new factor: from the time of King Edgar the king's will was made known not only *ore ad os* but also *meis litteris*. It seems unlikely that the written order was known in Scotland in the time of Malcolm III, but under Edgar and Alexander I the writ or *breve* came to Scotland in the form in which it was known in contemporary England: it was in Latin and opened with the king's name and a greeting to the recipient, both in the third person. The rest of the text might be a brief command or a statement that land has been granted, but was in the first and second person. The writ was authenticated by the king's seal, of which Edgar's recalled that of Edward the Confessor; Alexander I and all his successors had two-faced seals, on the face the king enthroned, on the reverse the king as knight; this seal followed the fashion of the Anglo-Norman kings and had its origin in their dual authority as king and duke, but in Scotland this origin had been forgotten. During the reign of David I many such writs with informal commands were issued, but there is a marked tendency for grants of land to be recorded in stereotyped phrases and at greater length: to such documents the name of charter (*carta*) was already given. They, or most of them, were the product of an office known in Scotland in later times as the king's chapel, but perhaps more readily identifiable now as chancery.[70] It cannot have been a large office—two or three clerks at most—and it perambulated with the king. Some at least of its staff were English-speaking and some French in this period, or so at least the spelling of name forms in charters would suggest. And its head was the chancellor, a cleric sometimes of prominent family, as William Comyn, who had known the chancery of Henry I, sometimes obscure, like Jordan, who had been a subordinate clerk or chaplain in the chancery. Edward was chaplain to Earl David, chaplain and then chancellor to King David, and finally bishop of Aberdeen. Other chancellors—though not all—were similarly promoted and, like Edward, demitted royal office on becoming bishop. The surviving texts of documents issued under the king's seal—about 145 for David I (29 years), 160 for Malcolm IV (12½ years) indicate an increasing recourse to the written instrument. But these are an un-

---

[70] An important article on the *Capella Regis* by Professor G. W. S. Barrow is to appear in the forthcoming proceedings of the *IVᵉ Congrès internationale de diplomatique*, ed. R-H. Bautier and C. Brühl.

certain guide to the total number, and analysis shows that there has been a particularly heavy loss of documents issued in favour of laymen. Biassed and inadequate as our documentation is, without it we should know nothing of twelfth-century government. If resources make government effective, writing makes it possible.

Whether the peaceful succession of three sons of Malcolm III in turn, the first two of whom were childless, created a law of kingship by the 1130s is a matter of some doubt. David I's only son, Henry probably born in 1115 or soon after, was reasonably adult by c. 1135, after which date his name began to be associated occasionally with his father's in authority. This might be done in various ways, usually in the context of important confirmations of title to land. Henry might be described at the end of the charter as 'bearing witness and agreeing'; the charter might run in the name of King David and Henry his son; or two separate charters might be issued almost identical save that one was given by King David, the other by Henry. This last was not markedly different from the situation in southern Scotland under Alexander I and his brother Earl David; but when David became king, Henry had no known appanage until 1136 and then it was in England. He did, however, act as regent during his father's absence in 1141.[71]

In 1144–5, however, a new and striking title was given to Henry: he appears as son of King David and 'designated king'.[72] The title is so close to that used in France that a borrowing seems unquestionable; it was the custom there for the king to have his oldest son accepted, crowned and anointed king so that his succession would be uncontested. But Earl Henry appears in this style only thrice in Bishop Robert's charter to St Andrew's cathedral priory, and in King David's and Earl Henry's simultaneous charters; all three were pretty certainly composed by a canon of St Andrews at the time, and do not amount to independent confirmation of each other. Indeed, unlike the Capetian 'designated king', Henry was never called simply 'king' but always 'earl' or 'son of King David', and it is therefore tempting to reject *rex designatus* as the whim of a St Andrews scribe. On the other hand, even without this phrase, his position clearly was unusually prominent and though he had not been made king some move had apparently been made to have him accepted as heir to the throne.[73]

---

[71] Lawrie, *E.S.C.*, no CXXX.       [72] rex designatus.
[73] Lawrie, *E.S.C.*, nos. CLXII–CLXIV.

What this may have been is suggested by events at his death in 1152 when David I took Henry's younger son to be accepted as earl of Northumbria, and Duncan, Earl of Fife, to whom belonged a prominent rôle in the royal inauguration at Scone, took the elder son, Malcolm (IV) with a numerous army and 'conducted him round the provinces of Scotland and proclaimed him to be heir to the kingdom'.[74] Although this action was not repeated by any subsequent king, an assembly was held in 1201 to recognise the three-year-old Alexander (II) as heir and, even on his deathbed in 1214, King William secured promises that his son would be accepted as king. Earl Henry may have been taken round the provinces and proclaimed similarly, but, if not, it is likely that he had been recognisèd as future king at an assembly and that an oath of fealty to him had been widely taken. If we contrast the English precedent in which no king for two centuries before 1189 was the heir of his predecessor, and each came to the throne by force, with the French precedent of hereditary succession secured by previous enkinging, there can be no doubt that the former brought more able men to the throne. The Scots, after a taste of succession by force between 1093 and 1097, shifted, or allowed their kings to shift, to something like pre-selection from 1097 onwards, though never going as far as to allow previous enkinging. Whether this was a perpetuation of earlier tanistry or simply a successful example of the smooth succession which every king, Plantagenet, Capetian or Hohenstaufen, sought for his heir, is uncertain.[75]

[74] Anderson, *Scottish Annals*, 228 from John of Hexham.
[75] J. Dhondt 'Élection et hérédité sous les Carolingiens et les premiers Capétiens', *Révue Belge de Philologie et d'Histoire*, xviii (1939), 913–53.

# 8

## WISE IN THE WAYS OF THE WORLD? WILLIAM THE LION[1]

King William succeeded his brother Malcolm IV without disturbance in December 1165. He had been born in 1143 and so was about twenty-two years old on his accession. His mother, the Countess Ada de Warenne, enjoyed her dower lands at Haddington and Crail until her death in 1178; she appears in King William's charters as a not infrequent witness, but she does not seem to have borne much responsibility for his policies. According to an English chronicler of the next generation she had tempted Malcolm IV (unsuccessfully) to abandon his vow of celibacy. With her younger sons she had no need of such temptations, but King William did not marry until 1186, Earl David until 1190. King William died on 4 December 1214 after a reign of forty-nine years and aged about seventy-one; Earl David died in June 1219, probably at a still greater age. Contemporary clerical writers give conventional obituaries of the king, including such absurd valedictions as 'the holy' and mild exaggerations as 'the lion of justice' whence later writers seem to have derived his by-name: the Lion. An Irish chronicler calls him *garbh*—brawny—and this seems a not unfair assessment of his bravery and intellectual stature.

In 1174 he was taken prisoner by an English army, at the moment (it was said) when Henry II was doing penance at the tomb of St Thomas Becket for the latter's murder. By the summer of 1178 King William had achieved interim solutions of the secular problems consequent on his folly. Its spiritual implications he now sought to meet by the foundation of a new abbey of Tironensian monks

---

[1] *ad usum mundi aptior*, Lawrie, *Annals*, 107, from William of Newburgh. It is correct to refer to this King as William I.

brought from Kelso to the coast of Angus at Arbroath, the foundations of whose enormous wealth were laid in the thirty years after 1178. At the Reformation it was exceeded in wealth only by St Andrews Priory and approached only by Dunfermline Abbey. Initially the king yielded from his demesne in Angus no fewer than five shires and seven churches, with one church in Mar and another in Tynedale and many miscellaneous revenues, but this was only the beginning of a stream of gifts not only from the king but also from his earls and barons. Thus the abbacy of the Culdee house of Abernethy had been given—or more probably confirmed—by the king to Orm, grandson of Gillemichael, Earl of Fife, to be held as a lay fief for ten pounds annually; Orm's son now gave to Arbroath from this abbacy the patronage of a number of churches on the south shores of the Tay and divided his personal teinds between Arbroath Abbey and the Abernethy Culdees. In this way the secularised revenues of a decayed college of clergy were once more diverted to ecclesiastical purposes, and Abernethy survived to become in turn an Augustinian priory and a secular collegiate church. The earl of Angus gave to Arbroath Abbey four churches, Robert de London (the king's illegitimate son) and Walter de Berkeley one each, all in Angus, while other gifts from the valley of the Dee, Mearns or Angus came from Earl David, the king's brother, Thomas de Lundin, the king's usher, Richard de Friville, John de Montfort, Philip de Melville and a family called Abbot who possessed Edzell. From these and other charters, notably those relating to Coupar Angus Abbey, we discover that in the first half of King William's reign there was an immigration of new families to whom the king gave fiefs in return for military service, a rapid colonisation which showed the continuing vigour of Anglo-French feudal society in Scotland. Let us look in turn at three men before considering the general features of this settlement.

William de Hay (de Haia or de la Haie) was the nephew of Ranulf de Soules, who came to Scotland by way of Northamptonshire; their families were neighbours in Normandy. They were jointly butlers (*panetarius*) to Malcolm IV and William, apparently as a life office, but in the thirteenth century the de Soules family—essentially now landowners in the west march—held the office alone. William de Hay is found as a landowner first at Pitmilly near Crail in Fife, perhaps in right of a wife of native stock. He was a hostage for the king in 1174 and between 1178 and 1182 received Errol

from the king to be held 'by the service of two knights'. His lordship passed fairly intact to the eldest of his five sons, but another
became lord of Naughton in northern Fife and was sheriff of Perth
and Fife at different times. Two other sons were jointly parsons
of Errol, which probably means that without taking holy orders they
shared the rich teinds in grain, animals and fish of this wealthy
parish and lordship. Coupar Abbey received from William de Hay
the land of Edirpolls ('between the pows') in Errol Parish, now
known from the manner in which it was exploited as Carsegrange.[2]

Walter de Berkeley came not from the Gloucestershire family
which has represented the name in England since the twelfth
century, but from a small Somerset village of Berkley, whence he
migrated to Scotland in the train of the Lovels who became lords
of Hawick. Robert de Berkeley, probably his brother, became lord
of Makerstoun in Roxburghshire, it is thought by marriage to an
heiress. The stages by which King William extended his favour
to Walter are not clear but he appears as a landowner in Galloway
before 1174, a hostage for the king in 1174, and before 1182 had a
grant from the king of 'Newtun' to be held for the service of half
a knight—the place is unidentified but if it lies in Angus or Perthshire, as seems likely, it is evidence of the spreading use of English
speech north of Tay. Further grants of Inverkeilor on the Angus
coast for the service of one knight and of lands in the parishes of
Fordoun and Laurencekirk in Mearns completed Walter's rapid
rise to wealth and were matched by the office of sole royal chamberlain which he held from c. 1171 until his death about 1193.
Walter's inheritance passed to the husbands of his two daughters,
Ingram de Balliol (the Galloway lands and Inverkeilor) and Humphrey fitz Theobald (the Mearns lands). Humphrey took Berkeley
as his surname and served the king as sheriff of Mearns; a Robert
the Steward, perhaps an illegitimate son of Walter de Berkeley,
farmed Inverkeilor for Ingram de Balliol and also served the king as
sheriff of Mearns.

The first witness to many of King William's charters was
'David, my brother', sometimes found agreeing to as well as witness-
ing a royal act because he stood for many years as heir presumptive
to the throne. About 1180 he received a charter listing his possession
of the lordships of Garioch (Aberdeenshire), Dundee, Newtyle
(Angus), Longforgan, Pitmiddle (Gowrie), Lindores (Fife) and

[2] See below p. 320 for the exploitation of these lands.

Morton (by Edinburgh). Along with these he was given the earldom of Lennox, but this he can have held for only a short time and he does not appear to have used the style of earl until in 1185 he became earl of Huntingdon.[3] The total service imposed upon him was that of ten knights. Later we find that he was possessed of rights in St Cyrus (Mearns). In 1195 he founded a Tironensian abbey at Lindores, generously endowed not only in Fife but also in the Garioch, whence it drew revenues from all the parish churches. To the Garioch he introduced Hugh Gifford of Yester (East Lothian) and Northamptonshire to hold half a knight's fee and other tenants with the English or French surnames de Billingham, de Boyville, de Aldri. Malcolm, son of Bertolf, received Leslie for the service of one knight; his son was the earl's constable at the motte-castle of Inverurie and his grandson had assumed the surname of Leslie, at which place he had a motte castle. The Bass of Inverurie was a natural mound sculptured into a motte, while at Dundee the earl probably built his motte from the ground; beside each he had a burgh before the end of the twelfth century. Some of these lands David probably held from early in the reign, but it seems fairly clear that the subinfeudation of Garioch was carried out after he had received an English earldom and through his relationship with the knights of Northamptonshire.[4]

As King William gave Errol to William de Hay and Inverkeilor to Walter de Berkeley, so he brought de Mortimer to Fowlis Easter (Gowrie), de Montfiquet (Mushet) to Cargill (Perthshire) and Kincardine (Menteith), Valognes to Benvie and Panmure (Angus), Carnall to Guthrie (Angus), Montford to Kinneff (Mearns), Gifford to Tealing (Angus) and Powgavie (Gowrie), all by grants of fiefs to be held for military service; it was surely on the same terms that the Olifards of Bothwell received Arbuthnott (Mearns), the Melvilles Tannadice (Angus), the Hastings Dun (Angus) and Robert de London, Ruthven (Angus). Henry the clerk received Rossie (Angus) for the service of one knight; it was later held by Hugh Malherbe, presumably on similar terms. It is not, however, enough to stress the fact that there was a wholesale distribution of land—

[3] *R.R.S.*, ii, no. 190 is exceptional being witnessed by 'earl David my brother' but dateable otherwise to 1175 × 78. The word *comite* may be an error inserted by the cartulary scribe. When David gave churches in Lennox to Kelso Abbey he did not call himself 'earl', *Kelso Liber* no. 226.

[4] Dr Keith Stringer has a book on David, Earl of Huntingdon in preparation.

and in the main of the king's thanages—to immigrant families, to be held as military fiefs. In some cases these were not the original Scottish endowments of the incomers: the Giffords and Melvilles were well established in Lothian and even Hay and Berkeley held land elsewhere. The grant of Ogilvy (Angus) to the son of the earl of Angus, of Rossie (Angus) to a cleric and Benholm (Mearns) to the brother of a native cleric, all for military service, underline the fact that the king's aim was not so much to introduce Anglo-French families to this 'Celtic' region, as to secure knight service. Feudalisation was the cost rather than the aim.

The king must have hoped that his new tenants, some of whom would of necessity be absentee landlords, would in turn subinfeudate for military service. One or perhaps two of them in fact departed on crusade (Osbert Olifard and David 'Rufus' of Forfar) so that the Olifard lordship passed to the main branch of the family, already settled in Lanarkshire. Arbuthnott was then fermed and sub-infeudated to a small landholder of native stock from the Merse, Hugh of Swinton, 'for his service'. But this does not seem typical of the region, and the smaller men of these fiefs remain of plainly Celtic name and origin and do not seem to have become knightly tenants. Earl David's lordship of Garioch alone had, after 1185, a subinfeudation for military service which, if we stretch the frag-ments of evidence, we may call systematic.

The line of the Allan Water and the Tay valley so far as Dunkeld seem to be the limits of this feudalisation. The earls of Atholl with their chief place at Rait and churches, lands and thanages in the valleys of the Upper Tay and Tummel, were not strangers to the court of King William, but their charters are wit-nessed either there by a group of the king's barons or at home by a group of Athollmen of Celtic name and origin. It seems clear that Atholl was not feudalised, though the earldom itself passed from Earl Matad to his son and his grandson without intermission. On the death of Earl Henry about 1200, leaving an illegitimate son and two lawful daughters, the earldom was probably held by the crown in wardship until c. 1209 when it was given with Earl Henry's elder daughter in marriage to Thomas, brother of Alan of Galloway, a mercenary captain of King John, who perhaps secured the marriage for him. His right was subsequently contested by Earl Henry's younger daughter, apparently on the ground that the lands of an earldom were partible among daughters but not sons, an argument which the court repelled.[5] Thus the heritability of the earldom was unquestioned and in this it was like a fief; but it was not partible among co-heiresses and in this still retained something of the character of a public office in a province.

Similarly the earldom of Strathearn passed in the male line without intervention by the crown even after the rebellion of Earl Ferteth in 1160. Earl Gilbert, who succeeded in 1171, married an Anglo-French lady, Maud de Aubigny, and before 1178 had granted Muthill and six other places in his earldom to Malise, his younger brother, to be held for the service of one knight, while the king gave him land in Strathtay on the same terms. He enjoyed cains and the profits of justice in wheat, meal, bere, cheese, fish and venison, and some of his rents came from the thanage of Dunning. He spoke rightly of his 'thanes and knights' for he had a steward, marshal, and *rannaire* or food-divider.[6] The honour of Huntingdon came even to Strathearn in the person of Nigel de Lovetoft, called de Dolpatrick after his new estate. Perhaps in 1179, when helping the king in Ross, the earl received lands in Strathspey to hold as he held his earldom,[7] but not long afterwards, when Gillecolm the marshal committed treason and forfeited Madderty, the king gave this as a knight's fief to the earl.[8] Royal policy which sought to make the earldom of Strathearn yield knights had a moderate degree of success by the early thirteenth century; among those who then appear as knights and landholders in the earldom are the survivors of Earl Gilbert's seven sons.

He was also responsible for bringing the rule of the Augustinian canons to a community of clergy headed by a hermit at Inchaffray, not far from another 'unreformed' community at Muthill. Upon Inchaffray Abbey the earls lavished lands and churches, while the see of Dunblane, of which also they were patrons, was filled by a succession of their chaplains and its cathedral church left without a college of clergy or worthy liturgical observance. We may contrast

---

[5] For Thomas of Galloway, Earl of Atholl see *Scots Peerage*, i, 420–2. His earliest appearance as earl is in *R.R.S.* ii, no. 489, of 7 January 1210. He appears as earl in English sources until 1212, then as T. of G. *simpliciter* until July 1213 when he is found with and without the title in the same week: *Cal. Docs. Scot.* i, nos. 585, 586. There are similar irregularities in the following years and Thomas, who supported King John in 1215, may have lost his Scottish possessions until 1217 or even later. He was an agent of Henry III in Ireland in 1219–20. See Genealogical Trees Nos. 3 and 6.

[6] See below pp. 432, 449.        [7] *R.R.S.*, ii, nos. 206, 474.

[8] *R.R.S.*, ii, no. 258.

Atholl, where knight and abbey are virtually absent, with Strathearn, where both were created by the earl. Yet personal names in Strathearn do not show Anglo-French family origins: on the contrary, feudalism for the earl's tenants and a regular monastic order for his anchorites seem to have been adopted on a moderate scale. The old order was scarcely touched in Atholl and only modified in Strathearn.

South of the Tay, in Fife, Lothian, the Merse and Strathclyde, feudalisation continued, though almost certainly at a slower pace. Sub-infeudation by Stewart, Brus, de Moreville, de Quincy, de Soules and others proceeded apace, and perhaps more rapidly than grants by the crown. A number of knights can be shown to have accepted fiefs in different honours as well as from the king, so that they were bound by homage and fealty to two, three or even more lords. The religious orders which had found their outstanding benefactor in David I now began to find his barons as generous as King William. Between 1163 and 1169 Walter the Steward settled a priory of twenty-five Cluniac monks from Wenlock at Paisley and endowed it generously. Before his death he had given his demesne at Mauchline to Melrose Abbey. His grandson, early in the thirteenth century, founded a Gilbertine house at Dalmilling which, however, had a brief life. The earls of Dunbar founded two nunneries in Berwickshire between 1153 and 1166. The Bruces gave churches and lands in Annandale to their priory of Guisborough in Yorkshire. For the most part, however, baronial grants were made to already existing religious houses and new foundations were smaller and less numerous between 1165 and 1214 than between 1115 and 1165.

Yet in these provinces the king did further the introduction of new families so far as he was able. He endowed with land such incomers as his marshal, Hervey, in East Lothian and the Fraser family in Peeblesshire and Stirlingshire; land in West Lothian was given to Duncan, Earl of Fife, for knight service such as was presumably specified in the other infeftments. A particular puzzle is presented by the king's grant of one hundred pounds of land with twenty infeft knights to his sister, Margaret, now a widow. Her second husband held Ratho and Bathgate (west of Edinburgh), which represent this grant, but which can scarcely have yielded £100 annually or provided twenty knights' fiefs. It is possible that Henry II compelled King William to promise provision for Margaret in this fashion in order to diminish the king's military resources in Lothian and that William was correspondingly sparing in fulfilling his promise. Although the Flemings Tancred and Simon were brought to Clydesdale in Malcolm IV's reign, their acquisition of lands further west in Ayrshire, where their names are also preserved in place-names, perhaps took place after 1165. There seems to have been some subdivision of fiefs and little new infeftment in this region.

In the last two years of his reign King William gave to Robert de Aubigny the 20 merks which were paid annually by Coldingham priory as wayting, 'until I or my heirs give to him 20 merks' worth of land on the south side of the Scottish sea or between the Mounth and the Scottish sea'.[9] The reason behind this grant and unfulfilled promise we shall never know, but it does suggest that the king no longer had a ready supply of land either in Lothian or north of Forth with which he could attract new settlers or entrepreneurs of settlement. It looks as if a phase in the history of Scotland had ended.

This was perhaps least true in Galloway, where risings took place, the lords of Galloway in revolt against their king, the men of Galloway in revolt against the first Anglo-French newcomers with whom the king could be associated. As a consequence, while alien settlement in Bruce's Annandale was extensive by 1186, in Galloway its real beginnings are found after that date. The two lords of Galloway in 1165 were Uhtred and Gilbert, who were sons of Fergus, but probably not by the same mother, for Uhtred was related to King Henry II of England while Gilbert, it seems, was not. The partition of an inheritance was customary in Galloway— it is found with the sons of Fergus and those of Dunegal of Niths-dale—and though Uhtred seems to have been the elder son, yet it was Gilbert who coveted his brother's inheritance; even before 1160 their relations were bad. (See page 215.)

Ralph, son of Dunegal, was Lord of Dumfries and Caerlaverock and probably of much of lower Nithsdale to the east of the river; he was alive until 1165 but apparently died about then and his lands passed to King William. His brother's issue, the macDonalds (*Duvenaldi*) seem to have held upper Nithsdale. Across the Nith lay the lordship of Uhtred, which stretched at least as far as the Fleet, and to the west of that (we must assume) lay the lordship of Gilbert.

[9] *R.R.S.*, ii, no. 514.

Uhtred undoubtedly began the feudalisation of Galloway for we know of a boundary dispute in Kirkgunzeon between Walter de Berkeley and Holm Cultram Abbey which indicates that Uhtred had already given Urr to Walter. It is to this period and this Anglo-Scot that we can with most probability ascribe the building of Mote of Urr, the largest motte in Scotland, a huge inverted basin of earth standing 80 feet (24 m) high with a vast bailey more than two acres (·80 ha) in area, whose strategic purpose is obscured by the modern shift of the Urr river course from west to east of the motte. Uhtred had married a Cumbrian lady and his surviving grant to a layman is of what later became New Abbey, to be held by a Cumbrian knight for military service. Yet his charters suggest that his following was native Galwegian rather than immigrant, and we can perhaps see his state of mind in the fact that his son appears in two guises in his charters—the Gael as 'Lachlan' and the French as 'Roland'. From the events of 1174 it seems possible that Uhtred was forced by the king to infeft Walter de Berkeley.[10]

The king's interest in the area was represented by the old castle—a motte—at Dumfries, which was doubtless overrun when the king was taken prisoner in 1174 and the two lords of Galloway returned home to expel royal officers, kill all the English and French, destroy the king's castles and invite Henry II to accept their allegiance. This revolt is reported by Roger Howden, who in November 1174 was in Galloway as Henry II's ambassador, and, although it conveys a greatly exaggerated idea of the extent of foreign settlement in the lordship, the stratum of fire and destruction discovered in the preliminary excavation of Mote of Urr may belong to this year and provide some justification for Howden's words. It is possible that Annandale as well as Nithsdale was attacked; it is certain that Gilbert was the leading spirit in the rising for between July and November he had procured the murder of Uhtred and in November offered 200 merks and an annual tribute in beasts to hold his province as a fief of England.

Against this tempting offer Henry II had to set the fact that his cousin had been murdered, that he had made peace with King William who was now his vassal, and that Gilbert did not appear to do homage to Henry with the other Scottish barons in August 1175. King William was sent to subdue Gilbert for all his offences.

[10] For 'feudalisation' of Scotia and Galloway see Barrow, *Kingdom of the Scots*, chapter 10. See Genealogical Tree No. 3 for the Galloway succession.

At some date thereafter, and before the end of 1177, the king had reoccupied Nithsdale and was at Dumfries and it was probably on this occasion that a new castle was thrown up there.[11] Subsequently—and we do not know what number or kind of campaigns were fought—the Scottish king brought Gilbert to Henry II who received homage, fealty and £1000 'for his goodwill' from him.[12] The only known term of this settlement was the surrender of Duncan fitzGilbert as a hostage to Henry II, but the statement of Howden that Gilbert returned to command the expulsion from Galloway under threat of death of 'all foreigners who had any holding in Galloway through the king of Scotland' may most plausibly be explained as Henry II's agreement that those expelled in 1174 would not be restored.

It is indeed generally assumed that Gilbert ruled the whole of Galloway until his death but another interpretation seems more consistent with the evidence. According to Howden, in the summer of 1184 because King Henry had returned to England, King William disbanded an army gathered to crush Gilbert 'who had wasted his land and killed his vassals but would not make peace with him'. Gilbert's activities must go back to 1183 or even 1182 and are probably the explanation of King William's failure to tackle the rebellion which broke out in Ross in 1181. The same source tells us that immediately upon Gilbert's death (1 January 1185) his land and that of other barons of Galloway was invaded and conquered by Roland against the prohibition of King Henry and his justiciars, which followed. On 4 July 1185 Gillepatrick (Dunegal of Nithsdale had a son of that name) was killed in battle by Roland and on 30 September 1185 perished Gillecolm, a freebooter (possibly but not probably the betrayer of Auldearn Castle of whom we shall hear), who had plundered in Lothian and then seized some of Gilbert's territory.

The extent of King William's complicity is unknown. He and

[11] *R.R.S.*, ii, no. 189. *Ibid*, no. 216 refers to the *vetus castellarium* of Dumfries and is our evidence that two castle sites then existed. Its date was said by Dr G. Neilson (*Transactions of the Dumfriesshire and Galloway Natural History and Antiquarian Society*, third series, ii (1913–14), 167, 170) to be 1186, but it must be 1179–85 and is probably of 1179; thus the new castle was probably erected before 1179.

[12] The date according to Howden was 9 October 1176 and the sum 1000 merks, but the debt appears as new in the English exchequer in the year 1178–79 and was £1000. The date may have been October 1176 or October 1178 but not October 1177, when Henry II was in France.

his barons were summoned to the English court at the end of May
1186 to discuss a suggested bride for the king, whose marriage was
long overdue. She was accepted, and while William was kept waiting for her at Henry's court the Scottish barons were compelled to
give hostages and then were sent to bring Roland to judgement for
his contempt—it would almost seem that the lady was a bait, the
marriage an excuse. Roland barred the approaches to Galloway and
Henry II prepared to subdue him in person. In July or August
1186 he was at Carlisle, and twice sent King William to fetch
Roland, the second time successfully. It was agreed that Roland
should keep his father's land and when summoned should answer in
King Henry's court the claim of Duncan fitzGilbert to Gilbert's
land. Roland swore fealty to King Henry and gave his sons as hostages; King William and his barons swore to support King Henry
if Roland broke his engagement. It seems that Duncan did not
press his claim and that Carrick was allowed to him by King
William in compensation, so that Roland kept the whole lordship of
Galloway.

In the chronicles it is nowhere stated that Roland conquered
Galloway in 1185; the phrase used is 'the land of Gilbert'. That
'he should retain the land of his father as the latter held it on
the day he died'—the terms of the 1186 peace—meant not that
he had just recovered this land, but that he had inherited it. There
is nothing in the contemporary sources to contradict the inherent
probability that when Gilbert made peace with Henry II in 1176 or
1178 Roland received his inheritance; this, moreover, would explain
Gilbert's renewed violence from c. 1182; he was seeking to expel
Roland from his moiety of Galloway. Roland gave the lands of
Kirkgunzeon to Holm Cultram Abbey, and, since this gift is mentioned in a papal bull of 2 May 1185, it was probably made in 1184
or earlier, thus indicating that Roland held his inheritance at that
time.[13] The case is not conclusive but it does more to explain
Gilbert's behaviour than the alternative account.

After 1186 the south-west was certainly the scene of further
feudal settlement, and a fair amount of land must have been at
Roland's disposal. Of the new families the larger element came
across the Solway from Cumbria—men such as David fitz Teri,
lord of Over Denton, who received Anwoth and perhaps built
the motte there, and Thomas fitz Gospatrick of Workington who

13 *Holm Cultram Register*, 21, no. 50a.

held Colvend at the mouth of Urr where there was a *castellum*. There are some twenty-eight mottes in Annandale and on the eastern side of the Nith, twenty-six between Nith and Cree and eleven to the west of the Cree, and without the guidance of excavation we can only hazard the guess that most of them were thrown up in the fifty years after 1186 and that they illustrate the discomfort of mind of incoming landlords in a province where the blood feud was still permitted and which was still notorious for the barbarity of its men in war.

Among the problems presented to the historian by the reign of King William is the measure of credit to be given to the 'assizes' or laws of his reign. We can, however, trust a royal writ (of 1195× 98) which shows that Galloway was a refuge for criminals and that the king in his 'assize of Galloway' had enjoined the lords of that land to help in tracking thieves.[14] Such broken men were doubtless one source of the army which Galloway could produce. The assizes relating to Galloway which have survived do not include the assize referred to in the writ; can an occasion be found for the following assize which has come down to us?

> At Dumfries it was adjudged by the *iudices* of Galloway that if anyone is convicted in Galloway, either by combat or in any other way, of breaking the king's peace, he shall give twelve score cows and three geldings (or for each gelding nine cows). Likewise in the same place and on the same day it was adjudged by the same *iudices* that if anyone within the barras where the combat takes place (apart from those who must keep the barras) should speak, the king will have a forfeiture of ten cows from him.[15]

This judgement belongs, we suggest, to the late summer of 1186, when the king was at Dumfries, and shows the restoration of royal authority over Galloway through the punishment of those who had broken the king's peace. The penalty imposed was of a size intended

[14] *R.R.S.*, ii, no. 406.

[15] *Palacia* = barras. The barras was the area set aside for the *duellum* or judicial combat. The text here translated is taken from the Berne manuscript, fo. 61, in preference to the text in *A.P.S.*, i, 378, c. XXII, where the middle paragraph is clearly a later gloss. The printed text has a final sentence taken from other manuscripts: 'And if he raises a hand he shall be in the king's mercy for life and limb'. This seems to me to argue the authenticity of the text in the Berne MS which suggests a judgement *ad hominem* (a man had spoken within the barras) and therefore a real occasion which would produce this circumstantial judgement. To this the later manuscripts add a much more obvious rule about interfering in the *duellum* which is unlikely to have needed statement by the *iudices*.

for substantial landholders and not peasants, who would presumably not be punished for following their lords against the king. In this way, perhaps, Roland was able to put the resources of Galwegian manpower once more at the service of the king and in the following July (1187) he and his men were at Inverness in the royal army and brought the rebel Donald mac William to book. The muster for that campaign may have begun at Lanark about 1 May, for the *judices* of Galloway were there in the king's court with Roland on that day in some year between 1187 and 1200 to adjudge the king's right to collect his cain in Galloway through the mairs (or serjeants) of Galloway and to lay down the penalties for delay or refusal in making payment; the wealth of Galloway once more made its contribution to the king's chamber.[16]

Roland had married the sister of William de Moreville, lord of Lauder and Cunningham and constable of the king of Scotland, and she had borne him three sons by 1186. Ten years later, by the death without issue of his brother-in-law, Roland was able to purchase succession to the vast de Moreville inheritance for a relief of something like 700 merks.[17] The extent of his family's power may be adjudged by the patronage of prelacies exercised by himself and his son, Alan: in Wigtownshire the Cistercian abbey of Glenluce (founded by Roland in 1191), the ancient see of Galloway, the Premonstratensian abbey of Soulseat (founded by Fergus), in the stewartry of Kirkcudbright the Premonstratensian abbey of Tongland (founded by Alan in 1218), perhaps the Augustinian priory of Trail, the Benedictine nunnery of Lincluden (founded by Uhtred), in Dumfriesshire perhaps the Premonstratensian abbey of Dercongal or Holywood (founded before 1225) and outside Galloway the abbeys of Dryburgh and Kilwinning (founded by the de Morevilles). Although the Galwegian abbeys were of only middling rank and wealth even among Scottish houses, and although their history is almost undocumented, yet this sustained investment of the resources of the lords of Galloway is remarkable testimony to their wealth and piety, and bears comparison with the scale of endowment by the royal house itself. It is also testimony to the peace which the lords of Galloway other than Gilbert held in their

[16] *A.P.S.*, i, 378, c. XXIII, the text of which is found only in the Berne MS. The king was at Lanark with Roland between March 1187 and March 1189; *R.R.S.*, ii, no. 260. I suggest that this too may be dated *c.* 1 May, 1187.

[17] The figure is given by Bower and like all money-sums in chronicles should not be taken literally; *Chron. Bower*, i, 509.

province. Alan fitzRoland and his brother were wooed by John, King of England, and lavishly endowed with lands in Ulster with the intention that they should help in the reduction of that province; it is clear that Galloway in 1212 was still an important source of infantry in large numbers. A decade later it was reported in Norway that 'an earl in Scotland was called Alan fitzRoland, earl of Galloway, the greatest warrior at that time, who had a great army and many ships and who plundered about the Hebrides and Ireland and made great warfare through the western lands'. On the eve of its dissolution the lordship of Galloway remained something of a kingdom within a kingdom, knowing its own customs and its own officers, devoid of sheriff and other agents appointed by the king.

In the 1190s the king must have recognised that he had permitted a drastic alteration of the territorial balance of power in western Scotland by investing Duncan fitzGilbert with Carrick and Roland with the de Moreville inheritance. It cannot be coincidence that in the year after the death of William de Moreville 'a new strength (*opidum*) was made between Doon and Ayr' (1197), and that we soon hear of sheriff and burgh at the new castle upon the Ayr, a dramatic affirmation of the king's authority in a province which seems to have been left much upon its own previously, for no surviving charters of King William are dated at places west of the Clyde. The new royal centre may have had another strategic purpose—to control the western seas and the routes sailed by the king of Man, to whom William had just committed the province of Caithness. Unfortunately, we are if anything less well informed about Ayrshire than about Galloway at this period and have little chance of recovering conditions there before and after the creation of the sheriffdom.

North of the Mounth between Dee and Spey the ancient earldoms of Mar and Buchan received very differing treatments from the king. Morgrund, who seems to have had some connection with the earls of Fife, was earl of Mar before 1152 and left several sons when he died at an unknown date before 1183[18] but probably some years before. No earl is attested for the 1170s and this may have strengthened the king's hold on the area and facilitated the grant

[18] The statement in the Peerages that he appears along with Earl Patrick of Dunbar (succeeded 1182) in a charter, *Dunfermline Registrum*, no. 147, is erroneous. See Genealogical Tree No. 6 for the earldom of Mar.

of Garioch to Earl David. In the 1180s the sons of Morgrund were ignored and the earldom given to a Gilchrist who is last recorded in the years 1203×11, when he had evidently given land in marriage with his daughter to an Angus laird, Malcolm of Lundie, the king's usher or door-ward (whence the name now given to the family, Durward). Gilchrist had begun the transformation of the Culdee house of Monymusk into an Augustinian priory and his grandson Thomas Durward probably helped to complete the change, for upon Gilchrist's death none of his sons received the earldom, vacant until 1222×28, when Duncan, son of Earl Morgrund, succeeded. During that vacancy Thomas Durward pressed his claim but had to be content with a substantial lordship between Dee and Don, dependent upon the motte at Lumphanan which he, perhaps, built. To the north, in Strathdon, lay the earl's motte, the Doune of Invernochty, comparable in size with Earl David's motte at Inverurie, and surely built by Morgrund or Gilchrist. It was per-haps—we may not say probably—the competing claims of their families which created another great lordship on the borders of Mar, Buchan and Moray, for it is at the very end of King William's reign that David, younger son of Earl Duncan of Fife, appears as lord of Strathbogie, a remote and landlocked group of parishes of great strategic importance lying athwart a main route into Moray.

In the north-eastern corner the earldom of Buchan with its chief place at Ellon on the Ythan was least affected by land-hungry settlers from England or southern Scotland. The earls are shadowy figures save for Colban who led the men of Buchan in 1174, but there seems to have been no break in their tenure until the end of the twelfth century. After a brief delay, Marjory, the daughter of the last earl, was married about 1212 to the justiciar of Scotia, William Comyn, who became earl. Other new families are found in this region 'beyond the Mounth' but in the main they appear in the sources after 1214 and it is only a probability that some of them settled in the north in the last years of King William. Perhaps the most noteworthy was the Bisset family which seems to have come from Nottinghamshire to Selkirkshire before 1200. By *c.* 1220 Walter Bisset was undoubtedly possessed of a lordship based upon Aboyne and was a neighbour to Durward, while his nephew John Bisset was lord of the Aird (west of Inverness). Three of the families we have mentioned, Comyn, Durward and Bisset, were to play critical parts in politics between 1237 and 1286.

Perhaps the most influential factor in the king's attitude to Mar, Garioch and Strathbogie was their strategic significance as the gateway to Moray. The route from Atholl to Strathspey followed by the modern road existed, but its remote, infertile and uninhabited character meant that it was of small use to the horse-borne and fodder-bound medieval traveller. The main routes lay further east from Aberdeen by Kintore, Inverurie and Fyvie to the coast at Banff or from Upper Donside to Strathbogie and thence to the lower Spey and Elgin. And the province of Moray had a particular importance to the crown as an area of early and planned settlement in which Flemings played an important part. The Freskin who received Duffus near Elgin, along with lands in Lothian, from David I was without doubt the most important of these settlers. Not only was his family responsible for the building of the greatest motte in the province at Duffus, but early in the thirteenth century they took to themselves the surname 'Moray', *de Moravia,* as a sign that they were greatest in that land. Their early history requires further study for there can be no doubt that they were closely related to a Clydesdale-Flemish family which by 1200 had taken the name Douglas from its lands.

The Laigh of Moray from Banff in the east to Inverness in the west exhibits the vestiges of early settlement only in the reign of King William, when it is already subject to change. Perhaps at Banff, Invercullen and Cromarty, certainly at Elgin, Forres, Auldearn and Inverness, there were royal castles, mottes which formed an integral part of the burgh which on one side stretched away from them. These burghs were regularly spaced and for the most part strategically situated on the lower reaches of the fast-flowing rivers which run into the Firth. At each of them we know—though sometimes from much later evidence—of the existence of a burgh *prepositura* or grieveship which has survived as the name of neighbouring lands. At Inverness the *terra prepositure* lay to the east of the burgh, but to the west there was another *prepositura,* 'Kinmyly', which was feued by the king to the Bishop of Moray in 1232 'excepting all the tofts and lands held by barons, knights and other good men of our land within the said *prepositura,* . . . so however that the men dwelling in the tofts and lands of barons, knights and other good men shall have the pasturing which they were accustomed to have in the same *prepositura*. . . . Saving to us all the pleas and plaints which may arise from the said *prepositura* and the men dwelling in it, except those which pertain to a (*or* the) thane'.[19] This, our largest glimpse of a grieveship, shows an estate with arable land and pasture exploited through a peasantry dependent in part upon the king, in part upon barons and other lords. Part of the grieveship had been given recently to the burgesses of Inverness, but before this it had clearly had no urban connection, and this was probably true of other *prepositure* such as that of 'Invereren'. Unfortunately, neither here nor elsewhere do we discover anything of the grieve. Was he the thane under another name, perhaps held more closely accountable to the king and not hereditary in office? Kinmyly might suggest so, for it lay in the Aird, which had been a royal thanage and was now apparently divided into this grieveship and Bisset's lordship, while the pleas reserved to the thane may have been the judicial authority of the grieve.

Yet what are we to make of the 'land of Invereren' and the separate 'land of the grieveship of Invereren', both of which were given by King William to Kinloss Abbey—for even the identity of the place is uncertain though it must have lain north of Forres?[20] In 1238 Alexander II listed his tithable revenues in the bishopric of Moray under four headings—the bailiwicks of Inverness, Invernairn, Forres and Elgin. Among the many lands listed, there are only two grieveships and both are associated not with burgh but with castle: *prepositura castelli de Vlerin* (Forres), *prepositura castelli de burgo de Elgin* (Elgin). 'Vlerin' has been plausibly identified with Blervie, to the south of Forres. Are we then to see in King William's time grieveship land and other royal land at Invereren; to the south the king's castle and burgh of Forres and southwards again the king's castle (site unknown) and grieveship land of Blervie—and all this in a four-mile walk? It may be that there was only one castle—Forres—whose grieve drew revenues from part of Invereren and from Blervie, where his grieveship lands lay. If this suggestion be valid, then Kinmyly would most naturally have been the lands of the grieve of Inverness Castle excised from the thanage of the Aird, while the burgh of Elgin would have yielded its rents to the *prepositus* of Elgin Castle as part of his grieveship. At other burghs the castle-grieve probably once drew burgh rents similarly; if so, either they were not tithable and so not listed here, or else had passed along with some of the extra-burgal grieveship lands to a separate, burgh, grieve or provost. We cannot forget that other

Fleming, Berowald, to whom Malcolm IV gave an extensive fief in the 'province of Elgin' to do knight-service in the castle of Elgin, along with a toft in Elgin burgh to be held with that fief 'as any of his peers holds his toft', for that suggests that in the middle of the twelfth century the castles of Moray were the foundation of the feudal and urban structure instituted by the king. The king's grieve in his castle must have been of far greater importance than the lowly title of his office suggests.

There are other traces of the settlement of Moray in the tofts in Elgin, Forres and Inverness held by the Steward, and in the lordship of Rothes held by Muriel of Pollock and, doubtless, also by her father Peter of Pollok, who was a prominent Moray baron under King William but who had surely come north in the Steward's train. Unfortunately, we have no other evidence so informative as Berowald's charter and for the area to the east, lying outside the diocese of Moray, we do not even have hints to verify a guess that some similar 'grieveship' and castle-province existed at Invercullen and Banff.

From the fourteenth century onwards there persisted a view that four cryptic words in the Holyrood Chronicle under 1163, 'King Malcolm moved Moray-men',[21] represented a removal of native peoples from Moray. Such a view cannot be disproved but it seems at least as likely that the words record a removal of the see of Moray by King Malcolm. It was not until King William's time that the north once more became a political and military problem for the Scottish king.

In 1168 Malcolm macHeth died holding the earldom of Ross, it is suggested as the rump of that greater province of Moray which had been the possession of his family. His earldom is not known to have passed to any of his sons and so far as can be told his sons played no further active part in Scottish politics. Yet his name survived in Caithness as Mackay and it seems possible that the family already held lands in Strathnaver. Certainly, if we would understand events in the north in William's reign we must look also to the provinces of Cat and (outside the kingdom) Orc.

The historian who struggles with the laconic and pathetically meagre words of the contemporary Scottish Latin chronicles must be enviously aware that for one province—Orkney—there exists for the middle years of the twelfth century a brilliant contemporary

---

[21] rex Malcolmus Muravienses transtulit, *Chron. Holyrood*, 142.

portrayal in a living tongue with remarkable narrative power of
the deeds and attitudes of all save the lowest in society. The
*Orkneyinga Saga*, with all its gaps and chronological uncertainties,
shows how in the time of David I and Malcolm IV the earl or
earls of Orkney were almost independent of the weakened Norwegian monarchy, ruling an aristocracy of farmers who still sailed
on summer expeditions but who followed Rognvald, their earl, to
Jerusalem, Constantinople and Rome in 1151–3. Although the behaviour of Orkney's aristocracy might be called 'heroic' rather than
'feudal', the northern earldom had come far from the times of
Harald Fairhair. The castles or halls, houses, churches and jetties
named in the saga can sometimes be pointed out today and show
how the violent behaviour of the Viking age had been eroded by
the adoption of Christianity and by traffic with the south. The
finest large Romanesque church north of the Tweed is at Kirkwall
and was begun by Earl Rognvald.

Frequent disputes and consequent partitioning of the earldom
reveal that Caithness, which had been colonised by Norse from
Orkney, had a very similar society, over which, however, the earl
had less effective control; Caithness was the most likely refuge or
home for an exiled earl of Orkney or for an unsuccessful claimant
to the earldom. At the same time, the earl of Orkney could usually
rely upon the ships and manpower of Caithness for a major expedition, and indeed it was the habit of two earls to hunt the red deer
on the Sutherland moors each summer. The province of Cat was
surely recognised as being Scottish yet as coming under the earl's
authority when, for example, David I commended the monks at
Dornoch to the protection of 'Rognvald earl of Orkney and the
earl and all goodmen of Caithness and Orkney'. 'The earl' of this
writ can have been not Rognvald but Harald, whose mother was of
Orkney but whose father was Matad, Earl of Atholl, and who
had gone at the tender age of five in 1139 to become nominal
ruler of half the Orkney earldom. This Harald Maddadson took as
his first wife the daughter of Earl Duncan (?I) of Fife, so that his
family relationships were with Orkney and also with the greatest of
Scotia.

David I and Malcolm IV had become involved in northern
affairs rarely, though one or other had 'given' half the earldom of
Caithness to a claimant, Erlend, to whom the Norwegian king had
then 'given' half of Orkney and who had temporarily ousted

Harald Maddadson.[22] From 1159 Harald was sole earl in Orkney and Caithness but the saga here turns to the rumbustious career of Sweyn Asleifson who had earlier charmed David I at Edinburgh and Malcolm IV at Aberdeen into supporting his dubious activities on behalf of Erlend. At some unknown date, but presumably not far from 1168, when Malcolm macHeth died, Earl Harald put away his wife and married a daughter of Malcolm, thereby associating himself with the latter's claims. Then in 1179 King William and his brother took an army into Easter Ross and established two new castles, one at Redcastle or Edirdour (p. 625) on the Black Isle peninsula, the other at Dunskeath on the northern side of the Cromarty Firth. Among unnamed enemies we can be fairly certain that Earl Harald was prominent, for the castles make little strategic sense except as a protection of the land (Redcastle) and sea (Dunskeath) approaches to Moray from the north.

In 1181 a much more serious threat arose in the person of Donald, son of William, son of King Duncan II. According to the chronicler he had 'often laid claim to the kingdom of Scotland'; Donald's claim remains concealed behind the unsolved problem of his legitimacy. Modern writers, including the present one, have regarded him as a bastard, but Professor Barrow offers the 'plausible' conjecture that his father had an earlier wife than his known one, a daughter of the house of Lulach and of the mormaers of Moray, and that she was mother of (a legitimate) Donald mac William.[23] No judgement is offered on this novel suggestion which is given colour by the statement that Donald invaded with a large army at the invitation of certain powerful men of the kingdom. Several previous 'furtive attacks' had left no serious mark upon the kingdom, but this was a different affair and clearly drew fighting men from the peripheral regions which King William did not control. The attack itself must have fallen upon Ross and Moray, and all the circumstances point to Earl Harald Maddadson as one of the instigators. Among these circumstances must be accounted the appearance at the Norwegian court before 1184 of Harald Ungi (the Younger) grandson of Earl Rognvald; his purpose was to obtain at least half the earldom of Orkney and he seems to have arrived with a title to half Caithness from King

[22] The date of this attempt seems fairly secure, 1151–53, but the saga calls the Scottish king 'Malcolm', a typical saga error.
[23] R.R.S., ii, 12–13.

William. This copy-book imitation of Erlend's claim in 1151–53 looks remarkably like King William's work, but there was no Sweyn Asleifson to bring it to completion and Harald Maddadson was not yet seriously troubled in his possession of Orkney.

For six years Donald mac William wrought havoc in the north, and Ross was lost to the king. In November 1186 sixty outlaws led by Heth (latinised as Adam) son of Donald, were cornered and killed in Coupar Abbey by Malcolm, Earl of Atholl.[24] Adam's father was probably Donald macHeth and the spread of serious disorder to Gowrie is a mark of the danger in which royal authority lay in Scotia—while the king was preoccupied with holding Henry II at arm's length and ensuring that Galloway was not lost to the kingdom. In Moray the king may have taken special defensive measures, for the castle of Auldearn was commanded by Gillecolm, marshal of the earl of Strathearn. This was the only Moray castle to fall and it was betrayed by Gillecolm, who joined the king's 'mortal enemies' and so forfeited his lands of Madderty. In 1187 the king was at last able to march to Inverness, evidently now the limit of his control, with a large army. It was by the merest chance rather than firm royal command (which was notably absent) that Roland of Galloway, coming upon Donald at Mam Garbh—an unidentified place near Inverness—defeated and killed him on 31 July. The castle of Auldearn was probably slighted for we hear no more of it, and King William soon obtained land nearby to build the new castle and burgh of Invernairn. The re-establishment of the king's authority did not, perhaps, extend to Ross and it seems likely that Earl Harald Maddadson lay far beyond his reach.

Earl Harald delivered himself to the king in the 1190s—a disastrous decade for the ancient earldom. In 1195 he had to humble himself before the Norwegian king and accept the loss of Shetland and some of his Orcadian revenues. In the summer of 1197 King William invaded the province of Cat so that his army (but not the king) reached and destroyed Thurso on the northern-most coast. Harald Maddadson submitted to King William's conditions that Thorfinn, his son, should be surrendered as a hostage and that half of Caithness should go to Earl Harald Ungi. Thorfinn had no mind for this fate and, probably soon after King William left the north, Thorfinn and his army suffered a defeat from royal forces near Inverness. In the autumn of the same year Harald

[24] *R.R.S.*, ii, 24 n. 47.

Maddadson, unable or unwilling to produce Thorfinn, came once more to King William, who was at Invernairn, presumably building his new castle. From there Harald was removed to Edinburgh or Roxburgh castle in chains and deprived of Caithness until Thorfinn surrendered himself soon afterwards. In the following year Harald Ungi made his bid for half of Orkney: whichever of the two accounts of the war is correct, the outcome is not in doubt. Harald Ungi was killed in battle at Wick and Earl Harald Maddadson once more controlled Caithness. The saga version of these events concludes that the earl returned to Orkney 'to boast of a great victory'. But Howden tells us that he went to King William offering gold and silver for Caithness and that the king demanded in addition that he should take back his first wife and surrender hostages. Doubtless on this occasion the earl gave an annual merk of silver to the canons of Scone, but he would go no further to propitiate King William. He returned to Orkney, Thorfinn to prison, and perhaps in 1198 or 1199 Caithness was given to the king of Man who placed it under stewards and paid an annual tribute to King William.[25]

The earl was probably little inclined to accept the loss of his mainland possessions, and may have been incited by John, King of England, to invade Caithness in 1201. The mutilation of the bishop of Caithness by some of the earl's army may not have been intended by the earl but it gave King William an excuse to blind and castrate Thorfinn. Early in 1202 a royal expedition brought Earl Harald once more into submission and for a payment of £2000 the king restored Caithness to him. In 1206 he died and his earldom passed to his two other sons.[26]

Among the uncertainties in this narrative we may discern one

[25] This narrative is based upon Howden, *Chron. Melrose, Orkneyinga Saga*, and one Icelandic annal recording the death of Harald Ungi in 1198—a date which seems certainly correct. Howden puts the whole tale under 1196, but this seems quite arbitrary, and *Chron. Melrose*, which places William's first invasion of Caithness in 1197, seems preferable. On the other hand, Professor Barrow attributes to 1196 a number of royal charters dated in Moray in the summer and autumn, *R.R.S.*, ii, 100, and nos. 388–95. Earl Harald's gift to Scone is *Scone Liber*, no. 58 and is witnessed by Laurence his chancellor, one of the hostages demanded by King William, See Genealogical Tree No. 6 for the earldom of Orkney.

[26] The saga and Fordun give quite different accounts of these events of 1201–2. The reconstruction in this paragraph is tentative but one hard fact may be offered: on 6 January 1201 King John ordered Earl Harald to visit him, and an Orcadian embassy did visit England in 1201–2; Lawrie, *Annals*, 341.

important strand—the macHeth claim to the earldom of Moray or at least Ross, inherited by the wife and son of Earl Harald. It was perhaps a reason for the activities which we have imputed to the earl in 1179–81. Certainly King William's anxiety to possess Thorfinn's person, to have him bastardised by his father's repudiation of his mother, and finally to unfit him for his inheritance suggests that it was not Caithness but Ross and even Moray and the vulnerable royal position there which guided the king's acts. This would also explain why in 1202 Caithness was tamely restored to the earl, for even though his sons David and John were full brothers of Thorfinn and therefore inherited the macHeth claim, warned by his fate they showed no inclination to urge it.

For some eight years the north was left to raiding parties from Norway while the western seaboard was racked by feuds. In 1210 King John invaded Ireland and was perhaps responsible for expelling Guthred, son of Donald mac William, who landed in Ross with local support in January 1211. By midsummer the king himself was on his way north and ordered the building of two castles in Ross in an attempt to come to grips with the rising—most probably a rebuilding of Redcastle and Dunskeath.[27] An army was sent under the earls of Atholl and Buchan and Malcolm, son of Morgrund, and Thomas Durward (representing the two lines claiming the earldom of Mar), which did much damage before an inconclusive engagement with Guthred. In September the king went south, leaving Malcolm, Earl of Fife, in charge of Moray; shortly afterwards one of the Ross castles was besieged and surrendered to Guthred and most of the king's work had to be redone. Early in 1212 he negotiated a treaty of mutual security with King John and sent his son Alexander to Westminster to be knighted, probably in preparation for the boy's first campaign as commander. But the crisis passed, Guthred was betrayed, brought to Alexander at Kincardine and beheaded, since the king did not wish to see him alive. Two years later (1214) the king is said to have gone again to Moray to make peace with John, Earl of Caithness (and Orkney), and at his death six months later King William seemed to have established his authority as far as the Pentland Firth. In fact the accession of the

---

[27] At Invernairn on 18 August, almost certainly in 1211, the king gave exemption from castle-work to Dunfermline Abbey and referred to *quando firmare feci castella mea in Ros* as if the current works were on his only castles in Ross. And, as in 1179, two castles were built. *R.R.S.*, ii, no. 500.

young Alexander II was the signal for the last great northern ?
In 1215 Donald, of the mac William kin, and Kenneth, of the
Heth kin, with Irish help invaded Moray—probably Ro~~ is
meant—and were defeated and killed by mid-June by a magnate of
Western Ross, Farquhar 'Machentagar'.[27a] He presented their heads
to the king and was knighted for his pains. And, indeed, he was
something of a phenomenon—a magnate of native stock prepared
and able to support the king's authority against the pretensions of
mac William to the throne and macHeth to Moray.

It seems clear that King William failed to consolidate his intermittent control over Ross and Cat, and it may be that the new
landowners whom we find there by 1230 were introduced after
1215. Yet the Bisset lordship of the Aird included Redcastle and
seems likely to have been established with that castle. Similarly the
Mowat lordship of Cromarty fits logically with the castle of Dunskeath. Moreover, King William had certainly made Hugh, grandson of Freskyn, lord of much and perhaps all Sutherland, for between 1211 and 1214 the king confirmed a gift by Hugh to Master
Gilbert, Archdeacon of Moray, and Hugh's kin, of Skelbo, Invershin
and all land westward thereof to the bounds of Ross—a huge territory to be held for the service of one archer. This grant may not
have been wholly effective but it is at least a strong indication that
John Bisset and Farquhar mac Taggart were already in Easter Ross.
Again, when Thomas of Thirlestane, an Anglian by descent and
tenant of the honour of Lauder, appears as lord of Abertarff on
Loch Ness side in 1228, it would seem not unlikely that he had
come north with Roland or Alan of Galloway in one of King
William's expeditions.

The contrast between this peaceful settlement of Moray and
penetration of Ross told to us by the charters, and the strife
narrated by chronicles and saga is not without its contemporary
comment, for the Barnwell annalist blamed the mac William risings
with Scots and Irish support on 'the more recent kings of Scots
(who) profess themselves to be rather Frenchmen in race, manners,
language and outlook; and after reducing the Scots to utter servitude they admit only Frenchmen to their friendship and service'.[28]

---

[27a] Macc an t-sacairt, son of the priest. He is thought to have been lord of
the secularised monastery of Applecross.

[28] Anderson, *Scottish Annals*, 330 n. The comment was made specifically in
the context of the mac William risings.

Taken out of its context this is much too extreme an assessment of King William's policy, but it is a valuable indication of the feelings aroused by the gradual transformation of Moray and Ross into another feudalised province. At Abertarff the king's cain ceased when the land was given as a fief. Yet Thomas of Thirlestane must needs lay hands also upon the half davach of land there which belonged to the church, leaving the priest with only toft and croft. In the Aird (twenty davachs), John Bisset seems to have owed the king an annual ferme of ten pounds until he was given the land as a fief—in other words he seems to have been eased into the thanage which subsequently became his lordship. It seems likely that these changes involved a more rigorous exploitation of the land and its native peasantry, for in one decade John Bisset founded a leper-house at Rathven (near Banff) and a Valliscaulian priory (at Beauly) from his own resources. Such factors must have played a part in bringing about risings against 'servitude'. The chroniclers dwell upon the huge royal armies in the north, with contingents from Galloway and some earldoms in 1187, from Atholl, Buchan, Mar and Fife in 1211 and with Brabantine mercenaries in 1212. Although these risings all collapsed in ignominy, the kings took them very seriously indeed and they must have enjoyed a good measure of local support. They may not be accounted simply a 'Celtic reaction' for the armies which the king sent against them were equally Celtic. They were rather a reaction of provincial particularisms against the more immediate royal presence manifested in castles and feudatories.

The western regions of Scotland remained divided between Scottish and Norse suzerainty, with the Manx king ruling Skye and the Outer Hebrides (or possibly only Lewis and Harris) and the sons of Somerled ruling mainland Argyll and the Inner Isles from Islay to Rum or Uist. One of them, Dugald, was sufficiently a baron of King William to attend and do homage to Henry II at York in 1175,[29] but another, Reginald, lord of Islay, styled himself king in the Irish manner and made a career on the western seas and not in Scotland. Reginald or his father brought Cistercian monks to Saddell in Kintyre and Reginald brought Augustinian nuns to Iona; we should be wrong to accept him as just the pirate depicted by the jejune annals which notice his life.

In the Firth of Clyde there seems no doubt that by 1200 Bute

[29] This is a deduction from his subsequent presence at Durham.

had passed into Scottish hands and that it was held by Walter the Steward. Possibly it was recovered on the death of Somerled in 1164, and with it the Cumbraes and even Arran. Although tucked away behind the protective apron of Kintyre, it was not so secure that its defence could be neglected. No later than the first quarter of the thirteenth century the Stewarts constructed on the water's edge of the northward-facing bay of Rothesay a round stone castle consisting of a battlemented curtain wall with internal wooden buildings. Much of this fine structure still stands with the addition of four round bastions; when put to the test in 1230 it fell to invading Norsemen, but it had proved a successful deterrent to any lesser invasion.

About two provinces of Scotland in King William's time we are poorly informed. The Lennox, stretching from the eastern shore of Loch Long to the Endrick Water and southward to the outskirts of Glasgow, remained free of Anglo-Norman incomers, even though it passed for a time from its line of native earls to David, the king's brother. The history of Menteith was probably no different, though not a single charter of a twelfth-century earl survives and only an occasional document suggests the absence of Anglo-French settlement. Then in 1213 the earldom itself became the subject of puzzling litigation which may help us to a fuller understanding of the earldoms of twelfth-century Scotland.

If we look back over our survey of Scotland we see the earldom of Lennox given to David the king's brother 'and his heirs' and yet reverting to the native line of earls; Mar passed from one family to another and back again, Ross reverted to the crown although its earl probably had heirs. In the time of David I it seems clear that the earls of Fife were not simply three successive generations but that the earldom became an hereditary fief and dignity when given by David I to Earl Duncan. It is not improbable that hereditary earldoms were created by David I in the Merse (Dunbar), Strathearn, Atholl and Angus, and by King William in the Lennox and Buchan, so that they descended from father to eldest son, and failing a son from father to daughter and her husband.

In Atholl we have seen that so late as the end of William's reign and in an earldom which was probably held as an hereditary fief, the English and later Scottish rule of descent of the dignity to the elder coheiress, and partition of the lands among coheiresses, was not applied. Now in the king's court in 1213 Earl Maurice the elder of Menteith resigned his earldom in favour of his brother, Maurice the younger, who claimed it as his right and heritage. The elder kept a liferent of some lands and other lands were given to provide a tocher for his daughters. Was he of doubtful legitimacy, as peerage writers suggest? Or was it that having no son but only daughters who stood small chance of succeeding, he resigned in favour of his brother and heir male who undertook to provide for his daughters? The history of the earldom after the death of Earl Maurice between 1226 and 1234 is a troubled one of legal battles inadequately reported in our sources, and we may not be too definite about the course of events. Yet this litigation makes best sense on the assumption that generations which knew only the laws of feudal inheritance were puzzled at the consequences of the settlement in 1213 which followed other principles. We suggest that, even where not feudalised by a royal charter, earldoms in King William's reign normally descended from father to son. The king could, however, vary the succession where there were claims for competing families. When a claim descended to a woman it was usually transmitted to her husband and acknowledged by the crown. When a claim descended to women there was still uncertainty, which might allow the claim of one or of a male relative to prevail. Earldoms still had something of the character of a public office and had not yet become wholly subject to the law of private inheritance of land.

King William, as a result either of policy or of a series of compromises with necessity, brought a new landed aristocracy to parts of Scotia and in varying measure the native aristocracy accepted new ways of thought. All this was achieved without rebellion save in the most outlying parts, for King William also multiplied and developed the instruments of his government, and sought to impose a firmer peace upon his realm. A number of his 'assizes' or statements of the law are derived from varying texts differently arranged and attributed to differing kings in different collections, contained in one thirteenth-century, two fourteenth-century and several later manuscripts. But although we are far from King William in these sources, it is possible to distinguish and discard the dross of apocryphal 'statutes', leaving assizes of which some are probably and some possibly genuine law-making of King William, his barons and his *iudices*.[30] Some assizes are mainly preoccupied with punishment

[30] *A.P.S.*, i, 371–84 and notes on 282–4, 42 chapters in all. I would accept

of theft, providing that a man followed and caught with the goods, or one accused and without a lord to offer surety for him, or one testified against by three older men, should be hanged; they seem to belong to the period 1170–5 and to owe something to the assize of Clarendon (1166). A group which can be dated at Perth on 30 October 1184 is quite the converse in intent. It seeks to protect the accused so that he might have time to produce warrantors to his title to possess the goods, and at the same time circumscribes the way in which a priest may act as warrantor. These groups of assizes seem to deal with presumption of unusually obvious guilt or innocence and suggest that theft was frequent and difficult to control.

At Perth on 26 May 1197 the king laid down that his prelates, earls, barons and thanes should swear an elaborate oath, 'that they will not receive nor maintain thieves, man-slayers, murderers nor robbers, but wherever they can find them, among their own men or among another's, with all their power they will bring them to a (*or* the) justice; that with all their power they will maintain the justice of the land; that after judgement of water, iron or duel be made they will take no consideration (*pecunia*) whereby justice is left undone; that to their utmost endeavours they will be helpers to the king to seek out misdoers and take compensation (*vindicta*) of them; and that, when the king asks, each will give true testimony concerning the court of another according to his knowledge. And the lord king has put their courts in pledge so that if any of them is convicted of breaking this assize, he shall lose his [right to hold a] court in perpetuity.'[31]

This assize owes an obvious verbal debt to Hubert Walter's oath

cc. 1, 2, 10, 11, 12, 16–8, 20, 22, 23, as probably genuine, because associated with particular dates and found in the earliest MS. I would accept cc. 6–7, 19 (first half, in Berne MS text), 26, 27 as possibly genuine.

[31] A Scottish assize is mentioned under 1197 by Howden, who uses words taken from the English assize of 1195. The law collections contain the above text, which is surely the assize intended by Howden and is self-dated Perth, 26 May. A charter which might be dated to the same occasion is *R.R.S.*, ii, no. 389 (Perth, 1 June, 1196 x 99). I have translated the text from the Berne MS which lacks the anachronistic *et tota communitas* and gives *nec latrones nec interfectores in murthedrices nec raptores* (lacking *nec alios malefactores*) where the word *murthedrices* has puzzled a scribe and caused him to write *in* for *nec* or *vel*. In turn the words *in murthedrices* became in the Ayr MS *in Moravia vel alibi*—or so I suggest we explain this curious reading. I have translated *vindictam* as 'compensation' because this is a meaning allowed by the *Medieval Latin Word List*; it may have the sense of 'surety' here. I doubt if the translation 'vengeance' is meaningful in this context.

'for the keeping of peace' taken generally by the people through England in 1195; it led there to an increase in the number of vagabond outlaws; to a lesser extent the Scottish version probably had the same effect for, by 1200, the king had sought such guidance from Pope Innocent III on criminals who took sanctuary in churches as to suggest that this had become a serious problem. The English edict sought to improve the system of arresting criminals; that is only the first provision of the Scottish assize, which goes on to insist that judgements must be made and must be carried out and that malefactors, too, should be sought out, and concludes with stating the sanction of destruction of a franchise. Are we to see here a distinction between such serious criminals as thieves, robbers and murderers, and less serious misdoers? If so, for which group are the franchise courts held responsible (for the assize clearly blames much upon their inadequacies)?

An assize of 1180 had laid down that franchise courts were to be held in the presence of a royal officer, presumably to ensure their proper working, but had then admitted that this was not always practicable though it is found in practice.[32] The same assize speaks of the four reserved pleas of the crown—rape, robbery, arson and murder—named also a decade earlier with treasure trove and forethought assault, when the king had confirmed Annandale to Bruce to be held as in the time of David I and Malcolm IV except for the *regalia* belonging to the king's royalty (*regalitas*) namely these six pleas, which were to be tried before the king's justices. The 'four' pleas of the crown, although mentioned occasionally in the thirteenth century, frequently in the later Middle Ages, were probably never more than a lawyer's catchphrase, those important and frequently occurring pleas which the king would not allow to a franchise. Other pleas—treasure trove, wreck, false coining, the whole field of urban privileges—remained pleas of the crown, but over these, we may take it, the crown had no difficulty in preserving jurisdiction. The delimitation of the border between franchisal pleas and royal pleas such as we see in the Annandale charter and such as is implied by 'the four pleas' seems to have been the result of King William's need to control disorders and serious crime. Supervision by royal officers, the naming of certain criminal matters as specifically crown pleas, the taking of the oath of 1197 with its threat of 'loss of court', are all part of the same

[32] Barrow, *Kingdom of the Scots*, 95; *Dunfermline Registrum*, no. 230.

policy. We may not call this an attack upon the franchises, for it
was probably rather defensive of the king's jurisdiction, an attempt
to limit their growth. And (to return to our questions in the previous
paragraph) the oath of 1197 deals with those criminals—thieves,
robbers, killers, murderers—who strike at the security of society.
They are indeed more dangerous than other malefactors and the
king is especially concerned to search them out; some will be tried
in franchises, some in the king's courts, and they do not exactly
correspond to offenders who were covered by the phrase 'pleas of
the crown'.

The definition of crimes and jurisdictions which took place in the
later twelfth century was not limited to crown pleas, but development there undoubtedly caused the emergence from anonymity of
the king's justices; fifteen men are explicitly so described. For most
of King William's reign their area of jurisdiction and term of office
are alike uncertain. The earliest to appear are David Olifard, lord
of Bothwell, Duncan, Earl of Fife, and Robert Avenel, lord of
Eskdale, two of whom may have been joint justices in Lothian and
Strathclyde while Robert de Quincy may have been justice in Fife.
In the 1190s William de Lindsay, lord of Crawford, was a justice
in Lothian, while a decade later his son held similar office. Gilbert,
Earl of Strathearn, Patrick, Earl of Dunbar, Roland of Galloway,
Richard and William Comyn, Geoffrey de Melville and Matthew,
Bishop of Aberdeen, complete the roll of King William's justices.
Earls Duncan and Gilbert acted in Scotia; both Earl Duncan and
William Comyn were styled justice or justiciar of Scotia and it has
been cogently argued these two were in succession 'chief' justices of
Scotia, acting along with a number of junior colleagues including
Earl Gilbert, Bishop Matthew and Robert de Quincy. The earliest
naming of a justiciar as 'of Lothian' does not occur until 1221,
probably because until about that date there were two or three
justices south of Forth, but certainly Earl Patrick and possibly the
Olifards and Lindsays held a 'chief' justiceship there in succession.
It has also been suggested that Roland was the first justiciar of
Galloway, with unnamed successors filling the gap between 1200
and the first expressly named justiciar of Galloway, in 1258,[33] yet
his three known appearances as *justicia* relate to Loudoun (Ayrshire), the lands of Melrose in or near Galloway (? Maybole in
Carrick), and Soutra hospital (East Lothian), together with the

[33] *R.R.S.*, ii, 45.

gatherings at Lanark in 1187.[34] Thus his remit may have been the shires of Dumfries, Lanark and Ayr rather than his own Galloway. Furthermore, royal writs which elsewhere are addressed to 'justices and sheriffs' are in Moray addressed only to sheriffs, so that in Moray there was probably no justice to aid or supervise the sheriff. We must seek some explanation why the duties of a justice should be heavy in the south, so that several justices were necessary, while north of the Tay the justice is encountered comparatively rarely.

The king's sheriffs and sheriffdoms achieve a greater regularity under King William than under his predecessors. The sheriffdom of Lothian was partitioned into Haddington, Edinburgh and Linlithgow and, in 1178 with the death of the Countess Ada, the sheriff of Haddington once more became a royal official. Linlithgow had a sheriff for most of William's reign but at the very end seems to have been reunited with Edinburgh.[35] The office of the king's forester was expanded to that of sheriff probably in Ettrick (Selkirk) and certainly in the Mearns (unique in not being named after the sheriff's administrative centre), while in the north sheriffs were instituted unspecifically 'in Moray' (early in the reign), at Inverness and Invernairn and perhaps at Elgin and Forres by the end of the reign. Ayr appears at the end of the reign and may have existed as a sheriffdom of Carrick c. 1195.[36] Contrary to this process was the amalgamation of some of the small sheriffdoms: early in the reign Clackmannan was united to Stirling, Dunfermline to Crail when the latter fell to the crown in 1178. Perth and Scone, however, remained distinct until c. 1220 or 1230.[37] In general sheriffdoms during King William's reign were of the same order of size. They had come to cover much of the non-Highland part of the

---

[34] Above p. 186.

[35] It is possible that during the English occupation 1174–86 there was no sheriff of Edinburgh and that the sheriff at Linlithgow or Haddington had authority over the sheriffdom.

[36] *R.R.S.*, ii, no. 374, addressed to the sheriff(s) and bailies of Carrick, Galloway and Lennox. But there is no other evidence for sheriffs in any of these provinces. One may compare *R.R.S.*, ii, no. 80, referring to the *comitatus*, earldom, of (Ro)xb(urgh), and *ibid*. nos. 132, 312, referring to sheriffs of Moray. I am inclined to doubt if we may take any of these documents literally, for scholars are agreed that there was no earldom of Roxburgh. One would like some corroboration of the sheriffdoms, for example a writ addressed to a sheriff of a royal centre in Carrick or Moray.

[37] Randolph was sheriff of Scone, still distinct in 1216 x 1219 (*Scone Liber*, no. 68). A royal charter of 12 April 1228 ends its list of witnesses with *vicec' de Perth et de Scone*, where *vicec'* might be singular or plural (*St Andrews Liber*, 237).

country, only the north-east remaining, so far as our knowledge goes, without a sheriff. Even here it may be that the lack is in our documentation rather than in King William's sheriffs. When we hear of a sheriff of Aberdeen, Philip de Melville, in 1222, he was also sheriff of Mearns, and perhaps the two were established by King William.[38]

The families which served the king in these offices were remarkably few and almost exclusively Anglo-French in origin. Macbeth, thane of Strathardle and sheriff of Scone, and Gillebride, sheriff of Dunfermline, were two examples of a native lord as sheriff; another example might be the descendants of Thor(ald), David I's probably native sheriff of Lothian, for William, his son, and Alexander, his grandson, were both sheriffs of Stirling. Yet, as the reign progresses there is growing evidence that the king chose his justices and some of his sheriffs from the great landholders. The very greatest became justices, the others sheriffs in their own locality, de Moravia at Invernairn, Melville in the Mearns, Comyn and Hay in Angus, Mortimer at Perth, fitzThorald at Stirling, Melville at Linlithgow, Lindsay at Berwick, Crawford at Ayr. In the reign of King William the succession of son to father as justice is plainly marked; for sheriffs the evidence is fragmentary, but similar succession was common under Alexander II, and probably therefore earlier. In Selkirk the sheriff was indeed an hereditary office, and while this was still formally rare, in practice the son of a sheriff would probably find himself holding the same office for a spell. Thus we may speak of ministerial families in Scotland, drawn from the baronial class, their official position strengthening the identity of interest between king and baronage.[39]

King William's writs are almost invariably 'generally' addressed —that is, addressed to 'all good men'—even when continuing with an administrative command. One or two writs addressed to a sheriff are concerned with burgal matters; the sheriff and *prepositi* of Haddington are commanded to fulfil a royal charter by making an annual payment from the burgh ferme.[40] Another commands the sheriff to permit the prior of Coldingham to remove those men (presumably unfree peasants) whom the prior has the right to

[38] There is a discussion of this in J. G. Dunbar and A. A. M. Duncan, 'Tarbert Castle', *Sc. Hist. Rev.*, 1 (1972), 8–12.
[39] There is a full and important discussion of the shrieval personnel in *R.R.S.*, ii, 39–42 and a list there on p. 64.
[40] *R.R.S.*, ii, no. 305; see also no. 98.

remove.[41] If, however, we examine those writs addressed to 'justices and sheriffs', (bailiary usually unspecified) we discover a much wider responsibility: to maintain the landed possessions of a church, to enforce its freedom from toll, its rents, its teinds, to secure its peasants; similar responsibilities are also indicated by royal precepts which are 'generally' addressed to all good men but which were surely a charge to 'justices and sheriffs'. The discharge of these duties in particular instances is rarely illustrated by our sources. There is record of a surprising number of land pleas held before the king himself and in only a few recorded cases was such a matter remitted by royal precept to justice or sheriff. For the rest, we must take the king's writs as evidence that these officers did hear particular pleas on the matters which they were generally commanded to enforce.

In Berwickshire justices and sheriff were commanded between 1165 and 1171 that the king's serjeants were to take exactions only at the rate found in other sheriffdoms when they moved pleas in the lands of Coldingham Priory, and subsequently the priory's men were acquitted of the two shillings exacted from them by the king's serjeants 'for (de) the pleas which they can find'.[42] The pleas referred to are those we should call criminal and it seems to be implied that they were brought before justice or sheriff by the serjeants after they had collected indictments through the sheriffdom. Among the assizes attributable to King William are two which have late manuscript authority but which agree well with this procedure. The first, an assize made at Roxburgh for Lothian provided that the sheriff or serjeants should secure, from the grieve and three men of the toun where stolen cattle were found, an oath that the toun was ignorant of the theft; the second, dated about Lent 1175, provided that anyone accused of theft or reset on the oath of the grieve and three good men of the toun should go to the ordeal, but the additional evidence of three 'senior' men against him should hang him at once.[43] Thus in each toun of Lothian four men spoke for the tounship to say to the king's sergeant 'in this toun there is knowledge of such-and-such a theft and so-and-so is defamed of it by common repute' but also to say 'in this toun there

[41] R.R.S., ii, no. 380.
[42] Raine, North Durham, nos. XXV, XXXVIII.
[43] A.P.S., i, 371, chapters 1 and 2 from the Bute MS. The first chapter occurs also in a curtailed version in the Ayr MS. of c. 1330.

is no knowledge of the theft of which one, our fellow tounsman, stands indicted by another'. In this second there is the clear implication that the toun would be punished if it knowingly failed to report or present a misdeed to the king's serjeant. Here then, in Lothian, was not only private indictment, familiar in England and in later Scottish criminal procedure, but also a tounship group whose presentments in the King's court were made by the king's serjeant.

The four of the tounship is a part, and the only part known in Scotland, of the English jury of presentment. It is known only in Lothian. The serjeant of the peace with a right to board and lodging from each vill or barony and duties of arrest is found in Wales, Cheshire and the three northern English counties; he is close kin to the serjeant of Lothian with his right to two shillings from each toun or barony and duties of public indictment and arrest, and his equivalent north of Forth, the mair, is not known to have enjoyed the right of indictment. Here, then, is an important difference between Lothian and Scotia—a whole system of presentment of criminals which, whatever its origin, created business for the king's judges. This, we may think, was the reason for the generous provision of justices in Lothian and their comparative scarcity in Scotia. Moreover it may explain the different frequency which has recently been remarked in grants of criminal franchises between Scotia and Lothian: 'sac soc and infangenthief' (giving the right to hang a thief caught red-handed) was usually granted in Scotia, but with lesser frequency south of Forth. If the right to pit and gallows (implying the use of the ordeal) is taken into account, the contrast is even more striking.[44] The royal assize of 1197 seeking to make the franchise courts more effective[45] was issued at Perth and this, together with its reference to thanes, implies a special relevance to Scotia; and so in many ways it complements the earlier assizes of King William relating to presentments in Lothian. It may be concluded tentatively that the justices of Lothian had to undertake a jurisdiction which in Scotia was often enjoyed by private lords. Whether this was also true of sheriffs is a more difficult question, since there is no evidence of the existence of a sheriff's court in the twelfth century, but only of pleas referred to a sheriff by the king.[46] Yet the early development of the sheriff's office in

[44] *R.R.S.*, ii, 49.     [45] Above p. 201.
[46] *R.R.S.*, ii, 42, an important discussion to which I may not have done full justice.

Lothian into something more than a demesne officer of the king (and this seems to have taken place by the late twelfth century) may well be explained by the existence of a court, meeting regularly and presided over by the sheriff, to deal with offenders presented and charged with lesser crimes than the justice would hear.

The sheriff was the king's principal local financial agent, responsible for his fermes from both landward and burgh, yet by no means the only source of royal income. Thanages and thanes must have provided demesne revenues which could be consumed by an itinerant king. Here, however, the records of central government suggest a rapid transformation, with the commutation of produce-renders for money rents, and probably the local sale of surplus produce. Thus, the thane often became more clearly a tenant at ferme, as the priory of Coldingham, for example, commuted its wayting for an annual rent of twenty merks, or the abbey of Cambuskenneth its teind of the profits of justice for the parish kirk of Forteviot.

It has been stressed that the chamberlain as holder of David I's money-bag had had a limited function. Under King William the responsibilities of the chamberlain, though remaining the same in kind, became much more onerous as the proportion of royal income in money steadily increased. Yet the king had only two chamberlains, Philip de Valognes, who yielded office to Walter de Berkeley about 1171 and took office again on Walter's death about 1193, and these great barons can scarcely have exercised the supervision to be expected even from a household knight. Among the witnesses to royal charters from the 1130s until the end of the century were the members of a number of lay families using the by-name *de Camera*; these probably discharged the routine non-clerical work of the chamber, including keeping the door of the chamber and the king's hall. The chamberlain also had the services of professional clerks. There may be significance in the fact that for some years after 1175 royal acts dated at Stirling seem to be witnessed with unusual frequency by Richard the king's cleric *de prebenda*. His function was to manage the king's household, keeping track of income in kind and of its use, either as 'liverance' (payment) or 'dispense' (consumption). Stirling would seem a likely place for a royal treasury holding reserves of cash and other valuables, but towards the end of the reign the evidence ceases to suggest where any such treasury may have been kept. On the other hand, the earliest document stored in the treasury in Edinburgh Castle a century later was a bull of Lucius III (1181–5); evidently the Register House of the Scottish kings was first established there on the withdrawal of the English in 1186. The rest of the treasury may have gone there also.[47]

The king's government acted at his will expressed either orally—and of this we have no record—or under his seal. Some five hundred texts once issued under this mark of authenticity have come down to us, four-fifths of them in favour of ecclesiastical bodies. We know of some sixty more of which we have no texts, and thirty-seven of these were for lay beneficiaries. Plainly, a great mass of documents in favour of laymen has been lost, and the total output of the king's chapel or chancery must have been well over the thousand figure which is a logical minimum. Yet even if we guess at an issue of almost ten thousand, over the forty-nine year reign this would represent only two hundred annually and suggests that while government was available in the form of confirmation of title to land and privilege, or of brieve to enquire into services or boundaries, it was not aggressive government intent upon pressing royal rights wherever they might lead. The staff of the king's chancery was small; about a dozen men served in it as clerks during the reign, that is, perhaps about three of four at any one time. Five can be identified by name, of whom one, William de Bosco, became chancellor, and three became bishops.[48] Before 1178 the office of chancellor was held by men who had been chancellors under Malcolm IV. For a decade from 1178 no chancellor is named and the office was on offer to an ambitious cleric as compensation for the loss of the bishopric of St Andrews. When in 1189 the king's cousin Roger, son of the Earl of Leicester, was appointed bishop of St Andrews, he was said to have been chancellor, probably for the preceding year or two. During these years the seal was probably managed by a royal cleric, Hugh, who became chancellor from 1189 until his death in 1199. This return to administrative regularity was continued until 1202 under William Malvoisin, a royal cleric who had come to Scotland with Queen Ermengarde, and in 1199 was made bishop of Glasgow; he resigned the chancellorship only on his translation to St Andrews. Until 1210 the king's nephew, Florence of Holland, seems to have been chancellor but in name only. The seal was managed by the

[47] *A.P.S.*, i, 107.          [48] *R.R.S.*, ii, 31–2.

experienced royal cleric, William de Bosco, who became chancellor from 1211 until 1224. Thus during two periods, each of about a decade, the chancellorship was treated as an honorific title to be conferred upon clerics of distinguished birth, or for other non-administrative reasons. Of those who held the office no fewer than four (including the absentee Florence of Holland) were promoted to the bishopric of Glasgow. For the most part, however, the chancellor was a serving royal cleric, both before and after his elevation a very frequent witness to royal documents. Did he follow the king from the hunting grounds of Selkirk to those of Alyth, to the north to humble Donald mac William and to the south to be humbled before John of England? Much depended upon who the chancellor was; the most assiduous were undoubtedly the professionals, notably Hugh (1189–99). The royal seal probably stayed with the king in the charge of a cleric even when the chancellor was away from court, and this would make possible those periods when the chancellorship was vacant or as good as vacant. The documents issued show an increasing but still controlled prolixity in the case of charters, an infinite flexibility of succinct phraseology for administrative matters. One sample can illustrate only the historical problems presented by such documents and not the wide range of matters they cover.

> William, by the grace of God king of Scots, to all good men of his whole land, cleric and lay, greeting. Let present and future persons know that I have granted and by this my charter confirmed to the canons of Scone that on the death of their abbot they shall be allowed to choose freely with my assent and counsel one of their convent as abbot, if a person suitable for this can be found in the house of Scone. Witnesses: Richard, Bishop of St Andrews, Arnald, Abbot of Coupar, Henry, Abbot of Arbroath, Hugh de Mortimer, Prior of May, Earl Duncan, justiciar, Robert de Quinci, William Comyn, William de Hay, John de Hastings. At Forfar, 29 May.[49]

The formal address in the third person is followed by notice of a grant, still in the first person singular but soon to use the regal plural; the invariable use of *Dei gratia* in the king's style had begun in the 1170s. The gist of a grant of land would include many clauses about easements such as woods, ponds, mills, inserted only because it now seemed wise not to omit them lest the beneficiary find himself denied them. In this case an unusual grant is made,

[49] *R.R.S.*, ii, no. 398.

carefully circumscribed so that the king still has a substantial if limited right of appointment, and there are no superfluous words—indeed the charter omits to say that this is a perpetual grant. In England a document of this kind would probably be drafted and classed as a letter patent; in Scotland it is a charter with full record of witnesses present when the grant was made, for the Scottish chancery made few distinctions between kinds of letters issued. There is a date of place, day and month as introduced by chancery in the summer of 1195 on the English model, but as yet, and until 1225, no indication of year. The introduction of a time date in 1195 was pretty certainly the work of William de Bosco, who had entered the service of chancery a year or two earlier; it has been suggested that this new feature was linked to the keeping of copies of charters on a chancery roll, one for each year, but the Scottish archives a century later showed traces of only the most desultory keeping of chancery rolls.[50] Fortunately, a chronicle tells us that in 1198 the cellarer of Holyrood was elected abbot of Scone at Forfar 'as pleased the king's men',[51] and we can surely identify the document with the occasion, discovering that the king intruded an outsider on this 1198 occasion but guardedly promised not to do so in future. We conclude also that the copy on which we rely for the text of this charter has a mistaken guess at the bishop's name, Roger not Richard, presumably from *R.* in the original.

Some of the 'king's men' or *curiales* of the chronicler, though not necessarily all, would be found among the witnesses. The number of monastic heads is unusually high, which is explicable by the nature of the business; it may have become unusual for the king to intervene in monastic elections (civil servants sought to become bishops, not abbots) and hence on this occasion amenable religious, Cistercian, Tironensian and Cluniac, were brought in to lend respectability to pressure upon the Augustinians. Of the laymen the first two were justices, and Comyn, Hay and Hastings were sheriff of Forfar, royal butler and sheriff of the Mearns, respectively. In the king's grant made at Edinburgh to the bishop of Glasgow of the annual Glasgow fair (1189×95), the witnesses are the king's former enemy John, Bishop of Dunkeld, Hugh the chancellor, Archibald, Abbot of Dunfermline (royal factotum), the abbot of Kelso, three laymen who were justices and six of whom five were the sheriffs of

---

[50] *R.R.S.*, ii, 58 presents the arguments for the existence of such rolls.
[51] *Chron. Bower*, i, 513.

Roxburgh, Forfar, Lanark, Stirling, and Edinburgh. Of the nine laymen the office of only one is given, *Alexandro vicecomite de Strivelin*, because, it seems, he had no accustomed by-name[52] and chancery therefore filled out his name with his office. This principle was observed only generally, and often departed from, but it explains why so many known royal officers are named without office and suggests that other officers are lurking unrecognised among the witnesses.[53] The occasion for such a gathering is unknown but it would be fair to conjecture that the business they had in common was to audit (the first seven plus the bishop of Glasgow) and be audited (the last six), and that from a session of the king's counsellors in his court at the exchequer board arose the request for Glasgow fair, the discussion and grant of it.

The king's *curia* thus performed many other functions than the judicial, and his counsellors were probably a body of changing composition, though it is remarkable that a relatively small group of men, including William Hay, William Comyn, the Berkeleys, and perhaps a dozen other such, seem to turn up in charters fairly regularly and without regard to the part of the country in which the charter is dated or with which it deals. The existence of a parallel group of clerical *curiales* is more certain and much less surprising. Upon occasion—and we do not know how frequent the occasions were—much larger councils were called together. The size of such gatherings may be indicated by the court which in December 1213 gave judgement on the earldom of Menteith: two earls, the chancellor and nineteen barons. Doubtless we could add a dozen or so prelates who were present but did not participate in this business. Probably in 1190 an aid was agreed at Musselburgh or at Holyrood for the payment of 10,000 merks to Richard I.[54] In 1201 there was a great assembly at Musselburgh to do homage to the king's son, and in 1209 another at Stirling (though transferred from Perth) to grant a further aid to meet payments due under treaty with England. This last was perhaps a council of laymen only. Unfortunately, our information about these aids is late and unreliable

---

[52] Cf. *Rollando filio Ucdredi, Willelmo de Lindesi*.

[53] *R.R.S.*, ii, no. 308 and pp. 45–6. It may also explain why a charter (such as the one translated above) often describes Earl Duncan as 'justiciar'.

[54] *R.R.S.*, ii, no. 326 shows that an aid was agreed at Musselburgh, but Fordun places the assembly at Holyrood. It seems possible that these represent separate grants by prelates and barons, though it would be curious if the clergy assembled at Musselburgh, the barons at Holyrood Abbey.

and we do not know whether they were payable by tenants-in-chief only or by all free tenants. But there was consent for them and it is not surprising that a feudal community should assume a theory of assent to taxation; it is nonetheless disappointing that we cannot tell how sophisticated that theory was.

Between 1171 and 1178 the king confirmed a gift of a ploughgate of land to the hospital of St Andrews to be held quit of army and works but paying 'royal geld which is taken *communiter* from lands and alms through the kingdom of Scotland.'[55] This right to a geld on the basis of each unit of land was presumably akin to the gelds and carrucates of twelfth-century England, but taken infrequently and perhaps at no heavy rate. From 1189, however, charters mention with increasing frequency common aid or forinsec aid which are also associated with army and are geld under two new names. The establishment of a right to geld on the English model was a mark of the growing power of the monarchy in society while its transmutation into 'aid' suggests that when sudden and large lump sums became necessary in 1189 and 1209 the king found it important to secure the assent of his barons. The concern among private persons about aid due to the king lasted well into the reign of Alexander II, but in the later thirteenth century the mention of aid in charters seems somewhat mechanical.

In 1188, a tenth of the revenues of king and barons seems to have been estimated at 1000 merks, while the kingdom was ransomed in 1189 for 10,000 merks, perhaps a year's income. If so, royal revenue might be guessed at a half or third of that figure—but this is only a guess. Even those substantial sums raised for extraordinary occasions may have been borrowed in order that they might be repaid as an aid became effective. We can be sure, however, that the king's income was subjected to a new and careful scrutiny when an audit of accounts at an exchequer board was instituted. In inventories drawn up at the end of the thirteenth century there is ample evidence of the existence of accounts of all kinds of royal officers. In 1292 there seem to have been a bag with twenty-three 'great and small' rolls of accounts and another, mixed, bag of 185 rolls of accounts and memoranda. By 1296, when these were handed over to the new Treasurer, King John's administrators had turned them into three rolls of 89, 89 and seven 'pieces' each, and more than twelve separate rolls of one piece each.

[55] *R.R.S.*, ii, no. 169.

This work of record-preservation seems to have been attempted in chronological order and the two long rolls begin in 1218. The short roll was described as 'containing seven pieces of accounts from the third year of the nineteen-year cycle to the year of grace 1215 and beginning "the twentieth account of Philip..."' (the last words are lost). The last 'third year' of the lunar cycle before 1215 was 1202; if accounts were annual (and this was by no means the rule later in the century) and if Philip's twentieth account had been correctly stitched at the beginning of the roll, then accounts had been rendered since about 1182. One of the miscellaneous rolls 'containing three pieces, called the roll of Abbot Archibald, of ancient rents in money and ancient waytings' points to registration of the king's income at the same period, for Archibald was abbot of Dunfermline between 1178 and 1198 and was active on the king's business, perhaps as a justice.[56] We may suspect that Archibald played a greater part in the financial administration of the reign than the records reveal, but we should be on surer ground in concluding that an exchequer audit was instituted in Scotland during the last two decades of the twelfth century. Although much less effective as an instrument of government than the exchequer of contemporary England, this innovation cannot have been without effect on the size of the king's income and the behaviour of his officials.

An assessment of King William's reign cannot deny the king some merits, for he weathered two decades of crisis in every aspect of policy. Reduced to vassalage by Henry II in 1174, he had to cope not only with the demands of his lord but also with persistent rebellion in Galloway and Ross. His grip on the church was challenged and for years he quarrelled bitterly with a pope who was not to be trifled with; he was excommunicated and his kingdom placed under an interdict at a time when secular problems pressed hard upon him. At the same time, the infiltration of Scotia by incomers, the setting up there of new organs of administration and the development of the king's finances were signs that the king was master not only of his problems but also of the further development of government along the lines laid down by David I. King William was a man of energy but his outlook was very much that of Anglo-French baronial society. His judgement in problems of foreign policy operated within the narrow confines of feudal right and propriety and was therefore defective in his dealings with Henry II and John.

[56] *R.R.S.*, ii, 59.

At home this weakness became a strength in his relations with the baronage whose influence he did much to spread. As a feudal lord William seems to have observed the limits of reasonableness in his demands on his barons, and it is likely that many of the 'rules' of feudal tenure came to be established in his reign. Only on the fringes of the kingdom did the Frankish outlook of the king and ruling class provoke a resentment which was released in rebellion. For the rest, William was successful in surrounding himself with a court whose baronial officers, Steward, Constable, Marshal, Butler and Door-keeper were an echo of Capetian France—like so much else about King William. The first two officers were hereditary and honorary at the beginning of the reign; by 1214 all five were.

*Addendum to 1978 impression.* Gilbert of Galloway may have been related to Henry II (cf. page 181) as his son was called 'cousin' by King John (*Cal. Docs. Scot.*, i, no. 480).

# TWO KINGDOMS: SCOTLAND AND ENGLAND

The relations of the Scottish kings with other princes are in the main a story of relations with the kings of England. But this dictate of geography involved Scotland in the complex rivalries of the English king brought about by his continental domains. Of the two kings—French and Scottish—to whom he was neighbour, the former was his inveterate enemy, while from the latter he sought only an enduring peace and a modicum of the respect due to a greater and wealthier ruler. From Westminster or Rouen the king of Scots seemed one of a company of princes of whom account must be taken, the counts of Anjou, Brittany, Toulouse and Flanders, the dukes of Aquitaine and Saxony, the princes of the Rhineland and the emperor himself but, unlike them, he could play no part in the continental policy of the English king. And so, while on the continent two means were employed for securing the king's domains, war and marriage, marriage was the only instrument of feudal policy used with the Scottish king.

Long before the Norman Conquest Scottish kings had become the 'helpers' of the kings of England; Malcolm III was the defeated foe of the Norman kings but his sons found a helper in William II. The Scottish king recognised in these different circumstances that he was the less powerful partner, a recognition formally marked, at least after 1066, by a bowing or homage. Such an acknowledgement of inferior position did not carry with it obligations or rights which could have been catalogued. It was doubtless the duty of these Scottish kings to act in the interests of their lords, but there is no sign that the right of an English king to such help gave him a right in or over the kingdom of Scotland. In commending himself

to the English king, the king of Scots commended neither his
dom nor his heirs.

For the reign of Henry I our evidence is tenuous but does
suggest that Alexander I (who was in no such need of help as Edgar
had known in 1094-7 when Rufus 'gave' him the kingdom) succeeded with Henry's consent and acknowledged his lordship. There
is no such suggestion about the succession of David I, but David
must already have done homage to Henry I. In 1113 King Henry
gave to him in marriage Maud, daughter and senior co-heiress of
Waltheof (son of Siward), Earl of Northumbria, executed by
William I in 1076, and of Judith (daughter of Adela), niece of
William I. It would be rash to seek to delineate the character of the
office of earl in eleventh-century England from the turbulent history
of the Northumbrian earldom. In 1055, when Siward died, Waltheof was too young to succeed, and when Earl Tostig was expelled
in 1065 the Northumbrians asked for a Mercian as earl. Probably
on this occasion Waltheof was compensated with an earldom in the
east Midlands. That the Norman kings did not consider Northumbria to be an hereditary earldom seems obvious, yet in granting it
to Waltheof along with his niece, Judith, the Conqueror was at
least in part acknowledging an hereditary claim, about which the
chronicler Symeon of Durham is quite explicit. Waltheof lost the
office and his head for some uncertain treason, but Judith retained
his Midland earldom. Early in the reign of William II, their
daughter Maud was married to Simon de Senlis, who in anticipation
had been given the earldom which she inherited. On her marriage
to David, Maud was a middle-aged widow with three sons, but she
brought with her the office of earl in the shires of Huntingdon,
Northampton, Bedford and Cambridge with lands in these and
seven more shires.[1] If she also brought a claim to the defunct
comital dignity of Northumbria, Earl David showed no disposition
to stretch his good fortune by exploiting it. Until 1135 his position
did not change. He must have done homage to Henry I when he
became earl; in 1118 his sister, Maud, Queen of England, died, in
1120 his nephew the Atheling William; in 1124 David himself
became king but without any further mark of subjection to King
Henry. He was the greatest of the English earls when, in the
autumn of 1126, he came to Henry I's court 'and King Henry

[1] Forrest S. Scott, 'Earl Waltheof of Northumbria', *Archaeologia Aeliana*, 4th
series, xxx (1952), 149-215 with map.

received him with great honour'. His purposes may have been ecclesiastical—to curb the pretensions of the archbishop of York— but he could not remain aloof from the dynastic problem of King Henry. Robert Curthose, formerly Duke of Normandy and eldest son of the Conqueror, was now removed by King Henry to a straiter prison at Bristol 'through his daughter's counsel and through David, King of Scots, her uncle'. It has been suggested that they urged a softer regime for the old man; it seems more likely that they wished him remote from the centres of power when King Henry should die.

The rivals for the English succession were on the one hand Matilda, widow of Henry V, King of the Romans, and usually called 'the Empress'; she was a daughter of King Henry and niece of David I. Stephen, Count of Mortain and lord of the honour of Lancaster on the other hand, a younger son of the count of Blois and Champagne and of Adela, daughter of William I, had married Matilda, daughter of Mary, the sister of David I, who therefore might have assumed neutrality between the rivals. Henry I favoured Stephen for the English succession until the Empress became a widow in 1125; thereafter he was persuaded that the kingdom could pass to his daughter and King David seems to have encouraged this delusion. On 1 January 1127 the prelates and magnates of England swore to be loyal to the Empress and to secure the succession to her; first to swear among the magnates was King David.

There is much to suggest that David I went to some lengths to secure the trust of King Henry; he was, for example, employed in investigating a conspiracy in England when the men of Moray rose against him in Scotland. Such assiduity was rewarded when Queen Maud of Scotland died in 1130–1, for her earldom continued to be enjoyed by David I to the exclusion of her eldest son, Simon de Senlis; this can only have been a mark of the favour of the English king, a favour which could interfere very readily with hereditary 'right'. The history of England between 1066 and 1154 seems at times a history of forfeiture, escheat and surrender of fiefs, and we shall not understand the problem of Anglo-Scottish relations unless we realise that inheritance by primogeniture was only a broadly established principle readily defeasible by the royal will. It has been shown that the barons of King Stephen's reign were seeking the establishment of unambiguous hereditary right and their success (by 1154) is exemplified in the introduction of the writ of *mort d'ancestor* in 1176.

On 1 December 1135 the solvent which David I had probably been awaiting, the death of Henry I, brought to the throne not the Empress (now married to Geoffrey Plantagenet, Count of Anjou) but Stephen. Most English magnates, other than King David, had disliked their oath of 1127 (which the Pope was shortly to annul) and Stephen secured speedy acceptance as king. So rapid was the Scottish response to his coronation (which occurred three weeks after Henry I's death) that there must be some suspicion that David I had planned to act whoever should succeed. He occupied Cumberland and Northumbria, taking Carlisle and Newcastle by subterfuge—claiming to act in the interests of Stephen—and he brought an army to besiege Durham. King Stephen gathered a large army with vigour and speed and on 5 February 1136 met King David at Durham. Their negotiations dragged on for two weeks and their 'peace' was transient. King David saved his principles (the oath of 1127) by refusing homage to King Stephen, but swallowed substantial gains through the person of his son Henry, who performed homage and received the earldom of Huntingdon with Carlisle and Doncaster and a promise that, if there was to be an earl of Northumbria, his claim thereto would receive justice. If Stephen had hoped that this promise and procrastination would satisfy King David, he discovered his error in the following year. The Scots assembled to invade Northumbria but made a truce in the face of determined opposition; on the expiry of the truce Northumbria was again demanded for Henry and firmly refused.

At this point King David recalled his duty to the Empress and, in January 1138, opened a sustained attack upon Northumberland, an attack marked by atrocities from which the priory of Tynemouth purchased exemption for 27 marks. In February Stephen reciprocated by a devastating raid into Lothian, in April David was back in Northumberland, and a section of his army, led by William fitz Duncan, was sent across Yorkshire and Lancashire. On 10 June 1138, it defeated an English force at Clitheroe; King David himself had unwonted success in securing the castles which, at any rate in the future, were to defy Scottish invaders successfully. This serious threat to the kingdom was met by the northern barons under the leadership of Thurstan, Archbishop of York. Strenuous efforts were made, particularly by Robert de Brus, to persuade David to withdraw on a promise that the barons would seek from Stephen the Northumbrian earldom for Henry. The Scottish king was not to be persuaded, and, on 22 August 1138, fought and lost to the northerners the battle of the Standard at Cowton moor near North-allerton in the North Riding of Yorkshire. Descriptions are English and rhetorical; they speak of bare-bottomed Scots, but also of a controversy among their leaders whether the mailed knights or wild Galwegians should hold the van. Two northern English were with King David—Alan, bastard son of Alan de Percy, and Eustace fitz John—and he had a bodyguard of English and French knights two hundred in number according to one chronicler. But the bulk of the army was composed of Galwegians, men from Teviotdale under Henry, son of the king, from Lothian probably under Earl Gospatrick and from the Gaelic west; the earl of Strathearn probably led a contingent from his earldom. This large army was defeated by the arrows and steady spears of the English infantry, whose losses were slight; King David saw his men break and turn after heavy losses and in the end he too was persuaded to slip from the battlefield. That the Scots were not pursued into a *débâcle* might have been due to the interests of northern English barons in Scottish fiefs.[2]

King David in spite of his defeat would not relax his efforts. The siege of Wark Castle was pressed unrelentingly, though the court was usually at Carlisle. There the papal legate Alberic sought a peace for King Stephen but came away with only a brief truce from which Wark was excluded; it surrendered to David early in November 1138. Since midsummer the party of the Empress had been in open revolt in south-western England; its successes were not striking but Stephen could not afford to carry on the war on two fronts. His queen urged her husband to make peace with her uncle and early in 1139 Stephen yielded to Henry those territories granted in 1136, together with the earldom of Northumbria in which Stephen reserved to himself the two chief castles—Newcastle and Bamburgh. The earldom was carefully defined to exclude the lands of St Cuthbert, that is, the later County Durham, between Tyne and Tees, and the conditions of Henry's tenure were carefully hedged. On 9 April 1139, before Queen Matilda, he swore to maintain the customs of Northumbria of the time of Henry I and he received the homage of the Northumbrian barons, saving their fealty to King

[2] H. A. Cronne, *The Reign of Stephen* (1970) 180–1.

Stephen. King David had undertaken to remain at peace with Stephen and in warranty of his loyalty he handed over as hostages on this occasion the sons of five magnates of Scotland: Malise, Earl of Strathearn, Matad, Earl of Atholl, Gospatrick, Earl of Dunbar, Fergus, Lord of Galloway, and Hugh de Moreville. The new earl of Northumbria joined King Stephen in prosecuting the war against the Empress and in the same year was married to Ada de Warenne, sister or half-sister to three powerful earls who supported King Stephen.[3]

On 2 February 1141, King Stephen was defeated and captured at Lincoln by the forces of the Empress, who moved to Winchester to be elected queen and then in June to London for her coronation. King David judged it prudent to break his word and joined her; he took the opportunity to secure her support for the appointment of William Cumin, formerly his chancellor, to the see of Durham. But the Empress was not destined to become queen; ignominiously she and King David were expelled from London. At Winchester they besieged the bishop's palace, only to find themselves surrounded by the army of Stephen's queen, Matilda. Their retreat (14 September) became a rout, and King David escaped only with the aid of David Olifard; by 29 September 1141 he was back at Durham, doubtless thankful that his only intervention in aid of the Empress had not resulted in his capture. Until 1144 William Cumin persisted in his efforts to become bishop of Durham and was abetted by David I and Earl Henry; otherwise their ambitions were stilled, their tergiversations over. The earldom of Huntingdon-Northampton was lost to them, given by King Stephen to Simon de Senlis (II) in or soon after 1141. The Empress had awarded King Stephen's personal honour of Lancaster to King David but this too was lost, after a brief possession, to the earl of Chester.[4] King David had burned his boats in 1141 and remained thereafter a nominal supporter of the Empress, but in Carlisle and Newcastle a Scottish peace reigned, a remarkable and remarked contrast to the misery of the civil war in southern England.

This northern peace persisted after 1148 when the Empress left England, and civil disturbance in the south took on a more sinister character. In 1149 her son by Geoffrey Plantagenet Count of

[3] Davis, *King Stephen*, 135.
[4] G. W. S. Barrow, 'King David I and the Honour of Lancaster', *Eng. Hist. Rev.*, lxix (1955), 85-9.

Anjou, Henry, later Duke of Normandy and king as Henry II, came to Carlisle to secure knighthood from David I. The significance of this ceremony in contemporary eyes was great; Henry was sixteen when his supporters urged him 'to get the emblems of a knight's rank from his father (the count of Anjou) or else from the king of Scots'.[5] But as heir to a duchy and a kingdom Henry knew that propriety demanded that he be knighted by a king; the opinion of society placed him at the mercy of his great-uncle, who, before he would dub Henry knight, obtained from him an oath that if he became king he would give to King David Northumbria from Tyne to Tweed, including Newcastle. In the ensuing campaign of Henry fitz Empress, which lasted for six months, King David took no part, and his forceable infeftment of William fitz Duncan in the honour of Skipton and Craven in Yorkshire in 1151 was a contribution to the anarchy of Stephen's kingdom but not to the Plantagenet cause. When Henry, Earl of Northumbria, died in 1152 the old king took his younger grandson, William de Warenne (later king) to Newcastle to be acknowledged as earl, and there, too, took hostages from the leading men of the earldom, a sign that the Scottish peace had not reconciled the Northumbrians to Scottish lordship.

David I died on 24 May 1153 at Carlisle, his favoured residence; did he die within a kingdom which now 'stretched far into Northern England?'[6] It may be true that as son of a 'son of the king of the Cumbrians' David had a claim as king to Cumberland and Westmorland, though it is unlikely that the Strathclyde which Duncan I ruled had stretched beyond the Solway. It is certainly true that David I had coins struck at Carlisle in his own name, as had Earl Henry in his own name at Corbridge. Since Earl Henry already held Northumberland, either the oath of Henry fitz Empress meant that he would be confirmed in it as an English earl, or that it would be handed over to David to become part of Scotland with Henry as a Scottish earl. It should not be assumed that Northumbria from Tyne to Tweed as Howden described it excluded the northwestern countries; they were often and rightly regarded as dependencies of Northumbria. William of Newburgh gave a rather

---

[5] *Gesta Stephani*, ed. K. R. Potter (1955), 142. The concluding section of this chronicle, from 1148, was first published in this edition and is not included in Anderson, *Scottish Annals*.

[6] Poole, *Domesday Book to Magna Carta*, 274.

different version: that Henry fitz Empress would not deprive David's heirs of lands which had passed from England to the lordship of that King. Moreover, in 1149 David bought out the claim of Ranulf, Earl of Chester, to Carlisle by yielding his own claim to the honour of Lancaster.

On the other hand, it is abundantly clear that Carlisle and Cumberland were ceded in 1136 to be held by Earl Henry of King Stephen, and that Northumberland was similarly yielded in 1139. From 1141 Stephen's lordship was rejected because King David was committed to supporting the Empress and by 1149, it seems, he had hopes that Siward's and Waltheof's Northumbrian earldom including the two western counties could be transferred to the Scottish kingdom, if his and his son's occupation could be sufficiently protracted and consolidated. There is, therefore, no simple answer to the question whether when David died Carlisle was in his kingdom; he seems to have hoped that it would be, but we cannot be sure that Henry fitz Empress had been told of his hope or had agreed to fulfil it. And these hopes or intentions of David I, which were certainly not fulfilled, did not invalidate the claim with which he started off in 1136, on behalf of his son, Earl Henry. This claim on the earldom of Northumbria must have derived from David's queen; in terms of hereditary succession it had little to commend it, for Queen Maud's heir was her eldest son Simon de Senlis, in 1149 holding her Midland earldom as earl of Northampton.[7] But such niceties did not greatly concern King David who valued the northern counties, because they were contiguous to Scotland, much more than the Midland earldom which he had lost and which he does not seem to have had the face to demand from Henry fitz Empress in 1149. On his deathbed David I must have seen the descendants of Malcolm (IV) as kings, the descendants of William (de Warenne) as earls of Northumbria. At the very least the latter would be vassals of the English king, at most of the Scottish king.

The chroniclers' harping upon David's commitment to the Empress's cause is more than generous to him. It is true that only once, in 1139, did he formally abandon her, but twice before that he had made a peace in which he maintained his oath of 1127, wept for the Empress, but graciously took what he wanted from King Stephen. It is also true that only once, in 1141, did he help the

[7] When held by the Scottish royal house this was called the earldom of Huntingdon, when by the de Senlis family the earldom of Northampton.

Empress; thereafter she was left to struggle on as best she might. It did not require a very cynical eye to discern in King David's acts a greater concern for the Northumbrian earldom than for the Plantagenet cause. Nonetheless, for eighteen years Henry and his son William held that earldom. That gave them some right to it, but it should always be remembered that, even if it had been based on an impeccable hereditary claim, it was still defeasible by the will of the English king.

In 1157, Earl William de Warenne was about fourteen years old, his brother King Malcolm about sixteen. Unlike his grandfather, the king does not seem to have resided at Carlisle; neither had done homage to Henry II, now aged twenty-four, and neither had become his ward. But his authority was now firm in England and he offered them his justice. King Malcolm came, probably by invitation to meet Henry II at Chester in July 1157; he was confronted with the arguments that David I had acquired the northern distiricts in the name of the Empress and that the English king should not be defrauded of so great a part of his kingdom— assertions, that is, that these were English provinces. He was asked to resign them and 'prudently judging that in this matter the king of England had the better of the case because of the strength of his resources' he yielded them up.[8] If King Henry had not fulfilled his oath of 1149 to confirm David I's northern possessions, neither had he quite broken it, for these lands were not seized but resigned. Malcolm IV then did homage 'as his grandfather had been the vassal of the old King Henry saving all his dignities'[9] and received the earldom of Huntingdon, now taken away from the luckless Simon de Senlis; William was now or a little later given a derisory fief of ten pounds annual value in the Tyne valley. If he felt anger towards Henry II, he must surely have resented even more the opportunism of Malcolm IV, who surrendered William's patrimony in order to increase his own.

The insistence of Henry II upon a return to the authority of his grandfather in church and state extended naturally enough to relations with the Scottish king. It is likely that the words of the *Chronicle of Melrose* represent fairly closely the very terms of Malcolm IV's homage, and the question arises whether they were deliberately vague. As his grandfather in 1113, so Malcolm IV in

[8] Anderson, *Scottish Annals*, 239 from the chronicle of William of Newburgh.
[9] *Chron. Melrose*, 35.

1157 did homage for his earldom, and naturally on the latter occasion reference would be made to the former, for there had been no homage between.[10] But the fealty of King Malcolm could not be unqualified as that of Earl David doubtless was, for Malcolm had responsibilities as king for his kingdom and these responsibilities were not to Henry II. Even if the dignities reserved were only customary rights of hospitality in England they signified Malcolm's entitlement to be treated as a king of Scotland as well as a baron of England. But they seem to be 'all the dignities' enjoyed by Malcolm IV before he did homage; of these the throne and kingdom of Scotland were pre-eminent, and the reservation of such dignities was a natural consequence of homage in these circumstances, carrying no implication that Henry II sought to become overlord of Scotland.[11] King Henry II set out to restore the rights of his grandfather, not to found the pretensions of his great-grandson.

It seems that King Henry feared the reaction of the Scottish king and kingdom to the surrender at Chester, for he immediately began the reconstruction of Wark Castle and (probably at the same time) commanded Hugh, Bishop of Durham, to refortify Norham Castle. Future events were to justify King Henry's caution, and in 1158 Malcolm IV came to Carlisle, possibly to protest at the fortifications. We know only that he parted on bad terms with King Henry, so that he was not knighted—which looks like a result, not a cause, of the ill feeling between them. In 1159 King Henry's expedition against the count of Toulouse was joined at Poitiers by the Scottish king and a number of his barons; shortly afterwards, on 30 June, Henry II knighted Malcolm IV, who remained with him for some three months and returned to Scotland only at the beginning of 1160. The rebellion which he then encountered and mastered arose 'because he had gone to Toulouse'—because, it has been suggested, he thereby compromised the independence of Scotland. But there is no evidence that he went at King Henry's summons and, in view of his concern to be admitted to knighthood,

[10] It would be necessary for Malcolm IV to accept the obligations of his earldom, e.g. in knight service and payment of geld. These would be summarised conveniently by reference to some previous holder of the earldom—i.e. Earl David.

[11] W. L. Warren, *Henry II* (1973), 178 is another and to my mind thoughtful account of this homage, though I do not agree with its argument for 'a deliberate quality of vagueness'.

it seems more likely that his expedition was voluntary and that his abandonment of the kingdom aroused resentment.

Far from being a complaisant vassal of Henry II, King Malcolm was establishing marriage connections which may have pleased his cousin little. In 1160 his sister Margaret married Conon, Duke of Brittany and Earl of Richmond, whose sister, Constance, was, it seems, to marry Malcolm. In view of King Henry's aim to lay hold upon the Breton duchy it seems unlikely that this alliance was of his making, though it was probably negotiated during the Toulouse expedition. In 1162 Malcolm IV's elder sister, Ada, was married to Florence, Count of Holland, who visited Scotland in order to convey her to the Low Country. It may have been these continental ties which decided Henry II that King Malcolm had showed too many signs of independence.

In 1163 Henry II found time to deal with pressing English problems; he took an expedition to South Wales and returned with the troublesome prince Rhys as captive. After a visit to Carlisle, he met all the leaders of the Welsh and King Malcolm at Woodstock on 1 July where each went through a ceremony of homage. Unfortunately, the chronicles scarcely clarify either the sequence or the significance of these events. The *Chronicle of Melrose* tells us that Malcolm IV recovered from serious illness at Doncaster 'and there is firm peace' between Malcolm and Henry, implying the resolution of a dispute. According to Ralph de Diceto the Welsh and Malcolm did homage to Henry II and to his son the Young Henry, and this will certainly have been true of the Welsh who had been in rebellion. But Robert de Torigni is clear that Malcolm did homage only to the Young Henry and that he gave as hostages his brother David and some other baronial heirs, 'for the preservation of peace and for his castles which the king wished to have;'[12] the *Chronicle of Holyrood*, which seems to be independent, confirms that hostages were given.[13]

How shall we understand these testimonies? It would seem a reasonable conjecture that Henry II went to Carlisle in order to make of King Malcolm demands which, Torigni suggests, were for castles, most probably in Lothian. Such demands were a means of testing a vassal's loyalty, even of provoking any lurking disloyalty, but Malcolm betrayed neither of his responsibilities. As king he

---

[12] *de pace tenenda et pro castellis suis quos rex volebat habere.*
[13] *Chron. Holyrood,* 141.

kept his castles; as earl he followed or more probably accompanied his lord south to Woodstock and reassured him there by agreeing to hand over hostages.[14] Diceto is probably wrong in ascribing to Malcolm a new homage to Henry II, for the fealty and homage of 1157 stood unbroken, and men did not cheapen the act by needless repetitions of it. Already concerned about the succession should he die, Henry II demanded and obtained homage to his heir from the Welsh and Scots who might disturb the peace as David I had done in 1135; this ceremony however stood distinct from any Welsh homage to the elder king and both had different roots from the demands for castles and hostages made of Malcolm IV. His illness and recovery took place, probably, on his return journey to Scotland with Henry II's precarious peace.

In any fief the castle was usually the chief place, possession of which constituted sasine of the fief; to have yielded Scottish castles would have been to yield the kingdom. Nor did King Malcolm give up as a hostage his heir, William.[15] We are left without any obvious cause for Henry II's dissatisfaction and trip to Carlisle; in view of the later sensitivity on the part of the English crown about marriages contracted by the Scottish royal house, it is not impossible that those of Malcolm IV's sisters were the cause of Henry's demands— but the explanation does not seem quite to measure up to the events, and a dissatisfaction with it remains.

If Anglo-Scottish relations are viewed legalistically, the reign of Malcolm IV is critical for their understanding, since in 1189 the conditions of that reign were deliberately restored and obtained until 1209 or even 1291. There can be little doubt that Malcolm IV yielded twice to King Henry, but contemporary sources do not suggest that he compromised his kingship or his kingdom; what Henry II recovered from him were the unjustified acquisitions of David I.

From 1165 Scottish policies were guided by a hand more determined but far less sensitive to the realities of political power. Unfortunately, our evidence for the years 1165–73 is scanty; we know that by the autumn of 1166 King William had crossed to join Henry II at Mont S. Michel in Normandy 'upon his lord's affairs',

[14] The Pipe Rolls for 1163–5 record no increase in the number of royal hostages most of whom seem to have been Welsh; but the hostages yielded in 1174–5 do not show up in the Pipe Rolls either.

[15] 'William the king's brother' who was present at Woodstock was Henry II's brother.

returning *statim* after participating in the tournament season. From a letter otherwise unconnected with Scotland, we learn that a word favourable to King William spoken on this occasion reduced Henry II to an animal-like fury. Fordun tells a story which, when stripped of embellishments, is consistent with this evidence—that William came to Henry at Windsor to discuss peace, and 'in order to get back Northumberland', when Henry departed for the Continent. Against advice William followed him to join in the knightly exploits and returned to Scotland without the peace. This is our only evidence of a preliminary meeting at Windsor (King Henry was briefly there in March 1166) and suggests that Fordun was using a lost twelfth-century source. His 'peace' is an embellishment but his statement that William sought the return of Northumberland accords well with King Henry's blinding rage and King William's return *statim*, as it were 'with a flea in his ear'. It seems likely that William did homage to Henry II on this occasion, but no source mentions it. King William never forgot that he had inherited the earldom of Northumberland from his father and that he had been deprived of it by his brother and King Henry; for almost fifty years he devoted no insignificant part of his energies to vindicating a right in which he believed with some passion.

In 1168 the Scottish king was clearly regarded as hostile to King Henry, for it was rumoured that his envoys were with those of Henry's other enemies at the court of King Louis, 'promising help and offering hostages' to secure a continuance of Anglo-French war. By 1170 peace had been made, and Henry II returned to England to secure the coronation of the Young Henry as king in spite of his quarrel with the archbishop of Canterbury. King William and his brother David were present at the Easter court which considered the matter; on 31 May Henry II knighted David and on 15 June 1170, the day after his coronation, the young king received the homage of King William, David and the other English barons. Fordun suppresses the homage but tells us that King William again unsuccessfully demanded Northumberland.

In face of the silence of contemporary chronicles we may be rash to trust the word of Fordun. Nonetheless in 1173 King William, who had done homage to the young king saving his fealty to the old king, joined in the rebellion of the former after demanding Northumberland as the price of his loyalty to the latter. The young king first offered Northumberland, Cumberland and Westmorland;

the old king then refused William's demand of Northumberland; the young king finally conceded this earldom and William mustered an army at Caddonlea, crossing the Tweed to lay siege to Wark. The castellan of Wark obtained a truce and the Scots moved to besiege Alnwick and then to take Warkworth. From there King William, reinforced now by a Flemish contingent, moved against Newcastle, which he decided would not fall, and then across country to besiege Carlisle. There word was brought of an approaching English army and King William briskly packed his equipment and retired to Roxburgh; he did not seek to defend Berwick nor protect the surrounding country when they were laid waste by the enemy. In ignorance of the invasion of England by other supporters of the young king (29th September 1173), he made a truce to last till 13 January 1174, subsequently extended to 31 March.

Thereafter Earl David (who had received an augmented earldom of Huntingdon from the young king) came south to join the rebels at Leicester, and King William once more set siege to Wark.[16] Direct assault, siege engines and fire were alike unsuccessful and the Scots moved to besiege Carlisle. Leaving most of his army there, King William set about the reduction of other castles in Cumberland, Westmorland and Tynedale, returning to grant a truce to the Carlisle garrison until 29 September, when the town and castle would be surrendered unless previously relieved. King William then set siege to the castle of Prudhoe on the Tyne for several days until forced to withdraw by the threat of an army of Yorkshire barons. His next target was the castle of Alnwick, where he supervised the investment by a force of cavalry, while most of his army ravaged Northumberland. The force with him numbered sixty in one account, five hundred in another. Most accounts say that he at first mistook the approaching enemy for his own troops, but discovered his mistake and led an attack upon them. Jordan Fantosme, who was there, is more convincing in saying that King William was caught wholly unprepared and unarmed at a meal when he first heard the war-cries of his attackers. He was armed and ready when the battle was joined, but his Flemings suffered heavily, and early on the king's horse was killed, pinning him to the ground. Thus, on 13 July 1174, he was taken prisoner and led hastily to Newcastle.

16 This is narrated only by Jordan Fantosme.

It is difficult to find sympathy for a king of whom Jordan said 'woe to Richard Melville, that he ever saw King William and his wild rashness'.[17] The catalogue of sieges begun and abandoned, of decisions to stand firm followed by headlong retreat, more than justified the view that 'he was too much accustomed to follow the last word in his ear';[18] but also suggests that he had no idea of strategy and embarked upon a war without any consideration of its relevance to his political aims. The alliance with the French king (for whom the young King Henry was a convenient pawn) and the count of Flanders marked the beginning of the 'Auld Alliance' and did bring significant mercenary aid. But it had no real support within England and, even if successful, was unlikely to win territorial concessions anywhere except in France.

On 26 July 1174, King William was brought to Henry II at Northampton with his feet ignominiously shackled beneath the belly of his horse; Huntingdon had surrendered after Earl David had fled to Scotland, and King Henry crossed to France in August with King William and other prisoners of state in close confinement in his train. Imprisoned honourably at Falaise, William must have heard of the rising which had broken out in Galloway after his capture, and of the approaches made by Henry II to the Galwegians with a view to attaching them to his service. On 30 September 1174, the sons of Henry II came to their father's peace, leaving King William at his mercy. He had no alternative but to accept the terms offered, the so called Treaty of Falaise, which was sealed at Valognes on 8 December. On 11 December, leaving hostages for the execution of the treaty, the king sailed from Normandy for England; on 15 February 1175 he was released, presumably after some of his castles had been surrendered. He had lost Huntingdon and Tynedale and all chance of recovering Northumberland.

But he had lost more than these. Probably at Falaise he had done homage to the English king 'for Scotland and for all his other lands' and had sworn fealty to him. He had undertaken that his barons would do homage likewise, and his and their heirs in perpetuity. His barons were explicitly bound to observe their fealty to King Henry should King William rebel against him. He had placed the castles of Roxburgh, Berwick, Jedburgh, Edinburgh and Stirling at the mercy of King Henry and undertaken to pay for garrisoning them. He had surrendered hostages and was bound to

17 Lawrie, *Annals*, 177.          18 *trop fud acustume de cunseilz noveler.*

surrender more if required; these baronial hostages would not be released until their heirs had been surrendered in their places.[19] There is more to the treaty—ecclesiastical provisions which fall to be discussed elsewhere[20] and mutual provision for the extradition of offenders—but this is enough to show that Henry II knew how to solve a political problem. No attempt was made to deprive William of his kingdom or to demand castles north of the Forth; security from attack on England was King Henry's aim, and for this the southern castles sufficed. At the same time, sasine of them marked his lordship over the kingdom. In August 1175, in the cathedral church of St Peter at York, King William and his brother, followed by the prelates and magnates of Scotland, did homage (the prelates excepted) and swore fealty to Henry II. He relied upon the moral effect of that act to bind the kingdom of Scotland to himself.

Yet these cords can scarcely have proved as irksome to King William as he had feared. Of the five castles which the English were entitled to garrison, only Berwick, Roxburgh and Edinburgh were occupied, but the towns were given up as well as the castles; evidently the garrisons were paid for from the burgal revenues. In 1186 Edinburgh was returned to King William on condition that he gave it to his new wife as part of her tocher. In 1188 four thousand merks were offered for the remaining two fortresses, but King Henry refused. There seems to be no evidence that the provisions for hostages were enforced, and presumably the same king relaxed them partially or even wholly. His right to arrange a marriage was acknowledged by William, who in 1185 had asked for the daughter of Henry the Lion, Duke of Saxony, a granddaughter of Henry II. Papal dispensation was not to be obtained, which suggests that the English king had no enthusiasm for the match but that he did not wish to earn the opprobrium of refusing it. In the following year, Henry made the offer to King William of Ermengard, daughter of Richard, Viscount of Beaumont sur Sarthe in Maine, and, after some discussion with his friends, he accepted her. The generosity of King Henry in providing part of her dowry and the cost of four days' wedding festivities at Woodstock (5 September 1186), could not have concealed the fact that King William had been disparaged; the new queen was of insignificant family, but it would be unfair to judge Henry too harshly

---

[19] The best edition is Stones, *Anglo-Scottish Relations*, no. 1.
[20] p. 262 ff.

for this. His aim was probably to arrange a match with as little political connection and significance as possible.

His interference in ecclesiastical matters was no more than a mild use of good offices. We have one document—a writ of protection in common form to Dunfermline Abbey—which assumes his direct authority in Scotland, and it may be significant that this omits the usual (but not invariable) clause forbidding the beneficiary to be brought to court except before the king or his justice.[21] In the years after 1291 a flood of English writs was let loose on Scotland, of which almost none survive; our knowledge of only one writ for the period 1174–89 is not a safe guide to the number issued, which may have been considerable. Although summoned to King Henry's court almost annually, King William was never required to provide his lord with military service: just as there seems to have been no right of appeal from Scotland to King Henry's courts, so no service was due from Scotland to his armies.

Amid the constantly shifting grounds of English claims (medieval and modern) to overlordship over Scotland, perhaps the most difficult to pin down is the notion that Lothian was held of the English king. Based upon the undoubted fact that when Lothian was acquired between 973 and 1027 the kings of Scotia became 'man' or 'helper' of the English king, this theory is given colour for the twelfth century by Robert de Torigni's references to homage for Lothian. The notion of vassalage 'for' some lands but not 'for' others is anachronistic in the tenth and eleventh centuries when vassalage was a personal bond requiring fidelity wherever, and however situated, the vassal might be; and it is quite clear that Torigni's 'Lòthian' was other men's Northumberland. A new argument, however, has been based upon the much more reliable Roger Howden, according to whom King William did homage at York in 1175 'expressly for Scotland and Galloway'—'the clear implication being that these two regions alone (and not Lothian) had previously been excluded from oaths of homage', because Scotia in the twelfth century always had its early 'north-of-Forth' meaning.[22] If correct this view would carry the consequence

[21] G. W. S. Barrow, 'A Writ of Henry II . . .,' *Sc. Hist. Rev.*, xxxvi (1957), 138–43.

[22] W. L. Warren, *Henry II* (1973), 179 and n.3. Professor Warren's account of Anglo-Scottish relations is sensitive and balanced, marred only by the unusual thesis that the kingdom of Scotland (*regnum Scotie*) lay to the north of Forth, and even this view, to my mind wholly mistaken, is advanced with due recog-

that when William submitted at Falaise and did homage 'for *Scotia* and all his other lands' the last words referred not only to Tynedale and such other English lands as Henry might allow him but to Lothian, Strathclyde and Galloway also. This was not the view taken by Richard I in 1189 when the *regnum Scotie* had a common frontier with England; it does not seem to have been the view taken elsewhere by Howden who refers to William as *rex Scotie*, to the prelates of the *regnum Scotie* and, on occasion, to journeys to *Scotia*, with what is most naturally explained as its modern meaning. To Howden, and probably to most educated twelfth-century Englishmen, *Scotia* was the *regnum Scotie* with its Tweed-Solway bounds. If King William did homage at York 'expressly for Scotland and Galloway' this was surely to clarify the status of Galloway where Uhtred and Gilbert had rebelled against William, offering to transfer their fealty to England. Roger Howden had come to conduct the negotiations but found that Gilbert had murdered Uhtred; Henry would have nothing to do with Gilbert, who was therefore without any lord. In taking King William's homage specifically for Galloway Henry II renounced the annexation which he had contemplated in 1174, and gave William the task of reducing Galloway to obedience and of bringing Gilbert into Henry's fealty—which he did by 1178.[23]

In 1184, when the Galwegians were again in rebellion, William, on hearing of King Henry's arrival in England, hastily disbanded his army in order to visit the English court; the invasion of the deceased Gilbert's lands by Roland fitz Uhtred in 1185 put Henry II in a difficult position, for he owed support both to William and to Duncan, a hostage left by his father Gilbert, nor could he permit the tangled web to be cut by Roland's forcible dissasine of Duncan for, like Gilbert in 1174, Roland had done him no homage. The

nition of the uncertainties of the evidence. The notion that Lothian was a fief of England appears in A. O. Anderson, 'Anglo-Scottish Relations from Constantine II to William', *Sc. Hist. Rev.*, xlii (1963), 1–20 with the claim (p. 16) that the Scots 'did introduce this idea... at some time not later than 1216 and the evidence suggests that this must have been done in Malcolm IV's reign.' What evidence? I can discover only the report of Gerald the Welshman that although between 1174 and 1189 Scotland was held of England, recent (*c.* 1216) Scotsmen claimed that this feudal subjection had been for Lothian only. This piece of Scottish dishonesty, likely enough though it is, scarcely bears out either Professor Warren's or Dr Anderson's view. *Giraldi Cambrensis Opera*, ed. G. F. Warner (Rolls Series, 21) viii (1871), 156–7.

[23] See above p. 182 for this rebellion.

final solution saved Henry's face, for Roland was confirmed in his father's lands and promised to accept (on summons) the judgement of King Henry's court in his quarrel with Duncan over Gilbert's lands which in fact were in his hands. We do not know whether Roland was ever summoned to Henry's court; according to Fordun, King William finally settled the dispute, and this may have been after 1189. It has been suggested that King Henry's interference in Galloway 'is no guide to his attitude to Scotland proper'.[24] Henry played fair by William in 1174–6 in refusing the direct lordship of Galloway; William had every reason to dislike Gilbert, who chose to rebel while William was a prisoner, but neither in 1176 nor 1184 could he disinherit one who was also Henry's vassal. He undoubtedly wished Roland to succeed in Galloway and this Henry must have known when he detained William at his court in 1186. The issue of Galloway was the only test of the meaning of the fealty of 1175; was Duncan, ward of Henry II, to be disinherited by Roland, vassal of King William? The appropriate court to judge such an issue was undoubtedly Henry's. Roland was offered judgement first, force only when judgement was spurned; King Henry showed a notable reluctance to invade Scotland. His anxieties may have been sharpened by the proximity of Galloway to Carlisle, but his anxieties were to preserve the content of the submission of 1174–5 and he would have been forced to a similar intervention if the same circumstances had arisen elsewhere.

It is clear that King Henry rode Scotland much more lightly than he need have done. The sources which speak in uncomfortably stilted terms of earlier meetings between the kings are effusive in describing Henry's amiability towards William in the years 1175–1189. Most striking of all testimony to this favour was the king's action following on the death in 1184 of Simon de Senlis, Earl of Northampton since 1174. Earl Simon had no son but had other heirs and these were passed over in favour of King William's brother David, who was made earl of Huntingdon in 1185; he held the earldom of King William, who in turn held it of King Henry, a feudal detail of some significance later.

Yet in 1188 the Scottish magnates showed strong hostility to the requests of King Henry. We have two versions of this episode, both from the pen of Roger Howden, and both agreeing that, after the English magnates had granted a tenth of rents and moveables to

[24] G. W. S. Barrow in *Sc. Hist. Rev.*, xxxvi, 141.

Henry II to pay for a Crusade (Jerusalem had fallen to Saladin in 1187), a party under the bishop of Durham was sent to collect the tenth in Scotland. According to the earlier version, King Henry had replied to William's offer of 4000 merks for his castles by a promise of favourable consideration if King William granted a tithe. Anxious to accommodate Henry, William met the bishop's party at Birgham on the Tweed, with his barons. The English embassy was given a firm and reiterated refusal originating from the barons: 'even if the king of England and their lord the king of Scotland had sworn that they (the embassy) would have it, they (the barons) would never give it'.[25] The revised account, probably for good literary reasons, makes no mention of King William's preliminary offer for the castles. He heard of the approaching embassy, met it in Northumberland and, refusing it access to Scotland, offered it 5000 merks for the castles and the tithe. This King Henry refused. This discrepancy is a warning about taking our sources too literally on the course of negotiations; it is regrettable that we do not know whether the resistance to English demands originated from the barons or from King William, whether King William was pushed into refusal by his magnates or was shrewdly exploiting the new political difficulties of King Henry. The earlier account showing a complaisant William is more circumstantial and is not explicitly contradicted by the later, which leaves an impression of a 'tough' William.[26]

We know of no reaction by Henry II to this first sign of his vassal's insubordination; he had little time to give such matters before his miserable death at Chinon on 6 July 1189. By November King William had reached agreement with Richard I that the Treaty of Falaise would be cancelled.[27] He was received at the Tweed with the civilities and honours customary before 1174 and conducted to Canterbury, where, on Tuesday 5 December 1189, his two castles were restored to be held by him and his heirs and he was released from 'all agreements which our good father Henry...

[25] Anderson, *Scottish Annals*, 300–1; Lawrie, *Annals*, 271–3.

[26] The first account was written between August 1188 and early 1190; it is part of a section on Scottish affairs and the tithe asked of Scotland is not explicitly linked to the Saladin tithe. In the rewriting (between 1192 and 1201) the episode was transferred to follow on the grant of the tithe in England and the preliminary offer for the castles was deliberately written out.

[27] This I think was the 'promissory letter of King Richard to the king of Scotland that he would restore to him all his rights' which was in the Scottish treasury in 1282; *A.P.S.*, i, 108.

exacted from him by new charters and by his capture so that he shall do to us ... whatever his brother Malcolm, King of Scotland, did of right and ought to have done of right to our predecessors'. The Quit-claim of Canterbury[28] went on to provide for the converse restoration of rights; in particular an inquest was to determine the rights of hospitality in England enjoyed by King Malcolm, 'and all liberties, dignities and honours rightly due to him'. The Border lands, if they had been usurped anywhere by English landowners, were to be restored as they had been before the capture of King William. His lands in England, in Huntingdon and elsewhere, were to be possessed as freely as in King Malcolm's time, and he was to continue to possess the land (presumably in Tynedale) given to him by King Henry. The allegiance of his vassals was restored to him, and the document recorded that King William 'has become our liegeman for all the lands for which his predecessors were liegemen of our predecessors'.

One of the striking features of the document is the absence of any positive statement about the kingdom of Scotland: why was not the homage done by him for Scotland restored to him along with the castles and allegiances of his men? The words of 1174, 'became liegeman for Scotland and for all his other lands',[29] provide the answer, for in 1189 King Richard did not give up the homage of King William but received it anew on different terms: he became our liegeman for all the lands for which his ancestors were liegemen.[30] The lack of limiting date on the king's ancestors here is in contrast with the otherwise persistent use of King Malcolm's name, but this was carefully done. King Richard did not wish to restore William's claim to the earldom of Northumberland, and King William did not wish to lose it. Reference to King Malcolm suited the former since Malcolm had never held the earldom; homage as of his ancestors suited William since he and his father had held Northumbria and his father had done homage for it. The text of the Quit-claim was not left to chance and the mercies of an office clerk; it was studiously and delicately worded.

On the other hand it is persistently suggested by those who will not take the trouble to understand, that there was deliberate ambi-

28 Stones, *Anglo-Scottish Relations*, no. 2. The original of this document survives, albeit much decayed.

29 *devenit homo ligio de Scocia et de omnibus aliis terris suis.*

30 *leggius homo noster devenit de omnibus terris de quibus antecessores sui ... ligii homines fuerunt.*

guity in the 'studiously vague' definition of what the king of Scots was to do for the English king, in order to protect some vestigial but vague English lordship over him. This view is a remarkable tribute to Edward I who does not want for historical applause; it extracts from the Quit-claim the only possible ambiguity which might have been turned to his purposes had he not preferred to suppress all mention of this inconvenient document in his account (the first) of Anglo-Scottish relations. The Quit-claim is explicit enough about some of the obligations of King Richard to King William in regard to hospitality 'and all liberties, dignities and honours rightly due to him': those of the time of Malcolm IV were to be ascertained by an international inquest. Belatedly in 1194, King Richard, without recourse to this inquest, confirmed specified rights of hospitality of King William as his 'liberties, dignities and honours'. Where such care was taken to provide for clearing up the obligations of the English king to the Scottish, we should require some evidence that the converse obligations were not then well understood to be those familiar things which we find the grandsons of David I doing as tenants of the English crown—going to the English court when summoned, rendering counsel and aid. It was not until the crisis of Angevin government in 1215 that a king was forced to agree to definition and limitation of counsel and aid; it is anachronistic to expect these to be defined and thereby limited in the great charter of 1189, the Quit-claim of Canterbury. The Melrose chronicle, written not long thereafter, was in no doubt that he had paid for 'the removing of the yoke of his (Henry's) dominion and servitude from the kingdom of the Scots'[31] Roger Howden, the busy clerk who had travelled to Galloway for Henry II and who was to accompany Richard I to the Holy Land, was equally in no doubt of what the Quit-claim meant:

[31] *Chron. Melrose*, 47. *R.R.S.*, ii, no. 287 is a charter exempting the Cistercian order from the consequences of having contributed to 'the redeeming of myself and my capture and the restoring of my whole kingdom to pristine liberty'. As it existed, the original of this document was certainly forged within the following century, but the place date (Restalrig) and most of the witnesses are consonant with the first half of 1190. If this was a copy of a genuine original, William de Berkeley could have been a mistaken guess at W for Walter, and only *Ricardo Cumin Justicia* remains to query the authenticity of the text, as distinct from the surviving original. If the Cistercians were given such a confirmation of their exemption from taxation some of the houses founded later, e.g. Culross, Deer, Balmerino, might well have sought a copy. I am therefore inclined to go a little further than Professor Barrow towards accepting this text. But I would agree that no conclusions should be built upon it.

'... the king of Scots did him homage for the holding of his dignities in England as the kings of Scots his predecessors were accustomed to hold them ... and King Richard ... quit claimed him and all his heirs for ever ... from all allegiance and subjection for the kingdom of Scotland.'[32]

The same chronicler and others tell us of King William's successful bid for his kingdom—ten thousand merks. To find such a sum in Scotland was no easy task, and its rapid payment was a mark of the great significance of the Quit-claim. After fifteen years of accountability, King William was at last master of his own subjects in his own kingdom; he was master, too, of his thirty-year-old claim to the earldom of Northumbria, but King Richard had probably anticipated this pretension, for on 25 November 1189, a few days before King William's arrival at court, the earldom was granted to Hugh, Bishop of Durham, for 2000 merks.[33]

On 12 December 1189, Richard I crossed to Calais after selling Scotland, Northumbria and many other dignities to pay for his crusade. In his absence the kingdom was troubled by the ambitions first of William de Longchamp, then of Count John, the king's brother, and by uncertainty about the succession. Late in 1190, at Messina, King Richard acknowledged Arthur of Brittany as his heir; Longchamp accepted the idea with enthusiasm, since the chances of Richard's early death were acknowledged to be high and the child Arthur would serve Longchamp's ambitions well. In order to secure this succession he sought a firm alliance with King William, an alliance which, if made, marked William as the enemy of Count John.[34] In 1193, when Richard's capture was known and Count John sought to seize the throne, King William refused help to the latter, and shortly afterwards sent 2000 merks as a contribution to Richard's ransom of 150,000 merks. Fordun is vehement in his protestations that this was an *ex gratia* payment, but his word would carry little weight were it not that the Scottish treasury in 1282 contained 'a letter of the king of England concerning aid given to him in money by the lord king of Scotland which is not

---

[32] Lawrie, *Annals*, 281.

[33] G. V. Scammell, *Hugh du Puiset* (1956), 49–50.

[34] William Longchamp was bishop of Ely and papal legate. He had apparently found it necessary to admonish King William to make a payment (presumably part of the 10,000 merks) due to King Richard. A letter to this effect was in the Scottish treasury in 1282; *A.P.S.*, i, 108.

to be held a precedent'.[35] King William must have owed something for his Tynedale lands, but his payment was unusually generous.

On 13 March 1194 Richard returned to England; his second coronation at Winchester on 17 April was doubtless already planned and King William commanded to attend it. The kings met on 4 April and on the following day William asked for 'the dignities and honours which his predecessors had had in England. He also asked for the earldom of Northumbria, Cumberland, Westmorland and the "county" of Lancaster'. Richard's answer was deferred for consultations till 11 April, when William was refused the lands on the grounds that otherwise concessions would seem to have been made from fear of the French. This illogical answer to a perverse question satisfied William not one whit, even though he was given a charter confirming his rights of hospitality and expenses when bidden to England.[36] The very next day Hugh, Bishop of Durham and Earl of Northumberland, refused to yield the best lodgings at Brackley to him and he was able to pour out bitter complaints to King Richard, who considered them justified. On 17 April King William carried one of the swords at Richard's coronation, and on 19 April Bishop Hugh surrendered his earldom, probably to buy royal favour. King Richard now had an asset to auction and on the same day received a bid of 15,000 merks for the earldom from King William; provided that he retained strategic control through possession of the castles Richard was willing to accept, but William would not agree to such conditions. On 21 April he was still seeking to persuade Richard, who would only go so far as to give him some hope of a more favourable answer when he returned from Normandy. The next day the kings parted; they did not meet again, nor did Richard return from France. It was perhaps the nearest that King William came to the recovery of his inheritance.

Nonetheless this was not the end of their negotiations. It is not known at what time the scheme was hatched to marry William's eldest daughter Margaret to Otto, second son of Henry the Lion, exiled Duke of Saxony, but it must have been after April 1194; there can be no doubt that Richard I was involved in it, for he was an intimate friend of Otto, who was his nephew, whom he made count of Poitou and finally persuaded the electors to make king of

---

[35] *que non trahatur in consequenciam*; *A.P.S.*, i, 108–9.
[36] Stones, *Anglo-Scottish Relations*, no. 3.

the Romans in 1198.[37] In 1195, probably in the summer, William fell ill and tried to secure the acceptance of Otto as his heir; his recovery removed the pressure for an immediate decision—and Earl Patrick of Dunbar and many other magnates were strongly opposed—but did not end the proposal. By December the two kings had agreed that Northumberland, Cumberland and Lothian should be the endowment of the couple, with the keeping of Lothian and its castles in the hands of King Richard and of the northern English counties in the hands of King William.[38] How or when the young couple would enjoy their tocher is not clear, nor was the matter put to the test; hoping for a son (and perhaps because of opposition from the magnates), King William backed out from the scheme.

Apart from what they tell us about the Scottish throne, these events cast much light on King William's attitude to Northumbria. He had learned enough sense in 1174 to know that he could not take it by joining a rebellion in 1193. Short of this, however, he was prepared to try almost any means to recover the northern counties —a fine larger by half than that paid for Scotland's independence, an alteration of the line of succession, English occupation of Lothian. However preposterous these offers may seem and however much they may suggest that William had no sense of the proportions of the issue, we must accept them as evidence that his profound concern for the recovery of his rights was admitted in England to have some justification. The birth of Alexander (II) in August 1198 added the incentive of a son to whom the counties might descend, and with the death of Richard I on 6 April 1199 the opportunity was presented of exploiting a disputed succession. Count John's moves to secure the throne by taking oaths from possible baronial opponents were met by King William's familiar demand for the northern counties; let him but keep peace with John, he was told, and he would have satisfaction. William kept peace and when John had used that breathing space to have himself crowned, William again asked for his patrimony with something of a threat. King John demanded and awaited his presence before giving justice, but William, now in a strong position because of dangers to John in France, insisted on his counties first. He would wait forty days for

[37] Poole, *Domesday Book to Magna Carta*, 377.

[38] The proposals of 1195 seem to show that as the northern counties were English domains, so Lothian was Scottish.

an answer and then use his 'power'; but his army was disbanded when Queen Margaret (not yet a saint) warned him in a dream not to invade England—or perhaps, we may say, when discretion overcame courage.

Having resorted to threats, King William now feared the consequences. During a brief spring visit to England in 1200 John waited in vain for him at York, and not until a powerful English embassy had reassured him with a safe conduct was William persuaded to yield the point of principle. On 22 November 1200 at Lincoln, in presence of prelates and magnates from both kingdoms, he did homage to King John 'for his [John's] right, saving his [William's] right'.[39] His renewed demand for the three counties led to prolonged discussion, no agreement, a prorogation to Whitsunday and subsequently to Michaelmas, 1201, Soon thereafter Roger Howden, the chronicler who knew and wrote of the court of Henry II and Richard I, died. It cannot be emphasised too strongly that the surviving chronicles for the rest of John's reign are extremely jejune and ill-informed and that we therefore know little of the continuing negotiations which Howden had hitherto detailed. We are dependent upon fuller record sources which were not made the repository of detailed negotiations and which are missing at crucial points in the story. By July 1205 King John was writing in pleased terms of a draft agreement which included a provision whereby King William would as an exception retain his Tynedale lands;[40] the implication seems to be that his right to other lands in Northumbria was to be yielded to someone else. Various safe conducts for William were issued and the two kings certainly met for four days of vain negotiations at York in February 1206.

King William was now an elderly valetudinarian concerned for the succession to his kingdom, while King John had shown himself to be determined, fearless, unscrupulous, untrustworthy and of poor judgement. In 1209 their affairs reached a crisis which has never been explained and were resolved by a treaty which has not survived. At the beginning of the year William was ill but on 10 April John was insisting on a meeting which he had 'often commanded'; he sought 'to complete the business which has been under consideration between us for a long time'.[41] He moved rapidly north

[39] Lawrie, *Annals*, 323–5.
[40] Lawrie, *Annals*, 347–8; *Rot. Litt. Clausarum*, 43.
[41] Lawrie, *Annals*, 361; *Rot. Litt. Patentium*, I, i, 91.

and by 23 April was at Alnwick. From there he went on to Norham on the Tweed. In April 1208 the death of the bishop of Durham had placed his temporalities in John's hands, and work to strengthen the bishop's castle at Norham was immediately put in hand. Work had also begun on strong fortifications at Tweedmouth, another episcopal possession, where in 1199 the Scots had encountered obstruction from the bishop when they sought to replace the Tweed bridge; the new castle was seen by the Scots as a threat to Berwick, and perhaps because of it the English were able to take a galley with a crew of fifty-two up the Tweed to Norham. According to John of Fordun, the Scots twice attacked and killed the builders of the castle and demolished their work, but Walter Bower is a more reliable source (for reasons which we must discuss later) and speaks of the throwing down of the castle (presumably once) by King William as cause of the anger which brought King John north. Evidently forewarned, William mustered an army at Roxburgh.

When John was at Norham he sent across the Tweed to William at Roxburgh demands which were firmly refused as prejudicial to the king and his subjects. A meeting between the two at Newcastle was arranged after hostages had been given for William's safe return, but William fell ill there and John departed south evidently leaving his demands on the table. On 24 May the king held a great council at Stirling from which went the bishops of St Andrews and Glasgow, William Comyn, justiciar of Scotia, and Philip de Valognes, the chamberlain, as an embassy with the king's reply. It caused great offence to John whose loud threats sent the ambassadors scurrying back to their king at Forfar. William combined caution with security; he ordered his castles to be put in a state of preparedness and he sent the bishop of St Andrews and the abbot of Melrose on an embassy of conciliation to John. It crossed with one from the English king which reached William at Edinburgh; its members were Saier de Quincy, Earl of Winchester and lord of Leuchars, and Robert de Ros, both well known to William, the latter his son-in-law. What they said was enough to frighten him into sending William de Mortimer, sheriff of Perth and the royal almoner, a Templar, with further soothing words. But soon the bishop of St Andrews returned to the king at Traquair with news that John was on his way north with a large army. William at first thought to put up resistance, but when John was at Bamburgh and William at Melrose, wiser counsels prevailed. They came together about 25 July and on 7 August 1209, at Norham, William came to John's peace.

The brief glimpse of scurrying embassies in June and July comes (apart from the previous sentence) from a single source, the fifteenth-century chronicle of Walter Bower.[42] Its circumstantial detail could scarcely have been invented and, indeed, it is only part of an itinerary of William, with accounts of what befell him and his brother David, which covered the years 1209 to 1212 or perhaps to 1214, and which was available to Bower. Although this account is better informed about the embassies than about the matters they dealt with, we probably should not be far wrong if we conclude that John's border fortifications were begun in anticipation of a denial of William's claims for Northumbria. The exact place of the destruction of Tweedmouth in the sequence of events is, unfortunately, not certain but Bower shows that it gave John the opportunity to strike a righteous pose and to make demands for amends from William. John could safely retire from the first meeting at Newcastle with the upper hand and fall back again upon diplomacy. Yet, in the south, he hastened to Wales to recruit Llewelyn and the Welsh to the army with which he hurried north again in July. What had brought about this further deterioration in relations?

The key to understanding John's reign is his preoccupation with the recovery of Normandy from Philip II. Scottish affairs were a tiresome interference with continental plans; they would become dangerous only if Philip II and William should make common cause. The contemporary *Annals of Margam*, a good source for John's intentions, report that in 1209 the Scottish king 'was said to have entered a treaty with King John's enemies';[43] a number of chroniclers of the later thirteenth century, including Edward I's narrative of Anglo-Scottish relations sent to Boniface VIII, assert that there was a marriage between William's daughter and the count of Boulogne[44] (who at the time was a friend of John—and a married man). In fact the Scots in 1291 had 'a charter of King John sent to King William concerning a treaty of marriage between the King of France and King William's daughter'.[45] Now if this means a marriage with Philip II, he was already in deep

---

[42] *Chron. Bower*, i, 524–6; Lawrie, *Annals*, 363–5.

[43] Anderson, *Early Sources*, ii, 373.

[44] Anderson, *Early Sources*, ii, 372–5. Stones, *Anglo-Scottish Relations*, 206–9 [103–4].

[45] *A.P.S.*, i, 112, line 8.

trouble for bigamy and certainly was not in the marriage market; his elder son, Louis (VIII), was married to Blanche of Castille, but he also had a younger son, Philip Hurepel or 'Shock-hair.' In the cataloguing of letters in 1291 it would be a simple error to confuse references to father and son of the same name. Moreover, Philip Hurepel was betrothed in infancy in 1201 to the daughter of Renaud, Count of Boulogne, who in 1209 began to intrigue with King John, and, we suggest, informed him of Franco-Scottish negotiations for a marriage and alliance. He fled to England in 1212, but Philip Hurepel was then married by his father to Renaud's daughter and in 1223 was invested with the county of Boulogne;[46] hence the later garbled story that William's daughter married the count of Boulogne. King John had every reason to think that he faced the likelihood of a political alliance between his constant enemy, the French king, and the Scottish king, whom he had embittered by dilatory tactics for ten years, an alliance to be cemented (as all alliances were) by marriage. To meet the threat he must swiftly overawe William, give him some reason to hope for concessions, cripple his finances and so his power to make war, and like a sanctimonious tipstaff possess himself of William's daughters. All this he did in the treaty of 1209.[47]

The accounts given by various chroniclers of the treaty made by the kings at Norham early in August 1209 must stand or fall as they accord with some fragmentary but nonetheless firm documentary evidence.[48] There was, it should be noted, no war with, and no invasion of Scotland, in 1209;[49] there was a peace which sought to settle outstanding issues, namely King William's claims to the northern counties, the marriage proposed for his daughter, the castle at Tweedmouth. Over the last of these King John made a concession. According to the Melrose chronicle (which makes no

[46] Poole, *Domesday Book to Magna Carta*, 453.

[47] I am indebted for the identification of the French husband intended for William's daughter to my former pupil Mr Andrew Jackson.

[48] This is conveniently listed in Stones, *Anglo-Scottish Relations*, xlv–xlviii which however is very tentative, except where pointing out the papal view of the treaty in November 1219. Here Professor Stones and Sir Maurice Powicke, whom he cites as added authority, are wrong about the date of the bull (November 1218) and its contents.

[49] Poole, *Domesday Book to Magna Carta*, 282 is a superficial account while Powicke, *Thirteenth Century*, 586, 594 not only assigns the treaty to 1212 but makes King William father of David, Earl of Huntingdon. Secondary works by Scottish historians are little better when dealing with the treaty of 1209.

mention of the attacks made by the Scots before the treaty) William received permission to demolish the castle; Fordun makes the same statement and adds that the castle was never to be rebuilt. Bower states that the castle was not to be built and that the king of Scots was to pay £4000 as amends for the dishonour done to the English king when the Scottish king broke it down. The Scottish treasury in 1282 contained a letter of King John 'that he may not build a castle on the port of Tweedmouth' which confirms this concession; but it also contained 'a letter concerning three thousand pounds and more paid to the king of England' for which no other occasion than this can be found.[50]

Surviving contemporary accounts are almost equally inaccurate about the other arrangements made. John of Fordun saw evidence which probably told the whole contents of the treaty; he picked on the clauses about Tweedmouth and made a story out of them to explain the tense situation. He also suppressed the payment of £4000.[51] Walter Bower for once does not inflate Fordun merely with florid Latinity; his account of the preliminaries to the treaty is that of a very careful contemporary Scottish observer who recorded comings and goings but not what they were about. This lost source, it is clear, gave the terms of the treaty of August 1209, although Bower also saw a version of these in Fordun's chronicle. These two sources were conflated for his account of the 1209 terms, but, as we shall see, given separately for the terms of 1212.

William's obligation to pay 15,000 merks to John in four instalments[52] of 3750 merks 'for having the goodwill of King John and for the keeping of the agreements made between us' shows that hostages were to be given as security for the payment, and that the document was to be returned when payment was completed. This is the only part of the treaty which survives in a full text, a copy of a lost original. This text shows that William's two daughters were not hostages (as Roger Wendover, for example, said in his chronicle); it shows that the *Chronicle of Melrose* and the English chroniclers

[50] *A.P.S.*, i, 109, line 2. There is no trace of the payment of £4000 in the English records but there are several possible explanations of this, e.g. that William's messengers carried it direct to one of John's castle treasuries.

[51] Professor Barrow in the course of editing *R.R.S.*, ii, formed a very favourable opinion of Fordun's accuracy for William's reign. See also W. W. Scott, 'Fordun's description of the inauguration of Alexander II', *Sc. Hist. Rev.*, l (1971), 198–200.

[52] 30 November 1209, Whitsun and 30 November 1210, Whitsun 1211.

did not know the exact amount promised but that Fordun and Bower did.[53] An account of John's agents in charge of the bishopric of Durham *sede vacante*, covering June 1208–November 1211, show two separate payments of 7000 and 3050 merks and we may equate these with receipts (kept in the Scottish treasury in 1282) for 7500 and 3750 merks.[54] The former receipt for half the sum due contained provision for the remission of the final quarter. It would seem that King William had acquitted himself by 1211 of the 15,000 merks due, by paying 10,050 merks, accepted as discharge of a debt of 11,250 merks;[55] but he secured this remission only by allowing his hostages to remain in England. These hostages, the sons of Scottish magnates, numbered thirteen according to Bower, fifteen according to the summary made in 1291 of some part of the treaty (possibly thirteen hostages plus two daughters); the only list of their names to survive is of 1213, which is rather late to be reliable evidence for 1209 but adds up to fourteen, of whom one was 'quit' (had been exchanged), another dead.[56] Since the treaty contained the hostages' names, either report may have miscounted; the important thing is that they, and especially Bower, show knowledge of the detail of its contents.

We may therefore turn with some confidence to what Bower has to say on the main issues dealt with in the peace of Norham. King William's two daughters were handed over to King John to be married, the elder Margaret to his elder son Henry (born October 1207) when he (or she?) came of age, the younger Isabel to a nobleman of England, either, 'as some wish', to Richard, younger son of King John (born January 1209), or to an appropriate nobleman; provided that if Henry or Richard died unmarried the

---

[53] Anderson, *Scottish Annals*, 329 n 1. The *Chronicle of Melrose* gives £13,000; the total amount owed by William to John was £14,000, i.e. 15,000 merks plus £4,000.

[54] *A.P.S.*, i, 108; Lawrie, *Annals*, 371; *Pipe Roll 13 John*, ed. D. M. Stenton (1953), 40. The payment of 3050 merks was sent to the king with Robert de Braybrook. He was in London to collect other monies on 2 February 1210 and may have been in the north not long before; *Rot. de Liberate ac de Misis et Praestitis* ed. T. D. Hardy, (1844), 148.

[55] In *R.R.S.*, ii, 19, 26 n. 86, 446, Professor Barrow takes the view that only half the money was paid, half remitted. Presumably he considered the 3050 merks to be part of the 7000 received; but they seem to be distinct sums in the pipe roll account and there are receipts for two amounts in the inventory.

[56] Lawrie, *Annals*, 392. Among these hostages was a son of Thomas of Galloway who can scarcely be Patrick of Atholl, his heir at his death; Thomas may have had a wife before his marriage to the heiress of Atholl.

survivor was to marry the elder daughter and that if either daughter died unmarried the survivor was to marry the heir to the English throne. Fordun gives a slightly simpler account omitting the coming-of-age provisions and differs in saying that the marriages were to take place after the lapse of nine years; this may indeed have been a term of the treaty which Bower omitted, finding it difficult to reconcile with the coming-of-age provisions. Bower's uncertainty about whether both sisters were to marry John's sons arose from his conflation of two seemingly divergent accounts, one in Fordun, another known only to Bower. But the summary of the 1209 agreement given in the treaty of 1237 speaks of marriage between Henry *or* Richard and Margaret *or* Isabel and this we may take to be correct. The intention may have been that the heir of King John would by marriage be heir presumptive to the young Alexander. Bower is the only source which knows when the daughters and the hostages were handed over: at Carlisle on 16 August 1209.

In 1239 it was stated in the charges brought against Hubert de Burgh (who later married Margaret) that for the marriage of his two daughters King William quitclaimed to King John all the right which he claimed in the three northern counties and paid 15,000 merks; even more officially the Treaty of York in 1237 linked the Scottish king's claim to the northern counties with the payment and marriage proposals of 1209. Turning to Bower and Fordun we find that they use identical words: King William resigned all the lands which he held of the English king in favour of his son Alexander, who did homage for them at Alnwick; in future these lands should be held not by the king but by the heir to the kingdom of Scotland; but according to Bower homage was done 'for his father's lands, possessions and honours and in the most ample way in which his father or predecessors had done homage most freely to themselves and most honourably to King John or earlier English kings'.[57] This homage, according to the 1291 summary of a 1209 document, was 'for all the rights for which his father had done homage to King Henry II'.[58] In his lifetime King William had held the earldom of Northumberland, the liberty of Tynedale and the superiority (without any demesne or services) of the honour of

---

[57] *Chron. Bower*, i, 527.

[58] Palgrave, *Docs. Hist. Scot.*, 136. See below p. 255 for a note on the date of this homage.

Huntingdon; he certainly continued to hold Tynedale and the superiority, which were excepted from the resignation, as intended in 1205. No English source shows Alexander as a tenant of the English king before 1215, when he was king, but at the age of eleven in 1209[59] any lands to which he might have a right would still be in wardship.

In 1209, then, King William gave up his claim to the earldom of Northumberland in return for the marriages and a promise that the northern counties would form an English appanage for the heir to the Scottish throne, as they had done for Earl Henry before 1152. The treaty, however, did not mention the three counties explicitly; the intention was as well known as any part of the treaty and, when he came of age, Alexander should have been invested with those lands and have held them until his succession to the throne.

The source of Fordun's information, and even more remarkably, of Bower's, is something of a mystery. The documents of the treaty were returned to Scotland in 1237, or so the treaty of that year provided, and they were certainly not in London in the 1290s. Neither were they in Edinburgh, so the Scots had probably destroyed them, evidence of their disparaging character. King William's obligation for 15,000 merks survives in a copy, the wording of which suggests that it was drawn up in the English, not the Scottish, chancery. It had only four witnesses, William, Bishop of St Andrews and Philip de Valognes, both prominent men, and Robert de Ros (the king's son-in-law) and Robert de Vieuxpont, not men of standing in Scotland; Bower states that Robert de Vieuxpont, councillor of King John, swore adherence to the treaty for him, and William Comyn, who must also have been privy to its terms, for the Scottish king. All these circumstances suggest secrecy and haste,[60] conditions in which King William was evidently victim of a confidence trick by John. He allowed the northern earldom to pass unnamed in the treaty although it was probably the one subject which had secured his acceptance of the many other humiliations. There can be no doubt that King William had been forced into a disadvantageous peace, and into paying for the enjoyment of his own humiliation. Yet all was not loss. There was to be no castle at Tweedmouth. The marriage promised for at least one daughter may seem to a modern eye to be a grave infringement of his

[59] Born 24 August 1198.
[60] *R.R.S.*, ii, no. 488 and Professor Barrow's comment on 446.

paternal rights, but it was the most honourable and distinguished match that she could expect. For such husbands as were intended the English king could normally expect that they would bring with them large dowries in lands.[61] It is clear that the 15,000 merks owed by King William—and not fully paid—included the dowry of his daughters; their marriages redounded to their credit and his, and for this he must pay. His ancient honours—the hospitality due to him in England—were protected, and his merchants could once more come to trade freely 'in the accustomed way' in England.[62]

But the debit side of the account gave no cause for satisfaction. A huge sum of money was owed to King John, who had possession of hostages from the most important feudal families of Scotland. The problem of the northern counties was shelved, not solved, but King William had admitted defeat on this issue for his own person. If the treaty was, as the *Melrose Chronicle* reports, 'contrary to the wishes of the Scots', it must have been a bitter humiliation to their king. Yet we must see that humiliation in the context of King William's reiterated demand for the Northumbrian earldom; at no point was the kingdom of Scotland in question, King William performed no homage to John in 1209, and, we must conclude, the juridical position of king and kingdom remained unchanged.

In fact, King John had achieved that kind of settlement at which he was adept: he had terrified his adversary, bullied him into giving hostages, extracted a large sum of money from him, and left him subservient but surely bitterly resentful. For the rest of King William's life John had no cause to fear Scotland.

In November 1209, when England had lain under a papal interdict for eighteen months, two English bishops took refuge in Scotland from their now excommunicate king. Although this immediately suggests, and has usually been accepted as, a strain between William and John, recent work has suggested that we should believe the Dunstable annalist, who says that the bishops stayed in Scotland 'with the favour of the king of England'.[63] Again in 1210, when Matilda de Braose and her children, along with

[61] Thus in 1160 Henry II carried through the marriage of his son to the daughter of Louis VII and secured the surrender of the Vexin, a crucial border province of Normandy, which had been promised as dowry.

[62] The first of these two articles is known to Fordun and Bower, the second only to Bower; *Chron. Bower*, i, 526.

[63] Anderson, *Early Sources*, ii, 377 n. 2.

Hugh de Lacy (recently deprived of the earldom of Ulster), fled from King John in Ireland to Scotland, she and her children were arrested and handed over by Duncan of Carrick, to King John's serjeants, taken in cages to him at Carrickfergus and ultimately to a horrible death by starvation in Windsor Castle.[64] Hugh de Lacy went to St Andrews but, reflecting on the friendship between the kings of Scotland and England, soon fled abroad to escape the knights sent to take him. In the same year King John, doubtless to buy security for Ireland from Galwegian galleys and even to buy a ready supply of Galwegian levies for English armies gave one hundred and forty knights' fees in Ireland to Alan of Galloway,[65] who did homage to him by leave of the Scottish king. Such complaisance by King William is reminiscent of the years after 1175, yet the Scottish reaction seems to have been significantly different. In 1210 there was a conspiracy against King William for which Thomas de Colville was arrested but released on payment of a fine. Early in the following year John sent a force of 100 knights and 100 serjeants (some of whom were Brabançons) under an English nobleman, usually thought to be Saier de Quincy, earl of Winchester, to help in the suppression of the revolt by Guthred mac William, a move which suggests that King William was as close to King John as to his own barons.[66]

Almost certainly there had been talk at the time of the 1209 treaty of a marriage between the Lord Alexander and a daughter of King John, should he have one. The birth of Joanna on 22 July 1210 now made it desirable to complete this understanding. At the end of January 1212 King John again came north to meet William at Durham on 2 February. From there they moved to Norham and made a further agreement during the first week of February. Again

[64] The evidence is well summarised in Anderson, *Early Sources*, ii, 383–6. Presumably the cages were kinder than the manacles which would be put on a man.

[65] This gift was not fulfilled 'on the ground' until 1213.

[66] The date of this expedition, narrated by the annals of St Edmunds (which do not mention Saier) is slightly puzzling. Guthred's rising took place in 1211–12. The annals place it in 1212 in which case the force would probably have accompanied or followed the Lord Alexander back from London in March 1212 and set out for Ross in June, to be met by a captive Guthred at Kincardine. Saier de Quincy may have led the contingent but the 200 marks paid to him by John on 24 February 1211 for the men who were (*fuerunt*) with him in Scotland must relate to another occasion, perhaps the 'army of Scotland' raised by King John in July 1209. *Rot. de Liberate*, 240. Cf. *Curia Regis Rolls*, vi, 290–1; *Pipe Roll 13 John*, 40; *R.R.S.*, ii, 26 n 96.

English sources are remarkably silent about this treaty. It is recorded by Fordun, who mentions the mediation of Queen Ermengarde, and describes it as a renewal of the 1209 treaty with the sending of Alexander to be knighted at London by John as a mark of the strength of the alliance. Bower follows this account verbatim but a few pages later (under 1211) has another account of what is clearly the same treaty. Each king, Bower tells us, swore to maintain the other in his just quarrels; the survivor of them would protect, help and cause to be invested in his kingdom the heir of the first who died. This agreement was sealed with the kings' and prelates' and barons' seals and sworn to on behalf of the kings by William de Harcourt and Alan of Galloway. Moreover, it was agreed that within six years John would give to Alexander a wife who would please him and honour the kingdom.[67] Again Bower is confirmed by a document which survives in the English archives; it is written in a hand of the mid-thirteenth century and bears no seals. It purports to be a charter by King William granting to his lord King John 'that he may marry off without disparagement Alexander our son as his liege man' within six years after 8 February 1212; whatever may happen to King John, William and Alexander will maintain fealty to, and help, Henry (III) as liege lord; William and Alexander have sworn to maintain this agreement and procured the affixing of the seals of the king, three bishops, an earl and three barons; when Alexander is knighted he will affix his seal. There can be no doubt that some of this document represents the treaty of 1212, but it is incredible that King William was called upon to swear in person, and it seems likely that the text was forged to secure homage from, and an English marriage by, the boy Alexander in 1244 or Alexander III in 1251, but that it was based upon a genuine text of 1212 which is accurately reported by Bower.[68]

[67] Lawrie, *Annals*, 379–80; *Chron. Bower*, i, 527, 533. 2 February 1212 would fall in '1212' by the reckoning of most chroniclers who began the year at Christmas 1211 or 1 January 1212. But it would fall in '1211' if the year was begun at 25 March 1212.

[68] The reasons for rejecting this document must be clearly understood. It is not rejected because it uses English formulae, for the surviving part of the 1209 treaty does that. It is not rejected because William calls John 'our liege lord' for John was his lord entitled to his homage and was called 'lord' in the 1209 treaty. It is rejected because whoever wrote it knew that of John's children Henry survived to become king of England. And because it provides meaninglessly that *whatever happens to John*, William and Alexander will be faithful to their lord, Henry, his son, *saving the faith which they owe to John*. One detail rings falsely, though it is not impossible: the use of *dominus* before the

As yet John was unaware of the conspiracy, incipient revolt and foreign invasion which threatened him. It may be that, although a vigorous 44 years old, he feared for the succession of Henry; but it is infinitely more likely that King William, a chronic invalid of 69, feared for the succession of Alexander should he die (as he must soon do) while the mac William revolt persisted, and while the unscrupulous John ruled England and Ireland. The purpose of the treaty and the marriage was surely to secure John's support for Alexander's succession, not William's for the succession of Henry— in 1212 the very idea must have seemed ridiculous. This time, however, William's humiliating dependence upon John's goodwill was distinguished by the form of reciprocal promises, as described by Bower. On 4 March 1212, in London, Alexander was knighted by King John and immediately returned home. Many years later[69] he was to urge upon Henry III that King John had promised him his daughter Joanna as wife, with Northumbria as tocher, and this promise, if correctly reported, would most probably be made in the first quarter of 1212. There is no likelihood that it was given in writing or that John intended to honour it, but it does suggest that the treaty of 1209 was regarded as incomplete when it was made: the rest of the transaction had to await Alexander's fourteenth year, when he could be knighted and could contract marriage irreversibly.[70] King William and his son continued to be deluded by John's suggestion that the earldom of Northumbria would be theirs one day. The sons of major Scottish barons remained in King John's hands, though committed to the keeping of relatives in England. Without any outright assault upon Scottish independence, John had bound King William and his heir hand and foot; they had delivered themselves to him in the quest for their English inheritance.[71]

Subsequent events are none too certain. In June 1212 King John was at Carlisle, evidently to see Alan of Galloway. One chronicler says that John set out for Durham 'to have a discussion' with William, and John was certainly at or near Durham on 28

---

name of each bishop. Texts are in *R.R.S.*, ii, no. 505 and Stones, *Anglo-Scottish Relations*, no. 4. See also below p. 537.   [69] In 1236.

[70] Alexander II completed his fourteenth year on 24 August 1212.

[71] Gerald the Welshman evidently regarded the treaties of 1209 and 1212 as tantamount to a restoration of English overlordship; but Gerald the Welshman, particularly in his *Fürstenspiegel*, had no great regard for historical accuracy. Anderson, *Early Sources*, ii, 400-2.

June but it is not said that a discussion took place. John had summoned an army for a campaign on the Continent, and the kings probably did not meet. A Welsh revolt took John south in haste and from there he wrote on 20 July to Alan of Galloway, recalling their previous discussion and asking for the service of 1000 Galwegians, preferably at Alan's cost. On 14 August, at Nottingham, twenty-eight Welsh boys, hostages since 1211, were hanged for their parents' revolt, chastening news for the Scottish court.[72] Shortly afterwards, if the credulous Roger Wendover is to be believed, King William warned John of the baronial conspiracy which surrounded him and John abandoned his Welsh campaign to meet this new danger. A leading conspirator, Eustace de Vesci, lord of Alnwick, certainly fled to his father-in-law, King William in mid-August, and in the first week of September 1212 John again came to Durham, this time to overawe the northern barons. By the end of 1212 he seems to have thought that the danger of rebellion was over. Once more he turned to the recovery of Normandy, planning to sail across in the spring, once more he visited the north, doubtless seeking military aid from King William, at the end of January 1213, and it is to this occasion that we might assign Bower's narrative of a planned meeting in '1212'; William was unable to travel further than Haddington and when John asked for Alexander's presence his father was persuaded to refuse the suggestion for fear that Alexander might be held hostage for the delivery of Eustace de Vescy. Although followed by the untrue statement that William married his daughter to the count of Boulogne the story of this failed meeting is probably true. There is little other evidence of mutual suspicion unless in June 1213, when King John intended to take the Scottish hostages with him to France. He had improved his fortunes by submitting to the pope in May 1213 and as part of that submission Eustace de Vesci had to be restored to his English lands. King William and Alexander (like the barons of England and Ireland) were enjoined by Innocent III to return to the fealty of

---

[72] It has been accepted that the kings met in June 1212, and even that they rode across England together, a feat then probably beyond King William's strength. The evidence is a payment of 30s. made on 25 June to the clerk of the Scottish chamberlain for the kitchen and stable costs of the Scottish king. This shows only that a meeting was intended. Professor Barrow however accepts the meeting, and Queen Ermengarde does seem to be prominent in Scotland in May and July (*Dunfermline Registrum*, nos. 166, 211) perhaps because the king was ill.

King John, a remarkable misrepresentation of a position in which John had hitherto had his way with them and yet had not established a right to their homage for Scotland. This letter was doubtless issued on the information of English ambassadors; it shows the direction in which John's policy was working and an interpretation which he could place upon the concessions extracted from King William. It is the first example of many from the thirteenth century of the presentation and credulous acceptance of an *ex parte* statement at the papal curia prejudicial to the liberties of the Scottish king. It was not inconvenient that he should be accounted a vassal of the pope's own vassal, the English king, yet King John did not put forward such a claim to King William, still less did William acknowledge it. For two years after mid-1213 our sources give no indication of Anglo-Scottish difficulties. On several occasions King John intervened with his officers in favour of Scottish merchants, and there was certainly no open hostility between the kings. The death of William (4 December 1214) made no apparent difference, though the new king could look for the fulfilment of many promises made by King John; since June 1212, however, John had ceased to be master of events, was unable to exploit any further the concessions he had wrung from William and was prepared to let drift the matters unsettled or uncompleted in 1209 and 1212.

The conduct of Anglo-Scottish relations in the century under discussion was marred by brutalities and unscrupulous behaviour on each side; the modern reader should not find it difficult to withhold his sympathies from all concerned and may see the course of events as a narrative of dynasticism and aggression. Certainly we are dealing with personal relationships untouched by the more modern concepts of patriotism and nationalism. Yet if we contrast the long Anglo-Welsh struggle we see the advantages of a situation in which the freedom of Scotland was seen only as the rights and liberties of its king. Because 'the more recent kings of Scots profess themselves to be Frenchmen in race and manners language and culture, and, after reducing the Scots to utter servitude, admit only Frenchmen to their friendship and service' the two kings not only spoke a common language but understood its vocabulary in the same way. For good or ill King William had far more in common with John 'sans terre' than with Guthred mac William, and the area of misunderstanding, the opportunity of conflict, was correspondingly restricted. If the wild Galwegians descended on Cumberland it would be in the service of their king's feudal claims and not as a revolt against Anglo-French knights, castles and fiefs. And therefore the English king needed peace (by fear or by friendship) with the Scottish king but he did not need conquest of the provinces of Scotland. The patience with which the claim to the northern counties was pursued by the Scottish king and entertained by the English king is much more remarkable than the foolish outburst of 1173–4. On the other hand Henry I, Henry II and his sons showed no very active desire to reduce the Scottish king to a client status. Absorbed in their continental ambitions they sought only a peaceful northern frontier, and although Henry II took a not unreasonable advantage of William's capture in 1174, his interpretation of the Treaty of Falaise could hardly be called exploitation of William's misfortunes. The policy of King John may seem a contrast with that of his predecessors, and so it was, not because John sought to impose again the shackles of Falaise upon Scotland but because he sought to squeeze money and men from Scotland as from England.

*Note on the homage of the Lord Alexander at Alnwick in 1209 (above p. 247).*

King John was in the north in 1210 only very briefly; he came to Durham on 8 April 1210 and seems to have turned south again at once, so that he can scarcely have been at Alnwick; *Rot. Litterarum Patentium*, I part 1, itinerary following p. xlviii, under date. Bower has caused much confusion by giving as date for this homage at Alnwick the year 1210. He is otherwise following Fordun almost verbatim who places the homage 'in these days', i.e. of the August 1209 treaty, and who goes on to tell how 'in the third following year, namely 1212' a further agreement was made. Seeking certainty, Bower evidently counted three back from 1212 and replaced 'in these days' with the result, '1210,' at his account of the homage. This had the further consequence of putting a year too late the Michaelmas (29 September) council at Perth which was held to raise the 15,000 merks, but was washed out by floods and adjourned to Stirling. This too happened in 1209 and not 1210 (cf. *R.R.S.*, ii, 104). Bower alone knows of this council, which he evidently got from his itinerary–chronicle for 1209–1212 or –1214; but in that source there cannot have been a clear indication of the year-date.

Further confusion has been caused by *Melrose Liber*, no. 168, a charter of the king's son-in-law, Eustace de Vescy, dated 'in the year after' Alexander's homage 'on the morrow of the Finding of the Holy Cross' i.e. 4 May. This date has been taken to apply to the homage whereas it is the date of the document (i.e. 4 May 1210); and the homage has been confused with the knighting of Alexander on 4 March 1212 according to chronicles which are then accused of error in mistaking 4 March for 4 May. E.g. *Melrose Liber*, i, xxx; Anderson, *Early Sources*, ii, 390.

# 10

# THE CHURCH I: BISHOPS, KING
# AND POPE

The history of the twelfth-century church can be written round several themes: the parish and diocese, intellectual and spiritual life, the relationship of the church and secular authority, canon law. In any one of these (or other) themes the story would reveal that changes of scale and quality transformed the church during the century so that individual churches which had shared almost unchanging doctrine, observances and obedience had, by the end of the century, been claimed as parts of an organisation governed hierarchically according to rules administered with professional advice. We may fix upon the definition of canon law as the sign of a change which was common to the churches of western Europe but which took place imperceptibly and at a different pace in each of them. Compiled about 1140, the *Decretum* of Gratian codified decrees of previous church councils and papal letters from which a new or refined legal definition could be drawn. The *Decretum* was not the first such collection but it was up-to-date at a time when bishops and their advisers stood in need of rules which would protect the liberties of each church against the claims of others and against the prescriptive authority of secular powers; hence it was accepted as the law of the church, and the pope was drawn further into judicial law-making (the *ius novum*) in order to refine its conditions and remedy its omissions. The growth of effective papal authority was in the main a response to a demand from the lower ranges of the church; only to a lesser, even marginal, degree was it the result of papal initiative or aggression. The decretals which made up the *ius novum* were in their turn codified at the orders of Gregory IX in 1234, by which date the church possessed not merely a code of law, new and evangelistic religious orders and, in the universities, intellectual training grounds, but also its traditional hierarchy, now with defined or definable rights and bound in obedience to the Apostolic See in a much more real (though still far from complete) way than had been the case in the early twelfth century.[1]

The development of the church's institutions in the particular case of Scotland is more fully recorded than that of parallel lay institutions but the evidence is still thin and patchy. Peaceful changes, recorded only incidentally, are never explained. Disputed changes are usually recorded when the parties reach agreement and wish to pass over in silence the points formerly at issue. In general the Scottish church gradually lost its peculiar features and, where the church tolerated variety, adopted English ecclesiastical custom. But at its most important level, the episcopate, the ecclesiastical polity was subject to rather unusual pressures which to some extent distorted its shape.

In the nineteenth century historians generally held that eleventh-century Scotland had one or a very small number of episcopal sees, and that David I was responsible for founding at least half the bishoprics of Scotland. This view is now wholly discounted but it remains uncertain just how many bishoprics were founded or revived by him;[2] the long vacancies at St Andrews after 1093 show that kings could keep a see vacant partly because of difficulty in securing consecration, partly, no doubt, to enjoy its revenues. 'Dunblane' or Strathearn had almost certainly been without a bishop perhaps for a century, and there may not have been a bishop of Caithness before David's reign—the see had no cathedral church of ancient dedication, and the bishop lived, it seems, at David's court. Other sees may have had protracted vacancies but only Glasgow is well documented. There, in 1123 or 1124, David as 'prince of the Cumbrian region' carried out an inquest by the *judices* of Cumbria into the ancient possessions of St Kentigern's church, to which he had appointed his chaplain, John, as bishop,

---

[1] For a recent account and introduction to the literature, C. Duggan, *Twelfth Century Decretal Collections* (1963); W. Ullmann, 'A Scottish Charter and its Place in Medieval Canon Law', *Juridical Review*, lxi (1949), 225–41 shows that *Melrose Liber*, no. 66 gave rise to a letter of Innocent III which entered the decretal collections.

[2] G. Donaldson, 'Scottish Bishops' sees before the Reign of David I', *Proc. Soc. Antiq. Sc.*, lxxxvii (1952–3), 106–18.

after a very long (*diutius*) vacancy. The bishops of Glasgow known to exist in the 1050s and a little before John's time were suffragans of York, titulars who may well never have crossed the Solway into Scotland.[3] Glasgow cathedral may have lacked a pastor for up to a century before 1123, but the vacancy cannot have been much longer since the *judices* were able to recall the possessions of the see. We know that some of the lands listed there were subsequently taken from the church by King Malcolm to endow Flemish knights in Clydesdale, and so we may see the restoration of endowments to this see as an early and enthusiastic move which the king in time reversed. In sum, we are not now disposed to regard the earlier silence about a number of our bishoprics as evidence that they were founded by David I. On the contrary, since each new bishopric must be carved from an already-existing one and so arouse comment if not resistance, we should treat the silence of our sources as an indication that all save the remotest sees (Caithness and Argyll) had an earlier existence. Like other royal patrons of monasteries in Europe, King David saw no need, spiritual or secular, to tamper with the diocesan partition of his kingdom, which in any case had fewer inadequacies than that of contemporary England—inadequacies, that is, which would interfere with episcopal ministrations. St Andrews and Glasgow were manifestly too large for all but the most active bishop, but neither was in the same class as the monstrous diocese of Lincoln.

When David I became king,[4] there was no bishop of St Andrews who might (if needed) hallow his inauguration ceremonies. Robert Prior of Scone, had been appointed by King Alexander but either he or some of his colleagues were now unwilling to accept a consecration otherwise than as prescribed by the law of the church—by his archbishop (to whom obedience must first be professed) with two assisting bishops. York had long claimed this metropolitan right in Scotland, and it had been explicitly acknowledged by Canterbury in 1072, but the Scots' king and bishops would have none of it. Unfortunately, York had only one other suffragan bishop, Durham, and for the consecration of a bishop thereof must call for the help of bishops outside his own province. In order not to be blackmailed

[3] N. F. Shead, 'The Origins of the Medieval Diocese of Glasgow', *Sc. Hist. Rev.*, xlviii (1969), 220–5.

[4] For much of what follows the evidence is collected in A. W. Haddan and W. Stubbs, *Councils and Ecclesiastical Documents relating to Great Britain and Ireland*, ii, part 1 (1873).

by Canterbury on these occasions, the archbishop of York maintained two tame bishops *in remotis* in his household, nominally of
Orkney and the Isles,[5] and struggled to secure the obedience of the
reluctant Scottish bishops and of their determined king.

At first York had called up the support of the papacy without
any challenge from Scotland. Several papal letters had been
addressed to the Scottish bishops as suffragans of York, along lines
suggested by the archbishop.[6] From 1124, however, matters went
decreasingly in favour of York; every passing year in which the
archbishop failed to establish his rights strengthened a little more
the likelihood that the Scots would convince the pope of their
prescriptive right to be a province of the church. The plainest sign
of that provincial status would be the creation of a Scottish archbishopric. In preventing this, and in establishing his claims over the
bishop of Whithorn and over part of the see of Glasgow, the archbishop of York won a limited victory. Otherwise the Scottish bishops
won their independence.[7]

These wider issues were explicit in the problem of the consecration of Robert to St Andrews. In 1125 a papal legate, Cardinal
John of Crema (probably sent at York's instigation), came by sea
to King David at Roxburgh to investigate the dispute between the
Scottish bishops and York; but no legatine council of bishops was
held, for King David was determined to secure an archbishopric
for St Andrews and to that end sent John, Bishop of Glasgow, to
the curia. John had been consecrated by the pope before 1118 and
had consistently refused obedience to York; it was now demanded
of him at the curia not only by York but also by Canterbury, who
sought to go back on his predecessor's concession of 1072. King
David's request was set aside and a hearing of the English archbishops' claims fixed for the spring of 1127. Now David I was probably prepared to allow limited and occasional recourse to Rome as
Henry I had allowed his archbishops to take their quarrel there

[5] This somewhat simplifies a complex situation. See Dowden, *Bishops of
Scotland*, 252–5, 272–3; Watt, *Fasti*, 197–200, 247–9.

[6] Lawrie, *E.S.C.*, nos. XLIV, XLV, LXIII. In addition to works on the
Scottish church see D. Nicholl, *Thurstan, Archbishop of York*, 1114–40 (1964),
and the first two chapters in R. J. Brentano, *York Metropolitan Jurisdiction and
Papal Judges Delegate, 1279–1296* (1959).

[7] The long introduction to Robertson, *Concilia*, is a mine of information
upon Scottish ecclesiastical history, and deals with, among other unrelated
topics, the attempts to secure an archbishop, moves to secure coronation and
unction for the king, and legatine visits and councils.

under the strictest conditions, for he must admit the papal claim to final jurisdiction in spiritual matters. But in practice his control of the church in his kingdom was as absolute as that of his brother-in-law, and in this matter he was not prepared to let his bishops attend the curia so that the pope might instruct them to given obedience to one or other English archbishop. At the end of 1126 King David secured through Henry I a concession from the archbishop of York, who asked the pope for a year's postponement of the case. Shortly afterwards, Robert was consecrated at York by the archbishop without profession of obedience and without prejudice to the right of York to such a profession in future. It seems that with this concession by York David I gave up his pursuit of an archbishopric for St Andrews; both sides may have been frightened when the pope (in 1126) at the request of Henry I gave legatine powers to the archbishop of Canterbury in both England and Scotland, for, suitably drawn and exercised, these powers might give Canterbury the substance while York struggled for the shadow.

During these same years a new bishop of Whithorn, probably appointed by the lord of Galloway, professed obedience to, and was consecrated by, the archbishop of York, while between 1130 and 1133 Henry I negotiated the erection of that part of the diocese of Glasgow which lay in his kingdom into the see of Carlisle, suffragan of York. David I made no effort to undo this work after 1138, and it is curious that when the first bishop, Athelwulf, died in 1157 (the year when the Scottish king gave up Cumberland), the see was left vacant by successive English kings until 1203.

If he had momentarily set aside his claims over St Andrews, the archbishop of York was the more determined to press his more reputable cause against John, Bishop of Glasgow. The Roman curia seems to have given judgement in his favour and by 1134 Bishop John was under heavy pressure from that source to yield obedience to York. In obscure circumstances John transferred his obedience to the anti-pope Anacletus II, perhaps a sufficient threat by David I that his other bishops might do likewise if York's similar demands over them were accepted by the pope. Perhaps as a consequence of the changed political situation from 1135, John felt himself out of favour and in 1136 or 1137 abandoned his see to become a monk at Tiron. In 1138, when the schism had ended, Innocent II sent a legate, Alberic, Bishop of Ostia, who found David I and his court at Carlisle in September licking their wounds after the drubbing given them by the archbishop of York at the battle of the Standard. Chastened, perhaps, King David acknowledged his devotion to Pope Innocent, and the legate recalled Bishop John, presumably with absolution for his schismatic actions. When John died in 1147 the king immediately appointed another Tironensian, Herbert, Abbot of Kelso, to the see of Glasgow; he was consecrated at Auxerre by Eugenius III, the see of York being then vacant. Papal consecration of two successive bishops was ample precedent when in 1164 Malcolm IV promoted Engelram, his chancellor, to Glasgow; Pope Alexander III, ignoring the expostulations of York, consecrated him at Sens. His successor, Jocelyn, Abbot of Melrose (a Cistercian house), was consecrated in 1175 at (Cistercian) Clairvaux at papal command and by a papal legate. Thus the see of Glasgow in its gradual escape from the unwelcome attentions of York found a canonical refuge at the Roman curia; as the English king struggled to limit the jurisdiction of church courts, forbidding his clergy to appeal to Rome and engaging in explosive contest with the archbishop of Canterbury and the pope, the claims of York (whose archbishops were complaisant royalists) over bishops in Scotland must have appeared less obviously just to the pope. The discretion of Scottish kings in sending their bishops of Glasgow to the curia paid dividends.

In 1159 Robert, Bishop of St Andrews, died and the king appointed his father's stepbrother, Waltheof (de Senlis), Abbot of Melrose, who refused the office. The king then dispatched Nicholas, his chamberlain, and William, Bishop of Moray, to the curia to secure archiepiscopal status for the vacant see, but although the unsympathetic Adrian IV had just died,[8] Pope Alexander III was unable to agree lest he offend York and Henry II. In 1160 Bishop William returned with the office of legate, a papal request that he should be appointed to St Andrews and a papal promise that whoever was appointed would be given the office of legate. The king, ignoring the suggestion, chose Arnald, Abbot of Kelso, who was consecrated by William and in due course succeeded him as legate; by that authority he in turn consecrated the new bishop of Ross. When Arnald died in 1162 the king chose his chaplain, Richard, to succeed. For two years the papal court was the scene of strenuous and unsuccessful efforts by York to secure obedience from the

---

[8] In 1155 he had commanded the Scottish bishops by name to give obedience to the new archbishop of York.

bishops-elect of Glasgow (consecrated on 28 October 1164 by the pope) and St Andrews (consecrated at his cathedral on 28 March 1165). In the summer of 1164, fortified with a commission as legate in his province, the archbishop appeared at Norham demanding admission as legate in Scotland, a blatant attempt to usurp the office of legate through which the Scots might otherwise escape his clutches. He was repelled by royal authority under colour of an appeal to the curia against his legatine authority by the dean of Glasgow and prior of Kelso. This may have been enough to prevent a renewed grant of legatine powers to the bishop of St Andrews, for the pope would be careful not to prejudice a cause which was *sub judice*. Richard was consecrated not by the pope or his legate, but by his fellow bishops on papal authority. Was each bishop to be in the like necessity of procuring papal letters to authorise his consecration, thus extending the vacancy in his see and effectively submitting his appointment for papal approval? In the end the answer to this question was affirmative, but the end, which should have been in sight, was postponed for almost forty years by one of those cases which periodically tested the power and authority of the church.

From the preceding account it is apparent that the bishoprics of Glasgow and St Andrews were regarded by the contestants as critical in their disputes, since York had a strong case against Glasgow, and St Andrews had a strong claim to metropolitan status. Between *c.* 1124 and 1165 in the sees of Dunblane, Dunkeld, Brechin, Aberdeen, Moray, Ross and Caithness some nine bishops must have been consecrated, yet we know who conferred the order in only one case and, while there may be a suspicion that some irregular consecration (complained of by the pope in 1119) continued to occur, the absence of papal complaint thereafter suggests that these bishops were consecrated by their fellows with papal authority, and perhaps without protest from York.

When the political settlement of 1174 placed the Scottish king at the mercy of Henry II, feudal subjection was accompanied by ecclesiastical terms. King William promised that 'the church of Scotland shall henceforward make (*faciet*) such subjection to the church of England as it should do and was accustomed to do in the time of (Henry II's) predecessors'; two bishops and two heads of Benedictine houses promised as Henry II's vassals that 'the church of England shall have the right in the church of Scotland which it lawfully should and that they will not oppose the right of the church of England' and King William agreed that his other prelates should adhere to this measure. These terms were deliberately ambiguous in specifying neither York nor Canterbury but the English church, which could only mean both archbishops or the one who had authority over the other. But in describing the subjection as 'customary' the English revealed another weakness in their position. The pope would throw out angrily any supplication to give York or Canterbury authority over Scottish bishops which told the truth—that Henry II had captured King William and extorted this concession from him; the concession had to be represented as the renewal of an old custom. At York in August 1175 six Scottish bishops and a number of abbots swore fealty to Henry II, but the fulfilment of the ecclesiastical terms was postponed until a legatine council in January 1176 at Northampton. Henry II demanded the obedience due by the same bishops to the English church, and received, predictably, their answer that none was due. Roger, Archbishop of York, then produced his evidence that bishops of Glasgow and Whithorn had been subject to his predecessors, but the new bishop of Glasgow was fortified with the bulls of his see; Alexander III had twice taken it into his protection[9] and in a new bull, issued for Bishop Jocelyn (30 April 1175), the words 'our special daughter, no-one between'[10] had been inserted. It seems unlikely that York would accept this as conclusive, but for unknown reasons the two English archbishops now opened their quarrel over which was entitled to Scotland's obedience and King William secured permission for his bishops to leave the council.

The parties now turned to Rome. The archbishop of York transmitted letters from King William to the pope begging him to place the Scottish bishops under York; the messengers of York were insistent that the letters should be returned to them by the curia, clear confirmation that they were forged.[11] King William and his bishops asked for a legate, and the pope sent Cardinal Vivian, who, to secure transit to Scotland, was compelled to swear that he would

[9] *Glasguensem ecclesiam. . . . sub beati Petri et nostra proteccione suscipimus.*
[10] *specialem filiam nostram nullo mediante*; Glasgow Registrum, nos. 26, 28, 32. Haddan and Stubbs, *Councils,* ii, part 1, 37–43 notes this important addition and subsequent confirmations on 43n.
[11] Haddan and Stubbs, *Councils*, ii part 1, 244–5; R.R.S., ii, no. 157; R. Somerville, 'Pope Alexander III and King William I', *Innes Review*, xxiv (1973), 121–4.

do nothing hostile to Henry II. He probably arrived in Scotland in August 1176, about the same time as a papal bull, *Super anxietatibus,* denouncing as lay interference the oath of obedience to the English church extorted by Henry II from the Scottish bishops and forbidding the archbishop of York to exercise any metropolitical right over the Scottish bishops until he had proved it (if he wished to do so) in the papal curia.[12] The Scots had exploited the weakness of their opponent's position brilliantly, identifying him to the pope as Henry II, author of the Constitutions of Clarendon and of the murder of Becket; Alexander III had no wish to put ten more dioceses (those of mainland Scotland, including Whithorn) into his masterful control. After 1176 the Scottish church was in a far stronger position than before 1174; once commanded to obey York, they were now forbidden to do so. In this respect at least, the treaty of Falaise had backfired. This bull effected the freedom of the Scottish church; the more famous *Cum universi* of 1192 merely amplified and confirmed it.

In December 1176, Cardinal Vivian went to Ireland, returning in July 1177 to hold a legatine council at Edinburgh at which, among other statutes, full payment of teinds was enjoined. When the bishop of Whithorn, long obedient to York but now forbidden by the pope to be so refused to attend, he was excommunicated by the cardinal; York was in some danger of losing the one see to whose obedience he was, by very ancient custom, entitled. Vivian was shortly recalled, accused of cupidity; certainly his visits, six months in Ireland, six in Scotland, must have cost his host bishops and abbots much expensive entertainment; the Scots with their bull of protection from Alexander III did not need him now and could well do without his reforming zeal. Yet within a year his place was taken by another legate, summoning the prelates of the realm to the third Lateran council in March 1179. Six bishops went from Ireland, six from England, but only Gregory, Bishop of Ross, is named as having attended from Scotland. A German chronicler thought that two Scots were consecrated at the council, one who came on a horse, the other on foot;[13] Turpin, Bishop of Brechin, and Simon, Bishop of Dunblane, were

---

[12] *Glasgow Registrum,* no. 38; Haddan and Stubbs, *Councils,* ii part 1, 245–6; Anderson, *Scottish Annals,* 267–8; Lawrie, *Annals,* 213–4.

[13] The point evidently was that a bishop should keep greater state than did these two.

consecrated about this time, presumably at the council, but we do not know which of them travelled with greater humility.

From the investiture dispute early in the century until Alexander III's bull of 1176, the question of secular authority within the Scottish church had remained dormant, for crown and bishops could not afford the luxury of a quarrel whose price might have to be paid at York. The bishops whose consecration aroused such tensions had all been appointed by the king, or, in the case of Dunblane and Whithorn, by a local magnate. But good bishops were the key to all else in the secular church, even in the church as a whole, for within each diocese the bishop was charged with overseeing the fitness of his clergy and their kirks, with the spiritual welfare of all the faithful. He must be personally responsible for the ordination of clerics, consecration of kirks and altars and confirmation of the laity; none of these could be delegated. He might use deputies to discharge his responsibilities as *doctor,* teacher and preacher to both clergy and laity, and as legislator and judge in a wide variety of spiritual causes: the creation of graveyards, chapels, parishes, the furnishings of kirks, the life of his clergy and their livings, the material obligations of their flocks to them. But only a good bishop would choose and supervise good officials; only a good bishop would by the discharge of his office maintain the ecclesiastical peace and good order in which the Christian life in his diocese would flourish. The best of kings—and we may include here David I—would recognise the qualities needed if the church in his kingdom was to flourish, but such royal discrimination was imperfect and transient, and in the view of ecclesiastical reformers (a growing body in the twelfth-century church) the church must deny such lay control in law and theory and, while mitigating it in practice, must take issue with blatant examples of its misuse. Hence a series of twelfth-century decretals redefining the episcopal electorate (the clergy and people) so as to restrict it to a few clergy; hence a careful observance of the formalities of election in each diocese in Scotland often by a 'chapter' or meeting of the leading clergy of the diocese; and hence, too, an improvement in the general quality of bishops in the western church.

Yet in Scotland as in England, the king continued to appoint bishops. We cannot compare the mid-twelfth century episcopate with Malcolm III's, but can scarcely doubt that it was Anglo-French instead of Celtic, knowledgeable of the ways of the western church instead of isolated. The two largest and wealthiest dioceses, St Andrews and Glasgow, each had two monastic bishops, who indicate the king's desire to promote reformers within the Scottish church. We are ignorant of the antecedents of Gregory, Bishop of Dunkeld (×1147–1169), who attended the Council of Tours in 1163, of Simon and Gregory, Bishops of Ross (×1150–*c.* 1160, 1161–1195), and others, but some we find in the king's court and chapel. Edward, Bishop of Aberdeen (×1150–1171), had been chancellor to David I, Engelram, Bishop of Glasgow (1164–1174), to Malcolm IV. Andrew, Bishop of Caithness, is of particular interest because he was a Scot and had been a monk of Dunfermline. David I 'gave' him lands in Longforgan parish (near Dundee), which may however have been royal confirmation of inherited land, and he witnessed no fewer than eighteen of that king's charters after appointment to his see in 1146 or a little earlier. Clearly he was much about the court and correspondingly inattentive to his see, much of which was under Orcadian domination; in him the monk and the curialist combined.[14]

By 1165 Bishop Robert of St Andrews had held diocesan synods of which at least two fragments survive, one confirming a long-disputed lay grant to Durham Priory, the other a church to Holyrood Abbey. As early as 1127 he had ventured upon the delicate adjustment of relationships between himself, the monastery of Durham and its parochial kirks, in a gathering at Roxburgh attended by English and Scottish bishops as well as the king—clearly no diocesan synod, though the business would later seem synodal. He gave up payments which represent hospitality on a visitation— visitation was not new—but he retained his episcopal 'right', his jurisdiction over the kirks, to see that they were fitly maintained and served. Thirty or forty years later the customary payments remitted or reserved by the bishop—and we find this in both St Andrews and Glasgow dioceses—include *synodalia*, clear evidence of not infrequent episcopal synods in which the bishop would exercise his jurisdiction.

In only four dioceses do we know of the existence of archdeacons before or about 1165: the bishop of Glasgow had an archdeacon of Glasgow or Teviotdale, the large and remote eastern spur of his diocese, as early as *c.* 1126, the bishop of St Andrews an archdeacon of Lothian by 1144. Plainly the office was first instituted for those

14   For Andrew see *R.R.S.*, i, 6, 7n. 42.

parts which were more difficult of access to the bishop, so that the archdeacon might exercise all those episcopal functions for which episcopal orders were not necessary. By 1152 there was a parallel archdeaconry of St Andrews, not improbably because the bishop was already 'oppressed by age and infirmity'.[15] By about 1165 there were archdeaconries at Whithorn and Dunblane, two sees which were effectively in private patronage. Other sees from Moray to Dunkeld acquired their archdeacons (one each) probably in the 1170s, the northern sees some time later. The archdeacon was an administrative officer and judicial deputy of the bishop; his appearance indicates that his bishop was following the means usual in the western church for government of the church.

It is apparent in the names of the Scottish dioceses that in almost all cases the church in which the bishop had his throne was already fixed by the end of David I's reign. The bishop of Ross was often 'of Rosemarkie'; bishop 'of Strathearn' and 'of Dunblane' were interchangeable. Only in Moray is there no known church and early in the thirteenth century it was asserted that the bishop's seat had until then moved among three churches near Elgin. With the possible exception of Aberdeen (perhaps moved from Mortlach) there is no evidence of a move to new and populous centres such as is found in Norman England. The old cathedral centres and sometimes the old saints were adhered to. But churchmen of Western Europe now looked for a cathedral with a building of suitable magnificence, with a well-endowed table to maintain adequate clergy for liturgical uses which would be an example to the parish priests. Where in Scotland would this be found? At Brechin the Culdee community with its abbot continued to minister in the cathedral. At St Andrews the long-delayed foundation of the Augustinian community took place in 1144 alongside a similar Culdee community, but King David intended that the Culdees' portions should pass to the canons through their either becoming canons or being replaced at death by canons. This scheme was ignored and both communities continued to exist until the end of the century when they made an elaborate division of certain disputed revenues. In 1147 Eugenius III repeated his predecessor's bull of privileges and possessions to the Augustinian priory and added: 'on the death of Bishop Robert a successor shall not be promoted bishop by

[15] Dowden, *Bishops*, 6.

subterfuge or violence, but shall be chosen by you or the wiser part of you.'[16] That was the ideal—it was a phrase inserted in many such bulls in contemporary Christendom; Bishop Arnald was indeed represented as 'elected', for the king must pay some regard to the ideal, but the appointment was really his.

At Dunkeld it seems that Bishop Cormac[17] tried to wind up a Culdee community and introduce canons;[18] the curious arrangements made by David I, which resulted in Gregory, Bishop of Dunkeld, founding in the 1160s an Augustinian priory dedicated to St Columba on an island in the Forth (Inchcolm), were a salvaging of the wreckage of some scheme of Alexander I. The circumstances, so like those at St Andrews, seem good reason for believing that Alexander I had sought unsuccessfully to introduce Augustinian canons in place of Culdees at St Columba's church, Dunkeld. For long Inchcolm, a distant and disjoined portion of their diocese, was the favoured church of the bishops of Dunkeld and, although Bishop Gregory obtained a bull in favour of the canons of Dunkeld, later evidence suggests that his cathedral was served by one or two priests who had no collegiate status.

Bishop Edward envisaged the introduction of 'canons or monks' at Aberdeen, but the scheme seems to have gone no further. Before 1153 there were Benedictines from Dunfermline at Dornoch in Caithness, whose bishop, Andrew, the former monk of Dunfermline, was here probably attempting to establish a monastic cathedral church. If so the attempt failed and the kirk was later served by a priest or two. Probably in 1177 Premonstratensian canons from Soulseat were introduced to Whithorn Cathedral by Bishop Christian. St Andrews and Whithorn were the only successfully established monastic cathedrals, but elsewhere attempts were certainly made to institute regular clergy so that cathedrals might be fittingly served. These attempts were unsuccessful in the main because cathedrals were poor, the bishop engrossing most of their revenues and looking for new endowments for his cathedral clergy. With the exception of Glasgow and perhaps Brechin, no secular cathedral had adequate clergy, still less an organised chapter. Glasgow alone had prebends

---

[16] I have paraphrased slightly. On the Culdees of St Andrews see Barrow, *Kingdom of the Scots*, chapter 7; Watt, *Fasti*, 289–93, 299–302.

[17] Bishop in the 1120s.

[18] According to a sixteenth-century writer who knew the archives of the see (A. Myln, *Vitae Dunkeldensis Ecclesiae Episcoporum*, 1831, p. 6).

for some seven canonries as well as common revenues; Glasgow alone had a chapter in the full sense with, by *c.* 1170, a dean, but no other dignitaries.

In contrast to monastic remains, the surviving Scottish cathedrals have almost nothing to show which is identifiably twelfth century. A doorway at Whithorn is elaborate with romanesque mouldings; rebuilding or decay and destruction have removed the traces of Bishop John's new cathedral at Glasgow, and of the twelfth-century Augustinian kirk at St Andrews only the east end now stands. There is no reason to think that the bishops of Dunkeld devoted to their cathedral the affection they clearly had for Inchcolm Priory. If there was building at Dunblane, Brechin, Aberdeen or Rosemarkie, it has left no trace. All this evidence points to St Andrews and, some way behind, Glasgow, as in all respects the most advanced sees in the Scottish church, Whithorn trailing behind and the others with few or no developments in organisation. If much was due to the size and wealth of St Andrews, resources cannot be the whole explanation, and much credit must be given to the bishops, especially to the long-serving Robert.

It is no coincidence that in his charters we first find a professional group of administrators identifiable by the title 'master' which denotes their academic background and hence their acquaintance with other provinces of the church. They and their like continued to serve Robert's successors and appear early in the *familia* of the bishops of Glasgow, for they contributed the expertise increasingly necessary in the business of being a bishop. They were not yet able, however, to break into the ranks of the episcopate, where Malcolm IV promoted his chaplain Richard to St Andrews (1163) and King William his chaplain Richard to Dunkeld (1170). When the latter died in 1178 the king appointed to the see Walter de Bidun, his own, as well as his grandfather's, chancellor; Walter died in the same year, before consecration, a faithful servant who did not live to enjoy his pension. Such men made undistinguished bishops; but they were complemented by two Cistercians who may have improved matters: Simon de Toeni, Bishop of Moray (1171), and Jocelyn, Bishop of Glasgow (1174), who gave unremitting attention to the affairs of his diocese and rebuilt some of his cathedral, which was consecrated in 1197. Jocelyn was elected at Perth, clear evidence of royal influence, but clear evidence too that the *formalities* of election by the chapter were now being observed, in spite of the fact that the king had plundered the revenues of the see during the preceding vacancy.

In 1178 two other bishoprics were vacant besides Dunkeld. Brechin was perhaps first to be filled, by a master who occurs occasionally and humbly in the royal court. Bishop Richard of St Andrews died in the infirmary of his canons in May. Without the king's leave but after a vacancy during which the great abbey of Arbroath, founded by the king, was dedicated to St Thomas who had died for ecclesiastical liberties, Master John the Scot, a familiar of three bishops, was elected.[19] As early as 1127 Bishop Robert's brother[20] had come to Scotland and *his* wife's brothers, probably also incomers, prospered under the bishop's patronage One of them, Matthew, was archdeacon of St Andrews until in 1172 he was appointed to the see of Aberdeen; Odo was steward of three bishops and ancestor of the lords of Kininmonth; Simon was of the bishops' *familia* until taken to Aberdeen by his brother and appointed archdeacon.[21] John the Scot was the son of their sister and of Bishop Robert's brother; doubtless given a university education at their expense, he returned to St Andrews, establishing an authoritative place in the bishops' *familia* and receiving parochial revenues.[22]

It is not obvious why the canons should have risked such an election, for John was not one of themselves. It may be that they sought to anticipate an election by the archdeacons and Culdees, who claimed elective rights in the thirteenth century; it may be, however, that Howden guessed and guessed wrongly in attributing John's election to them, that he was in fact elected by the archdeacons and Culdees. King William now intruded his chaplain Hugh, a civil servant, and John appealed to the pope. Thereupon the king secured the consecration of Hugh at St Andrews, to present the pope with a *fait accompli*. The form of Hugh's election was

[19] Any account of the ecclesiastical events of 1178–88 depends on two sources, the *Chronicle of Melrose* and the chronicles written by Roger Howden. I have relied for my narrative upon the papal bulls quoted by Howden. Only occasionally and for details have I used the commentary written by Howden, since that commentary seems to have had no source other than the bulls.

[20] His name was Robert.

[21] On the family see G. W. S. Barrow, 'The Early Charters of the Family of Kinninmonth of that Ilk', *The Study of Medieval Records*, ed. D. A. Bullough and R. L. Storey, 107–31.

[22] Dowden, *Bishops*, 8–9 is derived from Bower who is almost wholly erroneous. The details given belong to John of Leicester, Bishop of Dunkeld.

apparently observed under royal pressure; there can scarcely have been papal permission to consecrate and Hugh, uncanonically elected after appeal, was also uncanonically consecrated; the date is unknown but was probably late in 1178 or early in 1179.

Pope Alexander III quashed Hugh's election and sent his legate, Alexius, to ascertain whether the election of John the Scot had been canonical. Unable to exclude the two from Lothian, King William could not prevent the consecration of John at Holyrood, under English protection, in mid-June 1180. Matthew, Bishop of Aberdeen (John's uncle), and three other bishops participated, including Hugh du Puiset of Durham, who excommunicated the contumacious.[23] Hugh did not cease to exercise episcopal functions, and was first excommunicated, and his bishopric ultimately laid under an interdict by Alexius. One or other of these steps so angered King William that he seized the revenues of the see and harried the property of John, Matthew and their numerous kin. Alexius Matthew and John hastily withdrew and crossed to Henry II in Normandy, whence the pope was informed of their proceedings; other St Andrews clergy and laity took refuge in England. The pope's first step seems to have been the invocation of King Henry's authority over his vassal. King William was summoned and arrived in Normandy about April 1181. A settlement was then patched up whereby Matthew was allowed to return to his bishopric, and John was to give up St Andrews in return for another bishopric (only Dunkeld was vacant), the king's chancellorship, his income before consecration and forty merks from St Andrews. If this reflects Henry II's mediation, it is interesting in that it maintains the royal intrusion in St Andrews which had been quashed by the pope. Neither king was able or willing to see that the days of such bludgeoning were over.

The settlement, referred for papal approval, aroused a strong reaction. John was forbidden by Alexander III to accept any see other than St Andrews. Roger, Archbishop of York, was made papal legate in Scotland with orders to impose an interdict upon the kingdom and to excommunicate the king if he obdurately refused to accept John as bishop of St Andrews. The masterful pope knew

[23] Howden states that John was consecrated by Scottish bishops, but the only other one likely to have participated is Christian of Galloway (the rebellious province). The fourth bishop may have been one of those extraneous bishops who 'flit across the English dioceses' (C. R. Cheney, *From Becket to Langton*, 148).

what he was about in using York as his legate; as he grimly warned King William, 'be assured that if you persist in your violence then as we once worked to give your kingdom freedom so we will devote ourselves to bringing it back to its previous subjection'.[24] The king returned to England on 26 July 1181; both he and Archbishop Roger seem to have been unaware of the pope's reaction when they attended Henry II at Nottingham in August. William set out for Scotland to deal with the mac William rising; at Redden on the Border he was met by Hugh du Puiset and John the Scot, but their negotiations only exacerbated matters, for John excommunicated those of William's court whom he considered his enemies, including Richard de Moreville, the constable, and Richard de Prebenda.[25] Having failed to secure John's entry to Scotland, Hugh du Puiset and Archbishop Roger (whose part in all this was secondary probably because he was ill) summoned the clergy of St Andrews to come to their bishop (John) to render obedience. Those who tried to do so were impeded and persecuted by the king, and the bishop of Durham and archbishop of York now excommunicated him and laid the kingdom under interdict. The date is unknown but would be of critical importance since Alexander III had died on 30 August 1181 and the legatine powers of Roger thereby expired—though he would not know this for some weeks.

In November 1181 the archbishop died; York remained vacant until 1191, a factor of considerable importance in allowing the Scots to extricate themselves from King William's intransigence without loss of ecclesiastical freedom. The 'five elderly men' who were popes between 1181 and 1198 'were not nonentities, but they could not compare as rulers of the Church Universal with those two great lawyers and theologians' Alexander III and Innocent III.[26] These changes eased the task of Jocelyn, Bishop of Glasgow, and the three or four religious sent by King William to the curia in that winter of 1181–2. How they argued, what bags of gold they may have opened, we do not know, but on 11 March 1182 Lucius III absolved the king and lifted the interdict. In a gesture of unusual favour, the pope sent to King William the golden rose which he had carried on Laetare Sunday (7 March) and which was usually presented for his services to the prefect of Rome as secular governor

---

[24] Haddan and Stubbs, *Councils*, ii part 1, 255.
[25] In 1203 Richard de Prebenda succeeded John the Scot as bishop of Dunkeld.    [26] C. R. Cheney, *From Becket to Langton*, 11.

of the city; but between the absolution on 11 March and the bull recording it dated 15 March, Lucius left the city with which he had quarrelled ever more bitterly—and the golden rose was awarded to the favourite of the day, King William.[27]

Lucius also appointed two legates to look into the cause of St Andrews, and during the summer they held a three-day council with the king which reached agreement: Hugh and John were to renounce St Andrews and to receive Glasgow and Dunkeld respectively, with the same perquisites as in the previous abortive agreement. (Presumably Jocelyn of Glasgow would first be translated to St Andrews.) The quality of William's political chess may be judged from the fact that, having agreed to these moves, he saw that he had yielded the principle at stake and hence might lose the game. He then suggested to the legates that Hugh might stay at St Andrews, and that if John insisted on Hugh's resignation then he would still be agreeable but 'would not love Bishop John so much nor restore him to his full favour'. The legates reported the king as saying 'I believe well that from the time when master John returns to my peace and affection he will permit [Hugh to remain as bishop of St Andrews] . . . out of consideration for my affection and and from the persistence of my requests, and I would gladly speak with him about it'.[28] John, housed under the protection of Henry II's soldiers at Roxburgh, knew well what bullying and intimidation the persistence of the king's requests might mean and would not come although the king sent for him three times. Let the king swear to the terms agreed, was his answer, and the king, hardening as John hardened, found an escape from the agreed terms: Hugh of St Andrews appealed to Rome with the king's permission, and the legates fixed 1 October 1182 for the two 'bishops' to appear there. The cause came up in the first half of 1183 when the pope secured a resignation of St Andrews from both contestants and a few days later conferred St Andrews upon Hugh, Dunkeld and the various revenues upon John. It is difficult not to believe that King William's influence dictated a settlement which so defeated John. We know that John did not receive the royal chancellorship, but he seems to have enjoyed some at least of the revenues from St Andrews diocese which were his due and which

[27] For a further suggestion about the Golden Rose see below p. 557.
[28] Anderson, *Scottish Annals*, 285, from Roger Howden's text of the legates' letter.

are mentioned in a papal bull of January 1185. For two or three years the quarrel was stilled.

We are unfortunately in ignorance of the precise date of a bull granted by Lucius III 'confirmatory of the liberties of the Scottish church',[29] but it was the earliest document preserved in the king's treasury at Edinburgh Castle in 1282. That castle was restored to King William in 1186, which suggests that the bull came to the king's hands about that time. Some lost text confirming *Super anxietatibus* seems the most likely content of a grant by Lucius, but it may have had a wider significance which allowed the Scottish bishops to consecrate one another without awaiting papal approval. These suggestions are made because in July 1186 John and Hugh were again pursuing their vendetta at the curia in Verona. They seem to have gone thither on the king's business, business which may have procured from Lucius III (who died in November 1185) his bull confirmatory of the liberties of the Scottish church: the see of Moray had been vacant since 1184 but on 1 March 1187 a royal clerk was elected, on 15 March consecrated: a similar vacancy in Caithness was also terminated. (See page 280.)

In July 1186 Pope Urban III, who had announced that he would reopen the case of St Andrews, fixed a date for the hearing and commanded a group of Scottish prelates headed by Jocelyn Bishop of Glasgow, to ensure that the two appeared. Both seem to have returned to Scotland,[30] but only John went back to the curia. Hugh was suspended and excommunicated by the Scottish prelates and deprived early in January 1188 by Clement III who, in instructing a new election, urged John as a suitable candidate for St Andrews. It was a notable but unwise victory for John. Returning to Scotland he submitted to King William, gave up St Andrews and received Dunkeld and the revenues held before his consecration— without the chancellorship and the forty merks from St Andrews. Hugh went to Rome for absolution and on 4 August 1188, a few days after receiving it, died in the plague-ridden city. In April 1189 the king, summoning his prelates and barons to Perth, gave the bishopric of St Andrews to Roger, his cousin and chancellor; the chancellorship went to Hugh of Roxburgh. John, Bishop of Dunkeld was present and said nothing.

[29] *A.P.S.*, i, 107.
[30] Hugh was at St Andrews to consecrate the bishop of Moray on 15 March 1187.

The claims of Canterbury over Scotland had never been a serious threat and since the bull of 30 July 1176 the Scottish church had been free of subjection to York; since then, however, Archbishop Roger had enjoyed legatine powers and had pronounced an interdict and the pope had threatened to end the liberty of the Scottish church. The long-delayed consecration of an archbishop of York in August 1191 was surely the occasion which prompted King William to request further safeguards, specifically against the threat posed by an English legate with authority over Scotland; it may be, too, that the new archbishop was reviving moves against the Scots. And so on 13 March 1192 King William was conceded a papal bull, *Cum universi*, which declared the Scottish church (*Scoticana ecclesia*), containing nine named bishoprics, to be immediately subject, none mediating, to the Holy See.[31] None save the pope or a papal legate might pronounce an interdict, and only a Scot or someone specially deputed from the curia might be a legate in Scotland. Appeals might go out of the realm only to the curia. This bull *Cum universi* gave the Scottish bishops no more freedom than they had enjoyed since the death of Archbishop Roger and, in the matter of metropolitan authority, since 1176 when the front door, as it were, had been shut against York. In 1192 the back door was slammed shut against legatine powers, and York was effectively prevented from ever exercising its alleged rights again—though this did not prevent it from trying to do so after 1296. *Cum universi* is rightly regarded as the guarantee of the freedom of the Scottish church, but without it the church would have enjoyed little less freedom.

One or two incidental points are worth notice. The bishop of Whithorn had defied the bull of 1176 and gave obedience to York both before and after *Cum universi*. Contrary to what is often said, that bull did not acknowledge the rights of York in the see of Whithorn, and these rights, though well grounded in prescription, remained a violation of the 1176 bull.[32] The dioceses of Orkney and Sodor were now well established in the province of Trondheim and were recognised as such in the treaty of Perth in 1266. The diocese of Argyll, formerly part of Dunkeld diocese, had already been created when Cardinal Albinus drew up his list of dioceses

---

[31] The bishoprics were St Andrews, Glasgow, Dunkeld, Dunblane, Brechin, Aberdeen, Moray, Ross, Caithness.

[32] R. J. Brentano, 'Whithorn and York', *Sc. Hist. Rev.*, xxxii (1953), 144–6.

between October 1188 and May 1189 and is also included in the
list of the papal chamberlain, Cencius, written between 1191 and
1193.[33] Both include it with the sees immediately dependent upon
Rome, yet it is not named in *Cum universi*. According to the
fifteenth-century Bower it was created at the request of John the
Scot out of his diocese of Dunkeld because he could not understand
its language, and its first bishop was his chaplain, Harald. Bower
has otherwise confused John with his namesake, bishop of Dunkeld from 1211 to 1214, and since Harald did not die until *c.* 1230
it seems likely that he was chaplain to this second John. Nor, on
the showing of his previous career, is John the Scot likely to have
given away a part, however poor, of his diocese. It may be suggested,
therefore, that about 1181-3 the king, faced with accepting a
bishop of Dunkeld whom he disliked, permitted the lord or lords
of Argyll to procure the creation of the diocese by the pope. After
1183 Bishop John would certainly struggle to reverse that act; if the
see was *sub judice* we would have an explanation, and the only
good explanation, of its absence from *Cum universi*.[34] Presumably
when the dispute was settled in favour of the new see, the right of
presenting to it was allowed to the bishop of Dunkeld as some compensation, so that the second Bishop John appointed Harald.

The Scottish church at no time received from the king a definition of its liberties in any one of the areas where conflict could (and
in England did) arise. The removal of interdict by Lucius III in
1182, so markedly in contrast to Innocent III's treatment of John
of England on much the same issue, remains the weakness of an old
man running from the Roman mob. But even if the pope had prevailed, King William would have lost only in the cause of *John the
Scot* v. *Hugh*; there is no sign that the Scottish church would have
gained a royal charter of liberties in the matter of episcopal elections
or of anything else. As though to point the situation plainly for
posterity, the king allowed his cousin Roger to delay his consecration
as bishop of St Andrews for ten years. During his four years as

[33] *Le Liber Censuum de l'Eglise Romaine*, ed. P. Fabre (Paris, 1889), ii, 101
for Albinus, the earlier list. Albinus states that York had only one suffragan,
Durham (ignoring Carlisle); he places Orkney *in regione Granellandia*, Green-
land; and he makes no mention of Sodor. But his inclusion of Argyll cannot be
explained away by ignorance or carelessness; the diocese must have been created
before he wrote. *Ibid*, i, 232 for Cencius, the later and more correct list. *Ibid*, i,
1-8 for the dates of these collections.

[34] *Chron. Bower*, i, 356-7. Although Argyll is not mentioned in the reissues
of *Cum universi*, it seems always to have been included in its scope.

bishop he spent long periods at the English court.[35] His successor was translated from Glasgow, where the king now appointed his own nephew, Florence of Holland; five years later Florence resigned, still unconsecrated and after a brief visit to Scotland.[36] Such aristocratic disdain for the welfare of the church—and this during the pontificate of Innocent III—could only prevail where the king's control was unchallenged.[37] Unlike Becket and Langton, therefore, John the Scot struggled in vain. Yet his selfish concern for revenues should not blind us to the courage of his stand; when he had accepted his own demotion to Dunkeld he continued to oppose the promotion of Hugh and so risk losing all livelihood. It was a small stand for canonical regularity but significant at least of this: that the days of undisguised control were numbered.

There can be little doubt that episcopal appointments were made more circumspectly in the thirteenth century. The electing chapter had first to seek royal permission to make an election and this was without doubt usually the occasion of a royal nomination. There seem to be no further examples of election by *compromissarii* in the royal chapel.[38] In 1219 a disgruntled canon or vicar choral of Glasgow complained to the pope that in 1207 Bishop Walter, then a royal chaplain, had bribed the king's chamberlain and the queen to procure his promotion and that he practised corruption and nepotism; charges of extortion and immorality were brought against other bishops at the end of the interdict in 1218. None of these complaints (in which there may have been some justice) was sustained and from the time of the interdict the Scottish king and the pope co-operated to ensure a smooth episcopal succession and a secure and compliant episcopate.

Without an archbishop, the Scots had still either to go to the curia for consecration or send for a bull permitting Scottish bishops to examine as to fitness and then consecrate. It was easy for the king

---

[35] *Rot. Chartarum* I, i, 9b, 32a (in France, 3 Aug.–28 Dec. 1199); *ibid*, 77b, 99a (in England, Oct. 1200); *ibid*, 81b, 85a (in England Dec. 1200–Feb. 1201). He was also in England at some time between May 1198 and June 1199, and for King William's homage at Lincoln, 21–23 Nov. 1200; Anderson, *Scottish Annals*, 321, 324.

[36] *R.R.S.*, ii, 60 nll.

[37] Giraldus Cambrensis commented upon William's tyranny in episcopal elections; Anderson, *Early Sources*, ii, 401.

[38] *Compromissarii* were members of the chapter to whom the whole chapter had delegated the right to make the choice. Jocelyn of Glasgow was elected in 1174 at Perth probably in this way.

to lodge objections to the elect at the curia: wiser for the chapter to elect his nominee, or at least to consult him informally about an acceptable election; sometimes, it seems, these 'established channels' broke down. In 1238 the chapter of St Andrews postulated Geoffrey, Bishop of Dunkeld, a former civil servant, but the pope refused the translation apparently at the king's instance; usually the pope would provide in these circumstances, but somewhat unusually the chapter was allowed to make another election, this time of David de Bernham, a university master and royal chamberlain and surely a royal nominee. In 1253 the government opposed the election to St Andrews of Robert de Stuteville, dean of Dunkeld, sending master Abel, archdeacon of St Andrews, to the curia to have the election quashed and Gamelin provided. Abel returned as bishop to a frosty reception in Scotland. In Moray the election of a canon of Lincoln in 1252 has left no trace in Scottish record.

The most notorious case of an appointment opposed by the king occurred in Glasgow, where about December 1258 Nicholas de Moffat, Archdeacon of Teviotdale, was postulated and in due course rejected by the pope; one of the electing canons who accompanied him to the curia successfully urged his unfitness in the hope (unsuccessful) of falling heir to the bishopric. About October 1259 the pope provided and consecrated an officious English pluralist John de Cheam,[39] who had been active at the curia on behalf of the suffragans of Canterbury and against their archbishop. King Alexander III protested, especially when the pope used English bishops as executors of his mandate, but eventually gave way on receipt of certain papal assurances. Cheam was as busy in his see as he had been at the curia. He demanded residence of his cathedral canons and put forward a ludicrous claim which would have added the diocese of Carlisle to his own. For reasons which are not clear he left Scotland for the curia in 1267 but died in France a year later.[40] Nicholas de Moffat was elected again in 1268 but died unconsecrated (with a reputation as 'the laughing archdeacon') in 1270. In both 1258 and 1268 the chapter (including Moffat) made a compact that if one of their number was elected bishop, he would hand over certain episcopal property to the chapter. This may have incited the election of Moffat against royal wishes, which in turn would explain

[39] Cheam is in Surrey.
[40] E. W. M. Balfour-Melville, 'John de Cheam, Bishop of Glasgow', *Sc. Hist. Rev.*, xxvii (1948), 176–86.

why the pope sacrificed him in 1258 and then appointed Cheam as a rare demonstration of his independence and *plenitudo potestatis*.

Such tiffs were the exception, and it must be remarked that they occurred in the politically disturbed decade 1249–59. In St Andrews, Dunkeld and Glasgow the rule from 1210 until 1286 or later was a comfortable succession of royal servants, often with an earlier career in a university and in ecclesiastical administration. In Moray three out of four bishops seem to have been related to the Moray family, and towards the end of the century this aristocratic tendency may have been at work elsewhere—a Comyn at Brechin, a Cheyne at Aberdeen. But it would be facile to characterise bishops as 'university', 'civil servant', 'ecclesiastical official' or 'aristocrat', for many rose through the church with a combination of these qualities. Nearly all were native Scots but the few Englishmen promoted were in no way distinctive, and there was little or none of the xenophobia which might have arisen if Frenchmen such as Malvoisin had continued to be appointed. Four at least were monks, two of them abbots of Arbroath, but one, Brice, Prior of Lesmahagow and Bishop of Moray, presumably owed both his offices to his kinship with the lords of Douglas and, more remotely, with the lords of Duffus. The aristocratic Comyn at Brechin was also a Dominican friar; the first Dominican bishop in Britain indeed was Clement at Dunblane. His episcopal predecessor had, it seems, lived a refugee's life at Holyrood Abbey for some years before his death in 1231. The ensuing delay was doubtless caused by the reluctance of king and pope to allow the earl of Strathearn to nominate, and in 1233 three other bishops, by virtue of a papal commission, chose Clement, doubtless at the king's insistence; there was no cathedral chapter to object, but when Clement died his cathedral was a flourishing religious centre for the diocese.[41]

Whithorn has not been taken into account in the foregoing discussion since it remained ecclesiastically a part of York and in the matter of appointments the king did not have it all his own way. Both elections, in 1235 and 1253–5, were contested: the 'clergy and people' it seems successfully maintained their right to elect against the Premonstratensian canons of the cathedral, and chose a monk on both occasions. The successors of the lords of Galloway, the cathedral chapter and the archbishop of York were all compelled

[41] The see of Argyll was held by three Dominicans in turn from 1264 till 1362. There were no Franciscan bishops in thirteenth-century Scotland.

to acquiesce, though the struggle took over six years in the first case, over two years in the second. Yet it should also be noticed that these bishops do not seem to have been nominated by the king, who took up their causes and fought them through, presumably to destroy the lord of Galloway's patronage and, as far as possible, the archbishop of York's jurisdiction. It was surely to one of these occasions, more probably the later, that there should be attributed the lost bulls of Innocent IV (1243–54) 'that election and other causes shall not be examined outwith the kingdom of Scotland especially in the diocese of York' and 'that no one of the kingdom of Scotland, cleric or layman, shall be taken outside the kingdom by apostolic letters', that is, to York. In fact, both bishops acted as suffragans of York within the diocese of York: 'if you come to our region you shall have some churches to consecrate' wrote one of the archbishops, 'which will profit you something'.[42]

[42] R. J. Brentano, *York Metropolitan Jurisdiction and Papal Judges Delegate, 1274–98*, (1959), has a valuable chapter on Whithorn. For the quotation see Haddan and Stubbs, *Councils*, ii part 1, 59.

*Addendum to 1978 impression.* An important bull of Pope Alexander III, (Wilkins, *Concilia*, i, 416; Migne, *Patrologia Latina*, cc, 1093) has been drawn to my attention by Mr Robert Somerville. Addressed to R bishop of St Andrews and the other bishops *per Scotiam* it confirms 'the ancient liberties and reasonable customs hitherto used in consecrating bishops and other matters'. Anyone gainsaying these liberties is to be answered only before the pope or a legate *a latere*, and any new and serious problem is to be brought to the apostolic see. The bull from its date, (Anagni, 24 December) must belong to 1159, 1160, 1173, 1175 or 1177 and because of the submission of Falaise, 1175 and 1177 are unlikely. It is just possible that the initial R ( = Richard, bishop 1165–78) is a copyist's insertion and that the bull was issued to the mission of William bishop of Moray to Rome at the end of 1159 (above p. 261) when he hoped to succeed to St Andrews. The point of the bull is not immediately obvious, but it is probably designed to protect the custom whereby *per Scotiam* (i.e. except for Glasgow and Whithorn) consecration of a bishop was given by the bishop of St Andrews (acting as quasi-metropolitan), a matter which may have become a live issue for Bishop Richard with two consecrations in 1172. This supports the date 1173 and explains why Lucius III, having settled the dispute over St Andrews in 1183, should have issued a bull 'confirmatory' of this one, after the deaths of two bishops in 1184. The suggestions above, page 274, are misdirected.

# 11

# THE CHURCH II: REFORM

I f in general the thirteenth-century bishops were complaisant to
both king and pope and more or less attentive to their dioceses,
they were always jealous of their episcopal rights and privileges.
In the first half of the century it is possible to trace the establishment of cathedral chapters with common revenues and individual
prebends at one cathedral after another. The Culdees of Brechin
lost their prior and their 'name was changed to canons'. At Dunblane from the beginning of record c. 1170 until 1237 the bishops
had consulted, and secured the assent to acts affecting the see of, a
motley but canonical group: the archdeacon, the heads of religious
houses in the diocese (the priors of the Culdees of Muthil and
Abernethy, and the prior of Inchaffray) or of houses with appropriated kirks in the diocese (the abbots of Arbroath and Cambuskenneth), the dean of Christianity and a selection of parochial
clergy and clerks of the bishop. This was at once the chapter and
the synod of the diocese, the 'whole clergy' by whom the bishop
was elected. It was not enough for Bishop Clement who, in 1237,
was authorised by the pope to lift a quarter of the parochial teinds
from his diocese in order to endow his own table and to provide
for a chapter of dean and canons at Dunblane, a task which was
well begun by 1240, though perhaps not completed by the addition
of a chancellor until after 1274. Dunkeld under John the Scot and
his successors had a similar chapter of diocesan clergy, especially
deans of Christianity, regulars and episcopal clerks, the latter sometimes styled canons of Dunkeld, and these are known to have elected
the bishop in 1211. Dunblane and Dunkeld cathedrals about 1200
each had one or, at most, two resident chaplains. Under Bishop

Hugh (1214–29) the canons come to number seven and achieve collegiate standing with a common seal. The first cathedral dignitary to appear is a precentor and apparently under Bishop Gilbert (1229–36) other dignitaries were instituted along with the constitution of Salisbury Cathedral. By 1238 Dunkeld had dean, precentor, archdeacon, treasurer, subdean, succentor and a number (probably small) of canons.

Similar provision can be traced at other cathedrals, most notably Moray and Glasgow, whose records have survived and which adopted the constitutions of Lincoln and Salisbury respectively—with minor departures. These colleges of canons were small: at Aberdeen in 1256 thirteen canons, in Moray about 1220 eight canons, but thirty years later twenty-three. At St Andrews the Culdee clergy seem to have retained their place in the cathedral until almost the end of the twelfth century; under Bishops Roger and William Malvoisin, however, their endowments were transferred to form the collegiate kirk of St Mary of the Rock, whose canons were often clerks of the bishop. These bishops may have intended thereby the creation of a secular chapter, for in the mid-thirteenth century the king secured for the canons of St Mary's a temporary voice in episcopal elections, and the archdeacons allied with them to the same end.[1] There is evidence that diocesan clergy participated in elections in Whithorn, St Andrews, Dunkeld, Dunblane, Aberdeen, Argyll and Sodor, but, in all dioceses save the last two, fully organised chapters existed and monopolised the right of election by 1300.[2]

These chapters were generously endowed, in the main by the episcopate, in order to maintain the liturgy with fitting splendour. Liturgical uses were related more closely to those of English cathedrals than of any other part of the church, just as the 'four-square' chapter was derived directly thence. The thirteenth century was also a great age of cathedral building and, so far as later additions, alterations, ruinations and restorations permit us to say, Scotland was no exception. The two cathedrals which are generally esteemed to have been the finest were St Andrews and Elgin, the former dedicated in 1318, the latter begun after 1224 and continued, doubtless sporadically, through the thirteenth century; but

---

[1] Barrow, *Kingdom of the Scots*, chapter 7.
[2] I. B. Cowan, 'The Organisation of Scottish Secular Cathedral Chapters', *Recs. Sc. Ch. Hist. Soc.*, xiv (1960–2), 19–47.

their remains are fragmentary. Other cathedrals show a nineteenth-century face—Brechin, Dornoch and in some part Dunkeld and Dunblane. They are and were modest by most cathedral standards, the number of their altars small, but they were not insignificant achievements for the cities and dioceses which decade by decade, bay by bay, created them to the greater glory of God. The west front of Dunblane is the eroded wreck, the choir of Dunkeld a Victorian botch, of modest pieces of thirteenth-century pointed architecture, and if their simple formulae do not make the spirit soar, in their environment they have dignity and peace. The finest thirteenth-century church in Scotland is the now blackened cathedral of St Kentigern at Glasgow, built mostly during the episcopate of William de Bondington (1232–58) to replace Bishop Jocelyn's church. The ground plan is rectangular but the absence of transepts gives this magnificent Gothic essay a rare unity and strength. The architectural detail is English in inspiration, but the church has its own unique characteristics. Because the site slopes down to the east—an inconvenience to be explained by continuous occupation since sub-Roman times—the eastern arm is two-storied, an under church or crypt containing the tomb of St Kentigern round which pilgrims could make a complete circuit, and directly above it the high altar in the choir which also contained the feretry or shrine of the saint in the form of a stone base bearing a life-size and jewelled image of the saint's shoulders and head. The importance of Glasgow as a centre of pilgrimage was great but the bishops and chapter over-strained their resources in providing so magnificent a setting for the cult of St Kentigern. In 1240 a loan of 1400 merks was repaid to a Florentine banker, contracted in part, doubtless, to pay debts at the curia but partly also for the cathedral fabric. A provincial council of the Scottish church had the building fund proclaimed in all parish churches from Lent to Easter and Bishop John de Cheam devoted the canons' fines for non-residence to it. Probably the most important source of income was the offerings of pilgrims at the shrine. Thus the cult of St Kentigern was housed in a cathedral whose architecture was reminiscent of Salisbury, whose liturgy and constitution derived thence; on the whole, the Scottish church derived its most immediate experience of Latin Christianity from the church in England.

Outside his cathedral the late twelfth-century bishop had the services of his archdeacon (or archdeacons) and deans of Chris-

tianity; the latter were beneficed parochial clergy nominated either
by the bishop or the archdeacon as executive and even perhaps
judicial officers. Bishop and archdeacon could each assemble the
clergy within their jurisdiction and in such synods or chapters could
exercise oversight and jurisdiction.[3] At this time the dean of Christianity was more prominent and more active as executive or
administrative officer, and enjoyed probably a greater discretion,
than at any subsequent period in the history of the medieval church.
Thus the deans of Dunkeld and Dunblane dioceses become more
difficult to trace as the thirteenth century progresses and vanish al-
together for the fourteenth and fifteenth centuries; even in Glasgow
and St Andrews they become remarkably obscure from the late
thirteenth century. This change can be linked with the multiplication of *magistri* among the episcopal familiars and the appearance
about 1200 of a specifically judicial deputy of the bishop, the
Official.[4] The *magistri* were a trained clerical staff sometimes related
to the bishop and moving with him, more often settling at a
cathedral where they had been provided with canonries and serving
a succession of bishops. Gradually, under the influence of such
professionals, there was a new regard for the beauties of correct
procedure which replaced the earlier casual litigation in the synod.
The bishop was expected by the pope to govern his church and
diocese more intensively and this he could do only by using the
professional services of his deputies. The official may have shared
these judicial functions but initially, at any rate, he appears, like
the deans of Christianity, rather as an executive officer. It may be
that the official was executive of the bishop, the deans executives of
the archdeacon; we have no indication of how ecclesiastical jurisdiction was divided between these two, and almost none on any
matrimonial or testamentary causes or causes arising because a
cleric was party.

Our records are eloquent, however, of the problems arising from
ecclesiastical property, problems which in their turn arose from the
bishop's more intensive government. Case after case concerns the
division of revenues between parson or appropriator and vicar,
between mother-church and chapel, between two parishes divided

---

[3] Colin Morris, 'From Synod to Consistory', *Journal of Ecclesiastical History*,
xxii (1971), 115–23; Jean Scammell, 'The Rural Chapter in England ...', *Eng.
Hist. Rev.*, lxxxvi (1971), 1–21.
[4] At St Andrews by 1194, Aberdeen by 1199, Glasgow by 1202, Brechin and
Dunkeld by 1210.

by a fish-yielding stream; case after case concerns revenues from land, wood and water, and occasionally the right to present to a benefice—this last a matter which in England was claimed exclusively for the secular courts. Under King William there was, perhaps, some resistance to the widening scope of ecclesiastical jurisdiction, but it had little effect and the church was able to bring laymen freely before its tribunals while the crown supported the ecclesiastical sanction of excommunication. The tribunals which heard these causes consisted of three clergy, secular or regular, appointed by the pope (at the suggestion of the parties) sometimes with power to pronounce judgement, sometimes to report back. These judges delegate were undoubtedly the most important factor in encouraging the study and observance of canon law in Scotland. They are evidence of a steady traffic between Scotland and the Roman curia by clerics of low and high standing and of the total integration of the Scottish church into the centralised machinery of the western church. From the late twelfth century a Scottish bishop was in an everyday sense the harassed agent of popes, busy in the exercise of papal plenitude of power. Misrepresentation, procedural dodges and delays, blackmail and bribery by the parties, ignorance, vacillation and arbitrary judgement by the popes, all these vitiate the claim of ecclesiastical justice to a favourable verdict from the historian. The worst sufferers were the clergy themselves.

Yet the centralisation of the church had a purpose—reform, especially reform of the life and conduct of the clergy. The multifarious activities of Pope Alexander III and his successors, the legislation of the Third Lateran Council, were an attempt to 'stiffen' the bishops in their resistance to lay encroachment and their insistence upon a literate unsimoniacal and active clergy. In 1215 Innocent III convened the Fourth Lateran Council, attended from Scotland by four bishops, to 'make wise laws for the higher and lower clergy'. The decrees of that council were wide ranging, even miscellaneous and ill-assorted; a number of them, such as those aimed at the Greek church and the Jews, had no relevance to Scotland. Others dealing with such matters as the law of marriage, teinds, the obligation on bishops to reform the morals of the clergy, clerical incontinence, worldliness and ignorance, had much need to be enforced in Scotland. Perhaps their precise scope was not the important thing: what mattered was that the spirit behind them should inspire the episcopate and infuse the whole church. To this end the council included a decree that metropolitans should hold provincial councils annually and that their statutes should be published in annual diocesan synods. From this time the diocesan synod became a statute-promulgating body, an activity hitherto almost unknown to it. In England reforming statutes for the province of Canterbury were promulgated at the council of Oxford in 1222, but a very detailed and influential set of diocesan statutes had been drawn up for Salisbury by Bishop Richard le Poore by 1219. Thus in England provincial canons came second in time and perhaps in importance to diocesan statutes. The complex history of subsequent sets of statutes has recently been elucidated and shows much borrowing and modification—and reliance upon a wide range of ecclesiastical law besides the Fourth Lateran decrees, copies of which were scarce. The legislation of the Scottish church has not yet been examined in this critical way to disentangle provincial from diocesan, but it seems that the Scots adhered to the suggestion of the Lateran Council. In 1225 Honorius III, responding to a petition from some Scottish bishops which pointed out that no provincial councils could be celebrated in Scotland, commanded that they hold a provincial council by his authority.[5] At what dates and with what regularity such councils were held is unknown, but the assumption that provincial councils immediately or soon became annual is unlikely. One council which made statutes was held before 1232 possibly that held in Dundee in 1230.[6] On 1 July 1238 another was held at Perth, recorded in the settlement of a plea, but the authority for holding it is unknown. The death of Bishop William Malvoisin of St Andrews about this time—it is attributed to 9 July but this could be an error for 9 June—may be connected with the council, for the king certainly had to oppose the choice by the regular chapter of the ex-civil servant Geoffrey, Bishop of Dunkeld, who, the king evidently considered, had had his run at the *cursus honorum*. The king may have turned first to a provincial council to influence the canons, just as in 1239 and 1255 he evidently backed the claims of the collegiate kirk of St Mary of the Rock. If this suggestion for the council of 1238 be correct, then the inspiration, if not the authority, for it came from the king.

[5] The papal letter uses the singular *concilium* because all the bishops were to come together in one council. But it was intended there should be a succession of such councils.

[6] *Scottish History Society Miscellany*, viii, 5–6. This is a curious place to hold such a council as there was no friary or other religious house there.

In fact the papal commission to the legate Otto (1237) suggests that a legatine council was desirable because provincial ones could not be held. Again, such legatine councils had a turbulent history, and were associated with resistance to the king. In 1201, however, Innocent III had sent Cardinal John de Salerno to Scotland, and he held a three-day council at Perth which is said to have 'removed from the office of the altar those who were ordained priest on a Sunday'. During his two stays in Scotland the legate dealt with a number of disputes between religious houses or between them and their bishops, and one of these was left for King William to unravel. This legation seems to have been remarkably uncontentious and was perhaps mainly devoted to the cause of ecclesiastical reform. A poorly attested council of 1212 was held by the bishops of St Andrews and Glasgow as legates but 'at the king's command' and to preach the crusade. A four-day council under the legate James in 1221, again at Perth, is known only to have dealt with a matrimonial cause. Thus there was comparatively recent precedent for the legation of Otto and it is the more difficult to give credence to Alexander II's snub to him at York in 1237 as reported by Matthew Paris: 'I do not remember that I have ever seen a legate in my land . . . neither in the time of my father nor of any of my predecessors'. According to the same source, Alexander II warned in 1237 that in Scotland 'wild men dwell, thirsting for human blood', then blithely carolled in 1239 that no legate was needed for 'Christianity flourished there, the church did prosperously'.[7] Certainly, Otto's council at Holyrood in October 1239 was interpreted as a royal restriction upon his crossing the Forth, and royal hostility can probably be accepted and attributed to the legate's purpose of raising money for the pope. Taxation of the clergy seems to have been accepted by the Scots in 1220, when a legate persuaded the Scottish prelates to pay the twentieth for three years imposed by the Fourth Lateran Council for the recovery of the Holy Land. Otto was not in Scotland long enough to levy a subsidy, but a twentieth was collected after his departure by an agent, Pietro Rossi, for the crusade against Frederick II. It is clear that Otto also persuaded the clergy to accept statutes, one of which dealt with the residence and ordination of vicars, and some of the canons of Otto's council at London for the English church turn up in the Scottish collections of thirteenth-century statutes. These canons and some of 1268 have

[7] Anderson, *Scottish Annals*, 344, 346.

been described as 'the most important and authoritative legislation of its kind issued in medieval England',[8] and if the Scottish statutes of 1239 had survived, they might have deserved more certainly a similar verdict as the inspiration of the reforms of subsequent bishops.[9]

There has, unfortunately, been no modern enquiry into the tangled history of papal taxation in Scotland, so that, for example, we do not know the outcome of Urban IV's bull (1263) to Bishop Gamelin of St Andrews commissioning him to collect a yearly hundredth of church revenues in Scotland for five years for the Crusade. Certainly, Scotland never knew anything like the mess of Henry III's preposterous involvement in the pope's Sicilian business in the 1250s, but as papal needs grew and the genuine Crusade replaced papal vendettas with the Hohenstaufen, Scotland could not long escape demands to participate and finance. On this issue the clergy would look for support to the king in resisting papal demands, and it is perhaps for this reason that the complaints of the clergy in the 1240s against the crown's infringment of clerical liberties abated in the second half of the century; it is said that in 1242 at a provincial council Alexander II forbade the laity to withhold teinds and otherwise harm the church, but such assurances were probably already common form—mere pious platitudes.

It requires a mind trained in the subtleties of canon law to discover in the equally subtle papal letters the issues over which church and layman fell out in relation to jurisdiction, especially jurisdiction over land in ecclesiastical possession. There seems to be no twelfth-century evidence, but it may be that the decade after 1178 was unfavourable to ecclesiastical claims. In 1207 when Patrick, Earl of Dunbar, fell out with Melrose Abbey over some part of the land between Gala and Leader he denied ecclesiastical jurisdiction on the grounds that a layman might not be called to a church court for a 'lay holding', while the abbey claimed that a layman could be so cited for 'free alms'. The problem (solved in England by the assize *Utrum* heard in secular courts) was that to admit ecclesiastical jurisdiction meant admitting tenure in free alms which, in effect, was Melrose Abbey's case. The pope remitted the cause to the bishop of Moray as judge delegate, but in the

---

[8] Powicke, *Thirteenth Century*, 451.
[9] D. M. Williamson, 'The Legate Otto in Scotland and Ireland', *Sc. Hist. Rev.*, xxviii 1949), 12–30.

end the ecclesiastical judges had to take the 'amicable composition' which settled the matter to the king's court for confirmation, perhaps because some of the land was apportioned to the earl (the lay fee), some to the abbey (free alms).[10]

A dispute over land at Stobo was brought before papal judges delegate in 1223; again it was settled out of court but again with secular participation, before Walter Olifard, justiciar of Lothian. In this case the bishop of Glasgow was the pursuer; he was defender about ten years later when brought 'by royal letters' before the sheriff of Traquair and although successful he had to buy off the pursuer with a pension of ten marks.[11] It seems almost certain that this happened after the bishop had tried to wriggle out of lay jurisdiction by invoking papal commands, one a letter forbidding him to appear in the lay *forum* for land held in free alms, the other a letter to Alexander II cozening him to support the bishop's stand. Evidently it was unsuccessful.[12] In the diocese of Moray ecclesiastical jurisdiction was in similar trouble in the 1220s. Cases were heard before judges delegate,[13] but, in another instance in a secular court, the king intervened in a case which had been taken to judges delegate 'asserting that the manor (in dispute) was a barony and therefore ought to be litigated over in a royal court and not an ecclesiastical one'.[14]

After this tussle in the 1220s, the matter seems to have lain dormant until the death of Alexander II. Soon thereafter the prelates seem to have obtained from a secular council a promise of observance of their old liberties (the usual thirteenth century prelude to new claims), because in 1250 they complained bitterly of new infringements and spoliation of the church. Various letters of the 1250s,[15] of which the most wide-ranging was addressed to Robert Grosseteste, Bishop of Lincoln, and the bishops of Worcester and Lichfield on 31 May 1251, show the clergy on the offensive again. It is likely that the bishop of Moray had petitioned for the letter to Grosseteste, for Moray had ecclesiastical ties with Lincoln

---

[10] *Melrose Liber*, nos. 101–5, 133; *R.R.S.*,ii, nos 482–3.

[11] *Glasgow Registrum*, nos. 126–31, 172.

[12] *Glasgow Registrum*, nos. 158, 161. See also *Scone Liber* no. 120, of 23 December 1228 (Gregory IX, not Gregory X) which is a strong plea to Alexander II to protect ecclesiastical jurisdiction.

[13] *Moray Registrum*, nos. 28, 73, 74, 75, Orig. Charters no. 6.

[14] *Moray Registrum*, Orig. Charters no. 6.

[15] *Glasgow Registrum*, nos. 106, 197, 198; *Scone Liber,* nos. 105, 112.

and the bull is preserved in the Moray cartulary. Like the prelates'
complaint of 1250 it blamed the new advisers of the boy king, but it
is unlikely that Alexander II was wholly innocent: royal commands
revoke excommunications, cases about ecclesiastical possessions are
brought to lay courts, clauses in charters about liability to
common army and common aid are made the pretext to impose
other secular burdens on church lands, cases of patronage are taken
to lay courts, pecuniary penalties imposed by church courts are now
forbidden by the magnates, married clergy are denied benefit of
clergy, persons are forbidden to have their cases committed to papal
judges delegate.[16]

The pretensions of the clerical order embodied here may just
possibly have been acknowledged by Alexander II and denied
by Alan Durward. But it is much more likely that the critical battle
between church and state was fought in the 1220s over a large
number of individual cases each presenting its own problems, and
that the victor, at least in substance if not in principle and appearances, had been the king. The renewed troubles of the 1250s would
then be an attempt by the clergy, after the removal of the king's
strong hand, to reoccupy the field they had lost thirty years
before. The subject is complex and this conclusion can be tentative
only, for as late as 1273 the pope sharply reproved the king for
taking patronage causes to lay courts. An investigation is required
not only of cases heard before judges delegate but also of the many
amicable compositions which probably mark the conclusion of
litigation in the lay *forum*. The shrill protestations of the church,
Scottish and Roman, are only one factor in the history of civil
justice, and they are by no means the most reliable guide down the
twisted path to the session of the fifteenth century.[17]

The main function of the legation of Ottobuono in the British
Isles between 1265 and 1268 (the pontificate also of Clement IV)
was to restore peace in England and to preach the crusade; he
discharged both with conspicuous success and has rightly been
characterised as a great churchman who, as pope for only one
month (1276), had no chance to give to the universal church the
talents he had displayed in England. That he was unpopular was

---

[16] Robertson, *Concilia*, 242–6; *Moray Registrum*, no. 260.
[17] Lord (T. M.) Cooper, *Select Scottish Cases of the XIII Century* (1944)
treats this subject. Its reports are interesting but a far more systematic approach
is required before valid conclusions can be drawn.

the inevitable fate of a legate. His dealings with Scotland, which he never visited, are related by the chronicler Bower and, but unfortunately, by no means clearly. In 1266 he asked the Scottish church for procurations at four merks from each parish kirk, double the usual figure. A royal refusal and appeal to Rome were backed by an ecclesiastical contribution of 2000 merks, but in the following year the clergy pacified the legate by paying him 'sixpence for each merk and fivepence for each merk to Cardinal Hubert'. The obscurity of this episode is matched by that of the circumstances in which the legate sought and was refused (by the king) entry to Scotland, and then sought and secured the presence of four Scottish prelates at his legatine council in London (1268). The importance of the canons of this council for English church order has already been mentioned; there is some evidence that they were known in Scotland and perhaps used in synodal legislation, but to what effect is unknown. Fordun states that the Scottish clergy rejected them but this seems less likely than that they were ignored. Ottobuono's services to the king of England included the levying of a tenth for three years imposed by Clement IV upon the English church for Henry III's benefit in 1266. This tax was to be extended to Scotland if King Alexander agreed, which he plainly did not do for compensation to Henry III was commanded in 1267. It seems possible that the grants of sixpence and fivepence on the merk (just over a fourteenth) were an escape from the tenth, paid to the legate and a papal official. Whatever the truth of this matter, there seems little doubt that demands of the Scottish church from pope, legate and king and corporate resistance by the church were all compelling it to a more frequent use of provincial assemblies.

A further provincial council was apparently held in 1273 to receive the papal summons to the Council of Lyons, and those who attended—their number is uncertain—had to bring back the unwelcome news of a crusading tenth for six years imposed upon the church. The papal collector for Scotland, master Boiamund de Vicci, traditionally known as Bagimond, was sent by another Scottish council back to the curia with a plea against the proposed revaluation of benefices but in vain, and probably from 1275 the clergy of Scotland paid taxation almost annually (when the exaction of arrears is allowed for) until the outbreak of war in 1296. Accounts for Bagimond's activities were drawn up about 1287 and fragments survive which show that by then some £18,000 had been collected, approximately a seventh of the amount for England, but that almost certainly there were still unpaid arrears. This tangle of arrears from clergy to sub-collectors, from them to collectors (and the pope thought to stimulate Bagimond by granting to the English collector a commission for Scotland) and from collectors to Italian bankers became too much for ecclesiastical business methods. About 1285 Bagimond had sent to Rome, on demand, accounts for all six years: that for Moray diocese shows not one case of unpaid arrears in six years. But when he went to the curia in 1287 this comforting mirage suddenly vanished. Apparently real accounts for only the first three years were available and those for Moray reveal that in 1285 he had optimistically multiplied the first year's takings sixfold, so that his 'account' had not even been a realistic budget. Early in 1282 he had sought to be recalled to the curia because his work was (he claimed) finished, but the pope sternly bade him do his duty, and curse for arrears. Unfortunately, the destination of the large sum collected remains obscure. From the beginning the crusading ardour of Edward I had been stimulated by the prospect not only of the English tenth but also of the Scottish one, and various bulls had been issued (one by the legate Ottobuono, now pope) which, had he actually left for the Holy Land, would have made it difficult for the Scots to deny him whatever was in Bagimond's deposit account. By 1283 opposition was mounting: Bagimond was accused of usury in lending out his funds and of refusing to pay the bankers. Alexander III had certainly forbidden the export of the deposit and had even arrested some bankers who sought to evade his regulation. In 1286, however, the king's strong hand was removed and the money may have been shifted to England, where doubtless it would help to pay for the Christian purposes of Edward I. When a renewed papal teind was imposed for six years in 1291 the Scots were reassessed by an English bishop and found themselves liable for a fifth of the amount due from England—and again the beneficiary would be Edward I. This background to the stand of churchmen against English occupation after 1296 should not be forgotten, but it should also be seen as the background to another, and institutional, development—that of regular provincial councils of the church.[18]

Canons uncertainly attributed to the later thirteenth century

[18] For Bagimond's taxation see *Scottish History Society Miscellany*, volumes v, vi, x, where the accounts are edited by Dr A. I. Dunlop and Charles Burns.

speak of absolution for despoiling the clergy 'by the Conservator of the Council' only; the oldest fragment of conciliar legislation, two leaves which seem to be of the same period, provide for annual councils and for one of the bishops to enforce the statutes between councils. He is not as yet conservator of the privileges of the church nor does he moderate the assembly; his office is an interim one only, concerned with ecclesiastical discipline when the council is not meeting. Since there is no evidence nor likelihood that the conservator was to usurp episcopal discipline in removing evils, his functions would seem to have been pre-eminently defence of the bishops and of ecclesiastical discipline, particularly against lay interference. Bower relates that in 1267 Bishop Gamelin of St Andrews came into conflict with Alexander III over this very issue by refusing the king's request (backed by seizure of episcopal property) to absolve a knight, John de Dunmore, who had been excommunicated in a quarrel with St Andrews Priory. The bishop, on the contrary, extended the excommunication to all who had counselled the king to his action and the king seems to have yielded at least to the extent of procuring an act of contrition from Dunmore. From episodes such as this, and perhaps even from this very case, the office of conservator of statutes could well have arisen, for the thirteenth-century canons which begin by defining the office end by insisting that 'if the secular power compel anyone to relax sentences by meddling with the possessions of the church then let the diocesan by authority of canon and council punish the person who offends thus'. A diocesan who ventured to such boldness would need the full support of his fellow bishops.

The financial demands of the papacy were common to England and Scotland, as was the clergy's resistance to them. Different, however, from Henry III's capacity to squeeze pope and clergy was the Scottish king's exclusion from the benefits of such proposed taxation and his consequent alignment with his clergy. Yet he could not forbid taxation, only export of the money, nor could the clergy refuse a grant, only delay it. Almost certainly, the clergy found themselves encouraged by the king to corporate (that is, conciliar) resistance and at the same time much weakened by the absence of an effective leader, an archbishop, and by the dependence of a 'special daughter' upon her mother church of Rome. In such circumstances the king might well have accepted the development of what the conservator in effect was: a rotating office of metropolitan, able to call successive provincial councils to meet the needs of the king as well as of the clerical order.

Provincial and legatine councils seem to have been of limited importance in Scotland, but there is reason to think that at least the council of the legate Otto in 1239 did stimulate the Scottish episcopate to diocesan synods and legislation such as the reform of the church seemed to demand. The evidence is clearest for David de Bernham, Bishop of St Andrews from 1240 until 1253, who had obtained his see after the quashing of another's election, almost certainly as a result of royal influence. David was of a family of Berwick burgesses and by 1225 had attended a university or universities long enough to become Master of Arts. Where and how he was supported is unknown but he returned to become a member of the familia of William Malvoisin, Bishop of St Andrews, for a decade. Between 1233 and 1235 he shifted his career into the royal service, the first cleric for many years to become the king's chamberlain, an appointment perhaps owed to his Berwick connections.[19] William de Bondington, the chancellor, who became bishop of Glasgow in 1233, probably gave David his first ecclesiastical preferment, the precentorship of Glasgow Cathedral. Unlike Bondington, who clung to his chancellorship as well as his bishopric, David resigned from the royal service on his promotion to a see and devoted his energies to his diocese and the church universal.

As bishop-elect he may have attended Otto's council in 1239. Within a year of his consecration he had set off with Bondington for an abortive council at Rome which took the pair as far as the Rhône valley; in 1245 he attended the Council of Lyons and his seal is appended to the final communiqué issued on 17 July. In May 1242 he held a synod for the archdeaconry of Lothian at Musselburgh at which were promulgated some thirty statutes regulating the life of the church. Their concern with discipline, decency, order and charity is not expressed in orderly fashion, though the manner of administering the sacraments is logically expounded. Monastic apostasy is condemned, but the statutes on a canonical life at parochial level tumble forth in a way which shows how numerous, pressing and intractable were the problems which faced a conscientious bishop there. Clerics must not keep wives or concubines nor trade, but above all they must be ordained and reside or must make adequate alternative provision for their benefices. That such

19 Below p. 495.

things needed saying is a measure of the distance between the church as it was and the standards to which it aspired.

That Bishop David took his responsibilities for these standards very seriously is borne out by the record he has left in his service-book of the discharge of a statute (*Basilicarum*) made in London in 1237 and presumably at Holyrood in 1239. Between 1240 and 1249 he carried out the formal consecration of 140 kirks (ninety of them between October 1241 and October 1243), out of some 300 in his diocese.[20] Such activity was not merely ceremonial, for it behoved the bishop to assure himself before consecration that each kirk was sound of roof and adequately provided with vestments, books, lights, chalice, paten and font, a task which David is unlikely to have shirked. It can be shown that he visited some kirks at least once before consecration and these were doubtless occasions for enquiry, examination and the ordering of remedy before consecration was granted. In the memory of his cathedral priory he was a relentless persecutor who laid harsh burdens upon them, but this may reflect his insistence that their kirks too should be decently repaired and served and not just milked to build an extravagant Augustinian cathedral. The parish kirk of Inchture, consecrated on 11 August 1243, was later seized by him from the priory (for reasons unknown but most likely because no incumbent was being provided) and given first as a benefice to keep his nephew William at Paris Univer-sity and then as a pension to the bishop of Aberdeen. He turned the hospital (always liable to vacancy, neglect and dilapidation) at Scotlandwell over to the Trinitarian order (which could more readily be held accountable), and so threatened other parochial revenues of the priory, as they claimed. The basis of their hostility, however, is most likely to have been his support for the kirk of St Mary of the Rock in their struggle with the priory to effect a permanent division of rights and revenues.

We have already remarked that at a provincial council of 1242 (held at Perth on 2 June) lay interference with teinds and ecclesiastical immunities was forbidden by the king.[21] It is likely that the first twenty-five chapters of the collected statutes of provincial councils were made on this occasion, for some are more generalised versions of the Musselburgh clauses dealing with ecclesiastical

[20] *Pontificale Ecclesiae S. Andreae*, ed. C. Wordsworth (1885), x–xx; *St Andrews Liber*, 28–39.
[21] Above p. 288.

decency. Others, however, reflected a wider range of problems. The minimum endowment of vicarages was fixed at ten merks, and provisions were made concerning entry to the monastic order, the appointment of confessors, intrusion into benefices without the bishop's consent, and other matters.[22]

Among men so different in their careers as David de Bernham, Clement the Dominican, and John de Cheam the Englishman, there is no easy generalisation about the thirteenth-century episcopate. Yet close investigation might suggest that unpopularity was a measure of effectiveness. The long struggle of Cheam with the canons of Glasgow over residence showed up a vice which was widespread in the thirteenth-century church: plurality and non-residence. The cosy family relationships and other forms of familiarity among those holding major benefices in the Scottish church by the end of the thirteenth century certainly show that the church was not dominated by a few aristocratic families but that there was room at the top for those with the talents fostered by the schoolroom. Through the schools those of moderate means furthered their careers; whether they furthered the spiritual life of the church is another question.

About 1105 Thor, a Lothian follower, perhaps an immigrant knight infeft of the king, described how the king 'gave me Ednam[23] deserted, which I occupied with his help and my own stock. And I built a church in honour of St Cuthbert, and this church I have given, with a ploughgate of land, to God and St Cuthbert and his monks[24] to be possessed for ever'. There was probably nothing unusual about the transactions save their being recorded, but there is warning of the care with which such pious words must be received in a later letter of Thor which makes it clear that King Edgar had chosen the dedication to St Cuthbert and given the ploughgate of land, presumably from Thor's fief. How far the early twelfth-century kings demanded of their barons and knights, particularly those newly infeft, that they should build and endow

---

[22] I am indebted to Dr D. E. R. Watt for lending me his biography of David de Bernham; I have also used for his career the thesis of Dr Marinell Ash, 'The Administration of the Diocese of St Andrews, 1202-1328' (University of Newcastle-upon-Tyne 1972), which is full of good things on the thirteenth-century church; publication is most desirable and I have restricted my debt to the career of this bishop. See now *Innes Review*, XXV (1974), 3–14.

[23] In Roxburghshire.          [24] Of Durham.

kirks on their lands, cannot now be known, but such stimulus may have been quite common. As episcopal property was sometimes raided by the king to infeft his new vassals, kirks established on episcopal estates passed to new owners and were recovered by bishops later in the twelfth century only with difficulty (and with restricted rights); but as a result of this recovery it is possible to distinguish the old-established from the new Brus-established kirks in Annandale (and similar cases elsewhere in the well-documented Glasgow diocese). The king and his vassals must often have seen such foundations as partial amends to the saints for the losses inflicted upon too-often vacant episcopal chairs. The reality and close interrelationship of the intercession of saints, the offering upon the altar, and the welfare of souls is written time and again into charters and we may not deny to the early twelfth-century generation a spiritual motive for its acceleration of the process of founding and endowing local kirks. In the large areas served by mother kirks or minsters, others were built sometimes as the chapel attached to the landlord's court and hall, sometimes as the kirk for a toun in which he had a strong proprietary interest. Always it was landowner and saint who met at the new altar as, with sod, stone, knife or charter the one gave to the other fabric and glebe, and when immediately a third party, the priest, was introduced into the relationship, he served two lords, the earthly one who gave him the kirk, and the heavenly one who received his intercessions. That the kirk was still the property of the landowner is true in the sense that he retained rights and duties in it while the priest was in no position socially or economically to challenge his command. But what had been given as alms could not rightfully be taken back, and the priest was perhaps already secure in a lifetime's possession of which he could not be deprived.

Thor acted with King Edgar and secured Earl David's approval, but three things are notably absent from his version of events: bishop, parish, teind. About 1150 Bishop Robert of St Andrews recorded an agreement between the mother church of Ednam and the chapel of Newton, whereby the new lords of Ednam kirk, the monks of Coldingham, would cause mass to be sung three days weekly and on most feasts at the chapel, but on two feasts at the mother kirk. If, however, the teinds of Newton should be diverted from Ednam, divine office was to cease at the chapel until it was reconciled (a euphemism for 'had disgorged the teinds') to the mother kirk. The part of the bishop in arranging this settlement is noteworthy evidence of the spread of the bishop's activity as judge throughout his diocese; but he is still sharing this function with the secular power, at least in a cause which was essentially about teinds.

Payment of teinds was general in western Europe by the eleventh century, and there was well-understood local custom about what was titheable as 'increase' or produce and what was not titheable as stock or capital. Growing crops, the year's offspring of animals, the yield of milk or its man-made products, all these were liable to be tithed, in accordance with biblical precept, for the benefit of the church, and more particularly of the local kirk, owned along with its priest by the landlord who might divert these offerings into his own barns. Since the tenth century the state had enforced payment of tithes in England, and even where lay authority was more fragmented, they were still rigorously exacted. Each church drew these offerings from a defined area, its parish—a word which could also still be used of his diocese by the bishop. It is striking that in the gifts made before 1124 by Scottish kings and Earl David to monasteries there is mention neither of kirks (which may have been comprehended as secular possessions within the manor or toun or estate of X, nor of teinds, but that from the beginning of his reign David I systematically diverted a tenth of his own income to major churches, and then gave burgh kirks and their teinds to monasteries. Soon after his death his successors were referring to the payment of teinds according to King David's decision (*assisa*) and to a method of enforcement attributed to his time.

It seems certain that David I greatly extended, even if he did not completely generalise, the payment of teinds to local kirks within his realm, by making them enforceable by king, sheriff and landowner. By that stroke he effectively created the parochial system, for the parish could soon be defined as a district paying teinds to a local kirk; the mother church (a term still used of Ednam by Bishop Robert) became the parish kirk, endowed not merely with the ploughgate of priest's glebe but also with the compulsory 'offerings' of the tenth of all produce by the faithful. The parish priest had not only a plough for his furlongs, which made him a peasant among peasants, but also a barn for the teind sheaves of his flock, and a purse for the sale-price of their teinds of livestock. And these made him not only a Christian minister but also an economic burden upon all who worked the land. Fiercely

he defended the parochial rights of his kirk, pitting himself against
those landowners who sought to carve out parishes for their chapels;
he would yield mass and the congregation on most days but would
insist (as Ednam did over Newton) on the right to both on key feast
days, in token of his right to teinds. Thus teinds slowed down the
fragmentation of over-large parishes, but they could not halt it
entirely. Chapels and chapel priests with the support of a landowner could make a good case to the bishop for receiving at least
some teinds, especially where the priest of the parish kirk no
longer received them. For teinds had also become the enemy of
the parochial system by making kirks worth-while property in the
pockets of others.

Most grants of a kirk to an ecclesiastical corporation, such as
that of Ednam, were intended as a grant of the patronage, of the
appointment of the parson. But there was only a thin line between
this right and the right to become a parson, the corporation diverting
the revenues to its own uses (*in proprios usus*) and making other provision for the cure of souls. This 'appropriation' of kirks may have
begun as early as the grant of Ednam to St Cuthbert, but the formula
'I grant the kirk of X' could have been either a grant of patronage
or an appropriation.[25] The church struggled, from 1179 generally
successfully, to insist that a layman could grant only patronage,
and that appropriation was a matter requiring the bishop's approval,
but by that date many kirks had already been given by David I
and his grandsons as a means of sustaining the revival in the monastic and secular church which they sought. It is true that Cistercian
houses were not as yet allowed to receive such endowments, but
they were far outnumbered by other monasteries and by the
cathedrals for which a fitting maintenance must be provided. The
numbers of kirks so appropriated are strikingly high: Arbroath
Abbey when founded in 1178 possessed nine kirks (one of them in
England) but by 1214 the number had risen to thirty-five. Lindores
Abbey was endowed by its founder, David, Earl of Huntingdon,
with ten kirks, all that he had in gift in Scotland; Glasgow Cathedral
had some thirty-five by *c*. 1200; and similar numbers were held by
major abbeys such as Kelso, Paisley and Holyrood by the mid-
thirteenth century. It is likely that by the end of that century the
endowment of abbeys and remote cathedral chapters such as Ross
and Caithness had brought the proportion of kirks appropriated to

[25] F. Barlow, *Durham Jurisdictional Peculiars* (1950) ch. III.

over half of all parishes. In general the royal house had been generous to the religious, bishops and private laymen (some of whose gifts may be disguised sales) to cathedral chapters. The greatest spate of such appropriations came in the second half of the twelfth century, when rising productivity made teinds a gilt-edged investment.[26]

Charters of appropriation occasionally reserved the life-rent of the benefice to the priest in occupation, which makes it clear that his revenues would go in time to his corporate successor. Other appropriations were probably made when the priest died and the kirk was vacant. From 1179 the Third Lateran's decree that episcopal consent was needed was always observed and a few years later Jocelyn, Bishop of Glasgow, was directed by Lucius III (1181–5) to fill vacant appropriated, and other, kirks within three months—and it is likely that Jocelyn requested this bull to strengthen his hand in dealing with greedy appropriators and patrons. In truth, the episcopate was not so much reluctant as powerless to improve a situation which was deteriorating rapidly, for of the appropriators only Augustinian and Premonstratensian canons were able and occasionally willing to serve the parishes whose teinds they drew. It is thought that no priest was provided in some parishes and a 'mercenary' one in others but the degree of neglect is unknown. Characteristically, the complaints we hear of are not normally those of bereft parishioners but of the 'mercenary' priests, now called vicars because they served 'instead of' (*vice*) a parson, at the inadequacy and uncertainty of their income.

Historians may have too readily taken at face value the despairing cries of the 'mercenary' chaplains and have judged the thirteenth-century monastic appropriator by the behaviour of his sixteenth century successor. Thus the convent at Durham provided a chaplain for the parishioners at Coldingham, where the priory nave was the parish kirk, but in 1214, because this was inadequate and souls were thereby in danger, a second chaplain was added. One was parochial chaplain; the other helped him and said masses daily for the dead with *Commendacio, Placebo* and *Dirige,* and specifically he prayed for master Roger de Melsonby, canon of Beverley, 'who gave many goods to the house of Coldingham,' for deceased monks, the monks' fathers and mothers, their debtors,

²⁶ I. B. Cowan, 'The Religious and the Cure of Souls in Medieval Scotland', *Recs. Sc. Ch. Hist. Soc.*, xiv (1960–2), 215–29.

and all the deceased. The two lived together 'in one house and at one table', were given each day three loaves (a monk's loaf, a knight's loaf and an oaten loaf), and as many dishes as two monks would receive, two 'justices' of ale and two stones of salt at Easter. The second chaplain had for his 'reward' ten shillings from the baker's oven at Old Cambus and four shillings from the rent of a toft. The parochial chaplain's fee is not given since it had long been secured on some similar revenue.[27] Doubtless, to these chaplains the lot of the monks was a source of continuing envy, and there would be much complaining about the chaplains' miserable lot. But the parish was provided with the offices and the chaplains were not really badly off.

The church responded to the uncertain lot of such men at first piecemeal, then generally by a statute of the Fourth Lateran Council in 1215 for 'a perpetual vicar canonically instituted who . . . should have a fit portion of the profits of the church'. Their hand strengthened from outside, the bishops at an ecclesiastical council defined this portion in Scotland as ten merks and pursued elaborate vicarage settlements with the religious corporations of their diocese. Because the importance of commodities (for example, fish, flax) varied in different parts of the country, great care had to be taken in the definition of what was assigned to the vicar, who might otherwise delay or refuse payment to the appropriator. But in general, and with many minor variations, the agricultural teinds (called 'garbal', that is, of corn) were assigned to the appropriator, the parson or *rector*, while the pastoral teinds (called 'lesser' and including milk, cheese, wool, lambs, calves) went to the vicar. Offerings by the faithful were probably insignificant except in burgh churches but together with the lesser teinds seem to have been included in the term 'altarage', used also loosely for the vicar's portion. Often the adequacy of that portion was contested even when it had been settled and had become 'perpetual', but the validity of such complaints in the thirteenth century is doubtful. Poor kirks, in Ross or Argyll, would have very poor vicars, but the evidence of Bagimond's valuation does not suggest that most vicars were as yet poorly paid. On the other hand, that valuation also reveals that the parish of Ednam as given by Thor to St Cuthbert had now become three parishes: Ednam, Stichil and Nenthorn (with Newton). The objections of Coldingham Priory (for St Cuthbert) to division and

[27] *Coldingham Correspondence*, 239–40.

parochial status for dependent chapels had stemmed from the
threat to an appropriator's teinds. When these teinds had to be
divided, however, Coldingham, secure in its greater teinds from the
whole original parish, was willing to recognise the dependent
chapels, each doubtless served like Ednam by a 'mercenary' priest,
as vicarages receiving the lesser teinds from the divided parish.[28]
It is likely that many dependent chapels held in bondage by a
parish kirk anxious not to lose any teinds were emancipated and
received parochial status in this way, for the number of recognised
parishes certainly grew markedly in the thirteenth century. Of
course, the resultant vicarages were small, but their pastoral care
should have been more effective.[29]

The burgh kirk of Berwick, appropriated to Coldingham Priory,
had a vicarage revenue of 20 merks and we are allowed one glimpse
of that settlement in the mid-thirteenth century, by which time
the twenty merks were secured on the white (that is other than
salmon) fish teinds of Berwick. In 1263 the prior and convent of
Durham (who allowed Coldingham to draw the parsonage teinds
but not to exercise patronage of the vicarage) notified the bishop of
St Andrews of the death of master John de Barton, the vicar, and
presented master Patrick de Hartlepool 'to the vicarage of our
church of Berwick, namely to the teind of white fish'. The reason
for this phrase, so revealing of the appropriator's neglect of cure
of souls, is not far to seek, for Patrick, who happened to be brother
of the official of Durham, had already appointed proctors to take all
steps needful to secure any benefice given to him while he studied at
Cambridge.[30] Perhaps it did not greatly matter that Berwick never
saw its vicar for several years on end, for there would be several
altars and chaplains paid by the gild and perhaps by individuals.

The role of the episcopate in the moves to provide a more
effective cure of souls was of great importance, but the papacy had
also played a key part. The church had come a long way from the
days of lay proprietorship (and piety) in the early twelfth century,
defining carefully what it meant by parson, vicar, parish and teinds
and regulating their relationships. Over a century the church had

---

[28] For a presentation by the prior and convent as parson and patron to the
vicarage of Ednam, *Durham Annals and Documents*, ed. F. Barlow (Surtees Soc.
1945), 157–8.

[29] I. B. Cowan, 'Vicarages and the Cure of Souls in Medieval Scotland', *Recs.
Sc. Ch. Hist. Soc.*, xvi (1967), 111–27.

[30] *Durham Annals*, ed. Barlow, 156–7.

effectively obtained control of the use of its own parochial revenues and had limited the layman to a right of patronage of an un-appropriated kirk (that is, the minority of kirks). A patron should present to the bishop a candidate for a vacant benefice; the bishop could not refuse to induct unless the candidate was grotesquely unsuitable, and often chose not to refuse even when the candidate was. The early twelfth-century church had probably been staffed by married priests who had inherited a kirk, or who had been given one by a related landlord. The stages of ordination were not care-fully observed, and even where a priest was fully ordained his literacy was as open to question as his celibacy. During the twelfth century the bishops in effect made whores of the wives, and bastards of the children, of parish priests in their search for a celibate and literate clergy. If to us literacy (that is, education, whence under-standing and compassion) seems more important than continence, the twelfth-century church had a different priority: for incontinence was sinful (and illiteracy was not) and the priesthood could not discharge its widening responsibilities for lay conduct in the sight of God if its own behaviour was maculate, and hence a danger to souls. The clerical wife and mother was ousted by the clerical housekeeper and mother; the bishops set their hands to further improvement but failed to make much impact.

At the same time it is likely that educational standards for ordination became rather higher. The growth of the universities brought a crop of masters of arts to help episcopal administration, and there were doubtless many others who benefited from the primary schooling available even in the twelfth century at cathedrals and in burghs. Again, it was the schools of Oxford, Cambridge and Paris which posed a threat to parochial life, for many scholars were maintained there by diversion of the revenues of parishes mean-while served by a 'mercenary' priest.

William de Bernham, the nephew of bishop David, was parson of Inchture while at Paris and Oxford. He pursued his revenues by post like a true remittance man with bitter persistence. To his chaplain: 'I have had only 9 chalders of flour, 39 bolls of oats and 4 of wheat, and teinds of Inchture worth 9 merks have been adjudged to the rustics of the place against all justice. . . . I sent you my letters of attorney to seek my debts' (amounting to over 18 merks). Osbert the clerk paid him £4 annually for the altarage of the chapel of Kinnaird in the parish, an arrangement made for three years with guarantors for payment, and collected by the chaplain, who kept half a merk for his trouble. 'Moreover the year is almost over for which [a local small landowner] should have paid me four merks [as teinds] as he promised on oath.' Cheated by the 'traitor' who sold his garbal teinds for him, William's trouble was his absence and the claims of the bishop of Aberdeen to a pension of 60 merks, so that his careful arrangements for farming out the teinds to local small landowners broke down. Such farming was probably common, especially where the parson or vicar was non-resident, in spite of the fact that it was condemned by canon law; whoever lost through crop-failures or poor prices, it was unlikely to be the farmer. William arranged for the vicar of neighbouring Longforgan to send his rents: 'don't accept a penny unless it is monetised [current] silver or, if you must, weighed silver, but charge a [commission on] exchange. You know that for the half year just ended I am owed 16 merks from Inchture and 30 from Kinneff, except 5 which you are to give to my brother, and I am owed 10 merks from Arbroath of which you are to give 5 to my lady mother. Don't delay to send the money and remember to tell me how much the spiritual revenues of Inchture amount to.' Once he had to excuse himself for welshing on the price of a horse, because his money had not come forward, and on another occasion he pawned his books to go to the papal curia. He could not find anyone (fellow Scots?) to share his lodgings in Paris, his money was spurned as 'weak'—of inadequate silver content—and, as he told his uncle the bishop, 'I have lost the best of my horses on which I had hoped to realise a good price. Please send me money.' Though the loss of his horses seems a relative deprivation only, one may sympathise with William over the delays and tribulations of the banking system, over the unreliability of all his agents except Gilbert the Chaplain, Robert the cook, and Osbert, over his care for his mother (who also got his begging letters), but our greater sympathy should surely be reserved for the poor rustics of Inchture, caught between the upper millstone of William de Bernham and his farmers and the nether one of the bishop of Aberdeen. It was small consolation to them that a chaplain was provided for a few merks annually to say mass so that their parson could study art and law under fashionable masters in foreign countries, living well with his *socii* on bread, meat, peas, mustard, salt, soup and wine.[31]

[31] N. R. Ker and W. A. Pantin, 'Letters of a Scottish Student', *Oxford*

William de Bernham and the few like him were accepted without rancour compared with the strength of feeling over attempts to give benefices to absentee foreigners. The generally blamed villain of this piece was the mid-thirteenth-century papacy, which responded weakly to pressures by curial officials and some other clergy, notably at the universities, for benefices, by granting letters of provision conferring a benefice upon the suppliant. Yet the papacy was weak rather than malevolent; the safeguards it wrote into provisions about suitability seemed adequate but gave no real protection to the faithful from the educated and determined benefice hunter. When Innocent IV gave William Wishart an indult to hold his archdeaconry and benefices with yet another benefice worth up to 100 merks annually (and few benefices were worth so much) he weakened the whole fabric of the church; but all he gave was permission to acquire and Wishart must do the rest. Such indults and more straightforward provisions were useless if the lawful patron presented a suitable candidate in due time to the bishop, but if there were delays or other flaws, the person provided would be harder to resist, most of all where the patron was not a layman, but an ecclesiastical corporation or even the bishop himself. He could scarcely ignore the papal bull, however much he disliked it, and in consequence it is likely that provisions trenched most heavily upon ecclesiastical patronage. Their consequences were a rapid spread of the abuse of pluralism in kirks with cure of souls, which reached its height in the thirteenth century among vicars as well as parsons, and an exaggerated hostility to the few foreigners who were thought to be taking over the church in Scotland.

So much of the evidence for the medieval church is of the ceaseless pursuit of rents, teinds and benefices by ecclesiastics of all ranks that one is tempted to forget the office for which benefice was given; it was a hard world for the exercise of such office. A child would probably die before baptism at the kirk font and the priest must hurry through the night to save the soul of the newly born or to hear the last confession of the dying. Marriage was made by man and woman taking each other as spouses; solemnisation before the priest might or might not follow when fertility was proven. Confession was probably rare, for communion certainly was, and we may doubt if mass was really said three times weekly at the chapel

*Formularies*, ed. H. E. Salter, W. A. Pantin, H. G. Richardson (Oxford Historical Soc.), ii (1942), 472–91, especially p. 491.

of Newton. The dead were buried with a distribution of alms for the soul which could produce a drunken riot in the kirkyard. The parish priest should keep rain out of his chancel and water in his font. There was little time for spirituality when the priest must plough his acre, and perhaps little love for a spiritual estate so desperately committed to the worship of the tenth penny.

Was the church more 'effective' in 1286 than in 1124? As a political power in Scotland, undoubtedly it was, but this may be attributed to its greater wealth. It may also have achieved a stronger hold over the minds of ordinary men, but on this there is little evidence. Many landowners showed their devotion by building kirks, whose romanesque remains are still found in some Scottish villages, inconspicuous now but once surely outstanding among the huts of the cottars. Inside, the aids to devotion now accepted in a Roman Catholic country would be far scantier, and gifts of wax suggest that the faithful did not regularly provide candles at altar or shrine. The homily of the priest was more likely to be an annual than a weekly event and the men of the village can have had little comprehension of what went on at font or altar. The exception to this gloomy picture might have been found in the major towns, where schools are occasionally mentioned, schools which cannot have been wholly ecclesiastical in the training which they gave and which probably produced a literate urban class. Most burgh kirks were appropriated by the king (as Perth to Dunfermline Abbey, Edinburgh to the order of St Lazarus), but townsmen seem to have obtained effective control of them at an early date and were perhaps better served by and more responsive to the priesthood than the rural populace.

Thus it was presumably conventional piety, his king's generosity to St Thomas at Arbroath, and the eloquence of the vicar of St John's kirk which in 1208 sent a citizen, William, from Perth, on the pilgrimage to the tomb of St Thomas Becket at Canterbury, to secure remission for some of the sins which had made him a well-off baker. Whether he went by land or sea to London is unknown but from there he took the road later made famous by Chaucer. On Watling Street, outside Chatham, he was set upon, robbed and murdered; his body was taken for burial to the cathedral church of (appropriately, enough) St Andrew at Rochester. For a generation the monks of Rochester had watched pilgrims going past their doors laden with offerings for the shrine of St Thomas and returning considerably lighter; now their patience was rewarded. William, it was discovered, had been a man of un-gild-like saintliness who gave to the poor every tenth loaf he had baked; William, it was discovered, had been bound for the parvenu Canterbury shrine only on his way to the Holy Places themselves; William, it was discovered, performed such miraculous works in death as the purity of his life inevitably justified. And so in time the pilgrims to his tomb paid for a new aisled choir at Rochester and in 1256 William was canonised. He is the least known but by no means the least interesting of the small company of medieval Scottish saints.

About 1230 the new religious orders, the Franciscans and Dominicans, came to Scotland and were endowed by the king at the towns where their evangelism was likely to be particularly effective. The Franciscans had houses before 1250 at Berwick, Haddington and Roxburgh; the Dominicans enjoyed greater royal favour. Their mission to England had progressed very slowly in the years 1217–30, when only five houses were established. In that last year the first English chapter of the order was held and was perhaps responsible for sending a mission to Scotland under Clement, probably a Scot, certainly a friend (very likely at Oxford) of the great teacher St Edmund of Abingdon. Clement's rapid promotion to a bishopric (1233, the first Dominican bishop in Britain) must be a mark of his influence over Alexander II, further testified by the conveyance of royal town residences to the order as sites for their houses at Perth and Edinburgh. Other Dominican houses existed by 1250 at Berwick, Ayr, Glasgow, Stirling, Aberdeen, Elgin and Inverness. The preponderance of the Dominican order, which emphasised preaching, teaching and hence learning, may have been beneficial in that a sufficiency of friars existed to support theological schools at Perth and Ayr (presumably ended by the Wars of Independence), the nearest thing to a university available in Scotland.[32] The only scholar of originality produced by Scotland before 1300 was John of Duns in Berwickshire, who entered the Franciscan order perhaps at Berwick, but whose career was effectively outside Scotland.[33] In

[32] *Chron. Melrose*, 144. William Comyn was *lector* of the Dominicans of Perth. The pope called him a regent in the faculty of theology in the Dominican house at Perth. He became bishop of Brechin in 1275; Theiner, *Vet. Mon.*, no. CCLXII. For Ayr see *Paisley Registrum*, 164.

[33] Nothing is known of John Duns Scotus' origins or life in Scotland apart from what his name tells us. Any secondary work which purports to recount his early life is relying upon the seventeenth-century forgeries of Fr Brockie.

truth the kingdom lacked the intellectual centres which might have held Duns or attracted other scholars in the way Oxford and Paris did. There were no great thinkers just as there were no great men of spirituality in medieval Scotland.

*Addendum to 1978 impression.* I was unjustified in doubting the saying of mass where it was prescribed, as at Newton (pp. 305–6), and in describing the homily as more likely annual than weekly (p. 306). A more sensitive analysis would acknowledge the assiduity of many parish priests and the devotion of the faithful, especially women.

# 12

# THE LAND

In the absence of relevant evidence it is wildly misleading to guess at a figure for the population of 'medieval' Scotland. The significant evidence from England and north-western Europe generally points to a population increase at least in the three centuries after A.D. 1000, uncertain and probably uneven in pace, but nonetheless a significant factor in social and economic change. About 1300 the population of England or France was probably as high as it had ever been or was to be again until the late eighteenth century; whether the population of Scotland was half a million or a million at the same date is unknown but population declined after the mid-fourteenth century, so that the very concept of a 'medieval' figure is nonsense, obscuring the important characteristics of change, its speed and its relationship to other factors, most notably the ability of the aggregate wealth of the country to grow and hence to sustain continued demographic rise.

It seems generally accepted that a climatic optimum was reached in western Europe between 1000 and 1300 and, while archaeological evidence has not confirmed directly that it affected Scotland also (for example by raising the upper forest limit), such changes would not usually be halted at national boundaries. Even if the balance of diet was not improved by the growing of more varied crops, higher mean and average temperatures should have improved the fecundity of the soil, and hence supported just that increase in population which these centuries reveal.[1] The simplest

[1] H. H. Lamb, *The Changing Climate* (1966) chapters 6 and 7; E. Le Roy Ladurie, *Times of Feast, Times of Famine: a History of Climate since the year 1000*, trans. Barbara Bray (1971).

indicator of increasing population is increasing cultivation, the use of better ploughs and the ploughing of more land.

Archaeology might also be more revealing about cultivation implements, or about the age of those already known. Quartzite pebbles worn convex and heavily striated across the worn face, found in the Border counties, the Lothians, Bute and Shetland, mostly in fairly low-lying ground, postulate the use there of a heavy wooden plough (into which the pebbles were embedded) with mould-board, probably before the fourteenth century and perhaps since Viking times. A remarkable document of 1162×1189 provides that the brethren of the hospital of Lauder might send their ploughs to the lord's smith who 'shall make all the irons of their ploughs and those things of iron which pertain to their ploughs'—presumably for the traces or harness.[2] This probably implies the use of a wheeled plough such as is commonly associated with communal ploughing, and an eight-ox team or its equivalent; whether it also implies long rigs in large fields is an open question, and we are in any case now taught to beware any simple equation of plough-types with field-shapes and soil conditions, for in agriculture there was an infinitely variable response to local conditions, traditional practices putting up stubborn resistance to change.

The sources speak not of the plough, but of the ploughgate, the land cultivable by a plough and team of eight oxen in a year. The eight-ox team is suggested by grants of pasture for that number in areas as far apart as Roxburghshire, Moray, Argyll and Lennox[3] and it is likely that such teams were widely used. In 1962 the scholarly world was presented with a powerful argument—the evidence was a good deal less powerful—that horses were taking over the plough from oxen in the twelfth and thirteenth century and that this was directly connected with the change to a triennial rotation of crops and to a three field system.[4] Unfortunately, there are weak links in the chain of this argument which could not in any case be tested on the limited evidence available for Scotland; its premise is unsound—oxen were overwhelmingly in use as draught animals in both England and Scotland throughout the Middle Ages. But not

---

[2] A. Fenton, 'Early Cultivating Implements in Scotland,' *Proc. Soc. Antiq. Scot.* xcvi (1962–3), 278–9; *Tools and Tillage*, ii (1972), 50–1; *Dryburgh Liber*, 269.

[3] *Kelso Liber*, no. 367; *Moray Reg.* no. 37; *Paisley Registrum*, 126, 212.

[4] L. White, *Medieval Technology and Social Change*, Oxford, 1962.

exclusively so. The team of six oxen and two horses is attested for England and something similar may well have been used in parts of Scotland. The argument that horses were not generally adopted for drawing the plough because the horse was a much more expensive source of power surely has the corollory that where a horse was kept (as a cart-horse or pack-horse) it would be good economics to yoke it to the plough also. The problem needs further investigation, but there is surely some evidence for the use of a mixed team of oxen and horses in the grazings for sheep, ten or twelve oxen and four horses found as far apart as Mow in Roxburghshire and Garvock in Mearns and in other not infrequent grants of pasture for *animalia* (cattle or oxen) and horses.[5] The point is of some importance, since even the partial use of plough horses argues some change in agricultural techniques: perhaps longer and straighter furrows were possible, or perhaps the ploughing of poorer land, broken out from the grazings, capable only of producing oats, was possible only when some of the draught animals were horses fed on oats and husks, rather than oxen pastured on the grazing. The horse before the plough, then, is not a negligible change, but he is a modification of the traditional eight-ox team, probably to be linked with an expansion of arable.[6]

The common use of the traditional eight-ox team or of a modified version of it is most likely where the land unit of the ploughgate (or carrucate) is commonly made up of eight oxgangs (or bovates). Thus, although the ploughgate is widely distributed throughout thirteenth-century Scotland, and even occurs in Moray, the oxgang is of more limited but more significant distribution: it is found in the regions of 'vill' or toun where land is described as rigs (rarely), acres, oxgangs or ploughgates lying in the 'territory' of a named toun. Such phraseology is used so commonly in Lothian that this was clearly a zone in which there was a common pattern of cultivation, traceable to the early twelfth century when it was evidently not new. Each toun—and in this zone the translation 'village' would not be misleading—consisted of tofts and crofts (sometimes called *maisura* in earlier documents), peasant holdings with house or cottage and a small piece of land for special cultivation,

---

[5] *Kelso Liber*, no. 157; *ibid*, ii, pp. 458, 463, where the word *afros* or *affros* means plough-horses; *Arbroath Liber*, i, no. 314.

[6] This very tentative paragraph was suggested by J. Z. Titow, *English Rural Society, 1200-1350* (London, 1969), 38-40.

for barn or byre; near the toun was its 'territory', the arable and meadow.[7]

The unit of superficial measurement which was measured upon the ground was the acre, whose origins as a unit of arable did not prevent its being used as a superficial measure generally. Thus David I gave to Kelso Abbey 'in Sprouston a ploughgate *and three acres of meadow*'.[8] These phrases suggest not only that the acre was independent of arable, but also that the ploughgate was an abstraction, a conventional number of acres, so that a group of tofts producing a plough team might have ten more acres than that conventional number. Similarly, when Holyrood Abbey acquired St Cuthbert's kirk at Edinburgh with its dependencies, the chapel of Corstorphine had two oxgangs and six acres, that of Liberton two oxgangs only, suggesting that while each was endowed with enough land to require a quarter of the time of a ploughteam (and to produce two oxen for that team), the surface measurement of arable at Corstorphine in fact showed a total acreage yielding six acres in addition to two conventional oxgangs.[9]

The relationship of acres to large units is already hinted at in the early twelfth century, when David I gave to Holyrood Abbey the kirk of Airth with twenty-six acres (equal to the two oxgangs of the dependencies of St Cuthbert's kirk), and 'fifty-two acres of the land of Dalkeith between the wood and the open land', which is to say, apparently, fifty-two acres some of which are open or arable but the rest to be broken out from the woodland;[10] a relationship between the acreage and the plough-team is likely in such circumstances. It is explicit in Geoffrey de Percy's grant in 1152–3 to Kelso Abbey of a ploughgate in Heton (Roxburghshire) of five score and four acres;[11] this assumption that 104 acres make a ploughgate is widespread throughout south-eastern Scotland in the twelfth and thirteenth centuries[12] and carries the corollary that thirteen acres make an oxgang.

When the estates of Coldingham Priory were surveyed and

---

[7] An excellent discussion of field systems with a good chapter on Scotland appeared after this chapter was written: *Studies of Field Systems in the British Isles*, ed. A. R. H. Baker and R. A. Butlin (Cambridge, 1973).

[8] Lawrie, *E.S.C.*, no. CXCIV.

[9] Lawrie, *E.S.C.*, no. CLIII.

[10] Lawrie, *E.S.C.*, nos. CLIII, CLX.

[11] Lawrie, *E.S.C.*, no. CCLI.

[12] See for example, *Newbattle Registrum*, no. 38, where one ploughgate and five acres were exchanged for 110 acres.

extended about 1300, however, the realities of agrarian life could not be concealed: there were certainly thirteen acres to an oxgang at the chief touns of Ayton, Lumsden, Coldingham, Old Cambus and at West Renton, but at Swinton there were thirteen and a half acres in an oxgang, at Fishwick twelve and a half, at Edrom ten, at Lower Ayton fourteen, at Flemington fourteen, at Renton eight.[13] These variations represent the maturing of the village communities under the influence of population increase, the availability of new arable, the demands of the landlord, and they are not to be regarded as unique to eastern Berwickshire. It is likely that the conveyancing clerk's uniform ploughgate of 104 acres concealed the reality of plough-teams co-operatively ploughing the non-fallow part of between 60 and 120 acres annually, in the zone in which acres, oxgangs and ploughgates are recorded in charters.

What is that zone? Most clearly and without evidence of other agrarian arrangements, the south-east from Forth to Tweed. In the late twelfth and thirteenth centuries, however, the oxgang is also widely distributed from the Forth to the border of Mar; thus the abbey of Lindores received an oxgang in the donor's manor of For-gandenny (southern Perthshire), but the detail suggests that nine of the thirteen acres were assessed rather than measured on the ground. The same abbey acquired an oxgang in the toun of Newtyle (in Angus) not, it seems, scattered rigs but acres lying together, as a later grant of an acre 'below that oxgang' bears out.[11] In or just before 1214, Arbroath Abbey acquired two oxgangs called Rath in the 'territory' (arable) of Catterline on the sea coast of the Mearns as perambulated. Yet there was evidently dispute over the land, which a few years later was given again as 'two oxgangs in the territory of Catterline, namely seven acres of land joined and bounding with their land called Rath on the north and nineteen acres next to and joined to these seven acres on the sea shore to the east, namely within that *cultura* (arable or field) called *Treiglas* as they were perambulated by the sheriff' and others.[15] These oxgangs each contained thirteen acres, but they were evidently acres conjoined or consolidated in two parcels whose bounds could be walked round; the acres first acquired had a name, *Rath,* and on the second occasion were part of arable with a name. These circumstances are

[13] *Coldingham Correspondence,* no. LXVII, pp. lxxv–c.
[14] *Lindores Chartulary,* nos. LXVIII, XXXVII, XXXIX.
[15] *Arbroath Liber,* i, nos. 67, 124.

not found in south-eastern Scotland and suggest that, despite the use of the acre, we are concerned with different agricultural arrangements, with rigs scattered through large fields in the south, with acres lying together in smaller fields in the northern zone.

Unfortunately, this can stand only as a generalisation to which there were many local modifications. Thus the best early evidence (in a charter of Malcolm IV) of rigs 'scattered about the field' goes on to consolidate the holding 'in one piece' for greater convenience, without making it clear whether this holding was to be in the existing fields or newly broken out. The abbey of Newbattle, late in the twelfth century, received a half-ploughgate which was perambulated and marked out by stones as well as by an existing stone cross, ditch, highway and stream; significantly this land, which was evidently consolidated, was described as lying not in the 'territory' of a village (that is, scattered among the present rigs) but in the donor's fief of (West) Fortune (East Lothian). A little later the same abbey received another half-ploughgate only a few miles distant 'called Southrig in the tenement of South Hailes, land which lies divided into four places, as the stones placed for boundaries in these places bear witness.'[16] We seem to be treating in the first case of land still unploughed but intended for the plough, in the second of rigs dispersed across the ploughed 'territory' of the village.

Was this territory divided into fields, two or three in number and enclosed by hedge and/or ditch; were the fields themselves made up of strips whose length and line was dictated by contours and by the length of furrow which the team could plough? Certainly there were hedges and ditches, for not only do the sources refer to them, but the practice of livestock husbandry would make them absolutely essential. But it is doubtful whether each field was a continuous expanse of ploughed land broken only by the balks between holdings.

Old Cambus in Berwickshire, a dependent toun of the shire of Coldingham as granted by Edgar and David I to St Cuthbert had its own mill and, therefore, arable; its territory lay below Penmanshiel moor on ground sloping northwards to the sea or westwards to the Pease Burn, called in the charters *Aksideburn*. Early in the thirteenth century much of it was evidently held in demesne by the monks, since the earl of Dunbar gave them the right to drive the mill by the burns of *Akside* and *Elmedene* 'as long as they hold the

[16] *Newbattle Registrum*, nos. 107, 77.

toun of Old Cambus in their own demesne'.[17] But the monks were not the only landowners, for David de Quixwood made provision for his brother with seven acres 'in the field of Old Cambus', in eight amounts of between 1½ acres and 1½ roods scattered in *Langedales* (Langwards), on *Stele,* in *Heseldale,* in *Mideop,* in *Oggeslaudale* (Hogslaw dale) at the wood, under *Dailing,* in *Lange-toftes,* at *Brerilaue* rood. He gave twenty-six acres to Coldingham Priory with two parts of six acres and the rest in pieces of between four acres and half an acre. In another charter he described the boundaries by the *Aksideburn* of 'all my land with wood, in the field of Old Cambus', exchanged with the priory for two oxgangs at Coldingham; apparently this was a single tract of land, the arable of which was presumably divided into rigs. The priory of Coldingham acquired not only all these lands but also the half-ploughgate given to a leper hospital by the same David, apparently in order to extend its forest or hunting coverts, from which David was to take only four cartloads of stakes and wattles for building.[18] It is significant that a number of the acres are at places with *-dale* and *-law* names which must have been formed after Scandinavian settlements in the tenth century made these common elements in northern English speech. Thus we are again dealing with an area of cultivation which had been extended in very recent centuries. The names quoted show that oak, elm, hawthorn and hazel had once flourished in the places sheltered from the salt winds of the North Sea. While the modern map reveals some of the *-law* names still attached to hills, the burns run through steepsided valleys called cleughs (represented in charters by *-clow* names); it has not been possible to identify a single *-dale* name, and all seem to have been lost, presumably after eighteenth-century agricultural reorganisation; for it seems most likely that *-dale* was a hollow or slope, sometimes cleared of bushes and trees, on which arable was practised.

At Ayton land lay 'in the fields of the said village namely in Faulaueslat towards the north';[19] here as at Quixwood arable seems to be identified by lying not in a single north field but in some smaller group of furlongs with its own name, and making up the territory (here exceptionally called 'fields') of the toun. The

[17] Raine, *North Durham,* no. CXX.
[18] Raine, *North Durham,* nos. CLXXIX–CLXXXVI.
[19] Raine, *North Durham,* no. CXVII.

management of such acres must, however, have imposed at least a grouping for the needs of crop rotation, a subject on which we are almost wholly ignorant even in the well-documented thirteenth century. In the haughs by the Tweed at Paxton, Coldingham Priory received a half-ploughgate made up of two oxgangs of 'wheat-land' and two of 'oats-land', phrases which indicate a two-crop rotation with no fallowing presumably because silt-deposits kept the land in good heart.[20] It would follow that where fallowing was necessary, as it usually was, land would be under oats, under wheat, or fallow, grouped, that is, into three embryonic 'fields'. Each field was made up of parcels of furlongs; each parcel probably lay reasonably close to others but with waste (that is, moor and moss) intervening. It is in this sense that we should probably understand that south-east Scotland was a land of large open fields.

The origins of such a field system are to be found in a continual process of clearing and breaking out new land over many centuries. No doubt the nucleus of arable of any toun such as Ayton or Paxton may have been communal fields created at the time of settlement, say in the sixth or seventh century. But what the charters of Coldingham Priory reveal is too complex to go back to a single root of this kind. It is rather the product of assarting by individual or group effort to accommodate rising population over several centuries by successive accretions of cleared land to the village territory at places suitable for arable, laws (hillsides), dales, cleughs and haughs.[21]

How extensive was that arable? The former parish of Old Cambus had some 3000 or 4000 acres (1200–1600 ha) including moorland and the rocky hinterland of Fast Castle. By 1300 the prior of Coldingham had in his own hands two ploughgates each valued at 33s. 4d. annually, a good figure; there were also thirty oxgangs in the hands of others and valued at £1 per ploughgate.[22] Thus the village of Old Cambus had arable totalling some 600 acres (240 ha), and while this was probably an expansion of the amount available a century earlier, at both times we must admit of far more widespread cultivation than charter evidence alone tells of. Certainly,

[20] Raine, *North Durham*, no. CCCLVII.

[21] See the excellent recent discussion in *Studies of Field Systems in the British Isles*, ed. A. R. H. Baker and R. A. Butlin (1973) especially chapters 2, 3, 4, 12.

[22] *Coldingham Correspondence*, pp. xcix–c.

not all this land was ploughed each year, and perhaps a third or even a half lay fallow. But the presence of large open fields on this scale at a place not markedly suited by nature to the plough implies social and economic pressures which could not be relieved by improving the quality of cultivation but only by extending it quantitatively. What is now required is an investigation of the distribution and pattern of rigs observed (fossilised as ridges) on the ground and from the air, at those places where complementary documentary information is available in reasonable quantity. At Old Cambus aerial photography suggests, as a first impression, that most of what is now arable once lay in the rigs of medieval fields.

Such a study would be even more valuable in the area between Forth and Mounth, where by the thirteenth century the intermingling of Anglian nomenclature (for instance, ploughgate represented by *carrucata*) with Celtic, was widespread, and in the south of which the Celtic unit, the davach, is rarer than in the north. It has, however, been cogently argued that more attention should be paid to the form of land description than to the measurement units. Thus the 'two davachs in the territory of Lintrathen, namely Clintlaw and Balcasky', in Angus[23] combines the southern formula of 'arable in the village territory' with the 'arable with a name' formula which is almost unknown in the south, but is general in Scotia. Beyond the Mounth and especially in Moray this usual form is seen in such a grant as: 'the church of Arndilly with all pertaining thereto except the corn teinds of two davachs which are next to my castle of Boharm, namely Boharm and *Adthelnachorth*'.[24] This illustrates not only that the davach and northern ploughgate were commonly named but also that the davach with its corn tiends was essentially a measurement or unit of arable.

When the bishop of Moray gave up certain revenues and rents in Badenoch, Walter Comyn, lord of Badenoch, granted in exchange one davach in two named places (that is, made up of two half-davachs) and another davach at the Insh which the bishop was to choose from two named davachs, provided he took the half davach in which the church of Insh was situated.[25] This document makes it fairly certain that at least in Moray the half-davach was commonly a unit of agricultural land readily defined by its own

[23] *Coupar Charters*, no. LV.
[24] *Moray Registrum*, no. 23.
[25] *Moray Registrum*, no. 76.

name, and sometimes physically separate from the other half davach with which it went to make up a named davach. Moreover, although a davach is sometimes said to have 'rightful bounds' we do not seem to have an instance in which the boundaries of a davach or half-davach were perambulated and defined. The problem of understanding the agrarian arrangements by which this unit was cultivated is not made easier by the assortment of name-types by which it can be known. A davach in Strathardle was known as *Petcarane* and Tullochcurran, that is as a settlement and a natural feature (a knoll). There are settlement davach-names (Pit- and Bal-) and field davach-names (Ach-), but the word davach itself rarely enters into place-names except in the form of a fraction: Haddo and Lettoch both mean half-davach. There are thirds (Trin- or Tirn-names), quarters (Kirrie- names) and fifths (Coig- names), which refer to davachs though not using the word.

The word 'davach', although Gaelic, is not found in Ireland but only in the Pictish area of Scotland and is likely to represent fairly archaic agricultural arrangements. It means a tub or vat and is generally thought to refer to the land sown by such a measure of seed, or to the land required to produce so much grain. In either case, it seems that we are looking at the land from the point of view of the lord who gives seed and exacts tribute from peasantry and not, as with ploughgate and oxgang, from the point of view of the peasant community concerned with their labour input. A difficult twelfth-century Gaelic *notitia* in the *Book of Deer* bears this out, for the mormaer of Buchan and his wife freed 'all the grants to the church of Deer from all burdens on the share of (or, in exchange for the dues of) four davachs of that which should fall in (or on) the chief districts of Alba generally and the chief churches'.[26] In the present writer's view this meant a grant of freedom from burdens on an estate of four davachs in the usual commodities. If no interpretation is wholly convincing, it will nonetheless be common ground that the davach is seen as a source of tribute or dues throughout Scotia, and it may well be that the word was applied to land as a measure of the tribute or render which would arise from it.

It has been seen that davachs, and commonly half-davachs as

---

[26] Jackson, *Gaelic Notes in the Book of Deer*, no. VI, pp. 32, 35. My English version is not Professor Jackson's. His interpretation will be found *ibid*, pp. 77–8, 116, 119, 121.

well as lesser fractions, would have names and would therefore be identified portions of land. These davachs, halfs, thirds and so on were units of arable as were the furlongs of the south; but they must have differed from the large fields in their relationship to each other and to human settlements. Perhaps we should see a landscape of small enclosed units of arable often not marching with each other (and hence not producing boundary disputes and the need to perambulate) but separated by areas of moor and moss. Such small fields would suit dispersed settlement, so that the large village of Lothian was uncommon in the zone of the davach where the unit of settlement was the small hamlet or isolated farmstead grouped around or beside the arable. To establish whether or not this was so is of prime importance for the social and economic history of early Scotland, yet little progress has been made to test the various hypotheses which have been offered over the last century about the relationships between settlements and fields and their names. Aerial survey has not so far led to study of traces (if any) of earlier field systems, whether the larger open fields (and their rigs) of the south, or the possibly smaller fields (often called 'Celtic' in an English context) which may have survived in Scotia and may have formed named portions of a davach.

Such smaller fields would be cultivated by something lighter than the heavy wheeled plough of the south east, and it is probably significant that later plough-types do indeed seem to conform to a distinction between south and north in this respect. Nor should the possibility of cultivation by spade be overlooked. In one area of Scotland, the Lennox, the use of a light plough is implied by the survival of the ploughgate under the guise of the Celtic word 'arachor', which had a smaller acreage and presumably took its name from the light *aratrum*. Yet much later, in the eighteenth century, cultivation by a team of delvers by spade is described as being usual at Luss and Arrochar—which were measured in 'arachors'. Probably both plough and spade were in use, even in the Middle Ages. But the superior productivity of cultivation by the spade is well attested, and it may have spread, ousting the light plough, in order to feed a rising population in regions where the heavy plough and large fields were unsuitable.

Between the zone of the davach, north of the Mounth, and the open-field zone south of Forth lies a zone of intermingled plough-gates and oxgangs on the one hand and davachs on the other.

THE LAND

Since the ploughgates are often named like davachs, there is a
strong likelihood that in this zone they are not abstract units made
up of scattered rigs, but compact pieces of arable—in other words
the davach under another name, perhaps chosen by a clerk reluctant
to employ the 'uncouth and strongly vernacular' Gaelic word.[27]
In some cases at least, however, the ploughgate is accompanied by
the oxgang, as in the grant of two oxgangs in the territory of
Catterline (Mearns) already mentioned (above p. 313); and there is
also an instance of oxgang and half-davach being found in one
document about the same parish, Conveth in Mearns[28] and an
instance of ten acres in the field of an Angus village, Kinblethmont.[29]
If some of these, and other examples which could be given, represent rigs in a large open territory of arable, then not all 'carrucatae'
in documents from the zone are merely the davach or small fields
under a more respectable name. On the contrary, some must surely
represent the spread of the open field and open-field agriculture
beyond the Forth, with all that that implies in terms of breaking out new arable to link up the small fields represented by the
davach.

Edirpolles 'between the pows' at Errol in the Carse of Gowrie
lay close to and pointing like a wedge at the Tay, in the heavy clay
of the carse so inadequately drained by the sluggish pows that it was
later described as 'spouting'; but the monks at Coupar established
that Grange which soon ousted 'Edirpolles' as the name of the
place. By the end of the twelfth century the teinds of Edirpolles,
worth at least two merks annually, imply arable of some extent;
while David de Hay in confirming this land about 1200 reserved the
stank for a mill which had probably been recently established for
the grain of peasantry and lord.[30] About 1240 the monks built a
causeway across the spouting lands from Inchture to Carsegrange,
presumably for carts journeying to the abbey.[31] Their immediate
lord, David de Hay, endowed his brother William with the flat
land south-west of Carsegrange between it and the river, and
William seems soon to have wadset some of this estate to the
monks and paid off the debt by parting with some arable, 'a

[27] G. W. S. Barrow, 'Rural Settlement in Central and Eastern Scotland',
chapter 9 in The Kingdom of the Scots.
[28] Arbroath Liber, i, no. 272, of 1242.
[29] Arbroath Liber, i, no. 143, 1185 x c. 1200.
[30] Coupar Rental, i, 337, ii, 286, 288.
[31] Coupar Charters, i, p. xxxiv; nos. III, XXXVII.

ploughgate in the fief of Errol, on the south of the monk's grange, called *le Murehouse*... with all the pasture of my moor of *Admure*'. About the same time Coupar Abbey bought out two other neighbours, Roger, son of Baldric, from an oxgang to the south of Carsegrange and Richard de la Batail from land to the north. Their names strongly suggest that both these men were burgesses, presumably of Perth. In the first case, full possession was deferred by a lease current for five years during which the abbey was given another oxgang 'near to the mill', probably the mill of Aithmuir belonging to the Hays which was there a little later when Roger sold his other lands to them; that mill tells of grain and arable.[32] This substantial arable on the low ground, at least partly drained by the two pows and measured in ploughgate and oxgang, belonged to an immigrant family and colonising monks. It was associated with a settlement (albeit only a single toft), Muirhouse, whose English name must be recent, as was Carsegrange itself. The name for the uncultivated land, Aithmuir, may have been Gaelic in origin but seems to have assumed an English guise (Oat-moor), as the neighbouring 'Leys', if not an English word, had an English plural. There can be little doubt that between 1170 and 1230 substantial inroads were made into the wet ground, hitherto grazing, of Aithmuir and 'Edirpolles' to break out new arable and that this took the form of an open tract cultivated in rigs; it seems unlikely that the heavy plough would be used on the clay of the carse, but even a light plough might have required a full team of oxen for draught. Further, since no village developed at Aithmuir, the labour which this new arable represents must be seen as an expansion of the existing settlements, and especially of Errol and Inchture. The ploughgates of Errol were not davachs but a form of open field cultivation in Scotia, an increase in agrarian efficiency and production to meet the needs of rising population through the agency of a more effective market in country and town.

But the contrast between large and small fields, between ploughgate and davach, was not merely a matter of plough types and draught-teams. A song whose known form dates to *c.* 1550 evokes vividly a four-sided plough drawn by a team of eight oxen with ploughman and gadsman (or driver of the team). The singer asks

---

[32] *Coupar Charters*, nos. **XLII, XLVII, LVII**; *Coupar Rental*, i, 338; *Spalding Miscellany*, ii, 309, no. **XI**.

the laird to call the hinds to him to produce their oxen and the parts of the plough—and no fewer than twenty-five peasants are named, some with occupational names like 'mawer' and 'tasker', mower and thresher.[33] The *carruca* and the large team were only part of a means of production which the specialist must investigate but which in sum demanded co-operation in cultivation and management. They therefore imposed, or at least encouraged, a particular kind of settlement, village rather than hamlet, and a way of life in which no man might neglect his neighbours' needs and rights nor fear that his own would be ignored.

The crops grown in the fields, whether large or small, must have suited the climate and soils as well as the techniques of cultivation. Plainly in Scotland the limitations imposed by an Atlantic climate in our fairly northern latitudes would be much greater than in the midlands or south of England; the older reader should recall that in this century before the general introduction of the combine harvester sheaves would rot in the stook during a wet September, and he might multiply several-fold such disadvantages of a wet and cold climate for the age of the sickle and winnowing flail. There is little direct, but some indirect, evidence of crops grown in the fields. Thus, Malcolm IV entitled Scone Abbey to take from each ploughgate for hospitality various products, including sacks of meal or flour (*farina*) and ten thraves of oats (*avena*), but at Longforgan in Gowrie the thane's ferme to the crown was payable in wheat though it was foreseen that this might be changed to another commodity.[34] Teinds were payable on corn, *annona*, but in the case of the king's rents this was defined as wheat, bere (barley) and oats, and among the charters of King William there are many more references to wheat than to bere or oats.[35]

In the royal accounts for the 1260s the sheriff of Perth received rents in oatmeal, bere and oats, but bought wheat for the king's service. At Craigie, however, just outside the town of Perth, the king's farmer was enjoined to pay to the Blackfriars five chalders of wheat and ten of bere—rents presumably grown in the first place for the king's needs. The thanages of Forfar and Glamis paid cows, pigs, cheese, eels and hens, with thirty-two chalders of bere, ten

---

[33] A. Fenton, 'The Plough Song', *Tools and Tillage*, i (1970), 175–88.

[34] *R.R.S.*, i, nos. 243, 248; *ibid*, ii, no. 16.

[35] *R.R.S.*, ii, nos. 17, 107; index of subjects under 'oats', 'prebenda' and 'wheat'.

chalders of oatmeal and ninety-one chalders of oats; the thanage of Fettercairn, the crown lands of Elgin, Forres and Kinross paid in the same grains but the quantities are not given.[36] Wheat, however, is mentioned along with other grain by the sheriffs of Roxburgh and Stirling and in Galloway,[37] and a half-ploughgate of arable by the Tweed had two oxgangs under wheat and two under oats.[38] Rye scarcely seems to be mentioned but it was certainly grown on a small scale in the central belt of Scotland in the early fourteenth century.[39] In general, therefore, wheat was grown more widely in southern Scotland, the land of open fields, where it had perhaps taken over some acreage devoted earlier (in the twelfth century) to rye; it was, however, still grown only in lesser amounts than oats or bere. North of Tay the land of smaller fields was also the land of oats and bere and almost exclusively so.

Much of the grain imported to thirteenth-century Berwick and Perth from Lynn was wheat to supplement inadequate native production. Significantly, the great western monasteries, Glenluce, Dundrennan and Kilwinning, bought grain in Ireland or England under licences mainly of the 1220s (after which the issuing of licences fell into disuse though not presumably the buying of grain). These corporate landlords with twenty to forty monks each would consume larger quantities of such fine fare as wheaten bread than their demesnes and rents would produce. In the east this demand was met by the imports of merchants but in the west the landowners bought directly, at least until Ayr developed as the grain trading port which it certainly was by 1300.[40] The diet of a monastic community and its dependents is illustrated by corrodies at Coldingham Priory: in 1263 the priory's baker was promised a daily monks' loaf, a flagon of monks' ale and three dishes of meat, three of fish weekly; in 1279 in return for some eleven merks annually a small laird received daily a monks' loaf and a loaf of oats or rye, a flagon and a half of 'ordinary' ale, and the same weekly dishes, together with an annual clothing allowance.[41] Thus it would seem that the monks ate special bread, which can only have been wheaten, while bread

---

[36] *Exch. Rolls*, i, 1–2, 6–7, 12, 13, 15, 16; *Perth Blackfriars*, p. 2., no. III.
[37] *Exch. Rolls*, i, 22–3.
[38] Raine, *North Durham*, no. CCCLVII.
[39] *Exch. Rolls*, i, 146, 173, 328, 405.
[40] *Cal. Docs. Scot.*, i, nos. 765, 933, 974, (Glenluce); 982, 1889 (Kilwinning); 2414 (Dundrennan). No. 1889 is explicitly for wheat.
[41] Barlow, *Durham Annals*, 118; Raine, *North Durham*, no, DCLIII.

made from coarser grain was baked for their dependants and servants.[42]

The surviving records of agrarian production have come to us from landlords and represent a compromise between what they wanted and what the cultivator could produce for them. The ratios of commodities grown by the cultivator for himself and his family could and generally would differ from those grown to pay the rent; in particular the peasant could not afford for himself the luxury of growing wheat, of milling it and of baking it into bread. This was part of the more varied diet of landowners, large and small, of burgesses and perhaps of the wealthiest among the peasantry; it was not for the cottar and certainly not for the wage labourer.

The monotony of agricultural production is remarkable: there is no evidence, for example, that leguminous crops were grown in Scotland. Like wheat, peas and beans were certainly imported in the thirteenth century and even in the fourteenth they occur among purchases but not in rents. Thus these crops, with high protein content and with an important contribution to make to better cultivation by restoring the nitrogen content of the soil, were generally ignored.

The absence of heavy-yield strains of oats and bere may be taken as axiomatic. The peasant relied for his seed upon the grain harvested in the previous year and, even if that did not lead to deterioration of the crop, it certainly did not encourage a husbandry of improvement. Each ear scattered by the sower would yield (on evidence drawn from outside Scotland and from Scotland in later centuries) something between three and five ears threshed, of which one must be kept for the following spring sowing. Thus the acreage required to produce a chalder of grain free for the mill or available to pay the rent was very considerable, and explains why a comparatively modest increase in population created pressure to break out large tracts of new arable. In part, the poor yield ratios of grains may be attributed to the soils which could be cultivated: heavy soils with a high water-table could not be drained, yet when drained in the nineteenth century those fields became the heaviest croppers on the farm. Soils which could be ploughed were not turned over to sufficient depth to bury and kill weeds. After the

[42] Ten acres were given to Melrose Abbey to provide white (wheaten) bread at Easter for the monks, *Melrose Liber*, no. 302; and a chalder of wheat was paid annually from Leuchars in Fife to Coupar Angus Abbey, *Coupar Charters*, no. XVIII.

harvest, arable was turned over to grazing,[43] and this was not necessarily feeding on the stubble only, but perhaps also on the tares which (all literary sources imply) infested the cornfield. The object of this grazing was to manure the field, and probably the most important restriction upon agrarian productivity was inability to keep the soil in good heart. Dung was the only fertiliser and dung was limited by the number of animals grazed, itself directly in ratio to the pasture and rough grazing available. When new arable was broken out it must either be abandoned as exhausted after two or three years, or it must be manured. Yet the new arable itself reduced the better pasture and hence the manure available. Moreover, it is possible that sometimes the peasants' stock was compulsorily grazed on the lord's arable so that peasant acres lost what limited manure was available.[44] What we cannot assess is the total effect of such agricultural practices upon the land and its produce. The picture seems gloomy; and very much later, in seventeenth-century Scotland, when we have articulate comment upon Scottish agriculture, the picture is no less gloomy. It is unlikely that halcyon medieval days had given way to harsher times through lost techniques or some subtler process of decline. The probability is that the conditions of life for a thirteenth-century peasant were harsher and less remediable than those of his successor four hundred years later.

[43] *Newbattle Registrum*, no. 77, *blado asportato*.
[44] *Kelso Liber*, ii, 458, *possunt faldas suas ponere*.

# 13

## THE SORTS OF MEN

Few men thought it worth while to comment on the life and obligations of a medieval Scottish peasant.[1] He is the 'man' of someone else, apparently a chattel, his rights and duties a matter between him and his lord, rarely the concern of another unless he be a peasant also. Those few who do comment are without exception the lords of peasants; from such men we can expect only a partial view, to complement which we must use comparative evidence and liberal conjectures.

Fortunately the church was ever solicitous lest the peasant imperil his soul through failure to pay teind, and that to the right kirk. Alexander I, it was recalled about 1150, had given to the chapel of Stirling Castle the teinds of his demesnes in the soke or shire of Stirling, but teinds from 'hurdmen, bonders and gresmen' were owed to the parish kirk (St Ninian's); mortuary dues were payable to the parish kirk whether the dead were from the *mancipia* of the demesnes of (*or?* from) the parish. Our bonders are well enough known in Northumbria as peasants, villagers, paying food-rents in respect of hospitality due to a lord, but burdened with only seasonal works (boon-works) of one to four days at ploughing, hay-making and harvesting, together with an obligation to do carrying for the lord. Near by, at the shire of Callendar, the king's bonders

---

[1] I give little significance to the story told by the Lanercost chronicle of Alan Durward. Commenting that agricultural land in Scotland is not given as elsewhere for a perpetual return, but that the ferme is renewed at the same amount or increased annually, he tells of a rustic who paid an increasing rent for several years, each year with a promise, sealed by a handshake, that there would be no further increase. Finally, when offered his lord's hand again the peasant said 'No, give me the other one because that one has told me lies so often that I don't believe it any more.' *Chron. Lanercost*, 84–5: this chronicle has a fund of merry jests and moral tales of the like quality.

were the occupiers of arable with sufficient title to require the abbey
of Newbattle to pay them a rent of four shillings annually when
the king dispossessed them in favour of the Cistercians.[2] The hurdmen or 'hired-men' were more substantial and honourable retainers,
perhaps the equivalent of the drengs found in Lothian, less burdened with agricultural services, but expected to ride with, fetch
and carry for, their lord; their successors are found in the early
thirteenth century as small free tenants owing mixed services to the
king, and described as 'sergeants'. It would seem that they, or the
better-off among them, escaped from the peasantry to the ranks of
freeholders. Gresmen too are found in Northumbria, and in Angus
there is an isolated reference to 'grass-cain' payable to the landlord
which suggests that the 'gresman' had a pastoral holding and paid
rents (?in hay) appropriate thereto; the place-name 'gres-man's (or
-men's) toun' is also found in thanages in central Scotland, and
suggests that men with these burdens were not uncommon at least
in the early twelfth century; but as late as 1220 we read of the
crofts and *delues* of six gresmen at Airthrey near Stirling, where
*delues* is certainly cultivated, and probably spade-dug, land. The
gresman was perhaps the man with a toft or garden, no share in the
arable but a share in the grazing.[3]

It would seem that these three descending grades of peasant,
albeit they pay food rents and do some labour services, are accounted *mancipia* along with others who work the king's demesne and
who are therefore more heavily burdened with services. That the
word *mancipia* has implications of servility is undoubted, but these
men are not described as *servi*. Probably we may equate with them
the *rustici* who had land at Ruthven near Perth and at Nydie in Fife,
where there was a Bond Nydie;[4] and Boyndes in Garioch (Bondes
in the thirteenth century) may have been a settlement of bonders,[5]
a geographical 'outlier' to be explained like the 'Inglistons' of
Galloway, by colonisation under the landlord's guidance. The
geographically limited use of the term *bondi* is striking, for even
though it is clearly of Northumbrian origin and has its roots in the
Norse word for a cultivator of the soil, it seems to survive in the
twelfth century only on the fringe of the Anglian zone.

[2] *R.R.S.*, i, no. 109. The marginal note seems to mean 'this is worth nothing'.
[3] Barrow, *Kingdom of the Scots*, 38–9, 50 and references cited there; see also
*A.P.S.*, i, 404, c. XV.
[4] *St. Andrews Liber*, 315.
[5] Barrow, *Kingdom of the Scots*, 270.

A survey of the sources, indeed, reveals no single term (other than *homines,* men) or group of terms for 'peasants' which has wide contemporary authority. The most frequently used word is *nativi,* neyfs,[6] but in Scotia an earlier word, probably widely used despite its few appearances in Latin charters, was *cumelache.* As early as *c.* 1130 David I was commanding the landowners of Scotia and Lothian to return at once the *cumelache* of Dunfermline Abbey given since King Edgar's time and all *servi* given since Malcolm III's time, with all chattels.[7] The distinction in prescription, implying that it was more difficult for *servi* than for *cumelache* to escape from one lordship to another, points not merely to degrees of servitude but also to one characteristic of that servitude: association with, being thirled to, a particular lord or owner. In a similar brieve to Restennet Priory Malcolm IV commanded all men who had lived in the priory lands to return with their chattels, forbade anyone to detain them and authorised the priory to have 'all *cumelagas* and *cumherbas* and all its fugitives, wherever they are, wherever discovered'.[8] Effectively, the brieve says the same thing thrice over: that cumelache and co-arbs, and fugitives, belong to the landlord and may not move unless he wills it; so, too, in an early writ of King William to Scone Abbey. The co-arb is a servile tenant in Gaelic guise, but a satisfactory etymology for *cumelache* has not been established; that it also has a servile significance is certain.

The distaste for such 'barbarous words' as *cumelache* and *bondi* doubtless explains the more frequent use in documents of *nativi* (neyfs) and *fugitivi* for peasants. In the 1140s David I ordered landholders to deliver up to the lady Leofgifu any of her fugitives wherever she might find them, and a decade later the prior of St Andrews was to have his fugitives of Kinninmonth in whosesoever 'power' they might be—fugitives, that is, thirled to Kinninmonth, but, perhaps, drawn into the service or soke of another lord.[9] In the same way the abbot of Holyrood must have 'the native men of his land or his fugitives', and brieves to this effect, sometimes for neyfs, sometimes fugitives, sometimes both, are found throughout the reigns of Malcolm IV and William. Earl Patrick (I) of Dunbar

[6] 'Neyf' is the usual rendering. I find it difficult to regard it as a translation, but no better suggests itself.

[7] Lawrie, *E.S.C.,* no. LXX.

[8] *R.R.S.,* i, no. 195, embodying a previous brieve; *ibid,* pp. 62–4, where there is an important discussion.

[9] Lawrie, *E.S.C.,* no. CLVIII; *R.R.S.,* no. 167.

ordered the handing back of the *servi nativi* of Coldingham Priory and, as late as 1269 the earl of Strathearn gave to his sister Mary 'leave and power of seeking collecting and having all the native men justly pertaining to her lands . . . wherever they are found within our land, to dwell in her lands perpetually and to serve and answer to the lady Mary and her heirs with all their goods and chattels and their issue (*sequela*) as seems best to her and her heirs'.[10] King Alexander II freed from toll the bishops of Glasgow and their *nativi* and *servi,* the latter meaning the same as *fugitivi* to the bishop's archivist.[11] Although we find 'fugitives' so often in the context of a brieve ordering that they be restored, the same brieves also suggest that they are not men who have 'fled' from their lords but men who are being detained, the ownership of whom is in dispute. They are either more lowly than neyfs or lowly among neyfs, and are generally called *fugitivi* in the twelfth century, *servi* in the thirteenth. The primary meaning of *fugitivus,* 'one who runs away', had yielded to the secondary meaning of a servile tenant or serf; and the use of such unusual terms as *mancipia* and *fugitivi* prompts the conjecture that in the twelfth century *servus* had still the meaning of 'slave'. It is possible that slaves still survived in small numbers but that by the thirteenth century they had lost their chattel-status and become indistinguishable from the poorest class of neyf, to which accordingly the word *servi* was now applied.[12]

The category of 'neyf' probably covered a wide range of peasant wealth, sometimes including *servus,* serf, sometimes in contrast with it; although our information is all too slight, it makes sufficiently clear the same variation in nomenclature among scribes as is found in England. Nonetheless, all sources are agreed that the neyf was thirled to his lord by reason of his place of birth (hence *nativus*) and blood. Perhaps the most interesting description of his position comes from an enquiry in 1206 into the Kirkton of Arbuthnott, where hospitality was owed to the bishop as landlord but where the neighbouring thane and his landlord successor also enjoyed rights. Witnesses saw there in the twelfth century eight peasants called 'scolocs' or 'persons' having others 'under' them with houses and animals on the grazing. Each house in the kirkton owed to the thane, and later the laird, ten cheeses and three men for one day at

[10] Raine, *North Durham,* no. CXXI; *Inchaffray Charters,* Appx. no. V.
[11] *Glasgow Registrum,* no. 174.
[12] Cf. e.g. F. W. Maitland, *Domesday and Beyond,* 26–36.

the harvest along with service in the king's army, and the basis of this assessment, the house rather than a unit of arable, underlines the largely pastoral character of the toun; but the 'scolocs' had arable for they had once had a mill and now used the thane's. 'Scolocs' are found elsewhere in Scotia as peasants on kirklands; at Ellon in Aberdeenshire they claimed to have had succession to their lands without the need for a letter of inquest, and as tenants of the bishop of St Andrews they were largely free. They seem very comparable to the bonders of the king's demesnes a century earlier, just as at Arbuthnott the men 'under' them seem to have much in common with gresmen as pastoralists.[13]

One of the peasants of Arbuthnott, Gillandres the one-footed, was particularly reluctant to pay his dues to the thane, who, having been told that the bishop was lord of the Kirkton and could confer the land and houses on whom he chose, offered the bishop a fine horse to evict Gillandres. But the bishop utterly refused when told he was *nativus de terra,* native to the land. We do not know whether Gillandres was a scoloc, but it is more likely that he was not, for in due course a more pliant bishop acquiesced in the removal of 'scolocs and neyfs' (as the clerk wrote twice, once simply 'neyfs') by the laird who thereafter put plough to the land. Thus the neyf, and probably also the scoloc, enjoyed in his lands a customary security given to him by his ecclesiastical landlord and taken away by a secular landlord in pursuit of greater production. In the breaking out of this new arable we may hazard seeing the davach yield to the ploughgate, and certainly this is a good example of assarting and its social effects. In the description of the soke and parish of Stirling in 1150 the king's barons were much concerned with the same phenomenon: the king's demesnes and the lands of other men (bonders) might increase either by assarts (here new clearing in forest or waste) or by breaking out old unploughed ground, and the teinds of these should go to the appropriate kirk; but 'if more men than used to be the case now dwell on the demesne the chapel shall have the teinds of them and of all the men who cultivate that demesne, and the parish kirk shall have the corpses of those who dwell on the demesne'. It would appear that as cultivation of demesne lands increased, labour services there were imposed upon some who were not dwellers on (perhaps neyfs of) the demesne. Unfortunately, we do not know how heavy these services were, any

---

[13] *Spalding Misc.,* v, 210–13; *Aberdeen Banff Collections,* 310–12.

more than we know who laboured on the newly ploughed rigs at Kirkton of Arbuthnott or what became of the evicted peasants.

But we should pause before assuming that the fate of those peasants was typical of the twelfth or thirteenth centuries, for generally newly ploughed land would require more, not less, labour. The laird who expelled them took the view that the land was his but that the neyfs were thirled to the bishop: they were *nativi episcopi* as well as *nativi de terra*. Such was the general view implied by royal brieves entitling a landowner to recover his neyfs or fugitives, and it is borne out by the surviving sales of 'men' and their issue. In a by no-means exhaustive survey I have counted over twenty of these sales or grants from the middle of the twelfth century to the third quarter of the thirteenth: rarely do they categorise the man who is given, but his issue, *secta, sequela, proles* or *liberi* are always mentioned and his chattels sufficiently often to suggest that they were always implied. So far as his lord was concerned the neyf and his family enjoyed no rights (except perhaps the human ones of life and limb) and with his goods were at the lord's disposal.

Yet close examination of the largest single group, gifts or sales to Coldingham Priory, suggests that these documents may be only one factor in an otherwise complex situation. Perhaps about 1220 or 1230 Robert of Prenderguest gave to the priory Patrick, son of Waltheof of Prenderguest; 'and as many as come out of him' giving up the right to anything 'in' Patrick or his issue. We might see the man labouring now on the priory's lands—but this is not a sale, and indeed Robert not only gave Patrick but also a payment (*reddendo*) along with him of a pound of cumin annually. What became of Patrick? In 1247 a man of his name (and there is no reason to think it was anyone else), now calling himself 'burgess of Berwick', bought for twenty merks from Adam, laird of Prenderguest (with consent of his heir and in his great need), his neyf Renald, the grieve of Prenderguest: 'I (Adam) wish and grant that Renald, his wife, little ones and all sequel descending from him with all their goods movable and immovable may come and go and stay wherever they wish like other free men so that from henceforth I, Adam, and all my heirs can have no claim or challenge of neyfty against them.' The sale took place formally in the prior's court and there is no gainsaying its clear intention to free Renald (as Patrick had evidently been freed), for the sum paid is seven times or more the usual price for a Coldingham serf. We do not know for sure

why Patrick took this step, since Renald, 'son of Erneway', was
not obviously related to him. But it looks very much as if Patrick
treated the money as a loan which Renald was obliged to repay,
and that Renald failed to do so, for after an unknown interval
despite the emancipation Patrick gave Renald 'whom I bought
from Adam of Prenderguest' to the priory 'to serve the monks for
ever with his sequel'. He also delivered to the priory the title of
sale and manumission given by Adam of Prenderguest.[14]

Taken together these documents suggest that Coldingham
Priory was acquiring expertise, first of a man of business for the
town, Patrick, son of Waltheof, and secondly of a grieve. The
priory's other purchases of men and their sequels were always made
in the seller's 'great need', a phrase also used fairly frequently in
sales of land, and sometimes accompanied by the consent of heirs; to
alienate either 'men' or land was clearly a serious diminution of the
family's (often slender) stock of capital. The value of a serf (at three
merks) was considerable, so that even King William took the trouble
to have an action raised in his own court by the abbot of Dunfermline on the king's behalf to recover two men from the abbey
of Scone—unsuccessfully. In granting Gillandreas mac Suthen and
his children to Dunfermline Abbey in the 1170s, the king also issued
to the abbey a brieve for the recovery of *fugitivi* 'if they are found
outside my demesnes'[15] and this phrase became usual in the brieve
for recovery of neyfs. Thus neyfs on the king's demesnes were privileged and it would be necessary to bring an action in the king's court
to recover them; such an action perhaps lay behind the grant of
Gillandreas.

Moreover, except where neyfs were given or sold with their
issue, we find them on or in land; the brieve for recovery of neyfs
implies that they will be found settled somewhere and thirled to
another landlord. Conveyances of the land in the thirteenth century
so commonly include 'men' as to imply that they were always
understood to be included even in the more reticent twelfth century;
thus in the late twelfth century the posterity were named of men
given 'with Carberry' to Dunfermline Abbey by David I, yet that
king's charter gives Carberry alone and in the briefest terms.[16]
Unless Scottish usage departed far from that of England (where

---

[14] Raine, *North Durham*, nos. CCCXXX–CCCXLI.
[15] *R.R.S.*, ii, nos. 353, 163, 164.
[16] Lawrie, *E.S.C.*, no. CLVII; *Dunfermline Registrum*, nos. 5, 302.

'neyf' and 'villein' were generally equivalent), 'neyfs' were among the 'men' conveyed with the land. About 1200, the bishop of Moray leased for his own lifetime lands in Stratha'an in Banffshire to the earl of Fife but agreed that while he might take away his men who were on the lands on the day of the agreement 'the earl shall acquire by the bishop's help to inhabit the lands other men who are natural to these lands to whom the bishop has not proved a title.'[17] A neyf, that is, belongs to someone, and his lord keeps him on the land; his issue who inherit his neifty and his lord are therefore 'natural' to that land even if they leave and take another lord; it is such men as this whom the earl hopes to recover with the bishop's help. They will probably not have escaped their neifty, but will have become neyf to another lord, 'native' to another place. The assumption behind such an agreement and behind the royal brieve of recovery is that neyfs inhabit and cultivate land, and that it may be difficult to prevent them or their issue from seeking out the land which they will cultivate, and from choosing the lord to whom they are thirled. Perhaps the most unusual illustration of pressures like this also comes from the first quarter of the thirteenth century, when Scone Abbey and Adam fitz Odo (of Kinninmonth, steward of St Andrews Priory) agreed that Samson, son of Gilbert, with his issue, 'has this liberty' from the abbey: whenever they—it is noteworthy that the issue are evidently the point of contention—want they might go to Adam, staying as long as they like but the eldest paying annually to the abbey a pound of pepper and each of the others who is twenty years old a pound of cumin. They might also return, and indeed come and go as often as they like, saving always the right of the two lords to make another agreement. It is likely that this was a settlement of a dispute over ownership between the abbey and Adam, and difficult to see the outcome as other than an acceptance of the facts insisted upon by the sons of Samson.[18]

But the lawyers would doubtless insist upon the rights of lords in all dealings with their servile tenants. In the Register of Dunfermline Abbey are recorded the genealogies of some of its 'men', apparently those on more distant Fife properties, with a careful note for each man of either his dwelling—or burial—place; thereby were estab-

---

[17] *Moray Registrum*, no. 16: *alios vero homines qui naturales sunt ad terras predictas quos episcopus non diracionavit adquiret predictus comes.*
[18] *Scone Liber*, no. 84, 1206 x 27.

lished (it was hoped) the servile blood of each, and the place to which
the abbey had thirled him.[19] In gifts and sales of neyfs it was the
right to this thirlage which was transferred, the right to determine
where the neyf should dwell and by which lord he should be justici-
able. In a late (1253) and unique example, a donor gave the right of
bondage or thirlage (*ius ligiacio*) in a man and his issue to Lindores
Abbey, carefully reserving his ownership of the rest of his kindred.[20]
This right is personal to the lord just as the bondage is personal to
the neyf.

In Scotland there is no known medieval legal debate on freedom
and unfreedom, and 'unfree' is (outside the burghs) a wholly modern
term; it is used here in the sense of those held in personal bondage
and includes neyfs. But it can scarcely be defined realistically
in terms of the lord's right of disposal, for this would be a rarely
and exceptionally exercised right. More significant was the lord's
right to discipline his men. It has been shown that the extensive
jurisdiction of *furca et fossa*, gallows and ordeal-pit, commonly
granted by the king to barons and knights as well as ecclesiastical
corporations in the twelfth century, probably had its roots in earlier
centuries and in the rights of a thane as the king's *minister* responsible for his estate.[21] Thus Orm of Abernethy, confirmed in possession of the secularised Celtic minster of Abernethy, was to have
common army, common aid, common work, soc, sac, toll, team,
infangenthief, but gallows and pit in only two places, Abernethy and
Inverarity (perhaps for men from lands south and north of Tay
respectively).[22] Such jurisdiction entitled the landowner to try and
inflict capital punishment for theft, and to recover the chattels of
the man punished. Subinfeudation, however, made for a complex
situation and there are several instances of a division of these capital
rights. The earl of Strathearn in the early thirteenth century gave
no explicit jurisdiction to Inchaffray Abbey and difficulty soon
arose; in resolution the earl provided that if any man of the abbey
were tried in the earl's court for theft 'or any plea which belongs to
my court' and condemned, the earl would keep his (dead) body to
preserve his jurisdiction, but the abbey would obtain his chattels;
should the man make a fine—that is, buy off the earl's justice—that

19 *Dunfermline Registrum*, nos. 325-31; these entries were made not long
after 'the arrival of Balliol in Scotland' probably 1332 rather than 1292.
20 *Lindores Chartulary*, no. LXXXIV.
21 *R.R.S.*, ii, 49-50; Barrow, *Kingdom of the Scots*, 41.
22 *R.R.S.*, ii, no. 152.

payment would go to the abbey. His son gave an oxgang at Meikleour to Coupar Abbey and allowed them the fines and forfeitures made by their men in his court, but insisted on his own agents carrying out the ordeal and any punishment by lopping off limbs or head; presumably again the chattels went to the abbey.[23]

Yet these instances bring out very clearly that major and capital offences were not the stuff of a lord's jurisdiction over his peasants—as we might expect; far more important were the lesser offences and quarrels which led to 'forfeiture' (a fine in modern parlance) or 'fine' (an 'end' or out-of-court settlement): flyting, brawling, and similar releases of social tensions now confined to the terraces of football grounds. In feuing out its Lanarkshire estates Kelso Abbey gave to each tenant—and these were men paying as little as twenty shillings yearly—'a court of bloodwite and birthinsake and other such small pleas', sometimes adding that if blood was spilt on his land the tenant should have the forfeiture of his men, the abbey of its.[24] It is possible that a grant of sac and soc without pit and gallows—and this is quite common—was the more usual form for this limited jurisdiction to deal with anything as serious as a brawl in which blood was split, for 'bloodwite' is an unusual word in early sources. The evidence suggests that the 'forfeitures' of his men so frequently reserved by a smaller landowner were connected with, but less than, bloodwite. Thus a Peeblesshire laird gave a half-ploughgate to Simon of Scroggs because his father had died in the laird's service, and after laying down conditions about use and repair of the mill, he provided that if Simon owed forfeiture he would give twelve pence, if bloodwite two shillings; if Simon's men were guilty, Simon (and not the laird) would have their forfeiture.[25] In another instance, from Catterline in Mearns, men were again bound to use and repair the mill of the tenant's laird, but it is explicit that failure to do so would lead to a 'forfeiture'—the amount is not stated.[26] 'Forfeiture' was a payment to the lord exacted to enforce his seignieural monopolies such as the right to a mill and mill-dues. It was also taken for offences which are not

[23] *Inchaffray Charters*, nos. IX, XXV, XLIII; *Coupar Charters*, no. XXV.
[24] *Kelso Liber*, nos. 102–14.
[25] *Glasgow Registrum*, no. 85, *c.* 1200 x 1220.
[26] *Arbroath Liber*, i, no. 127. For another elaborate agreement over mill-rights followed by the provision that pleas against the men of one party are to be heard in the court of the other and the forfeitures divided see *Coupar Charters*, no. X, *c.* 1200.

defined but were less serious than brawling and bloodshed; perhaps any offence in which blood was not shed led to this payment fixed in relation to the wealth and status of the offender and not to the precise character of the offence. Where blood was shed an additional payment (perhaps double the offender's 'forfeiture', as with Simon of Scroggs) was exacted by the lord.

Other examples of the fixing of forfeiture by charter relate to the peasants of Coldingham Priory. For a mere acre and rood William Freeman owed a rent of twelve pence and the same amount for forfeiture, heriot and merchet; another tenant with three acres paid only sixpence as rent but his forfeiture, heriot and merchet were twelve pence.[27] In other cases the formula adopted to the same end was rather different: Adam Marshall gave to the priory 'my homage and service which William Brown and his heirs owed me, for the land which I gave him' for a rent to the priory of sixpence, heriot and forfeiture of twelve pence 'unless the offence is greater' (perhaps meaning unless blood is shed).[28] Simon, Prior of Coldingham, freed Haldan, son of Dune, and his heirs from bondage so that they might hold the toft and croft which Haldan previously held and twenty acres in the 'field' of Coldingham for a rent of four shillings; the forfeiture, merchet and heriot were fixed at three shillings.[29]

These men were considered free, capable of entering into the contractual relationship which each document implies. Yet the last example shows that the recipient had just been released from bondage, and the 'homage' owed by William Brown is best explained as the obligation of a bondman. These obligations of personal bondage were quickly listed: the lord's permission to send a son into the priesthood (or otherwise to free him); merchet: payment for the lord's permission to marry off a daughter (who thereby passed from the issue of one 'man' and the property of his lord to become the means of breeding issue for another 'man' and his lord); and heriot, a payment, usually the best animal, for succession of heirs to the man's land, chattels and obligations on his decease. The man who owed these things we might expect to be at the will of his lord, and punishable by him at will by 'forfeiture' (in English usage, 'amercement') for offences of which the lord's court found

[27] Raine, *North Durham*, nos. CCIV, CCCLXXVI*.
[28] Raine, *North Durham*, no. CCCXL.
[29] Raine, *North Durham*, no. DLXXV.

him guilty. In the instances cited in the preceding paragraph the men concerned were all burdened with the marks of unfreedom but their character has changed for they are fixed and certain and not imposed at the lord's will. In a more remarkable example, Adam de Lamberton gave a third of his land in Berwickshire to his nephew and his heirs, imposing six burdens: a pound of pepper annually to Adam, forinsec service (army and aids) to the king and regular service (presumably in work and carrying service) proportional to the land to the prior of Coldingham; to Adam for forfeiture twelve pence, for merchet twelve pence and for relief on succeeding to the land half a merk.[30] Here one of the marks of bondage, heriot, gave place to the free tenant's equivalent, relief, presumably because the amount of land concerned was substantial, and we are even more clearly in transition from the tenure of a bondman to free tenure in which it has been possible to modify but not to eliminate the marks of personal bondage.

This transition seems to arise as men from bond families enter the market to buy land which was usually held freely, obtaining heritable titles from other (but free) peasants; this the overlord, Coldingham Priory, saw as a danger, since heritable tenure, not being at the lord's will, implied freedom. In at least some cases the priory seems to insist that the land be held directly of it, and, while recognising the heritable and free tenure, seems to insist also upon the incidents of merchet and heriot. Possibly the rent was raised at the same time. It was not perhaps a consistent stand and it left the door wide open to the argument that merchet and heriot were no longer inescapable marks of bondage. Moreover, the recurrence of an identical payment of one shilling for merchet, heriot and forfeiture strongly suggests that in custom, though not by charter, the priory had allowed these payments to become fixed for its bondmen and that the step out of bondage may therefore not have been very great.

Indeed, while the term 'amercement' meant being at the mercy of the lord in the amount of fine which might be imposed, the Scottish equivalent, 'forfeiture', may have had the contrary implication of a fixed penalty. It is striking that King William imposed upon the neyf a forfeiture for non-payment of teinds of one cow and one sheep, which was customary in David I's time in the bishopric of St Andrews, and that in the later thirteenth century the same

---

[30] *Hist. MSS. Comm., Milne Home of Wedderburn Report*, 224, no. 495.

forfeiture appears as a standard penalty in the court of the abbey of Dunfermline.[31] It also appears in the law collections of the fourteenth century as the penalty to be exacted from a serf who will not put plough or spade to his land and from a rustic who stays away from the king's host; however doubtful these may be as legislation of Alexander II, it can hardly be denied that this 'forfeiture' was a widespread thirteenth-century customary payment for all kinds of offence not involving the drawing of blood.[32]

Moreover 'cow and sheep' suggests that forfeiture was, like heriot, an ancient payment, customary in eastern Scotland at least as early as the twelfth century. In that case we may see in the money forfeitures and heriots of Coldingham Priory not merely the effect of a large town (Berwick) upon rural customs but also perhaps the consequences of expansion of the cultivated area by peasants encouraged by their lord to take a toft, build a house and break out a new acre or two in return for money rent and money liabilities. There must be a strong suspicion that by the end of the thirteenth century these liabilities were difficult to enforce. In 1294 the merchets of the earl of Fife's estates were leased for 40s per annum, the oxen collected as heriots were worth 33s and the perquisites of the court ('forfeitures') came to a princely 16s.,[33] trivial amounts to an earl whose gross income was £10 weekly; with the possible exception of heriot, the burden even upon the peasant was probably not heavy—not as troublesome as the exaction of the priest's teinds nor even the miller's multure.

Behind the fixed merchet, heriot and forfeiture in money, which we meet in the limited sources for south-east Scotland in the thirteenth century, must have lain much more arbitrary exactions taken in animals, to mark the subjection of the bondman to the lord's will. But this earlier phase seems to lie in a very distant past, and may not have lasted into the twelfth century; these were only a part of his obligations. For neifty also, surely, involved the peasant in tenure of acre or acres given him by the lord in return for labour and rent to the lord. Heriot had its origins in the seed and stock loaned by lord to peasant with this land, but little or nothing is known of the extent of these holdings nor of the obligations in

[31] R.R.S., ii, no. 281; Dunfermline Registrum, nos. 317 (1256 x 75), 322, (1282).

[32] A.P.S., i, 397 c. I (taken from the late fourteenth-century Bute MS), 398 c. II (taken from the early fourteenth-century Ayr MS).

[33] Stevenson, Documents, i, 408, 413.

labour which they carried. The point is of some importance since most societies judged the freedom of the peasant by the degree of freedom which he enjoyed from weekly work in his lord's fields. Burdens such as those discussed in the preceding paragraphs were irregular and incidental when compared with the routine from ploughing to harvesting which the lord might demand if he chose to exploit his demesnes directly rather than farm them out.

By its very nature the evidence of charters can only be indirect since charters deal with free men. The Osbern who was 'our man' —in bondage—when he took a ploughgate of Midlem from Kelso Abbey, became by the abbey's charter 'our lawful man'—free— paying eight shillings annually and doing as boon-works (*precaria*) three days with two men at harvest and giving his plough thrice (that is, on three days) a year;[34] the eight-shilling ferme pre- sumably replaced a variety of services, including work. At Spynie in Moray, a similar combination of half a merk in money, plough, harrow and cart each thrice, and six man-days at harvest was agreed between a laird and the bishop as ferme for a half-davach.[35] In neither of these instances would the service demanded seem un- becoming of a free man.

It is in fact very difficult to find evidence of heavy labour services by bondmen even upon the estates of a great religious house which had demesnes of quite considerable extent. Certainly the extents made of the lands of Coldingham Priory and Kelso Abbey about 1300 show demesne cultivation on the wane but still im- portant; but they do not show labour services markedly different from those in the preceding paragraph. Since they are the only account of the rural economy in the high Middle Ages which we have, the complexity of tenures which they reveal in the different villages gives another dimension to the generalities about peasant status gleaned from charters.

At Swinton the priory had almost 500 acres (200 ha) of arable in demesne, and peasant land described in various categories. Alto- gether there were over 1100 acres (twelve ploughgates) of arable divided into twenty-four holdings of husbandmen. It is uncertain whether this 'bondman with house' did hold the very substantial amount of land, four oxgangs, implied for each. But it seems unlikely that such holdings were preserved intact while in the same

[34] *Kelso Liber*, nos. 117, 470, 1160 x 1180.
[35] *Moray Registrum*, no. 27, 1222 x 42.

village nine holdings of cottars (bondsmen with a more modest home or 'cot') had a mere twelve acres among them. This pattern of peasant tenures is seen through the eye of the lord; it is too neat to belong to the real world of the struggle for subsistence. The extent bears this out by adding the names of eighteen 'farmers' holding anything from half an acre to two oxgangs (significantly the wealthiest is the miller) for money rents, holdings which are most likely to be new land broken out to increase the village field, the tenants themselves husbandmen or cottars. The only trace of labour for the lord comes from the holding of three women, joint tenants of 22 acres (9 ha), owing money and four harvest works. Described as 'free',[36] they have evidently accepted this burden as part of the rent for the land. Finally, one aspect of Swinton is striking: it was poorly endowed with grazing, a mere 100 acres (40 ha) of waste with common meadow of 19 acres (7 ha) and a 'separate' demesne meadow of 24 acres (10 ha). Both meadows were worth 20s., implying that the demesne meadow was on inferior ground and had been enclosed later. The effect of the limitation upon stock imposed by the village resources may have been to make available for hire and labour on the demesne under-employed cottars and those peasants who worked for the husbandmen and more substantial farmers. But there would also be marked lack of dung for the arable of such a village.

At Fishwick on the Tweed the prior had a house with garden and dovecot, sometimes leased to a farmer (presumably by those priors who had no taste for country-house living), and 200 acres (80 ha) of demesne with 500 acres (200 ha) of peasant arable. While there was unmeasured common grazing and peat cutting upon the moor, the size of meadow was insignificant: a mere 2½ acres (1 ha) of common meadow (but separate pasture for the priory's stock) of 50 acres (20 ha); the peasant stock was evidently a small fraction of that of the priory. Among the peasantry were sixteen husbandmen, each with thirty acres of arable; upon each ploughgate (and each husbandman had only a third of a ploughgate) lay the obligation to plough and harrow one acre (the 'bondacres') of demesne for which, with his two companions, he would have a meal of three dishes with cheese and ale. Each week in the season he owed two days' mowing with two men, each day receiving two ploughmen's loaves, three salt herring and cheese—a stone of cheese each day.

[36] *liberi* not *libere*.

He had to bring in the lord's harvest, cut peats for a day, hoe for a day, bring in six cartloads of peat, cart teinds and corn from Berwick, and wash and shear (with others) two 'flokkis' of sheep. Carefully examined, these details suggest that the bondacres were a customary obligation making scant contribution to cultivation of the lord's arable and perhaps retained only as a token of bondage. Otherwise the husbandman was involved in carrying services and the maintenance of the lord's stock. Even the six cottars of Fishwick, each with six acres of land had similar duties: two days' mowing weekly with one man (one meal daily), stacking the corn (two meals), cutting peats for a day (one meal), stacking them (two meals) when the bondmen carry them (for the husbandman has a cart but not the cottar), and driving the sheep to be dipped and shorn.

The explanation for this balance of services is clear when we turn to neighbouring Paxton, where there was no demesne and three portioners or joint-farmers had taken the village at ferme from the prior for 66s. 8d., and 60 'works' at Fishwick at harvest; harvest works are lacking at Paxton itself. Under the farmers there were fifteen husbandmen, each with fifteen acres and paying 6s. rent but not said to be burdened with the boon works which had once perhaps lain upon them (four days each) but were now to be found by the farmers.

In Fishwick and Paxton (taken together) we come nearest in these texts to the classical manorial organisation found south of the Trent, with demesnes round the lord's hall or manor (for in medieval Scotland 'manor' had its modern English sense of house) and a fairly substantial contribution of peasant work to the lord's labour needs, with money rents running at a half or less of those found at some other villages. But even so it will be noted that ploughing, the really important and skilled task requiring co-operative hard labour, the one task which, left undone or badly done, will put an end to the others, is given in a mere fraction of what the demesne acreage would require. And the other services required were, no doubt, an important contribution to the labour required for seasonal tasks but cannot have met the whole requirement of the landlord, except possibly in dipping and shearing his sheep; it is probably significant that the lord had so engrossed the pasture that he could demand the undivided attention of husbandmen and cottars to his flocks.

At Edrom, Renton, Old Cambus, Upper and Nether Ayton the

demesne existed in substantial measure but was always less than peasant land. Thus, at Coldingham itself the priory had over 1000 acres (400 ha) in arable, the peasants almost 1500 acres (600 ha). At Lumsdain and Flemington all land seems to be at ferme; Swinewood had five ploughgates of demesne, four of peasant land and one at ferme; from its name this village was probably a true assart, newly created in cleared woodland—but this had already happened by the early twelfth century. In these and other village territories the extent makes almost no mention of services. The exceptions are an oxgang at Ayton held by Sir Ingram de Guines worth 5s. paying 16d. and doing three harvest boons with one man (food provided), work on the stank and various carrying services. At Auchencrew, where the prior's demesne of five oxgangs was recently acquired and where two of the three portioners of Paxton seem to have held most of the land at ferme, the husbandmen paid a money rent with unspecified services. And, finally, at Lamberton four men, including Sir Ingram de Guines, held the land, paying a money rent and ploughing bondacres and doing harvest boonworks at the manor of Ayton. All these exceptions, the three ladies of Swinton, and Fishwick and Paxton had in common not merely labour, however light, but also the tenure of the land by a free intermediary; which is to say that we hear of labour services owed where the prior's tenant is free, or even, at Lamberton, knightly.[37]

Unless the record misleads us by concealing labour in the money valuation—and this is unlikely—this paradox is best attributed to a very recent change in the management of the priory's resources and the commutation of labour services for money, a change to be attributed to the outbreak of war in 1296. The same extent reveals a catastrophic recent (in 1300–1) drop in values which must have been reflected in rents; presumably to recoup itself and meet the duns of its Lombard bankers, the priory has hastily sold its labour dues to the peasants who owed them. It was left with those dues which were owed from free tenures and which therefore could not be modified with such speed. May we, therefore, take the burdens found at Fishwick, Paxton and Lamberton as typical of the Tweed valley peasantry in the reign of Alexander III?

The survey of Kelso Abbey's properties made late in the thir-

---

37 *Coldingham Correspondence*, lxxxv–cii.

teenth century would suggest that we may. It is subsequent to 1285[38] and to 1299 when Abbot Richard (who is not referred to as 'deceased') was deposed as a rebel Scot; it is unlikely to be more than a year or two later, since some detail is incomplete and since conditions which Richard abolished were worth recording in detail; thus the Kelso survey seems to be almost exactly contemporaneous with the Coldingham one. Its purpose was not merely to record the abbey's lands but also those rights to labour services which Richard had commuted for money; the abbey doubtless hoped to recover them in more favourable times.

The abbey had granges (extensive demesne lands) at Redden, Elisheugh in Mow, Faldon, Whitmuir, Whitelaw, Holydean, and 'Newton'. At Redden the demesne of five ploughgates was balanced by eight husbandlands (each probably two oxgangs, hence two ploughgates in all), each husbandland owing carrying service from Berwick with a horse once per week to bring grain, salt or coal, and labour on one day weekly. On those weeks when no carriage was done, two days weekly were enjoined; at harvest no carriage was done, but three days weekly in the lord's field. Each husbandman received with his land ploughing and carrying stock (two oxen and a horse) and seed in oats, bere and wheat and this was returned to the abbey when Abbot Richard commuted all these services into a money rent of 18s. for each husbandland. The services of the nineteen cottars remained; how much land they held is not stated but each paid a shilling and did six days' work at harvest as well as help at the sheep-shearing, in return for food. At Elisheugh the abbey's grange had two ploughgates but only six days' service from fourteen cottars of Mow.

The granges of Faldon and Whitmuir had been farmed for £10 and 10 merks respectively, but the other granges in the barony of Bowden showed a fairly uniform pattern of services. At Bowden itself twenty-eight husbandlands and as many at Midlem owed a combination of money rent (6s. 8d.) and labour services: each husbandman must give four days at the harvest with his wife and household and a fifth day with two men; he must help to bring in the harvest, carry peats and wool to the abbey and bring goods from Berwick (one day each); he must plough one and a half bondacres at

[38] *Kelso Liber*, no. 219, a resignation by Hugh of Redden in May 1285 of his land in Redden and Home. Cf. *ibid*, ii, 456, which refers to land at Redden *que fuit Hugonis Reueden*.

Newton, harrow for a day with his horse, and help with the sheep-shearing. The cottars with holdings of various sizes owed various money rents but uniform labour: one man doing nine days' harvest work[39] and help at sheep-shearing. The abbey had no demesne at Bowden nor at Midlem but the services of these men were done at the grange of Newton, a place whose history presents problems. The very full Kelso Cartulary shows no abbey title for land there, whereas Bowden and Midlem are possessions documented from 1115; but the kirk (and by implication, the toun) of Newton of Lessudden, now Longnewton, existed by the mid-twelfth century, possibly long before.[40] Perhaps the abbey's grange was in Bowden parish, contiguous with Longnewton; alternatively, and more probably, Kelso Abbey's Newton is a lost small settlement represented now by Newhall on the Ale Water. The survey shows that it had seven demesne ploughgates with extensive grazings and that the nearest peasant holdings were at Clarilaw where twenty-one cottars, each with three acres, owed two bolls of meal yearly and the communal duty of hoeing the abbey's grain. These services complemented those of the husbandmen of Bowden and Midlem, but once again ploughing and harrowing duties at each bond tenement, even though six times heavier than on Coldingham Priory's estates, would make only a nominal contribution to the cultivation of the demesne.[41]

Both surveys take us behind the rapid commutation of the 1290s to conditions rather earlier, and reveal two broad categories of tenants—husbandmen and cottars. At each toun the distinction in size between the two holdings is considerable but the differences are only slightly more marked than the variations among the husbandlands at the various touns. This does not emerge so clearly from the Kelso survey which is reticent on the size of peasant holdings and speaks of the husbandland as a well understood measurement; apparently each was two oxgangs (the English term 'virgate' seems to be largely unknown in Scotland) except in Selkirk Abbatis where the size is given as one oxgang, so that wide difference was known there also. Nonetheless in these documents we are looking at peasant holdings rather than peasants; the burdens lay upon the holdings and the surveys are little concerned to tell us who discharged them. If we equate the bondmen of occasional

[39] *nouem dietas per vnum hominem.*
[40] *Dryburgh Liber,* no. 57.
[41] *Kelso Liber,* ii, 455–64.

charters with the husbandmen of the surveys it must always be on the understanding that there could have been even wider variations between the Tweed and, say, Fife than we have already found in the Tweed valley. But it is probably significant that late in the reign of Alexander III the bondman by that name begins to make his way into documents. In 1278 Dunfermline Abbey received land in its own parish 'with all men and cottars dwelling therein on that day', a grant which the king phrased slightly differently as 'with all bondmen' (*homines ligii*).[42] Under Robert I it became quite usual to list 'bondmen and bondage holdings' among the pertinents of land, where 'bond' (usually meaning husbandmen) had to do duty in a wider sense to include cottars also. The evidence, though tenuous in the thirteenth century, is much stronger in the fourteenth, when their labour services had largely disappeared, that husbandmen and cottars were to be found widely throughout Lowland Scotland.

In this discussion we have moved from the bonders and scolocs of the twelfth century to the neyfs and *fugitivi* of the late twelfth and early thirteenth centuries and finally to the husbandmen and cottars of the late thirteenth, passing many an uncategorised 'man' on the way. But this kind of change of nomenclature, with an English-derived term prevailing in the fourteenth century, can be paralleled in other fields, and we may cautiously accept that the neyfs whose personal unfreedom is reiterated in earlier documents and of whose land we know so very little, are the ancestors and predecessors of the bondmen with their holdings of the late thirteenth century. Of course, no strict equivalence is permissible: neyf is not always nor only husbandman, *fugitivus* not cottar. And while the scolocs may be categorised as neyfs, where shall we fit in the twelfth century bonders and gresmen of central Scotland? There are many questions which require further study and doubtless the conclusions suggested here will, in some degree, fall to the ground.

But we do have a model with which a beginning is possible in the Kelso and Coldingham extents. Around or among the bondage holdings were numerous holdings for rent ranging in size from half an acre to a ploughgate, held by farmers and evidently 'free' even though the land was occasionally burdened with boon-works. The larger of these tenancies represent, perhaps, early ministerial holdings, and might have been categorised as sergeanties. The smaller were perhaps new holdings broken out by landless peasants

[42] *Dunfermline Registrum*, nos. 86, 87.

in return for a rent to the lord. But it is the cottar holdings which are of greatest interest, for the services lying upon them are sometimes imposed equally without regard to the size of the individual holding, as though an obligation upon the whole village to perform a task had been divided into so many equal shares. The occasional requirement that the cottar shall come with a man to a task, becomes in the case of some husbandmen an obligation to produce two or three men, a requirement which can only be explained if the husbandman was the head of a quite extended household, and even the cottar was able to procure additional labour. Unfortunately, we simply do not know what security of tenure a bondman had with his holding, but if payment of heriot implies that bondage holdings in fact descended within the family, the evidence of charters of free peasant land shows that some tenants regarded all sons as co-heirs.[43] This may have been the custom of servile tenures in some places, where the husbandland would in fact be subjected to division although the lord might regard the eldest son as the husbandman responsible for all services. Where charters show small free tenants, themselves indistinguishable from peasants, bargaining for acres, half-acres and even roods of land (and it must be admitted that this is revealed only by the fine Coldingham collection), it is unlikely that the integrity of a twenty-six acre husbandland was easily maintained.

The husbandman is therefore likely to be the tenant as seen by the lord who, by 1300, had no eyes for the other men who dwelt on the husbandland, men with fragments of land for a 'cot' taken from bondagers, selling their labour to him and to their lord. On Coldingham estates, and even more markedly on Kelso estates, husbandmen (with larger holdings) had heavier labour services than cottars, implying the existence of a rural proletariat which figures in no charter and only incidentally in surveys as 'work with so many men', but which was employed by husbandmen and even by cottars. The demand on Kelso lands for weekly work of between one and five days seems heavy and servile until it is recognised as a burden upon the holding and probably, therefore, performed on many occasions by hired floating labour. The cottar with between one and six acres who was burdened with modest labour services had more capacity spare to work for another, yet at harvest often had to produce a second man for boon work; it seems that at

[43] Raine, *North Durham*, nos CCLXXV, CCCLXXXVIII.

some times he hired himself out for wage labour, at others was himself an employer. Moreover, the heaviest labour services sketched in the Kelso survey were not enough to have cultivated the abbey's demesnes: they were no more than a contribution which the abbey must have complemented by extensive hiring of labour. The scale and detail of meals found in the Coldingham extent (and mentioned in the Kelso survey) are appropriate to payment for labour where food is important; which is to say that these meals are likely to have been defined for hired labour and given of necessity also to boon workers.

Finally, it is to be noted that boon work was generally due at times of great pressure upon all labour resources, notably haymaking and harvest; this underlines the advantage of compulsory labour services: that they were available when labour was scarce and its cost in the free market doubtless high. But in saying that, are we not also saying that the landlord recognised the converse: that compulsory services were for the most part and at most times a less efficient and more expensive form of input of labour than hiring at need? At least this was true where the lord concerned himself with demesne production such as the larger Benedictine houses practised; their purpose in doing so was to feed the convent and to produce a surplus for cash sale, and the latter motive would also apply to secular landowners.

Two hundred years earlier this was a small and unimportant factor in the economy of Scotland and exploitation of demesnes was correspondingly unimportant. The owner of land was also the owner of peasants from whom he demanded in return for their land a rent in produce; this ferme was adequate to sustain his household and while services such as carrying, 'work' on buildings, and hospitality for his steward were certainly demanded, demesnes and demesne labours at plough and harrow seem to have been slight. There is much to suggest that in an even more primitive age the rent may have been imposed upon the toun, that all peasants dwelling there owed a rent for it which was broken down into a unit upon each house, and that this represented a predominantly pastoral economy, for we find it at the Kirkton of Arbuthnott, where there was no demesne, and in parts of Lennox, where agriculture remained unimportant. But the breaking out of ploughed land in increasing quantities at first increased the number of peasants taking arable at ferme and playing larger produce rents;

such were the eight scolocs of Arbuthnott in whom we may see the ancestor of the husbandman, while the others of that toun look like the predecessors of cottars. By the time (*c.* 1200) when this economy at Arbuthnott was swept away by the laird in his search for demesne, it is likely to have yielded elsewhere in more peaceable fashion, the peasants retaining and even increasing their lands and rents but burdened also with work on the lord's increasing acres. The search for neyfs which the brieve of recovery implies could be a search for tenants to take lands largely for food-rents or it could be a search for a labour force. It is most likely to have been both: a search for tenants for lands burdened with rents and labour dues. It represents an increase in the lord's income both from rents and from demesne. But we have no evidence to suggest a thorough-going 'manorial' economy with heavy labour dues at any period of the twelfth or thirteenth centuries; there was probably only a phase of some seventy years during which modest labour services spread as demesne exploitation spread. And there is the suspicion that lords may have experienced difficulty in retaining unfree tenants burdened with rent and labour because of the increase in peasant arable which offered new and less burdened holdings. In fact, the situation revealed in the surveys of 1300 is likely to have been arrived at as the amount of available labour (that is, the population) continued to increase after the increase in cultivation had slowed down or stopped because all land available to the techniques of the time had been brought under the plough.

In sum, it is suggested that there was widespread servility in twelfth-century Scotland but not widespread labour services; the introduction of labour services and the breakdown of personal servility were both the product of increasing demesne exploitation; once this increase faltered, even though demesne did not contract, labour services and unfree tenures also began to be commuted for rents in money and kind. By the late thirteenth century personal servility and labour services were much on the wane, leaving merchet, heriot, thirlage to mill and brewhouse and the lord's justice as the marks of peasant status. Finally, the royal courts in Scotland were not busily asking in the thirteenth century whether a man was 'free' or 'unfree' and thereby creating a legal buttress against economic change.

# 14

# THE CONDITIONS OF MEN

The enormous range of peasant wealth into which the sources give us a brief insight indicates that in Scotland as elsewhere there were peasant families which prospered and others which fell on evil days: among the Coldingham charters are many examples of peasant holdings surrendered 'for failure of service' and although these were free tenements their owners could equally well have held unfree land and found themselves in the same situation—unable to produce the rent because a run of bad harvests, gales, deaths in the family (whence heriots), had eroded the narrow margin which lay between peasant prosperity and destitution. In later centuries dearth brought high prices, but poor roads prevented the entry of supplies to mitigate misfortune attracted by high prices; almost certainly this would be equally true in the thirteenth century, and the *Melrose Chronicle* begins to comment on the 'hard' years in 1271. Whether the peasant benefited from any communal insurance—help shared among those in a village in common distress—we cannot say because the village community is a shadowy factor in the sociology of medieval Scotland. The village of the south-east seems to have had a grieve to speak for his fellow peasants but since the royal courts took little cognisance of the village community, it made no coherent statement in the sources. In the later Middle Ages, the barony courts could refer matters to the 'burlaw men' responsible for the keeping of 'good neighbourhood' among the peasantry by the holding of separate burlaw courts. They dealt with the maintenance of hedges and dikes, the damages caused by straying cattle, boundary disputes and problems of joint tenancy—with the whole fabric of peasant life in a village in fact. The antiquity of this institution is uncertain but the derivation of its name from Old Norse suggests that it developed between the ninth century and the twelfth. We must be chary of assuming that it arose among the peasantry rather than by the landlord's command, but nonetheless it is the nearest we shall get to a 'popular' institution in Scottish society. It could explain how the elaborate problems of the daily routine of a village in the fields and on the hills were resolved.

The complexity of that routine and of the 'custom' which supposedly governed it extended far beyond the peasant acres and the problems of ploughing and harvesting. Upon his acres the peasant grew bere and oats. From the former he made ale at the brewhouse to which his blood or later his holding thirled him. About 1300 the abbey of Kelso had on its temporalities numerous breweries paying it rents varying from five shillings to a mark; in some villages the abbey (not the only lord there) had two or four breweries, and occasionally land was attached to one; clearly these breweries were farmed out, presumably to a brewster. But in every case they are listed after but associated with the *cotagia,* holdings of cottars, who, it is implied, are thirled to use them.[1] The case is less clear with the survey of Coldingham Priory's estates, where three breweries are mentioned, two said to have been worth 25s and 30s;[2] one is described as 'a brew-house for the members of the village community with freedom to brew for outsiders.'[3] When the laird of Leitholm near the Tweed gave some of his land to a son in the 1270s he gave also 'a brewhouse on his land wherever seems best to him. And I wish that my men shall drink and buy as a matter of course from the ale of his men as they do from the ale of my men'; and to ensure the adequacy of this ale he insisted that each group of men might buy bere and other victuals from the other, at need.[4] It is implied that such freedom was not usual but that peasants were in the main thirled to the brew-house, while the brewster made his living from his rake-off in bere or ale. It is not possible to produce for Scotland even an echo of the sources for F. W. Maitland's famous passage on the twelfth-century Englishman as beer-drinker,[5] but equally it is not in doubt that each year in Scotland a large proportion, perhaps as much as a third, of the grain grown was

[1] *Kelso Liber,* ii, pp. 456–65.
[2] *Coldingham Correspondence,* pp. lxxxvi, lxxxviii, xc.
[3] *bracina communis cum libera bracina.*
[4] *Hist. MSS. Comm. Twelfth Report.* viii, (Earl of Home), 173, no. 291.
[5] F. W. Maitland, *Domesday Book and Beyond,* 439–40.

brewed into ale and drunk by cottars, husbandmen, lairds and lords. For the first of these at least it was the only alternative to water.

And the only cakes which it washed down are likely to have been oatcakes, for, as we have seen, much the greater part of the arable was sown with oats, and, as English evidence would suggest, oatmeal was the staple diet of the peasantry. We are introduced therewith to the man whom most peasants hated and who yet was indispensable to them: the miller. If our sources say little of the brew-house, there is scarcely a quire of published thirteenth-century charters which does not mention the mill, or stank or lade, and almost always in the context of the lord's proprietorial rights in it. Although a windmill is mentioned[6] almost all mills were water-driven, perhaps by undershot wheels, as the 'back flood' which we shall meet shortly seems to imply. Lades outside towns commonly powered several mills and perhaps this happened equally frequently in the country. Probably the energy generated was not efficiently transferred to the millstones, which would be limited in size, limiting production and requiring a multiplicity of mills.

There is abundant evidence of elaborate agreements among landowners to provide for the creation of a new millstank and to secure wayleave for a lade to a new mill.[7] Peasants were also bound in some places, and probably generally, to maintain the lade (stone-lined in some cases) in good order,[8] and elaborate agreements could be entered into to provide that a favoured party should have access to the hopper with his grain immediately after the lord—though the value of this precedence is not obvious. Mills were an important source of revenue to landlords, and jealously protected by strict legal sanctions for the thirling of the peasantry to the use of a particular mill, politely termed the suit or following (*secta*) of the mill. The founder of Lindores Abbey (*c.* 1199) was fortunately explicit in giving 'the mill of the toun of Lindores with all its suit and multure, so that my men shall do all the things which pertain to a mill', and in 1261 the abbey was fully entitled to the 33s. 4d. compensation which it obtained for surrendering its right to suit and multure from the men of his descendant, Sir William Brechin; they were evidently already being driven by Brechin to his mill, perhaps a new one, itself worked by a stream or lade from

---

[6] *Coldingham Correspondence*, p. lxxxv.
[7] E.g. *Arbroath Liber*, i, no. 127.
[8] *Coldingham Correspondence*, p. lxxxviii.

Lindores Loch, which further down its course drove the abbey's mill. Brechin undertook not to interfere with the abbey mill's source of power.[9]

Probably in the 1230s, Alan de Sinton, sheriff of Selkirk, took land at feuferme for one merk annually from Dunfermline Abbey to build a mill on the water of Esk (near Edinburgh) below the abbey's mill. He took pasture nearby for the horses carrying the sacks of grain in and meal out and had to promise that his mill would not impede the abbey's mill by 'back flood'—presumably interfering with the head of water in the lade. When the abbey's mill could not grind because of the lack of water, 'the men of Elphinstone who owe me mill-work along with the monks' men of Invereskshire' (who presumably also owed mill-work) were to repair the defects in the lade and stank; if the abbey's millstones broke, then the abbey's millers must not divert the lade maliciously but until it was repaired must allow their men to come to Alan's mill to grind.[10] The obligation to keep the lord's mill and lade in good repair is referred to in many similar charters and in the survey of monastic lands.

The difficulties of mill-owning with thirteenth-century engineering techniques are well illustrated by these sources; yet it was all worth while—indeed so worth while that the rents payable to Lindores and Dunfermline abbeys are too low to represent the value of the mills and there must be a strong suspicion that a lump sum also changed hands. In 1232 various mills in Moray were worth between £8 and £11 annually and about 1300 Kelso Abbey had mills of 8 to 10 merks value, while in a more agricultural region the Coldingham Priory survey of 1300 tells of similar values but of many more mills.[11]

The very considerable assessments or rents of mills represent the landlord's power to exploit this source of revenue. But he is only a rentier, his rake-off a fraction, albeit a large one, of the income of the miller, who, to cover his labour and rent, was entitled to a proportion of the flour or meal leaving his mill. This payment was

9 *Lindores Chartulary*, nos. II, CXIV; see also the compensation for a new mill to the old mill in *Kelso Liber*, ii, p. 457.

10 *Dunfermline Registrum*, nos. 197, 231. It was the sheriff's mill which broke down, *ibid*, no. 229.

11 *Moray Registrum*, no. 34; *Kelso Liber*, ii, pp. 456–63; *Coldingham Correspondence*, pp. lxxxv, xc xcix; at some of these villages there may well have been the mills of other landowners.

the ubiquitous multure. Sad to say, despite the frequency with which mills and multures crop up in medieval documents, there is no evidence of the incidence of multures save a somewhat obscure royal assize attributed to 1209.[12] Yet it seems that multures were measured in the grasping fist of the miller, that their incidence varied according to the grain and according to the miller's size and that they were the cause of the frequent dispute and endless ill-feeling, the miller intent upon his rights, the hapless peasant upon the wherewithal to feed his household. Of the village entrepreneurs in western medieval society the miller was most consistently unpopular, a reputation which cannot have been wholly groundless and for which there is a vivid illustration in Scotland.

It comes from about 1260, from a town, Dumfries, but one with strong links with the landward, and is told to us by an enquiry drawn from both the town and the surrounding baronies, evidently because one of the two men concerned was a countryman, the other—probably the miller, though this is not certain—a townsman. Let the record of the inquest upon Richard, son of Robert, the survivor, speak for itself: Richard and Adam the miller met at the church of St Michael on the Sunday after Michaelmas, and in the cemetery there Adam defamed Richard, calling him a thief, that is *Galuuet,* and saying that he would have him run out of town. Then it happened that on the following Thursday, when Adam was standing in the doorway of a house, Richard came down the street. A woman said to Adam: 'Clear off, look, Richard is coming'. Adam answered 'I won't clear off; I have a knife as sharp as his' and then Adam went into a house and brought out a knife to carve up Richard. Richard drew his sword to defend himself and struck Adam with the flat of it; when Adam put his arm around the sword, Richard pulled it away wounding Adam so that he died. Richard said 'Look, I didn't kill you, you killed yourself.' The burgesses and others of the baronies say that Richard is faithful in all matters, but Adam was a thief and of ill repute.[13] No doubt the enquiry wished to save the survivor from further unpleasantness, but surely Adam, however rash and quarrelsome, was defamed by the final irrelevant taunt—he was a thief—because he was a miller.

[12] *A.P.S.,* i, 381, c. xxxv. This is the last clause in these assizes for which there is manuscript authority, the earliest being the Bute MS.
[13] *A.P.S.,* i, 97–8.

With the meal which he could call his own after paying the miller and the lord, the peasant must feed his family. We should not assume that he baked loaves with it, for private peasant ovens would be prohibitively expensive to build and fire, and the common oven is a rare find; there is only one, at Coldingham itself, in the survey of the priory's lands in 1300, and it appears to have been a monopoly like brew-house and mill; it is worth only three shillings annually.[14] When the peasant, or at least the cottar, ate bread, it came as wages for his work, or perhaps on a rare occasion by purchase from the baxter of the lord or near-by town. The staple of his diet was oatmeal, and he might ring the changes on porridge, gruel, or brose (uncooked meal and water). The food which he might buy would rarely be fine bread but rather the meal to which he was accustomed and such protein as he could afford. The Coldingham survey has already shown the importance of herring in this rôle, and there are other indications that the peasant diet was supplemented by landlords in this way. River fishings were jealously guarded, but the value of salt works and salt imports indicates that curing of fish and meat were important activities, and the slowness of means of transport imposed upon sea fisheries the use of salting and drying if their catch was ever to reach the landward market in edible form. Lindores Abbey took a rent of half a load of dried herring annually for a ploughgate at Crail,[15] but this arrangement was rare; dried herring, and indeed other fish, do not figure in the tithing of income by which kings and others endowed the religious. All forms of animal income however did, and we may conclude that meat (and on Fridays fresh fish) went in the main to the lord's table but that salt fish was bought in to feed as wages to the peasantry—because that was the form of protein to which the peasantry was accustomed.

It is sometimes implied that Scotland had a largely pastoral economy whereas in England only the northern shires showed a similar balance. The judgement may well be correct over the whole country, but to the local community the local balance created the conditions of everyday life, not a gross national product. Not all non-arable land was used for grazing; in quality it varied widely—the water-logged clay soils of the Carse of Gowrie, the peat mosses

14 *Coldingham Correspondence*, p. xcv.
15 *Lindores Chartulary*, no. LXXV.

of Coldingham moor, the grassy slopes of the Cheviots or Sidlaws, and the rough heather-clad hillsides of the Grampians. Yet on almost all of it the peasant and his lord sought to graze their sheep and cattle, practising transhumance on the higher or more distant slopes when the summer grass invited.

Many of the money rents recorded in documents must have been paid in kind, and particularly in livestock. In the king's thanages in the 1260s, payments of cows and pigs are recorded though not, curiously, that characteristically Scottish rent, 'marts', beasts slain before the grass began to die, and paid as rent at Martinmas (11 November), whence their name. These beasts were grazed on the stubble of the arable field, upon the meadow from which hay was also taken, and on the 'waste', the rough ground around the arable. The extent of the meadow in most cases is not specified, but where it is it is a small fraction of the arable. The most detailed evidence again comes from the extent of Coldingham Priory's lands made about 1300, where we have seen at Swinton a very small grazing, at Fishwick a larger one, both much engrossed by the priory. At some villages no account of grazing is given but at Coldingham itself there were eighty acres of 'separate' pasture for the priory's stock but the waste was of unknown value 'because numberless'. This would certainly provide extensive grazing for peasant stock, and it is not without significance that Coldingham was the largest of the priory's villages. But neither here nor elsewhere do we have any indication of the size of peasant herds and flocks.

Since 1945 techniques of survey should have brought the archaeologist to the assistance of the historian by identifying the steadings and shiels which the documentary sources locate, sometimes within detailed bounds. In the Isle of Man some 350 medieval turf-built shielings have been identified, but only one in the northern English counties, where 135 stone-built shielings are thought to be post medieval.[16] Other turf shielings are considered to have been destroyed without trace, although this thesis is contrary to the general experience that the landscape is a palimpsest from which no work of man can be wholly erased except by subsequent work of man. In Roxburghshire a number of enclosures associated with traces of buildings and with field systems have been tentatively ascribed to the Middle Ages, including one at Kelsocleuch in Mow

[16] H. G. Ramon, R. W. McDowell, E. Mercer, *Shielings and Bastles*, London, 1970.

which was excavated and which revealed habitation, apparently
Iron or Dark Age and medieval, as well as enclosures which appear
to be connected with sheep-farming rather than arable. In southern
Scotland a number of 'scooped' enclosures in upland areas might
have served well enough as the dwellings or lodgings in hill pastures
to which medieval written sources refer; but these are now re-dated
to the early Iron Age and archaeologists have dotted the hills with
the remains of prehistoric pastoral economies but can find almost
nothing from the intensive sheep farming of the Middle Ages.[17]
Excavation may change the picture, for it is difficult to believe that
'the work of man's hand', to which charters refer, has left no surviving trace.

Variation in the ratio of pasture to arable can also be found
both north and south of the Forth. Unfortunately, the charters
of Coupar Angus Abbey, which produced the best wool in Scotland,
tell us far less of its grazing than do those of Melrose, but Coupar
was certainly well endowed with arable in Strathmore and with
grazings in Strathardle, Glenisla, and Glenshee.[18] Further east the
abbey of Arbroath acquired 10 acres of arable at Kinblethmont with
a souming which, if the arable had been an oxgang (that is, 1.3
times larger), would have been 52 sheep, 5 cows, 2 oxen and a
horse; nearby at Newtyle, Lindores Abbey, with an oxgang of
arable, acquired a souming of 30 sheep, 10 oxen and a horse, while
a little further north at Garvock, near Laurencekirk, the same
amount of arable had grazing for 100 sheep, 20 cows and a bull,
10 oxen and 4 horses, some three times greater than the first two
examples.[19] Perhaps, like the parishes bounding Lammermuir and
the Cheviots, the parish of Laurencekirk was well endowed with
grazings in the Grampians, and transhumance is well enough
attested in Perthshire, Angus and Mearns.

Beyond the Mounth, however, there is a difference at least in the
nature of the evidence: detailed specification of the souming granted
with arable is almost wholly absent.[20] This change might be attri-

---

[17] *Inventory of Roxburghshire*, p. 48; nos. 641, 666; *Inventory of Peebleshire*,
pp. 24–6, 49; nos. 672–6 .

[18] *Coupar Charters*, i, xxx–xxxiv.

[19] *Arbroath Liber*, i, nos. 143, 314; *Lindores Chartulary*, nos. X, XXXVII.

[20] The only examples I have noted are *Moray Registrum*, no 37, a modest
souming in the royal forest for a 'solitary chaplain' or hermit who might be
expected to eschew common grazings; and *St. Andrews Liber*, 362–3, Leochel
in Mar.

buted to the rather less plentiful evidence for the north, but this argument is not weighty. It is unlikely to be coincidence that prescribed soumings are found in the zone of the ploughgate and that of both ploughgate and davach, but are absent from the zone of the davach alone, and the simplest explanation would seem to be a difference in the human pressure on resources. If, as has been argued, the ploughgate must represent in many cases north of Forth an extension of arable and of the smaller fields and homesteads represented by the davach, then it would also represent increased pressure on pastoral resources which it simultaneously diminished; hence the tendency to define the numbers of stock which might be grazed. North of the Mounth the rarity of the ploughgate argues conversely for lesser demand for both arable and grazing.

The importance of the pastoral element in the economy of Scotland has long been recognised. Yet too much of the grazing was at an altitude which in winter made it useless for anything but sheep, and in consequence the stocks of cattle raised over the summer had to be reduced by the butcher in the autumn. Such carcases were frequently paid as marts and, when salted, provided winter meat for the tables of landlords and their households. It is less certain that any sizeable part of the peasantry had either beef or mutton to eat at any season of the year, though in view of the fairly large flocks of sheep which the sources reveal, some mutton may have found its way into the peasant diet. Yet both sheep and lambs were valued most of all for the wool on their backs and for the contribution which they made to the wool trade and to the cloth industry, rural and urban, Scottish and foreign.

But the moors and mosses of Scotland were important to the economy for other reasons. The migration to upper pastures was not one of stock alone: in pastoral areas a large part of the village or hamlet must have moved also, and it was this fact which made necessary the dwellings or lodgings and shielings to which written sources make reference. Oxen and horses are named in the soumings because they were needed to transport to the shielings the living-equipment of those who accompanied the stock, and access routes to the moors were carefully specified not only for grazing stock but also for beasts of burden, sledges and carts.[21] In the summer months,

---

[21] *Coupar Charters*, no. XLV shows that beasts of burden were marked or branded and would stray.

the moors and hills were a hive of rural industry, and especially of female industry. Spinning was doubtless the 'spare-time' occupation of the womenfolk for much of the year, but after the shearing there must have been a spurt in this activity. Much more important, however, was the making of cheese. Cattle and ewes were driven with their followers to hill or moor after calving and lambing and for weeks were milked for cheesemaking, presumably by the womenfolk. There are few if any references to transportation of the cheese back from shielings, but the importance of the commodity is not in doubt. True, it is best attested outside the prosperous east and south-east: in Lennox as a form of tribute which suggests that that province, or at least Lomond-side, was pre-eminently pastoral.[22] In 1212, when the bishop of St Andrews gave the abbacy lands (perhaps of the Culdees of St Andrews) at Airlie to Coupar Abbey on a twenty-year lease he imposed a rent of 2 bezants, 10 stones of cheese, and 12 'Scottish sacks' of bere, an annual so exotic that it must have been a survival from much earlier times.[23] About the same time the earl of Fife and bishop of Moray settled up the lands which the earl was to hold in Stratha'an, one lot heritably for a money annual rent, one for life similarly, and the third for life for 40 stones of cheese annually. In Badenoch the bishop took as his teind of the king's rents 4 merks, 6 pigs, 8 'cogals' of cheese and $2\frac{1}{2}$ chalders of oats.[24] In the 1260s the king received from the thanage of Forfar among other rents 404 cogals and from the thanage of Glamis 81 cogals, selling 223 cogals for £36.[25] These figures give some scale to the many twelfth-century royal grants of teinds of royal cain or rents in cheeses from all parts of Scotland[26] and suggests that, while thirteenth-century charters between Tweed and Mounth have little to say of cheeses,[27] this is to be attributed to the general commutation of twelfth-century renders to money in the thirteenth and not to a decline in cheese-production. In fact the Berwickshire peasants who did boon-works at ploughing, haymaking or harvest received among their food a stone of cheese daily. They and other lowland peasants produced cheese from the

22 *Lennox Cartularium*, 20, 23, 45–6.
23 *Coupar Charters*, no. XXI.
24 *Moray Registrum*, nos. 16, 76; see also the cheese rents of Monymusk Priory in *St. Andrews Liber*, 361, 369–70.
25 *Exch. Rolls*, i, 6–7; see *ibid*, index under 'cheese'.
26 E.g. subject index to *R.R.S.*, ii, under 'cheese'.
27 Cf. *St. Andrews Liber*, 43, 316–8 for Fife.

milk of their lords' flocks and herds, and, it seems safe to assume, from the milk of their own—though whether the latter cheese was adequate to feed the family for a year or whether there was generally a marketed surplus, are questions to which the answers, if known, could well show variation from parish to parish.

In many places the summer visits to shielings were used not only for grazing and cheese-making but also for peat-cutting. Peat figures so frequently as a right or easement which the donee is to enjoy that we are undoubtedly entitled to conjure up in these places the picture which can still be seen in parts of the west and in the isles: men and women labouring together to cut peats, leaving them to dry near by and weeks later moving them, in two or even three laborious stages, since wheels could not come close to the cuttings, down to the township. The turbary or peatery was the site of a labour-intensive, short-season, industry, but a valuable site nonetheless. From the many examples in documentary sources the grant by Robert de Quincy of a grange at Preston near Tranent to Newbattle Abbey, in the late twelfth century, is rather fuller than the more typical 'commoning in my peatery' phrase. Robert defined the bounds of the grange carefully, freed it from secular exactions and added common pasture of his land at Tranent and free passage (not to be impeded by ploughing) to use the pasture for 700 sheep and for the oxen needed to work the grange. He gave six acres of meadow at Tranent and twenty cartloads of peats in his demesne peatery with fuel (heather or brushwood) for the grange.[28] The structure of a Cistercian grange and, it might be said, of the thirteenth-century rural economy of Scotland, is revealed here: arable, pasture, stock, access, meadow, and fuel—and fuel was as essential as each of the other elements. Some fifty years later Roger de Quincy, Lord of Leuchars and grandson of Robert, allowed the monks of Lindores and their men, with oxen, horses and carts, free access through the middle of his wood of Kinloch to the moor of Eden for heather and through the moor of Eden to the peatery called 'Monagrey' for peats.[29] Subsequently, Roger agreed that from Kinloch (probably Eden) moor the monks were to take 200 cartloads of heather or more if they wanted, and from the peatery as many peats as they needed but only for their own use, not for resale. They had an acre (.4 ha) near by for drying their peats and

[28] *Newbattle Registrum*, no. 64.
[29] *Lindores Chartulary*, no. CXXXV, 1256 x 64.

two acres (.8 ha) close to the nearest ford on which to store the heather and peats in the custody of a peasant who might graze two cows and ten sheep on Kinloch moor—this was his living. The draught oxen of the monks which drew the fuel (but not their other draught oxen) might graze on the same moor from the beginning of the carrying until 8 September.[30]

These detailed provisions were perhaps necessary because Roger's first grant had been abused by the taking of peats for sale and by the grazing of too many oxen upon the moor. On the other hand, the abbey did not have the carts and men to move the fuel in the quantity they required from the moss to the convent before harvest time and so negotiated a half-way storage ground. The problem should not surprise us since an ox-drawn cart would move few miles in a day, and though heather and peat are not heavy, they are required in large quantities by bulk to maintain adequate firing, especially of conventual buildings; thus almost identical provisions were made in the late twelfth century in Midlothian for Newbattle Abbey at a peatery with two acres (.8 ha) where their man would 'procure the digging and drying of their peats', an arrangement which was itself an improvement upon an earlier 'little house next the peatery to house those cutting peat'.[31] Among their labours for the prior of Coldingham the wealthier peasants of Fishwick must cut turves for a day annually and carry six cartloads of them, while the cottars must cut and stack.[32] The fact that a landowner would invest in storehouses, as well as divert men, carts and beasts to transportation, emphasises the importance of this fuel to the maintenance of the household; whether monastic or lay, all large households must have used large stocks of peat annually.

The peasant, too, must have enjoyed peat-cutting rights, and although the individual quantities removed by him were small, cumulatively the effect of centuries of exploitation was surely considerable. Thus, when in the 1220s Coupar and Dunfermline abbeys fell out over the latter's townships lying between Coupar and the moss to the south of Blairgowrie, which Coupar had received from King William about 1200, the settlement insisted that Coupar have unimpeded access to its peatmoss but must assign annually to

30 *Lindores Chartulary*, no. CXXXVII. It seems that *ibid*, no. CXL comes chronologically between the two grants by Roger de Quincy and represents a first attempt to find a two-acre storage ground near Collessie.
31 *Newbattle Registrum*, nos. 36, 35.
32 *Coldingham Correspondence*, lxxxvii–lxxxviii.

the men of Dunfermline's townships two hundred cartloads of peat in due time and place.[33] These townships and others were farmed in 1282 for five merks annually[34] which suggests that each was of modest size; yet men were as heedless in the thirteenth century as later of the limits to nature's resources and between them the abbey and the peasantry stripped the moss until only the name, *blàr*, survives. It would be instructive to plot the peateries to which our sources refer and to examine the soils there today for it is likely that in many places a carpet of peat has been stripped from the ground. Much would have been burned on domestic hearths, and made tolerable the climate and temperatures of the Scottish winter; indeed we might guess that peat fires were one factor which lengthened the expectation of life and hence increased the population.

But this was not the only use to which peat was put. In the 1230s Walter Bisset, Lord of Aboyne, gave to Coupar Abbey his saltwork near Aberdeen 'with sufficient peatery to make salt' as the king had granted this to him.[35] The abbey had no other property there but it would value a source of salt so close to the great fishing port, for salt fish was an important part of rural diet. Many—perhaps most—of the saltworks named so frequently in documents from tidal regions must have had pans fired by peat like those of the archdeacon just outside the town of St Andrews in 1212.[36] The carse of Stirling was particularly well suited to the collection of sea water by tidal action, and saltworks there belonged to the abbeys of Jedburgh, Cambuskenneth, Holyrood, Kelso, Dunfermline and Newbattle.[37] That of Newbattle Abbey was given by David I, Malcolm IV adding the right to fuel from the wood of Callendar; in 1233 Alexander II seems to have handed over some or all the remaining royal saltworks and the abbey also took over those of Dunfermline and Kelso abbeys and of private individuals there. One of these yielded well over four chalders of salt a year, since that was the rent which the abbey paid for it. In 1237 Newbattle Abbey feued most of these to Holyrood Abbey for something over £40

---

[33] *Coupar Charters*, no. XXXIII; *Dunfermline Registrum*, no. 217; *R.R.S.*, ii, no. 420.

[34] *Dunfermline Registrum*, no. 322.

[35] *Coupar Charters*, no. XLVIII.

[36] *St. Andrews Liber*, 315–6.

[37] Lawrie, *E.S.C.*, nos. CLXXXIX, CLXXIX; *Holyrood Liber*, nos. 13, 61; *R.R.S.*, i, no. 131.

yearly, the latter having also taken at a ferme of over £50 the king's lands of Callendar in 1234.[38] Clearly the production of salt in this area was very big business, yet we hear only once, and that very early, of an easement of firewood to evaporate the saltwater, and it seems likely that local peat was at least as important for the purpose, although this peat must be included in the land granted with the saltworks since it is not mentioned explicitly. It has been suggested that at Bannockburn over the past millenium very large quantities of peat have been stripped from the carse, a fact which must be connected with the multiplicity of saltworks. Perhaps it should be added that there is no clear example of the granting of turves for use in building.

Many settlements had no access (or only a restricted one) to peat-mosses, and depended upon woodland for firing, so that commoning of firewood (*focale*) was frequently and widely granted for both landlord and peasant.[39] The same could be said of the right to take wood for building (*materies, meremium*), sometimes linked with grazing rights or with taking firewood. The danger of such building is well shown by 'one of the best granges in Coupar full of grain which was burned through the carelessness of a badly fixed candle' in 1215.[40] As early as the reign of David I, St Andrews Priory was taking timber from the king's forest of Clackmannan for its new building; in 1277 the chapter of Glasgow Cathedral acquired free access to the woods of Luss to take all kinds of wood necessary for the building of the cathedral steeple and treasury, and carted the timber away by horse and ox.[41] Between those two works a great deal of ecclesiastical and domestic building had gone on in Scotland behind a web of timber scaffolding and crowned by timber roofing. But most 'material' was probably used not for building of this kind but for wattle and clay walls, partitions and the simple roofs of the peasant cot or house which gave cottar and husbandman their names. A big house made of wattle (*de virgis*) beside the kirk of Old Kilpatrick on the Clyde was run by its occupant in the 1170s as a small guest house;[42] the wording might suggest that it was unusual to have a wattle house of such size. The shepherds of

[38] *Newbattle Registrum*, nos. 160, 171; *Holyrood Liber*, no. 65.
[39] E.g. *Arbroath Liber*, i, nos. 89, 142, 306, 314.
[40] Anderson, *Early Sources*, ii, 404.
[41] *St. Andrews Liber*, 183–4; *Glasgow Registrum*, no. 229.
[42] *Paisley Registrum*, 166–7.

Melrose Abbey had to shelter under wattled huts on the edge of Whitelee forest and not under anything more substantial—and these *claias wiscatas* seem to have been of dug-out or lean-to construction rather than buildings.[43] At Dirleton in the east the canons of Dryburgh were given 'roofing of bent or other roofing for their houses', and it is likely that heather and turf were much used for this purpose.[44]

When the right to take wood was granted, the sources scarcely ever specify the quantities; but the four cartloads of stakes and rods taken annually at Quixwood were subsequently bought up by the landlord (Coldingham Priory) for four merks so that the tenant could take the wood only when the priory allowed.[45] Assuming a twenty years' purchase price, a cartload was worth between sixteen and eight pence, which was probably fairly cheap in comparison with prices obtaining in England or France. There are indeed few signs that, away from the environs of the larger towns, wood was the precious commodity in Scotland which it had generally become in those countries,[46] perhaps because a deal of the woodland of Scotland would have been unsuitable for cultivation after clearing.

Yet at Mow we shall meet one example of the erosion of woodland by the taking of timber for sheepfolds (below p. 418). In Atholl the monks of Coupar allowed the local peasantry to take timber for making ploughs, carts, harrows and fencing (or hedges) so long as they made no waste, denuding or destruction[47] and the monks of Lindores took 'dry timber which is called 'dead wood' for fuel, and the wood called *wrawes* of alder and birch, a hundred loads of hazelrods for making sleds and a hundred long rods for making *circulos'*—perhaps wheels.[48] It would be interesting to know whether alder and birch were used for making or repairing ploughs and harrows; the repair of implements must have been frequent and expensive, and there would be a steady demand for timber for these and similar uses. The wood to which this text takes us was perhaps little different from the self-regenerating scrubland which can still be found in those parts of Scotland neglected by modern afforesters,

---

43 *Melrose Liber*, no. 106.
44 *Dryburgh Liber*, nos. 104, 105.
45 Raine, *North Durham*, no. CCXLV.
46 G. Duby, *Rural Economy and Country Life*, 143–5.
47 *Coupar Charters*, no. LXII.
48 *Lindores Chartulary*, no. LXXIII.

and it is likely that a great deal of woodland was of this kind. Oak and elm also grew but were perhaps difficult to come by—or so the purchase of building timber from Luss for Glasgow Cathedral would suggest.

Competition for woodland resources came from two other uses: grazing and hunting. In Moray the bishop had woodland in the king's forest around Elgin, Forres and Inverness; it must yield timber and fuel to the bishop's men without impediment by the king's forester and without their neighbours (presumably the peasants of other lords) enjoying the same privilege; and in it the bishop had pannage for himself and his men. Similarly, though more briefly, Melrose Abbey had easements of wood, timber and pannage in Ettrick Forest.[49] Pannage was the right to graze pigs and horses among the trees, as the Steward allowed Paisley Abbey to take a hundred pigs into his forest for a month in the autumn or as Kelso Abbey took its mares over the Border into the d'Umphraville forest in Northumberland.[50] Often the two were combined, as in Balfeith in the Mearns, where Arbroath Abbey had 'common pasture both of the donor's wood for their building needs and of other easements of peatery and pasture, so that they have grazing for a hundred cattle with their followers, as many pigs as they want and a stud (*equicium*) likewise.'[51] These animals were pastured on grass and moor as well as in woodland, but it seems to have been general practice for at least part of the year to graze them apart from the sheep upon woodland mast,[52] a practice which probably goes back into the Dark Ages or earlier. The place-name Swinewood in Berwickshire occurs at the end of the eleventh century and the priory of Coldingham had a swineherd nearby early in the thirteenth—although he had retired on the profits of a venture as champion in trial by battle on behalf of another peasant.[53] Rents in pigs were tithed by David I and occur in the king's accounts of the 1260s, but the numbers of swine pastured seem to have been only a fraction of the cattle, and a yet smaller one of the sheep, reared in most parts. Excavation (for instance of dateable ringworks) may throw more light upon the relative importance of pork and other

[49] *R.R.S.*, ii, nos. 362, 175.
[50] *Paisley Registrum*, 17; *Kelso Liber*, nos. 325–9. The former document, in the phrase 'season of *pessun*', uses an Old French word for pasture or grazing.
[51] *Arbroath Liber*, i, no. 89.
[52] E.g. *Coldstream Chartulary*, no. 35.
[53] Lawrie, *E.S.C.*, no. XIX; Raine, *North Durham*, no. CCCXCVII.

meat in medieval diet.[54] The mares and their foals were perhaps cart or pack horses in some cases, especially when grazed by the village community; but in many cases the lord's stud was kept for his hunting. Clearly there was much concern that the taking of timber for fuel and building would trench on hunting reserves, but the right of forest precluded commoning of green (building) wood only and not of the dead wood which was so valuable for firing.

In the west, Walter the Steward about 1220, granted land to Paisley Abbey carved out of his forest between the Black and White Cart rivers, within which they might 'assart, plough and build, make hedges and enclosures saving my wildfowl and beasts'. If within the winter close season for hunting their animals crossed into the forest they were heavily fined, but outside the close season less heavily so. From the forest they might take green timber for their own building needs and fuel, and in it they might pasture 100 pigs, but beyond these rights 'the said monks shall have nothing',[55] which is to say that they had no grazing rights for sheep there.

The process of assarting, which is illustrated particularly fully by this grant, went on intensively in moorland and forest from the late twelfth century. Sometimes we learn of pressure for it because it is forbidden, as in the great stretch of moor between Braco and Muthill.[56] In the forest between Gala and Leader David I gave part of the land of Blainslie to his foresters, but King William gave it to a small landowner who was perhaps responsible for breaking it out. By c. 1185 Melrose Abbey acquired it with permission to build, but was forbidden to cultivate any more than was already under the plough.[57] About the same time the abbey acquired from the de Morevilles the right to plough and sow 'the land of Blainslie and the whole clearing outside the wood' except that in one part of the land they might make no assart.[58] While in the early twelfth century forest areas for hunting were doubtless being extended, particularly in southern Scotland, by the latter part of the century these rights

[54] 'Excavations at Kildrummy Castle,' *Proc. Soc. Antiq. Scot.*, xcvi (1962–3, but 1963–4 on running titles), 223–4.

[55] *Paisley Registrum*, 17.

[56] *Lindores Chartulary*, no. XXVIII.

[57] *R.R.S.*, ii, no. 265.

[58] *Melrose Liber*, nos. 94–6; in the royal confirmation (*R.R.S.*, ii, no. 301) there is some departure from the wording of the grant, so that it reads contradictorily or at least oddly: the clearing of Blainslie to plough and cultivate without making an assart. The last four words should apply to part of Blainslie only.

were on the defensive against the remorseless demand that suitable land should feed more sheep and more humans.

Sometimes assarting is not immediately obvious, as in the grants of ministerial tenures on moorland—land for the peat-keeper or shepherd. Sometimes we cannot date it with any precision, as in those early English place-names in Celtic areas, particularly in the region between Tay and Mounth, or early examples of 'Newton' in Anglian areas. The ploughgate of the region between Forth and Mounth is sometimes to be interpreted in the same way: it represents either the enlargement of existing arable or the breaking out of new, although the dates and details of this process are now lost to us. Another telling indicator is the stream of judgements and concords concerned with disputes over teinds, arising because old-established divisions of teinds or exemptions from them do not (in the view of the grasping party) take account of new income. And, most telling of all, the establishment of new mills which may often be suspected to underlie the documented tussles over multures, is in some cases overtly provided for.[59] What new acreage justified a new mill we do not know, but that there is a direct link between the multiplicity of thirteenth-century mills and an expanding arable is beyond doubt.

Taken as a whole, the documentary sources leave no doubt that the area of cultivated land was increasing at the expense of 'waste'— moor and forest—until the late thirteenth century at least, and that this breaking out of new land was particularly active from the last quarter of the twelfth century until the third quarter of the thirteenth; similarly, it is abundantly clear that grazing, particularly by sheep, was becoming more and more intensive during the same period to meet the needs of the cloth industry. Yet plainly this expansion was not uniform throughout Scotland and there is much need to investigate its incidence by detailed local studies. It was most intense in the east between the Tweed and the Mounth, where it was served and stimulated by the swift development of twelfth-century towns, notably Perth and Dundee. These urban centres, far from being pattern-book homes of 'merchants and craftsmen', varied greatly in space and time in the detailed functions they performed in rural society. Their inhabitants were a significant body of consumers stimulating rural production of food; but, more important, as centres of exchange their rôle can hardly be under-

59 E.g. *St. Andrews Liber*, 353, at Dairsie in Fife.

estimated, and it was this which made them an essential part of the great agrarian and pastoral boom of the twelfth and thirteenth centuries and which differentiated this boom from the slower expansion of settlement discernable from post-Roman times until the eleventh century.

In England, it has been argued, by the thirteenth century the extension of cultivation, and particularly of peasant cultivation, had reached its limit: the lands then being taken up were of the lowest possible quality, marginal land whose yields were disastrously low and whose fertility was all too soon exhausted. The process of assarting or internal colonisation ground to a halt and was replaced by the economic and social crises of the late fourteenth century and the regression of the fifteenth. Yet there are exceptions to this story, notably on the periphery of England, and if the expansion continued later in Northumberland, it would be reasonable to conclude that in Scotland too (contrary to the argument on labour services in this chapter) the possible limits of extension of arable had not yet been reached, except perhaps in the immediate environs of towns, by 1300. In other words, a great deal remains to be done in the interpretation of the rural economy of medieval Scotland, the serious social and economic history of which has scarcely begun to be written.[60]

[60] The exception is the seminal studies of Professor G. W. S. Barrow.

# 15

## FIEF AND SERVICE

In this chapter we shall be concerned with the various levels of a society which, however convenient a single label for it like 'feudal' may be on occasion to historians, changed significantly over the twelfth and thirteenth centuries. A rural community in the expansive circumstances outlined in the preceding chapters was clearly subject to a variety of economic pressures which in the outcome might alter its form and social structure—and the lot of many individuals—drastically. Unfortunately, the evidence at our disposal is of very restricted value. It may be fortunate that no lawyer in Scotland undertook to describe the laws and customs of the land, for the social observation of the legal fraternity is in general limited; lawyers seek categories, especially those defined by rights and duties, and their division of medieval society would be as real as a division of modern society into the local-authority housed and owner-occupiers.

Most of our documents deal with one group, or social class, marked off from the peasantry by its monopoly of land ownership, its power in the state and in local administration, and its exclusive social intercourse most readily indicated by intermarriage. This landowning or 'feudal' class, encompassing the younger sons of lairds toward the bottom[1] and earls at the top certainly had its own internal rankings and was keenly aware of 'peerage'—that some are more equal than others—yet as a whole it shared common standards and common interests. Its members, while they tended to marry only with those from their own social rank or immediately

---

[1] I have used this term while well aware of the anachronism. I mean by it a free landholder of less consequence than a knight; the word vavassor was used occasionally in the thirteenth century.

above or below, were linked one rank with another, by mutual ties of contract and service and, in general, by a social intercommunication of which the charters, virtually our only source, tell us all too little. For this reason, it is possible for historians to differ over, for example, the nature and closeness of the relationship between a magnate and his tenants in the thirteenth century, although it would be agreed that when their ancestors came together to Scotland in the twelfth the fealty of vassal to lord was grounded in their common material interests in a new environment—and material interest keeps such a relationship wonderfully adaptable and active. At no point within the landowning class was there anything like the gulf which separated it from the other, and numerically vastly larger class in society, the peasantry. Along with his arable, meadow, mills and brew-houses the landowner will sometimes speak of his 'men' as another of his assets which must not be damaged by third party interests, but such 'men' are no party to their lord's concern. They are the objects of it.

Perhaps the simplest definition of the landowning class was that used habitually by the king's clerks in his writs: they are addressed 'to all his worthy (*probi*) men', scarcely translatable since the 'worthiness' meant by *probis* was a compound of good birth and sound standing—property or prospects. From these men of standing the king might single out earls and barons for special mention, and earls indeed are the one group whom it is possible to identify and enumerate. Elsewhere it is argued that the public functions of the earl hung about him for long in Scotland and that as late as William the Lion's reign the king might interfere with the hereditary descent of the earldoms for good cause shown. Yet this was exceptional and probably disquieting. The English debate about earlier twelfth-century heritability among the landowning class seems now to be summed up in favour of a stronger hereditary principle than was recently in favour.[2] And the Scottish evidence accords with that summation. Thus, King David's charters to his knight Arnulf are so close in date that it would be a mistake to read a difference into the two phrases used: 'to him and his heir' and 'to him and heirs'[3] Both meant heritable tenure in perpetuity, and the first was not a restriction to two lifetimes. It should be understood as a

---

[2] J. C. Holt, 'Politics and Property in Early Medieval England', *Past and Present*, 57 (1972), 1–52, and the earlier literature cited there.

[3] Lawrie, *E.S.C.*, nos. C, CI.

restriction of descent to *one* child (a male heir) in each generation and against partition among children or sons as coheirs. The grant of Annandale to Bruce, probably of 1124, makes no mention of heritability and indeed refers to the customs which Ranulf Meschin had in Carlisle—a territory which Ranulph had lost several years earlier and which was therefore not heritable. Yet it is difficult to believe that Annandale was to be other than patrimony, for as such it was certainly treated; when Robert Bruce died in 1141 his lands had been divided, the inherited lands in England going to one son Adam and the 'conquest'—his acquisition, Annandale in Scotland—together with lands in County Durham to the second, Robert. Thus a form of heritability was practised, partition of the individual fief or honour was ruled out, but not partition of the whole patrimony, at least where it lay in two realms. In this case primogeniture was clearly not practised but this can be attributed to the circumstances of the English civil war, King David accepting a different heir in Scotland and in the territory of Durham which he had effectively neutralised, from the heir accepted by King Stephen. When David I confirmed Annandale to the younger Robert 'and his heir', this is to be read also as a refusal to countenance partition; when King William confirmed it about 1170, the donee was Robert 'and his heirs' so that by this time (when 'and his heirs' was common form) the phrase must mean 'each heir successively' and not 'all sons in each generation in partition'.[4] By the late twelfth century most land in Lowland Scotland and in the great straths of the Grampians, held 'in feu and heritage' (*in feodo et hereditate*) was understood to pass from father to eldest son provided that the son met certain prior obligations—the widow's portion and the lord's relief.

It cannot be emphasised strongly enough that such a custom was the product not of enforcing a rule-book, but of the interplay of social forces among which the authority of the ruler was only one—and not necessarily the strongest. In his charter to Bruce of 1124, David I addresses 'all his barons and men and friends, French and English' and the concepts behind these words, of social standing, service and personal friendship, doubtless informed the grants of

---

4 Lawrie, *E.S.C.*, nos. LIX, CXCIX; *R.R.S.*, ii, no. 80; *Scots Peerage*, ii, 428–30; *Monasticon Anglicanum*, ed. R. Dodsworth and W. Dugdale, ii (1661), 148 or in the re-edition, VI part i (1830), 267; *Cartularium Prioratus de Gyseburne*, ed. W. Brown, ii, (Surtees Soc. no. 89, 1891), no. MCXLVIII.

land which he made to Bruce, de Moreville, the Steward and many others and which they made in turn to knights and lairds. Part of that relationship was the lord's friendship and generosity but another part was the reverence and service which he might expect in return and which indeed his generosity sought to sustain. It is most simply seen where the service due was military that succession by partition of the vassal's lands could, and almost certainly would, lead to an inability to perform that service. The diminished wealth of the individual in each successive generation would not sustain the cost of arms, armour and horse, especially as this rose in the late twelfth century. It was, therefore, plainly in the interest of the lord to insist upon impartible and male succession. Similar but more circumstantial pressures would be at work where the services expected were not military or where they were of the service of a number of knights (to which partition is not necessarily inimical so long as a holding was large enough to support at least one knight). The vassal must sustain not merely an intermittent service but a continuing social presence and status by which, in turn, his lord's standing is supported. Sometimes he must carry out continuing service as a *ministerialis* or administrator of lands or castle, paying a ferme and pocketing the profits, an arrangement which may cause his lord less trouble if it is not fragmented. Let the eldest son, therefore, succeed.

Yet surely the vassal must also have a concern for the destination of his estate, or rather a concern for his progeny as a whole and not just for the oldest son. To make provision for all children in order to assure that the family as a whole retains its place in society was probably as important in the twelfth century as any 'natural' desire of father to provide for his flesh and blood. Thus, the daughter must not be married beneath the family—disparaged—but to find a suitable husband she must bring a tocher in land (as well, no doubt, as goods) to him. In 1293 the earl of Strathearn made a marriage settlement on behalf of his daughter with her prospective father-in-law, Ralph de Thony, who promised two English manors and three advowsons to the couple. For five years the income therefrom was to go to Earl Malise who would maintain the young couple in a becoming manner; but in return he must pay to Ralph 1200 merks, of which half was returnable should his daughter die before the age of twenty. The delicate balance of provision reflects the superior social standing of an earl and his daughter, and his comparative poverty (in English terms), so that Ralph's son was expected to remain an English baron and sought no Scottish lands.[5] The tocher was usually given by the woman's father or brother and in land. Already Malcolm IV in 1160, giving lands as tocher to his niece and her husband Duncan, Earl of Fife, was careful to specify a limitation to land so given—that it should pass to their heir—if she bore no living child, that is, the land was not kept by her husband but returned to her family's patrimony.[6] This limitation on lands granted 'in frank marriage' was customary by the late twelfth century, and is the clearest evidence that provision was expected for all the children but that no obligation existed beyond kindred by blood. The family was the countervailing pressure to the lord's interest and by the late twelfth century the family had won the substance of control over land, leaving only incidental rights to the lord.

To be sure, the rule of impartibility remained for male descent, but, where no son survived, descent was to daughters, which is to say that the family lands passed not to a brother but by partition to sons-in-law, holding in right of their wives. Male tenure was invariable, but the striking aspect of this custom is that it defeats the family as a large group including brothers, uncles and cousins, it defeats the lord in so far as he is not allowed to take back the lands permanently, and it defeats them in the interests of others connected only by marriage to the family. The custom of descent to heirs general (that is, to sons, whom failing daughters) was indeed disliked by many of the landowning class, who looked upon the family as an agnatial group only, and in the fourteenth century the tailzie was developed to limit descent to heirs male. Why and when, then, did descent to heirs general become customary?

It is known that in England during the reign of David I's contemporary, Stephen, partition among daughters as co-heiresses was established by royal edict. The same rule may have been adopted in Scotland by the mid-twelfth century and there are clear examples that it was accepted in the later twelfth century. Thus, when the powerful Walter de Berkeley, King William's chamberlain, died about 1193 his estates passed equally to the Balliol husband of one daughter and to Humphrey fitz Theobald de Adeville, husband of another. Humphrey appears only once as his father's son, but many

[5] Stevenson, *Documents*, no. CCCVIII.
[6] *R.R.S.*, i, no. 190.

times as Humphrey de Berkeley, so that with his rich heiress he took her father's name—an indication that already name was a recognised mark of descent, that is, was closely linked with blood, and that where a family rose socially by marriage it would accept the obligation to take the more prestigious name for its own progeny. Partibility among co-heiresses was perhaps a consequence, at least in part, of the general desire of landowners to marry off such daughters well, but this cannot be the whole story, for such marriages often took place in the father's lifetime, when the birth of a son might yet defeat female.succession. It is much more likely that the custom arose as a compromise between lord and vassal: when the former accepted that heritable succession was indefeasible in the male line and insisted upon primogeniture there; he must also have insisted upon the return or 'escheat' of land when such heirs failed. Yet when no sons but a daughter survived the temptation was obvious—to confer the lady and the lands upon the highest bidder. And where several daughters survived it made sense to partition the lands and sell each individually in marriage: partition, that is, looks like the price of female succession, and was imposed even when the daughters were married before succession.

No policy along these lines was argued or imposed. If it happened this way, it happened through a multiplicity of individual instances cumulating into a general practice or custom. But the reader will notice that part of the argument assumes that land escheated would be sold by grant of the lord, and will ask why he should not retain the land, resisting inducements which would certainly be less than the long-term value of the land. Yet twelfth-century society seems to have expected just this: that a landlord would divest himself again within reasonable time of the lands which fell to him by reason of escheat or forfeiture. There is no law to this effect in Britain to measure beside the *Leihezwang* of Barbarossa's Germany,[7] yet tacit acceptance of some such principle is signified by the many grants of escheated property and by occasions of restlessness among relatives of a man to whose property the lord (especially the king in England) seemed intent on clinging. We should like to know, when a landlord had an heiress for disposal, the extent of involvement of the wider family (such as uncles and cousins) in the choice of her husband, and therefore of the destination of her patrimony. A better

[7] K. Hampe, *Germany under the Salian and Hohenstaufen Emperors* trans. R. Bennett (1973), 18, 21, 30, 204.

understanding of customs in these matters might explain more fully, for example, the descent of the earldom of Atholl in the mid-thirteenth century.

Yet in the vast majority of cases, land descended from father to eldest son to be held by each of the lord, by him of another and so on, perhaps for numerous steps, until held ultimately by someone of the king. Most of these men enjoyed the homage of the man on the rung beneath them on the 'feudal' ladder; only the man on the bottom rung enjoyed exploitation of the land, and it was a serious limitation that the vassal might not provide for all his sons by partition of his capital. In fact the very existence of the ladder and its many rungs is to be explained by the social pressure to provide for the whole family. If a man might not divide on his death, then he must needs divide in his lifetime, carve a fraction from his holding and pass it to his younger son to be held of the elder line as that line in turn holds the whole of the lord. Thus for part of the land at least a rung has been added to the tenurial ladder, and in the next generation another. The earls of Lothian or Dunbar were comparatively fortunate in that each generation assured direct succession but was not over-provided with younger sons. Earl Gospatrick (II), 'brother of Dolfin', who was killed at Northallerton in 1138, had acquired by royal grant extensive lands in Northumberland formerly belonging to his uncle, and these passed with other English lands to his younger sons, Edward and Edgar. Each of these three appears as a 'benefactor' of the church and especially of the religious, yet a closer examination reveals that the documents to which they are party are probably compromises, the outcome of struggles or negotiations with monastic houses, Earl Gospatrick with Durham Priory over Edrom and Nesbit, Edward with the monks of Melrose over Hartside and Spot, and Edgar with the monks of Tynemouth; their sister was married off with a generous tocher to the lord of Morpeth. Edward certainly retained lands near Dunbar, perhaps so that he might serve (and shine in the reflected prestige of) his brother the earl; but Edgar married very well and became sufficiently independent to cut loose from Scotland and even to quarrel with Edward, whose English lands he tried to seize, probably in the war of 1173-4. Edgar then joined King William and had to flee to Scotland, losing much of his property in consequence.

The effect of Gospatrick (II)'s generous support for his younger

sons was to leave Earl Gospatrick (III) as lord in England of little
but homages. He in his turn, therefore, had to provide for his
second son, Patrick, with a fief at Greenlaw in Berwickshire, but
with his wife he also endowed the nunnery of Coldstream and perhaps also that of Eccles. Patrick, who held the earldom for fifty
years after 1182, had at least two younger sons: William was lord
of Fogo, presumably by his father's gift, married the Corbet heiress
of Makerston and begat three sons, all calling themselves Corbet.
Robert was steward to his brother the earl but is not known to have
held any land.[8]

Although the earl probably had only a very small income from
England he retained a nominal allegiance to the English king, and
in this was typical of many 'Anglo-Scottish' barons who appear
in English records but whose real commitment was to the realm of
Scotland. The present value of this instance is the capital cost to
each generation of the endowment of the next, a dissolution of
wealth which may have been necessary to inhibit unrest among the
group of younger sons who could have given leadership to wider
social discontent among the land hungry. But if dissolution of
capital had been the only process at work, even earls would have
been socially demoted in the long run and the declining generosity
of the thirteenth-century earls of Dunbar may mark their aware-
ness of this threat; other factors, however, acted in mitigation or
even compensation. Land may have been granted at ferme (that is,
capital reinvestment); remaining resources were exploited more
effectively so as to yield higher returns; and some of these returns
might be invested in new purchases of land. But all this was conducted, or has survived, in the forms of feudal conveyancing and
produces an impression of tenurial complexity.

Sometimes this complexity was ironed out. Thus the abbey of
Kelso, in its anxiety to obtain arable and grazing by the Lammer-
muirs, entered into an elaborate series of agreements with the
vassals of the Steward who were his tenants there. In 1190 it took
the land on lease for thirty-three years for a ferme of 20s. annually
and with an undertaking that the three knights would not grant
a title to anyone else. The Steward confirmed their act and promised
that if the land reverted to him he, too, would grant it only to the
abbey. This arrangement was probably a wadset to the abbey in
return for a capital sum, for the three knights also granted the

<hr />

[8] *Scots Peerage*, iii, 241–57; *History of Northumberland*, vii, 30–65.

land individually in fractions ($\frac{2}{3}$, $\frac{1}{6}$, $\frac{1}{6}$) in feu-ferme (that is, per-petually), for rents adding up to 20s. and three *bothas*,[9] while a fourth knight granted a further sixth for 3s. 4d. and the fourth *botha*. Forty years later the abbey held the land of the Steward, paying 20s. and two pairs of *bothae* to him annually, so that the knights and their descendants (who would have fragmented the fief if they had not alienated it) were bought out of the tenurial hier-archy.[10]

This legal simplification was unusual, and neither church nor layman had much hesitation in accepting and giving land by con-veyances which seemed to pay little regard to the obligations already laid upon the holder of the land by some earlier donor. For it is difficult to discover in Scotland much evidence of the period when a vassal was first and foremost a client or vassal and only secondarily a tenant of his lord. True, Arnulf, the knight of David I, may be an example of the 'man' who loved and was loyal to his lord, as the homage which he did on bended knee and the oath of fealty which he swore on holy relics foretold that he would be, and who, be-cause of his loyal service as a mounted retainer, was rewarded with land (to which the church had a title!) on which he might live and for which he might continue to serve. But the same king's grant of land to Alexander of St Martin together with an annual money fee until such time as the king could give enough land to maintain his service as a knight, indicates that already loyalty, service and payment were inextricably mingled. 'Fee' and 'feu' are derived from the same root and have the same connotation of payment, even of payment in land, *Anglice* 'fief'—and this radical sense of pay-ment explains why grants of land will be either in (that is, as) feu or in alms but rarely (and really nonsensically) in both.[11] (Later 'feu' meant a non-military tenure, especially for an annual 'feu-duty'.)

Our earliest documents granting land in feu either do not specify the service which the recipient gives (as in the case of Robert Bruce in Annandale), or specify service as that of a knight. Cases of the former kind, where they are associated with a great magnate, have been understood to show reticence only on what everyone knew—the number of knights whose service was expected, in the

[9] I take it these are not booths nor casks (*butta*) but boots or archery butts, more probably the latter.
[10] *Kelso Liber*, nos. 247–61.
[11] Lawrie, *E.S.C.*, no. CXI.

case of Bruce the ten whom King William specified later. But this assumption may be unduly influenced by the fixed *servitium debitum* (service due) imposed by the English king, William I, upon the religious and barons of his kingdom as a means of spreading among them the cost of keeping a standing army of occupation amid a hostile populace. Circumstances in Scotland were not of this kind, but rather that the king favoured his friends, and it may be that the same amicable spirit informed the service which he expected in return. In a version of admitted lateness and some unreliability, King William described the lands granted to Duncan, Earl of Fife (some by David I), as held 'by the service of knights',[12] and this phrase may represent early practice: that a major baron was expected to come to the king when summoned with all his knights. If so, the unsatisfactory nature of an undefined responsibility must soon have been clear and from the time of Malcolm IV the number of knights expected was specified.

The striking feature of these *servitia debita* even of the heaviest, is their slightness: five knights for the Stewart fief, ten for Annandale, ten for the earldom of Lennox, the Garioch and other lands. King William indeed granted 100 librates of land and twenty infeft knights (presumably infeft on the 100 librates) to his sister Margaret, Countess of Britanny, on her second marriage to Humphrey de Bohun, but even this brief entry in the inventories of Scottish records makes it clear that this may have been something very different from a tenure by the service of twenty knights. Among the grants this was the only example to exceed the service of ten knights; some royal grants were for the service of half a knight, and fractional service was more common than integral service in the case of subinfeudations.[13] The number of such subinfeudations is small but since most of our records are ecclesiastical and knight service was not imposed upon the church, the survival rate was bound to be low, and it is more significant that among the non-ecclesiastical collections the military service charters seem to be a significant proportion of the whole.[14]

[12] *R.R.S.*, ii, no. 472.

[13] Barrow, *Kingdom of the Scots*, 311–14 lists all grants for military service before 1214.

[14] The classical literature on knight service and feudalism in England is best studied in F. M. Stenton *The First Century of English Feudalism* (1932, 2nd edn. 1961); A. L. Poole, *The Obligations of Society in the XII and XIII Centuries* (1946); C. Warren Hollister, *The Military Organisation of Norman*

Uninfeft household knights are not revealed by the sources as an important element in society, and the smallness of the *servitia debita* is best explained by the cost of subinfeudating to support a knight. This was undoubtedly done, for example by the Stewarts or Earl David, who brought obvious coteries of immigrants to Scotland. But the de Morevilles seem to have imposed knight service upon existing tenants or, as the king did, to have exploited the wealth of the church. In 1170, for a single payment of 300 merks, the bishop of Glasgow leased 'Gillemureston' to Richard de Moreville for fifteen years with the most solemn undertaking that it would be returned at the end of that time. But Richard did not hesitate to grant it heritably for a knight's service to a native tenant, Edulf, whence comes its name, Eddleston, and only after the de Moreville male line died out was the bishop able to recover his land.[15] We do not know what service was imposed on the extensive de Moreville lands, but the fact that they were reduced, apparently, to this chicanery, suggests that they did not find easy to pin upon their tenants the burden of knight service owed to the king.

Most land in Scotland was held not for knightly or other military service to the superior, but for money, or, much less important, for prayers or masses. Yet on all land, or nearly all, there was a military obligation to be discharged to the king whether the donor had specified service of knight or archer, money ferme or prayers. The *communis exercitus* and *expeditio* of the first half of the twelfth century due to the king[16] imply a burden on everyone with land which, if *expeditio* be understood literally, would be on foot.[17] This right to army service has its roots in the remote past, for it was clearly present in Dal Riata in the age of migration, and it may be presumed to have evolved its own customary rules in the centuries before David I. That in the twelfth century it furnished provincial armies under the earls north of Forth and under the lord of Galloway in that province is well attested by chronicle accounts of the invasions of England in 1138 and 1173-4 and of the expeditions against the mac Williams between 1181 and 1215. The army of

*England* (1965). But there are two important papers with refreshingly different approaches in *Past and Present* for 1970: E. King, 'Large and Small Landowners in Thirteenth Century England', xlvii, 26–50; S. Harvey, 'The Knight and Knight's Fee in England', xlix, 3–43.

[15] *Glasgow Registrum*, nos. 44, 45, 173.
[16] E.g. Lawrie, *E.S.C.*, nos. CLXXVIII, CCXXI.
[17] But cf. *Glasgow Registrum*, no. 85.

Mar was used to handle the predicament over the Bissets in 1242–3 and a hosting was part of the expeditions planned to go to Man in 1264 and 1275. It was local levies, *pedisequos patrie*, 'footsloggers of Cunningham' we might translate, who attacked King Haakon's similarly levied force on the shore of Largs in 1263.

Such provincial armies consisted of contingents produced by major landowners, of whom prelates are most clearly attested by our largely ecclesiastical sources. The 'freedom from mormaer' by which the religious of Deer sought to escape from producing its quota for the army was no defence against the king's demand for such service. In the 1120s the army of Fife led by the earl[18] included the army of the bishop whose leaders were Budadh and Sluadach; the name of the latter means 'one who has an army.'[19] In his general charters to Dunfermline, Cambuskenneth and Arbroath Abbeys, in Scotia, the king excepted from their immunities the defence of the kingdom, and thereby implied their liability to send a contingent to the host at least for limited purposes. By the reign of William it was usual for the king in confirming a private transaction in land to add a rider 'saving my service' (*saluo seruicio meo*), to impose army service upon the tenant of the land (or the donor if he had explicitly undertaken to do this service for his tenant). Thus the phrase occurs at the end of the king's confirmation of Arbroath Abbey's grant of Inverpeffer in Angus to the king's brewer.[20] His status as a royal domestic may have obscured his obligations, for in 1251 a jury found that his descendant Nicholas attended the abbot's court, paid annual rent to the abbot, and gave aid and army with the abbot's men, but that 'in the army which the lord king last had with him in Argyll, namely in 1248 (an error for 1249) . . . Nicholas sent his men in the army with the men of the lord king of the bailiary of Forfar' because he was at law with the abbot over his lands and wanted the king as his 'defender' in the action.[21] By this date it is likely that the earl's leadership was often ignored, but the weight and frequency of army service indicated by the jury's linking it with presence at court cannot be denied.

And indeed the conveyances of the late twelfth and thirteenth centuries deal regularly with this obligation, though usually under

[18] *Proc. Soc. Antiq. Scot.*, xc (1956–7), 74.
[19] Lawrie, *E.S.C.*, no. LXXX; *R.R.S.*, i, 75, 223.
[20] *R.R.S.*, ii, no. 209, 1178 x 1195.
[21] *Arbroath Liber*, i, no. 250.

the French-derived name of *seruitium forinsecum,* service, that is, outside (*forein*) or additional to whatever is due to the immediate lord, and sometimes identified explicitly with army service.[22] It is widespread and can be found due from fiefs held by knight service[23] as well as from kirk lands and lands held in feu.[24] Occasionally it is to be provided for by another party as when, settling its dispute over Exmagirdle, Lindores Abbey agreed to pay six merks annually to the bishop of Dunblane to be free of all aids, armies and other burdens which the bishop would discharge, except that, significantly, the earl of Strathearn would undertake the burden of army.[25] Other evidence suggests that these earls were particularly conscientious over forinsec service.[26]

But, in general, forinsec service was quite simply specified as being that due 'from so much land,' 'from *x* ploughgates' or 'from *y* davachs' and it is spelled out as the service of so many persons on only a very few occasions, as in 1271 when the tenure of Draffen (held of Kelso Abbey) was specified as including 'finding a man and a half in forinsec service'[27] or, a little later when two pennylands in Argyll were held for providing 'in the congregations of Argyll, when there is need, two men with their victuals as long as it (? the army) shall last, as is customary in that part (*patria*)'.[28] Presumably these obligations limited the usual more open-ended liability proportional to the amount of land in the same way as Inchaffray Abbey received land near Fowlis Wester in feu ferme, paying 'three pence for aid or army when the king exacted common aid or common army from the whole realm'. However forinsec service and common army were not consistently a burden fixed in manpower, but a liability whose incidence could vary: say, one, two or three men were demanded from each ploughgate or ten, twenty or thirty from each toun according to royal need. The clearest example of such a levy was for the abortive expedition planned by Alexander III to go to the help of Henry III in 1264–5; according to Fordun 'he enumerated (*connumeravit*) three men from each hide for the campaign'—where the hide is presumably a synonym for plough-

---

[22] E.g. *Moray Registrum,* no. 37; *Arbroath Liber,* i, no. 102.

[23] *Brechin Registrum,* i, no. 2; *Banff Charters,* no. 1, both of 1232.

[24] E.g. *Arbroath Liber,* i, nos. 257, 261.

[25] *Lindores Chartulary,* no. XLII, of 1210 x 1223.

[26] E.g. *Inchaffray Charters,* no. LII.

[27] *Kelso Liber,* no. 474.

[28] *Lamont Papers,* 7.

gate or davach.[29] And even total mobilisation had its exemptions
and alleviations: one of the tenants of Dunfermline Abbey in the
late twelfth century was granted with his feu 'leave to stay away
from the king's armies unless the army is so general (*communis*)
that the men of Inveresk and Monkton may not stay at home, and
then he shall find only one man'.[30] To the same effect, Robert Bruce,
Earl of Carrick, acknowledged in March 1302 that Melrose Abbey
held its Ayrshire lands free from forinsec service 'except common
army occurring for the defence of the kingdom and gathered from
the whole kingdom' and that he had dragged their men in his
army of Carrick to various places without any summons of the
common army. He promised to exact no more 'forinsec service or
army' except for common army of the whole realm, for its defence,
'which service all dwellers in the kingdom (*regnicole*) are bound
to do in duty'.[31] Evidence drawn from the period after 1296 in this
matter is to be treated with caution, but this document records old
custom as well as recent abuse and we may not doubt that on rare
occasions a common army of the kingdom's inhabitants had been
proclaimed so that 'every man should go forth to defend his
head.'[32] But forinsec service was usually more limited, that is, not
necessarily imposed upon all provinces of the kingdom and demanding only a certain number of men for each unit of land.

If common army from the whole realm is attested both north
and south of Forth, and this service was well known in both Celtic
and Anglian areas, yet in the thirteenth century there was sufficient
difference between the two for a fairly frequent distinction to be
made: north of Forth we hear of Scottish service, Scottish army,
forinsec Scottish service. Thus, in Strathearn, forinsec service to the
earl is Scottish service;[33] it is 'Scottish army and common aid of the
lord king,[34] or 'forinsec Scottish service of the king in defence of the
kingdom by power of armed men, horses and arms'[35] and in Argyll
the king granted land in 1240 for the service of half a knight in the
army and as much as pertains to one knight in aids and doing
'Scottish service as our barons and knights on the northern side of

29 *Chron. Fordun*, i, 302. Perhaps this mobilisation was exceptional.
30 *Dunfermline Registrum*, no. 301.
31 *Melrose Liber*, no. 351.
32 *R.R.S.*, ii, 57.
33 *Moray Registrum*, Cart. Orig. nos, 13, 16.
34 Fraser, *Grandtully*, i, 125, no. 69.
35 *Moray Registrum*, Cart. Orig. no. 17.

the Scottish sea do it for their lands'—where it is probably the
barons and knights which are northern and not the doing of service,
though we cannot be sure.[36] This last example seems to introduce
the customs of Scotia into Argyll which had its own 'congregations'
and basis of service.[37] Lennox also knew forinsec service, often
assessed according to the ploughgate in the usual way,[38] but where
the arachor was in use along the shores of Loch Lomond, this earldom produced such oddities as 'in the common army of the king
two cheeses from each house in which there is cheese or in which
cheese is made.'[39] This food-service may represent earlier practices
in the kingdom of Strathclyde or simply the best contribution which
the largely pastoral parish of Luss could make to the Lennox contingent; it should not be taken as illustrating forinsec service in
either Scotia or Lothian.

The difference between these regions is unlikely to reside in their
units of land measurement, for the ploughgate was widely used in
Scotia; the arms and armour required would seem an improbable
variable in geographical terms simply because these things developed so much in time. We are left with the possibility that there
was a well-understood difference in the zone in which service was to
be discharged, the Forth being the significant border for this purpose. That is, Scottish service was the defence of Scotia, and is
*prima facie* likely to have been defined or regularised during the
Norse incursions of the ninth and tenth centuries. Forinsec service
south of the Forth had its origins in the defence of the earldom of
Northumbria and had roots in common with the 'common army
in the earldom' found there in the twelfth century.[40] Undoubtedly
the 'defence' of the twelfth and thirteenth century realm did on
occasion require the army of Buchan or Atholl to traipse across the
moors of Northumberland in pursuit of King William's lost heritage, and the men of Galloway to seek out mac William and his
caterans in distant Ross, but in each case the incidence of 'call-up'
may have been light because of the distance involved. Common
army for all the inhabitants of the realm as the earl of Carrick

[36] *Highland Papers*, ii, 121–3; photograph at 227; 227–45.
[37] Above p. 380, referring to *Lamont Papers*, 7.
[38] *Lennox Cartularium*, 32, 40–41 etc.
[39] *Lennox Cartularium*, 19, 23, 85; *Reg. Mag. Sig.*, ii, no. 187.
[40] *Victoria County History, Cumberland*, i, 319–26; F. W. Maitland,
'Northumbrian Tenures', *Eng. Hist. Rev.*, v (1890), 626, 629; J. E. A. Jolliffe,
'Northumbrian Tenures,' *ibid.* xli (1926), 29–30.

recognised it in 1302 may still have been limited to service either south or north of the Forth.

Further light upon the native and regional characteristics of military service is thrown by the duty of tenants by knight service to garrison castles.[41] The earliest example is found in Malcolm IV's charter to Berowald the Fleming at Elgin, but this is also the only evidence that an attempt was made to introduce this service north of Forth.[42] As David I granted Annandale to Bruce with its castle, his grandson confirmed it for the service of ten knights 'except the guard of my castles of which I have quit-claimed him', presumably because those knights stood guard in Bruce's castle of Annan. The linking of castle guard with tenure by knight service is confirmed by a royal charter of c. 1220 to the laird of Hadden in Roxburgh-shire so that he and his heirs paid 20s. annually 'for the guard which they are bound to do in Roxburgh Castle for what pertains to a knight's fief for which they ought to do guard'. There is strong evidence that the circumstances described here, including the rate of commutation, were generalised in the thirteenth century. Thus, the service of a twentieth of a knight is found along with eighths, quarters, thirds and halves—and all are easy fractions of a 20s. pay-ment. Payments are not found in the fragmentary royal accounts of 1263–6, when, however, castles were garrisoned and expeditions sent to the Isles. But in the accounts for 1288–90 the sheriff of Berwick charged himself with £76 6s. 8d. for castle guard for 1288, and in 1330 the following net payments were recorded: Stirling £4 10s; Dumfries £7 5s; Edinburgh £34 13s. 4d; Rox-burgh £20; Berwick £25 11s. 9½. In 1359 the guards of the sheriffdom of Lanark came to £13 plus those from baronies in the king's hands; the fiefs once held by Flemish settlers (Biggar, Coving-ton, Thankerton, Symington, Roberton, Lamington, Wiston) were assessed at a uniform 20s. and the Somerville barony of Carnwath at 60s.[43] In 1335–7 the English were gathering castle guard in the same round figures, £33 10s. for Roxburgh, £13 6s. 8d for Lanark, and from Berwick £45 of which £30 was owed by the earl of Dunbar. Dunbar Castle drew its own guard payments to the earl: the amounts ranged from £5 for Polwarth down to 4s. payments

[41] C. W. Hollister, *The Military Organization of Norman England* (1965) chapter V is the best account of castle guard as a feudal obligation in England.
[42] *R.R.S.*, i, no. 173; see also *A.P.S.*, i, 101.
[43] *Exch. Rolls*, i, 45, 205, 582; cf. *Exch. Rolls*, iii, 162, 164; *Exch. Rolls*, vi, 101–2.

for various lands, and virtually the same amount, £22 9s., was still being collected for this purpose in the mid-fifteenth century.[44] In 1455 the barony of Strathbrock paid £2 as castle guard; along with Duffus and other lands in Moray it had been granted to William fitz Freskin about 1170 for two knights' service, but it does not seem possible to associate other payments with knight service charters, nor admittedly is this example a very convincing demonstration of a 20s. payment for each knight owed.[45]

The subject would repay investigation and it can be only a tentative suggestion that castle guard, and therefore tenure by knight service, is found most intensively in the south east, a strongly Anglian area, less intensively in the three Lothians; and that in Lanarkshire and perhaps Dumfriesshire it is associated with twelfth-century immigrants probably holding by knight service. It was not, apparently, found in wider Galloway between the Clyde and Solway Firths, nor beyond the Forth. Clearly castle-guard was not part of knight service as that duty was imported and spread throughout Scotland by David I and his grandsons, but it became attached to knight service in Lothian and Clydesdale. Yet the terms of tenure of Annandale seem to push it back before 1171; the heavy burden associated with the castles of Berwick and Dunbar suggests that it was already known in the eleventh century as part of the tenure of some Anglian landholders, the wealthier thegns whose lands were converted to tenure by knight service, such as Elsi, son of Winter, who held Thirlestane for three merks annually but whose son was confirmed there for a knight's service. As the greater thanages were converted into baronies in English Northumbria, where 'it is rarely that even the tenures in knight service are found without some trace of pre-feudal incident,'[46] so their early disappearance in Lothian may be explained by recognition as knights' fiefs. The author of this comment on Northumbria was referring to the persistence of bondage services and not to military services such as castle guard which are generally assumed to be of 'Norman' feudal origin.

But the commutation of castle guard granted to the lairds of

[44] *Cal. Docs. Scot.*, iii, 317, 319, 320, 323–4, 368–9; *Exch. Rolls*, v, 487–8, 579, 642–3; vi, 55, 539.

[45] *Exch. Rolls*, vi, 90. See also *ibid*, 94, 96–7, 101–2; it should perhaps be remarked that castle guards were collected by the sheriff, and very few sheriffs' accounts survive even for the fifteenth century.

[46] J. E. A. Jolliffe in *Eng. Hist. Rev.*, xli, 24.

Hadden was by no means final. They did not pay their 20s. when in case of emergency or war they stood guard for forty days nor if they went in the king's army beyond the Forth or the Border. And even if they had paid or served in an army or castle, they must still do castle guard or army service in an emergency. Only if they contributed according to their fief to a common aid taken from the kingdom were they quit of both guard payment and guard (army is not mentioned here).[47] Thus castle guard represents that army service which did not cross the bounds of Lothian; it is the defence of the province which is found in both Northumbria and Scotia as forinsec service or its equivalent. It may be that those thegns of Lothian who were responsible for bringing out or leading the common army from their estates, and whose tenures were recognised or reorganised as knightly, were explicitly required to defend their province in the king's or earl's castle; only the obligation to serve as knights outside their province would have been new.

Whatever the validity of these conjectures, it may still be emphasised that there was no feudal army distinct from the common army of lairds and peasants, and that knight service was not intended as a modernising of tenures in the twelfth century but as a means of achieving the specialist arms and techniques of a cavalry force from among those by whom it could be afforded.

Our charters of knight service were kept by the knight, who was concerned with a title to his rights and less worried that his duties be stated; hence the jingle of 'wood and plain, land and water, meadow and pasture, mills and stanks', and the lame conclusion, 'by the service of a knight' with no word of notice due, equipment, mount, sustenance, period of service. Yet we know that in England between c. 1180 and c. 1210 the cost of maintaining a knight trebled because of changes in arms, armour and the techniques of war, and that the process of scaling-down the due quotas of knight-service began. In Scotland the parallel process was the granting of fiefs for fractional knight service on a wider scale than hitherto. King William's grant of Linlathen in Angus for the service of a third of a knight, confirmed by his son for the service of a quarter, is a modest example of the processes which in subinfeudation

---

[47] *Reg. Mag. Sig.*, i, app. 1, no. 55; this charter is printed with translation and a discussion of some value in George Neilson, 'Tenure by Knight Service in Scotland.' *Juridical Review*, xi (1899); for a translation, G. Donaldson, *Scottish Hist. Docs.*, 54; for the payment of 20s. from Hadden *Exch. Rolls*, vi, 55.

could produce the service of the twentieth of a knight,[48] although even in the reign of Alexander III the service of a whole or half knight could still be required.[49] In 1265, when Henry de Nevith resigned Lour in Angus (part of his lands) to the crown for having failed to do service, Alexander III granted it to Hugh de Abernethy for the appropriate proportion (unspecified) of the service of a knight due from all Henry's lands.[50] Such a grant, coming in the aftermath of campaigns prepared against King Haakon in 1263 and the Manx king in 1264, strongly suggests that knight 'service' was still done in the field and not merely by exchequer counters, just as castle guard commutation made provision for active service. But fractional service may have reached the field in different ways: the most obvious is through financial contribution not to the king or lord but among a number of tenants holding, perhaps, the portions of a fragmented knight's fief, an informal kind of 'parage'. Of such arrangements the only evidence is the charter just cited, where failure to name the fraction of service required can surely mean only that it was up to the two tenants to produce a knight at their jointly agreed cost or effort. But if some kind of 'parage' had been widely practised it would seem inevitable that such partitions would fragment further. This did not happen so far as the king was concerned; in fact castle guard even in the fifteenth century had rarely been broken into fractions of less than a fifth of the 20s. for a knight's service. This fraction is also very rarely exceeded in thirteenth-century royal charters[51] whereas smaller fractions are common in private subinfeudations.

But attention has recently been drawn to the significance of one of King William's infeftments (probably after 1190) of Michael Fleming (who was sheriff of Edinburgh) in Gilberton for the service of a serjeant on a horse with a haubergel. Confirmed at first by Alexander II in the same terms, when Michael's son Archibald succeeded he had a new charter in 1226 of the same lands for the service of a quarter of a knight.[52] Other royal charters

[48] Fraser, *Annandale*, i, no. 7; *Glasgow Registrum*, no. 173.
[49] *Reg. Mag. Sig.*, i, app. 1, no. 95; *Newbattle Registrum*, Cart. Orig. no. 6.
[50] Fraser, *Southesk*, ii, 479, no. 27.
[51] See the *Handlists* of the Acts of Alexander II—John, by G. G. Simpson and J. Scoullar. For service of 1/10 knight see *Cawdor Bk.* 2.
[52] Barrow, *Kingdom of the Scots*, 301, referring to *A.P.S.*, vii, 144. I refer Archibald's charter to Alexander II in 1226 and not to Alexander III because its place day and month date is the same as *Inchaffray Charters*, no. LIV, undoubtedly of Alexander II.

for the service of a serjeant, usually with horse and haubergel, are known from the second half of William's reign, but the last examples seem to be two to the same beneficiary from Alexander II in 1223. This service represents fairly closely what earlier in the twelfth century would have been called knight service and it seems likely that as knighthood and the more elaborate knightly equipment demanded increased resources, the king had to make do in many cases with less well armed and horsed men. Whether the service of a knight as demanded for a particular fief by David I remained, or was done by one, or more, mounted serjeants, in the thirteenth century is unknown. But with new infeftments after 1223 it does seem that the crown decided to disguise the mounted serjeanty services, with which King William had made do, as a third or quarter of a knight's service (the difference probably reflecting a distinction in arms). In 1304 the barony of Callendar was held for the service of a knight and that of Kilsyth held of the earl of Fife for the service of ten archers; fiefs held for a fifth of a knight's service may have produced an archer's service.

During the war of 1263–5 the men at arms are serjeants: 120 were hired to keep Ayr Castle because the burgesses failed to do so; the chamberlain spent £85 in serjeants' wages over eighteen months, taking 200 to the Isles in the summer of 1264 and spending £30 on their food; the king ordered eight to spend six months in the castle of 'Invery' in 1263 at a cost of 104s.[53] During the same period and in the same record knights were retained just as we find them retained at the end of the king's reign for annual payments; their number was evidently fairly small. For an effective military force the king relied both in offence and defence upon the service of serjeants, who can have been recruited only from the provincial lairds. In the protracted crisis of 1263 they were paid, but for a customary period, probably forty days, they would owe the king unpaid service because of their tenure.

Why should the service of such men be disguised in charters as a fraction of knight service? The financial alternatives to knights' service were castle guard in Lothian and aids throughout the realm; these financial burdens would be readily computed and collected if all military tenures were put upon a footing of knight service,

<hr>

[53] *Exch. Rolls*, i, 6, 10, 11, 18. The number of serjeants required for Ayr seems extraordinarily large, but in September 1263 King Haakon was probably expected to land at Ayr.

and we have already seen that castle guard was collected in units or simple fractions of a knight's commuted service. That aids were also collected on the basis of knight service emerges from those cases where the service and aid were differently rated, as in the case of lands near Dumfries granted by Alexander II to a layman for a quarter knight's service, passed on by him to Melrose Abbey, which obtained confirmation from the king 'for doing forinsec service in aids only as much as pertained to the quarter part of a knight', but quit of army service.[54] Such an aid from each fief held for knight service was clearly not distinguished from the 'common aids' taken in the thirteenth century.

In 1216, when Alexander II set out to besiege Carlisle, he took, says the *Melrose Chronicle,* his whole army 'except the Scots from whom he took *expensas*'; so far as Scotia was concerned, common army had become common finance. And this shift is widely reflected in charters; even before the great payments agreed in 1189 and 1209 King William could reserve to himself 'common aid common army, common work'.[55] But from the last decade of the twelfth century provision for common aids or for forinsec service in aids is almost as common as provision for common army service, and is usually linked thereto.[56] Whereas donors were sometimes persuaded that the burden of army service was inappropriate for the church, they usually saw no difficulty in passing on the burden of aids, and many documents make separate provision for army and aid at greater or lesser length.[57] Whether there were aids confined to one or two provinces is unknown but perhaps unlikely. There were probably aids confined to Scotia or to southern Scotland, especially when, as in 1216, the army served from one and aid in money was taken from the other. But common aids were also taken from the whole realm[58] and upon the same basis of ploughgates or davachs as forinsec service in the army, reaching down to the peasantry and their livestock.[59] The evidence directly contradicts the claim of Walter Bower that when Alexander II imposed an aid of £10,000 to marry off his sisters in 1224, *eleemosinae*—lands held in free alms—were exempt because that was the custom.[60] In particular

---

[54] *Melrose Liber,* nos. 205-7.                    [55] *R.R.S.,* ii, no. 152.
[56] E.g. *Aberdeen Registrum,* i, 31.
[57] See e.g. *Arbroath Liber,* i, no. 75; *Melrose Liber,* no. 207.
[58] *Inchaffray Charters,* no. LII.
[59] *Dunfermline Registrum,* no. 181, earlier 13th century.
[60] *Chron. Bower,* ii, 53; the sum mentioned seems absurdly large.

cases, however, this view was taken, notably with Arbroath Abbey, where the king's specific claim to 'defence of the realm' was interpreted to mean common army but not common aid, from which the abbey was accordingly free. The royal writ has a verbal similarity to Bower, and may have been his source.[61] Even so the abbey made 'voluntary' contributions in 1216 and at some date before 1240.[62]

The word 'aid' may suggest an innovation of Anglo-Norman origin; but it is likely that only the word was new. When army service was taken men must often have contributed arms and victuals to send with some of their number, which is to say that they paid (in kind) for the army.[63] Long before the twelfth century kings and mormaers may have learned to take such contributions, without men, from one part to subsidise war in another; the twelfth century turned this into aid in money and probably made it available for non-military purposes. And when it was taken, the tenant in knight service paid according to that service and was also responsible for raising the aid from his peasantry according to the acreage they held.

When this tenant served, his duty would likewise be complementary to the peasant common army, to provide with other serjeants perhaps a body of light-armed horsemen, or perhaps individually to lead (as the 'twentyman' of the Edwardian army did) an infantry company, disciplining their unmilitary spirits and doubtless rusty arms into a unit of command. Such at any rate was the tenure of the 'armed man' to be provided by a ploughgate in Priestfield to lead the thirty archers owed to the army by the barony of Bowden in 1327—a tenure possibly modified by the Anglo-Scottish wars, but instructive nonetheless.[64]

Subinfeudation for knight service produced in the thirteenth century, in addition to the larger fractions which might be understood as serjeanty service, small fractions of which an eighth, tenth or twentieth seem the most frequent. Thus at Eddleston about 1200 Adam, the son of its first tenant for one knight's service passed part of this fief to his son for the service of a twentieth part of a knight;[65] with the recognition of alternative forms of knight service (serjeanty

[61] *Arbroath Liber*, i, no. 109; cf. *ibid*, no. 102.
[62] *Arbroath Liber*, i, nos. 110, 246.
[63] See the interesting document of 1263 cited in Barrow, *Kingdom of the Scots*, 43-4.
[64] *Kelso Liber*, no. 471.
[65] *Glasgow Registrum*, no. 173.

and archer's service), the problems of providing the service were much reduced, since arms and equipment were so much less elaborate, and partition of the liability was possible among three or four tenants, as the 'armed man' to lead the archers of Bowden must have come from the four husbandmen holding that plough-gate. Thus even knight service, it would seem, was modified, frag-mented, in part commuted, but, remaining still an occasional service, could become the liability of a number of comparatively modest men.

Yet, as the knights' fiefs of the earlier twelfth century dis-integrated towards its end, a form of renewal took place which gave the king knights and knight service—but not necessarily from the holders of knights' fiefs. Thus the Bruce lords of Annandale owed the king ten knights and perhaps infeft that number. By the last quarter of the century, however, charters were granted for the service of eighths or even twentieths of a knight's service; these are much more likely to be the break-up of old infeftments than the creation of new ones. Yet some among Bruce's followers were buy-ing as others were selling, creating economic units held by men of wealth to replace the disintegrating fiefs held by knights. Such men of wealth were accorded the social distinction of knighthood. A small group of eight or nine knights, one usually named as steward, witnessed the fairly numerous thirteenth-century grants by and resignations to Bruce, along with some lesser Annandale land-holders. One of these documents certainly was, and several possibly were, made as the settlement in the lord's court for defect of ser-vice by a small Bruce tenant, and it is clear that Annandale had a group of worthy men, distinguished by being knighted, who would serve as the prominent members of their lord's court and as his retinue in war, fulfilling his *servitium debitum*; not all of these men held a fief for a knight's service.[66] But in August 1248 some of them would follow Bruce to Edinburgh, perhaps for the king's parlia-ment.[67] It was their sons, now knights of Bruce's son, who according to the chronicler were brought together by their lord's heir (later King Robert I) in 1297 to hear why they should back his treason to Edward I and be his 'counsellors and very dear friends'. They chose

[66] *Cal. Docs. Scot.*, i, nos. 635, 704–7, 1680–5. The dating offered by Bain for these documents is untrustworthy; e.g. no. 1682 is of *c.* 1260–80.

[67] *Lindores Chartulary*, no. LXI. Was this the occasion of Bruce's recognition as heir to the young Lord Alexander?

to slip away in dark of night and when in due course a small English cavalry force (taking revenge for raids into England) invaded Annandale, it was the common army, perhaps a leaderless rabble, which hooted 'tailed dogs' at them.[68] In 1541, when the men of Annandale were mustered under their lairds to show the readiness of their arms for the defence of the Border, they numbered 1,168 men—and the figure for 1286 is unlikely to have been smaller.[69] The leadership of men in such numbers must always have been the responsibility of their lairds just as the lairds owed to their lord the advice, support and service which the young Bruce craved of his father's knights in 1297.

Do the sources support the conclusion of an eminent historian that in thirteenth-century Scotland 'rents and services of all kinds existed, but not an articulated system of knight service?'[70] The retinue of knights, each a substantial tenant, recorded for Bruce can be paralleled for other magnates—the Steward, the earl of Atholl, the earl of Dunbar—and although the contingents of knights which each could produce would be small, probably between five and ten for the very greatest lords, and their arms possibly a little old-fashioned, some knight service surely remained as part of a system of military obligations. The men who witness Bruce's charters as knights make no appearance as prisoners after the battle of Dunbar, most having presumably followed their lord in Edward I's army, although some of his tenants joined the 'rebellion'. The same must be said of the earl of Dunbar's knights; the Steward 'kept' Roxburgh Castle for King John until it was wiser to surrender it: by the autumn he was a useful agent of Edward I and 'all of his *familia* and retinue' were admitted to the king's peace. The knights of John, Earl of Atholl, went, like their lord, into English prisons.[71] Without thirteenth-century knight service, we might say, for good or ill there was no cavalry cohort to fight battle of Dunbar.

Moreover, although the apparatus of commissions of array was unknown in Scotland, the obligation throughout society to do

---

[68] *Chron. Guisborough*, 296, 307–8.

[69] *Hist. MSS. Comm. Fifteenth Report*, viii (Duke of Buccleuch, Drumlanrig), no. 135.

[70] Powicke, *Thirteenth Century*, 576.

[71] *Paisley Registrum*, 254 (Sir Reginald Crawford was appointed sheriff of Ayr by Edward I); *SHS Misc.*, iv, 320–5; *Rotuli Scotiae*, i, 30, 32, 33; *Cal. Docs. Scot.*, ii, nos. 742, 853; but note a William de Kilpatrick esquire of Annandale taken prisoner.

military service was at least as vigorous as in England.[72] The effectiveness of the common army depended, it is suggested, upon those tenants for partial knight service who as serjeants gave sinews to the body of peasant levies. After the war effort of 1263–5 these military obligations were put into service only in a modest expedition to Man (1275) before the civil war of 1286–7, but the 'system' of forinsec service remained unimpaired. Without common army there were no schiltrons to fight the war of independence.

Although there is no Domesday survey of Scotland nor of any large part of it, there can be little doubt that in the thirteenth century most land held freely was in the hands of rent-paying tenants, knights among them. The origins of such tenure in, or at, ferme are probably remote. It is an indirect form of land management, an entrusting of parts of an estate to middlemen standing between the lord and the peasantry; these middlemen paid to the lord a fixed annual render in kind, later in cash or in both, for the term of their lease which might be a number of years or life. In England this system has been called 'age-long'[73] and its origin and structure in royal estates has now been demonstrated in both England and Scotland, most clearly in the Northumbrian shires or discrete estates with a chief manor and dependent rent-paying vills or touns, whose tribute was the responsibility of a *ministerialis*, the thegn or thane. This tribute represented hospitality and services due to the king or other lord—a sure sign of the great antiquity of the estate— but by or in the twelfth century it seems to have become fixed, a ferme.[74]

David I, as we have seen, tithed himself for the religious in province after province, commanding those who managed his estates to hand over a tenth of produce rents to this or that convent. The fixing of such rents, a 'ferme', is implied by his permission to Scone Abbey to take a (probably enhanced) rent from each plough- gate which is said to be for the canons' sustenance (conveth): a cow, two pigs, four measures of meal, ten thraves of oats, ten hens, two hundred eggs, candles, soap and cheese.[75] Such evidence is rare but fortunately we have also the description of Arbuthnott on the

[72] For a readable account see Michael Prestwich, *War, Politics and Finance under Edward I* (1972).

[73] F. R. H. Du Boulay, *The Lordship of Canterbury* (1966), 197.

[74] 'Pre-feudal Scotland: shires and thanes', chapter 1 in Barrow, *Kingdom of the Scots*, 7–68.

[75] *R.R.S.*, i, no. 243.

southern fringe of the Mearns, whose Kirkton had belonged to the
bishop of St Andrews since the time of Bishop Robert. The laird,
Osbert Olifard, having taken crusader's vows (perhaps in 1188),
leased his estate to Isaac of Benvie (near Dundee) who found in
the Kirkton eight tenants called *persone* or scolocs, and peasants
under them, each house owing a fixed food rent to Osbert, and
hospitality to the bishop. Isaac held the estate for six years and was
replaced by successively Hugh de Benne, Hugh de Swinton and his
son Duncan, who were able to take over the Kirkton during the
long period when Roger was absentee elect and bishop of St
Andrews. Gillandres, the leading peasant, having died, Duncan
expelled the scolocs after 1202 and ploughed the land, which no
thane had done previously. In the eyes of some witnesses the
Swintons and Benne were probably thanes like Isaac of Benvie and
the eight or ten men who preceded him in memory reaching back
to the 1150s. The tenure of each averaged only some three or four
years and the 'service' which they gave to the king or Olifard is
unspecified but, as 'thane' implies, it would be a rent in kind and
perhaps money.

At St Cyrus in Mearns the priory of St Andrews (and not, as at
Arbuthnott, the bishop) held the kirkton and paid a food rent to the
thane, who in turn paid one to the king and perhaps later to Earl
David. At Inverkeilor the same situation is found before the incoming of Walter de Berkeley.[76] In Moray it was expected that the
peasantry would be subject to either thane or lord who was held
responsible for the church's teinds in kind, and who was himself
subject to a forfeiture in kind for failure, a custom expressly said to
be observed in the bishopric of St Andrews also.[77] Teinds and forfeitures paid in kind surely imply food-rents also, and in the first
half of the thirteenth century the thane still existed in Moray
alongside farmers for a term and feu-farmers, the thane presumably
paying food-rent, the farmers money rents.[78]

The Cistercians of Coupar Angus established granges at Airlie,
Errol and Kincreich, which were distant, but not more than the
statutory day's journey, from the abbey. At these granges houses of
*conversi*, the lay brothers who were an integral part of the Cistercian

[76] *R.R.S.*, ii, no. 352; *St. Andrews Liber*, 238; *Arbroath Liber*, i, no. 56.
[77] *R.R.S.*, ii, no. 281.
[78] *Moray Registrum*, nos. 34, 40. See no. 76 for the king's cain in money
and kind from Badenoch. And for the thanage of Rathenech see Barrow,
*Kingdom of the Scots*, 48–9.

system, managed the attached lands, probably by the thirteenth century exploiting peasant labour which was forbidden by their rule, the *Carta Caritatis*. At Blair Atholl, Tulloch was farmed to a man of Celtic name but Innervack was apparently not—though the manner of exploitation is obscure.[79] Murthly, also in Atholl and granted by the earls, was held heritably by Malcolm, son of Ewen of Dunkeld, for three merks annually.[80]

Although shires and thanages are thick enough in Fife, there are fewer traces of thanes and farming for food-rent. Early in the thirteenth century, St Andrews Priory agreed to pay the successors of the Celtic college of 'poor scholars' of the city a portion of the 'ancient cain' in kind for certain lands which were farmed by *feodati* or *feodatarii* or were held in demesne and might change from one to the other. Two of these feu-farmers are named: Gille-girig, clearly a man of Celtic lineage, and Adam fitz Odo.[81] Odo himself was a knight and had been steward of the bishop until his death about 1196; he had received the shire of Kinninmonth (which had first belonged to his brother Matthew when archdeacon and therefore as a life tenure) heritably from the Augustinians for two merks annually, while Bishop Richard gave him another estate for 40s. annually and the Culdees gave him a third for a food rent. His son, Adam, was made heritable steward of the priory, a post which the father may have held along with the bishop's stewardships, and farmed a ploughgate given by the priory for life—but passed it on to a burgess of St Andrews for a merk yearly. This mixture of short-term, life and heritable tenures, of produce-rents for poor scholars and Culdees and money rents for Augustinians and bishop, of Celtic and English tenants, of thane and steward, belongs to the process of change from exploitation for subsistence to exploitation for exchange.[82] It was not a tidy process in individual instances but the general trend away from a ferme in produce fixed for a limited period to a ferme in money fixed and heritable is unmistakable.

In the south-east the spread of money rents took place on the

[79] *Coupar Charters*, i, xxxiv; nos. XXII, XXXIX, L; Anderson, *Oliphants*, No. 3.

[80] *Coupar Charters*, no. XL.

[81] See above p. 270.

[82] *St. Andrews Liber*, 316–18; G. W. S. Barrow, 'Early Charters of the Family of Kinninmonth of that Ilk', *The Study of Medieval Records*, ed. D. A. Bullough, R. L. Storey (1971), 107–31.

whole earlier. David I gave a toft in the village of Ednam to St Cuthbert for two shillings a year; a hundred years later his successor gave most of the thanage of Callendar to Holyrood Abbey for 160 merks annually.[83] Many examples of royal grants of land for money rent could illustrate the same process with rents small and large, in money and kind, to cleric and lay. On the whole there are few examples of what must have been the commonest form, a lease of limited duration, since the recipient had no long title to secure in writing. But King David is discovered leasing Partick to two Cumbrians, Ailsi and Tocca, for a merk of silver annually; the land was 'in my [the king's] demesne' so long as they had their (finite) lease, but it ceased to be 'demesne' when granted for the same ferme to the archdeacon and kirk of Glasgow.[84]

At some time before 1211 Uhtred of Bangour in West Lothian gave up Bangour to the king, perhaps because his title was poor; the king returned it to him as his right and heritage in what may be the earliest recorded tailzie, recognising Malcolm, Earl of Fife, as his heir. In 1211 the earl succeeded heritably, burdened with the rent 'pertaining to that land' namely four chalders of oatmeal, four merks, four pigs and eight shillings.[85] This rent seems fairly low but it would be appropriate if originally fixed to take account of other duties. Perhaps Uhtred was himself, or was the son of, Uhtred, sheriff of Linlithgow about 1160, and thus associated with management of the king's demesne revenues and himself in all probability a thane.[86]

The trend towards heritable tenures for money fermes seems irresistible among those who are better than peasants. The bishop of Glasgow's lease of Eddleston[87] illustrates the difficulty which the church, and probably also laymen, encountered in enforcing a finite term against a magnate. In 1212 the lands at Airlie of the ancient abbacy of St Andrews were farmed to Coupar Abbey for twenty years at a rent expressly described as traditional, but it was allowed that the lease might continue beyond that period.[88] Kelso Abbey had to bring ecclesiastical censures against the tenant of Paniel in

[83] Lawrie, *E.S.C.*, no. CXI; *Holyrood Liber*, no. 65.
[84] Lawrie, *E.S.C.*, no. CIX.
[85] *R.R.S.*, ii, no. 496. In *The Kingdom of the Scots*, 46, Professor Barrow places this rent 'before 1205'.
[86] Cf. *R.R.S.*, ii, no. 407.
[87] See above p. 378.
[88] *Coupar Charters*, no. XXI.

Clydesdale; in 1269 his son renounced the lands in the court of Lesmahagow for the sake of his father's soul. But the abbey may have invoked the aid of its powerful neighbour Sir William Douglas, to whom in 1270 it gave the lands for life at an annual ferme of two pounds of wax. They evidently knew well the character of the 'protection' which Sir William (later nicknamed *le hardi,* 'the tough') promised them in return, for they stipulated firmly that at his death they must have unimpeded entry to these lands. Although he died in an English prison his kin remained powerful and in 1316 the abbey was evidently seeking to recover its property.[89] Almost every example of a finite lease, therefore, suggests that they were recorded when there was a fear or expectation that they would be extended into perpetuity.

Among the many peasant charters preserved in the Coldingham Priory collection, finite leases are rare; when Patrick Hopper gave one acre to a fellow peasant for twelve years in 1290, the consideration was not an annual rent but a lump sum which, if repaid within five years, brought the return of the acre—the village pawnbroker at work.[90] But that there were finite leases of land in the thirteenth century is clear from the Coldingham extent of 1300 in which a number of *firmarii* hold for a term of years. Some, burdened with unfree services, must be classed among the peasantry, but others were clearly entrepreneurs making a profit for themselves and, they hoped, the priory. Such were William and Hugh de Paxton and John de Chisholm, who paid 66s. 8d. yearly for Paxton, and some 60s. for the demesne at Auchencrew.[91] At Upper Lamberton one and two ploughgates were leased to business men of baronial rank, Ingram de Guines and Henry de Haliburton; in this case there are two extents which give the rents as 4s. and 7s. 8d. (1 ploughgate), 5s. and 15s. 4d. (2 ploughgates). Although we do not know whether the higher rents represent pre- or post-war (1297–8) conditions, it is obvious that these rents were adjusted according to the current economic value of the land, and that leasing of this kind was a realistic method of exploiting landed resources.[92]

Just how widespread it remained in the thirteenth century is obscure; with but few exceptions (some already mentioned) recorded

[89] *Kelso Liber,* nos. 189, 202.

[90] Raine, *North Durham,* no. CCLXXXIV = Durham, Dean and Chapter, Misc. Charter no. 932.

[91] *Coldingham Correspondence,* lxxxviii, xcii, xciii.

[92] *Coldingham Correspondence,* ci, cii; see also *Rotuli Scotiae,* i, 312.

grants of land at ferme were heritable. As early as the 1150s Kelso Abbey was granting titles to its Clydeside lands to local landowners for substantial money fermes. Draffen went to Lambin Asa and his heirs and Paniel on the Douglas water to another Fleming, Theobald, and his heirs, in each case for two merks annually. Other grants in the 1160s and 1170s were of smaller extent and ferme and towards the end of the century such titles were given even to a tenant whose payment of merchet suggests that the tenement was previously an unfree tenure.[93] Other distant property granted at ferme was Easter Duddingston, resigned by one tenant and granted heritably to Reginald de Bosco, probably a kinsman of the king's chancellor, for 10 merks annually, between 1211 and 1226. The abbey was careful to insist that he should make no perpetual alienation of any part of the estate nor wadset more than a half of it without the abbey's consent,[94] and it is evident that religious houses struggled hard to restrict dealing in lands granted heritably by them. The term rarely used in these Kelso charters but widely elsewhere for such heritable grants is 'at feu-ferme', where the word 'feu' clearly had the sense of heritability.[95]

In the cartularies of Arbroath Abbey and the bishopric of Moray there are numerous thirteenth-century examples of the same process of feuing ecclesiastical lands, and most collections of documents will yield some.[96] The earliest Moray example is a grant about 1190 to William fitz Freskin, distantly related to Sir William Douglas, for a rent in wax (cf. Paniel).[97] Such rents were not nominal yet they were probably favourable to the baron paying them. A clearer instance is the farming of royal demesne at Banchory Devenick to Arbroath Abbey in 1244 for 100s. annually; only twelve years later the abbey farmed the same land to Alan Durward, justiciar and active in the council of regency, for a mere 40s. yearly.[98]

It is in the context of this kind of exploitation by baronial neighbours that we should understand the phrases sometimes written

[93] *Kelso Liber*, nos. 102, 107, 104, and generally nos. 102–17.
[94] *Kelso Liber*, nos. 456–7, 242.
[95] This tenure is now threatened with abolition.
[96] *Moray Registrum*, nos, 16, 28, 31, 33, 35, 79, (cf. *Coupar Charters*, no. XXXVIII), 80, 85, 86, 87, 123, 124, 126; *Arbroath Liber*, i, nos. 247, 250, 259, 272, 318, 320; *Dunfermline Registrum*, nos. 150, 201, 223, 314–17, 320, 322, 324.
[97] *Moray Registrum*, no. 113.
[98] *Arbroath Liber*, i, nos. 252, 251.

into feu-ferme charters that the beneficiary might not alienate 'to any man of great power' or riches,[99] and the religious of St Andrews and Dunfermline both vainly obtained bulls from Innocent IV forbidding their tenants to alienate without consent.[100] But of course most of those who feued land at ferme, whether from church or laity, were not men of great power or wealth but free tenants of modest means, often feuing from others of the same kind in the fiercely competitive environment of the thirteenth century.

As early as 1210 a grant by the earl of Buchan included with the beneficiary his heirs 'and assignees', and from this date the phrase becomes common form in feu-ferme charters.[101] It replaces the earlier practice whereby the superior issued a confirmation when his tenant alienated part of the feu, by giving to the tenant the power to assign (that is, alienate) along with the feu. If this meant that all restrictions on alienation were removed, then clearly the tenure had become a very loose relationship. But a restriction did remain: that the ferme must be paid; if the tenant alienated so much of his feu that he was unable to pay this rent, then the superior could recover the feu in law. There are many instances of humble tenants resigning their feu because they were unable to pay;[102] where the tenant was more substantial the transaction was probably rather more elaborate, involving a readjustment of the ferme. It is not clear what happened to the sub-tenants in this case but it seems likely that the superior could recover the land from them too. And certainly, where the king was superior, he could do so.

But this process was cumbrous and exceptional; for the most part superiors either gave their consent to alienation or were ignored. Land changed hands largely unimpeded by 'feudal' rules and to most intents a free market in land operated by the mid-thirteenth century and probably by 1200. True, certain customs were still effective which maintained some life in the relationship of tenant to superior. The homage and fealty done were at least a reminder of obligations wider than an annual feu duty. The right to wardships, marriages and reliefs from sub-tenants was usually granted (or implied) by superior to his tenant; occasionally it was reserved by the superior. These rights befell at irregular intervals,

[99] *Arbroath Liber*, i, no. 274; *Newbattle Registrum*, Carte Originales, no. XVII; *Dunfermline Registrum*, no. 229; *Paisley Registrum*, 52.

[100] *St. Andrews Liber*, 97 (1248); *Dunfermline Registrum*, no. 289 (1249).

[101] *Aberdeen-Banff Collections*, 407.

[102] Raine, *North Durham*, nos. CCX, CCXI, CCXV, CCXX, CCLXXII, etc.

and from the word for such an occasion, *casus,* they are known as casualties.

When the feu-farmer died leaving a minor or a woman as his heir then his superior could exercise wardship of the person and of the fief. In the 1240s Thomas de Bosco of Duddingston died leaving a young heir; for £20 the abbot of Kelso sold to the widow the custody of the boy and the right to marry him off.[103] The prior of Durham sold for an undisclosed sum wardship of the heir and of the lands of Flemington to the king's chancellor, William de Bondington, who would presumably have access to the king's list of eligible heiresses; and fifty years later the heir and lands of Paxton for 40 merks to Sir Thomas Randolph, then retiring from the office of king's chamberlain.[104] In 1261 the prior persuaded the earl of Dunbar to yield the vestiges of his right to wardship of East Nesbit but the earl was careful to stipulate that the heir should not be disparaged.[105] It is noteworthy that the mother-house, Durham, arranged with the daughter, Coldingham, to retain the more lucrative reliefs and marriages,[106] but that, lacking access to the Scottish marriage market, it sometimes hawked the business to prominent civil servants who were well placed to arrange matches at the right social level.

Wardship of lands, however, would usually be exercised with great care since it was evidence of the lord's superiority as well as a profitable source of income, and it is likely that only the greatest ecclesiastical and lay barons (and of course the king) would pass this asset on to someone else for favour or money. The royal accounts include many payments collected by sheriffs for the wardship of lands, from the 30s. 11d. collected annually from Easter Alyth to the £80 from the earldom of Angus.[107] The earldom of Fife fell into wardship in 1289 and was administered for the crown by the laird of Cambo, who thus collected the wardships of the earl's tenants; from one he gathered some 71s., almost exactly the amount at which these lands had previously been valued.[108] In the

---

[103] *Kelso Liber,* no. 458.

[104] Raine, *North Durham,* nos. CCCXLV (1230 x 33), DXLIX (1278).

[105] Raine, *North Durham,* nos. CXXXVI-VII.

[106] *Coldingham Correspondence,* 241, listing the tenants of Durham.

[107] *Exch. Rolls,* i, 3, 27, 28: in 1264 E. Alyth is given as only 30s., probably an error of transcription. *Ibid,* 9 for the earldom of Angus.

[108] Stevenson, *Documents,* i, 407-18, especially 409, 413, 417. There is a discrepancy of 2⅓d. in the amounts.

two years 1291–2 when Edward I ruled Scotland without the bitter distrust which soured Anglo-Scottish relations by 1296, wardships were entrusted to Scotsmen who either paid for or earned the privilege; sometimes the king warned that the heir must not be disparaged in marriage. The Guardians promised to Michael Scot a wardship or marriage appropriate to his standing for one of his children in return for his service in negotiating the return of the Maid of Norway. They sold another wardship for twenty merks annually, but Edward I remitted the payment.[109] The bishop of Glasgow received two wardships and the bishop of St Andrews the marriage of a widow[110] and, rather later, lands in wardship were actually entrusted to the minor to administer, paying the 'true value' or what anyone else was prepared to give.[111] There is every reason to think that before 1286 the Scottish crown made sensible compromises similar to these between maximising its revenue and living in harmony with its subjects.

In the last example, it is to be presumed that the heir was at least adolescent; at what age would he succeed to his inheritance? In the case of earldoms, for instance, Patrick of Atholl and Alexander Comyn of Buchan, the age of succession seems to have been twenty-one; and this age is explicitly mentioned in an inquest relating to a much humbler tenancy in 1263.[112] In the case of an heiress her land remained in wardship until her marriage, and should she be widowed, she, her land, and her *dos*, a third of her late husband's possessions, again became available for marriage. The older and more frequently married, the better endowed and more saleable a property the lady became. It is scarcely surprising that King William charged 700 merks for the de Moreville heiress, or that Alexander III was so enraged that the widowed Marjory, Countess of Carrick should to all intents have kidnapped Robert, the handsome heir to the Bruce inheritance, and married him secretly, that he seized her castle and property (which would have been committed to a royal agent to ferme) and surrendered them only for a substantial payment.

The relief was in origin a payment to a lord to allow the son of his vassal to 'take up again' (hence *relevium*) the father's fief; it was

109 *Rotuli Scotiae*, i, 6a, 15b.

110 *Rotuli Scotiae*, i, 10b, 14a, 7a.

111 *Rotuli Scotiae*, i, 39a. For other examples see *ibid*, 11b (a wardship granted for a fine of 100 merks payable over 4 years) 132.

112 *Cal. Docs. Scot.*, i, no. 2677.

therefore material evidence of the lord's rights in the fief. Of its origins when heritability was defeasible there are no traces in Scotland. But once the relief ceased to be an arbitrary bargain struck between lord and incoming vassal, once it was fixed by charter or by custom, then it was not only evidence of lordship but also a guarantee of the vassal's succession; so long as he undertook to pay he could not be excluded from the fief. The relief was entry-money, like the parallel 'gressuma' (from ingressus, entry) for peasant tenancies (whence the later Scots word 'grassum'). But if lordship was shown by the superior obtaining wardship of the land during a minority, and the profits therefrom, then the case for entry-money was much weaker; in fact wardship and relief were alternatives.[113]

There is evidence for the amount of relief in a number of cases, but it is usually difficult to identify the return (military service or feu-duty) for which the land was held and so to construct a scheme of tenures each with its associated rules of relief and wardship: the English barony with a relief of 100 marks, knight's fee 100s. (irrespective of size and value in both cases), serjeanty fixed by negotiation, socage the annual value. In Scotland the evidence shows that no tenure enjoyed the benefits of fixed relief nor the disadvantages of wardship at will. In the 1290s the earl of Fife (or the king on his behalf) was collecting reliefs of 20 merks, 53s. 4d. and 45s. from his tenants[114] and the account states that the first of them was the assessed annual value of the land, a statement which is a vital clue to the working of feudal casualties. It is clearly established that in 1256 after the death of Neil, Earl of Carrick, an assize of his neighbours assessed each individual piece of the earldom and made a retour (Anglice return) of the values, incorrectly totalled at £112 12s. 2d, to the king. In the royal accounts for 1263 the earldom was still in wardship and is shown committed to the earl of Buchan who is accountable annually for that total figure.[115] In exactly the same way, the earldom of Fife was carefully assessed in

[113] There is a case, in Exch. Rolls, i, 33, of Robert Mappar for whom 40s. 4d. was paid in wardship for a year et de cetero non debet solui eo quod etas sua probata est, and 40s. was then paid in relief. This is the only known example in the period of wardship plus relief being paid and it might be explained away if the relief was assessed at 80s. 4d. But this is to strain the evidence.

[114] Stevenson, Documents, i, 407.

[115] I. A. Milne, 'An extent of Carrick', Scot. Hist. Rev., xxxiv, 48-9; Exch. Rolls, i, 5, 28.

its components and committed to a local laird for those amounts, and men were appointed to assess the lands of Alexander, Earl of Buchan, and of Dervorguilla, lady of Galloway. In 1292 lands of Roger Burnet, assessed at £10 15s. 9½. (the amount demonstrates the particularity of the valuation), the wardship and marriage of the heir and the marriage of the widow were committed to the bishop of Glasgow.[116] The evidence seems to show that this kind of assessment was the basis of administration of all wardships and also of reliefs, unless an interested party made a previous arrangement with the superior and a payment to him to end (*finis*) the discussion—hence a 'fine'.

The danger that the man to whom wardship was committed would sell off stock and implements and present the heir with a wasted inheritance could have been a running sore (as it was in England) in feudal relationships; to base the wardship upon value as assessed by the neighbours was both to prevent abuses and offer rough justice to both heir and lord. In the case of reliefs it will be noted that a good number of our examples relate to tenures other than feu-ferme—earldoms or knights' fiefs. But in the case of feu-ferme it was often simple to find the value of the land—the feu-duty itself represented a valuation generally discoverable from the steward's accounts without the assistance of the neighbours. In general, feu-ferme tenants would pay a double feu-duty as entry money, the grassum of later feu-ferme tenures. Of course, there would be exceptions the reasons for which are not now obvious. When Adam fitz Odo was made heritable steward of St Andrews Priory in the 1190s, holding the shire of Kinninmonth for a feu-duty of two merks, the relief was fixed advantageously at one merk, presumably because a *ministerialis* was not treated like an ordinary tenant. After all, if exploited he could recoup himself too easily as a dishonest steward.[117] Another Fife charter of 1250 × 80 fixed the feu-duty at £3, the wardship at a lump sum of twenty merks and the relief at £6—it is not clear whether this relief included or was additional to the year's feu-duty.[118] Nor is it clear what was done in those cases where the annual ferme was not a feu-duty but an object—gloves, spurs, sparrowhawk—which may have borne

116 *Rotuli Scotiae*, i, 12b, 10b.
117 G. W. S. Barrow in D. A. Bullough, R. L. Storey (ed.), *The Study of Medieval Records* (1971), 124.
118 *Laing Charters*, no. 15.

little relationship to the value of the lands at ferme. In a number of these cases exemption from wardship and relief is specifically granted, and in others there is exemption from 'all other secular demand', which may well amount to the same thing;[119] out of such cases arose the tenure of blench ferme known to later lawyers but very rarely (and inconsistently) named before 1300. Exemption from wardship and relief presupposes, and is a logical consequence of, the custom of basing these casualties upon the annual value of the fief.

Sometimes it may have been necessary to value land held in feu-ferme in order to fix the relief. With military tenures the search for a method of assessment acceptable to lord and vassal may have persisted through the twelfth century. Early in the thirteenth century a Buchan fief held of the earl for the service of an archer had the very high relief of £20 fixed by charter, but a Moray fief held for half a knight's service was similarly fixed at £2 'when the casualty (casus) of wardship and relief shall happen' a phrase which identifies wardship and relief as equal burdens.[120] At the end of the century Gilbert de Hay, to whose ancestor Errol had been given for two knights' service, bemoaned the burden of his relief after the devastation of war; if he paid 'the extent' (that is, the assessment) he would have to sell his lands. He asked for remission of his relief, a favour his ancestors had enjoyed (there is evidence that Robert I was later persuaded of the truth of this claim) and Edward I remitted £100, the balance to be paid in instalments of twenty merks.[121] A decade earlier the Maules of Panmure, who had inherited the fief granted by King William to William de Valognes for half a knight's service (but who also had lands of their own), were in like case; of a total relief of £122 10s. the king remitted all but £40, payable in three, twenty-merk instalments.[122] The same balance would place the Hay relief at £140.

Unfortunately, the only relief of whose amount we can be certain is that of Maule of Panmure, where the figure suggests a valuation such as the Hay example refers to. In the case of three earldoms, we know of a balance due: £200 for Dunbar in 1293, £120 for Buchan in 1294 and 100 merks for Lennox in 1305,[123]

[119] Fraser, *Wemyss*, ii, no. 6; *Morton Registrum*, ii, no. 6.
[120] *Aberdeen-Banff Collections*, 407–9; *Moray Registrum*, Cart. Orig. no. 7.
[121] *Cal. Docs. Scot.*, ii, no. 1738.  [122] *Rotuli Scotiae*, i, 9.
[123] *Rotuli Scotiae*, i, 18b; Stevenson, *Documents*, i, 418; *Cal. Docs. Scot.*, iv, 375.

and these may be instances where the heir made a fine with the king to obtain more rapid possession of his inheritance, as Simon Fraser of Oliver Castle made a fine of 100 merks (the English figure for a barony) for his relief in 1292, his lands being worth 200 merks according to his wife in 1297 (when she had an interest in exaggerating their value).[124] Perhaps the most interesting of the claims put to Edward I related to lands in Wigtownshire. The owner sought mitigation of his relief, that it should be taken according to the present value of the lands, not the old valuation before the war which had devastated them. The king instructed that relief be taken in the customary way 'either by a new extent or by the old register'.[125] During the twelfth and thirteenth centuries rising land prices would favour landlords as long as reliefs were based on assessed value; by the same token, as long as the family property had not changed in extent it benefited tenants if they could appeal to a previous assessment, to the last relief, and persuade the superior to accept this *antiquus extentus,* 'auld extent', as fair. It seems that by the middle of the thirteenth century and perhaps much earlier there was a hardening of reliefs in this way, with appeals to the old accounts (the 'old register') for evidence; lords were hard put to it to justify reassessment unless, presumably, land had changed hands. But with war damage the situation could be reversed and some tenants made piteous pleas for a 'true value' (*verus valor*) to replace the old extent, which now worked in their disfavour.

Relief thus had become a matter of negotiation according to generally accepted rules: it was the annual value of the lands, sometimes according to a recent assessment, sometimes according to a traditional valuation. So far as we can tell, no distinction was made in the conditions of succession--wardship, relief, marriage— on account of the nature of the return, which might be military or monetary, and the 'knight's fief' did not become (as it did in England) a fossilised relic lovingly preserved by the crown's lawyers amid the free conveyancing necessary to the expanding society of the thirteenth century. It would be of great interest to know how the military fief and feu-ferme came so closely together, but twelfth-

---

124 *Rotuli Scotiae,* i, 9b; Stevenson, *Documents,* ii, 96; see also *Rotuli Scotiae,* i, 11b where Richard Fraser of Touch Fraser paid a fine of 100 merks for the wardship of lands in Peeblesshire.
125 *Cal. Docs. Scot.,* ii, no. 1984.

century evidence seems too slight to explain the process. It is, however, noteworthy that in consequence a source of friction between lords and tenants great and small was minimised. This was the more true since the essentially commercial attitude adopted towards feudal casualties in Scotland was modified by considerations of social degree, that marriage should not be contracted with, nor wardship entrusted to, someone of lower rank.

Almost any thirteenth-century charter granted between baron, knight or laird, in addition to making the grant for a service, will specify a demand for suit of court and an offer of warranty. The lawyers and those historians who are of legal cast of mind would perhaps make suit of court the keynote of social intercourse in medieval society. It was no more so than army service. In most infeftments with suit of court, attendance was required at the three head courts held annually but nothing is specified as to other meetings of the court, and attendance there may have been necessary only at special summons. In a charter of 1312, Hay of Leys, in Errol, took land on a thirty-year lease from Scone Abbey and among the conditions of his tenure was suit at the three head courts 'but their husbandmen shall make suit to all the pleas of the abbot held in the barony of Scone'.[126] The distinction between head and other courts was a social one, in attendance and presumably also in business, but already in the thirteenth century there is some evidence to suggest that the important suitors played a preponderant rôle on assizes, that is in civil suits among free tenants.[127]

Such men of standing are found describing the suit owed by Nicholas of Inverpeffer to the court of the abbot of Arbroath in 1251.[128] The very first document in the Chartulary of Coldstream Nunnery records a gift by the late thirteenth century earl of Dunbar of land resigned in his court and is witnessed by his three sons, three knights and his steward. His other charters show small groups of knights and lairds about his steward; in these we may recognise the 'worthy men' of the earl's court.[129] They are also found as witnesses to charters of many magnates, the names of lairds hurrying after the knights as though to catch and reflect the light

126 *Scone Liber*, no. 144.
127 *Fife Court Bk.* appendix E.
128 *Arbroath Liber*, i, no. 250.
129 *Coldstream Chartulary*, nos. 1–3, 9, 16; Raine, *North Durham*, no. CXXXVII.

of their betters. Sometimes the document is a resignation to the
lord, sometimes a grant by him of lands formerly held by another; in either case a judicial process is almost certain to have
taken place, and the presence of the steward's name bears out that
we are in presence of the lord's court and its assize of worthy men.
Among the deeds of religious houses these lairds are the leading
witnesses whose seals are appended when small tenants and peasants
resign lands in the lord's court for reasons of need or defect of service
(which amount to much the same thing). What part they played
in bringing about these resignations in favour of, for example, the
prior of Coldingham, is obscure, but it is possible that they were
there to ensure an assize responsible in serving the essential interests
of the landlord while guarding against an arbitrary exercise of his
economic power. We are all too ignorant of the working of courts
of freeholders as late even as the fifteenth century, but something
of the flavour may be preserved in the pleadings in 1288 by a man
whose status is unclear over twelve pence levied at Eyemouth in
virtue of a ship tying up there. The prior's steward no sooner
impeached him, probably claiming the money as petty custom due
to the prior, than William Sembland, burgess of Berwick, appeared
to stand warranty for him. William was unable and unwilling to
find a pledge that he would answer at a later term and the steward
'asked the consideration and judgement of the court and they (the
steward and William) went out; having called them back again, the
court judged' that the burgess was in mercy, that is, must pay an
amercement. The steward pressed his advantage: let him now
answer the principal charge. Again William's reluctance led to the
court reaching a judgement against him in the absence of the
parties: he should pay the twelve pence as well as his amercement.
And when again William would produce no pledge for payment
the steward asked the court 'what he ought to do and the court
adjudged that William's body should be arrested', and so it was.
In the outcome, the town of Berwick plucked their burgess from the
prior's grasp and, claiming that the twelve pence were the king's
customs, had the case called before the guardians of the realm
(which is why a record of it was drawn up).

But the interest of the plea is the reliance placed by the steward
upon the suitors of the court to uphold the rights of their lord.
Ten are named as witnesses to the document and explicitly described
as suitors; for the most part their names may be found among the

priory's charters as the more prosperous of its tenants.[130] They were
not knights (few priory tenants were) and it may be that by the
end of the thirteenth century knights would disdain such trivial
business. But these lairds carried a considerable responsibility which
the steward, as a party in the case, left upon their shoulders and
which could perhaps lead to their compearing upon a summons of
error before the king himself. Suit of court may have been regarded
as a burden by the peasantry vexed to come to all the pleas of their
lord's court, but it does not seem to have troubled worthy men for
the elaborate arrangements detailed in charters for other services
are not found for this one. To serve upon the assize was a recognition, then, of social distinction; at the court of an earl or a great
baron who did have knightly tenants it put the lairds with the
knights and separated them from the peasants.

Among the deeds of a religious house, the reader will almost
certainly come upon agreements settling disputes, drawn up in
contractual form to record the concessions made by each side. Yet
alongside these there will often be a charter by one party recording
the same concessions as a grant and concluding with a clause of
warranty. In any transaction the title of the recipient was only as
good as that of the donor, who must, therefore, be held responsible
to make good whatever was defective in what he gave or sold. In
the thirteenth century such warranty was so often specified in
documents that it is commonplace and often overlooked. There were
cases where it took a special form, as when William de Bruce
promised warranty in peacetime and land in England if he failed to
give warranty (that is, in war); sometimes any alternative lands
were to be to the same value 'according to the estimation of worthy
men'; and there are cases where the warranty had to be made
good.[131]

In the last resort, it can be argued, this is what thirteenth-
century 'feudalism' was all about. The personal relationship of
knights to barons, while it seems to depend upon tenure, was really
coincidental with it in that most knights had tenurial links with
several men; their special relationship with a great magnate arose
from the fact that he was a great magnate and that their holdings
lay within the geographical range of his influence. They served in

[130] Raine, *North Durham*, no. CCXXXII.
[131] Fraser, *Annandale*, i, 1–2 = *Hist. MSS. Comm., Fifteenth Report*, viii,
no. 67; *Arbroath Liber*, i, no. 99.

his court, his administration, his social circle (*familia*), his company of war (*comitiva*) and some of these things were made to look dependent upon the land they held of him and the homage and fealty which they did to him. But the tenure of land can be regarded as a part of these relationships, and not, as the lawyers would have it, a reason for them. Among lords, knights and lairds the appearance of a meaningful 'feudal' relationship was maintained over many years by, for example, the giving and taking of homage, by wardship and marriage of the person as well as wardship of the land, all of which reinforced the social relationships among these men, the clientage of one and protection of another. This appearance, however, was surely selective: it ignored the much greater legion of homages and fealties and tenures which led to no such relationship, which were devoid of any content except the payment of feu duty and relief and the giving of sasine. This tired structure was scarcely more significant of social relationships than the ruinous feudal pile which conceals lucrative legal incompetence today. It existed as a form to enable two basic kinds of transaction to take place: sale of land outright, and irredeemable loan of land at a fixed rate of interest, the feu duty. But in either transaction society had to afford protection to the buyer that the bargain was good, and hence it insisted that the seller guarantee his title. Such a guarantee might have to last for generations, since unless the state, decreed otherwise the limit of legal memory was the limit of man's memory; to these ends men had recourse to the written title in ever fuller form to spell out in careful detail exactly what the donor's intention had been. Yet there was reasonable distrust of the lawyer's parchment and the fragile seal, and a disinclination to let them weigh more in a court of law than what men had seen, heard and believed. So the conveyance was completed by the giving of homage and sasine and was renewed in each generation by the same ceremonies. Even better if it were renewed each year by a symbolic transaction, the handing over of gloves or spurs, to remind the parties and outsiders that a title and guarantee of title still existed. Hence, even with outright sales, there was point in preserving an empty or *blanche* feudal render.

It is significant that the church was the landowner most willing to discard this symbol. True, it regularly offered a return of prayers for the soul's welfare, but after the tenth or hundredth charter with these promises (and there are thousands of them), they appear a sop to the consciences of men here and to the judgement session here-after. In fact, the church bought outright when it could, and to guarantee its titles it placed its trust in a well organised charter chest, in cartularies, in its corporate wakefulness untroubled by the minorities and senilities which beset the security of family titles, in its powerful voice in the state and in the existence of its own alternative legal system.

The contrast between feu and alms, between secular and ecclesiastical conveyancing, underlines the changes which were taking place in the twelfth and thirteenth centuries. The paucity of charters recording transactions between laymen for the first three-quarters of the twelfth century is not merely a matter of the adverse survival-factor; it seems that such deeds were rarely drawn up, because the fief was only a part of the donor's relationship with the donee, involving real services and a real control by the donor over the use and disposition of the fief. It was he who held his vassal responsible for services fitly performed for an integral fief; but from c. 1170 this dominant position broke down as vassals first sought permission to alienate and then, early in the thirteenth century, assumed the right to fragment at will. Going into the market with their lands they found the need to assure buyers of a secure title— hence the growth and nature of the conveyancing industry, already flourishing in the ecclesiastical sector.

# 16

# LANDLORDS, WORTHY
# AND RELIGIOUS

Landlord, thane and peasant each contributed to increasing the total area of land exploited by new clearings, new grazings and hence new cains, a process which had gone on for some centuries before the twelfth. The change from food to cash rent, perhaps in the eleventh, certainly in the twelfth, century represents an increase in expectations among the landowning class, a desire for the more specialised techniques and goods which industry (both rural and urban) and commerce were making available. At the same time, village and town markets provided a means of turning into cash the surpluses which had been paid as food-rent.[1] The response to these opportunities and demands, by monastery, baron, knight and thane would certainly vary as did their needs. The monastic community with its host of domestics would require larger supplies of foodstuffs and cloth than any lay household and might be driven into large-scale cultivation both for consumption and for the market. Yet problems of management must have bulked large along with such rudimentary economic calculations as a convent might make.

We should expect to find those with distant estates leasing them for a money ferme which could be adjusted from time to time. Estates close to the landowner's dwelling might be exploited by more direct management through a steward accounting not for a ferme but for income, consumption, sales and showing a profit. Yet, as we have seen, from the middle or late twelfth century the spread of tenure in feu-ferme seems inexorable, an apparent

[1] E. Miller, 'The English Economy in the Thirteenth Century', *Past and Present*, xxviii (1964), 21–40.

dissipation of resources for returns which may sometimes be economic when fixed, but are always a bad bargain for the donor after a lapse of some time. A number of reasons can be advanced which may explain this, to us mistaken, calculation. In the first place, farming was a traditional means of exploitation and the weight of custom was heavy; at Arbuthnott, Isaac of Benvie did not dare remove Gillandres the Lame when he heard that he was a long-established neyf of the bishop, nor did he dare upset practices for use of the mill. In the second place, from the landlord's point of view the calculation was a social one, perhaps, more than an economic one. 'Feudal' tradition measured a magnate's significance by the number and socio-economic standing of his vassals. In the grant of a fief for a knight's service the donor's calculation had been almost wholly social and scarcely economic at all. In the same way, provision for the family—younger sons and brothers as well as female members—led to a great deal of feuing, usually for a ferme, and for social reasons. Thirdly, the continuing expansion of resources by the breaking out of new land, the extension of old and the making of new settlements, mitigated the dissipation of landed resources caused by feuing.

In the fourth place, in many cases there may have been a capital payment, unmentioned in the conveyance, which justified the feu economically and which was reinvested in the purchase of land elsewhere, again in feu-ferme, or which was spent in conspicuous consumption. Such sales are documented time and again with peasant feus which do not hesitate to mention payments for purchase. They are rare, indeed, at the level of magnate or laird. Yet, in 1231, Patrick of Dunbar (before he became earl), moved by divine piety for love of St Cuthbert and for the souls of himself and all his relatives, gave up the toun of Swinewood, which he admitted his ancestors had unjustly taken away from Coldingham Priory. It is a second document which tells us that he was persuaded of his duty in the king's court at Roxburgh, a third and fourth that he asked the king and his father to confirm the priory's title, and four more documents which reveal that this access of careful piety was brought on by a promise of 200 merks from the monastery, money collected (dare one say it?) religiously, at the due terms.[2] True, this is not a case of land held in feu-ferme, but it does suggest that

[2] Raine, *North Durham*, nos. CXXV–CXXXII.

pious words, whether Christian (*divine caritatis intuitu*) or secular (*dilecto fideli meo, pro homagio et servitio suo*), may often divert attention from the realities of the relationship.

But the most important reason for grants in feu-ferme was the security which they gave to the 'tenant'; his land was not merely heritable, but, and this was probably much more important, disponable. Together the land and its feu charter were a negotiable asset in the hands of the recipient, to be exploited as commercial opportunities widened. In the circumstance where a man of small consequence sought land from one of greater standing, once the decision to sell was taken, the ferme itself was the best the seller could do to provide himself with an economic return: since the ferme could not be tied to a cost-of-living index as a hedge against inflation, in questioning the policy of feuing we are really questioning the growth of an active land market and the entrepreneurial initiative of those who were busy taking and giving land at ferme.

There is much circumstantial evidence that landowners, great, middling and small, could run their affairs into debt. In 1170 Robert de Quincy, who had borrowed £80 from Abraham, a Jew, pawned land to Newbattle Abbey, who cleared the debt, acquiring the land outright from Robert before the term of their possession ran out, presumably for another payment. Robert was also in debt to Aaron of Lincoln, and both Melrose and Holyrood abbeys stood pledge for him there.[3] There is no evidence that Jews were active as money-lenders in Scotland, but every reason to think that the Cistercians, and probably religious of other orders, were frequently involved as money-lenders on the security of lands to which in consequence they ultimately acquired title. For example, why should the Cistercians of Coupar acquire property about 1210–1220 in Atholl, where they had had no interest hitherto? There must be a strong suspicion that they took land in Strathtay and Blair Atholl as security from Thomas of Galloway, Earl of Atholl, perhaps to help him to pay the king for marriage to an heiress. Wherever a thirteenth-century land transaction involves an ecclesiastical corporation and a layman it would be right to assume that a material consideration was important, and to discard that assumption only where the evidence of piety is plain. In England ecclesiastical corporations were bankers in the land-market, with large debts

[3] G. W. S. Barrow, 'A twelfth century Newbattle document', *Scot. Hist. Rev.*, xxx (1951), 41–9.

as well as huge assets, and there is every reason to think that they were at least as prominent in Scotland.[4]

As neither borrower nor lender made a cost-benefit analysis of his transaction, there was probably a great deal of improvidence in the management of resources, land, labour and cash, at all levels of the landholders' society. One clear instance stands out: the diversion of capital into a non-productive sector, the monastic orders. Moved by true piety, two noble ladies in the thirteenth century went to considerable lengths to amass the capital needed to found new houses: Queen Ermengade at Balmerino from 1225 to 1229 and Dervorguilla of Galloway at Sweetheart in 1273. But laymen were also active in a small wave of foundations which took place at the turn of the twelfth–thirteenth centuries. In 1191 Lindores Abbey (Tironensian) was founded by Earl David, in 1200 Inchaffray (Augustinian) by the earl of Strathearn. In the decade 1210–20 the earls of Fife and Buchan established Cistercian abbeys at Culross and Deer, the earl of Carrick tried to secure a Cluniac one at Crossraguel; in the following decade Fearn (Premonstratensian) was founded by the earl of Ross, and about 1240 the priory of Inchmahome (Augustinian) by the earl of Menteith. What this entailed, and the kind of expense which deferred the establishment of Crossraguel for many years, is delightfully revealed by the letter written by Walter the Steward in the 1220s to the Master of the Order of Sempringham explaining that he proposed

> 'for the souls' welfare of myself and of all my ancestors and successors, to found immediately at my own expense a house of your Order at .. Ayr ... and since prolixity is tiresome I set forth here as promptly as possible what I propose to assign for the support of the religious: the wainage of five ploughs[5] ... pasture stocked at the outset at my own expense with 300 cows; grazing similarly stocked with 2000 sheep; a convenient fishing; the kirk of Dundonald worth 100 merks yearly and the kirk of Sanquhar worth 20 merks; two mills worth 12 merks; part of my wood of Sanquhar and the buildings, ecclesiastical and domestic, which I shall put up at my own cost for the religious there.'[6]

It was not enough, or not enough of it was forthcoming, and after a decade of trial the cell at Dalmilling was closed down. Walter the Steward learned the hard way that grandiose plans

---

[4] *Inchcolm Charters*, no. XX.

[5] I.e. five ploughgates.

[6] G. W. S. Barrow, 'The Gilbertine House at Dalmilling', *Collections of the Ayrshire Archaeological and Natural History Society*, iv (1955–57), 50–67.

have a heavy cost and he pulled out with nothing worse than burnt fingers. Others, particularly among the earls, carried through their plans doubtless at considerable cost to their family fortunes. Lesser men diverted capital to nunneries, friaries, and (like David de Quixwood at Old Cambus) to hospitals. In general, if a quantitative judgement is possible, it might seem that great landowners were more liable than small to such irrational and uneconomic investment of a portion of their capital, but nonetheless the magnate with greater resources on which to fall back was better able than the laird to weather a financial crisis. And if religious considerations moved some laymen in their dealings with the church, it is equally likely that other men were moved by social considerations in dealings with their vassals and tenants, and not always by economic motives.

The references scattered through charters to 'demesne', *dominium,* are quite frequent; unfortunately, it is sometimes clear that demesne is land held at ferme contrasted with land at feu and not with peasant land. It is therefore difficult to discover the balance of demesne (kept in the lord's hands, cultivated by peasant labour, for the lord's profit) to peasant land but it is more important to discover how that balance was changing. Some signs of an increase in thirteenth-century high farming can be found. Thus the abbey of Inchaffray in Strathearn secured no fewer than four papal bulls, in 1248, 1252, 1256 and 1274, to recover if possible the possessions of the abbey granted to 'clergy and laity, religious and seculars, to some for not a short time, to others in perpetuity and to yet others for life at ferme or for annual rent'.[7] Probably ineffectual, they nonethe less suggest an interest in building up the abbey's demesne; if other religious obtained such bulls, they have not survived, and it seems unlikely that collections of charters will indicate the scale of any move towards demesne farming.

Yet the surveys of the monasteries of Kelso and Coldingham remind us that the arable demesne of a great landowning convent was perhaps less significant than wealth reckoned in flocks and herds. In this respect the priory of Coldingham is instructive for, although favoured with Coldingham moor, it did not have the vast stretches of hill grazing which allowed Melrose and Kelso abbeys to manage sheep ranches. Down by the Tweed at Fishwick and Paxton the priory had flocks of sheep, but the use of the 'innumerable' acres of Coldingham moor is perhaps indicated by the existence

[7] *Inchaffray Charters,* nos. LXXVIII, LXXXII, LXXXIV, CIV.

at Renton (on the other side of the moor) of 'separate moor of about 1000 acres to establish heather, but it is common grazing for cattle'.[8] Perhaps the priory took heath for fuel from a part enclosed for the purpose, and the village grazed its cattle on the rest; presumably the priory managed its grazing from the Coldingham side. But the entry may have a more sinister import: had a thousand acres been enclosed to exclude the stock which had destroyed the grazing? We are certainly examining a society clumsily trying to husband the natural resources which it was simultaneously exploiting to the point of exhaustion.

Among these villages the different balances of arable, meadow and waste is striking and warns us firmly against constructing a model village ecology even for the restricted area of east Berwickshire. In general there was an obvious link between the extent of meadow and the availability of waste since both served for grazing and livestock feeding, but the balance between arable and pastoral activity varied greatly and there was no notion that an acre of arable should be accompanied by grazing for so much stock. On the contrary, we can see in the separate pastures the careful attention of the landlord to his own stock and to the manuring of his own arable, and we can deduce the attrition of peasant grazings. In other words, we must consider the situation revealed by the Coldingham extent not as a fixed balance holding through the ages but as the outcome of shifting pressures to bring land into the most profitable uses. And this is surely also the significance of the loss of grazing to bring more land under the plough. The balance of arable and grazing at Swinton and Fishwick could scarcely shift any further in the direction of arable, and sums up the breaking out of new land, perhaps over several centuries and certainly during the thirteenth century. Again, the consequences of lack of manure for the extensive arable of these villages would be serious in the long term.

In large parts of Scotland, however, there was no lack of 'waste'—vast tracts of upland moor and hillside which, then as now, could carry large flocks of sheep. The parish boundaries of villages on the southern edge of the Lammermuir hills stretch far back into these hills so that each village would have its share of upland grazings; the survival of 'shiel' names there tells us that the grazings

[8] Est ibi una mora separalis circiter M acras ad radicandum brueras sed est communis pastura ad animalia.

were exploited by the village community or hamlet sending up its flocks and herds under the supervision of villagers dwelling in summer shanties. Yet the landlord also had his stock, and our evidence shows the ever more lively interest which landlords took in grazing rights of all kinds. Thus, when Humphrey de Berkeley gave Balfeith (Mearns) to Arbroath Abbey in 1199, he specified also common pasture in his fief for 100 cattle and their followers (calves) and as many pigs and horses as they needed, with the right for the monks and their men to have a shieling for these animals in named upland parts from Easter to All Saints (1 November).[9] This grant is unusual in its very specific terms, probably because it was the outcome of a formal process of perambulation; other landlords who admitted monastic sheep-farmers to their grazings were, however, equally careful to protect their interests, especially the interest of hunting. Thus Melrose Abbey took land in East Lothian from the earls of Dunbar with grazing for (or souming of) 1500 wedders, but after three generations the earl added five acres which the abbey was forbidden to plough but must enclose with a ditch to make a sheepfold so that controversy would not in future arise with the earls over whether the abbey was exceeding that souming. At nearby Innerwick the knightly tenants of Walter the Steward granted a piece of land, round which the abbey built a ditch, along with grazing. There was both sheepfold and meadow here,[10] but the earl of Dunbar was persuaded to add common pasture on Lammermuir, evidently as summer shielings, provided that 'if they give up their pasture of Innerwick, their sheepfolds shall follow their flocks with their dwellings which belong to these folds, without manual work (that is, without making permanent folds) and without using my own dwellings of Belton'.[11] The difficulty in separating and keeping count of flocks was evidently considerable and could lead to the abuse of overstocking.

Other landlords, and the religious who took grazings from them by gift or purchase, overestimated the stock—especially of sheep—which a stretch of land might carry. At Primside in Roxburghshire about 1180, Kelso Abbey received two oxgangs with grazing for 1000 sheep in two or three flocks, 24 cows and 8 oxen.[12] In 1204 the abbey, after intervention by a papal legate and King William

9 *Arbroath Liber*, i, no. 89; *R.R.S.*, ii, no. 413.
10 *Melrose Liber*, nos. 55, 56, 62.
11 *Melrose Liber*, no. 76.          12 *Kelso Liber*, no. 367.

himself, had yielded two oxgangs, two acres and grazing for 400 sheep there to Melrose Abbey in return for the favourable settlement of a boundary dispute elsewhere.[13] Evidently the arable had already been extended slightly, but in giving it away Kelso effectively ended the possibility of raising cattle and in 1290 the abbey's extent revealed that Primside had seven acres of arable (broken out from pasture, probably, to support the shepherd) and grazing for 300 sheep, not the 600 which might be expected had the original donor estimated correctly the stock which Primside would carry.[14]

The neighbouring parish of Mow, almost all of it 500 feet or more above sea level, is now deserted save for a few hill-farms; its village and kirk have disappeared, but about its economy in the twelfth and thirteenth centuries much is known. It was granted by Malcolm IV to Walter the Steward, who had married the heiress, Eschina, of an Anglian family; her ancestor, Uhtred, son of Liulf, gave the kirk of Mow to Kelso Abbey with Elisheugh and common grazing. When Eschina confirmed the gift in 1186 she specified more clearly a safeguard against the abbey's ever-growing flocks, namely that the chaplain and the peasants dependent on the kirk were to have common pasture and a reasonable souming along with her peasants.[15] The lady and this husband had already, between 1173 and 1177, given to Paisley Abbey a ploughgate of arable at *Blakedean* in Mow and pasture for 500 sheep with 'easement of other stock', that is, with appropriate common grazing,[16] but apparently after her second marriage to Henry of Mow she gave to Kelso Abbey not merely the kirk of Mow but also two oxgangs there and pasture for 400 sheep, 16 cattle, 2 oxen and 12 pigs.[17]

The religious looked at the land of Mow and found it fair. Kelso obtained (also before 1195) from the other big landowner there, Anselm of Mow, a stretch of 'arable and meadow and wood' on the west side of the parish, and Elisheugh in wood, plain and pasture.[18] He disposed of his peatmoss and a half-ploughgate of arable to Melrose Abbey,[19] but in none of these endowments was

[13] *Melrose Liber*, nos. 145–8; *R.R.S.*, ii, nos. 440, 441.
[14] *Kelso Liber*, ii, 459.
[15] *R.R.S.*, ii, 283; *Kelso Liber*, nos. 176, 146.
[16] *Paisley Registrum*, 74–6, 91; not found in *ibid*, 408–10, of 1173.
[17] *Kelso Liber*, no. 178; *R.R.S.*, ii, no. 367 × 1195) includes this gift.
[18] *Kelso Liber*, no. 154; *R.R.S.*, ii, no. 367.
[19] *Melrose Liber*, nos. 134–7.

grazing specifically defined. Controversy arose between Kelso Abbey on the one hand and Eschina and Anselm on the other over the grazings which the monks demanded by right of their kirk of Mow; and this was settled by almost identical agreements, grants to the abbey of grazing in 'my' lands for 700 sheep, and 120 cattle by Eschina but 100 (not 120) cattle by Anselm.[20] Unable to define the grazings by geographical bounds, the abbey had obtained a title to its souming from both its neighbours, though in some way Eschina made special provision for a further twenty cattle with their followers and a bull.[21]

Many of the place names in the complex documents are now lost, but it is clear that two reluctant landowners—and the obscurity lies principally in their relationship with each other—were steadily pushed by Kelso Abbey into yielding additional small pieces of arable with more and more extensive grazings. In the 1230s or 1240s this powerful new neighbour added to its extensive holdings by obtaining from Cecily, daughter of Eschina, three oxgangs of arable and eight acres of meadow, much scattered but near Atton Burn, with pasture for 300 sheep, 10 cattle and 4 horses 'anywhere in my demesne pastures'.[22] Evidently the arable was sufficiently extensive to impede access to the hill pastures, and in its agreement with Anselm, Kelso Abbey went carefully into the 'easements' of access which were necessary for the exploitation of its grazing rights on his hills, and obtained timber from Anselm's wood to make sheep folds; but there was a limitation on the grazing of one half of Anselm's lands, *Berehope*, from which all sheep but not cattle were excluded for seven weeks in the summer—sure evidence that shielings were occupied then by the cattle, and perhaps a recognition of the damage which continuous heavy grazing by sheep could do to the pastures.

In 1250, some fifty years after Anselm's grant, his descendant confirmed it with a significant reservation: that the abbey should take wood for its folds under the supervision of the donor's serjeant, reasonably and without destruction of the wood, that the folds must endure, that when repaired no additional timber should be taken and, indeed, that for twenty or thirty years no timber whatever should be taken 'until the said wood grows well again and is in

---

20  *Kelso Liber*, nos. 155, 166.
21  *Kelso Liber*, no. 147.
22  *Kelso Liber*, nos. 150, 148.

better state'.[23] Thus, the intensive exploitation of the Cheviot Hills by sheepruns had outrun the local timber resources for controlling the sheep and erosion of woodland was well advanced.

Finally, the abbey's extent of its lands reveals the state of affairs at Mow in 1300. The pasture of *Berehope* carried 700 sheep but the grazing of cattle had apparently stopped, and the exclusion of sheep was limited to four weeks, in which period the men of Anselm's descendant must graze his cattle and calves at the shielings and make their cheese. During those four weeks the abbey's sheep were folded on four acres at *Lathlade*, where the charters show the abbey had been given eight acres;[24] the abbey also had seven acres for its shepherd. At Atton Burn the abbey's arable and meadow had increased slightly from forty-seven to fifty acres, and the souming remained the same, 300 sheep, 10 oxen and 4 horses. There was also four acres of arable for the shepherd with pasture for the beasts of burden he needed for migration to the shielings. At Elisheugh the abbey had created a grange with arable for two ploughs and grazing for 20 cows, 20 oxen, 250 ewes and 200 wedders. Otherwise, the various stretches of arable which the abbey had held during the thirteenth century[25] and the quite extensive tract with grazing, the lease for which it had taken over from Jedburgh Abbey for ten years from 1255,[26] do not figure in the extent, and it it to be assumed that the former had been farmed out to the fourteen cottars of Mow who paid two shillings and did six days boon work each year. Kelso Abbey had turned markedly away from such opportunities for a mixed economy as this parish offered, and, abandoning the arable, also gave up the hill grazing of cattle which from autumn to spring grazed on the meadow and on the fields of stubble, manuring them both.[27]

The grants of arable with grazing rights discussed in the preceding paragraphs relate exclusively to landlords, occasionally specifying what is probably assumed in other charters: that these figures were the total of beasts which the lord and his peasants might put upon the grazing. The size of a peasant souming is given rarely, perhaps only when the peasant had a special function to perform

[23] *Kelso Liber*, no. 149.
[24] *Kelso Liber*, no. 161.
[25] *Kelso Liber*, nos. 162, 165.
[26] *Kelso Liber*, no. 160.
[27] A summary of the documents relating to Mow will be found in *Origines Parochiales Scotie*, i, 413–26.

for his lord, like the two fuel-keepers of Lindores Abbey who had grazing for 2 cows and 10 sheep, and for one horse, 2 cows and 20 sheep respectively near Collessie in Fife.[28] In most cases the soumings detailed were those of landlords, where the seller (for that is what the donor probably was) was in effect restricting the grazing available to himself and his peasants for the benefit of another landlord; he must then decide whether to cut the numbers of his own stock, the numbers of peasant stock or to allow overstocking.

In England the tendency, especially on the part of the peasantry, was to overstock pastures, but this may not have been so pronounced in Scotland, and in parts may not have been the case at all. Thus the very detailed provisions for controlling the size of flocks insisted upon by the earls of Dunbar, when admitting the rancher monks of Melrose to Lammermuir, were one response to the problem. Another was the struggle which the same monks had with the peasants (*homines*) of Wedale (the valley of the Gala Water) which was settled before the king in 1184 and in which, it has been suggested, 'the abbey was seeking to encroach upon or monopolise ancient shieling grazings', probably in the royal forest of Ettrick and between Gala and Leader.[29] Perhaps the men of Wedale had allies among the powerful; the leading member of the assize which swore to the bounds of the king's forest was Richard de Moreville, who four years earlier, in 1180, had himself quarrelled with Melrose Abbey over their respective rights in the forest between the Gala and Leader waters. In that settlement de Moreville kept the rights of hunting but could not build a lodging or shieling or fence nor any other work of man; the monks obtained the grazing rights and a site for a byre for 100 cows, at a cost of a hundred merks.[30] The fact that the Wedale decision was not recorded in a charter, while the de Moreville one was, confirms that the men of Wedale were of little social consequence; and both occasions show the abbey of Melrose in ruthless pursuit of grazing rights and, no doubt, of the profits of the wool trade. Arguably, the monks would be careful not to overstock as their knowledge of large-scale sheep farming increased. But the men of Wedale and the men of Richard de Moreville (who, if they interfered with the abbey's grazings, paid a fine to the abbey and a forfeiture to Richard) had little alternative

[28] *Lindores Chartulary*, nos. CXXXVII, CXL.
[29] Barrow, *Kingdom of the Scots*, 262; Anderson, *Early Sources*, ii, 307.
[30] *R.R.S.*, ii, no. 236.

as the abbey's hurdles progressively restricted the pastures for their sheep and cattle.

Moreover, by the 1290s the consequences of intensive sheep husbandry showed themselves in the form of disease among the animals. Known in England by 1272 and probably not much later in Scotland, sheep-scab by the names 'pluk' or 'pilsought' had become so dangerous that in the summer of 1294 King John ordered an inquest in each sheriffdom on each reported outbreak and forbade both the keeping and the movement of infected stock, which had to be slaughtered.[31] Such an extraordinary measure of government interference bespoke real alarm and a serious scourge, but the economic damage was not necessarily prolonged. 'The incident seems another indication of the human pressure upon natural resources in the late thirteenth century, this time upon the apparently limitless grazings of Scottish hills and mountains. There is also evidence of serious cattle disease in Lothian about 1270.[32]

Despite the conflict between rights of pasture and rights of hunting, considerable areas were designated hunting-forest. In the mid-twelfth century David I granted rights of forest to Robert Bruce in Annandale, forbidding anyone to hunt there except by Bruce's leave, or to travel there except by the highway.[33] Presumably such a grant entitled Bruce to demarcate his hunting grounds and to discipline those who took deer there. Other twelfth-century charters included in the prohibition not only hunting but also cutting of wood, and specified, as the penalty for infringement, the king's forfeiture of £10; later evidence shows that this penalty was exacted for each beast killed or each tree felled. But it seems to have applied only to the killing of deer, since in some cases the king added the right of warren, by which hares and rabbits were included in the landlord's game monopoly. Since the £10 forfeiture went to the king, the landlords had little incentive to enforce by harsh courts the rights granted to him; and even in the royal forests there is no trace of the notorious forest laws of England.

'Forest' was in fact a legal and recreational term rather than an ecological one, and in some parts, notably the Southern Uplands, it would by no means correspond to woodland. In the royal forest of Ettrick it has been argued that woods were situated in valleys, on

[31] *Reg. Brieves*, 59, no. 74; for the date, *Scot. Hist. Rev.*, xlv (1966), 43–4.
[32] *Chron. Lanercost*, 85; 'Lungessouth', lung-disease.
[33] Lawrie, *E.S.C.*, no. CXCIX.

broad or narrow banks along the sides of the main rivers with extensions up the tributary streams where soil and shelter were available, with a generous upper limit of some 1200 feet (365 m) above sea level; most of the forest is more than 1000 feet (305 m) above.[34] In other words, the contest here was between hunting rights and grazing rights for sheep, a contest well reflected in our sources by the difficulties which Melrose Abbey had with the de Moreville lords, particularly over the 'disputed wood', Threepwood. In effect, the monastery kept the timber and grazings but the de Morevilles had *saluaginam bestiarum et auium*—literally 'wildness of beasts and birds'. To one the pursuit of profit, to the other the pursuit of game; and each had a forester to look after their respective interests.[35]

What was understood by that Latin phrase we may learn from Robert Avenel, who gave to Melrose Abbey land in Eskdale, keeping for himself among animals only the *saluagina*—hart, hind, boar and roe. He would have no forester—an unusual privilege, since he could have little control over poaching by the monks' agents—but he would have a keeper to take thieves and those trespassing from the roads, and to look after the nests of falcons and tercels. The monks (their tenants are meant) might not hunt with horn and nets, nor set traps except for wolves. Seventy years later the monks and Roger Avenel went to the king's *colloquium*, to clarify these terms, for the monks, in their need for timber (perhaps to build the abbey) had been driving the falcons from their nests and then claiming that the trees might be felled because they did not return there to nest.[36] That such a matter could engage a gathering of the greatest in the land bears out the importance of hunting to those with wealth enough to indulge in it. It explains the careful attention to woodland grazing for horses and the thumping £10 forfeiture for each beast or tree, imposed upon anyone hunting or cutting wood in the forest without leave.

The Steward was also careful of his game rights with the monks of Melrose, granting them grazing rights in his forest of Mauchline with all easements except, as he sententiously observed, 'that neither monks nor lay brothers nor anyone else by their authority may hunt or hawk in that forest, for this does not suit their cloth nor do

---

[34] *Inventory of Selkirkshire*, 3, 17, 19.
[35] *R.R.S.*, ii, no. 236.
[36] *Melrose Liber*, nos. 39, 198.

we think it meet for them'.[37] But he was equally careful with his own foundation, Paisley Abbey, perambulating land in what is now Neilston parish to be given to the abbey with the right to assart, plough and enclose, but not the right to wild beasts or birds, and imposing an elaborate code of fines if their beasts strayed into the forest either within or outwith the closed season (*fermeisun*). A hundred years later, at the end of the century, James the Steward went into even greater detail, allowing the monks and their servants to cross his lands by the usual roads with swords, bows, arrows, grey-hounds and dogs, but forbidding them to cross his forest except with dogs on leash and bows unstrung.[38]

But, although hunting remained the passion of kings and mag-nates for centuries to come, the reserves of game on moors and mountains were sufficient to provide an alternative to the use of good pasture land, and forest was gradually limited to Ettrick, the Ochils and the foothills of the Grampians, where Alexander II already had castles—Clunie, Kinclaven, Kincardine—strategically spaced as hunting lodges. It is possible that worthy men spent more time with hawk, hound, bow and spear than at courts, councils and prayer. But at least they did not enforce a vindictive and cruel forest law of mutilation and death, and there is little sign that in the thirteenth century men thought forest law an oppression.

What was the gross value of the revenues of a great landowner, lay or ecclesiastical? Any venturer into the uncharted sea of ecclesiastical valuations is immediately aware of the dangers which surround the subject. A number of texts survive apparently from the decades 1290–1310, but none securely dated, giving figures which vary widely even where we can be sure that they relate to the same kirk and income-category. One assessment (p. 424) for Lothian and the Merse appears to belong to *c.* 1293, when the collectors were driven to be particularly exacting; its figures are high but it does give a unique and invaluable breakdown and there is no reason to think that one source of income is overvalued in relation to another.

These figures, it must be stressed, cannot claim to be the total in-come of the houses in question since they relate very roughly to the counties of Berwick and the three Lothians, and do not include the important lands of Kelso and Melrose Abbeys in Glasgow diocese.

[37] *Melrose Liber*, no. 73.
[38] *Paisley Registrum*, 17, 92–6.

The Cistercian monks, by maintaining their renunciation of appropriated kirks, had to invest in arable and sheepfarming, while the regular canons put the larger part of their capital into kirks, which they were allowed to serve; but, clearly, all orders invested much more heavily in a pastoral economy than in agriculture. The figures for calves and lambs represent a valuation of those born yearly, not

TABLE I

Monastic Incomes in the Archdeaconry of Lothian

| | Rents | Demesne | Demesne Plough-gates | Calves Lambs | Wool Lamb-skins | Appro-priated Kirks |
|---|---|---|---|---|---|---|
| | £ | £ | | £ | £ | £ |
| *Benedictine, Tironensian monks.* | | | | | | |
| Coldingham Priory | 216 (113+103) | 40 | 20 | 9 | 44 | 260 |
| Kelso Abbey | 108 | 16 | 7 | 10 | 37 | 232 |
| *Cistercian monks* | | | | | | |
| Newbattle Abbey | 91 | 50 | 19 | 37 | 66 | 24 |
| Melrose Abbey | 54 | 18 | 9 | 58 | 86 | — |
| *Augustinian, Premonstratensian canons* | | | | | | |
| Holyrood Abbey | 132 | 37 | 11 | 37 | | 570 |
| Dryburgh Abbey | 18 | 13 | 6 | 7 | 14 | 223 |
| *Cistercian nuns.* | | | | | | |
| Berwick Priory | ? 60 | 12 | 6 | 11 | 10 | 32 |
| Coldstream Priory | 34 | 20 | 7 | 6 | 9 | 49 |
| Eccles Priory | 73 | 12 | 6 | 3 | 10 | 10 |
| Haddington Priory | 78 | 29 | 10 | 12 | 71 | 26 |
| North Berwick Priory | 21 | 23 | 6 | 6 | 14 | 31 |
| St. Bothan's Priory | ? 5 | 4 | 2 | 4 | 22 | 8 |

the income from them, and the wool figures must also represent growth, not sales. Evidently the Cistercians no longer denied themselves peasant and mill fermes, but they invested much more heavily in livestock than in demesne agriculture; the difference between Newbattle and Melrose is therefore perhaps significant, the former retaining a quite substantial demesne which was of great value. One explanation suggests itself: the relationship of these houses to the feeding of towns. Newbattle was close to, Holyrood beside, Edinburgh, which, while it had Leith, was not a great seaport like

Berwick, importing grain from England. The fact that each retained a substantial demesne and that each ploughgate was worth £2 10s. (Newbattle) or £3 5s. (Holyrood) may be attributed to this relatively protected urban market. It is difficult to believe that the ploughgates of Coldingham Priory, assessed at £2 each, a figure borne out by the extent of 1300, were markedly less fertile, but competition of imported grain at Berwick may have kept the prices (and the valuation) down. Similarly Melrose Abbey, at a greater distance from Berwick, had much less incentive than Newbattle to go in for numerous granges and extensive demesne farming, when the Berwick market was open to sea-borne grain and there was a strong demand for wool.

The extent of Coldingham Priory lands *c.* 1300 reveals a demesne of at least thirty-five ploughgates, and it is likely that the *c.* 1293 valuation, which gives twenty ploughgates, generally understates revenues at about a half of their true value. But the Coldingham entry also has a unique feature in distinguishing between the priory rents, including mill or mills and fishings (£113) and 'lands set at ferme with the issues of the court' (£103), a distinction which it is difficult to perceive in the 1300 extent, but which may indicate that a considerable amount of demesne had recently been leased.[39]

In all these documents it is clear that demesnes played a fairly—but only fairly—important part in the economy of some monasteries; where we can discern movement, demesnes were shrinking in size and importance. Those still maintained show virtually no sign of cultivation by peasant week-work which would be an indication of high farming on the conventional model. More and more land seems to be going at ferme to the peasantry, and almost every religious house on our table is a rentier first and a manager of cultivation only a very poor second.

Early in the fourteenth century the process is visible in the disappearance of *conversi* and of the direct management of granges by the Cistercians, as at Coupar Abbey. The outburst of conveyancing among private persons and corporations which begins about 1160 tails off fairly markedly in the second half of the thirteenth century (especially if later confirmation of earlier transactions be discounted), indicating a rise and a levelling off or slight fall in the demand for

---

[39] *Coldingham Correspondence*, cviii–cxvii, no. LXX. For the date see *ibid*, preface pp. xi–xiii.

land in these two periods. The early phase of this activity coincides with the swift rise in prices which has been discerned in Angevin England and with the associated rapid development of town life and urban institutions, both features which can be traced in contemporary Scotland. An increased demand for land and rising prices are an indication of a marked increase in population and consequent pressure upon natural resources to increase production. This period probably saw an increase in the size of some demesnes and a move towards 'high farming' with the fairly extensive use of labour services, at least on the part of the greater landowners, but also possibly among the lesser barons, knights and lairds who trafficked so eagerly in the land-market. There is no means of measuring this movement, which would certainly not be uniform even in Lowland Scotland, but it may be suggested that it was less a matter of resuming demesnes once farmed out, than one of overall extension of cultivation by both peasants and lords. If this view is correct, then at some time after the middle of the thirteenth century the changes went into reverse, with a resumption of farming out and a general shift away from demesne exploitation as revealed by the various extents.

There is an almost total absence of evidence for secular estates, from the king downwards. In 1294–5 an extent of the lands of the earl of Fife in wardship assessed their annual worth at a total of £432; there is only one reference to a demesne, worth £23 annually, but the terminology varies between *villa, terra, manerium, feodum* and other land may have been demesne. In the accounts of the king's agent the lands are not itemised; income is from many sources, but the only significant one is land: £348 from fermes of tenants and £84 from grain coming from certain fermes, a total of £432 from Fife, to which might be added £21 for lands in Moray and £37 for land in Lothian. Since the granitar was paid for his services in 'setting the demesne lands at ferme and receiving the grain from them' it seems that the £84 may represent former demesnes which provisioned the earl's hall but were now leased for produce rents since the heir was a boy carefully guarded in England. If so, five-sixths of the earl's income was rents, one-sixth demesne exploitation. Moreover, deduction was made for £26 remitted by the king to some tenants on account of their poverty, while some (apparently demesne) lands 'lie waste and cannot be leased'; it may not have been easy to find tenants at the assessed rents because the demand for land was already slipping.[40] Few magnates, if any, were wealthier than the earl of Fife, the leading earl in Scotland, whose income at £500 was that of a modest English baron, thrice that of Neil, Earl of Carrick, who died in 1256, and six times that of the earldom of Angus in 1263. Such modest incomes were the product of modest endowments and, it may be suspected, of traditional, rather than unrelenting, exploitation of resources. 'High farming' was a less marked feature of the economy of a magnate's estates than careful collection of rents.

Further down the social scale it is even more difficult to assess the manner of exploitation and the relative importance of demesne, rents, and the wool crop. In the 1270s John of Leitholm, son of a knight of Earl Patrick (II) of Dunbar, passed on to his son Ketell a rag-bag of tofts and crofts and acres, including much that was purchased both from peasants and from another small laird, Duncan, son of Nicholas, including the latter's meadow 'in Hemmingleth, ploughed and unploughed' (that is, separate pasture, some of which was ploughed), with the right to pasture beasts in John's demesne (*dominicum*). The emphasis here is upon arable being garnered together, every fragment truly valuable; once more some of the better common grazing, having been enclosed as meadow for the lord, had in its turn been put under the plough to increase production.[41] It may be that at least in the south-east there was careful working of modest demesne by thirteenth-century knights and lairds, evidence for which might be found by meticulous gleaning in the sources. But without inquests, surveys or extents the evidence will probably never yield certain conclusions.

The exploitation of pasture was a less complex problem and for the large landowner, in particular, could be very profitable. The monks of Melrose were hawking their wool in Flanders in the twelfth century, and their pre-eminence, and the importance as a whole of the Cistercians in Scotland, in wool production and trade, have long been recognised. Yet it would certainly be wrong to see the Cistercians as producing the greater part of exported Scottish wool; they were merely the most important among many lay and

---

[40] Stevenson, *Documents*, i, 407–18. The printed text obscures the fact that the two accounts, nos. CCCXVII and CCCXIX, are in fact two versions of the same account, for 16 Feb. 1294—16 Feb. 1295; the dates in the modern headings and rubrics are misleading, since the account was obviously made after its closing date.

[41] *Hist. MSS. Comm. Twelfth Report*, viii (Earl of Home), 173, no. 291.

ecclesiastical entrepreneurs in large-scale sheep-farming to meet the apparently insatiable demand of Flemish and Italian looms for the short-woolled fleeces of northern English and Scottish moors. Secular landowners and the Benedictines, whose pastures were scattered among the villages (themselves often scattered) where they held land, were at a managerial disadvantage in comparison with houses like Melrose, Newbattle, Dundrennan and Dryburgh which were free, or freed themselves, of the constraints of village organisation and disposed of wide grazings on moor and hill where the wool crop could readily be estimated and graded. So, when the wool merchant rode up the banks of the Tweed and Teviot, he could learn at Melrose, as perhaps he could not at Coldingham, the quantity and quality of fleeces to be shorn; he could inspect them, discuss prices with the cellarer, the monk charged with conduct of the business of a Cistercian house, and perhaps enter upon a contract for delivery of so many sacks at such a date.

The early Cistercians, denied so many traditional sources of revenue—mills, appropriated kirks, demesne labour services—must have suffered severely from lack of cash; they made no stand against the woolmonger anxious to buy their surplus wool, and in the thirteenth century found it advantageous to enter into a contract for two or three or even ten years, a forward sale for which the broker might offer cash in advance for one or even more years. Of course it was to the mutual advantage of merchant and abbey to iron out the grosser leaps and tumbles of market prices, but where a convent took money in advance for more than one year's crop it was borrowing on the security of the wool and it paid interest in the form of a lower price. Such contracts were improvident whether the market was bull or bear, for they were almost always made in a spirit of unjustified optimism as to the size of the wool crop. To deliver his promise the abbot and his cellarer were driven to purchase wool (known as the 'collect') from the peasantry or lairds—an enterprise expressly forbidden by the general chapter of the order in 1157, just as forward selling was forbidden in 1181 and 1277. To no avail; the 'collect', was an important part of the annual turnover of any well-run Cistercian house by the late thirteenth century, when the financial situation worsened under the impact of papal taxation—Bagimond's tenth from 1274 to 1280 and that of Nicholas IV from 1291. It is significant that while Bagimond deposited some money at Melrose and transmitted the tax to Italian bankers, he employed secular clergy as sub-collectors and the religious had nothing to do with the collecting.[42] In the 1290s all was different: without exception the sub-collectors were abbots who banked the money with Italians, a conjunction which is unlikely to be co-incidence, for the latter were actively buying wool direct from abbeys.[43] In effect the abbeys paid their tax (at least in part) in wool which was remitted to Italy; secular clerics might sell their wool to an abbey to pay the tax, a paper transaction which increased the abbey's 'collect', enabling it to ask a better price and improve its profit margin as middleman.

As early as 1255 Coldingham Priory had financial dealings with Siennese merchants in London, presumably through wool sales, and in 1286 a Florentine firm took nineteen sacks of wool as the year's clip from the same priory. The second case was clearly an example of forward selling and the first may be so also. The Italians were well established at Coldingham, possibly through its link with Durham, and native merchants were not acting as middlemen there.[44]

The scale of monastic production is indicated by the handbook of Francesco Pegolotti, dating from the early fourteenth century with a passage on England beginning with convents 'di Scozia d'Inghilterra'. It gives, for three qualities of wool from each monastery, the price in Flanders in an unknown year which the latest commentator has suggested would be *c*. 1320 on the evidence of the price levels. Others have favoured a date some thirty years earlier, which might fit the presence of Scottish houses rather better. And we should note that the total English output of the list, 2650 sacks, was only a small fraction of the average annual export from England *c*. 1300 of 35,000 sacks.

It has been suggested that 1000 sheep would yield four or five sacks of wool; if the lower figure be accepted then Melrose Abbey had 12,000 sheep at least, and possibly a good many more, since, as noted, Pegolotti seems to underestimate production. The pre-eminence of the Cistercians with Italian merchants arose from their

[42] *SHS Misc.* vi, 27–30.
[43] *Register of John de Halton*, ed. W. N. Thompson and T. F. Tout, i (Canterbury and York Society, 1913), 13, 15–22, 28–9, 33–6, 41–6, 56–7, 60–5, 73–4, 150–61, 171, 259–61, 267–8, 300.
[44] Durham Dean and Chapter Muniments Misc. Charters nos. 3418, 3609. I owe these references and a sight of photostats of the documents to Dr Grant G. Simpson.

TABLE 2.

| 1 Pegolotti's Name | 2 Modern Name | 3 Order | Price in marks for | | | | 8[45] 1294 assessment of income from calves and lambs plus wool and lambskins (Lothian archdeaconry only) |
| | | | 4 Good | 5 Middle Wool | 6 Poor | 7 Sacks Annually | |
|---|---|---|---|---|---|---|---|
| Niobottali | Newbattle | Cist. | 14½ | 9 | 7½ | 30 | £103 |
| Mirososso | Melrose | Cist. | 16 | 10 | 8½ | 50 | 144 |
| Bermicciacche | Balmerino | Cist. | 10 | 7 | 4 | 14 | — |
| Cupero | Coupar | Cist. | 18½ | 10½ | 9 | 30 | — |
| Chilosola | ? Culross | Cist. | | | | | |
| | ? Kinloss | Cist. | 15 | 11 | 7½ | 15 | — |
| Donfermellino | Dunfermline | Ben. | 13 | 8½ | 6 | 15 | — |
| Dondarnane | Dundrennan | Cist. | 18 | 10½ | 8 | 15 | — |
| Grenellusso | Glenluce | Cist. | 18 | 11 | 5 | 15 | — |

Wool from the following houses fetched 9–10½ merks per sack:

| | | | | | | | |
|---|---|---|---|---|---|---|---|
| Balledirucco | Holyrood | August. | | | | | 36 |
| Guldingamo | Coldingham | Ben. | | | | | 53 |
| Ghelzo | Kelso | Tiron. | | | | | 47 |
| Norbonucche | North Berwick | Cist. nuns | | | | | 20 |
| Sansasano | ? Haddington | Cist. nuns | | | | | 83 |
| | ? St. Bothans | Cist. nuns | | | | | 26 |
| Gridegorda | Jedburgh | August. | | | | | — |
| Il Tenpo di Bratendocca | Balantrodoch | Templars | | | | | — |

careful and expert grading of wool, which other orders generally ignored. The presence of Dunfermline in the first list is mildly surprising for that reason; the presence of Kelso and Coldingham in the second means not that they produced less than fourteen or fifteen sacks—they were surely important producers—but that their wool was unsorted and included 'collect' mixed with the abbey's

---

45 Column 8 is from Table 1.

production.[46] Pegolotti unfortunately does not give a price for the collect of the Cistercians in either realm, but as middlemen they did take the clip of both magnate and peasant.

Among landowners the Cistercians had perhaps the best organisation to handle the business of their estates; those abbeys with arable relied upon direct exploitation or supervision, and even as late as 1243 Melrose had a monk to manage its affairs at Mauchline in Ayrshire, where its land which lay more than a day's journey from the abbey was discreetly not called a grange.[47] Other religious bought grazing for sheep, and arable for a shepherd; the Cistercians used hired men who could be kept close to the abbey. But even the Cistercians had only a rough-and-ready business capacity, and they rarely looked beyond the glint of merchants' gold and the immediate benefit of cash in hand.

Turn elsewhere and the inadequacy is even more striking. The extent of Coldingham Priory lands, and of the earl of Fife's lands, and the accounts for the latter, were all produced to satisfy the English government; the absence of such documents before 1286 may be a consequence not of the adverse survival factors alone, but of the lack of demand for them by Scottish landlords and their agents. There are no treatises on husbandry or estate management, no documentary references to an audit of accounts. Both the great Benedictine houses, Coldingham and Dunfermline, had a *terrarius* as well as the steward who is found on many great estates, ecclesiastical and lay. The function of the *terrarius* was to lease the monastic lands, but he also held a court (probably the non-head-court meetings of the barony court) and in both cases he seems to be the steward's deputy, dealing with peasants. The estate steward is a little-studied figure, most usually found presiding over the barony court. Early in the thirteenth century he is usually a laird in his own right, as was Robert, the steward to Walter de Berkeley and laird of Inverkeilor. The priory of St Andrews granted their seneschalcy to the son of a man who was nephew of Bishop Robert, marshal of Bishop Arnald and steward of later bishops—but

[46] Francesco Balducci Pegolotti, *La Practica della Mercatura*, ed. Allan Evans, xxviii–xxix, 258–9, 392–6; also in W. R. Cunningham, *Growth of English Industry and Commerce*, i (fourth edition, Cambridge, 1905), 629–30; T. H. Lloyd, *The Movement of Wool Prices in Medieval England* (Economic History Review Supplement no. 6, 1973) 8–10; David Knowles, *The Religious Orders in England*, i (1948), chapter VII.

[47] *Melrose Liber*, no. 191.

probably steward of the household rather than of estates since he is called *dapifer*, 'food bearer'; with the office went the lands of Kinnimonth. Gilbert, Earl of Strathearn, whose marshal, Gillecolm, betrayed the king's castle of Eren, still had a full college of officials in the 1190s: Constantine *judex*, Henry *rannaire* (food-divider), Gilleneve *dapifer*, Constantine butler, Abraham chaplain, Robert dispenser and Anecol thane. Gilleneve was succeeded as steward by his son Malise, after whom the family lost the office; their lands of Tullibardine, which they may already have held while stewards, passed by marriage in 1284 to a younger branch of the great northern family of Moray. The stewards in the 1230s and 1240s were the sons of Anecol, the thane of Dunning, now holding land at ferme of the earl.[48] By 1247 Earl Malise had a marshal called Alan and in 1257 and 1258 his cousin Nicholas, parson of Crieff, was his chamberlain, succeeded by 1266 by Master Richard of Stirling, official of Dunblane, and a little later by William of Ruthven, younger brother of a knight of the earl and ancestor of the earls of Gowrie. The unique feature of the Strathearn earldom is the collection of overlapping household dignitaries whose offices disappear after the death of Earl Gilbert; the marshal remains because the army of Strathearn is an important responsibility of the earl; the thane who becomes steward represents the tenacity of a ministerial family as well as the earl's attention to his revenues. This attention became more rigorous with the appointment of a chamberlain who had clerical experience, the seneschalcy apparently fading in importance, at least as a financial office. The earls of Dunbar, like most other magnates, had only a succession of clerical and lairdly stewards and, in general, signs of business methods or growing bureaucracy in estate administration are scanty. It seems reasonable to conclude that Scotland's wealth, limited by climate and soil, would not sustain a complex administration, that large-scale capitalist enterprise on the land was less efficient (from the landlord's point of view) than small-scale (peasant and rent-paying) enterprise.

Such a conclusion is not wholly satisfactory since it takes little account of the expectations and aims of the landowner in his manner and standard of life. The great ecclesiastical corporations, of whatever order, were devoted in the thirteenth century to grandeur and comfort first, to the services in kirk second and, a

[48] *Inchaffray Charters*, lxxv–lxxx; no. LXXVI.

long way behind, to solvency, or rather to controlled insolvency. Alms for the poor mattered very much less than decent entertainment for the rich, and the energies devoted by the Cistercians to sorting their wool were paralleled among the other regulars by the pursuit of teinds in their appropriated kirks. But could this be wrong if the glory of God was served by loftier walls and vaulted roofs for His kirk and more becoming quarters for His servants? The charge side of the monastic account is still visible at Melrose, Dundrennan and Glenluce in the most sophisticated dwellings which medieval Scotland has left to us.

The primitive kirks which served early monastic settlements have without exception disappeared; this is, fortunately, not true of the early strongholds which preceded later medieval stone castles, and in consequence it is possible to form some impression of the growing wealth of secular landowners over two centuries. Early ringworks in which a ditch is dug, and a palisade erected on the upcast dike, are now being recognised in increasing numbers. In the great Stewart fief of Renfrew there are now four known examples; that at Castlehead, a suburb of Paisley, may be the predecessor of the Blackhall (another suburb) which was a Stewart residence early in the thirteenth century. In the Queen's Park at Camphill there is a second, which might be the work of Renaud of Cathcart. Of a remarkable size, an irregular circle with maximum diameter of 390 feet (119 m) it includes the summit of the drumlin on which it was constructed but is not centred on it, lying mainly on one slope. So large a fortification may have included a whole village as well as a manor.[49] We are on surer ground with Pollok, the fief of Peter, son of Fulbert, and with Crookston, which took its name from the wealthy knight Robert Croc. Referred to as his 'close' and his *curia* within which he had an oratory, this earthwork is sited on a low hill with fine outlook over most approaches. It was perhaps occupied until the stone castle on the site was begun in the late fourteenth century.[50] Finally, to this list we might add Tarbolton in Kyle, the fief of Gilbert fitz Richer, where there are possibly traces of another ringwork. This small group of sites in a now heavily urbanised environment may suggest that others have been lost and that the fashion for this particular form of manor was

---

[49] H. Fairhurst and J. G. Scott 'The earthwork at Camphill in Glasgow', *Proc. Soc. Antiq. Sc.*, lxxxv (1950–51), 146–56.
[50] Plan in Macgibbon and Ross, *Castellated and Domestic Arch.* i, 533.

rather localised. It may have been so, yet, despite the prolonged
occupation which some of these sites may have had (and Paisley
Abbey regarded the oratory at Crookston as a permanent instal-
lation), they were the simplest form of defended residence which
might be thrown up quickly by an incomer with doubts about the
native inhabitants. In the east, there was in the early thirteenth
century an 'old castle with ditches' at Eldbottle on the mainland
opposite Fidra Isle.[51] It belonged to the de Vaux family and was of
some small strategic importance since the earl's ferry to Fife crossed
the Firth from there; but the family had abandoned it for a stone
castle by 1220. It is unfortunate that the document cannot be
married with the site (which is unknown) in this instance, but the
very disappearance of the castle suggests that it was a ringwork
rather than a motte.

It would be particularly valuable to identify this and other
ringworks in the east, where there is a marked scarcity of motte and
bailey castles. Some may pass as 'earthworks' of indeterminate
date,[52] and others have been incorporated into later structures,
perhaps as the bailey to a new motte. A particularly dramatic
example may be seen at the de Soules castle of Hermitage in Liddesdale. Work on a castle here caused friction with England in 1242–4,
a castle which may survive in a few courses of squared ashlar
masonry at the heart of the later fortress. Around that fortress is an
elaborate pentagonal ditch and bank, which has the appearance of
a ringwork modified on the north to serve as ditch to the stone
fortress. Outside this to the north is a contiguous but asymmetrically
placed 'base-court' or rectangular bailey, also of ditch and bank;
we must have here the remains of growth in several stages, but a
twelfth-century ringwork could well be the original nucleus.[53]

The de Soules family, however, created another strong-point
some four miles away on the Liddel Water, whether before or
after the early work at Hermitage is unknown. Across a bluff 100
feet (30 m) high in a loop of the river two ditches were dug, the
outer one broader, and between them a broad rampart rising about
6 feet (1.8 m) above the interior. The inner yard, irregular but about

[51] *Dryburgh Liber*, no. 104.

[52] See e.g. *Inventory of Roxburghshire*, no. 925, a ringwork which was the
predecessor of Smailholm Tower.

[53] *Inventory of Roxburghshire*, no. 63 especially plate 25. I am heavily in
debt to my colleague Mr Eric Talbot for pointing out these ringwork sites but
he must not be held responsible in any way for the discussion of them here.

150 by 180 feet (45 by 54 m) at its widest measurements, is large enough to take timber buildings for quite a large household, and since the nearby kirk is mentioned by 1165, we can date the occupation of this castle site from the mid-twelfth century till *c*. 1300. Only excavation could reveal whether there was only a single ditch originally, the second being strength added at a later date. If so, this improving upon nature is found in simpler form at Keir Knowe of Drum in Stirlingshire. On the edge of an ancient shore-line now midway between Stirling and Loch Lomond, the tip of a natural promontory formed by a burn was cut from the adjacent land by an artificial ditch leaving an irregular circular top some 72 feet (22 m) in diameter. The perimeter was defended by a stout wooden stockade, and inside that a second stockade except on the ditch side where a stone wall almost three feet (.85 m) high survives. In the centre a tower had been erected on nine wooden posts set in a square with sides of about fifteen feet (4.5 m).[54] A work of this size is clearly defensive, a look-out and a refuge for humans only, there being no evident access for stock. It has in common with Liddel Castle the nature of the site and underlying defensive notions. Both would be even speedier to erect than the ringwork and, given a suitably high promontory, both were easy to secure and defend. Such sites were often defended by ditches in prehistoric times and it is not impossible that early duns and forts were brought back into use for a period: an isolated example on the distant shores of Loch Broom recently gave up a purse of coins of King William's time from its latest occupation phase. Keir Knowe of Drum and Liddel Castle would best be designated promontory forts, and recognised as part of an evolution of different defensive and residential traditions which also produced the motte and bailey castle.

The motte may be defined as an earthen mound, round or oval, with timber palisaded defences at its upper or lower circumference (or perhaps both); the bailey is a lower enclosure of ditch and palisaded bank at one side of the motte, but sometimes wholly enclosing it, so that the motte sits asymmetrically close to one end of an oval bailey. Some baileys may have begun life as ringworks, with which tradition they have an obvious kinship. The motte is likewise akin to the promontory fort save that it is free-standing; both represent, it would seem, the concept of an elevated fortress, but this is to ignore the quite considerable number of simple mottes, low in profile

[54] *Inventory of Stirlingshire*, no. 187.

and either small (Wolfclyde in Lanarkshire) or large (Lumphanan in Aberdeenshire) in area. The latter might almost be a ringwork with raised enclosure. Discussion of the evolution of these structural types is only beginning; in Scotland the careful excavation required by prehistoric sites was for long denied to medieval remains which could produce no masonry, and analysis of the sites according to their surveyed structural features is virtually unpublished. We need to know which mottes are placed beside or on hills like a number of Dumfriesshire mottes utilising the slopes of hillsides to augment the defences of both motte and bailey,[55] and which are on the open plain, particularly at river crossings. The Somervilles' motte at Carnwath, apparently wholly artificial and with no bailey, stands high like a dumpling in the midst of flat and open upland country, but the mottes associated with Flemish settlement in the upper Clyde tend to overlook the river, and in one case, at Abington (as at the Bruce motte of Annan) both motte and bailey have been partly swept away. The range of size is great in each dimension; in Kirkcudbright none exceed 27 feet (8.25 m) from base to summit except when the natural elevation of the site is taken into consideration, yet great differences exist in the dimensions of the summit areas. Thus, the motte of Balmaclellan measures only some 38 feet (11.5 m) in diameter while the motte of Troqueer has a summit plateau measuring 127 feet by 131 (39 × 40 m).[56] The relationship of size to personal factors is obvious where, as at Annan, Lochmaben, Urr or Inverurie, the lord is known to have been a magnate of importance (Bruce, Bruce, de Berkeley, Earl David respectively). A relationship of size to strategic factors would be worth investigation; also the relationship of mottes to village and kirk and the character of nearby farm-names. In the south-west there are examples of 'Ingliston' near mottes, which suggest that an incoming Cumberland laird may have brought peasants with him. The place name Borland implies not merely land to sustain the castle, but land set aside by an English-speaking castle-community.

Some two hundred mottes have been plotted upon the map and perhaps fifty more might be added.[57] They are found in most

---

[55] *Inventory of Dumfriesshire*, lviii–lx.

[56] *Inventory of Kirkcudbright*, xxxix–xl.

[57] Grant G. Simpson and Bruce Webster, 'Charter evidence and the distribution of mottes in Scotland', *Château Gaillard*, v (1972), 175–92. The list of mottes and map in this article are by Geoffrey Stell. Additional mottes have been noted by Mr Eric Talbot, who is preparing a further paper on the subject.

parts of Scotland, including even Cowal, though there are only a few outliers in mountainous districts. The concentration in Dumfries-shire and Kirkcudbright is remarkable, but a glance at the comparable map for England suggests that this zone was akin to the Welsh march, also heavy with mottes: the populace was hostile and had a tradition of feuding, a native prince might rebel without warning, and central government was too far removed to maintain order by fear or decisive action. The same explanation loses some force in Kyle, and is unconvincing in the bleak moorland of Upper Clydesdale, which can never have been heavily populated. The castle of the earl of Lennox at Balloch or those in Carrick are an adoption of the motte by native lords, for particularly in Carrick the strongly Celtic character of society is attested by the names of the earls' *familia* until the mid-thirteenth century.

Since many mottes were retained as the sites of manors in the thirteenth century and some until even the sixteenth century (for instance Huntly and Edzell) it may be assumed that, even when their importance as points of security receded, they nonetheless remained symbols of prestige and power, and a fashion for erecting mottes may have succeeded need. This would explain the rather self-conscious oddities in Galloway, rectangular mottes with stepped sides, which must surely be late in the sequence of such forts in this region. And this explanation, working in reverse, would explain the almost total absence of mottes between Tweed and Forth. Here perhaps the settled Anglian society offered little threat to incoming landowners which could not be met by simpler earthwork and palisade, while the greatest magnates—the king and earl—had their castles, in part of stone, at natural strongholds, Edinburgh and Dunbar. Since they did not build mottes, neither did the lesser men who would ape them in other ways.

Yet it is surely instructive that while the king had no castle at Haddington or Linlithgow, demesne centres often visited by him and presumably provided with palisaded hall and offices, a motte was built at Peebles, perhaps by *c.* 1150 when a castle is documented there. The site is a steep-sided natural mound at the junction of the Eddleston Water and the Tweed, a site very like that of Roxburgh at the junction of Tweed and Teviot.[58] Peebles Castle was, therefore, a promontory fort and our attention is directed

[58] *Inventory of Peeblesshire*, p. 41 and nos. 523, 539; *Inventory of Roxburgh-shire*, no. 905.

again to the early motte as a variant of this type of castle, and to the marked distribution of mottes in river valleys where bluffs and confluences provided natural features sculptured into mottes with relative ease.

For a motte thrown up from the ground is more than a response to unsettled conditions and social envy. It is an investment of capital and, even more strikingly, of labour resources far greater than is needed by a ringwork or other defensive work. Arguably, therefore, the motte is a product of a society which, lacking the skills of readily available masons, could call upon a great deal of manual labour at low cost. In this view mottes indicate the availability of labour services, an unfree peasantry exploited at the will of the landlord and hence constrained to castle work, as we know the peasantry of Dunfermline Abbey, freed by David I, were constrained by King William in Ross.[59] It may be that we have the most important explanation of the absence of mottes from Lothian and their rarity in the Merse in the effect of early economic prosperity and the commutation of labour services, throwing lords back upon the alternative of a castle professionally built and financed by rents.

The advent of the stone castle and hall-house certainly represents rising production, incomes and expectations. Its date is as uncertain as the date of ringworks and mottes, which remained in use throughout the thirteenth century, and in Scotland there has been a notable reluctance to ascribe any secular stone building to the twelfth century. But it may have been at a comparatively early date (say, the second half of the twelfth century) that some mottes were provided with stone enclosure walls round their upper circumference, as in two northern examples, Doune of Invernochty and Peel of Lumphanan, where stone walls some six feet (1.8 m) and three feet thick respectively enclosed timber or timber-framed domestic buildings. Probably the best surviving example of a shell keep of this kind is the castle of Rothesay in Bute, where a simple circular wall with battlements was built in the manner of a ringwork surounded by a water-fed ditch and overlooking the landing shore; this work may be ascribed to the Steward in the later twelfth century. (See page 443.)

Stable ditches and earthen mounds must be rounded and therefore dictate a round or oval plan for a fortified site which is to

[59] *Dunfermline Registrum*, nos. 31, 54; *R.R.S.*, ii, no. 500.

contain rectangular structures. With stone walls it is simpler to build to greater height as a defence against missiles, and to use a rectangular plan, the external walls being used also as walls of internal structures whether in timber or stone. Such simple rectangular stone castles of enclosure were probably built from the late twelfth century also, but surviving examples show a marked Highland and West Highland distribution. Castle Roy at Nethybridge in Inverness-shire has a trapezoid curtain wall built of rubble (avoiding the expense of dressed stone except at the doorway and privy) enclosing timber lean-to buildings; like a number of other castles of this plan, it is some seventy feet (21 m) square. Castles on much the same plan but about 120 feet (36.5 m) square were built by the king at Kinclaven on the Tay and Kincardine in Mearns: they date, it has been argued, from the 1220s, but this argument ignores the evidence that King William was residing at Kincardine in the 1190s, to which decade it could well belong.[60] It may be that the most sophisticated example of this kind of castle is the Bruce strength at Lochmaben, built about a mile from the motte on a promontory in the loch. The castle itself was rectangular, some 190 by 120 feet (58 by 36.5 m) with walls nine or more feet (2.75 m) thick dressed in ashlar masonry; the side walls extend out over the innermost ditch of the defences turning it into a canal and haven for small boats. The outworks with three further ditches were extensive and may have been altered and strengthened during the wars of independence, but those nearest the castle were an integral part of its defences and must surely belong with it to the thirteenth century. Since the skills of stone masons were extensively used it represents a considerable investment, probably by Robert Bruce the Competitor.[61]

His rivals, the Balliols, adopted at Buittle the round-angled curtain wall which was the consequence of an artificial ditch but their curtain was provided with flanking towers, particularly at the entrance. The development of siege techniques, it is thought, was

---

[60] J. G. Dunbar and A. A. M. Duncan, 'Tarbert Castle', *Scot. Hist. Rev.* l, 8–11; *R.R.S.*, ii, nos. 358, 428, 494, 496; see also no. 410.

[61] *Inventory of Dumfriesshire*, no. 445(2); Cruden, *Scottish Castle*, 53–4. I cannot accept Mr Cruden's suggested date of the early fourteenth century for this castle, since the English wardrobe records are very plentiful and very informative on new castle work of this period, and they show no trace of work here, nor, be it said, at Kildrummy. In my submission both castles are pre-1306 and must therefore be pre-1296.

responsible for these flanking towers being semi-circular on plan; a simple example of such a curtain wall castle, essentially a strongly walled bailey without a tower, keep or motte, was the Comyn castle of Lochindorb, but at Inverlochy, belonging to the same family, one of the four corner towers, more massive than the others, is planned as a keep. The castle architect could offer his client the basic alternatives: extra strength either at the entrance or at an angle of the curtain–gatehouse or keep; either would be on a circular or semi-circular plan.

Perhaps the most powerful example of developed thirteenth century castle architecture in Scotland is the de Vaux castle erected upon a rocky outcrop at Dirleton, presumably deliberately chosen for its imposing eminence when the old castle at Eldbottle was to be abandoned by *c.* 1220. Here three large and one small circular towers were ranged on two sides of the enclosure, built of dressed ashlar and rising from the spreading bases necessary to support masonry of such weight and to defeat the miner. Within the largest, the donjon, whose exterior diameter is 36 feet (11 m), are the lord's living quarters with a hexagonal private room with vaulted and ribbed ceiling, fireplace and (down a passage) privy; with walls some ten feet (3 m) thick the room is only sixteen feet (5 m) in diameter, but the poor lighting by three narrow fish-tailed slits emphasises the importance of security in the minds of those who planned so elegant a chamber. And it seems that they did so in the first quarter of the thirteenth century.[62] At Bothwell, a castle was planned on truly extravagant lines, probably in the second half of the thirteenth century by the Morays, businesslike raiders from the north who took the great Olifard inheritance by a well timed marriage; the diameter of the donjon is 65 feet (20 m), its walls 15 feet (4.5 m) thick and 82 feet (25 m) high. The lord's chamber is octagonal and was provided with vaulting and ribs in timber to imitate stone, scarcely for cheapness and therefore for warmth; there is an adequate window, which must have been glazed, over-looking the courtyard. Although the courtyard originally planned, some 230 by 200 feet (70 m by 60 m) was sacrificed to something much more modest, the cost of the thirteenth-century work at which we may still look must have represented many years' income of the barony of Bothwell.

With this thought in mind the reader is urged to look at the

[62] *Inventory of East Lothian*, no. 27; Cruden, *Scottish Castle*, 81–3.

excellent modern works on Scottish castles, reflecting on the cost of such strengths as Yester (Gifford), the two Caerlaverocks (Maxwell), Roslin (Sinclair) and Kildrummy (earl of Mar), who devoted resources to strongholds against an unknown enemy, strongholds of a kind not found necessary by the king or most other magnates. That a national war did come and in some manner justify the castles is hindsight.[63] In the 1270s, the builder of Bothwell was declaring or enhancing his social prestige and flaunting his wealth; the gain in comfort and everyday security was marginal. Even the more modest efforts of the Comyns at Dalswinton, Inverlochy, Lochindorb and Blair Atholl, of the earls of Atholl at Moulin and of the builders of many other simple castles of enceinte were probably a heavy burden upon the estates which financed them, and some landowners, magnates even, were content with older fashions and long-lived structures. Thus, the earls of Strathearn towards the middle of the thirteenth century had a residence at a 'Kenmore' which can be identified with the flat promontory formed by Loch and River Earn opposite St Fillans. Palisaded, and probably with a ditch on the third side, it was secure enough to withstand the insults, slings and arrows of an outraged King Robert and his force in 1306; the earls of Menteith retained their ancient promontory fortification at Doune. Many modest manor houses, more or less well defended, served the second-rank barons of Alexander III.

Lest it be urged that the assumption of a peaceful society is invalid, the small number of recognised hall-houses of late thirteenth century date is worth mention. Essentially a compact dwelling house in stone with a timber-roofed hall set upon a domestic and storage undercroft, the hall-house was provided with slight defensive works; those at Morton (Dumfriesshire) and Rait (Nairn), for example, are lit by generous traceried windows and, although placed within enclosures, they have none of the forbidding character of the great castles of enclosure. They are rather to be thought of as conspicuous demonstrations of independence and wealth by knights or lairds, declaiming in expensive stone what most of their fellows must murmur in timber and clay. With these stone and timber halls we descend towards the simple moated homestead which was probably the home of the smaller free landowner. The name form 'Peel of' attached to some examples shows that they were stockaded, presumably to control both stock and men, but all that can now be

<hr/>

[63] Had castles not been there, Edward I would have had to build them.

seen is a rectangular or rounded ditch and bank enclosure of modest dimension, each side somewhat over or under 100 feet (30 m). Among the landowners who paid homage to Edward I in 1296 were the lairds of Gartfarren and Garchel in Stirlingshire, both places with homestead moats which can confidently be associated with the lairds. Their use, like that of mottes, went on for centuries and in place of excavation we may rely on Blind Harry's description in the 1470s of the nearby Peel of Gargunnock, with a drawbridge over the dike and within 'bathe closs, chawmer and hall'; the 'close' may have been a pound for stock.[64] Moated homesteads are found in most lowland parts of Scotland, but their numbers are still comparatively small.

Perhaps the most interesting part of any of these dwellings, from the largest donjon to the smallest peel, should be the midden. There we should find the bones of animals and fish, the shells of molluscs and traces of grains, in short the diet of the inhabitants, not perhaps in the balance in which they ate but at least revealing the variation in standard of nutrition between different social levels and different geographical zones. Unfortunately, there do not seem to be published accounts of such evidence where it has been found; exceptionally Kildrummy has yielded widely scattered deposits of animal bones, all fragmented but identifiable. Although bones of sheep and deer were found, they were greatly outweighed by those of pigs and oxen, sometimes chopped as for cooking (rather than split for extracting marrow). Some of these deposits may relate to the thirteenth century, and they aroused comment because the proportion of deer was so low.[65]

Much more attention has been paid to the fine collections of pottery recovered at Melrose and Glenluce Abbeys and Bothwell Castle. They suggest 'a remarkable variety and richness of medieval household effects pertaining to the kitchen and table'[66] but their forms also show that wares were imported, particularly from northern England, and influenced the shapes of native-produced

---

[64] *Inventory of Stirlingshire*, 41 and nos. 189–91; *Inventory of Roxburghshire*, 47–8 and no. 559. The last, at Moorhouselaw, may have belonged to the de Normanville family or their tenant. It is a double enclosure; was the smaller part a 'close' for stock? Dunbar, *Historic Architecture*. 35–6.

[65] See also the bones recorded at Coull castle, *Proc. Soc. Antiq. Sc.* lx (1923–1924) 91–2.

[66] See the excellent reports by S. H. Cruden in *Proc. Soc. Antiq. Sc.*, lxxxvi (1951–2), lxxxvii (1952–3), lxxxix (1955–6); *Dumfriesshire Trans.* xxix (1950–1).

pottery where a shape might outlive its English prototype. Wares imported from further afield are rare: eight jugs from Gascony were found at the royal castle of Kirkcudbright, probably an accompaniment of the wine trade; but most pottery was made in Scotland. A kiln has been found at Colston in East Lothian, another postulated at Leuchars in Fife, and it seems accepted that Bothwell had its own potter and kiln.[67] It would seem that wealthy Scottish landowners did not stint on their household utensils, and were able to command the techniques and fashions with which purchased imports familiarised them. What we should welcome now is the accumulation of a corpus of pottery finds from such humbler sites as may be excavated, with attention to what they represent and not just what they are. It would be valuable to compare the proportion of fine wares and sophisticated forms from this context with that from the context of castle and abbey.

Yet even the buildings themselves do suggest that the large landowner was able to provide himself, if he so chose, with a rapidly improving standard of living and ostentation to a much greater degree than the many smaller men whom we meet in documents and who can only rarely be associated with castles or homesteads. The profits of the economic boom of the thirteenth century found their way, it might seem, into the hands of the extensive landowner to a greater degree even than his land-holdings might warrant; in particular, this seems to be true of the south of Scotland where the thirteeenth-century commerce of Berwick, Edinburgh and perhaps Ayr would give many opportunities to the landowner who would traffic on a large scale. Yet more northerly towns, from St Andrews to Inverness, were also active, offering similar means and opportunities to the ambitious magnate of Scotia. Some certainly responded, as the remains at Red Castle in Angus and Coull Castle in Mar testify, and it may be that we shall do more justice to their efforts when a beginning is made on a survey of the ancient monuments of Scotia between the rivers Tay and Oykell.

[67] G. C. Dunning, H. W. M. Hodges, E. M. Jope, 'Kirkcudbright Castle, its pottery and ironwork', *Proc. Soc. Antiq. Sc.*, xci (1957–8), 117–38; M. R. Apted, 'Excavation at Kildrummy Castle', *ibid*, xcvi (1962–3), 208–36, especially the report by G. C. Dunning on pp. 233–6; Lloyd R. Laing, 'Excavations at Linlithgow Palace' *ibid*, xcix (1966–7), 111–47, especially the discussion on pp. 139–47.

*Addendum to 1978 impression.* The stone wall at Peel of Lumphanan (p. 438) was built *c.* 1782.

# 17

## IDEALS: THE CROSS
## AND THE CLOISTER

Even if we might assume—as we should not—that the different regions of Scotland were equally affected by the rapid economic expansion of these two centuries, it would still be difficult to assess the effect of economic change upon ways of life. More wine was drunk, more food and perhaps better balanced food eaten. To the lay eye there is *prima facie* evidence of an improvement in hygiene, and accommodation was surely more wind and water-tight; but there was also change in non-material ways which a brief contrast of, say, the 1070s and 1170s reveals. The greedy marauding of Malcolm III and his men in northern England, aiming at booty and the annexation of territory, the homages extorted from him by King William I's great might and the binding of Malcolm in loyalty to William, these are part of a lay world of exclusively masculine virtues—of 'bonnie fechters', loyal companions, men with unspoken obligations to each other, despising betrayal, trusting in the efficacy of their own saints and their relics, incurious about the wider world beyond the frontiers they knew. These are the virtues of the war bands which set out centuries before from Edinburgh to defeat at Catterick. At Alnwick, Malcolm III with his son was killed fighting in battle by Morel, a felon deed because he was Malcolm's sworn brother; at Alnwick eighty years later, King William was allowed and allowed himself to become prisoner, intervened against by St Thomas. Men had doubted King William the Lion's right and wisdom in invading England, distrusted his elaborate negotiations with the English and French; and while they would fight internal rebels, and invaders from outside, they showed genuine reluctance to embark upon the further pursuit of their king's rights by force. Perhaps they had learned the necessary wisdom of small battalions faced with big ones. But the growth of the tournament, whether practised in France, England or Scotland, suggests a changed attitude to fighting; formerly there had been knights, now there was knighthood, a complex of virtues including bravery, but not rashness; and loyalty, but to an ideal and not to a band of companions.

The change in literature has been well marked: the song of Roland depicts the epic virtues as do *The Battle of Maldon* and *The Gododdin*. The literature of the later twelfth century is concerned with the quests of an individual, often solitary, for knightly adventures, the point of which is not the bravery or comradely loyalty of the seeker, but the physical dangers and anguish of spirit which afflict him in his quest for a loved one; the court is certainly there as a place of companionship, but it is not the focus of knightly activity. That is within the knight himself, for knighthood is a life of the spirit, or, when we leave literature for the realities of life, knighthood is life according to a code of decent behaviour. Thus, a man may be knighted for good service but, by the late twelfth century, he is more likely to be knighted for a complex of social virtues, including good service, and for one economic virtue—the wealth necessary to sustain himself and his family in these social virtues. He is perhaps in the household of a baron, more probably he is of that small group who are the chief jurors and doomsmen of the baron's court, who, it is likely, counselled him and if necessary defended him with their oaths or their arms. He is married into another knightly family, his dwelling is substantial, his clothing and demeanour decorous. From early in the thirteenth century, rarely in the last years of the twelfth, charters tell us that some witnesses are knights, and by implication the rest are not; knighthood is a mark of belonging to the nobility among worthy men.

Yet, as we have seen, documents suggest that lairds also hastened along with knights to pass judgement in the baron's court, and the two groups served likewise in the king's host as part of the barony's contingent. Many a laird was the younger brother of a knight—the classic instance is William, brother of Sir Malcolm Wallace of Elderslie, to whom none can deny a concern with the local and political issues of the kingdom—and it would be false to conjure a mystique of knighthood as a barrier between lairds and their betters. Both lairds and knights were responsible men, as Edward I acknowledged when he took sealed oaths of fealty from two thousand of them in 1296; that occasion also reveals that they were not just vassals and clients of the great, but advisers to them, men of independence and influence. Magnates, knights and lairds seem linked by ties of mutual respect which are far removed from the rough vassalage of Malcolm III's war bands, and which, we might say, lead to a sharing and resolution of the political and social stresses felt by any one group.[1] It is perhaps significant that the word 'baron' was widely and freely used in documents to include many who would not be included by the historian's use of the word. A term for social status to which (unlike knighthood) there was no symbol of entry, it could be used to comprehend all those who were set apart from the peasantry, as by the right to discipline them, and in fourteenth-century Scotland this is what holding 'in barony' meant. But it was also acknowledged that there were 'small barons', lairds who nonetheless belonged to the society of worthy men. This use of 'baron' for a widely-drawn social category acknowledged the mutual dependence and ties of respect between the great and the middling in thirteenth-century society.

There were those whose knightly ideals and religious devotion took them on knightly adventures. The marked lack of enthusiasm in Scotland for the recovery of Jerusalem after its fall in 1187 was modified as the thirteenth century progressed and the spiritual benefits of the Crusade were preached assiduously by the church. Patrick (I), who had held the earldom of Dunbar for fifty years, spent Christmas in 1232 in a party with his sons and daughters, kinsmen and neighbours; four days later he had a stroke, received the Cistercian habit from the abbot of Melrose and died on the last day of the year, being buried in the Cistercian nunnery of Eccles. His son, Patrick (II), as the number of charters issued in his father's lifetime suggest, had for some years controlled the family fortune. Called *miles strenuus* by the Melrose chronicler, the *Lanercost Chronicle* tells of his setting fire to the kitchen to avoid disgrace when his steward told him that the food was not adequate to the number of guests, and of his appointing a pardoned thief as under-chamberlain, being rewarded with an attempt at murder, and offering the man a purse to go on a pilgrimage of expiation. Such

---

[1] Seen from below this solidarity doubtless might look very different: a coherent landowning class defending its right to exploit the peasantry; but when that analysis was made the situation itself had passed out of existence.

quixotic tales are probably the result of journalistic distortion, for in 1247 the earl set methodically about the fulfilment of his crusading vow. He sold his stud to Melrose Abbey, for he would need no horses till his return, spent Easter of 1248 with the king at Berwick or Coldingham and shortly afterwards set out through England to join Louis IX. He died, probably of disease, at Marseilles in the same year. Others took the crusading vow, from David Rufus of Forfar (in 1201)[2] who may have finished up scaling the walls of Constantinople, to the earl of Atholl who died at Carthage in 1269, Sir Alexander Seton whose squire was captured by the Saracens in 1270 and Adam de Kilconquhar, Earl of Carrick (by marriage), who died at Acre in 1270.

The contrast between the deaths of the two earls of Dunbar is observable (for example, among university professors) as the contrast between the serenity of old age and the wanderlust of advancing middle age. But the *Melrose Chronicle* records many burials of less exalted men who also felt the attraction of the Cistercian ideal to secular society in the first half of the thirteenth century. We must allow that men's actions, conduct, notions of decency, were ennobled by the teaching and example, however flawed, of the religious.

On the other hand, the number of known participants in the crusades is not large, and while those who went are a tribute to the effectiveness of the more militant preaching of the church upon men's consciences, their fewness suggests that considerable wealth was also necessary. Moreover, whether as a cause or an effect, their fewness also suggests an isolation of Scotsmen from the cosmopolitan junketings of later thirteenth-century Europe. A few accompanied their king to the English court, and some, like Malise, Earl of Strathearn, were friendly with Henry III, but Alan Durward, who served the Lord Edward in Gascony and visited Spain, was a rare bird (in this as in many other ways) among the Scottish baronage. No doubt geographical isolation had much to do with this, but it did not preclude influences in the other direction. Scotland received papal letters and papal legates; even though we must look for evidence at seals and other *fragmenta disjecta*, it would seem that artistic fashions spread with little lapse of time to Scotland.

Were the Scots then 'out of things', rustics, because they knew no French? The evidence for linguistic usage among lowland Scots

[2] *Coupar Charters*, nos. X, XI.

of the landlord class would be a matter of great interest. Late in the twelfth century and early in the thirteenth the strength of Anglo-Norman is hard to deny even though our sources are almost wholly in Latin. There is, it is true, only one romance, the *roman de Fergus*, which seems to have arisen from Scottish patronage, and it survives in a number of northern French manuscripts—perhaps because it suited the fashion for tales set in the backwoods of Europe. Other literature in French with episodes in Scotland was not written for Scotland though it was read there. Early in the twelfth century a Fleming could place King Arthur's palace in 'the land of the Picts', probably identifying it with a Roman shrine at Stenhouse in Stirlingshire. Geoffrey of Monmouth in his Arthurian fiction made plentiful use of Scotland, though it has been argued that his 'Castrum Puellarum' was not borrowed from Edinburgh, but rather loaned to it, and the Dolorous Mount loaned to the Eildons. Chrétien de Troyes borrowed Owen map Urien of sixth-century Rheged, transformed him in the 1170s into Yvain de Loenel (Lothian) and told a romance of him the tale of which occurs independently in the *Life of St Kentigern* written at or for Glasgow cathedral two decades earlier. In a later romance Chrétien made Gawain into a king of Galloway (an identity already suggested by William of Malmesbury in the 1120s), perhaps because he was writing for King William's ally and sought to improve on Gawain's usual kingdom—*Gales*, Wales. Geoffrey of Monmouth placed Merlin in the Caledonian Forest; and Drostan, son of Talorc, passed from eighth-century Pictland to Wales, where he picked up Esyllt, wife of March; in Cornwall, March became King Mark with his hall at Tintagel, and so the three crossed to Brittany by the early eleventh century, for the name Tristan was used there by 1050. The literary form which the legend of Tristan and Isolt took in twelfth-century France, including its association with the Arthurian cycle, doubtless ensured its wide distribution throughout western Europe; medieval Europe's ideal lover was a Pict.[3]

By the end of the twelfth century Tristan was back in Pictland, at the little court of Gilbert, Earl of Strathearn from 1171 until 1223, the founder with his Aubigni wife of Inchaffray Abbey. Tristram, 'son of Avicia', was laird of Gorthy, and although he had

[3] R. Bromwich, 'Celtic Dynastic Themes and the Breton Lays', *Études Celtiques*, ix (1960–1), 39–74; R. S. Loomis, 'Did Gawain, Perceval and Arthur hail from Britain?' *Études Celtiques*, xi (1964–7), 70–82.

probably a brother and certainly a son called Henry who held successively the office of the earl's *rannaire* or food-divider, his other sons had French names, Tristram and William, and his matronymic suggests a Breton origin for the family.[4] The influence of the countess may be seen in the names of her children—the first four alternately Celtic and French—and in the earl's similarly mixed college of officials, including a *dapifer* and a *dispensarius*; it is possible that Tristram's family reached Strathearn in the countess's train. No doubt French speech, Breton *lais* and French *romans* came also, though there are comparatively few traces of their influence in personal names. Bishop Arnald of St Andrews had two clerics, Masters Arthur and Merlin, and an Arthur was appealed of trying to kill Malcolm IV—though this last name is probably derived from Strathclyde Welsh rather than French. In the forms of names there are occasional examples of the prosthetic *e* which is characteristic of Anglo-Norman, and until early in the thirteenth century a few names occur in French form. The sixty years after 1140 were probably the highwater mark of French influence in Scotland, when the king and some of his magnates were attracted to France for tournaments and when migration of French-speaking barons and knights from England was on the whole welcomed by the king and native earls.[5] Yet, it is unlikely that the French tongue survived in aristocratic circles in Scotland for any length of time or that *roman* and *lai* were widely read or listened to even among the aristocracy after 1200. By the later thirteenth century, when the vernacular became permissible and English civil or military correspondence took place in Anglo-Norman, Scottish documents stick resolutely to Latin; there are only two or three documents from Scotland before 1290 written in French.

In the Latin charters of the twelfth and thirteenth centuries the linguistic influences which come through are English: the Celticisms of the twelfth century, such as *can* and *conveth*, yield to *firma* (from *feorm*) and *waiting*. We hear of *gresmanni* in Mearns early in the thirteenth century, and later in the century the terms 'husband' men and 'cottage' men or 'cottars' seem to have spread widely up to the Mounth. Among institutions, French-derived terms such as

---

[4] *Inchaffray Charters*, lxxxi–ii, 315.
[5] R. L. G. Ritchie, *Chrétien de Troyes and Scotland* (1952); his *The Normans in Scotland* (1954); R. S. Loomis 'The Arthurian Legend in Scotland', *Proc. Soc. Antiq. Sc.*, lxxxix (1955–6), 1–21.

*servitium forinsecum* are certainly found, but the context suggests
that they too were borrowed from England. Personal names were
largely the common stock of twelfth- and thirteenth-century
England and France but on the whole their forms are English. John,
William, Richard, Geoffrey parade through documents with such
regularity that one can only comment on the comparative unpopularity in Scotland of Henry who (in more than one sense) ruled in
England, and the appropriate popularity here of Alexander. Some
families retained the tradition of their own names, and in the second
half of the thirteenth century there are some grounds for thinking
that there was a revival of interest in things Celtic, including family
origins. But the zones of true Celtic survival are well marked out by
documents, and it is only necessary to look at a charter from
Duncan, lord and later Earl of Carrick (who died at a great age in
1250), to recognise the strength of Celtic families and therefore of
the Gaelic language in Galloway and Carrick.[6] It is more difficult to
strike a balance on the survival of a Celtic-speaking landowning
class in Atholl or Strathearn in the late thirteenth century; the
peasantry were doubtless Gaelic-speaking as in other straths, but it
seems generally agreed that from the borders of Galloway to the
Mounth and east of the Highland line the landowning class, from
laird to earl, spoke Scots, a version of northern English, by the
late thirteenth century. Some might also know Anglo-Norman,
others Gaelic.

The evidence for this conclusion lies mainly in the fourteenth
century, when ignorance of French can be demonstrated; the causes
of the spread of Scots are therefore difficult to elucidate. There can
be no doubt that the quickening pace of commerce was an important factor, for the towns were English-speaking and there is a
mighty incentive to know well the language in which business is
done. Until the arrival of television, trading was the greatest modern
enemy of the Gaelic language, though a second enemy was education through the medium of English. This phenomenon, ignorant
and arrogant though it may be, survived so long because where
landlords dominated a peasant society both accepted the 'superiority' of the landlord's language which came from a wealthier and
more powerful society—a reason which may also explain persistence

---

[6] See e.g. *Melrose Liber*, nos. 29–37, *North Berwick Carte*, nos. 1, 13, 14.
Note how the inheritance of Roger de Scalebroc passed in part to Ruairidh mac
Gillescop.

in the use of French in fourteenth-century English government and its ultimate disappearance. By the same token, English shared the prestige of the English kingdom, and to speak it was a mark of belonging to a society which was not remote and particular (the mark of Gaelic speech) but widespread and wealthy. It is remarkable that early in the fourteenth century, in documents relating to the Celtic areas, Gaelic words become admissible; thus *feachd* and *sluagh* sometimes push aside the *servitium forinsecum* in which the thirteenth century disguised them. It is as if the wars of independence ended the cultural dominance of England, allowing Scots and Gaelic to go their own roads.[7]

It would be a mistake to overstress the language cleavage in Scotland, if only because we are ill-informed about both languages in the period. Gaelic was the language of poetry and song, and bards flourished in Lennox and on the western seaboard and perhaps survived in Galloway. There were ballads in Scots, and Thomas the Rhymer is an historical figure in the Merse though none of his poetry is identifiable. The literary forms employed for each language were doubtless those it inherited but we should not assume that their matter had nothing in common.[8]

*Baron et feme*; integrated into the literary or 'romantic' view of knightly conduct was the changed attitude of society to the relationship of man and woman, even of husband and wife, of which earlier centuries took little acount. Increasingly men admitted sentiments such as compassion and love to a place in the values of secular society, sentiments which are best expressed by womankind and which were the basis not only of literary romances (in both meanings of the word), but also of family relationships where life was good enough to be more than an unrelenting struggle for adequate food and shelter. Compassion and love are Christian qualities and the change can best be seen in religious attitudes. It is no coincidence that as knighthood became a mark of settled wealth and therefore of nobility, to the dubbing of a knight was often added a vigil before his sword upon the altar, implying a sanctifying of knighthood, that it be used in pursuit of God's commandments, and notably in

[7] I fear that the inadequacy of this discussion is particularly plain. The reader is referred to·Derick S. Thomson, 'Gaelic Learned Orders and Literati in Medieval Scotland', *Scottish Studies*, xii (1968), 57–78.

[8] See Derick S. Thomson, 'The Macmhuirich Bardic Family', *Transactions of Gaelic Society of Inverness*, xliii (1963), 276–304.

protection of the weak, especially clerics and women. Marriage, too, the church insisted, must be solemnised in kirk before a priest; since the church rarely stepped far ahead of secular opinion, its distaste for marriage *per verba de futuro* was surely an acknowledgement that society on the whole recognised a spiritual and a social purpose in marriage as well as a sexual one.

In 1198 the Earl and Countess of Strathearn lost their eldest son and heir; when the clerk of the bishop of Dunblane put their commemorative intentions into words, he joined the countess with her husband and phrased their piety in a particular way. This too was surely part of their intentions:

> ✠ In the name of our lord Jesus Christ, who is coequal and coeternal with God the father and the Holy Spirit I, Gilbert son of Ferteth, by God's mercy Earl of Strathearn, and I Matilda, Countess, daughter of William de Aubigni, wishing by the inspiration of divine grace to exalt the church of God in our fief and patrimony and to sow the seeds of holy religion for the cultivation (*cultus*) of God there, with the assent of the bishops of Dunkeld and Dunblane and consent of our children, knights and thanes, give Inchaffray, which in Latin is called the Isle of Masses, to our Lord Jesus Christ and the blessed MARY his mother and St. John the apostle.... For this place is so dear to us that, having chosen to have ourselves and our successors buried in it and having just buried our eldest son there, we have given therefore the following possessions to God, St MARY ever virgin, and St John the apostle her procurator...[9]

It is true that the order which they introduced to the anchorites of Inchaffray was Augustinian and not Cistercian, but otherwise this is a fine expression of the spirituality which could come forth from secular love under the stress of bereavement. The earl's title by God's mercy, *Dei indulgentia*, is to be taken as humility, not arrogance; but the most striking feature of the document is the treatment of the deity, first placing Son before Father, then linking the Son to his mother and finally naming God and Mary in that order but visually emphasising the latter by majuscule letters.

The twelfth-century church found a new significance in the human sufferings of the Crucifixion, and, in preaching that redemption, the church preached devotion to the humanity of Christ and therefore also to his mother. The 'cult' of the Virgin took a decisive step forward in the twelfth century, when collections of miracles attributed to her intervention achieved immense popularity not only

[9] *Inchaffray Charters*, no. IX.

in ecclesiastical circles but also in popular devotion; there are many fugitive Scottish illustrations of this, as for example the stories in the *Melrose Chronicle* of miracles within the cloister. Its secular popularity shows that it reflected social attitudes to woman, marriage and motherhood. This devotion, particularly associated with the Cistercian order, was a part of the Cistercian ideal and experience which attracted support for the order, not just in the vigorous days of David I, but in the more relaxed early thirteenth century. Of particular significance in this respect were the Cistercian nunneries which, to be sure, were refuges for the disposal of well-off spinsters, but also show that society acknowledged a place for feminine ability, emotion and vocation, in this case of women who did not make homes through marriage. The interest taken by the royal house in Queen Margaret and the successful effort to procure her canonisation show an important part of male society recognising the unique power of feminine intercession, acknowledging thereby the compassion and love shown by women. King William could put alongside the many miracles of the Virgin the dream in which Queen Margaret miraculously warned him not to invade England.

Of course, there was a great gap between the ideals represented by the Cistercians and accepted by secular society, and the performance of that society. Yet we must understand why, having devoted much energy to the building of an earthly castle, it was important to a baron or knight that at the end of his days he should adopt the habit of a Cistercian monk, or at least be buried within a monastic precinct, often at considerable previous cost to himself. Abandoning the appetites of secular life including carnal love he finally adopted the Cistercian way toward salvation through spiritual love; abandoning the companionship of home and family he entered a spiritual home and family whose companionship nourished his soul. Family love is complemented by the love of God. The family is valued not just as a group of males who must secure landed wealth for each generation, but as an ongoing relationship among men and women over several generations, with an inheritance of attitudes and mutual responsibilities as well as of land.

We cannot tell whether the shift in the church's teachings or the rapid rise in material wealth came first, which was cause, which effect. But plainly the thirteenth-century baronial castle and knightly hall, its family apartments and domestic chapel or oratory, and the pursuit of secular and religious weal which made up life there, these things were all sustained by the order of an essentially peaceful society itself, the product of economic opportunity and growing wealth.

The pace of royal favour to the monastic orders slowed markedly after 1178, so that no further abbey was founded by the crown except Balmerino about 1230 and Pluscarden, one of three Valliscaulian houses founded in 1230–1; but as we have seen,[10] there was a steady progress of private monastic foundations from 1190 until the 1240s which showed the continuing hold of the monastic ideal in secular society. In what health was the monastic order?

It is true that fine monastic buildings were erected on an ambitious scale at most or all houses in the thirteenth century, though stone vaulting on a lavish scale was uncommon, and there was perhaps a conservative addiction to the Romanesque style when it had become unfashionable in England. At Melrose the abbey kirk was laid out in the mid-twelfth century, 221 feet (67 m) long in nine bays exactly as at the mother-church of Rievaulx, with narrow aisles and a nave slightly slimmer than at Rievaulx. The conventual buildings were placed, unusually, to the north to suit the water supply, which was brought by lade from the Tweed, driving the abbey mill as well as flushing the elaborate sewage system necessary for the two colleges living on the premises: the *conversi* or lay brothers and the monks. Each had dormitory, frater and cloister as well as cellarage, kitchen and other offices. The monks' cloister was approximately 125 feet (38 m) square and round it these buildings and the chapter house were ranged. Architectural evidence suggests that it was late in the twelfth century before these buildings were constructed in stone, but there could be no end to such work. The kirk itself may have been slowest to reach completion, with thirteenth-century work in the nave and a Galilee porch built early in that century on the west gable. About 1240, the chapter house was extended presumably to house the growing convent but with a grand new frontage in the cloister; and an elaborate novice house was added to the north-east corner of the cloister. In the second half of the century a new and larger frater for the monks was built over a vaulted undercroft, and an extension to the 'house of the lay-brothers', possibly built as a single-storey range, had a vaulted cellar and upper storey. The total length of this range from the west end of the kirk to its gable beyond the main drain was 358

10 Above p. 413.

feet (109 m.), longer even than the same range in the great Cistercian houses of Yorkshire.

Melrose Abbey kirk was largely rebuilt in the late Middle Ages so that we can say only a little about the earlier structures; Dundrennan Abbey was no less magnificent, its early kirk surviving in greater measure, 250 feet (76 m) long in restrained and dignified early Gothic, used elsewhere by the Cistercians in the later twelfth century, with round and pointed arches. The chapter house was almost as large as that of Melrose, pillared and vaulted and with a splendid entrance from the cloister, an elaborately moulded archway and windows of the thirteenth century. At Jedburgh, another abbey in the Border hills whose order did not forbid the decoration which Cistercians avoided in the twelfth century, the choir and crossing of the kirk were finished by the 1170s and work was begun upon an elaborate nave of nine bays, working eastward from a fine west front (less elaborate than the surviving fragment of the west door at Kelso Abbey). The elevation was changed early in the thirteenth century so as to give greater height, with nave arcade, triforium and clearstorey, and with the kirk completed by the mid-thirteenth century, the cloisters were (as necessary) remodelled. Later in the thirteenth century the chapter house was rebuilt with a lierne vault supported on a central column—an elaborate building effort essayed here for the first time in Scotland.[11]

This sketch tells of a steadily expanding business whose directors, the monks, were increasing in number and thereby engrossing more and more of the output of the labour-force (among the Cistercians) of lay brothers, whose numbers must also have risen. Meanwhile, income was also ploughed into housing the increased staff, but probably on a scale and at a cost wholly disproportionate to the use made of the buildings. Much was done for ostentation, not just in the kirk itself, where secular considerations must be suspended, but in the elaborate conventual ranges where the thirteenth century clearly brought immense improvements in comfort and healthiness. In spite of the subsequent dilapidation of all Scottish religious houses —the best preserved conventual buildings are in the small abbey of Inchcolm in the Forth—wherever we can test, the late twelfth and the thirteenth centuries are periods of major building effort by all orders on a scale which can fairly be described as grandiose.

[11] *Inventory of Roxburghshire*, nos. 567 (Melrose Abbey), 414 (Jedburgh Abbey); *Inventory of Kirkcudbright*, no. 398 (Dundrennan Abbey).

But building was an expensive form of spirituality if un-accompanied by life according to the rules of St Benedict or St Augustine. The writings of Adam, Abbot of Dryburgh (a house of White Canons sharing many Cistercian ideals) in the 1180s, go far to explain how, without becoming mercenary or even worldly, the monastic community could not maintain the standard of spirituality found in a new settlement. 'I beseech you that when you come to the election of an abbot you proceed to the election as in the sight of God.' But some come in a different inspiration: 'I wonder if they will choose me. They can hardly choose another when I'm about—they wouldn't dream of going past me.' But they do and jealousy runs round the disappointed: 'He's young, knows less than me, speaks poorly, not from a respectable family, no appearance', and so in the election 'what is utterly against God is irrevocably laid down'. A man of Adam's calibre required the wisdom of Solomon to measure up to his abbacy. He has little to say of the daily round of services but throws light on other aspects of monastic life. Despite the climate the canon must read, study and meditate in the cloister, a confinement which would pall so that the obedientiaries (cellarer, almoner, kitchener) going about their business became the object of envy and even the subject of (forbidden) chatter. Only in the parlour (a draughty corridor at Dryburgh) might there be conversa-tion: never more than two were to be in it together; and their con-versation was to be in the hearing of the prior or his deputy. They were to remain standing and to leave as soon as the necessary business was done. Why should this be? Adam explains. Conversa-tion might lead to quarrels among canons and grievances against superiors. The prior must be present to lead conversation along proper channels. Something is wrong with canons who wish to go to the parlour every now and then. It is a sign that their thoughts are not totally absorbed by the religious life. The only reason they have so much to say is that they do not know how to observe silence. It is better for them to cultivate the pleasure of silent meditation.[12] In the daily chapter of canons the sins of life were to be confessed, and penance was to be indicated by the abbot. But 'there is too little love and tenderness in those sitting round', for the negligence or sin not confessed is picked up and related by a comrade and, while a charge is not always made maliciously, when it is, the canon should remem-that 'the chapter is the place of humiliation not of exultation, of

[12] J. Bulloch, *Adam of Dryburgh*, (1958), 39.

accusation, not of defence'. Two of Adam's sermons for Christmas Day are concerned with relations between abbot and canons, exhortations to love and humility which were all too easily forgotten in the isolation of a monk with a horizon of his colleagues' backs in choir and their faces in chapter. As early as 1148 the first abbot of Melrose was deposed for undue severity; in 1230 Dunfermline was troubled by 'violent' monks; in 1320 the abbot of Dryburgh was roughed up in chapter by a canon.

The fundamental weakness of the monastic orders was their method of recruitment. While there is little direct evidence on this in Scotland, the novitiate was undoubtedly recruited there as elsewhere without certainty of vocation. 'It is abominable', writes Adam of Dryburgh, 'that the poor man in a monastery should have delicacies while a rich man there is devoting himself entirely to labour for the sake of food. But in fact we see this far too often'— that is monks with and monks without a vocation for the monastic life. Wealth has been blamed for this decline in that it attracted unsuitable recruits but the blame lay first with those regulars who accepted wealth, often in direct contradiction of their order; the weak vessels came before the bad wine. Perhaps we should recognise that the swift expansion of monasticism placed great strains upon regular life: in order to pay for a fine church to the glory of God was it not harmless to accept under safeguard a forbidden revenue? Yet the proper answer to that question was 'it is harmful', and the monastic orders in departing from purity of observance were yielding to a variety of pressures: insistent lay donors, abbatial authority in chapter, declining fervour in those monks who had mistaken their vocation. There was and is indeed, no way known to test the truth of a proclamation of vocation for it is not given to one man to see into the soul of another. Bishop David de Bernham's synodal statutes contain a brief provision that no one be received into a religious order 'for a stipulated sum'. This enactment rules out selling monastic places but not buying them with an 'offering'—which could be refused if not high enough. Selling was probably very common. The catechism of an illiterate age was at best a rough guide to honesty of purpose, and how far it failed may be seen in the commercial success of the monastic orders in the thirteenth century.

In 1159 Melrose Abbey received its first appropriated kirk, burdened with a pension, 'for the entertainment of the poor and pilgrims' coming to the abbey; this was in fact the solution of a dis-

pute over the kirk between the king and Jocelyn, Bishop of Glasgow
(once Abbot of Melrose). The first kirk given to Coupar was justified by a subsidy from it to the Cistercian general chapter. Churches
and mills, once forbidden, had long been accepted by the Cistercians, and by 1170 Melrose and Newbattle (and later Holyrood)
were in business, discounting pawn tickets for lands pledged by
barons in need. The strength of the acquisitive spirit is better
revealed in some monastic collections than in others: at Coldingham
the almoner used his funds to buy up the lands of bankrupt peasants,
and Paisley Abbey seems to have invested similarly in burghal tenements. It took Duncan, Earl of Carrick, thirty years to persuade the
same abbey to found a promised daughter house on lands he had
given at Crossraguel. In England, it has been estimated, thirteenth-
century wealth permitted a house to hire servants at least to the
same number as the monks.

The convent of Melrose in the first half of the century was not
devoid of the conventional sanctity of the time. Adam the Yorkshire-
man, a monk who found himself locked in the orchard when the
vespers bell sounded, was wonderfully released at a postern; in the
kirk he once saw a vision of the Virgin; at his tomb the blind
William of Duns, formerly sacristan, had his sight restored. Adam
of Lennox, whom none saw enter or leave a bed for twenty years,
spent his nights in winter in the kirk accompanying himself on the
harp in the songs to the Virgin which are called 'motets' and his
days by the abbey gate, psalter in hand, dispensing bread to the
poor, while the great of the land, even King Alexander himself,
sought him out to be their confessor. Or so, in the 1260s, the stories
went.[13] But there was another side to the life of the abbey.

Matthew of Newton had probably become cellarer of Melrose
in 1236;[14] the abbey had just acquired from the king's forest a vast
stretch of moorland 'waste' around the upper Ettrick and Yarrow
waters which can only have been devoted to sheep farming, and at
the end of May 1236 the king granted rights of forest in its Ettrick
and Mow estates which would enable it to exclude anyone without
rightful business there. In December 1236 three further royal
charters gave land in Nithsdale to provide a pittance for the monks,
disafforested their lands between Gala and Leader and south of the
Tweed, so that they might use them and everything above and

---

13 *Chron. Melrose*, 119–22.
14 *Chron. Melrose*, 85.

below them as they wished and gave the right of forest in the same lands which would allow the exclusion of strangers. The phrase 'above and below their land' strongly suggests that the convent intended quarrying stone and lime for building work.[15] It looks as if a new and more business-like era for the abbey's sheep-runs was in train, but we can trace the cellarer at this business only in 1243 when he went to Mauchline to watch the earl of Carrick define the bounds of the abbey's lands there and to pay twenty shillings to the earl's disgruntled knight for whatever he suffered thereby.[16] Abbot Adam ruled the convent from 1219, and when he died or resigned in 1246 Matthew the cellarer was elected his successor. His policy of furthering the abbey's economic welfare went on. In 1247 the earl of Dunbar sold out his stud and grazing rights in Lauderdale for 120 merks leaving the ground clear for the abbey's stock. In 1251 the bankrupt Nicholas Webster, burgess of Berwick, sold his houses in the Briggate of Berwick next to the abbey's existing houses for 100 merks and a life pension of wheat, oats and ten merks of money; the interest of a burgess of Haddington was also bought out.[17] In 1252, for thirty-five merks, the needy laird of Fairnington sold eight acres of meadow there, which the abbey had already enclosed for him with a ditch and bank and which could now be thrown in with its own surrounding possessions.[18]

The simple diet prescribed for the Cistercian order was still intact, unlike the elaborate meals consumed by the black monks which made nonsense of the Rule of St Benedict. But even the Cistercians were allowed sparing and discretionary additional dishes, or pittances, and we have seen Alexander II make such provision in 1236; his namesake Alexander the Steward, between 1251 and 1255, yielded all his grazing rights at Mauchline to provide a pittance annually on 25 July. It is intriguing to find Peter Haig of Bemerside persuaded in the 1270s that the five fresh and five old (!) salmon which he had paid annually to the convent in recompense for some injury done them, were inappropriate, so that he substituted Lenten lighting for the chapel of St Cuthbert at Old Melrose; the salmon may have made their way to the Lenten table of the monks, a pittance so far from the spirit of the order that it was

15 *Melrose Liber*, nos. 203, 257, 258, 264, Appx. no. 2.
16 *Melrose Liber*, no. 191.
17 *Melrose Liber*, nos. 230, 328, 312–15.
18 *Melrose Liber*, nos. 335, 240.

removed by a later abbot.[19] The climate was a valid reason for good sense in diet and clothing and there were as yet no excesses of gluttony or finery. But neither was there mortification of the flesh.

There is ample justification therefore for the valedictory comment of one of the authors of the *Melrose Chronicle* upon Abbot Matthew on his dimission of office in 1261: 'through this good reverend and generous man, and by his acquisition, the house of Melrose obtained several possessions and many pittances. Through him we have pittance loaves on Fridays in Lent when we fast on bread and water. He also made our great houses in Berwick and he built many byres for cows and oxen, and the abbot's great chamber which is on the bank of the lade, and not a few other buildings.' The great chamber's foundations may still be seen, 76 feet long, 33 feet broad (23 m by 10 m), showing a vaulted undercroft to support the long-vanished hall in which Matthew entertained the prelates, barons and knights who associated themselves with the abbey. Such an one was the ecclesiastical laird, Master William of Greenlaw, who gave or sold three ploughgates to the abbey shortly before his death and his burial in the chapter house in 1247.[20] He was one of six buried at the abbey in that year; at least one other had also paid his mortuary dues to the abbey in land.[21]

Abbot Matthew has also surely left his finger in the abbey chronicle. Untidily kept under his predecessor, it drifted into a pastiche of newsletters from the continent for 1244–5. What we have from 1246 is a fair copy, made in or just after 1258, of the chronicle of Matthew's abbacy, doubtless kept year by year in draft and beginning in ceremonious phrase and majestic lettering with the election and benediction of *Dompnus Matheus*—the title itself is unusual in the chronicle. In 1262 four more annals for 1259–62 were entered and we read that in 1261 '*Dompnus Matheus* the sixteenth abbot of Melrose because of the infirmity of his body committed his seal to the prior in the chapter' on 24 July and a week later his successor, formerly cellarer of Melrose, was chosen abbot. Matthew himself probably wrote these annals (his predecessor's dimission is nowhere mentioned), adding a final account of 1263 in his retirement; a separate chronicle section was already in draft

19 *Melrose Liber*, nos. 322, 334.
20 *Melrose Liber*, nos. 232–7.
21 *Melrose Liber*, nos. 218–22.

beginning with background, the pious tales of the abbey in the 1240s already mentioned[22] and then plunging into the year 1260 with quite new versions of the abbatial succession at Kelso and, under 1261, of the deposition of Abbot Matthew by the abbot of Rievaulx, without consultation of anyone in Scotland. The concealment of this deposition in the first version strengthens the case for Matthew's authorship thereof; but the favourable verdict upon him of the second version is also instructive, for in effect it says that his faults were not great enough to justify deposition. His care of the monastic diet excused, if any excuse was needed, his well-intentioned breaking the Cistercian rule by building separate abbatial quarters. Matthew was a good business man, author of a conspicuously wasteful but prestigious building which the abbey could still afford. So far, perhaps, all was well with Melrose.

But his successor won a reputation for arbitrary behaviour which led to his deposition in 1267[23] and the next abbot lasted only a year. His successor was none other than Robert of Kenleith, abbot of Dunfermline and chancellor until 1251; he had settled as a Cistercian at Newbattle, whence in his old age he came in 1268 to be abbot of Melrose, dying in 1273.[24] However able Patrick of Selkirk, the last thirteenth-century abbot, was, the business affairs of the convent are likely to have been in poor shape when the effects of sheep scab and of papal taxation began to be felt. The survival in wartime and the renewed life of the abbey in the fifteenth century are tribute to its enormous wealth and staying power, but as a landowner Melrose was entering a crisis in the late thirteenth century. The material expectations of the abbots and convent, constantly revised upwards, had engrossed in a programme of building and plenishing all the wealth produced by the abbey's carefully exploited sheep-runs.

Manual labour probably died out by the end of the twelfth century in most houses, to be replaced in theory by study and meditation but all too often, in other countries and probably also Scotland, by stravaiging, hunting for pleasure, or bargaining for business. The monastic libraries, so far as they have survived, were properly moralistic and theological save for their marked further interest in canon law—especially, the cartularies suggest, the law

22 See above p. 458.
23 *Melrose Liber*, no. 329, *irrequisito conventu*.
24 See below pp. 559, 562.

limiting the rights of the visiting, enquiring and supervising bishop. Neither illuminated manuscript nor stained glass testifies to the skill or patronage of monastic orders. The *Chronicle of Holyrood* is jejune even for a set of annals; that of Melrose is a better piece of work, sustained until 1266 and resumed even later through interest in the deeds of the saintly Simon de Montfort. We pay tribute to monastic historians and lawyers by using their two chronicles and dozen or so cartularies throughout these pages; but their spiritual qualities make no appearance in those works.

The system of visitations included in the Cistercian order was probably still active, though at irregular intervals; probably less active in Scotland was the Premonstratensian system which included Scottish houses (except Fearn) in the English *circaria*. The Fourth Lateran council commanded other monastic orders to form local chapters, and a Scottish chapter of the black monks, perhaps including Tironensians, met, though with what frequency is unknown. Such administrative devices doubtless helped to keep monastic life free from the excesses which later ruined it—abbatial isolation, individual property for monks, laxity and immorality. But they did not exclude the comfortable failings of leisured affluence; there is the suspicion that a postulant's pedigree counted for more than his vocation, and the material gifts he brought with him for more than the spiritual.

*Addendum to 1978 impression.* The censorious tone of passages in this chapter on the monastic order is misleading. The great building achievement is inadequately described as 'for ostentation' and 'grandiose' (p. 455). On the whole Adam's writings (p. 456) show that monastic observances were intact; and the stress on unmonastic pursuits at the foot of p. 461 is excessive.

# 18

# TOWNS AND TRAFFICKING

Although it is generally accepted that trade did not wholly die in dark age Europe, there seems little doubt that on the periphery it was comatose; archaeological finds do not suggest that in Scotland before the Viking period there were other than desultory trading links with England or the Continent. Nor do the finds indicate that sophistication in manufacture produced full-time specialised craftsmen. Until the eleventh century, it seems, Scotland was a land of peasants living in peasant touns, with part-time craftsmen producing pottery and crude artefacts (such as stone querns for grinding cereals) for peasant or landlord and, perhaps, with small pedlars operating within comparatively restricted areas to provide occasional variety within otherwise self-sufficient communities. Not only was there no regional or national coinage in Scotland before the twelfth century, but finds of coins from other countries dating from the fifth century to the eleventh are apparently rare and scattered; this was a society whose commerce cannot deserve any other name than 'primitive'.

It is likely that by the early eleventh century these circumstances were changing. A hoard of over 100 English coins was buried at Lindores about 1027, and provides evidence of the more intensive commercial activity which alone could lead to the accumulation of so much liquid capital. Unfortunately, there is nothing for this period to parallel the elaborately studied pottery finds of prehistoric times, nor indeed does prehistoric precedent suggest that if there were we should be much wiser about commodities and lines of commerce. Nonetheless, it would be valuable to have some guide to the quantity and sophistication of local craft products to support the conjecture that production was increasing and was more specialised. For some three hundred years from A.D. 1000 the population of western Europe was on the increase; the causes are more obscure than the trends and sometimes much emphasis is placed upon the great trade routes and mercantile cities. But the growth of local trade, craftsmanship and communities is at least as important; the number of people engaged in trade or craft grew both absolutely, and relatively to other groups, and they flourished also in wealth. Their communities were the towns which grew up beside monastery or castle in northern Europe, or flourished on old Roman city sites in southern Europe, and it has been cogently argued that, at least in northern Europe, these agglomerations of population flourished most where specialised production attracted foreign traders. Particularly important for Britain were circumstances in Flanders where population growth seems to have coincided with advances in the early or mid-eleventh century in the technology of weaving. It was now possible to produce cloths of uniform width and texture—and to feed Flemish looms with wool from the flocks of England and Scotland.[1] In the growth of Flemish towns industry came first, trade second, but these circumstances need not have been reproduced elsewhere; on the other hand the revival of economic activity in Flanders, and later elsewhere in northern Europe, was on a far greater scale than earlier revivals and marked a further step in the long transition from agrarian to industrial society.

At the very heart of the urban revival of the eleventh and twelfth centuries was not the new technology of Flemish cloth-making, important as that was, but the ready and widespread availability of silver cash; plentiful coinage, if not the cause (and to isolate a single cause is dangerous), was certainly an essential means for the growth of specialised production and marketing, and, therefore, of towns. A skilled evaluation of the numismatic evidence for urban history is not possible here but the scarcity of finds of Anglo-Saxon coins is striking—especially since there is one exception, Jedburgh, whose tenth- and eleventh-century hoards suggest that it was an important centre of exchange on a route from Northumbria to Lothian.[2] But should not isolated finds of individual coins weigh more as evidence of urban trade than deliberately concealed hoards,

[1] C. Verlinden, 'Marchands ou tisserands?' *Annales*, xxviii (1972), 396–406.
[2] *Sylloge of Coins of the British Isles, National Museum of Antiquities of Scotland*, i, (1966), ed. R. B. K. Stevenson, xiii–xvii, xx.

usually in rural places? Is the absence of reported finds at, say, Edinburgh or Perth rightly taken as evidence that they were not towns before the twelfth century?

If the negative evidence of numismatics is an uncertain guide to urban origins in Scotland, traditional documentary evidence suffers more certainly from the same limitations. It will not do to argue that because there is no written evidence of eleventh-century towns in Scotland, there were no such towns, for there is no documentary evidence at all for eleventh-century Scotland and very little written evidence of any kind. No surviving charter or other document to a town or townsmen corporately is earlier than the 1160s; before that date there are a very few grants to individual townsmen, many grants of urban property and of money from urban rents and tolls to monastic and secular clergy, and a very few grants to clerical bene-ficiaries of the right to burgh privileges for their town. All these illuminate urban development, albeit obliquely; after 1160 burgh charters survive, but only where fourteenth-century warfare has not brought destruction, as it did at Berwick, Roxburgh, Edinburgh, Perth, all important towns, and at many smaller towns south of Tay. On the other hand, although houses were constantly renewed, house plots, called tofts, pass down the centuries with unchanging bounds, the pattern of early settlement, market and roads is fos-silised and although undated it can still be studied in the modern map of the town centre.

Unfortunately, the replanning of Berwick and total disappear-ance of Roxburgh have deprived us of the morphology of the two towns which are described as burghs before 1124. Between 1124 and 1130 the sources show Edinburgh, Dunfermline, Perth and Stirling also as 'burghs', and this term is so closely associated with urban development in Scotland that its significance is worth con-sideration: an agglomeration of houses (not necessarily surrounded by walls) outside and dependent upon castle or monastery, and growing up around a market. Most historians of towns, at least in Europe, will look for one early indicator of urban development— the appearance of a market. In Scotland we should do well to give an equal place in our thinking to marketing.

To the west of the ancient crag fortress of Edinburgh lies the church of St Cuthbert 'under the castle' whose parish once stretched in all directions to include the crag and its eastward tail. (See plan, page 626.) On that tail lies the burgh of Edinburgh and its parish kirk of St Giles, the earliest reference to which is of *c.* 1200, although a kirk was presumably there somewhat earlier, so placed as not to obtrude into the line of the high street. The Dalkeith road from the south to Leith which crosses the tail to form the eastern boundary of the burgh at the Nether Bow seems to have been pushed eastward (the Pleasance) and a more direct line (Roxburgh Place) abandoned. Another route from the south pushed eastwards by the burgh loch (now the Meadows) thereafter swung north westerly to join routes from the west at the highest point in the valleys below the crag, the head of the Grassmarket, whence a road, the West Bow, wound up the slope to the head of the high street and the castle. This route from the south to the castle, presumably very ancient, can also be joined from the Dalkeith road by the Cross-causeway, and immediately thereafter a branch (Potterrow) runs directly to the burgh joining the high street at the mercat cross, almost equidistant between the West Bow and the Nether Bow. There is a twelfth-century reference to the south port, presumably the point at which this road entered the burgh. The high street itself is so wide that it is a market street for almost all its length; yet the line of toft-frontages on the north side was not straight, and thus was scarcely laid out at one time. It looks very much as if the Lawnmarket was the urban nucleus, developing where the old road from the West Bow climbed the slope to join the road up the 'tail' and so to enter the castle. Around this market grew up the first settlement; St Giles Kirk, and the frontage line from there down to the Nether Bow would then be later developments, together with the diverted Pleasance and the Potterrow road to the mercat cross.[3]

This chronology can only be conjectural, but it is suggested by the existence of a chapel in the castle which evidently had some parochial rights (conveyed to Holyrood Abbey), and which is paralleled by chapels in Stirling and Perth castles each evidently also the church of the early urban nucleus. St Giles succeeded this Edinburgh chapel as burgh kirk, its parish carved from that of St Cuthbert, as the outlying pendicles of St Cuthbert show. The Scottish towns lacked the multiple town churches of England because their growth began effectively only in the eleventh or twelfth centuries when parochial rights were hardening. But the distinction

---

[3] F. C. Mears, 'Primitive Edinburgh', *Scottish Geographical Magazine*, xxxv (1919), 298–316; there is little change in his 'The Growth of Edinburgh', *Edinburgh, 1329-1929* (no editor, 1929).

of urban community and way of life from the countryside was none-theless maintained by the creation of the urban parish.

Moreover, during his reign David I gave to the abbey of Holy-rood (whose foundation involved diversion of a road) the right to 'build a certain burgh between their church and my burgh', and the existence of this contiguous burgh, Canongate, since *c.* 1150 makes it certain that the Netherbow was already the eastern end of Edinburgh's High Street, where the tofts were not shorter to give the burgh an elliptical shape, but ran to full length parallel with the Pleasance, an unusual feature explained by the existence of this other burgh on the other side of the Pleasance. Thus by implication Edinburgh's High Street was already fixed and of market width for almost its whole length at this 'early' date.

Perth also repays a little detailed study, for in many respects it contrasts with Edinburgh, not least in that a fair number of fugi-tive documents illustrate its importance. Here there was a crossing of north-south and east-west routes, the former with castle and church, but the latter widening (as the High Street) to form a market street leading to the staked ford over the Tay, and so to the royal cult-centre of Scone. (See plan, page 627.) Some early fortification to guard the crossing is likely, and it may be that this was placed on the castle site because of the protection afforded there by the small streams flowing into the Tay. The castle had a chapel with teinds, which suggests that it was an early (even eleventh century) establish-ment with a dependent settlement. Perhaps the road from the south, which enters the town at an angle at the South Street port, once crossed the present burgh site to join the High Street near the bridge, as surviving alignment at each end suggests, but if so that line was swept away before 1128, presumably with royal consent, and replaced by the curious dog-leg route down South Street and along the Watergate. The importance of the river to Perth's development is suggested by Alexander I's letter to the merchants of England telling them that Scone Abbey might bring a ship to Scone custom-free, a writ which may mean that the Tay was already well familiar to them; if so they are unlikely to have sailed beyond Perth. Under David I, ships were attracted in such numbers that the customs were a major source of cash revenue, more significant, it seems, than burgh rents. So the Watergate is part of the nucleus of Perth, as the burgages running from it to the river would suggest.

The other part of the nucleus is the High Street itself, on either side of which, so far as the Meal Vennel, are burgages of roughly equal length, whereas the South Street burgages on the north side are short and, it is suggested, a later development. The area to the west of the Meal Vennel is also, perhaps, a later development. Thus, the early town would lie between the river and the Meal Vennel, and the back line of the burgages on either side of High Street.

About 1160, a Flemish lorimer or maker of military harness, who had been induced by David I to settle as a royal 'client' at a toft freed of burgess services except watch within the burgh and enclosure proportional to his toft, was granted a site for a booth, ten feet by twenty feet, 'in the street of the north, at the castle' (*in vico de north apud castellum*), at the corner of High Street and Skinnergate. The 'North' street implies South Street and its existence is confirmed by a grant to Arboath Abbey, *c.* 1180, of a toft 'outside the burgh of Perth as laid out between the two ports', a toft which nonetheless was to be held with burgess rights. Later evidence places this toft beyond the ditch or lade, between the High Street and South Street ports. A monastic toft of 1178×95 was granted 'in my new burgh of Perth', words which have been used as evidence for phases of expansion of Perth within its medieval walls; this view would seem to be erroneous, for the medieval bounds were fixed by the mid-twelfth century and King William's 'new burgh' was a suburb to the west, 'between the two ports'.

By about 1180, it would seem, tenements within Perth were fully taken up and the king could find none with which to endow his favoured abbey, Arbroath. The town had clearly expanded to fill its bounds (whenever these latter had been delineated), and this rapid development of the twelfth century is to be attributed to the favourable geographical circumstances which attracted local and inter-regional trade. When in 1174 the king lost control of Berwick, Roxburgh and Edinburgh, his charters show that the larger courts or councils were held at remaining centres such as Stirling, Aberdeen and Perth, at which, for example, a statute was made in 1184. The elections of bishops took place there, under the king's eye, in 1174, 1189 and doubtless on other occasions. An important factor was the existence of a town in which the prelates and magnates might lodge while in attendance upon the court. Thus the constable, who had important functions in lodging the king's court, had a toft in every burgh, and when in 1209 the Tay flooded and swept into Perth during a council held to raise the 15,000 merks due to England, the chronicler Bower records that many magnates escaped in little boats or upstairs into the solars of the burgess houses. This relationship between the court and town was probably important in another respect: the king's household itself must be provisioned, especially with those things which were imported to meet the tastes of the wealthy: wine, fine cloth, furs, spices. It may be that Stirling, where the king's chamber was apparently housed in the 1180s, benefited most from these needs, but Perth burgesses too were certainly involved: one of the key figures in King William's household, Richard, clerk of the provender, had a niece married to a Perth burgess.

The town grew wealthier and more status-conscious, more socially divided, in the second half of the twelfth century. Its gild merchant was recognised in 1209. By then there was a bridge over the Tay (and usually townsmen maintained such structures as well as contributing to their building) when the disastrous rainstorm and flood swept away 'a certain eminence' (*mons*), nearby, which in turn carried off the bridge; it was, nonetheless, rebuilt by 1219 when the town had a common seal to mark the autonomy of its government from the sheriff. The 'eminence' was the old royal castle, which was not re-established; the sheriff moved his storehouses to Kinclaven, and the burgesses could no doubt strengthen their independence through that removal. The decision to build stone walls around the town, whenever taken, may have arisen from the loss of the castle and again part of the cost would certainly fall on the townsfolk. They were men of success and importance among the burgesses of Scotland—of greater wealth and importance than any save those of Berwick.[4]

At Crail the original nucleus round the harbour developed first one market street and then, parallel with this and further from the sea, a High Street and Marketgate on a truly remarkable scale. (See plan, page 627.) Beyond this, at the opposite end of the town from the castle is the burgh kirk with surviving Romanesque, that is, twelfth-century, work; it is therefore difficult to date the streets between castle and kirk any later than the twelfth century.[5]

The consideration of these three places, Edinburgh, Perth and

[4] A. A. M. Duncan, 'Perth, the first century', *Transactions of the Perthshire Society of Natural Science, Special Issue* (1974), 30–50.

[5] R. G. Cant, *Historic Crail* (1967). There is an excellent discussion of the evolution of Ayr by William Dodd in *Ayrshire Archaeological and Natural History Society Collections*, x (1972).

Crail, offers one conclusion in common—that in the twelfth century, and even in the earlier twelfth century, they were already flourishing towns, even though they were not all burghs, for the growth which they show by the middle or third part of the century simply could not be the consequence of only fifty years, no matter how active the king in giving encouragement. The town churches whose patronage and teinds, the town houses whose store-rooms and solar, were eagerly sought by the religious, are symptoms of a well established life and prosperity whose roots lie in the eleventh century, where they must be investigated by archaeology.

When David I assured Holyrood Abbey that their men of neighbouring Canongate might freely trade in his burgh (Edinburgh) he meant that they were not provided with a market place and market day of their own; so he must needs also guarantee that no one would take forcibly in their burgh bread, ale, cloth or anything saleable—which is to say that Edinburgh might not interfere to prevent trading in the Canongate (even though it had no market place) in these staple goods. A great abbey like Scone would produce its own bread and ale and might sell a surplus; but it must buy cloth and must stitch it into the monastic habit. When Malcolm IV allowed the canons of Scone to have a smith, skinner and tailor for their business and service, enjoying the privileges of the burgesses of Perth, he was allowing the abbey to share in the division of labour and specialised production (albeit technically primitive) of the neighbouring town. The appointment of weekly market days at Brechin and at St Andrews was attributed to David I by King William[6] and it seems likely that the market days granted to some and perhaps to all important towns by *c.* 1200 were, in fact, kept from early in the burgh's history. The town, as all these examples reveal it, was a place for the making and marketing of the necessities of life, rather than the luxuries, for those within and outwith.

The weekly market threw the street open to the landward man and was designed to attract supplies of fuel and food to the town. In doing so on one day a week it created the maximum of competition and lowered prices to the benefit of the townsman, if only in the short term. Early in his reign King William allowed the abbot's villagers of Kelso to buy fuel and grain from those carting these commodities, to turn these into bread, ale and meat, and to sell these foods (and fish if imported by the villagers themselves) in their

[6] *R.R.S.*, ii, 115.

shops; but all these privileges were removed for the day of Roxburgh market.[7] This is a classic illustration of the function of the
market day, of the activity—indeed function—of the town in turning raw materials into consumer goods, however rudimentary, and
of the importance, even indispensibility, of roads and routes to the
development of trafficking and therefore of the town. What we are
here told of Kelso village is by implication even truer of Roxburgh;
but (to controvert those who would have the king as sole manufac-
turer of burghs) by 1237 the villagers were styling themselves burgesses, and were engaging in cloth-finishing, a trade usually reserved
jealously to the king's burghs. Evidently, under the protection of the
abbey they had flourished, and no amount of government regulation could deny them the advantages of their geographical situation.[8] Such illustrations of infra-local trade could be multiplied, and
would strengthen the argument that the towns were not alone in
meeting local needs, and that village markets must have flourished.
Every mill implied the right to multure, and to a surplus of which
the miller must dispose; not every family could bake or brew, most
would buy bread, oats for porridge, and ale at least occasionally and
all families must buy salt and sometimes cumin or pepper.

The need for protein was met most cheaply by fish, but fishing
rights were jealously guarded by landlords. Both sea and river fish
were salted in vast quantities (and landlords also valued their salt-
pan monopolies and sales of salt) for consumption in both hall and
hovel. The market in fish was a risky one, the cry of 'stinking fish'
easily raised, but for the most part it was a sellers' market flourishing in both town and village. Probably timber had become scarcer
near towns through rapid consumption and townsmen certainly had
to pay handsomely for their fuel supplies. Clothing was as important
as food and fuel, and we shall see that towns dealt in the finer cloths
but that coarse cloth was produced and sold rurally. In fact, of most
commodities there were finer versions available in the towns but
never ousting completely from localised trade the coarser products
of local craftsmen or—perhaps more important than the sources tell
—craftswomen.

To the more important or flourishing village markets the king
gave the status of burgh; such inland towns as Forres, Haddington,
Peebles, Linlithgow, Rutherglen, Jedburgh or Lanark, all burghs
of the king before 1175, must have been pre-eminently centres of

[7] *R.R.S*, ii, no. 64.   [8] *Kelso Liber*, no. 355.

infra-local trade to which inter-regional traders could be attracted only by special measures such as an annual fair.[9] Where the lord was a powerful ecclesiastic he might obtain or assume burghal privileges for his town, as we have seen at Kelso; in the twelfth century Glasgow was such a market village given burghal status, and in the mid-thirteenth the town or village of Newburgh in Fife was to be held by the abbey of Lindores 'as a free burgh and market'. Burghs of secular lords such as Renfrew, Prestwick, Inverurie, Dundee, Kirkintilloch, Dunbar and Irvine fall into the same pattern. There are market centres (Dunblane, Crawford, Urr) making a fleeting appearance as burghs, whose lords aspired to this privileged status—but in vain, since they are not heard of again. For each of these there must have been many other smaller, more intermittent and less efficient rural centres of production and sale, their turnover and importance increasing as the thirteenth century progressed, but never qualifying them to be called towns. The towns of Scotland were the more important centres of infra-local trade, as their fairly even distribution through the Lowland zone bears out, and a large part of their population was engaged in this trade and its associated manufactories of goods: cloth, leather goods and metal ware. We shall not deal again with the trade of lesser towns, but this is not to belittle their rôle in the economy; it is a consequence of the scarcity of evidence on localised trade.

It follows that if the market place was essential to the burgh, was perhaps its very *raison d'être*, then it was not intruded at the heart of the burgh; rather the town developed from a market nucleus which owed its existence to a crossing of routes of communication. At this crossing, for strategic or other reasons, the king may have placed his manor or castle which thereafter stimulated market and settlement, but without a communications factor there was no urban growth. Of the earliest burghs, Roxburgh was at the junction of Tweed and Teviot where each might be forded, Perth was at the point where the Tay became tidal and bore ships to sea, yet could be forded on the land route from south to north.[10] Stirling was similarly placed. Dunfermline was on the route from the Queen's Ferry to Perth, but the early town there had gone by the end of the twelfth century, probably for two reasons: the nearby attraction of the

[9] See below pp. 510–13.

[10] At Perth the Tay flows from north to south and the crossing is therefore east-west; but in a wider context this crossing is part of a north-south route.

abbey under whose walls a second town grew up, and the more distant attraction of Inverkeithing, whose market was at the junction of routes from Perth and eastern Fife to the Queen's Ferry. Harbours by themselves did not attract market and town, but when combined with land routes, such as the crossing (already a bridge by 1150) of the Tweed at Berwick or the ferry over the mouth of Montrose Basin, then exchange flourished there and exchange implied market and town. Some towns and town plans present problems not readily solved, problems such as the 'old town' and 'new town' found at both Peebles and Selkirk[11] and perhaps also at Aberdeen, but even in these cases the relevance of ford or bridge to trade and settlement cannot be denied. And since the town was a place to traffic, a place of access and welcome, our sources mention the gate perhaps as frequently as they mention the market place. Indeed they tell us more of the 'gate' than of the 'walls' which in the age of gunpowder and Tudor invasion came to surround most towns of size. The notion persists that medieval Scottish towns were defensive and defended, with the implication of a countryside in turmoil and of royal resources devoted in the twelfth century to the planning and erection of twenty to forty walled strengths.

The largest town, Berwick, had only a ditch and palisade in the 1290s; its burgesses were indeed 'bound to enclose the town'[12] but the fact is commented on as though rather exceptionally the king had insisted upon the provision or maintenance of defensive works at a place shown to be vulnerable in the war of 1216. Similarly at Inverness in the 1180s, provision was made for enclosure by a good ditch and stout palisade; here too military necessity—the mac William rising—dictated such expensive works. In most towns all that the evidence allows us to conjecture is an enclosing palisade, not necessarily of great height, serving to secure the inhabitants and their stock from thieves by night. If more was provided or needed, the burgh laws of the thirteenth century and the warfare of 1296–1318 have nothing to say of it.

Exceptionally, however, at Perth 'the wallis war all of stane'[13]

<hr />

[11] Introductions to the *Inventory of Peeblesshire*, and *Inventory of Selkirkshire*.

[12] *A.P.S.*, i, 112. Murage, a toll to pay for the upkeep of the town walls, was introduced at Berwick after 1296. It was unknown at other Scottish towns though widespread in England; H. L. Turner, *Town Defences in England and Wales* (1970) especially pp. 22–25.

[13] Barbour, *Bruce*, bk. ix, line 335.

in 1312 and probably so by the mid-thirteenth century, when they were called *muri*.[14] This is likely to have been a consequence of the destruction of Perth Castle in 1209 and it may be assumed that the twelfth-century defences were palisaded. Even so, in 1160, when Malcolm IV returned from Toulouse to what the *Melrose Chronicle* called the 'city' of Perth, the six earls who besieged the city to take him failed in their *coup*; the palisade was evidently stout. Perth was palisaded and walled, and Berwick and the towns of Moray were well palisaded as a communal responsibility for strategic reasons. For the rest, the obligation upon each burgess to enclose in proportion to his holding (*claustura*) was doubtless discharged in less sophisticated manner by a palisade of relatively simple style, and perhaps without ditch and bank. Archaeology will doubtless reveal the nature of this enclosing stockade; its purpose, however, is not in doubt. Within it there often ran the open path or back lane whose function is illustrated by the name of Edinburgh's Cowgate: it was a daily route for the livestock of the burgess from the burgh pasture (outside the town) to his toft and byre. The burgh made some contribution to feeding itself, and usually had an extensive muir or haugh for grazing in the surrounding countryside; burgess interests were agrarian and pastoral as well as mercantile and, especially in the smaller landward towns such as Peebles or Lanark, this rural interest must have been very strong. But even here the town was enclosed, marked off from the surrounding countryside, and yet welcoming its business in daylight hours through its open gates. On the seals of several towns is a castellated structure which (far from being the local castle as is usually said) may symbolise the gate giving access to the trafficking of the town. Here the early burgess owed his stint of watch (*vigilia*) during the hours of darkness.

That David I sought to enforce a marketing monopoly for burghs seems clear from an exemption such as that to the monks of May Isle and their men 'of the freedom of selling fish in their port as in a burgh. Therefore ... they are not to be impleaded for merchandise bought any more than for purchase in my own burgh;' The 'impleading' was perhaps a demand for tolls on which the king's charters throw such an emphasis as to leave no doubt that they were frequent and irritating if not heavy. Burgesses were cer-

---

[14] *Scone Liber*, no 80. *Chron. Melrose*, 36. *Murus* is rare; it was used of Roxburgh *c.* 1150, Lawrie, *E.S.C.*, no. CCXLI. For the *fossatum* of Roxburgh, *Kelso Liber*, no. 415.

tainly exempt from them, and special exemptions were also granted to many religious houses; they appear as a burden upon the landward man and by the 1180s they were collected by the burgesses whose ferme was presumably fixed to take account of them.

The close connection between a marketing monopoly and tolls is suggested by the privileges granted to Rutherglen's burgesses by David I, according to his grandson's charter of 1179×89: first, boundaries, apparently of the lower ward of Lanarkshire, second, the right to pursue those not paying toll or other right given by King David and to call for help from landowners; 'and I firmly forbid anyone to bring anything to sale within these boundaries unless he shall first have been to the burgh of Rutherglen'. In 1205 King William gave to his recently established burgh of Ayr boundaries which marched with those of Rutherglen, and laid down that toll owed to the burgh be paid at the boundaries, that it be not carried beyond the boundaries, and that if it were the defaulter be pursued and arrested. These documents reveal an obligation upon the landward inhabitant to market his goods in the king's burgh of his province or sheriffdom, and not to sell them by the wayside or in a village. He would pay a toll on entering either the burgh or its market. But if he chose to take his goods to another burgh, he must nonetheless pay the toll due to his local burgh when he crossed the provincial boundary—a proviso which suggests that the burghal trading monopoly was truly unenforceable, just as the proviso for pursuit of defaulters suggests that the border customs posts were ineffective.

Nonetheless, the tolls go far to explain the king's interest in urban development; even if paid in kind, in the town they could readily be turned into money. They were a means of providing him with a cash income such as was not forthcoming from his estates nor from other landward sources. The rents of burgesses were similarly important to him, and it is indeed from these sources that the whole of David I's known revenue in money is derived. It is not surprising therefore that so active a ruler, with many projects costly in capital on hand, should have actively promoted the growth of burghs. It seems likely that the drawing of town boundaries and the delimiting of individual burgage tofts would be the work of experienced *lineatores* brought in from other towns, and this and similar functions may explain the early royal interest in Flemish settlers. In the early thirteenth century the crown offered tofts in less attractive towns—Dumbarton and Dingwall—rent-free for a period of years (five and ten respectively) in order to attract settlers; similar concessions for one year at least were offered at an earlier date at some towns, though there can hardly have been a lack of willing rent-payers at Perth or Berwick.

Unfortunately, these burgesses of early days are elusive creatures; burgh laws of the late twelfth century describe the rights of a *rusticus* dwelling outside the town but owning a burgage,[15] and thereby imply significant immigration from countryside to town—and the term *rusticus* need not imply humble status. On the other hand, the names of Elfgar, Arnald and William the Cook, burgesses of St Andrews by *c.* 1150,[16] do not suggest Fife peasants attracted to the town but rather migrants from Lothian or England. There are no early burgesses with Celtic names, doubtless because of the hasty adoption of Teutonic names in Celtic families, but even so this confirms what all the other evidence suggests in the towns: a predominantly Teutonic culture, northern English with other influences from further afield. We will search vainly for evidence that prosperous peasants and minor landowners, officials perhaps of a magnate, were introduced into the towns by the king or by those barons and monasteries who owned tofts there. It has been argued that some landholders and baronial officials took to urban opportunities, put their capital into trade and so became part of the emerging town patriciate along with immigrant merchants;[17] but in Scotland we simply do not know whether those burgesses with rural surnames (and they are remarkably few in number) come from this freehold and ministerial setting or from much humbler peasantry.

An important element in the early burgh population were the Flemings, who figure large in modern discussions because they were beneficiaries in a number of surviving documents, whereas no documents survive for early native or English burgesses; their apparent importance may only reflect the king's need to give written assurances to valuable Flemings in order to persuade them to stay.

There is, indeed, an apparent contrast between Baldwin, the king's 'client' in Perth, who held his toft free of every service except

---

[15] *Leges Burgorum*, chapter 11; later twelfth century; there is no equivalent chapter in the Newcastle customs.

[16] *St. Andrews Liber*, 124.

[17] A. B. Hibbert, 'The origins of the Medieval Town Patriciate', *Past and Present*, iii (1953), 15-27; S. Reynolds, 'The Rulers of London in the Twelfth Century', *History*, lvii (1972), 337-53.

watch and ward and who, when he wished to leave the town, might sell his house and toft as a burgage, and Mainard, the king's own burgess in Berwick, whom the king gave (*tribuit*) to the bishop of St Andrews to be reeve there and who was among the first to build and stock that burgh. Clearly these burgesses were in a very real sense the king's, for although the 'client' enjoyed a liberty of movement denied to the 'burgess' who was shuttled from Berwick to St Andrews, he did so only because king explicitly permitted it. It looks very much as if David I valued Flemings as efficient agents in furthering the physical development of towns, and that their freedoms as burgesses were subordinated to their duties as clients. The same need not have been true of other early immigrant townsfolk, for instance from England.

There may have been particularly strong Flemish settlement in the north of Scotland. To be sure, only one townsman, Berowald at Elgin, can be named, and he was a landowner by knight service also. But about 1180 King William granted to his burgesses of Aberdeen, burgesses of Moray (that is, Inverness and possibly elsewhere) and burgesses north of Mounth, their free hanse as in David I's time, which they are to have 'where they wish and when they wish', so that no one is to 'vex or disturb them for it'.[18] Although variously interpreted since the charter was first printed, the hanse seems to be a due or rent, rather than a fellowship or meeting. An early sense in which the word is found in the Low Countries fits it well here: a payment for the right to traffic, due to the ruler but remitted by him to those who settle, and hence taken by them from those outsiders who come to share in commerce.[19] The charter, if correctly so interpreted, implies a settlement of traders from Flanders and Artois between the Don and the Ness, and on any interpretation implies close links and common interests among burgesses there. Of the king's four charters to Inverness, two mention the burgesses of Moray, once equated with Inverness but, nonetheless, a phrase which should give us pause since burgess loyalty is usually so emphatically to one burgh community that the use of a provincial name must signify an unusual degree of closeness among the burgesses there.

[18] *R.R.S.*, ii, no. 153, translating *inde* as 'for it'. The word for hanse is *ansum*, twice.

[19] E. Coornaert, 'Les Ghildes mediévales', *Révue Historique*, cxcix (1948), 22–55, 208–43, especially 225–6.

The Latin of royal charters is far from Ciceronian but in one of those given (about 1180), to the burgesses of Inverness we read of 'burgess or *stalagarius*', the permission, *grantum*, of the burgesses, the sustaining, *sustentamentum*, of the burgh, by the grant of *Burchhalev*, the burgh haugh, 'namely which is between the hill and the water' (perhaps an attempt to render burgh haugh into Latin). No one is to make *wannagium* there; the burgesses have agreed, *conventionauerunt*, with the king about a ditch, *fossatum*, with palisade, *palitio*, which they will maintain, *sustentabunt*.[20] The words for 'ditch' and 'palisade' by themselves would arouse no comment, but all in all this is an unusually macaronic text requiring some explanation. Undoubtedly it derives from a burghal draft but 'burgh' words tend to have an international usage and these suggest both Romance and Germanic origins. They could come from England or from Flanders, most probably from both. But it has been pointed out that another Inverness charter, granting exemption from judicial battle, resembles Flemish precedents rather more closely than English ones.[21]

The case for a substantial Flemish settlement in Inverness and the Moray Firth towns is strong though by no means conclusive. One point might be added: in the first half of the thirteenth century the count of St Pol caused to be constructed 'a wonderful ship in Inverness that is in Moray so that in it he could boldly cross the sea with ... the Flemings and those commonly called of the Low Countries'.[22] Inverness was unique among early towns in that it straddled its river, but this circumstance would be explained by a shipbuilding industry requiring not merely construction yards but also waterborne transport for the long keel timbers. In the sixteenth century trees were floated down from Loch Ness to Inverness for this purpose, and the siting of shipbuilding there, evidently famous by the thirteenth century, is to be explained by the availability of timber and transport, as well, perhaps, as skills imported from the Low Countries, with which links remained sufficiently strong to come to the notice of a neighbouring count.

The evidence so far reviewed has illustrated town activities and answered particular questions: why towns grew up at particular places; whether they were walled; whence their inhabitants came; what function their market served. But it has not answered the more

---

[20] *R.R.S.*, ii, no. 213.  [21] *R.R.S.*, ii, no. 388.
[22] Anderson, *Scottish Annals*, 295n.

fundamental question: why towns at all? Trade and rural manufacture had never wholly died, and it is possible to construct a model in which the village craftsman produced necessities while the merchant brought luxuries to the landowner, exchanged them for wool and departed for Flanders without contributing a jot to urban development in Scotland. The markets at Kelso and Brechin villages were examples of rural markets which probably existed widely but without the recognition and organisation achieved by these two exceptions; the market monopolies of burghs arose from a wish to end the rivalry from such landward exchanges. No doubt the growth of trade and manufacture were necessary for urban growth; but why were towns an invariable feature of developing trade and manufacture in the twelfth century? Security was one reason, but of limited importance since society was not inherently nor frequently in disorder; on the contrary, it adhered to an ideal of social immobility and unchanging function, with baron and knight enjoying their honours, lands and rights of exploitation, and *nativi* owned by them as the means of that exploitation. The restrictions imposed by the state and by the dominant landowning group upon rural society, on succession to land among the landowners, on personal freedom (to move, to own and to contract) among the peasantry, these were essentially contrary to the aims of men seeking to profit by trafficking. They must be free of restrictions on their means of livelihood, must be outside the feudal order of landward areas, and must develop their own rules of personal status, ownership, succession, and trafficking. For these reasons, men took to the collective security of towns and developed a way of life sometimes viewed with suspicion by some feudatories, but in general encouraged by rulers and their barons because the proliferation of trade and manufactories enhanced their wealth and status. Thus the privileges granted to towns by rulers are as essential a part of the history of urban growth as is trade. Urban market monopolies, from one point of view, sacrificed the peasantry (who would find the rural market convenient and adequate) to the pretensions of the landowner (who wanted the benefits of size and sophistication when he sold or bought). From another point of view, they represented the townsman's view that a bargain, whether good or bad, made outside the burgh law was without guarantee or remedy and therefore worthless: let all men traffic in towns.

Such urban liberties as a market-monopoly show an obvious

self-interest. Moreover, they are secondary, the consequence rather than the precondition of town settlements. The essentials of urban development were an acceptance of special, non-feudal, rules about personal status and property. From the reign of David I, the beginnings of recorded urban history in Scotland, the king gave his peace to all burgesses, that is the protection of his officers in maintaining their standing as burgesses and their holdings as burgages. It remains mighty difficult to find a definition of burgess and burgage which will serve alike in Caen, Norwich and Perth, or in 1150 as in 1250. To say that a burgess of 1150 was a free man is to apply the absolute categories of a rather later and legally-minded age and we may doubt how meaningful such freedom was to William Lunnock, who resigned his land, house and service in Berwick to King William and had them given to Melrose Abbey.[23] But perhaps the king was still a privileged lord of burgesses; among the customs borrowed from Newcastle for the burghs of Lothian in the late twelfth century was a law that the man of a baron or knight, or an unfree man who bought a burgage and lived in it for a year and a day, was to be free as a burgess and enjoy the liberty of the burgh. On the other hand (and this was not borrowed from Newcastle), a countryman buying a burgage but living in the country enjoyed the status of burgess only in his burgh;[24] the point is obscure but it seems that the rustic must not claim in the landward courts the privileged forms of trial open to a burgess. The freedom which a burgess enjoyed was in relation to the landward man who might claim to be his lord; 'town air makes free', but once assured of that freedom the burgess was guided, ruled, even shackled, by the regulations of his fellow burgesses.

'I have granted to my burgesses of Inverness who will inhabit my burgh of Inverness, all laws and rightful customs which my other burgesses dwelling in my other burghs of Scotland have.'[25] Dealing with a town far distant from Newcastle or Lothian, this charter of King William shows marked agreement with the burgh laws that a burgess must live in his town (that is, must share in loyalty to its community), and charter and law perhaps belong to a period of concern about 'upland men'—country dwellers—buying town tenements in order to share in urban privileges. But if it was assumed in the early twelfth century that burgess and tenement

---

23 *R.R.S.*, ii, no. 98.          24 *Leges Burgorum*, chapters 15, 11.
25 *R.R.S.*, ii, no. 475.

holder were equivalent terms, there must even then have been town dwellers who were not burgesses: women, servants, labourers, and hired workers of all sorts. By the late twelfth century, the freedom of a burgess was jealously guarded and a custumal—the first part of the *Leges Burgorum*—was drawn up or consulted to guide different towns on what was the best practice of neighbouring Newcastle on burgess freedoms. Thus the son of a burgess enjoyed his father's freedom to buy and sell so long as he lived in the parental home, but lost it on leaving unless he was (that is, had been admitted as) a burgess.[26] The same custumal shows the practical consequences of burgess freedom when, for example, it denied the right to a domestic oven to any save the king's burgess[27] and so protected the baxters' livelihood. By the late twelfth century, admittance to the burgesses' freedom and delineation of it had become a matter of domestic regulation by the town, so that by the mid-thirteenth century, none might become a king's burgess (a burgess in a royal town) unless he did service to the king for (that is, owned) a rood of land.

These regulations extended to the burgage tenement, where the burgh laws show a Scottish version of a common burghal limitation, namely that relatives could prevent a burgess from disposing of inherited, though not purchased, lands. Special provision had to be made for cases of bankruptcy, but in general the community was prepared to protect the social standing of property-owning families from the irresponsibility of one member. The range of burgh customs is wide and the custumal is particularly full on the complex subject of poinding—the taking of pledges or sureties in a legal action—which could interfere seriously with any tradesman's or trader's stock. From *c.* 1130 occasional royal writs refer to sasine of burgh lands and are addressed for example to *prepositi*[28] or to the sheriff and his officers.[29] Although there is no early reference to a burgh court, when it is mentioned in the thirteenth century it is as witness to changes in the possession of tofts, in terms which show that already the rights of the burgess's family to heritage were elaborately protected by burgh law. Such well-established custom means that the burgesses' court was of some antiquity, and may be

---

[26] *Leges Burgorum*, chapter 14.

[27] *Leges Burgorum*, chapter 18. I am inclined to think that this was aimed against non-burgesses rather than burgesses of other lords.

[28] Lawrie, *E.S.C.*, no. LXIX.

[29] *Aberdeen Burgh Recs.*, xx.

linked with or have arisen from the early interest of *prepositi* and
sheriff in sasine; already one or other presided over the court, and
probably the court was as old as the burgh.[30]

The law which that court administered was unwritten but its
elements had a far wider currency than the law and custom of landward parts. The urban settler would expect those conditions of
property-owning which elsewhere have proved necessary and
advantageous for the business community; the trader must know
with what speed his disputes will be settled and would discourage
his fellows from trafficking at a town in which the standards of commercial practice fell below those to be found in other towns in
north-western Europe. Thus, although the evidence nowhere speaks
of the laws of Breteuil or Newcastle being granted to a Scottish
town or towns, the privileges of Perth were explicitly granted to
Aberdeen, and in most burghal charters there are unacknowledged
borrowings which imply that all burghs had accepted a common
mercantile and burgh law. In those towns where commerce
flourished, a more sophisticated version of these common customs
developed and it is doubtless to this fact that we owe most of the
*Leges Burgorum*, a jumble of substantive rules and procedural
technicalities with a smattering of economic legislation probably
drawn up under the influence or even precisely for Berwick but
with no official standing so far as is known. But burgh law was only
a common minimum on which each town might improve with the
ruler's grant of speedier forms of trial or greater self-determination
in economic policies. That is, each town sought to increase its own
welfare by a privilege-differential over its fellows, and the wealthiest
towns were able to buy such differentials, which the less wealthy
must then seek to close; this familiar game of economic leapfrog
explains the transfer of liberties from one burgh to another, but its
earliest manifestation, the farming of the burgh by the burgesses,
was probably not recorded in charters.

Under David I the rents due to the king were referred to as the
*firma* (sometimes *census*) of the burgh, that is the lump sum predetermined as the amount payable by the king's officers into his
chamber. And already a writ on burgh affairs may be addressed
'*prepositis de Perth*', to reeves responsible for giving sasine of a toft
and an allowance from the custom on ships; at least in the larger

---

[30] W. Croft Dickinson (*Aberdeen Burgh Recs*, xx) is vague about the origins
of the burgh court.

(and probably in all) towns the sheriff had these special burghal reeves.[31] If the sheriff farmed the burgh under David I there must have been a point at which the burgesses took over this right, and it is likely that with this change there would be an accompanying change in the office of *prepositus*, for the burgesses and not the sheriff would now require an agent to collect rents and pay the ferme to the chamberlain. At Perth the *prepositi* were burgesses before 1162, at Inverkeithing by 1170; at the latter the *prepositi* and burgesses could hold land outside the burgh 'for the easement of the burgh communally' and could pay an annual rent for it. The wording is cautious, and 'communally' refers to common grazing rather than to an urban community, yet official recognition of the community has taken a large step forward since the time of David I, who granted no charter to burgh or community. The community of burgesses of Inverkeithing was then evidently headed by the *prepositi*; the only reasonable explanation is that the burgesses then farmed the burgh just as they rented fields outside it. Not long afterwards the same burgesses received a monopoly between the (Fife) Leven and Devon rivers: no one might trade or take toll there 'without their leave'—a phrase which implies the capacity as a community to give such leave, a phrase which is not found in the king's charter of monopoly, some ten years earlier, to Rutherglen, nor in that to the new burgh of Ayr in 1205. There were differences in the speed of urban development and it is apparent that the *prepositi* remained very much the king's 'reeves' in Rutherglen and Ayr, while in Inverkeithing their place was with the burgesses and the term might be translated 'provosts' for it is likely that already they were chosen by the burgesses.

Evidence elsewhere is equally tantalising. Payment from the ferme of Berwick is commanded to the *prepositi* (*c.* 1170), from the ferme of Haddington to the sheriff and *prepositi* (*c.* 1190),[32] so that the burgesses probably farmed Berwick but the sheriff farmed Haddington. If the word *ballivi* in a burghal context be shorthand for 'sheriff and reeves', then Rutherglen in the 1190s, Elgin, Crail and Linlithgow[33] were farmed by the sheriff, while in Rutherglen by 1201–2, Perth and Roxburgh[34] the provosts were addressed

[31] Lawrie, *E.S.C.*, no. LXIX, *R.R.S.*, i, no. 223.
[32] *R.R.S.*, ii, nos. 123, 289, 304–5.
[33] *R.R.S.*, ii, nos. 261, 360, 370, 407, 490.
[34] *R.R.S.*, ii, nos. 415, 426, 289.

directly by the king and the burgesses may have farmed the burgh. Elsewhere in Europe the decades after 1190 were marked by rapid advances in urban self-government, for which some parallel should be expected in Scotland; its exact form is sadly conjectural—that the burgesses of an increasing number of towns farmed the burgh and elected the provosts—but is confirmed by the appearance of burgh common seals (at Berwick, 1212; Perth, 1219; Elgin, 1244; St Andrews and Aberdeen c. 1250; Banff, 1290; Edinburgh, Roxburgh, Stirling, Arbroath, Dingwall, Glasgow, Jedburgh, Linlithgow and Montrose by the end of the thirteenth century),[35] associated in the earlier cases with the work of the burgesses' court yet carrying the name of the community of the burgesses. This new burghal self-confidence evidenced from 1200 must result from an altered relationship with the king such as would be brought by the right to farm the burgh.

Although the Scottish adaptor of the customs of Newcastle in the late twelfth century added two new clauses (that each man shall pay his rent for his burgage to the king and that anyone made a new burgess of the king shall swear fealty to the king, the bailies and the community of the burgh), there is good reason to think that these clauses describe a situation less simple than at first sight. For it is apparent that by the 1160s admission to burgess-ship was no longer (if it ever had been) a matter of burgh-residence and toft-holding, but was carefully regulated by the burgesses themselves through the oath. To be a king's burgess was a privilege not conferred merely by paying a rent; it brought freedom from tolls, a place in the burgh court, and perhaps in time a voice in the choice of the provosts. But above all it brought the right to do business in the burgh trading precinct. In c. 1179 two classes of inhabitants of Inverness might so trade: burgesses and stall-holders; but others were by implication excluded. Since early burgh charters tend to deal with matters in debate, rather than list the obvious and accepted, this is evidence of tension within the town and of the emergence of a burgess community within the burgh community. Thus, in Perth the king insisted in 1209 that 'those who dwell in Perth and want to have dealings (*communicare*) with my burgesses at market, shall have responsibility (*communicent*) with them to pay my aids, whose-so-ever men they are'. Not only are there second-class citizens, ex-

[35] *Aberdeen Burgh Recs*, p. 1; J. H. Stevenson and M. Wood, *Scottish Heraldic Seals*, i, (1940) under the burghs mentioned.

cluded from the burgesses' monopoly of trade in the landward
parts, often the men of someone else, perhaps the tenants of an
ecclesiastical or baronial toft, but they have claimed the privileges
of second-class citizenship, that is of not sharing in the burgesses'
responsibilities. They are sternly put in their place: if they dwell
and do business in the burgh, they pay with the burgh. This
provision, recurring in some other thirteenth-century burgh charters, shows clearly the restriction of burgess-ship within towns
both large and small and the tensions arising therefrom.[36] Perhaps so
long as the restriction operated against landward men it was justi-
fiable, but the burgh customs show[37] that when the son of a burgess
left his father's home, he was excluded from his father's privileges
until he became a burgess himself. It seems certain that domestic
servants, apprentices and even journeymen, who were much less
close to the burgess than his son, were excluded and that a majority
of the adult male inhabitants of a town were not burgesses.

What were the king's aids (*auxilia*) which all inhabitants must
pay at Perth (and later elsewhere)? English precedent, where
borough 'aid' was used interchangeably with 'gift' in the twelfth
century, yielding to 'tallage' from *c.* 1190, strongly suggests that aid
was first a payment taken in place of, or to pay for, military service,
but that in time it was also taken for other purposes.[38] Significantly,
the amounts were fixed in England by discussion between borough
and royal officers. It is likely that burgh aids in this sense taken from
the largest towns became necessary in Scotland in 1173-4 to pay for
Scottish armies, after 1174 to pay for English garrisons, and after
1189 to pay for their removal, in a period when rapidly increasing
urban prosperity made such aids possible and worthwhile. But their
appearance in this charter of King William to Perth has special
significance, for its date, Stirling, 10 October,[39] attaches it firmly to

---

[36] The passage in *Lanark Recs.* 309, a charter of 1285, is simpler than in the
Perth charter: *omnes manentes in burgo nostro de Lanark cum dictis burgensibus
nostris communicantes contribuant ad auxilium nostrum cum eisdem burgensibus
nostris de Lanark.* The Perth charter is *R.R.S.*, ii, no. 467, where a misplaced
(p. 431, line 13) comma obscures the meaning. Read: communicare voluerint ad
forum, communicent ... Cf. Ballard and Tait, *British Borough Ch., 1216-1307*,
138-9.

[37] *Leges Burgorum*, chapter 14.

[38] Carl Stephenson, 'The Aids of the English Boroughs', *Eng. Hist. Rev.*,
xxxiv (1919), especially 466-75.

[39] *R.R.S.*, ii, no. 467. Professor Barrow dates it '*c.* 1205 x 1210, probably
1205'. For the date of this episode, 1209 not 1210, see p. 255 above.

the year 1209 when the king and magnates met at Perth for a council on 29 September, were washed out by floods and adjourned to Stirling. There the king asked the magnates for 'aid' to pay the £14,000 which he owed to John of England and 'they promised they would give 10,000 merks apart from the burgesses of the kingdom who promised 6000 merks apart from the churches on which they did not dare to impose anything'.[40] This curiously worded statement arouses little trust by seeming to anticipate the three estates of the fifteenth century; yet we can be sure that burgesses of Perth were at Stirling bemoaning their sodden charters, craving a royal confirmation, and insisting that if burgesses must pay the aid, then all inhabitants of the burgh must pay. It is probable that 6000 merks was the unrealistic target which the king set himself to raise from the burghs by negotiating with them severally.

Although the verb *communicare* in its two contexts can have only a non-technical meaning, the phrase *communicent ad auxilia reddenda* must mean that the burgesses of Perth had made themselves responsible in common for producing a lump sum agreed with the king. A rudimentary communal organisation for these purposes implies some persons who will speak for the community— almost certainly elective provosts; indeed the king's need for aids may have been the bargaining point which secured elective provosts for many towns. In England royal reluctance to grant, and willingness to resume, urban liberties including elective officials caused a steady stream of borough charters of definition: charters are concerned with points at issue. The absence from Scottish charters of the right to elect the provosts (and it was still absent from feu-ferm charters in the fourteenth century) simply means that the points were not at issue, that the king had conceded gradually and silently the election of provosts and showed no disposition to question what (presumably) worked well enough.[41]

Yet a burgh could be granted land outside its walls 'to sustain the burgh farm' or 'to feu-farm',[42] so why did not the burgesses of Perth, Aberdeen and other large towns succeed in feuing the burgh ferme? Here was a liberty (widespread in England) which each

[40] *petito ab optimatibus auxilio ... promiserunt se daturos decem mille marcas praeter burgenses regni qui sex millia marcarum promiserunt, praeter ecclesias super quas nihil imponere praesumpserunt;* Chron. Bower, i, 529.

[41] The question of early town councils is discussed below, pp. 488, 496.

[42] Ballard and Tait, *British Borough Ch. 1216–1307*, 333, 336 (Inverness and Ayr).

town must have sought but which, with three exceptions, was denied until the later fourteenth century and for no apparent reason. The explanation is probably administrative: generally in England a borough's choice lay between the sheriff's responsibility for an adjustable farm and the burgesses' responsibility for a feu farm. To feu-farm the borough was to escape from the sheriff's rapacity. In Scotland, however, the sheriff seems to have lost the burgh farm to the provosts and burgh because the king's chamberlain had or took the task of negotiating (presumably on ayre) with the burgh the amount of the farm for a year or several years. Thus the sheriff's (presumed) rapacity was exchanged for the comparative mildness of the king's cupidity and a method of negotiating the farm satisfactory to king and burgh; if the fourteenth century is any guide, farms would not vary greatly from year to year, and the burghs therefore had no incentive, organisational or financial, to pay large sums for feu-farm status.

The limitation of burgess-ship to some inhabitants, especially the more established and propertied class, is not to be seen as an invasion of primitive urban democracy, which did not exist, but rather as a part of the ill-documented process in the twelfth century whereby the king's interest in the town (other than fiscal) was transferred to that element in it which was solvent, trustworthy, responsible, *probus*—and which was wealthy enough to pay for the privilege of responsibility for the farm.

Evidence has been found for the number of burgesses at Perth and Berwick in the submissions to Edward I made by those towns in 1291, naming some seventy and eighty persons respectively. Certainly the documents confirm the pre-eminence of the two towns over others, and perhaps indicate their relative size. Among the names are a tailor, carpenter, skinner and three baxters at Perth, two tanners and a skinner at Berwick, from which it might be concluded that a few artisans could still become burgesses. Unfortunately, it seems that not all named were burgesses, and there is no means of distinguishing those who were; the order of names is haphazard and might suggest that the town oligarchy was reluctant to betray the kingdom and that English agents swept in humbler folk as makeweight. Certainly in 1296 Berwick, despite its many English surnames, defied the English, was sacked, and hence was not called upon to acknowledge formally English rule. However at least ten other towns did so, and in nine cases, including Edinburgh,

Roxburgh and Stirling, twelve burgesses acted for the town; in Perth, the number was eighteen. The group of twelve chosen to safeguard and administer the common weal of the town was common in north-western Europe, and is found in Scotland in the later Middle Ages as the 'quest', 'assize', 'duodene' or 'doussan', evolving into the burgh council. A chapter in the *Leges Burgorum*, possibly of late thirteenth-century date, prescribes that the alderman shall cause twelve of the most substantial burgesses to swear an oath to preserve the burgh customs, and it seems likely that in the larger towns it was these twelve who were called upon by Edward I to swear *his* oath; they probably already carried out the functions of counsellors to the provost and bailies, and were, we might say, proto-councillors, but there was as yet no recognition of the existence of *a* council. The eighteen at Perth presumably reflect the greater wealth and commercial sophistication of that town; they would certainly be councillors, for their number is half way from the twelve of other towns to the twenty-four councillors recognised in thirteenth-century Berwick, and more conveniently discussed later.[43] At Perth, Edinburgh, Aberdeen and perhaps one or two other towns the councillors were probably recognised under that name in the early thirteenth century; elsewhere recognition came later, and in the smaller towns the twelve for long remained only an assize appointed by the burgh court to draw up regulations.

Perhaps the burgesses as a whole were too numerous to qualify for the description 'oligarchy', yet in the larger towns they were the seed-bed from which oligarchy grew: the gild. Although no Scottish gild is mentioned in the twelfth century, the regulations drawn up by the Berwick gild in the thirteenth suggest that it was an institution of some antiquity, since they frequently prescribe a cask of wine as a forfeiture for infringement[44] (wine, that is, for the conviviali-ties of the gildsmen). It has been argued persuasively that the origins of gilds in the Low Countries lie in the religious, charitable and social impulses of the business men and traders who could afford them; their early statutes, as at Valenciennes and St Omer, are much concerned with masses, alms, burial rites, with mutual assist-ance in court and with the brawls arising at convivialities (*potatio*). All these purposes are implied by the Berwick statutes, and the gild

---

[43] W. Croft Dickinson, *Aberdeen Burgh Recs*, lxxxii–lxxxviii; for Berwick see below p. 496.
[44] E.g. *Statuta Gilde*, chapters 26, 28, 35, 36.

there had, it seems, a similar origin in a fellowship for mutual aid and solidarity when the town was ruled by the unsympathetic agents of the king, before, say, 1174.[45] The same was probably true in Perth, Edinburgh, Aberdeen and perhaps one or two other towns.

When the gild is recognised and thus documented (from 1209) it no longer looks inwardly but is pursuing economic ends, and indeed comes to exercise administrative functions. The recorded liberties of early Scottish towns are almost exclusively economic and not institutional privileges; the king bolsters up the pretensions of those who think that the town's businessmen must be protected from the stunting cold blast of competitive winds, though of course for the businessmen of *other* towns and regions the keen air of competition in open marketing is not only healthy but necessary. And the gild is the businessman's mouthpiece and protection; it is a 'gild merchant'—not a gild of merchants (long distance traders) only, but of those who live by buying and selling, whether as merchants or as employers of craftsmen.

From the first half of the thirteenth century there survives a scatter of some thirty documents relating to the burgesses of Perth and their property.[46] They tell us the names of about a hundred inhabitants of the town, all with surnames: patronymics, place names, nicknames or trade names. Almost all the trade names— furbar, taillur, tenteman, *tinctor* (no fewer than four dyers), *tannator*, lorimer, *galeator* (helmet-maker), *faber* (smith)—seem to be descriptive and not inherited surnames and are concerned with a limited range of processes: cloth and clothing, leather-work, metal-work; they bring home to us that the materials and techniques available were limited. Thus, vessels and utensils must be made of iron or leather (which are represented) or of wood or pottery (which are not). The raw materials for leather bottles and pottery dishes and cooking-pots were cheaply to hand and these things were produced in quantity, but at both Perth and St Andrews the pottery factories were outside the town, presumably to be near clay and fuel and to remove fire risks.

[45] E. Coornaert, 'Les Ghildes mediévales', *Révue Historique*, cxcix (1948), 22–55, 208–43.
[46] The following passage is based on *Scone Liber*, nos. 21, 45, 46, 79, 80, 82, 86, 88, 89, 90, 95–7, 169; *Dunfermline Registrum*, nos. 144, 166, 149; *St. Andrews Liber*, 316; *Arbroath Liber*, i, no 215; *Inchaffray Chrs.*, nos. LXIX, LXX, LXXI, LXXIII; *Lindores Chartulary*, nos. LXVI, LXVII, LXVIII; *Balmerino Liber*, nos. 21, 22, 25, 27, 28, 30; *Coupar Charters*, no. XXV.

Notably missing from the trade-names are baxters, brewsters and other food tradesmen; but also two important cloth-making trades: webster and waulker (weaver and fuller). Moreover, except for two dyers who are met twice, our tradesmen each occur once only and all are therefore markedly less significant people than some of those with other name-forms. The clothing industry was important in Perth, yet those involved in cloth manufacture fell into different social and economic groups; at the bottom were the websters and waulkers, above them the tradesmen we have already met, tenteman and dyer. But both were subject to the government of the town patriciate.

As studies in England have shown, dyeing was of particular importance in the development of the cloth industry since dyestuffs must often be imported; woad, a blue dye also used as a foundation for other colours, was no longer produced in adequate quantities in Britain; brasil, vermilion and grain, each used to dye red, came from the East Indies, Red Sea and Mediterranean lands respectively; as mordants to fix the dyes, potash was often imported, and alum came from the Mediterranean. Thus, whereas the weaver had abundant supplies of home-grown and home-spun thread, the dyer must not only master a difficult craft, but must traffic for his raw materials abroad or with foreign merchants, and must lay out considerable sums for commodities of comparatively small bulk. The dyer thus became a merchant and business man, employing hired servants to work at his vats, and dominating the whole production-process of cloth by virtue of his key place in, and perhaps his organisation of, the industry.

In mid-thirteenth century Leicester the cloth industry was in the hands of such capitalist entrepreneurs, purchasing wool, having it dyed, parcelling it out to domestic carders and spinners and then employing weavers and fullers at fixed piece-work rates to produce cloth marketed from the merchants' own stalls at urban fairs.[47] The toll-lists show that dyes were imported to Scotland, and our Perth evidence implies a cloth industry structured much as was that of Leicester, though whether dyers fathered the entrepreneurial group to quite the same extent is a matter of speculation. Certainly the four dyers of Perth were not among the town's major capitalists; they may have operated small dye-sheds on a contract basis. But

[47] E. M. Carus Wilson, *Medieval Merchant Venturers*, chapter V; E. Miller in *Economic History Review*, xviii (1965), 64–82.

that there were such capitalists is put beyond cavil by the king's grant to the burgesses of privileges, including a gild, in 1209. Competition (and hence price cutting) in the market was limited since no merchant from outside Perth might sell goods anywhere in the sheriffdom but only at Perth market, nor cut cloth for sale there except for a few weeks between Ascension day (usually in May) and 1 August. The exemption may be accounted for by a desire to sell some of the season's wool clip to foreign merchants for export (probably to Flanders) and hence a need to accept some imports and sale of Flemish cloth in Scotland. And direct access to view wool and hides was prohibited to outsiders except in the burgh; that is, a special advantage was given to urban middlemen.

In granting to the burgesses that 'they' might have 'their' gild merchant, the king acknowledged a vested interest which probably had roots in the time of Perth's emergence as a burgh, and a long unofficial history. By 1209, the capitalists of the cloth industry were especially prominent in the gild, since weavers and fullers, the proletarians of cloth making (and fulling or waulking, pounding in a solution of fuller's earth, was especially hard labour), were expressly excluded from it; doubtless the gild was used to adjust and enforce the piece-rates for weaving and fulling. The pre-eminence of dyers among these capitalists is implied by a prohibition that no rural inhabitant of Perthshire might make dyed or shorn cloth nor cause it to be made, except burgesses of Perth who were in the gild; clearly there was an extensive rural weaving industry which was tolerable so long as it produced undyed and lower-cost cloths for peasant consumption. But production of the finer cloths (which had been dyed and/or finished by raising with teazles and then shorn) and all access to the finishing crafts, these were firmly in the hands of the entrepreneurs of Perth who thus controlled weavers both inside and outside the burgh.

But in the Perth of 1209 there was another vested interest: no one might have a tavern in any toun in Perthshire except where the lord of the toun was a knight and dwelt in that toun, and then there could be only one tavern. It is unlikely that this was concerned to protect urban brewers, since breweries were common in town and country; a tavern meant wine, and the burgesses of Perth, like those of Bristol in 1188 and of Irish towns, were anxious to take into their own hands so far as possible a monopoly of wine sales. This was 'quality' trade, and the gentry (to borrow the terms of another age) could not be denied a local tavern in which to buy (or perhaps to sell surplus?), but since the investment in a wine cargo was substantial and since, once the sea-hazard was over, profits could be considerable, the men who dealt in wine were as much capitalists as the cloth entrepreneurs. Once again, in this brief clause, adopted also at Inverness, Aberdeen and Stirling, a wealthy vested interest took steps to reduce competition and, it hoped, to maximise its own profits.[48]

The leading members of the gild, the capitalist entrepreneurs of Perth, stand out among our hundred named inhabitants of Perth by the frequency of their occurrence: seventeen men are named four or more times, and not one has a trade name; they are the patricians of the town. Henry Bald, however, who occurs seven times, has a trade description thrice as well as his name; he was a goldsmith, a trade involving large capital outlay, yielding high profits, and yet, probably because of the skills needed and the dangers of a dishonest employee, requiring his personal labours. He was therefore a wealthy man, but an exceptional one in that he was still a manual worker. The other sixteen surnames include one Scottish place-name, Dundee, and a number of foreign ones, Leicester, Bedford, Lynn, la Bataille, to which can be added, from the names of the less prominent, Scarborough and Stamford. The family of la Bataille or Battle is found also in Berwick, from which the Perth member may have come; in the next generation it held land in the Carse of Gowrie. Richard of Leicester proclaims himself the cousin of Master Robert of Leicester who had a long ecclesiastical career, appearing as 'of Perth' and 'of Craigie' (on the hill to the south-west of the town), where he must have owned some land. Together with their relative John of Leicester, Bishop of Dunkeld,[49] they were presumably active in Scotland through the patronage of Roger, son of the earl of Leicester, kinsman and chancellor of King William and Bishop of St Andrews; Richard of Leicester, then, is an example of a merchant whose initial capital probably came from a feudal source and whose business benefited from the migration of a branch of his family to a new country.

Many of the seventeen surnames are uninformative, such as John Cokyn or David Yeap, or patronymics like James, son of

[48] R.R.S., ii, nos. 467, 475; Ballard, British Borough Ch. 1042–1216, 216–7; Ballard and Tait, British Borough Ch. 1216–1307, 291.
[49] 1211 × 1212–14.

Uhtred. Their Anglo-Saxon character is modified in some cases: thus three brothers, Geoffrey, Alan and Osbert, were all called Redbeard, which is therefore a family name (there is also a William Whitebeard), but Alan appears in French guise once as Rouge-barbe.[50] But, although the prominent burgesses of Perth were of cosmopolitan origin, by the early thirteenth century they were forming a number of small dynasties or clans within the town, for among the hundred names relationships are sometimes stated, as with the Redbeards, or more frequently implied by a common surname such as Lynn. Burgh law, with its insistence that inherited land might not be sold, meant in fact that the heir was named as consenting to such sales; but brothers, uncles, nephews and cousins were also commonly named where burgage inheritance was not in question and the relationship is more likely to have had commercial significance. Thus William de Len (Lynn) has a *socius* or business partner called Richard who appears also as Richard de Len;[51] names of kinsmen or names taken from the same place-name may imply a similar *societas*, for this was the most usual form of venturing capital and sharing risk. Serlo the tally-cutter was a Perth tradesman who may have been much employed in recording the business transactions of such partnerships.

The most prominent kin in Perth was that of Henry, son of Geoffrey, son of Martin;[52] Alexander II had a clerk Geoffrey, son of Martin of Perth, to whom he gave the isle of Scone and who seems to have become clerk of the liverance in 1228 and bishop of Dunkeld in 1236.[53] Only his name suggests that he was related to Henry the burgess, but the prominence of both may be due to their working together in provisioning the king's household. Henry's business took him to be a witness to charters of Thomas, Earl of Atholl, and Abraham, Bishop of Dunblane, and presumably involved buying raw materials—wool or hides—from landowners, but as in the cases of his fellows among the prominent inhabitants of Perth, we have no indication of the exact nature of his business.

His standing, however, is unquestionable; he and John de la

---

[50] French influence is also denoted by the name of Malise Treisdeneris.
[51] For this family see *Inchaffray Chrs.*, 283.
[52] *Inchaffray Chrs.*, 283. Was he perhaps the Henry who married a niece of Bishop Richard (1203–10) of Dunkeld (*Balmerino Liber*, no. 28)?
[53] Anderson, *Early Sources*, ii, 500; *Dunfermline Registrum*, nos. 138, 140.

Bataille appear in 1240 leading the burgess witnesses, but distinguished from them by the prefix *dominus*;[54] both had been provosts, but so had others not distinguished thus. The provosts are to be found among the seventeen prominent witnesses; the only apparent exception, Simon of Crieff, may disappear if he is the same person as provost Simon de Camera. Twice the provosts appear as a threesome, and presumably three (not four as in Berwick) held office each year. But sometimes a provost appears by himself and this may be explained by his particular prominence as head of the gild rather than by the absence of his fellow provosts. For Henry, son of Geoffrey, was provost in the early 1220s, and first burgess witness to a charter sealed with the burgh seal; in a very similar charter of the same decade he appears as first witness and as alderman—head, that is, of the gild. As alderman he appends the burgh seal. It is the clearest evidence we are likely to get that the offices were held conjointly, so that one provost by virtue of being alderman outranked his fellow provosts and was perhaps accorded the courtesy of *dominus* before his name, like the pretentious Lord Provosts of a later age. His fellows, in a gradual way, varying from town to town, lost the style of 'provosts' for that of 'bailies', a general term for royal officers.[55] The change in style, itself unimportant, signifies the fact that the gild, a gild of the town's patricians, their kinsmen and partners, had secured control of the choice of head of the community, and in all probability of the bailies also.

The working of the gild is documented only in the statutes of the Berwick gild, whose evidence shows such remarkable congruence with the *Leges Burgorum* that it is scarcely in doubt that the *Leges* have a Berwick provenance. Their core is of the early thirteenth century and they show that the provosts at Berwick (and probably it was also so elsewhere) were to be chosen at the Michaelmas headcourt of the burgh by the advice of the worthy men, *probi homines*, a euphemism (on the analogy of English practice) for choice by the wealthy element in the gild; the burgh court was presented with a *fait accompli* to which it gave formal approval. At some date between 1212, when it had provosts, burgesses and a common seal, and 12 April 1238, when Alexander II wrote to the mayor and provosts, the government of Berwick was taken even more firmly and formally into the hands of the oligarchy of wealth, a commune,

[54] *Inchaffray Chrs.* no. LXIX.
[55] W. Croft Dickinson, *Aberdeen Burgh Recs*, cii *n*.

which the king acknowledged in an undated document mentioning mayor, provosts and commune.[56] The mayor of 1238 was Robert de Bernham, whose gift of a net-fishing at Berwick to Melrose Abbey before January 1240 was witnessed by 'the whole commune';[57] that fishing had first been bought by his brother David, the distinguished cleric and later bishop of St Andrews, who for five years from 1235 served the king as chamberlain, the first of two ecclesiastics to hold this office in the thirteenth century, and clearly a man of many-sided abilities. If we bear in mind that Berwick was burned in 1216 and that communal rights were granted slowly and to few towns in Henry III's domains, reaching his second capital, Dublin, for the cancellation of a debt in 1229, it seems likely that the Berwick commune would belong to the 1230s rather than the 1220s. Now in August 1235, after a doubtless costly campaign in Galloway, Alexander II married off one of his sisters to Gilbert, Earl Marshal, at Berwick, with a substantial dowry, and in the same month provided a belated dowry for another sister married in 1225; whence the money? We suggest that when Alexander II asked his court that question at Berwick in 1235, Master David de Bernham stepped forward from the following of the bishop of St Andrews to propose that his brother Robert and other leading Berwick burgesses would pay substantially for a grant of communal privileges. To bring this to a conclusion the king broke with the precedent of lay chamberlains since 1165 and appointed this cleric as his chief financial officer; he got his money within three years, and perhaps at once; Berwick had its commune and Robert de Bernham his mayoralty. Many unusual circumstances are explained if it happened then and thus.

The commune of Berwick, then, did not arise as did London's in 1191 in the tensions of political revolution, but like Dublin's it was undoubtedly modelled on the institutions of the London commune, which had acquired respectability in the interval. At its head was a new official, the mayor, to be chosen each year by the burgesses and required to take an oath of fealty before the king or his chamberlain. That oath summed up one aspect of the commune—that the burgesses pursued the notion that they held the whole town in chief of the king as a collective tenure, the mayor personifying their community. The king probably rejected that view of their status—there seems to be only one royal mention of 'commune'—

[56] Raine, *North Durham*, no. LXXII; *Kelso Liber* no. 38.
[57] *Melrose Liber*, no. 178.

but accepted the tenurial implications: it is probably from this date that the ferme of Berwick was fixed in feu at 500 merks annually.

Election of the four provosts by the 'worthy men' probably antedates the grant of the mayoralty and commune; later in the thirteenth century it was admitted that controversy might arise at the election of mayor and provosts, in which case their appointment was delegated to be made 'by the oaths of twenty-four worthy men chosen to choose a person to rule the burgh'. This regulation represents the tightening bonds of oligarchy; the sworn twenty-four did not differ much if at all from the personnel of the burgh council. The institution of this council of twenty-four worthy men must certainly date from the institution of the mayoralty, even though (on English analogy) the council was probably not explicitly mentioned in the king's grant of a commune. The members were to be chosen from the 'better, more discreet and more trustworthy', to govern the burgh with the mayor and provosts, but we know of their meetings only that there was a two shilling fine for non-attendance.[58] Not long after the grant of a commune, the town brought from Simon Maunsel, a burgess, a vacant plot of land on which it built 'a house called le Berefreit' for the custody of prisoners, and presumably in which to hang the bell which henceforth, as the *Leges Burgorum* and Gild Statutes show, tolled the hours and regulated, as the town government decreed, the opening and closing of trading.[59]

It was the custom in Alexander III's Berwick for the king or his justiciar to choose a burgess as coroner to keep the pleas of the crown, that is, to attach criminals and others to appear before the justiciar. Effectively this excluded the sheriff from the town, since it put into the hands of a burgess the one shrieval function not exercised in the burgh court; Berwick could not, like London, make the local sheriff a dependent elective official, but it was just as anxious as London to tame his authority within the town so as to complete the directness of the town's relations with the king. The burgess-coroner was instituted before 1286, possibly as early as the 1230s; the evidence for a firm date is lacking.[60]

Nor, unfortunately, can we tell whether the commune of Berwick ever used the widespread oath of loyalty to the town and its franchises which elsewhere made the commune feared as a con-

58 *Statuta Gilde*, chapters 37 and 38.
59 *Calendar of Inquisitions, Miscellaneous*, ii, no. 1553.
60 For the coroner see Robert I's charter to Berwick of 1320.

spiracy (*conjuratio*) aimed against the crown's authority. It is certain that the council would be sworn to secrecy in the town's business, and likely that the burgess oath would include loyalty to the mayor and the town's liberties, but it is perhaps unlikely that other inhabitants took such an oath, except in times of social and political stress.

It is possible that one such time of stress is recorded in the earliest eighteen clauses of the Berwick gild statutes, which could just belong to the period in which the commune was granted, but more probably belong to the later 1240s.[61] To secure, through 'many bodies gathered in one place' the unity, concord, and firm and sure love to one another, which should characterise the relationships of burgesses, the mayor and worthy men of the town had drawn up these statutes of the 'gild of burgesses' lest any burgesses meeting as a sectional interest (*particulariter*) should break the freedom or statutes of the 'general gild' or in any respect produce new counsels against it.[62] All particular gilds hitherto held were abrogated; what were these gilds? It seems unlikely that Berwick had had the weavers' and fullers' gilds recognised in a number of English towns from the early twelfth century, though it certainly had had a gild merchant. It is possible that one group in that gild, 'the worthy men' had dominated the new commune, leaving the moderately prosperous discontented. It is even more likely that, in the general intensification of commercial activity in the town, other economic interests had prospered into middle-class ambitions (say as certain prestigious crafts) but were excluded from the gild and the commune by the 'worthy men' and so were driven to form their obnoxious, but short-lived, particular gilds.[63]

The new gild of burgesses was almost certainly the old gild merchant writ a little larger. If the burgesses enforced the marketing monopoly in the burgh court, as the gild they claimed all forfeitures of more than eight shillings. The entry-fee to the gild was fixed at 40s. except in the case of sons and daughters of burgess gild-brethren, so that only those of some wealth could gain admittance.

[61] *Statuta Gilde*, preamble and c. 1–17. These chapters are found in the Bute MS without the subsequent clauses found in the earlier Ayr MS, and so I take them to be a unit. The date is indicated by the mention of Robert de Bernham, knight and mayor. He was both in 1249 and had ceased to be mayor by 1251.

[62] I read *in aliquo* with *possint elidere*.

[63] It would be interesting to know why Simon Maunsel is mentioned in the preamble. He had been a provost × 1226, *Newbattle Registrum*, no. 186; was he alderman or dean of gild?

The gild undertook charitable concern for its widows and those brethren who fell on hard times but expected also to be 'remembered' in a brother's will; it would have nothing to do with a brother who 'neglected' the gild. All in all these clauses are concerned with the welfare of the gild and, as might be expected in a reconciliation of particular interests, have remarkably little economic content. Of the remaining thirty-six clauses, the last ten belong to 1281–94, the remainder presumably to c. 1250–80; in general they show an increasing preoccupation with the conflicts of economic interest between one group in the community and another.[64]

Some attempt was made to maintain standards of manufacture, but for the most part the gild was concerned with limiting 'unfair' competition among merchants and regulating conditions of manufacture and sale among craftsmen. Only a gild-brother or a stranger merchant might trade in wool, hides and cloth, and the stranger merchant might not do so in company with a gild-brother, for evidently this would be a device to escape paying the higher price demanded from stranger merchants. He might commission a freeman as his agent (presumably to the same end) but that freeman must not take a profit, on pain of a fine or loss of gild. The ordinary townsman might buy wool or hides for his own domestic needs, as much as one servant could carry, but if he bought more he was presumed to be buying for resale and infringing the gild's liberty 'to the hurt of the community'. Two particular groups who might similarly infringe the privileges of the wool merchants were the skinners and glovers, buying fleeces for the skins and shearing the wool for resale; to do so when the wool market was active was to risk being deprived of the right to exercise their crafts for a year and a day.[65]

Perhaps the most interesting clauses relate to trade in food. Herring and other fish, salt, corn, beans or peas came by sea to the wharves but must on no account be sold before the ship was tied up. Yet the fishmongers and victuallers, who were forbidden by the gild to forestall, in order to assure to each a fair share of their com-

[64] I include in the Gild Statutes after clause 29, the statutes printed as *Fragmenta Collecta*, cc. 47, 45 in *A.P.S.*, i, 729, as cc. 44, 42 in *Ancient Burgh Laws*, i, 182, 181. In interpreting these statutes I have taken the man on whom a fine of wine to the gild is imposed as a gild brother, the man on whom a money fine is imposed as a non-freeman of gild and burgh.

[65] This clause (c. XL) brings out the particular difficulty of interpreting these texts since it first seems to speak of 'any skinner or glover or *other* burgess' but then goes on to impose different penalties for craftsmen and burgess. Hence *aliquis alius burgensis* must mean 'anyone else, a burgess'.

mon monopoly, were also a commercial necessity and therefore economically strong; the ship's master would have to dispose of his (sometimes perishable) cargo in order to load another and depart as quickly as possible. The native wholesale food merchant or middleman must shift the cargo to his warehouse between sunrise and sunset, and pay up the full price of the bargain struck without delay and without haggling over a deduction for God's penny. But he must also be prepared to part with up to three-quarters of his purchase without profit to neighbours present at the sale (or with scanty profit to neighbours not present) for their domestic needs. Such a rule makes sense only if the neighbours were in the same business—and we know that for social and economic reasons in most towns men in the same line of trade often bunched together— and, having been outbid for the cargo by their fellow, were without domestic supplies. Not for them the obligation to buy in open market which seemed so healthy for others; a gild-brother should make his profit from others, not those in his own class and trade.

These regulations show the native provision merchants as an important element in the gild, steadily securing their own interests and yet still viewed with some suspicion by other elements (presumably cloth and wool merchants) in the gild, fearful of inflated food prices. Of quite a different standing were those who, waylaying country suppliers, sought to buy fish, hay, oats or cheese coming to the burgh by road; they must wait till it reached the market-place and till the market-bell was rung, for they were not merchants but regrators, hucksters (a pejorative term, one who seeks to buy wholesale in order to retail at a profit) and they were not members of the gild. They were even more ill-regarded than the flesher, who must not buy beasts on the road into the town nor outside market hours on pain of losing his craft, for unlike him they performed no useful service; if the worthy butcher abjured his axe and ceased to practise his trade, he might deal in wool and hides, and presumably be admitted gild-brother and burgess. Until then he had no say in the gild, but the gild could, and did, fix a maximum price for meat at different seasons in the burgh. Such regulations have a close relationship with others affecting the food trade included in the rather earlier *Leges Burgorum* (which for the most part deal with property and status).[66]

Both texts assumed that brewsters would be women, and the gild

[66] *Leges Burgorum*, chapters 59–66.

evidently tried to fix maximum prices for their ale and to threaten them with loss of craft for disobedience. Office holders in the burgh might not brew for sale, but otherwise there was no limitation on those who might do so, so long as a rent of fourpence was paid and so long as the dyer, flesher and tanner used different vats for brewing and for their trades![67] The baxter must make his bread to the satisfaction of the worthy men of the town and sell it at his shop window or in the market, taking for his profit as much flour per chalder as the worthy men laid down, and not witholding any bread; the price was almost certainly fixed by worthy men, and there is a suspicion that the baxter was a tied worker dependent upon a victualler for supplies of flour. There were also commercial ovens to be hired; the worthy men regulated their staff and fees, as well as those of the burgh miller. The flesher sold his meat at prices fixed by the worthy men, but he must also make himself available to slaughter animals and salt them for the burgesses at Martinmas, and if a salted carcase should rot, he must make recompense to the burgess—who fed him at the servants' table and paid him a halfpenny for each ox or five sheep prepared.

The overlap between these clauses of the *Leges Burgorum* and the gild statutes is marked, especially in the role which they assign to the 'worthy' men: the two texts agree that they ruled the town by monopolising office, and that, while they shared the market monopoly with each other, they combined to impose upon craftsmen quality and price controls which, if effective, would cut deeply into the craftsman's living. It is true that the evidence of these texts is much concerned with the provisioning crafts and has almost nothing to tell of cloth-making, although charters reveal a Berwick weaver in 1250.[68] Dealing in hides was then regulated so that a stranger merchant could sell tanned hides only in open market and not in a house, while a souter might buy only the poorest hides if he meant to do his own tanning.[69] The implication is that tanning was firmly under the control of entrepreneurs, presumably also dealers in skins and wool, who maintained in their shed tanners on piece work, and who, it is likely, also dominated the finishing crafts, such as souters and lorimers, through control of supplies. In other words, the leather

---

[67] *Leges Burgorum*, chapter 94.

[68] *Melrose Liber*, nos. 312–4.

[69] *Leges Burgorum*, chapter 16, *Statuta Gilde*, 24, 25; in the Ayr MS of these statutes c. 24 is repeated after c. 45. I understand this clause to mean that the horns shall not have grown longer than the ears.

industry was so tightly controlled by 'worthy' entrepreneurs, traders in leather, that the only aspects on which legislation was necessary were those in which their interests clashed with the wool industry. Such domination of an industry is the most likely explanation for the few words in the texts on tanning, and for their almost total silence about weaving, fulling and the rest of cloth manufacture. Far from being absent, cloth was an important industry in Berwick, the foundation of the fortunes of many of the town's 'worthy men'.

The Berwick gild was reformed in mid-century tensions but rapidly became the means whereby the wealthiest inhabitants, having excluded much of the community from burgess-ship, also persuaded the middling-prosperous gildsmen to leave them a lion's share in town government. The gild was, indeed, troubled by those of its own number making 'a conspiracy against the community to separate or scatter it' and those who revealed the secrets of the gild contrary to their oath. These clauses are associated with others limiting the choice of mayor and councillors, and suggest that within the gild the rather less 'worthy' had a less effective voice and were prepared to encourage tumult in order to reinforce their own share in the town's oligarchy. They were firmly put in their place by the 'worthy' entrepreneurs, wool, cloth and leather merchants, fishmongers and victuallers, who had complete control of marketing in the town and exercised it firmly in their own interests; the resentments which must have built up among craftsmen and, perhaps, even among the urban poor never, to our knowledge, erupted into open turmoil.

*Addendum to 1978 impression.* An unprinted charter of Roger bishop of St Andrews of 1198-9 mentions the gilds of Roxburgh and Perth as well established, that of St Andrews as new (cf. pp. 488, 491). The absence of Berwick from this charter suggests that it had more than one gild.

# 19

# COMMERCE

In the previous chapter the nature of infra-local trade was briefly discussed with particular reference to the smaller market towns. Through an examination of Perth and Berwick, a few larger towns were shown to have been centres of local production and marketing but also of inter-regional trade. Both aspects contributed to the rise of capitalist entrepreneurs whose control of their towns was apparently well established by 1200 though its early stages are obscure; since the trade of Scotland was not conducted in a vacuum it is reasonable to conclude, from agreement of the limited evidence with English and continental developments, that Scotland also saw the rising curve of demand climb more steeply in the last quarter of the twelfth century, with a corresponding rise in production of food and wool in the countryside and of manufactured goods in the towns. Urban markets enabled supply to match demand; town wealth grew and consolidated urban institutions, including gilds, by about 1200. This expansion continued until the wars of independence, though probably at a diminished rate after c. 1250.

The wider economic and social significance of the elaborate restrictions designed to protect urban monopolies of trade and manufacture is as relevant to Scotland as to other parts of Europe. It bespeaks an undeveloped technology in which the craftsmen who flourished were specialists, such as goldsmiths, making large profits in a specialised market but contributing nothing to general industrial growth. The capital employed in industrial production was small, and the groupings of craftsmen in whose hands it lay were unable to fulfil the promises of opportunity which attracted poor and landless men from overcrowded villages and rural wage-slavery to the towns; the economy of Europe displays an increasing 'saturation', an over-provision with commercial and industrial services, as the thirteenth century advanced. In fact capital

> 'was significantly employed in the processes of exchange—linking together interrelated stages of production, bulking the produce of small men for sale, and joining producers to distant markets or consumers to distant sources of supply. Men throve therefore through trade rather than through manufacture; the avenue to civic power was most conspicuously open to the merchant; and in power the merchant naturally endeavoured to utilize the instruments of civic government in order to maintain or augment his profit margins.'[1]

But because in the absence of mass markets there was no opportunity to invest in industry and even investment in trade was limited, the merchant was tempted to invest in land. The urban oligarchies of Scotland were men of property like those of York or London, speculators and rentiers not only in their towns but also in the surrounding country. The appearance of the first mayor of Berwick as a Border knight and the links among the clerical, landed and urban members of the Leicester family at Perth have already been remarked. The Hay lords of Errol made provision for members of their family in different parts of the parish: John, laird of Inchyra on the Tay, a nephew of Gilbert, John and William de Hay of Errol, was a son of Duncan son of James, a prominent Perth burgess, whose father, James son of Simon was a provost of Perth before 1200 and a tenant of the prior of St Andrews at Rossie in Inchture parish (beside Errol) before 1190. William de Hay held Aithmuir in the parish as neighbour of Roger son of Baudric whose name has an urban ring, and Richard de la Bataille, a Hay tenant near Inchmartin, was presumably a member of the prominent burgess family of Berwick and Perth.[2] Careful study of the sources would certainly reveal a similar investment in land on the part of prominent Dundee burgesses and doubtless the process could also be illustrated around Edinburgh and Berwick. The oligarchies of Scottish towns were not 'closed' in that they still threw offshoots into the country and they could not exclude the merchant thriving elsewhere and with whom they traded and who chose to establish a son or brother as agent in a Scottish town. There was social migration even if social mobility was discouraged, but the very

---

[1] E. Miller, 'The English Economy in the Thirteenth Century', *Past and Present*, xxviii (1964), 21–40; the quotation is on p. 36.
[2] *Scone Liber*, no. 118; *Spalding Miscellany*, ii, 308–10, 317–18; *R.R.S.*, ii, 261, 396–7; *Coupar Rental*, i, 338, no. 50.

importance of trade in thirteenth-century towns is a sign of the failure of the industrial base of twelfth-century society to develop (through innovation) a parallel importance.

The inter-regional trade of earlier twelfth-century Scotland was perhaps of modest dimensions and seasonal. It is revealed by royal grants to religious of exemption from ship-custom, of the right to their own ship, and of sums of money from those customs at Perth, Stirling or Edinburgh. Almost all religious other than Cistercians were endowed with town houses, and many with town fishings or mill-dues; their main purpose was to victual the monastic community, which in many cases was not provided with adequate supplies of grain for bread and ale from its own estates. Yet to plot the town houses of religious would not necessarily tell us a great deal of early inter-regional trade. Probably the largest number was in Berwick, with Perth, Roxburgh, Edinburgh and Stirling not far behind. The wealthy priory of Coldingham had only one belated toft in Haddington,[3] presumably because of its proximity to Berwick, yet other abbeys had a house in their local town. Rutherglen attracted no monastic house until Kelso Abbey acquired a toft there, presumably for the needs of Lesmahagow Priory. The northern burghs had houses of northern religious only, save that at Aberdeen the abbey of Scone, alone of the southern houses, held a toft, given by Alexander I; evidently the northern towns did not attract customers from the south, and as a whole the sources suggest that an increasingly strong pull towards a few larger ports was felt in the later twelfth century. And the more southerly the larger.

The growth of trade with England in the twelfth century must be assumed for there are few illustrations of it. By the end of King William's reign, however, English royal letters, English place-names in Scottish burgess-names, and treaty provisions all show how important the southward trade had become to Scotland. Whereas in 1174 and 1189 nothing was said of trade, in the 1209 treaty it was agreed that 'in the accustomed way the merchants of Scotland might freely go to England to carry on their business';[4] when the Scots adhered to the 1217 peace, the English government immediately opened its ports to Scottish merchants, and the English records of the 1220s have evidence that Scottish ships passed regularly to English ports and English to Scottish.

To return to the twelfth century: the references in charters to

[3] *R.R.S.*, ii, no. 369.                    [4] *Chron. Bower*, i, 526

ports indicate a fairly flourishing coastwise trade which by the 1160s took in places such as Kinghorn or Dunbar, not yet burghs. David I had granted to the canons of St Andrews a fishing and house in Berwick, freedom from toll in burghs and leave to buy corn and flour for their needs wherever they wished—but by implication in burghs, and especially in Berwick. Thus, even in the reign of David I, town provision-merchants were selling grain, which, on later evidence, would surely be imported, and when under Malcolm IV the burgesses of St Andrews (in the earliest known royal charter to a burgh) were given the freedom of the king's burgesses, 'throughout my land, at whatever ports they put in' we might conjecture that the town of St Andrews, which was plainly much involved in coastwise trade, and whose first reeve came from Berwick, had become involved in provisioning its own priory.

The importance of the victualling trade must be gauged as much from negative evidence as positive. The burgh of Ayr, founded about 1198, was important in the Irish trade, especially in importing corn from Ireland; by 1203 Cambuskenneth Abbey had a house there, presumably to facilitate the buying of grain. Other monasteries, however, went direct to the Irish ports: in 1220, 1226, 1227 and 1252 Glenluce Abbey had leave to buy in Ireland a shipload annually for seven years; Kilwinning Abbey had similar leave in 1227 and 1252.[5] Other western abbeys probably did the same—Dundrennan was buying corn in England in 1266[6]—but it is striking that there is little trace of similar purchases by the religious houses of eastern Scotland, where grain was imported from England by sea to the larger towns not by monastic agents but by merchants of the two kingdoms. King John of England gave permission to Arbroath Abbey to trade in England quit of tolls, in 1207, but he also gave his protection to the merchants of Perth and Dundee, whose ships would carry the goods of the abbey; professional merchants were the past and the future of inter-regional trade.

A rank of flourishing towns second to Berwick and Perth existed by the late twelfth century: Edinburgh, Stirling, Aberdeen and Inverness. Edinburgh is the most enigmatic of these. The figure of its ferm in 1328, 52 merks (cf. Berwick 500 merks, Aberdeen 320 merks), suggests that it was then small and unimportant. But this

[5] *Cal. Docs. Scot.*, i, nos. 765, 933, 974, 982, 1889.
[6] *Cal. Docs. Scot.*, i, no. 2414.

figure must have been fixed artificially low because the importance
of Edinburgh is attested by its being given feu ferm status and by its
exports of wool and hides, then on the large scale of Berwick or
Aberdeen. The ferme included the port of Leith, which permitted
the business men on the tail of the crag to develop inter-regional as
well as local trade. In the pages of one collection of monastic charters after another the reader will find Peter, Edward and Thomas of
Restalrig feuing out tofts of land at Leith to the shrewd religious;
the rise of this commercial settlement at the mouth of the Water of
Leith began in the twelfth century and continued till the mid-
thirteenth when a merchant with a cloth-working surname, Tenteman, could describe himself as 'merchant of Leith'. Parallel in a
much smaller way was the rise of Blackness as a port for landlocked
Linlithgow.[7] Cattle and herring were shipped from Inverness to
Leith and wine imported to Edinburgh through that port in the
1260s, all for the needs of the king whose parliaments there
demanded special victualling.[8]

The thirteenth-century treatise on customs provides for imports
of corn, peas, beans and salt 'to Berwick or other town' by partnerships which might be English, continental, or native. Such imports
come first in the treatise, and the English record gives them equal
prominence during the brief periods when licences to export from
England were sought. In 1226, John of Dunwich was shipping corn
from Sandwich to William de la Bataille of Berwick; Hugh fitz Odo,
a Scottish merchant, and Godfrey Boxeneto and Geoffrey fitz Peter
were shipping corn to Scotland. Alexander of Dunwich was shipping to Scotland barley and beans in 1225 and with William, son
of Lambin, and Richard of Dieppe, corn, wine and salt in 1229.[9]
In all these cases except the first the port of departure was Lynn, at
which Scottish vessels were to be found in fairly large numbers
although their tunnage was small.[10] Lynn was the focus for shipping
the production of the cornfields of Midland England and East
Anglia, and in the thirteenth century it attracted the ships and
investment of London cornmongers who were probably also
involved in the trade to Scotland. Nonetheless, the surname Lynn at
Perth indicates that in the twelfth century the corn (and associated

[7] *Newbattle Registrum*, no. 48; *Holyrood Liber*, no. 41.
[8] *Exch. Rolls*, i, 13, 19, 25.
[9] *Cal. Docs. Scot.*, i, nos. 907, 932–7, 1044. See also nos. 850, 877.
[10] *Cal. Docs. Scot.*, i, no. 858.

victual) trade with Scotland was already growing and that it involved native as well as English merchants.

Probably the largest single customers for imported grain were the monastic houses, since they had large numbers of mouths to feed domestically. Melrose Abbey, perhaps the largest wool producer in the country, would have much wool to send to Berwick to pay for its purchases there. That the abbey's carts rumbled down Tweed-side to the port is indicated by their obtaining from the king a clear declaration that one night's free grazing for draught beasts with carts was the ancient custom of the countryside; documents of New-battle Abbey confirm this assertion and also show that convent sending carts to Berwick, a striking comment on how that town dominated the trade of southern Scotland, since the abbey was much closer to Leith.[11] But the clearest evidence comes from the extent of Kelso Abbey's lands made in 1300. At Redden the abbey's husbandmen were liable to take a pack-horse to Berwick weekly in the summer and return with three bolls of corn, or two of salt or one and a half of coal; in winter the loads were lighter, and in the autumn they were not required to go at all. At Bowden only one journey was required annually, and carriage of peats was required of the husbandmen instead.[12] There is no provision for the carriage of wool to Berwick, and we may presume that this was the respon-sibility of the purchasing merchant.

The *Customs* treatise also throws particular emphasis on salt, which was certainly purchased at Berwick by landowners and sent from there to Roxburgh.[13] Doubtless it was used to salt meat and fish; the catch of white fish landed at Berwick was worth 200 merks annually. Herring—by which salted herring were meant—were also a bulky but valuable import. Almost certainly they came from Yarmouth and Norway, which exported large quantities to England; this trade perhaps brought to Berwick the family of Norris (the Norwegian). The custom on a thousand herring was a penny, the same as that on a chalder of corn, meal or salt, but a further penny was payable on each horse-load of herring taken out of the town. We meet them at their destination in the toun of Fishwick, where each husbandman and cottar was given a meal of two loaves and three herring for a day's boonwork for the prior of

11 *Melrose Liber*, no. 309; *Newbattle Registrum*, nos. 202–6.
12 *Kelso Liber*, 456, 461, 462.
13 *Exch. Rolls*, i, 30.

Coldingham;[14] whatever multiplier we may use for all the husbandmen and cottars in Lowland Scotland and for all the days of the year
on which they found their own meals, the annual total of imported
herring is more likely to have been well over a million than a few
hundred thousand.[15]

Other imported foods were onions and garlic, pepper, cumin,
ginger, almonds and rice, of which the most important were probably pepper and cumin. They occur so frequently as commodities
in which rents must be paid that the demand for them to season
meat must have been great.

Native cloth manufacture brought imports of dyestuffs, of
which woad was particularly important, attracting a custom of 22
pence at entry and 25 pence on leaving the town or 18 pence on
woad taken away unsold after Martinmas. In contrast with this the
customs on brasil, on alum and barrels of ashes and on teazles, were
comparatively light. Manufactured goods also appear in the
customs lists: pans, cauldrons, locks, keys, iron-bound chests, and
also the raw materials, timber and iron; hides are included among
customable exports, but shoemakers' leather was evidently imported.

The thirteenth-century northerner might choose his drink from
water or ale, and doubtless he consumed a deal of both. But for his
betters the monotony of this fare was broken each year by wines,
expensive because always imported and because the vintage lasted
only a few months before turning sour, but, like many expensive
consumer goods, much in demand for dietary reasons as well as
those of social prestige. As early as the mid-twelfth century wine
was being imported to Berwick for the uses of Jedburgh Abbey, at
whose town house it was poured from the casks in which it had been
shipped, presumably into skins for carriage overland.[16] In the thirteenth century, French wine was imported to Scotland, both from
Normandy and Maine and, of growing importance as the century
progressed, from Gascony through the great wine port of Bordeaux,
where by 1246 the merchants of Perth had had debts, doubtless
incurred in wine purchases.[17] It has been shown that wine merchants were so important an element within the patriciate of
London aldermen that there was what amounted to a 'patriciate of

[14] *Coldingham Correspondence*, p. lxxxvii.
[15] Herring may have been salted in Berwick; *Cal. Docs. Scot.,* i, no. 901.
[16] *R.R.S.*, i, no. 278.
[17] *Cal. Docs. Scot.*, i, nos. 331, 881, 935, 1044, 1694.

vintners'. Some at least extended their activities to sell in Scotland directly or through Scottish merchants, of whom the best documented is John Rufus of Berwick. In 1224 one of his ships was arrested at Sandwich along with various French ships, but ordered to be released along with its cargo of 'the wine of William Hardel', a London alderman and mayor at the time of Magna Carta who involved himself heavily in the Gascon wine trade; Rufus himself was on another of his ships when she was arrested at Southampton.[18] A number of Scottish cargoes were arrested in England at this time and in 1242 because during the war with France cargoes of French vessels were impounded;[19] it is likely that a major part of their imports to Scotland took the form of wine. The statutes of the Berwick gild, and the regulations at Perth and elsewhere about taverns, show how regular and valuable wine imports were, though there is not a great deal to tell how large a part Scottish merchants played in bringing the wine either from France or from the merchants of southern England.

The most important single customer in both England and Scotland was the royal household. In summer 1263 Alexander III bought 178 tuns (some at least Gascon) for £450 and in 1264 (when the grape harvest was presumably poor) 67 tuns for £374;[20] wine was carted from Perth to Kinclaven Castle for him[21] and doubtless the household arranged for a similar distribution of his other wine purchases at Aberdeen, Leith and Ayr.[22] By 1284 the king's council had contracted for a supply of wine with John Mazun, a merchant of Bordeaux, but the arrangement proved unsatisfactory and Mazun was imprisoned, claiming that he was owed over 200 merks. The government responded that the money it had offered in settlement had been claimed by a creditor of Mazun, whose wine business clearly had some ramifications in Scotland.[23] What the king expected in his cup was desired by an ever-widening circle of his subjects; wine upon the table was better living and required a higher income level of those who aspired to it. Hence wine was a stimulant

[18] *Rot. Litterarum Clausarum*, ii, 13b; Williams, *Medieval London*, 64; *Cal. Docs. Scot.*, i, nos. 883, 884. Could Rufus perhaps be a member of the Redbeard family at Perth?

[19] The ships captured by King John at Berwick in 1216 included one or two from France; *Rot. Litterarum Clausarum*, i, 254, 259, 260.

[20] *Exch. Rolls*, i, 10.

[21] *Exch. Rolls*, i, 3.

[22] *Exch. Rolls*, i, 12, 25, 28.

[23] *Cal. Docs. Scot.*, ii. nos. 252, 264.

to agrarian and pastoral expansion and to the growth of the Scottish economy.

The same significance has already been suggested for the making of good cloth. The finest cloths, however, were imported from Flanders and Italy, and in concluding this survey of imports we may return to the impact of such imports upon urban society, which strove hard to exclude competition from foreign (fine cloth) and rural (coarse cloth) looms in the early thirteenth century. The struggle against increasing demand is difficult enough for modern governments; with thirteenth-century resources it was hopeless. By the second half of the thirteenth century, population increase had greatly expanded the lower end of the market for cloth, while increased prosperity brought greater expectations at the upper end; the monopolistic claims of urban cloth merchants were under a double assault. First, Flemish high-quality cloth production reached its zenith in the thirteenth century; thanks to mass-production and advanced commercial techniques this end of the Scottish market could be supplied effectively and more cheaply from Flanders than by the class-ridden and restrictive native urban industry. Secondly, the same urban monopolies may have directed the attention of entrepreneurs to the opportunities of unrestricted development presented by the native rural industry where rough cloth had always been produced. In the late thirteenth century capital was invested in a technical advance, the water-driven mechanical fulling (or waulk) mill in the countryside, which implied not only that weavers were already nearby, but also that they were, or rather their landlord was, moving over to the production of better finished cloth.[24] It is not to be concluded that cloth production in Scottish towns necessarily declined in the later thirteenth century, but only that it failed to expand at its previous rate or perhaps at all.

Sales of cloth from all sources, native and foreign, however, probably continued to increase; some towns encouraged, and benefited from, this by the holding of fairs, periods of a week or more during which special protection and privilege was given to those doing business in the town. All restrictions upon those with whom a burgess might trade were then lifted, no man might be arrested, save

[24] The earliest waulk mill I have noted is at Kincreich in Angus, by *c.* 1260, belonging to Coupar Angus Abbey; *Coupar Charters*, no. LX. On this subject see E. Miller on 'The English Textile Industry', *Economic History Review*, xviii (1965), 64–82, and the literature cited there.

for heinous crime, not even a fugitive neyf, and no poinds (distraint) might be taken in a civil action; in other words, during fair time the trader coming to the town would not be troubled with the rigours of the law, whether justly or frivolously.[25]

Early fairs are more elusive in Scotland than historians have sometimes pretended. They were granted to Glasgow about 1190, Dumbarton in 1226, Ayr in 1260 and Aberdeen in 1273. There was also, certainly, a thirteenth-century fair at Roxburgh, Haddington, Lanark, Stirling, Dundee and Montrose, but there is no evidence of a fair at Inverness, Perth, St Andrews or Edinburgh. Berwick presents a special problem, since in 1302 Edward I granted a fair from 3 May to 24 June, while in 1319 Robert I set the period as from Easter to 29 September (half the year), but only the first forty days for foreign merchants. The Scottish king explicitly claimed to be restating pre-1286 privileges, but Edward I's charter, which makes no such claim, also seems at many points to be restating the findings of an inquest into ancient customs. But the fair comes towards the end of both charters (which are agreed on the market days) and may be a new grant; the silence of Berwick's gild statutes about a fair (whereas the market is mentioned) perhaps suggests that there was none in the thirteenth century. If this was also true generally of the other larger east-coast towns—and the very late (1273) grant to Aberdeen seems confirmation that hitherto it had no fair—then we are not dealing with an ubiquitous feature of urban history.

Despite the distance between the towns, the Dumbarton charter granted the customs used at Roxburgh fair and so implied that it was the most significant in Scotland; agreements to make payment at that fair confirm that it was an occasion of note, attracting folk from the surrounding country.[26] The town lay on an important land route from England to Edinburgh, and the fair may have arisen during the English occupation (1175–89) as an occasion when English merchants came to buy beasts, leather or wool for shipment through Berwick, from breeders in southern Scotland. The early part of the *Leges Burgorum* tell us that anyone identifying a stolen object at a fair must take the 'owner' of it to the bailies to name his lord and his home and to give a pledge to answer the claim to it;[27] although the object is *rem* not *catalla*, it is assumed that the 'owner' will be a

[25] *Leges Burgorum*, chapters 3, 54, 86, 88.
[26] *Kelso Liber*, nos. 34, 133.
[27] *Leges Burgorum*, chapter 87.

country dweller, probably a peasant. When Sir James Douglas lured
out the garrison of Douglas Castle in 1307 it was with fourteen men,
apparently taking pack horses (with bogus packs of victual) to
Lanark fair.[28] But they might have carried wood or yarn which was
sold in towns without restrictions on who might buy only in fair-
time.[29] At Stirling fair, horses of sufficient quality were to be had
for a valet of Edward I to send his squire to make purchases.[30] The
fair, then, was an occasion when local rural produce might be sold
to any buyer; it was a convenience to both buyers and sellers to
know when the other would congregate at this or that town, and the
town did well enough from customs at the gates and tron dues. The
east-coast ports had no difficulty in attracting merchants from elsewhere, and much difficulty in restricting their competitive activities
in the landward areas. In Perth or Berwick there was little point to a
fair, especially since the movements of overseas merchants were
governed by wind and tide and not the calendar. But trading in
beasts, which usually travelled on foot, was best organised in towns
which did not divert them over needless miles, and in short periods.
Hence the fair, perhaps, had something of the character of the
eighteenth-century cattle tryst, at least in its origins. A French writer
has drawn the same conclusion on much fuller evidence but for
circumstances not essentially different: 'The fairs were primarily
cattle, wool and leather fairs, whose occurrence was regulated by
the pastoral calendar, some taking place in the autumn [cf. Stirling,
8 September] and some in the spring [cf. Lanark, Whitsuntide].
The conditions of animal husbandry in fact forced small farmers to
sell their animals at the first of these seasons and to buy others at the
second; the growth of exchange and the requirements of traders
encouraged, particularly in the country, activities which were outside and parallel to the cultivation of cereals.'[31]

Thus fairs were a useful instrument to encourage the growth of
western towns, Glasgow, Dumbarton, Ayr, which were remote from
the eastern centres of foreign mercantile activity. But however
general it was—and there must be some uncertainty on the point—

[28] Barbour, *Bruce*, ed. Mackenzie, 145.
[29] *Leges Burgorum*, chapter 66.
[30] *Cal. Docs. Scot.*, ii, no. 78.
[31] Georges Duby, *Rural Economy and Country Life in the Medieval West*
(London, 1968), 134; Roxburgh fair was held about 25 July, those of Glasgow,
Dumbarton, Ayr and Aberdeen began on 6 July, 24 June, 24 June and Trinity
(which falls between 17 May and 20 June).

the thirteenth-century fair was also, doubtless, an occasion for the diffusion by foreign merchants of fine cloths, soft pelts and rare spices which raised the living standards somewhat, and the expectations even more, of at least some sections of the community.

The foundation of the inter-regional trade of Scotland was the export of hides and of wool to feed the looms of the industrial cities of Flanders which lived almost wholly by the manufacture of cloth; Flemish textile production increased throughout the twelfth and thirteenth centuries, though the fastest rate of growth probably came between 1150 and 1250. By the 1180s Scotland was already well integrated into the supply lines for raw wool, which must have been the 'goods' referred to by Philip of Alsace, Count of Flanders, in the exemption from tolls which he granted to Melrose Abbey: 'moreover', his writ says, 'if any dissension arise between merchants of England and Flanders, let no one dare to lay a hand on the brethren nor take their goods as pledge.'[32] The document may be related to the dislocation caused to the wool trade by the French king's seizure of Artois, including St Omer. If this indeed sent the monks to sell their wool in Flanders, then the writ implies that they would be found in the company of English merchants, although the wool would presumably have been shipped through Berwick. It may be that during the English occupation of Berwick (1175–89) numbers of English merchants (whose home towns are found later as burgess names) settled there and became involved in the export of wool. A brother or brethren of Melrose in Flanders would have travelled as supercargo, 'in charge of the abbot's money', as Henry III's licences to Melrose and Coupar abbeys put it in 1224,[33] and in 1225 and 1230 English licences were issued to a merchant and a monk to export wool and other merchandise to Flanders.[34] The linking of Melrose and Coupar in 1224 and 1225 suggests that the Cistercians may have had a system of collecting the wool for export from these and other houses in stores at Berwick and Perth, under the control of these abbeys. The need for such licences in 1224 and 1225, when foreign goods were liable to arrest in England, points plainly to regular exports on these lines, going back probably to the 1180s and earlier.

A similar danger of arrest in 1229–30 shows Melrose (but not

[32] *Melrose Liber*, nos. 14–5.
[33] *Cal. Docs Scot.*, i, no. 880.
[34] *Cal. Docs. Scot.*, i, nos. 904, 1086.

Coupar) still chartering a ship; a precious indication of cargo is given in a safe conduct of 1229 to Gervase le Cordwainer, a powerful London alderman, shipping wool and other merchandise from Berwick to London, probably intending the wool for Flanders, hides for London or Gascony, whence came the wine in which Gervase traded to London, Berwick and elsewhere.[35] Such safe conducts became rarer as the century advanced and in any case rarely mentioned the nature of merchandise for the obvious reason that they were granted in advance of the voyage. In 1242, however, the outbreak of Anglo-French war led to the arrest at Yarmouth of 28 sacks of Scottish wool and 17 of English, and at Dunwich of 41 sacks of Scottish wool and 15 dacres of hides, and to the recovery of six sacks of Scottish wool already sold to buyers at Ipswich. These goods belonged not to English or Scottish merchants but only to merchants of the king of France, presumably return cargoes after delivering wine to Scotland; William of Arras, merchant of Berwick, recovered his hides from arrest (that is from a French ship) at Yarmouth.[36] Clearly equal or much larger amounts of Scottish wool and hides must have reached East Anglia in ships from England and Scotland and the Low Countries, but these are revealed only when misfortune struck the ship, as it did that of Bernard de Alverstone, a Scot from Berwick, who, in 1229, claimed seven sacks of wool at Sandwich, asserting that they had been taken by piracy. In the same year Robert Stater, a burgess of Berwick who became mayor in 1255, had a last and a half of hides and three sacks of wool arrested at Romney, as part of the cargo of an English ship. By 1253 he had his own ship, for it was driven ashore by foul wind in Lincolnshire and plundered.[37] The part cargoes were ventured by one member of a *societas*; Stater's full cargo of 1253 is not described, but in 1273 we know what was in a ship going from Aberdeen to St Omer: 56½ sacks of wool, 5½ dacres of hides, 150 salmon (a characteristic Aberdeen export) deerhides, timber and lambskins.[38] The most valuable item was undoubtedly the wool, destined directly for Flanders.

It is particularly difficult to assess the part played by Flemish

[35] *Patent Rolls, 1225–32*, 261; Williams, *Medieval London*, 64, especially notes 4 and 5, 67.

[36] *Close Rolls, 1237–42*, 462, 466; *Cal. Pat. Rolls, 1232–47*, 303; *Cal. Docs. Scot.*, i, no. 1594.

[37] *Cal. Docs. Scot.*, i, nos. 1042, 1051, 1915, 1950, 2011.

[38] *Cal. Docs. Scot.*, ii, no. 9.

ships and merchants in this trade. It is likely that they were most active in the twelfth century, when there are virtually no documents to mention their voyages. In 1213 an English protection to go to Berwick was granted for a ship of Bruges, then the centre of the Flemish wool market; it was later displaced by Douai—and William of Douai, who held land in Berwick, was forbidden to go to Scotland in 1244, while the name of a merchant of Douai in 1246, John Bataill, suggests another connection with Scotland.[39] Later the Douai merchant, Hugh Bonbrook, was trading to—and presumably from—Scotland in 1268 and was described as the queen of Scotland's merchant in 1271.[40] It is likely that Henry Curwen, who was a merchant in Flanders and a man of affairs employed by Alexander III and the count of Flanders, had mercantile roots in Berwick.[41]

By 1296 the Flemish merchants had a place of business, the Red Hall, in the Seagate of Berwick. Monastic gossip put their number at thirty and claimed that they held it on condition of defending it at all times against the English king;[42] this most unlikely tale is perhaps a garbled version of conditions like those of the London steelyard where German merchants had a self-governing community whose members, forbidden social intercourse with native English, each kept a suit of armour for use in case of need.

The share of Flemish ships in the North Sea wool trade had declined markedly in the second half of the thirteenth century, and the Red Hall is therefore more likely to have its origins in the earlier part of the century. Whatever the true date, it is no less puzzling than that of the entry of German merchants into Scottish trade. In the early fourteenth century, merchants of Cologne and Hamburg were certainly active in carrying wool and hides to Flanders, and had a White Hall in the Seagate of Berwick—a name which may imply coexistence with Flemish Red Hall in the thirteenth century. But apart from one widow of Cologne in Berwick, there really is no strong evidence that they displaced Flemings from the Scottish trade before 1300 as they certainly did from English and Baltic trade.[43]

[39] *Rot. Litterarum Patentium*, I, i, 106; *Cal. Docs. Scot.*, i, no. 1634; *Cal. Liberate Rolls, 1245–51*, 91.

[40] *Cal. Docs. Scot.*, i, nos. 2496, 2615.

[41] *Révue Belge de Philologie et d'Histoire*, xxxiv (1956), 390–1.

[42] *Chron. Guisborough*, 275.

[43] James W. Dilley, 'German Merchants in Scotland, 1297–1327', *Scottish Hist. Rev.*, xxvii (1948), 142–55.

Almost as obscure is the entry of Italian merchants into the Scottish wool market, exporting to Flanders and Italy. It seems likely that papal taxation of the church, which brought Italians into the heart of English commerce from the mid-thirteenth century, would do the same in Scotland. Italians, it is argued in another chapter (above, p. 429), were active in the Scottish wool trade in the late thirteenth century but they did not dominate it. That fact must lie behind the extraordinary (and surely garbled) tale of Bower that the Lombards offered to Alexander III to build 'royal cities' at Queensferry, near Cramond or elsewhere if they were given special privileges.[44]

One of the most important factors in the development of twelfth- and thirteenth-century trade to Scotland was undoubtedly improvements in shipbuilding, including the introduction of the stern rudder, which greatly increased the size and carrying capacity of vessels. Early in the thirteenth century, Scottish vessels in English ports were expected to be small, taking fewer than ten horses, but the evidence of boat fragments of the thirteenth century found at Bergen suggests that a wealthy merchant could shift substantial bulk in the broad beamed vessels then used in the North Sea and Bay of Biscay; likewise the supply lines to armies in the Edwardian occupation of Scotland were maintained by large ships evidently well familiar with the routes to Berwick, Leith, Blackness and Perth.[45]

This increase in the scale of inter-regional commerce was accompanied by a parallel rise in rents, and apparently prices, in the thirteenth century. The survey of part of Berwick made about 1297 shows that burgages in the Hidegate paid rent varying in amount from half a merk (6s. 8d. or 33p.) to eight merks, or nearly £6, whereas holdings in the Seagate, many but not all of which were *placea vacua*, unbuilt-on, paid rents usually below 4s. (or 20p.). The abbot of Jedburgh had two holdings in Highgate, each paying half a merk, one with two shops, the other with six cellars and solars (stone vaults with timbered rooms above); on the other hand, Michael Spicer paid £1 for two cellars and a solar. In these variations in rents there were doubtless factors which cannot now be evaluated: the size of the holding and its commercial 'desirability'

---

[44] *Chron. Bower*, ii, 130. I amend 'spiritual' to 'special'.
[45] *A History of Seafaring*, ed. George F. Bass (1972); chapter 8, 'The Vikings and the Hanseatic merchants: 900–1450' by Ole Crumlin-Pedersen. This book is superbly illustrated.

(proximity to markets cutting transport costs); but the largest factor is likely to have been the size and condition of the buildings.[46] The description, 'cellar and solar' must cover as much variation as the modern house-agent's descriptive vocabulary, but there was certainly a free market for rents in thirteenth-century towns so that they would respond to economic forces; sometimes the town rentier or speculator burned his fingers and revealed how far the town had come from the ideal envisaged by the *Leges Burgorum* of each burgess in his burgage paying sixpence to the king.[47] Where rents were high it seems likely that this was a result of cost-push (in building trades), since the several large unbuilt-on tofts argue against a demand-pull explanation. If so, this is more likely to have been the situation in the later thirteenth century than in the late twelfth or earlier thirteenth, when the sources suggest a greater rate of expansion, for (an impressionistic judgement) rents seem to have risen steeply before about 1250 but much more slowly thereafter.

Expansion in both local and inter-regional trade required expansion in the means of exchange. The debts which the crown contracted to wine and cloth merchants, and which merchants were accused of leaving unpaid in foreign ports, point to some use of credit facilities, and possibly of discounting, but most trade, at least in Scotland, was for cash, that is, for silver pennies. And here the Scottish crown remained curiously conservative, even backward. The number of mints was small—Berwick, Roxburgh and Edinburgh at the end of David I's reign, with Berwick evidently the most active. Under William a mint was opened at Perth, apparently to compensate for the closing down of the other three, but many coins were isued without mint-names and were possibly struck at places like Stirling, Selkirk or Peebles. After 1189 the Roxburgh mint was especially active for a period, with Perth and Edinburgh also issuing coins and in the first half of the thirteenth century the pre-eminence of Roxburgh continued. Moreover, coins bearing the name of King William continued to be struck long after his death and only about 1240 or later were dies made in the name of Alexander II. During a whole century it seems that not only was the number of coins struck limited, but that the mints had only a partial coincidence with known centres of commercial importance, in that Berwick for a long period, and Perth apparently for some decades, lost their

[46] Stevenson, *Documents*, no. CCCCXVIII.
[47] *Aberdeen Registrum*, ii, 278–9.

mints. It is not impossible that until the 1230s mints were active only when the king recoined his own money income or part of it, and hence that mints were at a limited number of royal centres.

About 1240, however, with the first coins of Alexander II, the mint-name Berwick reappears (though still rare) and it probably struck all the coins for his son's first year. Then, in 1250, the coinage was reformed to conform with English long-cross pennies and for the first time earlier issues seem to have been withdrawn on a large scale and reminted. The first stage showed mints at Berwick and Roxburgh, Perth and Aberdeen, with Ayr, Glasgow and Lanark in the west, but by 1265 some sixteen mints had been active. Some of these were doubtless temporary, to carry out the recoinage, and as the reign advanced Berwick became more and more important in the issuing of what was evidently designed to be a coinage for Scotland in the same sense in which the English crown provided an English coinage. There was a further recoinage towards the end of Alexander III's reign which showed the same characteristics: a number of temporary mints but eventual concentration at Berwick.[48] Conclusions can be only tentative, but it does seem that a plentiful Scottish coinage did not exist until the later thirteenth century.

The predominance of English coins and the scarcity of Scottish ones among hoards concealed in Scotland, mostly in the troubled years after 1296, confirm the nature of Scotland's interregional trade—it was an extension of the interregional trade of England and depended greatly upon movements in London commercial circles. On the other hand after 1250, when Scottish coins became plentiful (presumably often recoined from English sterlings) they were concealed in fair numbers, though still as a tiny fraction of the total, in hoards at Brussels and Colchester, to show that commercial links were strongest with England and the Low Countries, while the growth of a pre-eminent mint at Berwick confirms that this was indeed the principal port of Scotland.

[48] Ian H. Stewart, *The Scottish Coinage* (1966), and his article 'Scottish Mints' in *Mints, Dies and Currency*, ed. R. A. G. Carson (1971).

TABLE 3

A Sample of Coin Hoards

| Site of Hoard | Date | Total Coins | Scottish | English | Low countries |
|---|---|---|---|---|---|
| Aberdeen | 1324 × | 12 000 | 123 | 11 414 | 133 |
| Ayr | × 1300 | 155 | 5 | 143 | 0 |
| Cleuchhead (Kirkcudb.) | c. 1307 | 155 | 0 | 0 | 138 |
| Galston (Ayr) | c. 1300 | 231 | 0 | 7 | 224 |
| Kirkcudbright | c. 1300 | 84 | 1 | 7 | 76 |
| Mellendean (Roxb.) | c. 1296 | 890 | 65 | 704 | 103 |
| Penicuik (Midlo.) | c. 1320 | 273 | 7 | 257 | 1 |
| Renfrew | c. 1320 | 674 | 151 | 479 | 1 |
| Brussels | c. 1264 | c. 150 000 | c. 1750 | 80 000+ | ? |
| Colchester | c. 1260 | 10 926 | 168 | 10 572 | 0 |

[Based on J. D. A. Thompson, *Inventory of British Coin Hoards, 600–1500* (1956). For Renfrew see *British Numismatic Journal*, xxxv (1966), 128–47 and for Brussels see *ibid*, xxix (1958–9), 91–7].

# 20

## A GREAT CHIEF AND
## SUFFICIENTLY AMBITIOUS:[1]
## ALEXANDER II, 1214–49

When Alexander II was placed upon the royal stone at Scone on 6 December 1214 he was sixteen years and three months old but had shared in royal authority for at least the last two years of his father's life. His personality, like that of any medieval king, is elusive, but his ability seems to have been above average. His reign was by no means peaceful, yet it would be difficult to regard it as other than a period of consolidation of royal authority during which the outlying provinces were brought under the control of the crown and one major problem in foreign relations was solved.

Probably within weeks of his accession the king was told of the northern rising of mac William and macHeth, doubtless designed to take advantage of the inexperience and lack of authority of a new king. Fortunately, the rising was quelled on 15 June 1215 by the northerner, Farquhar,[2] for on the same day six hundred miles to the south King John set his seal in agreement to the Articles put forward by his barons. Among his many concessions were two to individuals, the prince of Wales and the king of Scots; after a few days' discussion these promises emerged in Magna Carta in a fuller form: 'we shall act to King Alexander concerning his sisters, the return of his hostages, his liberties, his right, according to the form in which we shall act to our other barons of England unless it ought to be otherwise by the charters which we have from King William his father; and this shall be by judgment of his equals in our court'.

---

[1] Anderson, *Early Sources*, ii, 539 from Haakon's saga.
[2] p. 197 above.

The king's sisters do not appear in the Articles and neither document makes mention of the large sum of money paid for 'his right' in 1209. But these promises refer to other undertakings in Magna Carta—to give up hostages, to restore those disseised of lands without lawful judgement of peers—and makes it plain that they applied to King Alexander as an English baron unless in the judgement of other English barons King John could show written evidence under King William's seal why they should not.[3] The Scottish hostages seem to have been released but in the other matters nothing was done as England drifted into the civil war which broke out in September.

King Alexander was inactive in the months before June although the baronial leaders, Eustace de Vescy and Robert de Ros, were married to illegitimate daughters of his father. He could not ignore the concessions they had obtained for him and the mutual dependence so created. On 19 October 1215 the Scots laid siege to the castle of Norham, persisting (as King William had notably failed to do) for forty days. On 22 October the barons of Northumbria did homage to Alexander, and it is likely that the twenty-five English barons charged to see to the execution of the Great Charter had already adjudged the three northern counties to him.[4] Seisin was given by Eustace de Vescy, and the staff used in the ceremony carefully deposited in the king's treasury.[5] But at the end of November Alexander abandoned the siege of Norham; of the great strengths of northern England only Carlisle was in his hands. There was already a price to be paid. Perhaps later, but more probably at this time, the English barons undertook to subsidise King Alexander's army, for subsequently they had to present excuses for failure to pay;[6] the sum of money must have been large, probably running to several thousand marks.

[3] W. Stubbs, *Select Charters*, (9th edn. 1929), 290 c. 46; 300, c. 59. For the relevant 'form in which we shall act to our other barons of England' see Magna Carta cc. 6, 40, 49, 52.

[4] Magna Carta c. 60, *securitas pacis*. So far as I can tell this was the only instance of c. 60 being put formally into effect.

[5] There were numerous documents from the barons adjudging the three northern counties to Alexander II in the Scottish treasury 1282-96; *A.P.S.*, i, 108-12. The staff is *ibid*, 112. The only discussion of these events which is at all aware of King Alexander's existence is J. C. Holt, *The Northerners*, 131-5.

[6] *A.P.S.*, i, 108: *Item excusatio nunciorum regis Scocie facta per quosdam magnates Anglie et de alia securitate facta per eosdem super quadam summa pecunie deponenda ad Templum Lundonie.*

In December King John turned his attention to the north and on 4 January 1216 was at York. On 11 January the rebellious barons of Yorkshire, in fear of their king, did homage to Alexander II at Melrose. The wording of the chronicle suggests that they had come to implore the king's aid and protection and found themselves faced with the demand for homage, fealty and sureties which they were in no position to refuse. If the initiative came from the Scottish king it would seem that he had little to learn from John when it came to exploiting a favourable situation. Moreover, we should not return too firm an answer to the question whether Alexander was to hold the northern counties of the English king or as part of Scotland; doubtless he would turn any situation to his own best advantage.

He had little time to ponder these problems, for in mid-January King John entered Scotland, taking Berwick and advancing to Haddington and Dunbar. All three towns, together with Roxburgh, were burned within ten days and without interference from King Alexander. John had sworn that he would 'make the fox-cub enter his lair', and had indeed recovered all the northern counties, including Carlisle, and driven Alexander into his own kingdom, where he hastened to gather an army, perhaps at Edinburgh. Within weeks the 'red-headed lad'[7] had left his lair and launched a counter-raid into Cumberland which was as indecisive as King John's attack had been. During the following months many English barons submitted to their king, while the hard core of rebels continually urged Prince Louis, heir to the French king, to come to England as claimant to the throne. On 21 May he landed in Kent and the authority which John had recovered in the north vanished rapidly.

To the historian of England the events of 1215-17 present many problems; little consideration, however, has been given to the reasons for choosing Louis rather than Alexander II as future king of England. Alexander II was an ally who had actively helped the baronial cause and it may be thought that his acceptance of homage from the barons of Yorkshire showed him not unwilling to become ruler of England. In turning to a French prince the English barons

---

[7] The fox cub occurs in two versions: that he would be hunted from his lairs by John's invasion of Scotland (Anderson, *Scottish Annals*, 332 from Matthew Paris); that he would be driven from the northern English counties into his lair (Anderson, *Early Sources*, ii, 408 from the Histoire des Ducs de Normandie).

may have been showing their distrust of Alexander's motives and of their ability to influence him. More probably, they regarded him as ruler of a kingdom which had less to offer than France, whose king might be prepared to restore the Norman fiefs which some had lost when John lost the Duchy. It may be significant of English distrust of Celtic levies that in July King Alexander summoned his host from the southern parts of his kingdom, while from the 'the Scots' —and it is a monk of Melrose who calls them so—he took payments in place of service. It may be that knights from north of Forth served, but clearly native levies of footmen were not called thence to the host, perhaps because they would not be helpful in the king's purpose of securing the northern English counties and serving Prince Louis.

On 8 August 1216 the town of Carlisle fell to King Alexander, the castle at an unknown later date. From there he marched across to Barnard Castle and must then have sent a large part of his army home, because he now moved rapidly south along with the northern barons to join Louis at Dover. The mounting cost of war was making itself felt; to pay his way there the king had to sell hides belonging to his burgesses, perhaps seized in his 'great necessity', and he must have hoped for a rapid political solution.[8] About mid-September he did homage to the Frenchman for the northern counties, while Louis and his supporters in turn swore to make no peace with the English king which did not include Alexander. When King John retaliated by a raid across Midland England, the Scottish king and northern barons immediately feared for their own possessions and, abandoning Louis, hastened home, about the time of the death of King John on 19 October.

Those loyal to the Plantagenets were, in fact, strengthened by the death of an unpopular king, but their immediate assessment was probably of the weakness of their position. This would explain why an invitation was sent to Alexander II and the prince of North Wales to participate in the choice of a new king at Northampton, an attempt at conciliation which is not known to have received any response, and which was certainly overtaken by the coronation of the nine-year-old Henry III on 28 October at Gloucester.[9] During the following winter his supporters increased in number and

---

[8] *Arbroath Liber*, i, no. 110.
[9] *A.P.S.*, i, 112. This intended election does not seem to have been remarked by modern writers on the period.

gathered strength. As a measure of conciliation the regents reissued the Great Charter but without certain clauses: not only was the promise to do justice to the Scottish king dropped; it did not even appear among the doubtful matters postponed for consideration at a more appropriate time. The chief magnates of Henry III seem to have sworn before the papal legate to maintain for the king during his minority all lands held by his father, a promise which amounted to a refusal to consider Alexander II's claims. The same legate excommunicated the supporters of Louis, including the Scottish king, and placed their lands, including Scotland, under interdict. Although this sentence was not published in Scotland till 1217, it should have been a warning to the king that circumstances were no longer in his favour. The decisive trial of strength took place in the absence of the Scots at Lincoln on 20 May 1217, when the rebel forces were defeated and many leading supporters of Louis captured. During the same month Alexander II besieged Mitford Castle in Northumberland for a week, withdrawing perhaps on hearing news of the battle. Support for Louis trickled away further, and in June the northern agents of the English government threatened to invade Scotland. To forestall them Alexander II again invaded England on 5 July; it was the last hostile army to cross the Border for eighty years and it seems to have achieved nothing. Alexander was at Jedburgh with yet another force in September when he heard of peace negotiations between Louis and Henry. Wisely he disbanded his army and awaited the outcome. Louis made peace and sailed back to France. He did not ask King Alexander's consent, but at least secured for him the option of adhering to the treaty. On 1 December 1217, at Berwick, the Scottish king ordered that his agents give up Carlisle and in return received absolution from excommunication from the archbishop of York and bishop of Durham, whom he also had to permit to proclaim the legate's interdict. For a further year the Scottish church suffered the penalties of its subservience to the king in having ignored the interdict.

In the third week of December 1217, Alexander II did homage to Henry III at Northampton for the earldom of Huntingdon, which was held of him by his uncle, Earl David, and, from 1219, by his cousin, Earl John, and for the other lands (Tynedale) which he held of the English king. A turbulent episode was closed which had cost the Scottish king and his subjects a great deal of effort and money and had achieved nothing material. On the other hand, Alexander II had shown some, and perhaps learned more, military common sense, appreciating the limitations of the forces of which he disposed and by good luck or good judgement avoiding the battle at Lincoln which might have proved his Alnwick.

Prince Louis sailed away with ten thousand marks to which he had no right; King Alexander received back not a penny of the money which his father had paid to King John for favours promised but not performed. The Scottish king had no intention of allowing matters to rest, nor could he afford to do so since his kingdom lay under interdict, while the English regency sheltered behind the pope as feudal overlord (since 1213) of England and refused to do justice to the claim to the northern counties because it had promised to do nothing to diminish Henry III's inheritance before he came of age. In January 1218 messengers of the legate arrived in Scotland to receive submissions from priests and people and so lift the interdict. Unfortunately, the Cistercian abbeys, relying on the privileges of their order, had ignored the interdict even after it was promulgated in Scotland, and papal absolution for prelates was delayed until Cistercian pretensions had been quashed. During their journey the messengers of the legate had received at Edinburgh from the king and his men—presumably lay magnates—an oath to accept the judgement of the church and the mandates of the pope. The matter at judgement is not revealed but it can scarcely have been other than the treaties of 1209 and 1212 for, in November 1218, when Honorius III was lifting excommunication from the prelates and confirming the privileges of the Scottish church, he also remitted to his new legate, Pandulph, the question of the treaties between King William and King John.

It is curious that this episode has been regarded in modern times as evidence of the feudal lordship of the English king over Scotland, for the documents in the case make no mention whatever of that subject. On the contrary, they show the legate journeying to Norham at the end of July 1219, there to meet Alexander II on 2 August and to hear from him and from the procurators of Henry III, as judge over equal parties, the arguments for their positions. The case was debated for several days and then prorogued until 3 November when the search for a political settlement (rather than a judgement) doubtless continued. Next year Pandulph and the two kings met at York and on 15 June 1220 reached agreement; King

Alexander was to marry one of Henry III's sisters, while Henry III was to find suitable husbands in England for Alexander's two sisters before October 1221. No mention was made of the northern counties but it was perhaps part of the settlement that a papal legate should be sent to Scotland to act as mentor to the king.[10]

This settlement was very much less than the king of Scots had wanted, less, too, than the one for which King William had paid. Honorius III and his legate were clearly unwilling to do anything which might weaken the position of the young English king and the unique influence which they apparently enjoyed in English government as a result of the pope's feudal overlordship of the realm. In fact, it must have been increasingly apparent that the prisoner of this relationship was not England but the pope who had to accept and support the things done by the English government, and who preferred not to take a firm line with England for fear that his newly found lordship there be ignored. Pandulph, legate in England, was not replaced but in 1220 or 1221 the pope sent the chaplain and penitentiary James as legate to Scotland and Ireland. What King Alexander hoped to get out of this visit is uncertain, but he evidently required James to crown and anoint him. The request was referred to Honorius III whose answer clearly shows opposition from proctors of England in consistory: James was sternly told that the matter was none of his business 'since that king is said to be subject to the king of England'.[11]

On 19 June 1221 the marriage of Alexander II to Joanna, eldest sister of Henry III, was solemnised at York, and she was provided by her husband with a dower of lands worth £1000 yearly. In the same year, perhaps in the autumn, by agreement of both kings, Margaret, eldest sister to Alexander II, was married at York to Hubert de Burgh, justiciar and now effective ruler of England. It was later said that he had seduced the lady but a less dramatic explanation of the marriage is more likely. The departure of the legate Pandulph and the growth of Hubert's power explain

[10] *Foedera*, i, 154, 157 (The bull of Honorius is of 1218, not 1219), 160–1, 165.

[11] Robertson, *Statuta*, xlv = *Cal. Papal Letters*, i, 83. It appears that some historians think that this bull proceeded from a papal examination of the treaties of 1209 and 1212 and therefore represents the trend or substance of those treaties. Historians who read the bull will recognise 'it is said' as the indication of a contrary argument which has been put to the pope and which forbids him to alter the *status quo*.

the English decision, while Alexander II in agreeing may have hoped to further his claim on the northern counties through Hubert. In 1223, Isabel, second daughter of King William, was returned to Scotland unmarried, but in 1225 was married to Roger Bigod, Earl of Norfolk. In 1231 Henry III proposed his own marriage to Margaret, youngest daughter of King William. That William the Lion had two lawful (and it may be added, one illegitimate) daughters named after the ancestor and queen who was already regarded as a saint, has led to some confusion. It seems likely that the younger Margaret was born in or after 1209 when her sisters went to England and there was probably twenty years' difference in the ages of the namesakes. The treaty of 1237 referred not only to the marriage of the elder Margaret or Isabel promised by King John in 1209 but also to a promise by Henry III that he would marry Margaret. While this latter may refer to the treaty of 1220 and the older Margaret, it is also possible and indeed more likely that it refers to an agreement of 1231 and the younger Margaret.[12] There can be no doubt that a promise was made by Henry III in either 1220 or 1231 and that it was not kept. In 1231 Hubert de Burgh was politically isolated, his fall from power imminent, and the English barons persuaded King Henry that marriage to the younger sister of Hubert's wife would be unfitting. In the following year Hubert began divorce proceedings against his wife; their child died young in November 1237 but Margaret herself was alive in 1259. Isabel was alive in 1253 and the youngest sister, Margaret, having married Gilbert Earl Marshal in 1235, died in 1244. None of the sisters left issue. The marriage of the younger Margaret, celebrated at Berwick, may have amounted to a defiance of Henry III, whose approval was certified after the event, and who was precluded by it from fulfilment of the treaty of 1209 and subsequent agreements.[13]

The critical period of the reign of Alexander II came in the mid-1230s, when a serious rebellion in Galloway was followed by final difficulties and a solution in Anglo-Scottish relations. But in the earlier part of his reign disturbances in the more remote provinces showed that political unity by no means brought about social cohesion. In

[12] Stones, *Anglo-Scottish Relations*, no. 7. One small pointer that the preamble of the treaty deals with promises of marriage to two Margarets is the absence of (*pre*)*dicta* before the name of the second one. In modern reference works she is Marjorie but this of course is just a spelling of a French pronunciation of Margeret.

[13] See Appendix C in Powicke, *Henry III and the Lord Edward*.

March 1221 the king returned to Perth from being with his army at Inverness 'against Donald mac Neil' to make provision for stringent fines from those absenting themselves from the host.[14] Neither Donald nor his father has been identified. Fordun would have us believe that the king, after his marriage in June, gathered an army from Lothian, Galloway and other provinces and sailed against the men of Argyll. Driven back by a storm to Glasgow, he renewed the expedition in June 1222, receiving hostages from some who submitted and distributing the lands of others who fled. The expedition must have been brief, for the king was at Scone on 15 May and Jedburgh on 8 July, on the latter occasion granting a charter of burghal status to Dumbarton, which suggests that the expedition was based on the Clyde. It may have secured royal control of Cowal, Knapdale and even Kintyre, but is unlikely to have gone further afield. Probably after this the construction of a stone castle was begun for the king controlling the strategically vital porterage for ships at Tarbert (Loch Fyne).[15]

Later in the same year trouble broke out in Caithness, where the bishop, a Cistercian from Melrose, had returned from the Fourth Lateran council and set about the exaction of teinds with more zeal than discretion. According to one source, he increased the payment of a *spann* of butter for the customary twenty cows to a payment for fifteen, twelve and finally ten cows. There had been mediation before the king, who in August 1222 was planning a pilgrimage to Canterbury. On 11 September, at his manor of Halkirk,[16] the bishop was set upon by some of the peasant farmers of Caithness while the earl of Orkney stood ineffectually by. The bishop's *aide*, a Cistercian from Newbattle, was killed, and the bishop took refuge in his house. It was evidently well defended, for the men of Caithness had to burn it down and roasted their bishop to death. The king abandoned his pilgrimage and hurried north, gathering an army; the earl was heavily punished in his revenues, many of those involved lost hand and foot, and the peasants (*bondi*) as a whole had to pay a fine to be allowed to keep their lands. In January 1223 the pope wrote enthusiastically of Alexander's work as 'champion of God' in Caithness.[17]

---

[14] *A.P.S.*, i, 398, c. II.

[15] J. G. Dunbar and A. A. M. Duncan, 'Tarbert Castle', *Sc. Hist. Rev.*, l (1971), 1-17.

[16] Eight miles south of Thurso in Caithness.

[17] Anderson, *Early Sources*, ii, 449-52; *A.P.S.*, i, 110.

Trouble again broke out in Moray in 1228, when Thomas of Thirlestane, Lord of Abertarff, was killed in his wooden castle—presumably a motte—and part of Inverness burned early in September by a Gillescop. (It would seem that he was not the subject of a judgement in Holyrood Abbey against a Gillescop who had promised to deliver hostages to the king and failed to do so; the year is unknown, the patronymic uncertain, but Gillescop was no leader of a robber band surely, but a landowner of some substance.[18]) It is just possible that his activities lie behind the somewhat confused account of a mac William rising in remote parts in 1230 and its suppression, including the barbarous murder of an infant 'of the race of mac William' in Forfar market-place. For the suppression of Gillescop the king gave a copious army of footmen to his justiciar William Comyn, Earl of Buchan, and left him in charge of Moray. Not long afterwards the same earl's second son, Walter Comyn, appears as lord of Badenoch and (since his successors held it) was probably lord of Lochaber, which may have signified both the reward of the Comyns and the punishment of Gillescop.[19] The king spent Christmas 1230 at Elgin, perhaps in the company of Farquhar mac Taggart, upon whom the earldom of Ross was conferred about this time as a mark of the king's authority in the region and of the features which made it different and less suited to being placed under a royal sheriff. The pacification of the north was completed.

It is noteworthy that in these troubles we hear little of support for Alexander II such as his father had enjoyed from Roland of Galloway. No chronicler complains of wild Galwegians invading England in 1215–17 and, while much is known of Alan, Lord of Galloway from 1200, it is not as an active participant in Scottish affairs. Close to King John, whom he supported at Runnymede in 1215 and lord of extensive lands in Ireland, Alan became deeply involved in the maritime affairs of the western seaboard. As early as 1212 or 1214, his younger brother Thomas joined with Ranald, son of Somerled, in a piratical attack on Derry and, although given

[18] *Chron. Bower*, ii, 57–8; *A.P.S.*, i, 398–9, c. III. The date 1228 ascribed to this law seems to have been derived by the editor from Bower. For the charters of Abertarff see *A.P.S.*, i, 110.

[19] The judgement of Gillescop is dated in October (about 8th), but the editor is probably wrong in attributing it to 1228 since he is called Mahohegan and can be identified with Gileskop Macihacain, a Galloway-Carrick notable (*Melrose Liber*, no. 192), who is unlikely to have been at Abertarff. This erroneous identification is the only authority for the date 1228 for the judgment.

the heiress to, and the earldom of, Atholl about 1209, Thomas of Galloway appears frequently in English record as an Irish magnate, much more rarely in Scotland. Alan was King Alexander's constable, but scarcely appears at his court. He helped Henry III to suppress the rebellious Hugh de Lacy in Ireland (1223) and meddled in the fraternal strife which divided the kingdom of Man and the Isles, sailing with his brother to Man and to Lewis in support of King Reginald, to whose daughter his own illegitimate son, Thomas, was married. In 1230 a substantial Norwegian fleet descended upon the Hebrides and Bute but had to withdraw at the approach of Alan's fleet of 150 ships; 'He was the greatest warrior at that time. He had a great army and many ships. He plundered about the Hebrides for a long time.'[20] Alan may have commissioned the romance about the founder of his family which shows his acceptance of French chivalric ideals and the French language. Nonetheless, his career was that of a great sea-captain in the Gaelic society of the western seaboard, intent upon acquiring territories in Ireland, Man and the Isles, territories which must be linked by dominance of the sea-routes. Inevitably, he relied upon the sailor-warriors and ships of Galloway and of his other lands rather than upon the knights and mottes of his father's day, and inevitably, too, Galloway seemed to enjoy remarkable independence of the king of Scots. If Alexander II was tempted to take issue with Alan —and there is a hint that he quickly regretted confirming his constableship in 1214—he held his hand, perhaps because Alan had fathered only three daughters and an illegitimate son.

The lord of Galloway died in February 1234, predeceased by his brother, Thomas Earl of Atholl, in 1231. Alan's daughters were all married to English barons and only the eldest had a husband with strong Scottish connections. King Alexander does not seem to have hesitated to command a partition of the lordship among the coheiresses and to reject a request from the Galwegians that the unity of the lordship should be preserved. According to the *Melrose Chronicle*, they besought the king to take the lordship for himself, but it seems more likely that they foresaw the bastard Thomas as their lord; the royal refusal led to Galwegian raids into neighbouring territories. In July 1235 the king entered Galloway with an army which was attacked at an unknown place while pitching

[20] Anderson, *Early Sources*, ii, 464. See Genealogical Tree No. 3 for the Galloway inheritance.

camp. Fortunately, Earl Farquhar of Ross, a late arrival, took the Galwegians in the rear and routed them; the king left Walter Comyn in charge of the pacification of Galloway. The expedition took only days, because on 1 August the king and his barons were at Berwick for the marriage of his youngest sister, but the trouble was not yet ended. The army of occupation behaved badly and when Thomas returned with men from Ireland he seems to have recovered the lordship with no difficulty. The subsequent course of events is obscure; Patrick, Earl of Dunbar, seems to have secured the submission of Thomas's chief supporter and Thomas then sought the king's mercy. He was briefly detained in Edinburgh Castle and then according to the *Melrose Chronicle,* was released; this seems improbable and certainly he was subsequently in the charge of the Balliols at Barnard Castle. On the afternoon before Alexander III's death in 1286 his council was discussing the possible release of Thomas, who survived to a great age and was finally produced once more as champion of Galwegian liberties in 1296. Thomas's Irish mercenaries drifted northwards, were set upon by the burgesses of Glasgow, then unused to migrant Irishmen, and destroyed.

If this rebellion was no more than a pale shadow of the great rising of 1174, it had its own significance. The last great Celtic province of Scotland south of Ross had made its plea to the king for the preservation not merely of its individuality, but also of its unity and had failed, and failed conspicuously, to make any impression upon alien feudal custom. The laws of Galloway, with their primitive code of blood-payments commensurate with the injury complained of, probably remained intact for some time, but they were bound to yield eventually to the processes of royal justice. In 1237 Thomas Randolph was sheriff of Dumfries and in 1263 the earl of Buchan was sheriff of Wigtown, offices which were probably created in or just after 1235 and which marked the king's determination to exercise direct authority in the provinces; even more striking is the appearance in 1259 of John Comyn of Badenoch as justiciar of Galloway, an office which speaks even more plainly of the same royal purpose. With this office may have gone the introduction west of the Nith about 1235 of king's serjeants with the rights to indict criminals on their own word and to hang those caught red-handed, a right known as *surdit de serjeant* and doubtless justified by the absence of any kind of jury in Galwegian judicial procedures and by the need to protect the king's interests. Before 1286 the

Galwegians had persuaded the king to abolish *surdit de serjeant* as a custom which they hated for its oppressive use. It probably did much to silence opposition to royal policy in the years after 1235.[21]

The new lords of Galloway, de Quincy, Balliol, and de Fortibus may not have taken possession of the whole lands of Alan. In 1246 on his death without heirs, the de Fortibus inheritance passed to de Quincy and Balliol and it may have been this change which caused a final rebellion in 1247. Roger de Quincy was besieged in a Galwegian castle and was lucky to escape with his life to Alexander II, who reinstated him. In 1265 the de Quincy lands were in turn divided among co-heiresses, leaving the Balliols as the largest single landowners in Galloway. It seems likely, however, that some parts of the lordship were retained for the crown. Thus royal castles were built or existed at Kirkcudbright (chief place of Alan) and Wigtown. Even more striking is the prominence in Galloway after 1235 of the Comyn families, descendants of William Comyn, Earl of Buchan (died 1233), by his two marriages. Alexander Comyn, Earl of Buchan, was sheriff of Wigtown in 1263, that is, before he succeeded to part of the de Quincy lands in 1265; the office of sheriff was normally held by a local magnate and it seems likely that the earl had benefited from the dissolution of the lordship in 1234–5. Similarly, Comyn of Badenoch held land in Nithsdale as neighbour to Thomas Randolph, sheriff of Dumfries, and was justiciar. The ancestry of Thomas is uncertain but, allowing for the difficulty of equating Ralph and Randolph, it seems most probable that he was descended from Ralph fitz Dunegal, lord of upper Nithsdale in the mid-twelfth century, and thus represents a native family recalled to prominence by the disappearance of the lords of Galloway. (See page 551.)

The marriages being arranged for his sisters probably incited Alexander II to raise with Henry III in 1234 the question of the unfulfilled treaties and promises of the years since 1209, because in January 1235 the pope issued a bull which in effect commanded Alexander II to observe the treaty of Falaise (1174) and obey Henry III;[22] in April 1236 the Scottish king was upbraided for ignoring these English-inspired demands. If by this wholly characteristic move Henry III hoped to bury the claims of Alexander, he was sadly mistaken. In the same month Alexander's agent Master Abel pressed his claims and in September the two kings met at Newcastle, when Henry III is said to have offered annual revenues of eighty merks in acquittance to Alexander. The final conference and settlement took place a year later at York in the presence of the papal legate Otto, sent at Henry's request. Otto had the Scottish affair added to his commission as something secondary but of importance, and it is clear that the English king feared that a Scottish crisis would be added to his many other worries. In May 1237 he conjured up phantom Flemish mercenaries travelling through England to Scotland in disguise, a little later Scottish pirates in the Irish sea so that the Irish ports were closed to all Scottish ships; and, finally, a jittery watch was kept over the walls of Northumbrian castles for the Scottish enemy who never came. Much of this was probably the result of an overstrung imagination, but Alexander II did not discourage it and does seem to have encouraged piracy in the Irish sea.

In June 1237 the king's cousin, John, Earl of Huntingdon (and, through his mother, Earl of Chester), died, leaving three sisters as co-heiresses. He was heir male to the Scottish throne and his death gave both an opportunity and a problem for the Scots king. The opportunity was to claim the earldom of Huntingdon, of which Alexander was given seisin as lord; the problem was the succession in Scotland. King Henry made an arrangement with Earl John's co-heirs whereby they succeeded to his lands and in part sold them to the crown. Effectively the long Scottish connection with the earldom of Huntingdon was now ended.

For three days, in September 1237, the legate Otto conducted negotiations between the kings at York; on 25 September a treaty was sealed and the kings parted.[23] In return for yielding his claims to the northern counties, to the 15,000 merks paid (it was inaccurately said) by William to John, and to the marriages agreed for his sisters, Alexander II received two hundred pounds' worth of land, in Northumberland and Cumberland 'outside towns where there are castles', with extensive franchises. The documents of the marriage treaties between John and Henry III and William and Alexander II were to be handed back by each side to the other, but any matter there not covered by the 1237 treaty was to be renewed. In the simplest terms, Alexander II was bought off; to the modern historian the treaty must seem a wise and moderate compromise and he might point out that it is surprising that King Alexander II

[23] Stones, *Anglo-Scottish Relations*, no. 7.

settled for so little and that Henry III was persuaded to grant so much. As one of the terms of the treaty Alexander II and his barons besought the pope to constrain them to observe it by ecclesiastical censures, a gesture which suggests that Henry III feared that the Scots might still have an incentive to break the treaty. They had settled for what they could get, but what they were given scarcely represented the paper value of what they gave up.[24]

From York it seems that Queen Joanna went south to visit the shrine of St Thomas at Canterbury. At London she was taken ill and on 4 March 1238 she died there. Her influence over her husband and brother, the kings of Scotland and England, does not seem to have been great, and she is not mentioned as mediating in 1237 as Queen Ermengarde had done in 1209.[25] Her position was probably weakened by her failure to produce a child, and her death presented to Alexander II both the problem of the succession and the chance to solve it. In May 1239 he married the daughter of a French baron, Marie de Coucy, and on 4 September 1241 she presented him with a son, the future Alexander III, their only child. In 1291 it was urged by and on behalf of Robert Bruce that Alexander II had recognised him as heir, he being the nearest male relation to the king. Although the circumstantial details are untrustworthy it seems that between 1237 (when Earl John died) and 1241 Bruce was generally recognised as heir presumptive. No chronicler speaks of a council in which this was done, and, although negative evidence is dangerous, it seems likely that there was no formal recognition and no sealed document anent his rights such as Bruce claimed in 1291 to have existed; there was, I suggest, merely presumption.[26]

The attitude of Henry III to the remarriage of his brother-in-law

[24] The letter written by Alexander II and his barons to the pope in 1237 is preserved by Matthew Paris under the year 1244, with the pope's initial altered to 'I' to suit this date; *Chronica Majora*, iv, 383. It seems to me that this confusion may throw some light on the English 'paper constitution of 1244'.

[25] Queen Ermengarde had lived until 11 February 1233 and perhaps overshadowed her daughter-in-law.

[26] Palgrave, *Docs. Hist. Scot.*, 29. Bruce claimed that when Alexander II went on an expedition to the Isles (?1249) by assent of the prelates and barons, he recognised Bruce as his heir if he should die without a son, and that a sealed instrument to this effect was in the royal treasury. None was listed there in 1282–96. It is however just possible that Bruce was referring not to 1238–41 but to c. 1249 when the king did have a son, and that Bruce was recognised as heir should Alexander (III) die. See above p. 390n., and the discussion in Palgrave, *ibid*, xxi–xxix.

is unknown. For four years the kings negotiated touchily over the means to be adopted for choosing the manors to be given to King Alexander. The Scottish king would not have the pope's legate as arbiter in the event of disagreement and no alternative was acceptable to Henry III. At the end of 1241 Henry was compelled, in order to settle the Gascon business, to make concessions in the north. The bishop of Durham was told to assign 200 librates of land with, if Alexander was dissatisfied, a further ten pounds' worth, and on 22 April 1242 five manors in Cumberland were granted to King Alexander. Along with the manor of Wark in Tynedale they were valued in 1290 at £368 annually, so Alexander II seems to have been fairly dealt by.

Yet scarcely were these ancient issues settled when new ones brought the two kings to the edge of war. The immediate cause was information laid before Henry III in the autumn of 1243 by Walter Bisset, exiled from Scotland by the influence of the Comyns and the earl of Dunbar. In April 1244 the northern sheriffs were instructed to arrest any foreigner travelling to Scotland and to send him and any letters he might carry to the king; apparently intrigues with Louis IX were feared. A month later orders for a muster at Newcastle on 1 August were issued, 'because of certain trespasses done by the king of Scotland against us, to require amends of him', and King Alexander seems to have prepared to meet an invasion. In the event, he met Henry III under safe-conduct at Newcastle and on 14 August 1244 renewed the peace between them. The chronicler Matthew Paris presents a string of reasons for this outburst of distrust—Bisset, and his opposite number, the English outlaw Geoffrey Marsh, who had taken refuge in Scotland,[27] the de Coucy marriage, which entailed an alliance with a French enemy of King Henry, a reputed letter of Alexander II denying that he held a jot of Scotland from Henry III, and the fortification of two Border castles by the Comyns; Fordun specifies the making of Hermitage Castle, some of whose walls and outworks may well belong to this time. Certainly, the chroniclers are right to stress the meddling of the Bissets as the source of King Henry's knowledge of what was going on in Scotland. The English king was liable to unreasonable fits of antipathy, and in this case he seems to have exaggerated minor wrongs into a major suspicion that Alexander II was negotiating an alliance with

---

[27] He was related to the Comyns. See Appendix B in Powicke, *Henry III and the Lord Edward.*

Louis IX of France. There was probably nothing to this, for a settlement was reached quickly by the mediation of Henry's brother Richard and of other English barons, who were doubtless used to the phantoms conjured up by Henry III, and Alexander II gave easy assurances which suggest that he had no sinister plans. He promised to preserve faith and love to his lord Henry III, to make no treaty with his enemies and to stir up no trouble for him—all pointing to a suspected French alliance. The treaty, however, speaks of 'agreements about the contract of marriage' of Alexander (III) and Henry III's daughter, and most chroniclers are agreed that they were betrothed on this occasion, perhaps in order to preclude a French marriage for the young Alexander.[28] In 1282 the Scottish treasury contained Henry III's counterpart of the treaty of 1244 conceding that the agreement 'should not prejudice the king of Scotland in making marriages freely';[29] this price was perhaps exacted by the Scots because King Henry had cited the 1212 grant of the marriage of the young Alexander (II) in order to urge a similar grant for his son Alexander (III).

King Henry's insistence upon the loyalty owed to him by the Scottish king is underlined by the oath taken by four bishops and twenty-four barons of Scotland to uphold, and cause to be upheld, the treaty and to give neither help nor advice against it. The talebearing of the Bissets may be seen in the oaths exacted by King Henry from their opponents Patrick, Earl of Dunbar, and Walter Comyn, Earl of Menteith, with thirty-nine and forty compurgators respectively, that these earls had taken no share in the attacks on Ireland nor in providing refuge for William Marsh—both events of 1237. These oaths were an attempt to hold Scottish barons responsible for the activities or omissions, future and past respectively, of their king, and suggest that, whatever the relative importance of the various elements in it, the crisis of 1244 marked a new phase in Anglo-Scottish relations, a phase in which the English king could no longer use the carrot of the Northumbrian earldom but must find new means to manage the Scottish king. On this occasion he wielded the big stick; in 1235, 1251 and under Edward I in 1278, a more subtle weapon in the English armoury, a claim to

---

[28] Matthew Paris thought that their marriage was arranged in 1242 but his chronology for these years is unreliable. The marriage agreement was in the Scottish records in 1282.

[29] *A.P.S.*, i, 108 at middle.

homage for Scotland, was given an airing and put back in store once its potential had registered with the Scots.

In fact, it was not until December 1244 that King Henry took steps to deal with Earls Patrick and Walter, for he had been pre-occupied with a domestic crisis with his own barons since August. Either for this occasion, or for the marriage of Alexander (III) in 1251, was written the surviving text of the 1212 treaty which grants the marriage of Alexander (II) to the English king along with a pro-mise (which is not authentic as it stands) that 'we [William] and Alexander our son will maintain faith and fealty to his [King John's] son Henry as our liege lord against all mortals and will help him, so far as we have power, to support himself in his realm, saving the faith by which we are bound to our lord King John'. If it was Henry III's hope to secure maintenance from Alexander II against the nagging of English barons, then it was a vain hope, and for the remaining five years of Alexander II's reign relations between the kings were friendly but distant.

An attempt, in October 1245, to define the Border between the two kingdoms over a comparatively short stretch of moorland south of the Tweed produced a deadlock, and it is likely that there were similar disputes in the Esk valley on the west. Anxious to avoid encroachments, the men on both sides of the Border would take up 'immovable' positions over any issue and hence became defenders of conservative, not to say outdated, practices. In 1216 the pope condemned the usage of compelling ecclesiastics on the Border to participate in person in the judicial duel; twenty years later cham-pions were permitted for churchmen, but in the event of defeat both champion and prelate were supposed to perish, a fate which had befallen the prior of Canonbie (a house of canons lying just inside Scotland).

In April 1249, while King Alexander was preparing an expedi-tion to Argyll, formal codification of the laws of the Borders was undertaken by a mixed jury empanelled at the instance of both kings. They were much concerned with the problem of the fugitive offender, who might well be a free or unfree man escaping his lord by crossing the Border but was more likely to be a plain criminal guilty of theft, robbery or manslaughter; any man dwelling within the bounds of the two kingdoms could be called to the Border to answer his accuser from the other kingdom. Thus, if cattle or sheep were stolen and taken over the Border, the pursuer must appear in

the fief to which the supposed reiver belonged and recover them in
the court (of the reiver's lord, it seems) by the oath of six men willing to swear to his ownership. If the reiver swore they were his, the
debate was settled by combat, that is judicial duel, at the March.
Such provisions suggest a measure of 'rustling' but not one greater
than within Scotland itself, where the early assizes were verbose and
reiterative on the subject of stolen animals. The processes available
to March law were limited; an accusation on oath could be denied
on oath and judgement was by combat. In no circumstances was
there recourse to the jury, nor, it seems, could the accused place
himself in the mercy of his king to escape with restitution and fine.
Men of one kingdom would not trust either the jury or the king of
the other; only the finding of the truth by divine judgement in combat was trusted. As international law the code seems neither sophisticated nor, in all probability, very efficacious since it depended in
the last resort on getting two parties to appear simultaneously at the
Border, and even the elaborate system of 'wads' or pledges cannot
have secured this very readily. Nonetheless, this was a description of
working Border custom, not of new law and in some of its details it
has the appearance of great antiquity. It implies that men had
sought means of solving their disputes and distrustfully had come to
imperfect procedures, which reflected not only a political frontier
but also the peaceable society which lay on each side of that frontier. When Alexander II died the Border had been fixed at the same
line (apart from very minor deviations such as that discussed in
1245) for more than two centuries. Even during periods of warfare
neither kingdom seems to have sought to move it. No doubt the
shortness of this frontier helped to reduce the number of points of
tension, but it is unlikely that any other land frontier among the
states of feudal Europe was so completely stable during this period.
It divided communities with the same language (at least on the
east), the same social structure and agrarian practices, and we would
do them an injustice if we supposed that they wished to ignore these
ties for the endemic warfare such as was encouraged by the two
bellicose kingdoms of the late Middle Ages. The Border was peaceable because kings and Border folk wanted peace and the arts of
peace.[30]

It is rarely possible to say why on any particular occasion a king

[30] Barrow, *Kingdom of the Scots*, chapter 4; G. Neilson, 'The March Laws',
*Stair Society Miscellany*, i (1971), 11-77, especially pp. 15-24.

and his court sat down to agree to 'new' laws. When they did, the laws were usually of one of two kinds: the first was a decision of a general principle arising out of a particular case. When John of Burnwell died, his widowed mother still held her third of his father's estate; was John's widow to receive a third of John's estate only or also a third of his mother's third? The king's court decided on the latter and the king made this the law of the land.[31] The second kind of law was an assise, a general statement which did not alter the substantive law, the custom of the realm; it extended or contracted the remedies and procedures open to anyone seeking justice. And in the reign of Alexander II, the condemnation of the ordeal by the Fourth Lateran council in 1215 led to a rapid abandonment of this form of proof and an extension of the alternatives, trial by combat, and verdict of the neighbours, that is, the jury. By 1230 the latter was being used in circumstances where once ordeal or combat had been usual; the time had come to define its limits. There was no bench of learned judges, as at Westminster, to define and refine year by year and so build up the law without a statute; in Scotland the king and his court must give their authority to what the lawyers draft. Hence 'The king laid down', *Statuit dominus rex.*

Although the assizes made by the king with one bishop, two earls, a prior and three barons (two justiciars among them) at Stirling on 13 October 1230 first appear with the preamble giving that information in a comparatively late manuscript, the authenticity of some of them seems sure, of the rest fairly sure. The first forbade a prelate or baron to repledge (that is, call into his own court from that of another) an accused man, as had hitherto been done, merely to benefit from his amercement, that is, perhaps, his 'forfeiture',[32] unless the accused was his liege man, or neyf, dwelt on his land or was in his following. The lawful men of the country, a jury of either sheriff or baron court, were to lay bare any such abuse.[33] The same occasion produced one other statute (c. V), extending the rights of clerics, widows and other persons who could not fight. If such a person were despoiled of goods (and it is clear that theft is not meant) he could complain to the sheriff, who would empanel a jury made up of the grieve and four good men from three neighbouring baronies, to enquire 'who that malefactor was'. Only the accused could put himself on (that is, put his guilt or innocence to) the jury,

[31] *A.P.S.*, i, 401–2.          [32] Discussed above p. 335.
[33] *A.P.S.*, i, 399, c. IV.

and a guilty man might well feel his chances were better in combat. This statute gave a pursuer the right to put his loss to a jury, which in naming an accused was in effect giving a verdict upon the evidence. But, as is shown by royal letters of 1231-2 to two abbeys, the formality of judgement could not be denied to the accused. These letters echo the statute so clearly that they are welcome proof of its date, 1230; each instructs the sheriff to help the pursuer (i.e. the abbey) by finding a champion for it 'if perchance there is need' (that is, if the accused did not put himself on the jury), until the cause was completed 'in the estimation of discreet men or by compounding for the offence', leading to the malefactor being convicted or quasi-convicted respectively, 'in his malice'. The pursuer had restitution of his goods, and the king his forfeitures.[34] The statute shows the fumbling for new procedures as the old were rejected, for, while combat was clearly discouraged, the jury was asked to decide questions within its knowledge—'who is said to be malefactor?', 'is the cause completed?'—and not to form an opinion, 'is he guilty?' Moreover, in suggesting that the accused might compound and that the goods must be restored, the statute was treating such causes as quasi-civil actions, recognising that cattle and sheep might be taken not as theft but because the taker thought he had good title to them. We are here a step along the road leading to the action of spuilzie, parallel to the road which in England led to trespass.

The third statute (c. VI) attributable to 1230 turns to the question of theft; it did not introduce the jury (as is often suggested) but assumed that it was a regular recourse for those accused of theft and that the guilty would be punished. But what if found innocent? Then the accuser was to be in the king's mercy, that is, fined; this was the point of the statute, but it concludes by forbidding the ordeal, in brief and almost 'throw away' words which suggest that the ordeal had lingered on in a few obscure corners but could now be finally forbidden. In 1248 a large royal court at Stirling decided that no 'oath of loss of life and limb of a landholding man be made except by worthy men, freeholders by charter'.[35] The statement is brief but most probably referred to the possibility of clearing oneself of an accusation by oath-helpers, and evidently made this more diffi-

---

[34] *Melrose Liber*, no. 175; *Scottish History Society Miscellany*, viii, 8-9. There is a curious error in the latter, *anno regni octavi decimi* (which I have confirmed in the original). Was there a rush for brieves of this kind and carelessness in producing them?

[35] *A.P.S.*, i, 404, c. XV.

cult to achieve; the effect would be to encourage recourse to the jury.

A fourth statute of 1230 (c. VII) introduced an action for dissasine: anyone in full possession of lands who was expelled without judgement might put his cause to a jury and secure restitution if his complaint was found just. This does seem to be a new kind of action in the field of 'real' (landed) property. Significantly, it was confined to the courts of sheriff and justiciar, and was not available in franchises, which, if they had kept only the older forms of action, would have lost much business to the sheriff court.[36]

When that study of the early assizes and early judicial proceedings which is still a crying need has been made, the interpretations offered here may be discarded. On the other hand, the occasion of 1230 itself will surely be more remarked than hitherto as evidence of the maturity of attitudes to the law and especially of attitudes to forms of action. Perhaps they had always been more flexible than recent historians were prepared to allow; but when government recognised that its authority should be used to make forms of action responsive to social needs, then the stresses of feuding to settle wrongs, civil or criminal, were a thing of the past, and society had accepted the function of the ruler to punish and make restitution without respect to persons. The breakdown of this political attitude in 1242[37] is the exception which underlines its general success. Legal hacks of a later date persistently attributed to David I that innovatory and codifying rôle which belonged to Alexander II and his time. The nucleus of the various collections of assizes and *leges* included authentic instructions, such as the assize of 1197 (a drive against criminals), as well as brocards on a miscellany of subjects. The idea that such *written* material was relevant to the practice of law seems to have arisen in the reign of Alexander II and to have been complementary to the king's rôle in reforming judicial practice by 'statute'.[38]

The feudalisation of Scotia in the reign of King William reached its most westerly known limit in the grant of Lenzie, on the

[36] *A.P.S.*, i, 399–400, cc. IV–VII. In c. VII read in line 7 *per preceptum regis iuste recognosci faciat* with the Ayr MS.

[37] Below, pp. 544–5.

[38] In the printed statutes of Alexander II, c. VIII is probably an authentic judgement but of any date between 1170 and 1286, c. IX is of ecclesiastical origins, cc. XI–XIII are probably brocards. On all these statutes see George Neilson, *Trial by Combat* (1890), chapter 34.

borders of Lennox, to William Comyn. Descended from a daughter of Donald III and grand-nephew of David I's chancellor the would-be bishop of Durham, Comyn inherited lands in Tynedale and at West Linton in Peeblesshire from his father Richard Comyn, but the fortunes of the family were decisively improved by William himself. He already had two sons by his first marriage when, about 1212, he married Marjory, daughter of Fergus, Earl of Buchan, and was made earl of Buchan. He was justiciar of Scotia and suppressed rebellions against the king in 1211 and 1228-9, and we have seen that his second son, Walter, was apparently rewarded with the lordship of Badenoch where his descendants built a castle at Ruthven, now obliterated by a Hanoverian barracks. William seems to have intended that his eldest son, who scarcely occurs in Scottish record, would become pre-eminently an English baron, his second son a Scottish baron, while the earldom of Buchan would pass to his son by his second marriage. He died in 1233. In 1233-4 Walter Comyn of Badenoch succeeded to the earldom of Menteith, in the same way as his father had gained Buchan, and soon thereafter served the king in Galloway along with Patrick, Earl of Dunbar. In 1237 it was these two men whom Henry III regarded as responsible for the descents upon Ireland made from Scotland with official connivance or contrivance, a hint that they held lands or official position in Galloway. Although Walter's half-brother, Alexander Comyn, had not yet succeeded to the inheritance of his widowed mother, the countess of Buchan, the family was plainly as powerful as any (the king excepted) in Scotland, for while one cousin succeeded by marriage to the de Valognes fief of East Kilbride, another, a John Comyn whose descent is wholly unknown, married the heiress of Angus and died as earl of Angus in France in 1242. Although this marriage is something of a mystery and had no long-term effects, it is a mark of the standing of the Comyns.

Yet as the family fortunes were built by marriage, other connections were made by the need to find husbands for the daughters of the house. Now marriage could cement a friendship and lead to a political alliance, and was doubtless often made in that hope. On the other hand, it might also seek to heal a dispute which had still-rankling causes, it might lead to disputes over marriage portions and their return, and where the wife was an heiress it could put out of joint the nose of some male relative who hoped to succeed should she die childless. There was no close marriage alliance between the

Comyns and their ally, the earl of Dunbar; other marriages seem to knit the baronage of Scotland in the mid-thirteenth century in a close community which may indeed have shared the same social outlook but was certainly not always politically united.

There is reason to think that the earldom of Atholl was one of the divisive elements. As early as *c.* 1180 Malcolm, Earl of Atholl, had married the widow of Richard Comyn. She was not the mother of his son and successor, Earl Henry, but she may have borne Earl Malcolm's daughter, who married Thomas Durward and was the mother of Alan Durward. Earl Henry seems also to have married a Comyn, and had only two daughters, of whom one, Isabel, was married to Thomas of Galloway, son of Roland and younger brother of Alan of Galloway. Thomas, whose career we have touched on several times, was earl of Atholl from 1210 till 1231, when he was killed, probably accidentally, by a knight of the eastern march and client of the earl of Dunbar, Patrick of Goswick; his widow survived until 1232 and perhaps later. One of her acts in 1232 was to make a formal protest before relatives and friends of her capacity in 'free widowhood' to make a gift to Coupar Abbey which none of her heirs could gainsay.[39] This special protest must surely relate to the fact that in charters dated 25 December 1234 and 23 February 1235 Alan Durward appears as earl of Atholl, and that a charter which he granted as earl almost certainly belongs to the same occasion as a royal confirmation 'at the petition of Alan Durward' dated at Kintore on 12 October 1233. In September 1237 among the Scottish barons who wrote to the pope was an un-named earl of Atholl who can only have been Durward. Either he had married Isabel or else Isabel had died and Alan had advanced a claim to the earldom (or to the wardship of it) as nearest male heir of age, against Patrick, son of Isabel and Thomas, and against Isabel's sister; there are grounds for preferring the latter explanation in the uncertain recognition accorded to Alan's title by the royal chancery and the fact that Alan, unlike the husbands of Isabel and her sister, has left

---

[39] This document (*Coupar Rental*, i, 333) is dated on the vigil of St Laurence, 1232, which would mean 9 August 1232, 16 October 1232 or 2 February 1233 since there are three feasts of Saints Laurence. The first is the most probable. Among those present was Walter Comyn, Earl of Menteith, who lacks that title in royal charters as late as 30 June 1233 and first bears it on 9 January 1234. It is possible that the text of Countess Isabel's document has a miscopied date, but I am more inclined to think that Walter Comyn had married the Menteith heiress by 1232 and assumed the title but received sasine and royal recognition only in 1233-4. See Genealogical Tree No. 6 for the Atholl succession.

no trace of having sasine of the earldom. The young Patrick, whose only documentary appearance before his death is as witness to a charter of his namesake, the earl of Dunbar, seems to have been brought up in Comyn-Dunbar surroundings.[40]

In 1233 Alan of Galloway gave his sister as wife to Walter Bisset, lord of Aboyne and near neighbour to Durward. Bisset thus became uncle by marriage to Patrick of Atholl. In 1234 Alan of Galloway himself died leaving three co-heiresses, but it is a striking fact that they did not inherit his extensive Irish lands, which forty years later are found in the hands of the Bissets. Walter Bisset was extensively employed by Henry III in Ireland in the 1240s and we can only conjecture whether this was the cause or effect of his holding lands there. Furthermore, we know nothing of what happened to the lands of Thomas of Galloway in both Galloway and Ulster, lands which should have passed to his son Patrick if he had come of age. He died on an unknown day in 1242, when, on the night after a tournament, his lodging at Haddington was burned down, according to the *Melrose Chronicle* to conceal his having been murdered in bed. We cannot now discover the truth of the suspicions which seem to have fallen at once upon the Bissets, but of the choice of motives offered by the chroniclers one seems significant. Matthew Paris holds that Walter Bisset had received a fall in the tournament at Patrick's hand and was the murderer, the *Melrose Chronicle* (without any motive to offer) that John Bisset was the criminal, his uncle Walter Bisset an accomplice, Bower that William Bisset (an error for Walter) was responsible not in person but through his knights and that the motive was certain ancestral wrongs. John Bisset in fact betrayed guilt by fleeing shortly afterwards; Walter was widely regarded as guilty but impressed the king with his denials.[41] It is, therefore, of considerable interest that the *Lanercost Chronicle*, which knows nothing of the Bissets by name, says that

[40] The Peerages accept Patrick as an *earl* of Atholl, and he is so called by Bower. But thirteenth-century chronicles are agreed in calling him Patrick of Atholl and I now think that he neither received the earldom nor was belted earl. In 1213 a lawful son of Earl Thomas of Atholl, who can scarcely have been either Patrick or the bastard Alan, was one of the hostages in King John's hands. His name and fate are unknown.

[41] John Bisset was in Ireland probably by October 1242 because, on 17 December at Bordeaux, Henry III confirmed an agreement made by the justiciar of Ireland with John Bisset whereby the latter was to serve Henry III in Guienne in return for a fief in Ireland. This may explain how John Bisset later came to hold Galloway lands in Ireland.

Patrick of Atholl was murdered 'because he was expected to become great lord of a certain inheritance which descended to him and although he had been warned on that day by a letter from the wife of his murderer'. The inheritance was surely that of Thomas of Galloway, the lady who may have betrayed the death as a murder was surely his aunt, wife of Walter Bisset. In some way this senseless murder was, or was thought to be, about the Galloway inheritance.

For some time the king delayed acting against Walter Bisset, although pressed by the earls, including Patrick, Earl of Dunbar, and Walter Comyn, Earl of Menteith. Two young Comyn heirs, Alexander of Buchan and John of Badenoch, then took the law into their own hands and laid waste the Bisset lands while Walter was cooped up in Aboyne Castle.[42] Alexander II, greatly angered, caused the 'army of Mar' to escort Walter to Forfar, where he offered combat or compurgation to clear himself while his opponents demanded that he put himself upon the neighbourhood jury. In the outcome he placed himself in the king's mercy, and judgement of outlawry and abjuration of the realm was pronounced upon him and the other Bissets at Edinburgh on 26 November 1242. This account follows Bower in the main, and in one essential—outlawry —agrees with both Matthew Paris and the *Melrose Chronicle* although the latter places the sentence in 1243. Certainly, by August 1243 Walter Bisset was in England (having sworn, according to Bower, to go to the Holy Land) and for some five years he served Henry III, turning him against Alexander II by describing Scottish negotiations with France.

So far it would seem that the Comyn family had successfully compelled a reluctant king to punish an offence against their family. Yet this was by no means the end of the affair. In 1241 and 1242 respectively, Walter the Steward, justiciar of Scotia, and Walter Olifard, justiciar of Lothian, had died; the king appointed Robert de Mowat and Philip de Melville as joint justiciars of Scotia, David de Lindsay as justiciar of Lothian. Mowat was undoubtedly an ally or dependant of the Comyns, while Melville seems to have been a man of little importance. It should not have surprised the king, therefore, that little action was taken by the justiciars against those who had raised war against the Bissets. By 1244 both men had

[42] This castle was probably Coull castle on which see W. D. Simpson, 'The excavation at Coull Castle, Aberdeenshire', *Proc. Soc., Antiq. Sc.*, lviii (1923-4), 45-92.

been removed and Alan Durward was appointed in their place. How active he was we do not know; to some extent internal divisions may have been healed by the crisis in relations with England in 1244. Nonetheless, the king had turned to a man of consuming ambition who already can have had no love for the Comyns. The earldom of Atholl he could not have since it had gone to the aunt of the deceased Patrick and to her husband, David de Hastings, lord of Dun in Angus, but still he rose in royal favour and was given the king's illegitimate daughter in marriage.[43]

The murder of Patrick of Atholl is a reminder of the sombre side to thirteenth-century Scotland. The brutal death of an infant member of the mac William family, her brains dashed out against the stone pillar of the market cross of Forfar, was the work of a vengeful government. Irish gallowglasses, refugees from the Galwegian rising of 1235, were beheaded by the citizens of Glasgow, save two who were sent as prisoners to be torn limb from limb by horses for the entertainment of the burgesses of Edinburgh. Such rigour in the punishment of political offences emphasises the inadequate means of detection and proof available for the protection of society against the violence of private criminals.

There is some reason to think that after 1238 the justice ayres flagged for some years. In February 1245 a far-reaching royal assize, made with the consent of five prelates, seven earls (two of them English), and eight barons, laid down that each sheriff was to enquire from the presenting jury of the toun about malefactors who had committed offences since Christmas 1242 and to arrest any accused so that they might be put upon a jury before the justiciar of Lothian 'except Galloway which has its special laws'. Those convicted of pleas of the crown—'murder, robbery or similar felonies'—were to be punished by royal officers and their chattels escheated to the king, but for lesser offences, theft or homicide, punishment and escheat belong to the offender's lord. 'From henceforth' the king's officers were not to arrest anyone on the accusation of an individual unless he was indicted by the presenting jury, that is, in legal Scots, the dittay. There is a suggestion here that the justiciar's jurisdiction was to override that of the franchises, and also that private appeal (leading to judicial combat) was not to be used.[44] If so, these measures were ineffectual. It is quite clear that

---

[43] The year of this marriage is unknown. Hastings was lord of Abergavenny.
[44] A.P.S., i, 403, c. XIV.

this assize applied south of the Forth only, but the date chosen for the limit of legal memory of the inquest, Christmas 1242, probably refers to the troubles associated with the expulsion of the Bissets. According to Bower, Alan Durward was appointed justiciar of Scotia to deal with these troubles and it seems not unlikely that there was a parallel enquiry north of Forth, though whether it could have used the presenting jury is uncertain. By 1266 the dittay is known to have been in use in Aberdeenshire, and it probably came into general use in Scotia during the first half of the thirteenth century.[45]

The strengthening of royal authority in the far north, through creating the earldom of Sutherland and taking the earldom of Caithness from Orcadian into Scottish hands, was made easier by the growth of a strong Norwegian monarchy in the hands of Haakon IV, who reduced the power and independence of the earls of Orkney. The two kings, Scottish and Norwegian, also confronted each other on the western seaboard, where two semi-independent princelings had long ignored nominal royal authority. The isles were divided between those held by the king of Man—Man, Skye, Lewis —and those from Gigha to Mull or even to North Uist,[46] held by the descendants of Somerled: the mac Donalds of Islay and part of Kintyre; the mac Dougalls of Argyll, Mull, Coll, Tiree; and the lords of Garmoran (the most northerly territories). These three families held mainland (Scottish) as well as island (Norwegian) territories. From 1188 the kingdom of Man was ruled by King Reginald in Man and, under him, by his brother Olaf in the Outer Hebrides. In 1226 Reginald was ousted by Olaf and turned for help to Alan and Thomas of Galloway, who by reason of their lands in Galloway and Antrim were in a uniquely favourable position to subdue Man. In 1230, fearing conquest, Olaf set sail for the court of his lord, King Haakon, at Bergen.

He arrived to find that Haakon was already preparing an expedition under Uspak (a Norse attempt at 'Gillespec'), son of Dugald, son of Somerled, against Uspak's brothers, Duncan and Dugald mac Dougall, who were causing anarchy in the Isles, presumably by attacks upon neighbouring landholders. The expedition of Uspak

---

[45] Barrow, *Kingdom of the Scots*, 111–3.
[46] A. O. Johnsen, 'The Payments from the Hebrides and the Isle of Man to the crown of Norway, annual ferme or feudal casualty?' *Sc. Hist. Rev.*, xlviii (1969), 18–34. The status of the Outer Isles to the south of Lewis is uncertain.

and King Olaf was not strong in ships and its proceedings were somewhat curious. While Uspak and his brother Duncan had friendly negotiations, the Norwegians in the fleet attacked the other mac Dougalls, without Uspak's knowledge. In spite of this, the three brothers made a concerted attack upon Bute, which had passed into Scottish hands many years earlier. At Rothesay, under a tortoise-shell of shields they hacked with axes at the soft stonework of the castle—probably the circular shell which is the core of the present castle there—and in spite of boiling pitch from the wall-head they broke in and slew the 'steward' (perhaps a cadet of the Stewart family) who was in command. The news of an approaching Galwegian fleet and the death of Uspak, who had been wounded, caused the Norwegians to draw off and so to achieve their other objective, the restoration of Olaf, King of Man. The episode had no permanent effect, but it shows that King Haakon was prepared to intervene in the Isles and either that he sought the recovery of Bute or else that the lords of Argyll were prepared to use his interest to secure it for their family. It was only a matter of time before King Alexander reciprocated this interest.

Although these barons of Argyll and the Isles were lords of piratical fleets of swift longships, calling upon their dependents for naval service and probably owing the same service to the king, they were also familiar with the castles and monasteries in the landscape of contemporary Scotland. Since the late twelfth century Argyll had been a bishopric with its see at the site of the seventh-century monastery of St Moluag on Lismore. In the third quarter of the twelfth century, Somerled or his son Ranald founded a Cistercian abbey at Saddell in Kintyre, and about 1230 Duncan mac Dougall established a Valliscaulian priory at Ardchattan. This priory, and the bishop's seat, lay within a few miles of the strength of the mac Dougalls, Dunstaffnage Castle. The thirteenth-century stone castles of the western seaboard—Skipness, Sween, Duntroon, Dunstaffnage, Duart, Mingarry, Tioram, Innischonnel—survive tolerably complete; all save Skipness are by obvious anchorages and they have a family likeness which stamps them as the product of particular social and political circumstances. Among the scattered rocky islets of the same region were some whose sides, rising as cliffs from the sea, made them natural fortresses, strengthened by walls across gullies and gentler slopes; such were Cairnburgh and Dunchonnell, but these offered neither beaching nor anchorage. A mighty aristocracy was at the same time in contact with the military architecture of the 'Norman' and 'feudal' stone enceinte and sailed in its galleys supreme over the western seas. Although we have neither documentary nor archaeological evidence to ascribe these buildings to the mid-thirteenth century, there is no other period with which they are so congruous.[47]

Alexander II may have encouraged the 'great dispeace' caused by Duncan mac Dougall which brought about the Norse expedition of 1230; certainly Duncan was one of the select company of Scottish barons who informed the pope of the treaty with England in 1237. A royal charter of 1240 deals in lands at the south end of Loch Awe and on Loch Fyne side and shows that royal authority stretched to the boundaries of Lorn, while the history of the bishopric of Argyll also suggests the growth of royal influence. By c. 1230 the vacant see was given into the charge of the non-Scottish bishop of the Isles, but in 1236 (presumably on a royal petition) the bishop of Moray was instructed by the pope to secure an election, and by 1239 a dignitary of Moray was bishop. In 1241 the new bishop was drowned and the see was a little later given into the charge of Clement, Bishop of Dunblane. By 1248 the bishop, backed by the king, secured powers to end the vacancy in the see and to move the cathedral to the mainland. These moves mark a growing determination to end the influence over the see of the lord of Argyll into whose pocket the admittedly scanty revenues were probably flowing. Matthew Paris is clearly and well informed that Bishop Clement urged his king to act against the new lord of Argyll. His motives were doubtless ecclesiastical, his influence considerable.[48]

Ewen, the son of Duncan, had become lord of Argyll after 1237 and perhaps by 1240, and for unknown reasons turned, along with his cousin, Dugald, lord of Garmoran, to Haakon IV for support. In the spring of 1248 they arrived in Bergen, seeking the title of king, which was given to Ewen. Late in the same year, however, the king of Man was drowned and early in 1249 Ewen was sent west 'as quickly as possible to be ruler over the Isles until King Haakon made another plan for them'—that is, he was given a temporary commission to rule all the isles from Lewis to Man.

Since the settlement of his difficulties with Henry III in 1244

[47] *Inventory of Argyll*, i, no. 314; ii, nos. 287, 292.

[48] A. A. M. Duncan and A. L. Brown, 'Argyll and the Isles in the Earlier Middle Ages', *Proc. Soc. Antiq. Sc.*, xc (1956–7), 192–220.

Alexander II had been free to show a new interest in the western seaboard, and in that year he made his first known bid to Haakon IV to buy the Isles 'for refined silver'. Over the following five years repeated offers made no impression, but the Norwegians must have known that the logical consequence of their refusals would be to drive the Scots to force and the hasty commission for Ewen reflects this concern. At the same time, Henry III was not above meddling in these affairs for, in the spring of 1248, he had allowed Walter Bisset to buy stores in Ireland for Dunaverty Castle on the Mull of Kintyre (opposite the Bisset island, Rathlin) which he had seized and was fortifying—a sweet revenge for the hospitality given by Alexander II to William and Geoffrey Marsh. Sometime during 1248 Dunaverty Castle was stormed by Alan 'son of the earl', illegitimate son of Thomas of Galloway, and evidently Bisset was taken captive there, for on 13 January 1249 he reappeared in Scotland for the first time as witness to a royal charter.[49] It would seem likely that he owed his restoration to royal favour to the information he could disclose about the western seaboard. Alexander II moved in great anger that summer against Ewen of Argyll, who was expelled and restored in 1255 only at the instigation of Henry III—the only 'Scot' for whom he interceded. These facts suggest that the turncoat Bisset was able to disclose negotiations between the English king and Ewen and possibly other lords of the Isles. Finally, Walter Comyn, Earl of Menteith, is not found as a witness to royal charters from the beginning of 1248, and other Comyns are exceptionally rare, while their ally Patrick, Earl of Dunbar, went crusading in the summer of 1248 and died. There can be little doubt that, perhaps with the aid of Walter Bisset's disclosures, Alan Durward eclipsed the Comyns in the counsels of the king during 1248 and 1249.

Alexander II was surely perturbed by Ewen's commission from King Haakon, a greater concentration of authority in one pair of hands than had been known since the time of Thorfinn the Mighty, and yet enjoyed by one who was also a Scottish baron. Presumably the king knew that negotiations with Norway would be fruitless, because the expedition which he commanded must have been fairly long in preparation. We know that the host was called out from Angus, and therefore, it seems likely, from other provinces. The sources do not mention a land expedition through, say, Glendochart, but there may have been one, eclipsed in chronicles by the king's

[49] *Dunfermline Regitrum*, no. 77.

naval expedition. Matthew Paris tells of negotiations in which Ewen pleaded that he could serve two masters, and finally offered to give up some or all of his Norwegian territories, but met with a refusal from Alexander II. The saga of King Haakon speaks of a visit by Ewen to Alexander's court and a demand that he should give up to the king Cairnburgh and three other castles and all his island territories. We know only that while his fleet was anchored in Oban bay the king was taken ill with a 'fever' and died on the island of Kerrera, on 8 July 1249. On the same day his seal was put to a charter dated at Kerrera and granting to the vacant see of Argyll the kirk of St Bride in Lorn. The witnesses were Clement, Bishop of Dunblane, whose ecclesiastical motives we have examined already, Alan Durward and his fellow justiciar David de Lindsay, Alexander Stewart, Walter de Moray, William de Brechin, Walter Bisset and Robert de Menzies; these men may be seen as a group opposed to the Comyn influence preponderant until *c.* 1242. It would be wrong to conclude that the king was in any way dominated by a faction, or that he did not wholly control the choice of his own council. Among those prominent at court was William, Earl of Mar, whose right to his earldom certainly prejudiced claims of Alan Durward; the two were later politically opposed for this reason but as long as Alexander II lived their rivalry was stilled and they served him.

Within limits the expedition of 1249 was successful. Ewen was expelled from Argyll and fled to Lewis; when in 1250 he sought acceptance as 'king of the Isles' from the Manx, he was forced to withdraw. For a few years he made a career in Scandinavia as a mercenary captain to King Haakon, while his lands in Argyll were in the hands of a royal bailie and his bishopric was filled by a cleric Alan, who was perhaps a son of Duncan, earl of Carrick, or one of his clerks, a graduate. But though Argyll was his in a new sense, Alexander II had not united the Isles to Scotland. It remained to be seen whether he had taught the Islesmen a lesson.

*Addendum to 1978 impression.* The discussion of the south-west (pp. 531–2) requires correction on several points. The right of *surdit de serjeant* (p. 531) was ancient, is found elsewhere in Celtic Britain (cf. p. 76) and was not introduced in the thirteenth century (G. W. S. Barrow in *Northern History*, iv, 16). The death in 1246 (p. 532, line 5) was not of Alan but of the de Fortibus coheiress, Christine countess of Albemarle. And Professor Barrow has shown me his notes on the Fitz Randolph family which was clearly from Stichill, Roxburghshire and not connected (at least through the names Ralph, Randolph) with Ralph Fitz Dunegal of Nithsdale (p. 532).

# 21

## HIS LAND AT PEACE:[1]
## ALEXANDER III, 1249–86

Wh, no doubt that his son, Alexander, would be the next king. But as in other kingdoms (and most clearly documented in England, France and Germany) the absence of a formulated rule of succession had perpetuated the idea, understandable and necessary in, say, 1093, that a man became king only when given possession of the symbols of kingship. It was not until 1272 in England and 1329 in Scotland that a reign was reckoned to begin before (in each case, as it happened, months before) the inauguration of the king. Thus, on the day after King William died at Stirling on 4 December 1214 (having seen his son received as future king by prelates and magnates) two bishops, the queen and the chancellor stayed with the corpse, while early in the morning seven earls (Fife, Strathearn, Atholl, Angus, Menteith, Buchan and Dunbar) and the bishop of St Andrews took their new lord to Scone where he was elevated as king. On that and the two following days there were festivities, but on the fourth day after his death the old king's body was met at the bridge of Perth by the new king and conveyed to Arbroath for burial. However macabre the mixture may seem to us, there was sound sense in inaugurating the new king before the old was in his grave, for the period between the death of a king and the accession of his successor was an interregnum in which, for lack of a king, the king's peace had died.[2]

Nothing specific is known of the inauguration ceremony of

---

[1] Anderson, *Early Sources*, ii, 687 from the Chronicle of the Kings.
[2] W. W. Scott, 'Fordun's description of the Inauguration of Alexander II', *Sc. Hist. Rev.*, l (1971), 198–200.

1214. It is said to have been more uplifting and glorious than any previous one; the king 'took up the government', was 'elevated'. But no mention is made of the insignia used, and we must turn to other kinds of evidence for a fuller understanding of the symbolism of kingship in Scotland. Twelfth-century coins show a crown upon the head of the Scottish king; a miniature painting on Malcolm IV's charter to Kelso Abbey shows David I and his grandson with crowns and other insignia. Such evidence is untrustworthy because copied from exemplars, probably not Scottish. The royal seals are rather more informative. King Edgar's shows the influence of Edward the Confessor's: the king wears a lily crown and carries sceptre and sword, while the legend calls him *basileus*. That of Alexander I is more obviously derivative, in this case from William Rufus' seal: among several features in common are the sword and orb carried by the king. But there are differences. While Rufus wears an arched lily crown from which a jewelled pendant hangs over each ear (the *kataseistai* of a Byzantine emperor), Alexander I wears a simple hair-band with meaningless pendants. Rufus is *Dei gratia rex Anglorum*, Alexander I *Deo rectore rex Scottorum*. Whether the pendants disappeared in 1124 or 1153 is not certain; impressions of the seals of David I and Malcolm IV are few and poor but show that the design of Alexander I was closely followed. The seals of William and Alexander II were completely redrawn but follow earlier seals with sword, orb and legend, King William wears a cap, and his son is bare headed; there are no pendants.

This evidence is untrustworthy where it is derivative, but significance must be attached to those features which are unique. Alexander I used the words *Dei gratia* in the address of charters but they were plainly avoided in the legend of his seal. By itself this might mean little but in conjunction with the pointed omission of the crown it surely indicates that the designer of the seal had in mind the absence of anointing and coronation from the ceremony of royal inauguration.[3] Writing not long before 1214, Gerald the Welshman noted that the Scottish and Spanish kings were neither crowned nor anointed; in fact the Spanish kings were abandoning these ceremonies, while the Scottish Alexander II strove to secure the right to them from the pope. Whatever ceremony took place in 1214 at Scone we may be sure that it was neither coronation nor anointing;

---

[3] The English coronation order contained the words 'Anoint this king with the oil of the grace of thy Holy Spirit. . . .'

from the attendance of seven earls and one bishop it would seem to have been predominantly secular. Scone was the traditional place of inauguration; some of the ceremonies would be of ancient lineage.

We have seen that in 1221 Alexander II asked that he should be crowned and anointed, and that Honorius III preferred the representations of Henry III (his vassal) that Scotland was subject to the English king. The pope replied that unction would be permissible only with the consent of Henry, his councillors and his prelates.[4] In 1233 another application was successfully opposed by the archbishop of York on behalf of himself and his king. There may have been other approaches to the papacy, perhaps even in the twelfth century, but none was successful, and Alexander II must have tasted gall when he heard of the coronation and anointing of Haakon IV in 1247. The Scots failed where the Norse succeeded because they were bitterly opposed at the curia by the English. The opposition had the same roots as the Scottish desire—an acceptance of the ecclesiastical view that a true king was created only by these religious signs, that without them his kingship was defective, and hence, in the English view, subordinate.

The situation in 1249 was complicated by the youth of the new king, then well on in his eighth year. It was almost a century since a boy had succeeded in Scotland, though only thirty years since the nine-year-old Henry III had succeeded in England, when William Marshall, Earl of Pembroke was appointed 'governor (*rector*) of the king and kingdom', and the boy himself was entrusted to his widowed mother. Henry III, we may note, was crowned at once but waited for three years before a seal was struck in his name. Alexander (III) was probably with his mother, Marie de Coucy, at Scone or Dunfermline Abbey when word was brought of his father's death. On 13 July 1249, only five days after that event, two bishops (at least) and a number of magnates were gathered at Scone for the king's inauguration. The assembly cannot have been large but Alan Durward was there, having, we may presume, hurried overland from Argyll.

The ceremony was held up by a debate among the magnates, a party led by Durward urging that the king must first be knighted. This was indeed a growing convention in thirteenth-century Europe, and Henry III had been knighted by the *rector* before his corona-

4 Above, p. 526.

tion; it seems that Durward aimed to knight the king himself, thereby conferring the first of the insignia and probably staking a claim to be regent. At the urging of Walter Comyn, Earl of Menteith, this argument was rejected and the king was inaugurated: 'in the ancestral manner on 13 July, made king by the magnates, placed on the paternal throne and honoured by all as lawful heir'—these words of the *Melrose Chronicle*, written in the 1250s, stress the secular nature of a ceremony of which enthronement was the core and essence. Fordun (who tells us of the magnates' dispute) gives a rather fuller description, placing acceptance or acclamation at the beginning, not the end: after all those present had agreed to his immediate inauguration, the magnates, headed by the earls of Fife and Strathearn, led Alexander to a cross in the abbey graveyard where they placed him on a royal throne, and the bishop of St Andrews, with the others, consecrated him as king with the king sitting upon the throne, a stone, while the magnates on bended knees cast their garments before the throne. A Highland Scot on bended knee before the throne read the king's genealogy in Gaelic back to the eponymous Scota, daughter of Pharaoh.[5]

The earliest literary description of the stone throne, by the Yorkshire chronicler Walter of Guisborough, states that it was very large, concave and made to the shape (*ad modum*) of a round chair; the only depiction of a royal inauguration, upon a seal of Scone Abbey, shows the outline of a conventional throne without back, very much as seen upon earlier royal seals, but reduced in size to accommodate other figures. We must leave open the question whether the throne was a chair-shaped stone or the present stone enclosed in a wooden chair, for even Guisborough's description is not unambiguous. The seal clearly shows that the king was vested in his robe by a bishop and unmitred cleric, the bishop of St Andrews and the abbot of Scone respectively. Behind both of these are secular figures, two earls whose identities are indicated by the shields of arms under the king's feet—Fife, the king, Strathearn— and who had presumably enthroned him. Three figures are shown above them; one is a cleric offering to the king a small house, a reliquary-shrine, for the taking of an oath; another may be a layman and holds something long, narrow and two-dimensional, the

---

[5] *Chron. Fordun*, i, 293–5. M. D. Legge, 'The Inauguration of Alexander III', *Proc. Soc. Antiq. Sc.*, lxxx (1945–6), 73–82. Note that Fordun is explicit that the genealogy was read.

rolls of the king's genealogy; the function of the third figure is not clear. The king is youthful, wears an open lily crown, and carries in his right hand a sceptre terminating in a lily, while his left holds the fastening of his mantle. These insignia, the seal suggests, were worn by the king at his inauguration; it refrains from suggesting that he was invested with anything other than the mantle. The background is dappled to indicate an out-of-doors ceremony. No precise date can be put upon this seal, but stylistically it is of the thirteenth century, and several details, such as the king's youth, point to the inauguration of Alexander III as the ceremony which it depicts.

By June 1250 the king was provided with a seal which departs from the traditional in so many ways that its evidence is especially valuable. It was much smaller than usual; for this there was no parallel in England or France and we must presume that it was to mark the fact that the king was in his minority and that the acts to which it was appended could be rejected or confirmed when he came of age to rule. On one side is the king in majesty, wearing a crown for the first time since 1107 in Scottish royal seals, on the other a shield of his arms; this combination is without precedent. The dropping of the king on horseback from the reverse may be attributed to the fact that he was not yet a knight. Both sides have the same legend, a motto probably chosen because it included the word *columba*,[6] but around the enthroned king are also the words *Dei gratia rex Scottorum* (not as heretofore *Deo rectore*). The youthful king wears a lily crown, holds a sword lying horizontally on his knees[7] in his right hand and a foliated sceptre in his left hand. These symbols and words depict a king by God's grace; the stress is upon the nature of kingship, to the exclusion even of the king's name.

By the end of 1250 the king had a great seal on which he was shown crowned, holding sword and either orb or sceptre.[8] After a brief period the small seal was brought back into use for a decade until, about 1260, a second great seal was engraved closely following that made for Henry III at the end of 1259 and showing an

----

[6] *Esto prudens ut serpens et simplex sicut columba*, adapted from Matthew, x, 16, where the apostles are to go out as lambs among wolves, and be prudent etc. The relevance is obscure.

[7] Perhaps because he was not a knight.

[8] The surviving impressions are few and show the left arm outstretched but do not show what it holds.

elaborate throne (like the wooden chair in Westminster Abbey) and a bearded king. It varies only in what Alexander III holds—in his right hand a foliated sceptre, in his left the fastening of his mantle. Thus it may have provided the model for the Scone seal which also has these features but which shares a beardless king and stool-throne with the smaller seal. If their exact inter-relationships are not certain, four seals are agreed in introducing to Scottish royal iconography a crowned king, three in showing him holding a sceptre terminating in a flower or in branches. These were now the symbols of kingship in Scotland and we can hardly doubt that such articles existed. There is record of the existence of a crown of King John in 1296; the August 1291 inventory of the Scottish treasury lists *virga Aaron* among several miscellaneous but costly items from Alexander III's wardrobe—a rod blossoming just as the king's sceptre does upon his seal.[9] As in Irish inaugurations, twelfth-century and earlier kings had probably been invested with a staff of governance—a simple and obvious symbol of coercive authority. But in 1182 Pope Lucius III sent the golden rose to King William as a mark of favour: *rosam auream in virga etiam aurea erectam*.[10] Denied a crown and holy oil, William no doubt made the most of displaying his golden rose on ceremonial occasions, and in this way it came to be used, we suggest, as a royal sceptre and to be interpreted as a symbolic Aaron's rod, which, left in the tabernacle where it brought forth blooms, showed God's choice of the Levites as the kin set aside in Israel for the priesthood. So, too, King Alexander was marked by God to rule.

The king must also have possessed a sword, but the small seal shows it ineffectually at rest while the Scone Abbey seal and the second great seal, having put the sceptre in the king's right (sword) hand, omit the sword and leave the left hand clasping and drawing attention to the king's mantle with which the clergy invested him. The sword was perhaps not one of the insignia of kingship, or, if it was, was of lesser importance.

In pretending to crown, mantle and sceptre the Scottish king was going as far as he dared towards the coronation and anointing for which Alexander II had asked. Since the Scone seal and the small royal seal strongly suggest that Alexander III bore these insignia on 13 July 1249, they must already have existed under Alexander II, though not, of course, used at his inauguration. The

[9] *A.P.S.*, i, 112.                    [10] *Chron. Fordun*, i, 280.

crown-wearing Alexander III was enthroned by the earls and robed by the clergy, invested with sceptre by one or other, probably swore an oath, was acclaimed on bended knees and had his genealogy proclaimed. The order of these elements had probably changed since 1124, but they remained appropriate to a more primitive society than thirteenth-century Scotland. The king accepted the ecclesiastical view that his kingship would be of full stature only when conferred by churchmen in quasi-sacramental ceremonies. When Fordun speaks of the bishop and others consecrating Alexander III as king he is using an anachronistic term for ceremonies which were still essentially secular.

In May 1250[11] Alan Durward was at Inverurie with his knights, still justiciar of Scotia and engaged in founding a hospital at Kincardine O'Neil; for the next eighteen months he is frequently named in the office. On the other hand, David de Lindsay ceased to be justiciar of Lothian, presumably at Alexander II's death, and no replacement is found. Thus Fordun is correct when he calls Durward in July 1249 'justiciar of all Scotia', that is, all Scotland, an office surely comparable with the English justiciarship and singling him out as second only to the king in secular government. Early in June 1250 there was a council at Edinburgh and on 19 June, in fulfilment of negotiations which had been carried on at Rome since 1245, the king, his mother, the prelates and magnates gathered at Dunfermline to mark the canonisation of Margaret, queen of Malcolm III, by transferring her relics to a new and more splendid shrine. As a ceremony it could not compare with Henry III's rebuilding of Westminster Abbey for the relics of Edward the Confessor, but the devotion of the royal house to the cult of Margaret had something of the same significance: she was the kingdom's past, the devout wife of a semi-legendary and heroic king, a sign to Scotsmen of God's grace to the royal house. Her name was given to its daughters until the time of Alexander III (though by Alexander II only to his illegitimate daughter—and she was married to Alan Durward).

In the autumn of 1250 Queen Marie de Coucy left Scotland for France in enjoyment of a remarkably high terce, variously reported

---

[11] Powicke, *Thirteenth Century*, chapter XII is excellent. There is another excellent discussion of the 1250s differing from this one in some details and in emphasis by D. E. R. Watt, 'The Minority of Alexander III of Scotland', *Transactions of the Royal Historical Society*⁵, xxi (1971), 1–24.

as between 4000 and 7000 merks. Although she seems to have planned to return in the following spring, she did not see her son again till Christmas 1251 and did not return to Scotland till 1257. The two earliest original letters of Alexander III to survive bear in June 1250 the small seal or seal of minority, and in December 1250 the great seal which was a token that the king was now considered of age to grant secure titles and to be represented as exercising government. This change, taken with the queen's departure, represents a decisive shift of power towards the end of 1250 into the hands of Alan Durward, sole *justiciarius Scocie*. In 1250 the chamberlain under Alexander II, Richard of Inverkeithing, was promoted bishop of Dunkeld and by February 1251 Sir Robert Menzies, a supporter of Durward, held this office.

William de Bondington, Bishop of Glasgow since 1233, was chancellor from 1231 until 1247 and may have continued to hold office until Alexander II's death. At some point in the following two years the unusual step was taken of appointing a monastic chancellor—Robert de Kenleith, Abbot of Dunfermline since 1240. This man had shown his ability by securing the mitre and ring for the holder of his office, the canonisation of St Margaret for his abbey, and a papal chaplaincy for himself, besides a number of lesser privileges. His undoubted familiarity with the papal curia would suggest to the Scots his suitability to become chancellor, for they had important business with the pope. On 6 April 1251, Innocent IV refused an English petition that the Scottish king might not be crowned nor anointed without consent of Henry III, who claimed to be his liege lord, but at the same time promised to grant nothing prejudicial to the royal dignity (of England).[12] This refusal to renew the veto granted by Honorius III in 1221 makes it clear that the Scots had asked for coronation and anointing for their king and were then actively pressing the matter at the papal court in Lyons. We may hazard the conjecture that this business was set on foot in the autumn of 1250 and that Abbot Robert was then appointed chancellor and dispatched to accomplish it.[13] About the same time or a little later, however, the Scottish bishops or some of their number seem to have lodged bitter complaint at Rome against the 'new courtiers' who ruled the boy king and had attacked ecclesiastical

---

[12] Stones, *Anglo-Scottish Relations*, no. 9.

[13] There is no trace of his being in Scotland during 1251 but such negative evidence is inconclusive.

privileges and jurisdiction over a wide field, so that the pope issued a commission of investigation to three English bishops in May 1251. It is possible that these dissident Scots had found allies among English agents at the *curia*.

Although Henry III had gilded the lily by asking the pope for a tenth of Scottish ecclesiastical revenues—unsuccessfully—relations between the governments were sufficiently amicable in the summer of 1251 for agreement to be reached on the early conclusion of marriage between Alexander III and Margaret, daughter of Henry III; the need for good relations with England was presumably appreciated by all Scots. At York on Christmas day 1251, in the presence of his mother (on a visit from France) Alexander III was knighted by the English king along with twenty other young noblemen, and was married to Margaret on the following day, with the promise of a dowry of 5000 merks. Immediately thereafter he did homage to King Henry for his English lands and was requested to add homage also for the kingdom of Scotland. According to the *St Albans Chronicle*, which is our only source for this episode, King Alexander replied that he had come to marry and not 'to answer about so difficult a matter'; this refusal, which Henry could only accept, may not be accurately reported and we should not build too much upon the wording of it nor, for that matter, upon the wording of Henry's demand. When the Earl Marshal of England sought King Alexander's palfrey as his customary right on such occasions, he was firmly told that the Scottish king could be knighted by anyone—that is, that there was no English right to do so, though probably (and since 1153 certainly) no Scottish king had been knighted by anyone else. Like the elaborate precautions to provide adequate but separate quarters for the retinues of the two kings in order to minimise friction, these episodes are symptoms of the clearer nationality of Scotland, whose barons had fewer material interests in, and therefore fewer intellectual commitments to, England. The trickster English king was now prepared to jeopardise relations which, since 1237 or 1244, had been free from causes of conflict, by seeking to add to the other promises of good behaviour which he had from the Scottish king the general promise of homage and fealty. The Scots were clearly well aware of these pretensions and were prepared to reject them in whichever form they were served up.

Before or more probably on 27 December, Henry III gave his

support to those Scots who were moved to fear and jealousy by the growing power of Durward and by their own exclusion from government. The whole grounds are not known but Alexander III or Henry III in his name was able to demand and receive the resignation of all those royal officers (and their number is uncertain) who were present; some slipped away to Scotland, among them probably the chancellor, who had not resigned. Henry III conceded that these resignations on foreign soil should not prejudice the king or kingdom of Scotland and accepted exclusion from the appointment of new officials which seems to have been held over till the court was back in Scotland. Nonetheless, the Scots must have accepted his proposal to send 'a prudent counsellor' who would help to look after the affairs of the queen and king.[14] It has often been stressed that Henry III acquired the right to intervene in Scotland because of his concern for his daughter's welfare, but in normal times this would have allowed him to name (as he did) only some members of her household. The much wider scope of his concern and of his intervention stemmed from the internal Scottish crisis of December 1251 and from one party having called Henry III in to resolve it. He helped to get rid of Durward because Durward seemed a threat to Alexander III and Margaret; he had a reasonable claim to a representative at the Scottish court who would participate in the new government in order to ensure that the threat did not recur. There was probably an understanding that the new government would retain authority until the king's fourteenth birthday in September 1255.

What had Durward done? Our two sources, the *Melrose Chronicle* and Fordun, are slightly at variance but we cannot be far wrong in saying that he was charged with seeking the legitimation of his wife in order to make her and his daughters heiresses to the king, and with the intention of obtaining the throne by foul means. Fordun would have it that the chancellor was to legitimate under the great seal, but the *Melrose Chronicle* must be right in speaking of messengers to the pope who alone could legitimate in such circumstances. If the chancellor was such a messenger to the curia, Fordun's confusion and the treatment of the chancellor would alike be explained. On the king's return to Scotland at the beginning of January 1252, Abbot Robert surrendered the great seal,

[14] Perhaps on the grounds that the queen's interest in the assignment of her dowry must be protected by some powerful baron.

which was broken up. His convent accused him of embezzlement and he surrendered his abbacy on 2 February, subsequently becoming a Cistercian monk at Newbattle. This victimisation suggests that he was thought to be privy to Durward's plans, which may not have extended to treason, but, in view of his determination and ambition on other occasions, could well have amounted to legitimation of his wife as insurance against the king's death from natural causes. Whatever the justification, Durward must have created a mountain of suspicion and resentment. His treatment of the church, his sole justiciarship, his striking of a great seal, his rigorous exclusion of the Comyns from office and power, his marriage, which occurred before Alexander II's death, perhaps even the translation of St Margaret's remains, must have accumulated to suggest that there was no limit to his ambitions.

This revolution was almost certainly begun by the earls of Menteith and Mar, who returned to Scotland in control of the king and the government, immeasurably more powerful and prestigious than Durward and his supporters. Alexander Comyn, Earl of Buchan, became justiciar of Scotia, William, Earl of Mar, his brother-in-law, chamberlain, and Thomas de Normanville, lord of Maxton in Roxburghshire, justiciar of Lothian, while the king's small seal, now recalled to use as the only seal, was carried by a pushing university teacher Master Gamelin, illegitimate but probably the son of a Comyn. The Comyns (including Mar) formed outstandingly the most important and powerful group in the new government, but in December 1253 they counted upon the support of Alexander Stewart and Clement, Bishop of Dunblane, both of whom had previously been associated with, though not necessarily committed to, Alan Durward. Nicholas de Soules, lord of Liddesdale, and Thomas fitz Randolph, lord of Upper Nithsdale, more important Border lords than Normanville, were on the council and seem to have been Comyn supporters. Perhaps the most interesting 'inner' member of this government was David de Graham, representative of a junior branch of the Graham family, whose senior branch had been lords of Dalkeith and Eskdale in Midlothian since the mid-twelfth century. David held land in the Merse and appears as witness to charters of Patrick, Earl of Dunbar (died 1248), who was probably his most important lord. By 1253, however, he had acquired a string of lands lying just south of the Forth: a holding near West Calder, Eliston and Kinpunt in West Lothian, Dundaff and Strathcarron, holdings near Falkirk and Dunipace, a substantial barony (Kincaid, Killearn and Strathblane) in the east of the Lennox and bordering on the Comyn lordship of Lenzie. He held land also in the west, in Strathgryfe, Cunningham and Carrick. Most if not all of these extensive territories were acquired in the time of Alexander II, who in 1248 appointed Graham to be depute of the justiciar of Lothian. He was a 'new' man who had risen fast—one can only suspect that he speculated in land—and he took care to protect his acquisitions by securing a royal confirmation of eighteen separate donations in December 1253.

The two leading members of the government were undoubtedly Walter Comyn, Earl of Menteith, and Robert de Ros, lord of Wark on Tweed and one of King Henry's two representatives at the Scottish court. Ros was a son of the English baronial leader of 1215 and of an illegitimate daughter of King William, and was well enough known at Alexander II's court. His fellow representative was John Balliol of Barnard Castle, who had recently acquired part of the lordship of Galloway by marriage but who was less familiar with Scotland and allowed himself to be guided by Ros. Whatever King Henry's intentions, his two representatives seem to have identified themselves with the government of Scotland, and the young queen was soon complaining of her treatment in letters to her father. She and the king lived in Edinburgh Castle, where they were not allowed to cohabit as man and wife but had to suffer cramped conditions and inclement weather. A month before his departure to Gascony (on 6 August 1253), King Henry was begging the Scots for a visit from his daughter to her mother, but in vain. When in Gascony he fell victim to rumours of a Castilian invasion and sought help from the regency in England, which in its turn asked Alexander III to summon his prelates and magnates to be at Edinburgh Castle on 16 February to hear news from Gascony and to furnish 'counsel and aid'. If such a discussion was held it is unlikely to have offered the men and money requested but probably took grave offence at the request. One Scot went to the aid of Henry III: in May 1254 Alan Durward undertook to perform the service due in Gascony by the earl of Strathearn as an English baron. He may have gone in the company of King Henry's son Edward, whom he certainly accompanied to Burgos in Castille late in October 1254 for his marriage. For this Alan received £30 additional to the annual fee of £50 given to him by King Henry; 'he not only recovered the king's friendship, but also accused in many ways those that had accused him before the same king with their accomplices'.[15]

Henry III had already been deeply committed by the pope to another ploy—the conquest of the kingdom of Sicily for his younger son. From May 1254 the pope repeatedly demanded a tax of an annual twentieth of revenues for three years from the Scottish church, the money to go to a crusade which was in effect the Sicilian business. The refusal of the Scots was perhaps a further offence in Henry's eyes. In August and September 1254 he issued several commissions for embassies of great weight to preach his secrets to Alexander III, but there is no evidence that any of them visited Scotland to involve the Scots in support of the Sicilian business. When King Henry returned to England at the very end of 1254 he had many good reasons for dissatisfaction with the Scottish government, of which the best was probably the treatment of Queen Margaret.

Unfortunately, we know little of Scottish reaction to the behaviour of the Comyns and of Henry III. In 1253, when the see of St Andrews fell vacant and the convent made an election unauthorised by the government, an appeal was lodged at Rome through Master Abel, archdeacon of St Andrews, who had enjoyed the favour of Alexander II. He succeeded. in having the election quashed, but instead of procuring the appointment of Master Gamelin, now styled chancellor, as the government plainly intended, he was himself postulated and consecrated. He returned in June 1254—and the government at first thought to exclude him—but died on 1 December 1254. The government procured the election of Gamelin in February 1255. In a somewhat different case in 1253–4, the council overrode the rights of patronage in the see of Whithorn claimed by John Balliol, who seems to have called on the support of the archbishop of York in a protracted dispute which left strained relations between the Scots and this representative of King Henry. The government nominee, Henry, Abbot of Holyrood, is not known to have had any close connection with the Comyns, but so far as these episodes go they do suggest that the council had assumed the rights of the king in matters ecclesiastical, and so alienated a measure of baronial opinion.

At the end of August 1254 Henry III ordered Robert de Ros

[15] *Melrose Chronicle* in Anderson, *Early Sources*, ii, 576. See Genealogical Tree No. 4 for the Comyn family.

and John Balliol to withdraw from the council of the Scots king 'until it is otherwise reformed' but Ros, at least, seems to have ignored these instructions. It was a further year before King Henry acted and he probably did so because Alexander's fourteenth birthday was imminent. He sent the earl of Gloucester and John Mansel, an able diplomat, to Edinburgh in July 1255. They slipped quietly into Edinburgh Castle to interview the royal pair and on the basis of what they learned told Henry III that Robert de Ros was principally to blame for the unhappiness of the queen, and indicated the Scotsmen upon whom Henry could rely if the Comyns were ousted from power. That word had reached the English king by 10 August, when, on his way to York, he extended a promise of assurance to the earls of Dunbar, Strathearn and Carrick, Bruce, Stewart, Durward and several others and their supporters.

Unfortunately, the exact chronology of August 1255 is unknown to us, for while English sources speak fully of Ros and Balliol, the Scottish source, the *Melrose Chronicle*, tells us of a *coup d'état* carried out by Durward and the earl of Dunbar, who attended the king at Edinburgh 'for the restoration of peace' and then during an adjournment, ostensibly to Stirling, seized the king and Edinburgh Castle while the opposing magnates were absent. It seems that Mansel was already back at the Scottish court, and we may conjecture that Robert de Ros, who had promised to return to England, now took fright at the fall of his Comyn colleagues and went back on his word. For a brief time the king, queen, Dunbar, Durward, Gloucester and Mansel seem to have been confined to Edinburgh Castle by the Comyns and their supporters, but they were able to make their way to Roxburgh, and then over the Tweed to Wark to greet Henry III, leave Queen Margaret with him and return. On 8 September, King Henry visited Roxburgh and Kelso Abbey and began negotiations which lasted until 20 September, of such length that they must have been conducted not only between the kings but also with the Comyn party. King Henry failed to persuade the leading members of that party 'to put their seals to a certain most wicked document which the aforesaid conspirators (that is, Dunbar, Durward and their supporters) had drawn up and sealed, in which many things were contained that might result in the dishonour of the king and kingdom'.[16] Doubtless this document was a projected settlement of the government for the remaining seven years of royal

[16] *Melrose Chronicle* in Anderson, *Early Sources*, ii, 583.

minority, but its contents are wholly unknown; it seems likely that the Comyn party refused to participate because they had been ousted directly by Henry III, and were being called upon to make monetary 'amends' to him as well as to Alexander III.

The document[17] finally issued on 20 September in the name of Alexander III and at the instance of Henry III has all the appearance of an exasperated sweeping of the unco-operative Comyn party from all part in government. The bishops of Glasgow and Dunblane and the elect of St Andrews, the earls of Menteith, Buchan and Mar, John Balliol and Robert de Ros and a group of barons—Comyn, Soules, Normanville, Maxwell, fitz Randolph, Graham and eight others—with three clerics were removed as counsellors and from all office and favour, not to be restored until they had atoned for their offences to both kings, but liable to be called on for help if there was a foreign invasion of Scotland. The measure of the offences committed and of the atonement required are alike unknown, but the offices of state certainly changed hands at this juncture. Durward once again became justiciar of Scotia but this time with a justiciar of Lothian, Walter Moray of Bothwell, while a former holder of that office, David de Lindsay, became chamberlain. Richard of Inverkeithing, chamberlain in the 1240s and now bishop of Dunkeld, replaced Gamelin as chancellor but this office was clearly greatly reduced in importance since the new counsellors had effective disposal of wardships and escheats, of local offices and of 'reasonable grants'.

The new counsellors, who were to hold office for seven years from the king's fourteenth birthday, 4 September 1255, were appointed 'for our councils, the government of our kingdom and the keeping of the persons of ourselves and our queen',[18] unless discharged earlier by the two kings. Alexander III would be twenty-one years old at the end of seven years, but this provision for discharge of the council would enable him to declare himself of age at some earlier date—as Henry III did when he was nineteen. An individual counsellor could be removed by death or for manifest demerits, but effectively only the other counsellors or King Henry could pronounce upon such demerits, and King Alexander was really submitting to rule by a group of his own magnates backed by

---

17 Stones, *Anglo-Scottish Relations*, no. 10.
18 ad consilia nostra et gubernacionem regni nostri et custodiam corporis nostri et regine sponse nostre.

the English king. This group was undoubtedly headed by Patrick, Earl of Dunbar, son of the earl who had opposed Bisset and Durward in the 1240s, said to be unlike his father, and certainly at odds with his widowed mother. The Durward faction of 1249–51 was of this party, but its strength surely derived from the broad base of moderate opinion opposed to the monopolising of power by one family and its dependents. Malise, Earl of Strathearn, was closest to Henry III, having perhaps negotiated his support for the *coup d'état* during a visit to England in May 1255; Malcolm, Earl of Fife, Neil, Earl of Carrick, Stewart and Bruce came from the very top rank of the Scottish aristocracy, while William de Brechin (son of an illegitimate son of David, Earl of Huntingdon), Walter Moray of Petty and Bothwell, Gilbert de Hay and Hugh Gifford were important barons of the same quality as Durward and his supporters Menzies and Lindsay. The bishops of Dunkeld (chancellor) and of Aberdeen (Peter de Ramsey, formerly chancellor) completed the council. Examination of this party reveals no obvious or close links of family or territorial interest, though it is said that the earl of Dunbar's mother and the earl of Carrick's wife were sisters of Alexander Stewart. Several had lands in England, notably Bruce and, by his recent marriage, Moray, or in Ireland (Carrick), but only Bruce was an active and important member of the community of Henry III's barons, and it would be difficult, though not impossible, to justify the view that this party had closer links with England by way of English lands than the Comyn party had. If the Comyns were great northern lords, while Dunbar, Fife, Carrick, Stewart and Bruce were lords of the southern half of the kingdom, such a division breaks down when we turn to their supporters, for Balliol and fitz Randolph, the bishops of St Andrews and Glasgow from southern Scotland supported the Comyns, whereas Durward, Menzies and Hay,. the bishops of Dunkeld and Aberdeen, all northerners, were among their opponents.

Thus the new administration, whatever the help it had received from Henry III, drew its unity from its Scottish purpose to maintain firm and stable government until Alexander III came of age; it was not in any real sense an 'English' party, and it would indeed be difficult to find in the long history of the Fife, Dunbar or Stewart families evidence of pro-English leanings, though evidence of the contrary attitude may be detected. Henry III referred to himself as principal counsellor of the Scots king, called the Comyns 'rebels against our command' and said that he had appointed the new Scottish council, all 'to the honour and advantage' of Alexander III and Scotland; historians have accepted these *ex parte* statements without question but, while in their turn the king and the new council promised that they would not readmit the Comyns and their supporters to office or favour, they neither called the latter 'rebels' nor mentioned the initiatives in Scottish affairs which Henry had undoubtedly taken. King Alexander's constitutional settlement of 20 September was in fact an undertaking to Henry III, and was sent to him, but the Scots secured a reciprocal promise from him that it would not prejudice the freedom of the kingdom and would be returned in seven years time. It may fairly be said of Henry III in 1255 that he was an innocent mischief-maker, anxious to preserve a king and queen from a seemingly ambitious baronial family, but moved to unnecessary severity by further anxiety as father of the queen.

The new government lasted only two years. It tried to forbid the consecration of Gamelin, which took place at the hands of William de Bondington, Bishop of Glasgow, also politically disgraced, on 26 December 1255. Failure was followed by victimisation; money was demanded of Gamelin, perhaps for his predecessor's personal effects or for the revenues of the see during the vacancy, and this was predictably refused. He was then exiled, and, being refused a safe-conduct by Henry III, fled to France by sea; safe conducts were given to Mar and Buchan to visit Henry III in the first quarter of 1256, but there is no evidence that they were used, and the government seems to have made no effort to achieve a reconciliation. Henry III had indeed intervened with the Scots on behalf of Ewen of Argyll and secured his restoration at this period; only Gamelin seems to have suffered, while Ewen benefited from the turn-about of 1255. Once more Alan Durward sought personal profit from political power: a papal letter of 13 December 1255 ordered enquiry into Durward's claim (which must have been forwarded on the morrow of the September coup) that he was unjustly excluded from the earldom of Mar by Earl William, descended from the illegitimate (or so it was asserted) earls Morgrund and Duncan. The papal judges delegate could not afford a false procedural step and Earl William was able to spin matters out. In March 1257 he had secured a papal enquiry into the authenticity of the letter of 13 December 1255; the original judges delegate had reported to Rome.

There, in October 1257, all previous proceedings were annulled and a new enquiry was ordered into the legitimacy question only, 'judgment of the earldom being reserved to the king', probably at the instance of Durward, who must have realised that he might not outlive the processes of papal justice.[19] The fall of the government in 1257 ended the matter, evidence that Durward was exploiting his political position to make good a weak claim.

It is difficult to assess the state of Scotland in these years since almost all our evidence comes from English records. Only two documents are known to have been issued under the king's seal, one a letter to Henry III, the other, still bearing the small seal, a confirmation of a private land transaction in Tynedale. The government thus seems to have respected the king's minority by preserving his domains and revenues. The English view that Scotland was on the verge of civil war is represented by a safe-conduct of June 1256 for the king: no one was to trouble Alexander with unwanted conversation about himself or his kingdom, while if he was detained in his kingdom by war or otherwise the queen and her retinue received a safe-conduct which, however, did not extend to outlaws—namely the Comyns. In August the king and queen did visit King Henry and Alexander was paid 500 merks, perhaps part of his wife's overdue dowry but also in support of the régime. He was also given the 'honour of Huntingdon', which amounted to little or nothing in financial terms. On 1 September the four northern sheriffs were ordered to be ready to support King Alexander, and in the middle of the month John Mansel was sent to Scotland with two sets of credentials: one 'to treat' in Henry's place between Alexander and himself on the one hand and the 'rebels' on the other about the disagreements (*contentionibus*) between them: the other, for use if negotiations with the Comyns broke down, 'to provide, ordain and dispose' in Henry's place in business touching Alexander and to his advantage. The men of the northern shires were placed at Mansel's call. By the beginning of 1257 a 'formula for the good of peace and the tranquillity of our realm' had been drawn up with the Comyns, and Alexander III sent ambassadors to discuss this and his (Alexander's) complaints against them. Even this last phrase is not contrary to the view that the main obstacle to conciliation was

---

[19] Earl William had consumed two years in challenging a genuine papal letter; the bogus 'earldom of Mar' charter of King William belongs to the early 1290s; *R.R.S.*, ii, no. 119.

Henry III, who regarded Scotland as dangerously unstable throughout 1256. Even in June 1257, when Queen Marie de Coucy sought to return to Scotland with her second husband, she was compelled to swear to King Henry that she would do nothing to upset the government of 1255.

Nonetheless, matters were moving to a settlement and, in June or July 1257, a meeting was fixed for 29 August at Stirling at which the disputes might be ended: a powerful English embassy was appointed to attend, and Henry III at length forgave John Balliol his transgressions in Scotland between 1252 and 1255. Unfortunately, the affairs of Gamelin reached a crisis at the same juncture. During 1256 he had defended himself successfully at the papal curia against charges brought by the Scottish government, and on 20 July 1257 Alexander IV ordered his restitution and named a papal legate to see this carried out and when this had been done to relax the sentences of excommunication pronounced against his enemies. But the hostility of the Scottish government and of Henry III prevented Gamelin's return and had probably also prevented publication of this excommunication.[20] It was at Stirling that Clement, Bishop of Dunblane, and the abbots of Melrose and Jedburgh found courage to pronounce excommunication against the (unnamed) persecutors of Gamelin; since a secular centre, not one of the great churches, was used we may assume a secular occasion for this disruptive ceremony, probably the council of conciliation planned for 29 August. Later the contumacious opponents of Gamelin were excommunicated by name. It is unlikely that conciliation got very far in this atmosphere, and the Comyn party now fell back upon force, being joined by William, Earl of Ross, who, like the earl of Mar, had married a daughter of William Comyn, Earl of Buchan.

On the night 28–29 October 1257, headed by Walter Comyn, Earl of Menteith, they seized the king at Kinross and then, or shortly afterwards, took the king's seal from the dean of Dunkeld. who held it for his bishop, the chancellor. The government broke up in confusion but nothing further is known of events in Scotland over the following four months. For two months Henry III seems to have been either in ignorance or doubt about what had happened,

---

[20] There is some difficulty in reconciling the *Melrose Chronicle*, which places the Rome litigation in 1257 and gives one version of the judgement, with the version given in Alexander IV's letter of 20 July 1257. I have followed the letter, but for the upshot have fallen back on the chronicle

although Roger de Quincy, Earl of Winchester, was in Scotland on his behalf. In mid-January 1258, Henry ordered the northern barons to prepare their forces for the expedition he intended against the 'rebels' in Scotland, while at the other end of the country the arrest of Gamelin (if he should cross the Channel) was ordered. But the affairs of Henry III were now entering upon their great crisis: this was no time for a war with Scotland, and within a month Henry III was prepared to allow the return of Gamelin to Scotland. The sheriffs of York and Northumberland were supposed to go there to the help of the king's ousted friends but there is no evidence or likelihood that they did so, and early in April Durward and Moray were provided with refuges (if needed) in Norham and Wark castles. These two and David Lindsay might now operate on both sides of the Border.

Their opponents in Scotland were in a difficult position. On 18 March 1258[21] the Comyns and their associates made a treaty with the resurgent Llywelyn, Prince of Wales, and his allies that they would make no peace or truce with the English nor permit armed men to go from Scotland to be used against the Welsh but would be faithful to the Welsh alliance. But the Comyns had also to promise that if compelled into a truce with Henry III by their king they would try to procure its benefits for the Welsh, that they would not violate the agreement unless so compelled but rather would try to induce their king to enter it. This treaty, perhaps fortunately, was unknown to the English and came to nothing. But it is of great value in showing that while Alexander III did not control the Comyns, he was by the middle of March 1258 a free agent, and the Comyns were so far from controlling him that they imagined his relations with Henry III to be closer than ever—even extending to possible military help. That Alexander's purpose was to end the factions of the previous nine years emerges clearly from the embassy which he sent to Henry III in the same month, announcing (as Henry's reply explains) a parliament to be held at Stirling in mid-April at which 'the transgressions done to us [Henry III] and our queen or to [Alexander III] and his queen our daughter or to others, our friends, would be corrected and amended'. Henry claimed that he

[21] This document is self-dated 18 March 1258, i.e. usually meaning 1259 (cf. *Cal. Docs. Scot.*, i, 2155) but this year does not fit the political circumstances, and in any case Walter Comyn, Earl of Menteith, named in the document, died in 1258. The document has no place-date. *Littere Wallie*, ed. J. G. Edwards (1940), no. 317.

was unable to send the adequate embassy invited to this occasion and asked to have it postponed to a later day and more suitable place; he also urged his friends in Scotland to behave well as long as no harm was being done to them by their opponents, but told them to meet at Roxburgh on the same day as the Stirling parliament. Scotland was free of civil strife and Alexander III was looking for a settlement but it would not be easy to find one. He sought on the one hand to reconcile the Comyns to Henry III and himself in terms of his promise of 1255, and on the other to reconcile Henry's friends to himself and to the sharing of power with the Comyns. It is to this stage that the events described by the *Melrose Chronicle* may be ascribed: the king came (probably from the Stirling parliament) with his army to Roxburgh to subdue his 'rebels' (Durward and his allies), who under truce promised to meet the king and fix upon suitable amends on a stated day at Forfar. If this was designed to entice them far from Wark and Norham castles, it failed, for they fled to England. King Henry's request to the Stirling parliament had been more successful and the business of reconciling the Comyns was put off to a parliament at Edinburgh on 2 June. Once again Alexander III invited the English king to send a strong embassy and once again he received the answer 'it is too soon, the proper magnates are not available, I am too busy, it is too far away' with a request to postpone the parliament till 8 September. At the same time, the northern sheriffs were instructed to attend at Edinburgh on 2 June in case Henry's friends needed support.

Fortunately, the English king was at the end of his tether at home; on 2 May he promised reform to his barons and from 12 June he ceased to control the English government. On 4 August a powerful embassy was named to go to Scotland to 'treat of peace between the disputants and reform the state of the kingdom', a phrase which suggests that the new English council, unlike Henry III, considered itself a party outside the dispute, but thought that all kingdoms were, like England, in need of reform. This embassy crossed one from Scotland about the end of that month bringing unwelcome news from Alexander III, presumably announcing a measure of reconciliation with the Comyns. The final stage of the settlement began on 8 September when Alexander was at Melrose to bring Durward and his associates who were at Norham to their senses—by force according to the *Melrose Chronicle*, more probably by negotiation, because an English embassy now arrived to 'restore peace' between the two contending factions. Perhaps this was the parliament for which King Henry had asked in May.[22] After negotiations which lasted from 9 September till the end of the month, the parties reached an agreement which placed the *regimen* (rule) and *cura* (care or charge)[23] of the kingdom in the hands of Bishop Gamelin, Queen Marie and her husband, Menteith (who died a few days later), Buchan and Mar, Stewart, Durward, Menzies and Hay. King Henry's part was a promise to give aid and counsel, a promise from which he was to be released if these counsellors erred and did not mend their ways within three months of being called upon to do so by him; subsequently, he tried unsuccessfully to obtain an oath of good behaviour and of aid and counsel to himself from the counsellors and from Alexander III. And to the end he was worried about his daughter's health and welfare.[24]

So far as Scotland is concerned, the only part of the settlement known to us is the composition of the council and it has long been recognised that this represents a compromise between the two factions: Gamelin and the two earls from the Comyn party, the four barons from their opponents, Queen Marie and her husband uncommitted. But this is not the whole story, because a notable group of persons had been wholly ignored—the earls of Fife, Strathearn and Dunbar and Robert Bruce. Their ally of 1255, Neil, Earl of Carrick, had died in 1256, but his knight, Hector, was with the Comyn party in 1258. Strathearn was asked by Henry III, and on 6 May 1258 agreed, to keep a beneficent eye upon Queen Margaret, in words which suggest that he was not excluded from the court, not powerless against nor lacking influence with the Comyns. Fife and Dunbar simply drop out of sight, neither punished nor favoured by the king. The councillors of September 1258 were not so much a compromise as a union of two groups, Comyn and Durward, which had been pushed in turn into the isolation of royal displeasure. Moreover, Durward and his friends were there only as the price for English acceptance of the settlement. This becomes plain when we turn to the officers of state. In the treaty with the Welsh of

---

[22] The *Melrose Chronicle*, with characteristic claustral suspicion, says that their real purpose was to kidnap the king.

[23] These words are used in English documents.

[24] Stones, *Anglo-Scottish Relations*, no. 11. These documents recording promises by the Scottish council were drafted in England and sent to Scotland for acceptance—but they were not accepted and represent only a 'try-on' by Henry III.

March 1258, Buchan was justiciar of Scotia, another Comyn justiciar of Galloway and Maxwell was chamberlain. These offices they continued to hold after the compromise, Buchan indeed for the rest of the reign. The new chancellor (1258–73), William Wishart, archdeacon of St Andrews, a graduate of Oxford University and a dedicated pluralist, came of a family from the Mearns three of whom were ousted with the Comyns in 1255; Hugh de Berkeley, justiciar of Lothian from October 1258 for about twenty years, is a more obscure figure who nonetheless joined the Comyns in the Welsh treaty. Of the sheriffs, twenty-one of whom can be named either for the period 1264–6 or for a date nearer 1258, two were hereditary, six of unknown or no affiliations, one had been among those named as trustworthy by Henry III in 1255. The remaining thirteen sheriffdoms were held by ten men (Buchan and Maxwell each held two) who were on the list of Comyn supporters either in 1255 or 1258 and by one who was a close relation to a Comyn supporter. The only former supporters of Durward to flourish through public office in the 1260s were Gilbert de Hay, who had married a Comyn, and Alexander Stewart who rarely failed to find the winning side. Abbot Robert de Kenleith, the chancellor who had been relegated to Newbattle Abbey as a monk after the fall of Durward in 1251, must have emerged about 1255–7, for in 1260 he was in England acting as messenger for Henry III, perhaps an exile from Scotland; in 1268 he became abbot of Melrose.[25] Thus the compromise represented the substance of victory for the Comyns and their supporters, with reconciliation of Durward, Menzies and Lindsay as a token concession to their supporter, the English king. Fife, Dunbar and Strathearn were ignored because, when ousted from power, they accepted the situation and did nothing with the offers of help which Henry tried to make to them.

Around the crises of the decade 1249–59 a legend has grown of a 'native' party and an 'English' party, and of a simple but undefined English lordship, the latter a justification for the pretensions of Edward I in 1291, the former presaging the strength and weakness of the Scots when faced with those pretensions. Neither document nor chronicle suggests that Henry III claimed to interfere by virtue of lordship. He interfered as neighbour and father-in-law, and the sanction for his settlement was a promise by the Scottish king, limited to seven years. More difficult to dismiss are the 'native'

[25] Above, p. 461.

(Comyn) and 'English' parties, for these names derive from a contemporary, Matthew Paris, who says that Alexander III (not his counsellors, be it noted) promoted foreigners and neglected natives and so precipitated the coup of 1257. In fact, the promotion of Englishmen in 1255–7 was limited to Richard de Potton, a cleric who had become 'Scotticised' and was appointed to the see of Aberdeen; Matthew Paris, a noted xenophobe, is not to be trusted as an interpreter of these years. As we have seen, the 'native' Comyns came to power in 1251 with English help and co-operated for three years with two men, Ros and Balliol, who came to Scotland as King Henry's agents. Their opponents enjoyed a like favour after 1255, but there is every reason to think that the Comyns sought to be reconciled to Henry III and failed through no fault of their own. In 1257–8 they feared armed intervention from England and were forced into a posture more obviously directed against Henry III. At no point were they anti-English, and only of necessity became opposed to the English king because opposed by him.

The 'English' party dissolves into two groups, one consisting of Durward and his few supporters who won their way into the confidence of Alexander II, Henry III and ultimately even into acceptance by the Comyns. Durward was a power-seeker of uncertain political attitudes. The other group—four earls, Robert Bruce and Alexander Stewart—anticipate remarkably the Bruce party of the 1290s, a party which was undeniably to look more to England than did the Comyns. But when ousted from power in 1257 not one of these men sought the help of Henry III, and it seems unjust to label them as 'English' when from opposition to the Comyn regime they had loaned themselves to Henry III and Durward in the common purpose of changing the government in 1255. The remarkable feature of these years is not a bitter division in attitudes to England but a common regard for the English king and (until disillusioned) trust in his fairness towards Scotland. All the elements in the struggle were 'native and natural' counsellors, in a modern word, patriotic; to all of them the preservation of peace and harmony with the English king was desirable and probably instinctively so. There were, in fact, sympathisers with Henry III in Scotland, notably Roger de Quincy, Earl of Winchester, half of whose wealth lay in Scotland, half in England, and Robert Bruce, Robert de Ros and John Balliol, who were in a very similar position though Bruce had an ancient Scottish heritage while Balliol had only recently married one. Each of these four emerges from the English records as a go-between for Henry III and a Scottish government, and while Balliol and Ros joined the government and fell into disfavour for their actions all seem to have been regarded primarily as Englishmen who were entitled to a voice in Scottish affairs as Scottish landholders, men to be used in a difficulty. They were in Scotland at King Henry's command.

We have seen that in November 1258 Henry III sought an assurance from the Scottish government of good behaviour and help. This mission was entrusted to a monk of St Albans who spent three months in Scotland[26] and was charged to bring about a visit by Alexander III to England, according to Matthew Paris. The ambassador found King Alexander and the Scots in a parliament where, after considerable difficulty, he persuaded them to seal a document of agreement (apparently to the visit) on condition of the return of a document (which must be King Alexander's promise of September 1255). Following the returning monk (the chronicler claims) came a powerful embassy, Buchan, Durward, and the chancellor, which spoke with the monk and returned having accomplished nothing. There is no trace of this embassy in the English records and it probably did not leave Scotland but in May 1259 an ambassador, John de Dunmore, a Comyn supporter, asked Henry III for the overdue dowry of Queen Margaret, the return of a document (the 1255 promise), agreement to a Scottish coronation, and the abandonment of support for the king of Man, to each of which King Henry returned an evasive reply. These points strengthen the impression that Alexander III was now in control of his own kingdom, and by 1260, when he visited England still demanding his wife's dowry, he had gone so far as to raise a claim to Northumberland, if the St Albans chronicle is to be believed. So far as we know no documents were issued in the king's name between October 1258 and May 1260, but no fewer than five survive for May–December 1260, a fact which also suggests that in 1260, and perhaps in the spring, the king took full control of the government. This view is supported by a reversal which the Comyns suffered over the earldom of Menteith, to which we shall return.

The visit to England of November 1260 marks the renewal of friendly relations between the two kings. Queen Margaret was pregnant, and Alexander was persuaded to leave her in England for

[26] December 1258–February 1259.

the birth of her child, against King Henry's promise that they should not be detained and that if King Alexander were to die they would be delivered up to four bishops, five earls (two Comyns, three of their former opponents) and four barons 'notwithstanding the state of either kingdom'. This provision of a regency council indicates that the lesson of 1249–60 had been learned; moreover, it forms an interesting precedent for the experiment of guardianship in 1286. The Scots did not like the birth of Alexander's daughter, Margaret, taking place in England (February 1261) but in the summer the queen returned to Scotland, leaving King Henry to multiply his excuses for failing to pay more than two-thirds of a promised instalment of £1000 towards her dowry. Subsequently, he interceded for Scottish ambassadors who had been detained at the Norwegian court, and after 1265 was able to resume his personal interest in the welfare of Queen Margaret. When Alexander III proposed an expedition to the Isles, in 1264 or 1265, Henry wrote to the Scottish council to dissuade him from so dangerous an adventure when his heir was young—though his real reason was probably to discourage the Scottish annexation of Man at a time when he was powerless to stop it. The English king owed the Scots something, for in 1264 John Comyn of Badenoch, Balliol and Bruce had joined his army at Lewes and had been captured by Simon de Montfort while some hundreds of their followers, 'unimportant men of the common people, and especially of Scots' had died in this foreign quarrel. In the following year, when King Henry and the Lord Edward were prisoners of Earl Simon, they were visited by the abbot of Dryburgh and an appeal for help was sent to King Alexander by Edward probably after his escape from captivity.[27] There is some chronicle evidence that Alexander III intended to give that help but the battle of Evesham made it unnecessary. It is said that Guy de Balliol, 'a Scot by race' and an ambassador from King Alexander, died with Earl Simon in the battle as his standard-bearer; if so, not every Scot adhered to the conservative royalist side.

Henry III's difficulties encouraged the Scots to raise again with Haakon IV the question of ceding to them the Western Isles. In 1261 an embassy to Bergen met with no success and, indeed, was detained over the winter when it tried to slip away without permission. In 1262 the earl of Ross and Cormac Macmaghan attacked

[27] *A.P.S.*, i, 108: *Item littera Edwardi de succursu petendo a rege Scocie et est dupplicata.*

Skye, and the Islesmen so warned King Haakon that the Scots intended to subdue the Hebrides that he decided upon a summer expedition westwards 'to avenge the warfare that the Scots had made in his dominions'. Scottish aggression brought about this war. The history of his expedition is one of unrelieved misfortune for the Norwegian king, misfortune which can be explained in part by his late departure date—11 July 1263. The fleet is said to have been a very great one, perhaps about 150 ships including some commandeered English merchantmen, and its arrival in the northern isles was the subject of wild rumours, for the king of Denmark was said to be with Haakon and no one knew where they might strike. King Alexander took all possible precautions, filling his castles on both coasts with stores and calling upon his subjects for protracted spells of castle-duty.

Although he had given his subjects around Scotland ample warning of his arrival, Haakon encountered difficulty in raising the men and ships of the northern isles—he had made subjects but not friends of the Orcadians—and was compelled to sail to the west coast on 10 August without them, and to the news that Ewen of Lorne too would probably not support him. Near Skye he was joined by Magnus, king of Man, and at Kerrera by Dugald, Lord of Garmoran, and some Islesmen. While part of his fleet plundered the south of Kintyre, off Gigha King Haakon received Ewen, who resigned his island territories, preferring his fealty to Alexander III, but was kept in honourable captivity. His cousins the MacDonalds, lords of Islay, also stood out against Haakon until threatened with the devastation of their lands, when they submitted to a levy of a thousand cattle—or so the *Hakonar Saga* claims—securing from Haakon only a promise that he would include them in any peace he might make with the Scottish king. The raiding party was now withdrawn from Kintyre, much of which belonged to the MacDonalds, but another descended on Bute and took Rothesay Castle, while the main fleet sailed round to Lamlash Bay in Arran.

The length of this voyage and of the subsequent negotiations between Haakon IV and Alexander III, who seems to have come to Ayr, are alike unknown.[28] The negotiations seem to have been very protracted and to have broken down over the unwillingness of the Scots to cede Bute, Arran and the Cumbraes, which they had

---

[28] The situation of Alexander III is deduced from the saga which says he was in the market-town of *Norar* or *Noar*, necessarily on the Clyde coast.

retaken from the Norse a generation or two earlier: thus it was Haakon who felt that he had the upper hand and that he could demand concessions. Perhaps at the beginning of September—a date given by Fordun which seems too early—the main Norwegian fleet sailed across to the Cumbraes while a squadron of Islesmen, perhaps forty ships strong, went up Loch Long and by porterage into Loch Lomond, whence they burned and terrorised the Lennox, apparently in the hope of inducing a more amenable frame of mind in Alexander III.

Haakon seems to have felt unable to land his whole force on the mainland, and in consequence his supplies now ran short. On the night of Sunday 30 September 1263 the autumn gales blew up, raging for several days. Anchor after anchor was put out but ships drifted and on Monday morning a merchant ship (whose is unknown) and three longships and their crews were stranded on the shore below the steep slopes of the Cunningham hills—whence the name of the place, Largs, 'the slopes'. During Monday there was skirmishing with local Scotsmen, who fled when additional Norwegians landed. Both sides had their pickings of the merchantman, whose cargo was so precious that in a lull in the storm on Tuesday morning (2 October) King Haakon with a larger body of men—perhaps some hundreds—landed to empty her hold. Their task was interrupted by the arrival of a Scottish force which they thought at first to be commanded by Alexander III. Battle was joined and raged up and down the stony beach among the stranded ships, a knight of the Steward, Sir Peter Curry, distinguishing himself by such courage that his name found its way into the *Hakonar Saga*. How it ended we do not know, for the saga claim that the Scots, ten times more numerous than their opponents, were driven from a commanding eminence by Norwegians, is not very convincing. The battle was regarded by the Scots as their victory, though the Norwegians probably withdrew from the shore in orderly fashion.

The battle of Largs has been the subject of many unnecessary misconceptions. It is clear that the forces engaged were partial, and neither king participated. Haakon was (wisely) sent back to his ship when the Scots army appeared, and the forces he left on shore were only a fraction, perhaps as much as a quarter, of those he had with him. The Scottish commander was Alexander Stewart and the forces under his command were described by the contemporary Melrose chronicler as *pedisequi patrie*—the footsloggers of the locality. This description of the hosting of Ayrshire or Cunningham is a little unfair to the Stewart knights, who were numbered as high as five hundred by the Norwegians when they returned to the ale-houses of Bergen but who are unlikely to have exceeded one tenth of that.[29] The storm did not wreck Haakon's ships, nor was his army defeated on land; yet this was more than a skirmish and we may take it that it warned Haakon of what might happen if he tried foraging parties on land.

On Thursday 4 October the Islanders returned from Loch Long with a fleet depleted by the weather, and all anchors were weighed. On Friday the ships stranded at Largs were burned and the whole fleet sailed to Arran, probably very short of food. There Haakon thought of accepting an invitation from the native Irish to free them from English power but was strongly dis-suaded by his magnates—there was nothing for it but a return to Orkney. This return voyage was not like the retreat of a beaten armada: Islay was taxed 300 cattle, and men left behind to collect the tax; at Kerrera negotiations with Ewen (who had been released during the negotiations with Alexander III) ended when the men of Lorn attacked Mull. Ewen's territories were given to the lords of Garmoran, Bute and Arran to other Islesmen. Skye was taxed and the fleet arrived at Orkney on Monday 29 October, losing one ship in the Pentland Firth. Haakon decided to winter in Kirkwall, and after some weeks' illness died in the bishop's palace there in the early hours of Sunday 16 December. The expedition had made pláin that, faced with a choice between Norway and Scotland, the lords of those islands which lie to the south of Ardnamurchan preferred Alexander III who was already their lord on the mainland and that only blackmail would make them choose Haakon IV. The Norwegian hold would last only so long as the Norwegian fleet sailed in those waters.

An embassy from Orkney in the spring of 1264 found the Scots angry and unwilling to negotiate, but in the autumn messengers from King Magnus, Haakon's son, were told that in the following summer terms could be discussed in Scotland. It took two such embassies and one from Scotland to Norway before peace was con-cluded at Perth on 2 July 1266. During the years 1264 and 1265

[29] The figures usually assessed for Largs on the basis of the Haakonar Saga are probably much too high; a hundred or two men on each side is, in my view, a more likely estimate of those engaged.

the Scots had gone a long way towards their aim of annexing the Isles. A great army gathered in Galloway in the summer of 1264 to invade Man. Deprived of the protection of Henry III (who was a captive), the king of Man hastened to forestall it by submission, doing homage to Alexander III, from whom he was to hold his kingdom for the service of ten galleys. A year later he died and the isle of Man became a bailiary of the Scottish crown.[30] Also in the summer of 1264, there was an expedition to Caithness which took heavy fines in cattle from Ross (180 beasts) and Caithness (200 beasts), as well as hostages for payment, as a punishment for the blackmail paid to Haakon when he first arrived at Kirkwall; this expedition was commanded by Buchan and Durward, apparently a successful team, for in the following year the king visited Inverness and, perhaps at his instigation, they attacked Skye, returning with hostages. The Western Isles were attacked in 1264 by the earl of Mar, commanding two hundred serjeants and part of the fleet which had been gathered to invade Man; Angus MacDonald, lord of Islay, submitted, and the young MacDonald heir with his nurse was brought back to Ayr as a hostage. The importance of this submission is to be gauged by Angus's written recognition that he would be disinherited if his loyalty wavered again and by a written promise by the barons of Argyll that in these circumstances they would serve the king and rise against Angus; he was recognised as the man who carried the loyalty of the Argyllsmen with him—presumably the king now had no doubt of Ewen's loyalty to Scotland.[31] Only Dugald of Garmoran of the island kinglets held true to Norway; only the Outer Hebrides had not felt King Alexander's wrath. There were alternatives for the Norwegian king: to recognise the Scottish conquests or to set about their recovery. He was surely wise to choose the former.

The treaty of Perth (1266) amounted to a sale of Man and the Isles to the Scots for 4000 merks payable over four years, but with a

[30] It seems likely that had it not been for the civil war in England, the kingdom of Man would have survived by invoking English protection.

[31] *A.P.S.*, i, 109, 112. In the Scottish records there was an obligation by W. Earl of Mar, M. Earl of Fife and M. Earl of Atholl that Ewen would pay to the king 'CCCXX' merks 'for a certain ferme of land'. The first two earls give a possible date as 1244–66, but the third earl is incompatible with that. Perhaps 'Strathearn' not 'Atholl' was in the original document. The occasion may have been Ewen's restoration in 1255 but it could also have been 1264–5. The sum of money is very high and I suspect that there has been misreading of iii as CCC and that 'XX' means 'score'—i.e. 60 merks, not 320. *A.P.S.*, i, 115.

guarantee of security for the Islesmen who were now subjected to the law and custom of Scotland—a phrase which was to prove hard to· put into effect. Neither king was to harbour traitors from the other, and lesser criminals could have asylum for a year only. Shipwrecked sailors were to have their goods and ships for sale and not be deprived of them by the royal right to wreck. And the Scottish king undertook to pay in perpetuity one hundred merks annually to the Norwegian king. As seems to have been understood when the treaty was made, the Isle of Man later became the nominal appanage of the Lord Alexander, the elder son of the Scottish king, born in January 1264; in fact it was committed to a series of bailies, the first of whom has a name suggesting an insular or Galwegian origin. Unfortunately for the Manx, in 1275 Godfrey, the illegitimate son of the last Manx king, descended upon the island and established himself as its ruler. A 'large' Scottish army was assembled in Galloway under John de Vescy, an English baron who was lord of Alnwick in England and Sprouston in Scotland and had just returned from the Holy Land with Edward I, John Comyn of Badenoch, justiciar of Galloway, Alan 'son of the earl' (that is, son of Thomas of Galloway, Earl of Atholl), Alexander, son of Ewen of Lorn, and Alan of Garmoran, a collection of names in which we may see represented a small group of fully armed knights, the 'common army', footmen or serjeants of Galloway, and the ships of the Islesmen, all bent to the purposes of the king. The army landed in the south of Man, offered Godfrey the chance of submission, which was refused, and defeated him in an engagement which became a bloody slaughter. Thereafter Man paid its tribute to the Scottish crown, but was certainly not reconciled to Scottish rule.

The rest of the old kingdom of the Isles seems to have accepted the new situation without rebellion or regret. The descendants of Somerled were allowed to retain their lands as the treaty had specified and were accepted into the coterie of Scottish magnates, yet were leaders of a separate society, the 'barons of Argyll and the Isles'. Alexander of Lorn was appointed to the 'care and custody' of Kintyre, Argyll and Lorn, with responsibility for the king's revenues there. William, Earl of Ross, was perhaps given Skye and Lewis on the same terms, a special provision for an area which like Sutherland and Caithness, had as yet no sheriffs. Ewen of Lorn's daughter married the earl of Strathearn, his son a daughter of Sir John Comyn and Alan of Garmoran's heiress married a younger son of Donald, Earl of Mar; while these men were not frequenters of the royal court, they obeyed the king's command to turn up on a special occasion. Only the MacSweens of Knapdale seem to have been ousted at this time, to be replaced by Walter Stewart, Earl of Menteith. By the death of Alexander III there was every indication that the king's peace would prevail in the Isles as elsewhere in the kingdom.

The reality of this peace for the last twenty years of the reign is scarcely to be doubted, though it was broken by the Manx expedition in 1275. Something may be attributed to our ignorance, for the *Melrose Chronicle* dies to nearly all intents at 1266, but even the overheated imagination of the Franciscan friar who kept the *'Lanercost' Chronicle* can find little that was remarkable to relate about Scotland. The annals of Walter Bower pass from one pair of dead ecclesiastic's shoes to another, with occasional glimpses of secular controversies, as when Sir John Comyn of Badenoch built a castle at Blair in Atholl, to the great annoyance of the earl of Atholl; their dispute was settled by the king. The sorry story of the earldom of Menteith may have roused some political difficulties.[32] In 1259 Isabel, Countess in her own right and widow of Earl Walter Comyn, married an English knight, Sir John Russell, but shortly came under suspicion of having murdered Earl Walter. In circumstances very reminiscent of the suspicions against Walter Bisset in 1242, a large body of magnates, drawn, it was said, from both sides in recent controversies,[33] arrested the couple, extracted from them grants of lands and pensions and a resignation of the earldom in favour of Sir John Comyn, the heir of the late Earl Walter but not of his countess, in whose right Walter was earl. In 1260 they were expelled from Scotland, not to return unless prepared to stand to the judgement of their equals. One of these grants has survived, twenty librates of land at Aberfoyle for Sir Hugh Abernethy, and suggests that the earls of Fife and Strathearn indeed had cast in their lot with the Comyn faction, for together they form the witnesses to the deed. Although Durward and some of his followers were said by Countess Isabel and Russell to have joined in the arrest and to have

---

[32] *Scots Peerage*, vi, 127–31. See Genealogical Tree No. 5 for the earldom of Menteith.

[33] Mar, Buchan, Strathearn, Fife, Alan Durward, John Comyn, Alexander Stewart, Alan son of the earl (illegitimate son of Thomas of Galloway, Earl of Atholl) Hugh Berkeley, David Graham, David de Lochore, Reginald Cheyne, Hugh Abernethy, Freskin Moray.

benefited from it, it seems that they did not in fact join in the Comyn spoliation. Instead Walter, younger brother of Alexander Stewart, put forward a claim in right of his wife, Mary, probably a cousin of Countess Isabel, and this was acknowledged by the king with the concurrence of the magnates before 17 April 1261, when Walter appears as Earl of Menteith.[34] This represents a victory for Stewart (probably supported by Durward) over Comyn, which can only be explained by the new authority of the king himself. ·

For twenty-five years Earl Walter Stewart was questioned in his title. In September 1261 Countess Isabel and Russell obtained from Henry III an exemplification of the resignation of the earldom by Mary's father to Isabel's father in 1213. They appealed to Rome against Earl Walter and obtained a legate to hear their case. King Alexander and others were cited to appear before the legate, unfortunately in England, and on these grounds they appealed to Rome in their turn. In January 1264 the case was remitted to a group of Scottish prelates and there we lose sight of it. By 1273 Isabel and Russell were dead and their daughter (who can scarcely have been more than twelve years old) married to William, heir of Sir John Comyn, who now pled their cause at York on behalf of his son against Earl Walter! Finally, in April 1285 at Scone, Alexander III heard the plea of William Comyn and adjudged to him half the lands of the earldom, the other half with the title to remain with Earl Walter, whose wife was probably now dead. This was probably an innovation in Scottish custom, where all the lands of an earldom (but not of a 'barony') undoubtedly accompanied the title to the eldest daughter and her husband without partition. On the island of Inchmahome in the Lake of Menteith, in the choir of the priory founded by Countess Isabel and Earl Walter Comyn, lies the recumbent effigy of their successors, the arm of the Countess Mary clasped affectionately round the neck of a fully armed Earl Walter Stewart.[35]

In the later thirteenth century the changes seen in Menteith and in other earldoms are characteristic of what could happen at any

[34] Peerage writers have assumed that Mary was sister of Countess Isabel, but there is no evidence to that effect, and in the 1291-2 pleadings about the crown this earldom was not cited on the matter of co-heiresses. Countess Isabel based her right upon the resignation in 1213 of Earl Maurice in favour of his younger brother Earl Maurice: this suggests that Isabel was the daughter of the younger, Mary, a descendant of the elder. Hence Mary's claim was better than modern writers have assumed.

[35] This effigy has now been moved for protection from the weather.

point in baronial or knightly society. The earldom of Angus had gone by marriage in 1243 to the English family of d'Umfraville, and was in wardship for twenty years, when it was worth £80 annually. This was a fraction of the earl's total income and after coming of age in 1267 he took little interest in Scotland. The earldom of Carrick, worth about £170 annually, was also in wardship on the death of Earl Neil in 1256; his daughter Marjorie was first married (and the earldom given) to a member of a cadet branch of the Fife family, Adam of Kilconquhar, to whom she bore a daughter before his death in the Crusaders' camp at Acre in 1270. Before 1274 Robert Bruce, son of the lord of Annandale and Cleveland, was seized by the countess, who took him by force and for love to Turnberry Castle, where they were married. The king seized her lands and castle but on payment of a fine released them and acknowledged Bruce as earl; of their children two became kings, one queen, three daughters married Scottish barons and one married beneath her estate; three sons died at the hands of English executioners, a fourth in battle. The earldom of Atholl passed, in the course of the first half of the century, through the hands of two sisters and their husbands. From the death of Earl David de Hastings about 1247 a silence falls until about 1264, when we hear of a new earl, David de Strathbogie, an Aberdeenshire baron descended from the earls of Fife; his title to the earldom is quite unknown.[36] He, too, died on crusade at Tunis in 1270. The earldom of Fife, by contrast, passed in the male line from father to son, but each time after periods of nonage. Earl Colban, who succeeded in 1266 as a minor, died only four years later, leaving an eight-year-old son who obtained possession only in 1284, the revenues of his earldom having been enjoyed by the Lord Alexander. This earl was murdered in 1289 and his son and successor was born posthumously; once more the earldom was in wardship and this time we discover that its lands north of Forth lay for the most part in Fife and were worth over £500 annually. In all these cases, and in the majority of them where lands and dignity passed from father to adult son, the inheritance was preserved entire subject only to the attrition of providing for daughters and younger sons—a major qualification.[37]

[36] A. A. M. Duncan, 'The Earldom of Atholl in the thirteenth century', *The Scottish Genealogist*, vii (1960), 2–10.

[37] For these earldoms see the respective entries in the *Scots Peerage* and Genealogical Trees Nos. 3, 5 and 6.

Other honours, however, were subjected to the partition which afflicted Menteith. The great de Quincy inheritance, itself containing a moiety of the ancient Galloway and de Moreville lordships and the constableship, was divided among the three daughters of Roger de Quincy, Earl of Winchester, upon his death in 1264. Two were married to English barons, but the second to Alexander Comyn, Earl of Buchan, who now added to his already wide territories a substantial domain and the office of sheriff in Wigtownshire. The dignity of constable of Scotland seems to have lapsed for a few years; the son of Margaret, Countess of Derby, the eldest co-heiress, laid claim to it about 1270 but his mother was subsequently (probably in 1274 or 1275) induced to resign her right in favour of Buchan, who now became constable as well as justiciar of Scotland.[38] On the other hand, when Alan Durward died in 1275 his lands were divided among his three daughters and his 'palace' dignity was forgotten as though it had been only a surname.

When, in 1284, thirteen earls and twenty-four barons regulated the succession to the throne, their names reflected not only the physical expansion of the kingdom—the earl of Orkney (as earl of Caithness) and three leading Islesmen were there—but also the factors of marriage and royal favour which singly or together brought perhaps ability, certainly change, to the ranks of the baronage. Beside earls of ancient family are their constant baronial companions since the twelfth century—Stewart, de Soules, Moray, the Scottish Balliols, Lindsay, and Hay. Beside an English earl like Angus or Carrick is John de Balliol, son of the lord of Barnard Castle in County Durham and of Dervorguilla, one of the co-heiresses of Alan, lord of Galloway. By 1266 the father of this John Balliol had established bursaries for scholars at Oxford University and in 1282 Dervorguilla made provision for the college which his endowment had become. In 1273 she had already established in his memory the Cistercian Abbey of Sweetheart, near the mouth of the Nith, the first major religious house to be founded since Balmerino (c. 1230) and the last founded before the Charterhouse at Perth in the fifteenth century. Her home was Buittle Castle by the Urr, but her son, the future king, made his in England. A more unusual

---

[38] Buchan was still not constable on 1 August 1274 (*Arbroath Liber*, i, no. 246) but had the dignity on 20 May 1275 (*R.M.S.*, iii, no. 962). Margaret, Countess of Derby, resigned it personally to Alexander III (*A.P.S.*, i, 115) and was bound for Scotland in May 1276 (*Cal. Docs. Scot.*, ii, no. 73) perhaps to do so. It seems likely that she was bought out.

foreign recruit to the baronial class was Enguerrand de Guines (Guines, Pas de Calais), a nephew of Queen Marie de Coucy and ultimately (in 1311) lord of Coucy, who had come to Scotland by 1275 as a younger son but the king's cousin, and to whom the heiress of William de Lindsay, lord of Lamberton in Berwickshire and Kendal in Cumberland, was given in marriage.

There are signs that the Scots and their king were already sensitive to the problem of loyalties posed, mildly as yet, by these men. One of those signs is the acquisition by the king of the fief of Bathgate and Ratho, which had been given to Margaret, Duchess of Brittany and Countess of Hereford, by her brother King William as a hundred librates of land and had descended to the de Bohun earls of Hereford. The fief was resigned to a younger son of the earl, who in his turn sold it to King Alexander; in 1292 the Scottish treasury contained receipts from de Bohun to show that he had had from the crown the truly enormous sum of £989—and other receipts may not have survived.[39] Since it imposed so heavy a financial burden the buying-out of his interest was a major political decision which was surely shared by the king with the magnates. A similar instance, if less expensive, was the attempt made by the king and the bishop of St Andrews to purchase from Reading Abbey its dependent priory on the Isle of May, on grounds which seem to have been strongly tinged with xenophobia; and finally we might instance the diversion of the constableship to Buchan. It looks as though those northern Englishmen—Umfraville, Bruce, Balliol—whose proximity to Scotland permitted them to appear in Scotland reasonably often and who thereby maintained acquaintance and family ties with the Scots, were still acceptable, even unquestioned. But wholly absentee landlords were no longer so. The attitude seems not unreasonable, but at the moment of judgement in the 1290s those who were Scots only by reason of the technicality of their homage to King Alexander—Balliol and Umfraville—in one way or another took the English side—as did Bruce.

There remained a small number of families whose representatives achieved a new significance in the reign of Alexander III. This assessment is derived in the first place from the frequency with which they witnessed royal charters and other acts, but is borne out by the occasions on which they were employed by the king on missions to other rulers and by the public offices which they enjoyed.

[39] *A.P.S.*, i, 116.

Reginald Cheyne of Inverugie and Thomas fitz Randolph of Stich-ill were chamberlains in turn between 1266 and 1278, the one sheriff of Kincardine, the other sheriff of Roxburgh and then Berwick. William Comyn of Kilbride was sheriff of Ayr, Hugh de Berkeley justiciar of Lothian and sheriff of Berwick, John de Lamberton, with lands in East Lothian and Berwickshire, was sheriff of Stirling, Patrick Graham of Mugdock (son of David Graham and perhaps the builder of Mugdock Castle) his successor as sheriff of Stirling, David de Lochore, sheriff of Fife; all are found as frequent witnesses to royal charters. Two others, however, demand fuller notice.

Simon Fraser, lord of Oliver Castle in Tweeddale, and descen-dant of a family which came to Scotland in the reign of King Wil-liam, was son, and probably heir, of Sir Gilbert Fraser, sheriff of Traquair or Peebles by 1233 and for some years thereafter. Sir Simon acquired the same sheriffdom in 1263 and probably held it for some twenty years; along with other sheriffs from the Scottish side of the Border he acted as a justice in the king's franchise of Tynedale in Northumberland. In 1281 in Flanders, it was he who swore in the king's name that his master would observe the marriage treaty between the count and the king.[40] His younger brother, William, had entered the church, become a master at Paris or Oxford and by 1273 was dean of Glasgow Cathedral. In that year the king made him chancellor, when William Wishart the chancel-lor became bishop of St Andrews. In 1279 he succeeded Wishart as bishop and so became a more important man than his elder brother, whose influence must have procured his early advancement.

If we are not sure whether Simon Fraser was his father's eldest son, we must be even less certain about Sir William de St Clair or Sinclair when about 1263 he became sheriff of Edinburgh, Linlith-gow and Haddington in succession to Geoffrey de Mowbray.[41] By 1279 he was guardian of the Lord Alexander, heir to the throne, and this, together with his custodianship of Edinburgh Castle, which held the king's treasury, suggests that he was closer to Alexander III than any other Scot. In 1279 Henry of Roslin, the king's tenant of

[40] In 1261 an embassy of an archdeacon and a knight 'called Missel' went from Alexander III to Haakon IV seeking the transfer of the Isles. 'Missel' saw and was much impressed by the coronation of Magnus Haakonsson. He has never been identified. His name may be a version of 'Frisel', that is, Sir Simon Fraser.

[41] The statement in *Scots Peerage*, vi, 564, that he came from France, is given there on the authority of Father Hay, who makes no such suggestion.

that place (a few miles south of Edinburgh) resigned his lands in favour of Sir William Sinclair, who was to hold them for half a knight's service. Since Sir William's son was called Henry, he may well have obtained the lands by marriage to Roslin's daughter, yet more evidence of royal favour. Seven months later Sinclair was also given Inverleith below Edinburgh (no service was specified).

Neither Fraser nor Sinclair were 'new' men in the sense in which Enguerrand de Guines was a 'new' man, yet we must recognise their remarkable prominence as a sign of the political importance of their class to Alexander III. Even among the Comyns it was not Buchan or Badenoch who was most regularly at his court, but William Comyn of Kilbride, member of a recent and junior branch of the family. It is tempting to read in the events of 1286–1306, when the Comyns were the most important single family in Scotland, and when their every marriage added to the complex of their powers, a similar domination of the reign of Alexander III. There is no contemporary evidence of such dominance; on the contrary it seems that the king relied particularly upon the services of a fairly large group of barons of all ranks, including the earls of Buchan, Mar and Menteith, who served him as sheriffs. All were men of the king's choosing. There was little difference in social standing between Sir Simon Fraser and, say, Sir William Douglas, father and son. But the Douglases gave much thought to increasing their possessions by hook or by crook both in England and in Scotland; perhaps for that reason they enjoyed no public office and no known royal trust. Similarly, the name of Malcolm, Earl of Lennox, as lord of an earldom with easy access to the lowlands, might be expected in royal charters; the only evidence of the king's concern about him is to be found in the office of sheriff of Dumbarton, which the earls of Lennox resented and coveted and which the king gave to the earls of Mar, Menteith and Fife in turn, doubtless so that the peers of Lennox as earl could be his master as sheriff.

The strength of Alexander III's position was reflected in his relations with England. In 1274 he and the queen went to London to attend Edward I's delayed coronation, held on 19 August. Although his expenses were paid, the king was careful to obtain a written acknowledgement from Edward I that he would not be prejudiced for the future either by his attendance or by the service asked of him. If, as seems most likely, this service was the carrying of a sword of state, then Alexander must have refused to perform it. Not only this; he also returned without having done homage for his English lands. On 26 February 1275 Queen Margaret died, but her lands were released to her husband early in May; during the following three years embassies seem to have crossed the Border fairly frequently, concerned with the undischarged homage and whether King Alexander was entitled to his expenses when attending to perform it, and with Border disputes which during March or April 1278 took three Scottish bishops to Berwick for a fruitless conference with English negotiators. On 20 March 1278 a safe conduct was issued for a visit by Alexander III to England in the three weeks after Michaelmas (29 September), and on 5 June there was a further assurance demanded by the Scots that this would not be to his future prejudice. The tone of all this correspondence was friendly, even familiar, but throughout the Scottish king was careful to reserve his position, or even to state his terms; he agreed to come without payment of his expenses, and it is surely this fact which was in Edward's mind when his clerk used the words 'without any conditions' of the visit and homage.[42]

On 16 October the two kings met at Tewkesbury and Alexander III offered his homage. On the grounds that his council was not present and with a written assurance of 'without prejudice for the future' King Edward postponed the ceremony. It took place during parliament in the king's chamber at Westminster on 28 October and it was recorded contemporaneously in the English Close Roll and some fifty years later in the cartulary of Dunfermline Abbey, from an unknown but surely contemporaneous text. The English record is entirely credible so far as it goes. Alexander III said 'I ... become the liegeman of Lord Edward, King of England, against all men' and this was received by Edward reserving, however, (the document does not quote his words) his and his heirs' right and claim to homage for the kingdom of Scotland when they wished to speak of it. Alexander then asked to swear fealty by the mouth of the earl of Carrick and this was granted without prejudice for the future; the words of the oath—to keep good faith and perform services for the lands held of the English king—are both unspecific and innocuous.

Whoever wrote the Scottish account was composing a defence. The wording of the homage—'for the land which I hold ... in ... England ... saving my kingdom' is less probable than the English

[42] *absque condicione aliqua;* cf. Powicke, *Thirteenth Century,* 595n.

version, as is the wording of the fealty which harps on the same point. Both have been improved, sharpened or doctored. But the Scottish account explains that after the homage the bishop of Norwich interjected 'and let it [the kingdom] be reserved to the king of England if he has a right to your homage for the kingdom', to which the king replied 'to homage for my kingdom of Scotland no one has right except God alone, nor do I hold it except of God alone'. There is no reason to doubt the substance of these statements, which complement and explain the English account at the point at which it is coy. The postponement of the homage from Tewkesbury suggests that King Edward planned to take some advantage of the occasion. When Alexander III had spoken the formal words, the bishop stated Edward's reservation, to which King Alexander took strong exception but which he could not undo. When King Alexander offered his oath not as a vassal but as a king by the mouth of another, King Edward had to accept, but took exception for the future.[43]

Much has had to be made of this episode, as of so much else in Anglo-Scottish relations before 1286, as a signpost on the road to the last decade of the century. Yet this was not its purpose, and if it is examined not in the heat of later controversies but in the cooler light of the 1270s it is surely plain that Edward I can have had neither expectation nor hope that his claim would be allowed and that the English account represents exactly what he sought to achieve—the statement and registration of this claim. Doubtless Edward I was aware of the similar claim made in 1251 and of the precedents from before 1124 and from 1174–89 to justify it, but if we would seek a motive for the recollection of these dim memories they are not to be found in some long-term scheme to subvert Scottish independence. It seems much more likely that they were meant as a bargaining counter, something which the Scots and the English knew could be produced if the policy of co-operation and friendship was abandoned by Scotland; this is certainly the atmosphere of the negotiations in the years 1274–8.

In the remaining seven years of the reign relations between the kings and the kingdoms were cordial. Although Edward I might have urged a right to find a wife for the Lord Alexander and might have pressed the claims of his own daughters there is no evidence

---

[43] Stones, *Anglo-Scottish Relations*, no. 12.

that he did either. On the other hand, King Alexander may well have consulted Edward before choosing for his son Margaret, daughter of Guy de Dampierre, Count of Flanders and ally of England; the marriage was agreed in December 1281. With his daughter, Guy was to provide £11,000 of which half was to be repaid if she were to die childless. Alexander III promised her a dower (if her husband should die) of 1500 merks annually, made up of 1300 merks payable in cash at Berwick and the manor of Linlithgow with rents of 200 merks, and he also recognised specifically that the issue of his son and Margaret would be lawful heirs to the kingdom. Alexander and Margaret were married after a slight delay perhaps for the receipt of cash (Alexander III gave a receipt for about £5000 on 25 December 1282), at Roxburgh on 15 November 1282. There was, overall, little financial profit to the Scots since they had shortly before married off another Margaret, Alexander III's daughter, to Eric II of Norway. By a treaty concluded at Roxburgh on 25 July 1281, the Scottish king had to produce 7000 merks in money and rents of 700 merks annually. The former was paid in 1281 and 1282; the latter was assigned upon Bathgate and Ratho (formerly de Bohun lands and yielding, in 1288–9, 250 merks), Balhelvy and Rothiemay. The maid Margaret sailed with the earl and countess of Menteith, Bernard de Mowat and the abbot of Balmerino on 12 August, and married her fourteen-year-old husband immediately on her arrival. The Scottish ambassadors returned with all the appropriate Norwegian receipts and undertakings only to be shipwrecked off the coast; Mowat and the abbot were drowned, the documents recovered sodden with sea water.[44]

Alexander III had already lost his second son, David, in June 1281. Margaret, Queen of Norway, died on 9 April 1283, leaving an infant daughter and namesake. The Lord Alexander died childless at Lindores on 17 January 1284 after a long illness. Edward I wrote that although death had taken away his Scottish kinsfolk yet 'we are united together perpetually, God willing, by a link of indissolvable love' and Alexander III acknowledged this as the latest of 'the many kindnesses we have received' from his 'dearest brother, for which we ought deservedly to praise the constancy of your excel-

[44] *Collection de Chroniques Belges: Monuments pour servir à l'Histoire des Provinces de Namur, de Hainaut et de Luxembourg*, ed. Baron de Reiffenberg, i (Brussels, 1844), 177–82; *A.P.S.*, i, 421–4.

lency'.[45] The poignancy of these phrases surely represents real feeling as well as the technical skill of two Latin secretaries, but there was little point in dwelling on the tragedy of the situation; death was no stranger to a royal house, but this time had taken the mother and not the child. And so, with necessary, if unfeeling, practicality, King Alexander went on to indicate that 'much good may yet come to pass' through his granddaughter—that is, that she would be married into Edward's family. But the life of this baby was an inadequate and precarious insurance for a free kingdom and the sooner the forty-three year old king were to reinsure with a new wife and new children the better for all concerned. The lady settled upon was Yolande, daughter of the count of Dreux, a French vassal of Edward I, and in February 1285 Master Thomas Charteris (the chancellor), Patrick Graham, William Sinclair and William Soules set out to fetch her to Scotland.

The terms of the settlement are unknown; Yolande travelled through England in the autumn of 1285 and married the king at Jedburgh on either 14 October or 1 November 1285.[46] In five months she was a widow. Returning one stormy night from a council at Edinburgh to his wife at Kinghorn, the king crossed the Queen's ferry and became separated from his guides in Fife. The following morning, 19 March 1286, Alexander III was found dead on the shore, killed by a fall from his horse. No man knew the scale of the tragedy which this portended, but all who were conscious of politics knew that it must mean internal strains, and within the month knew that these strains were indeed to be severe. In the circumstances, they turned to the man with whom King Alexander had established such friendship and intimacy as was possible between brothers-in-law, kings and neighbours. Edward I had stated his claim to homage in 1278 and historians have, not improperly, judged him for this; but from 1274 until 1286 he had respected the integrity of Scotland and the status of its king. Border disputes, the occasional misconduct of a Scottish baron in England, the difficulties which inevitably arose over the franchises of the Scottish king in Northumberland and Cumberland, even an impudent Scottish claim for the earldom of Huntingdon, none of these produced the tensions which were familiar in the time of Henry

---

[45] Stones, *Anglo-Scottish Relations*, no. 13.

[46] Fordun says 14 October; Bower accepts this and adds Jedburgh; Lanercost gives 1 November and no place.

III. The reasons were twofold: the good sense which Edward I could show as long as his rights were not being challenged and the good sense of Alexander III in finding his alliances (that is, his marriages) among Edward's friends and in strengthening his authority within a unified kingdom.

# 22

# THE KING, THAT SCOTLAND HAD
# TO STEER AND LEAD[1]

Probably about 1292, and for the guidance of King John, some well-meaning Scottish court correspondent set down in writing his slightly tendentious version of the various functionaries who made up the government of the kingdom, both those within (*denzeins*) and those outwith (*foreins*) the royal household, so that the usual modern title, *The King's Household*, is rather misleading. To the prelates and magnates he assigned a voice in the choice of officials such as they had never enjoyed, but otherwise much of what he wrote was in accordance with thirteenth-century practice. This treatise, then, can be our guide to Alexander III's government.[2]

The office of justiciar is emerging in the light of modern study as perhaps the most significant bridge between the king's court and the localities.[3] The three justiciars or occasionally pairs of justiciars, of Scotia, Lothian and Galloway, were men of substance, often having a family connection with the office, as did the three Comyn earls of Buchan in the thirteenth century. Their presence at royal *colloquia*,[4] in international undertakings and on embassies stresses the dignity and central political rôle of the justiciars. But their central function in the thirteenth century emerges, in the words of

---

[1] Quhen Alexander the King was deid
That Scotland had to steyr and leid
(Barbour, *The Bruce*, ed. Mackenzie, 2).
[2] 'The Scottish King's Household Early in the Fourteenth Century', ed. M. Bateson, *Scottish History Society Miscellany*, ii, 31–43. For the date see the succinct note in Barrow, *Kingdom of the Scots*, 93.
[3] Barrow, *Kingdom of the Scots*, chapter 3, 'The Justiciar', replaces all earlier comments on this institution.
[4] Discussed below p. 610.

*The King's Household* as holding 'their sessions of the justice ayre twice a year, once at the season of the grass and a second time at the season of corn'. The known pleas before justices do seem to fall into summer and winter groups, but the claim of the treatise that the conduct of the sheriff was enquired into is belied by the long tenure of office of many sheriffs. From 1250, however, a fair number of recorded pleas before a justiciar show the increasing importance and formality of justiciary courts, and while the record usually gives the end of the action and is reticent about its roots, many of the pleas were about land, and were resolved either by an inquest, probably in consequence of a brieve of mortancestor or dissasine, or by a perambulation of disputed bounds. Such perambulations were by no means always made by a justiciar, but he does seem to have been the 'ordinary' for such actions. Their importance is underlined by the existence of royal enrolments for these and other 'recognitions' throughout the thirteenth century; it is likely that the 'roll of justiciary' of which there is late evidence was the same record under another name.[5] Essentially it was public record of the resolutions of private debates, the state offering its authority to hold the parties to the outcome of their pleas. The magnates who acted as justiciars for the king were men of such substance that none receiving their judgement could doubt the weight of royal authority. As for their criminal jurisdiction, far less can be said; as we shall see it yielded a trivial profit to the king but significantly more than the sheriff's justice.

In the badly transcribed fragments of the lost royal accounts for 1264–6 and 1288–90,[6] we have another invaluable supplement to the scanty light cast upon the king's administration by charters and kindred instruments. The ordinary unit of administration remained the sheriffdom, the number of which scarcely increased during the thirteenth century. There were thirteen south of the Forth,[7] seven between the Forth and the Mounth[8] and eight north of the Mounth.[9] Four of these, Cromarty, Dingwall, Kinross and Auchterarder were small and had probably—Kinross certainly—been created by turn-

[5] *A.P.S.*, i, 114; *Dunfermline Registrum*, nos. 83, 85, 196; *Arbroath Liber*, i, nos. 227–30, 294.

[6] I have used these accounts since they obviously continue Alexander III's administrative system.

[7] Berwick, Roxburgh, Selkirk, Peebles or Traquair, Haddington, Edinburgh, Linlithgow, Stirling, Dumbarton, Lanark, Ayr, Dumfries, Wigtown.

[8] Fife, Clackmannan, Kinross, Auchterarder, Perth, Forfar, Kincardine.

[9] Aberdeen, Banff, Elgin, Forres, Invernairn, Inverness, Cromarty, Dingwall.

ing a thanage into a sheriffdom. The three sheriffdoms of Linlithgow, Edinburgh and Haddington were all held by Roger de Mowbray and then by William Sinclair, and Clackmannan was incorporated in Stirling; somewhat inappropriately Dingwall and Wigtown were in the hands of Alexander Comyn, Earl of Buchan. In these cases, or where the sheriff was an important magnate, perhaps with other duties, for instance as a justiciar, he exercised his office by deputy; in several cases this deputy was the constable whom he appointed to the king's castle in the sheriffdom. It seems that even where there was no castle, as at Linlithgow and Haddington, he would nonetheless appoint a constable as deputy. Even when such deputies are included in their number, the sheriffs are a cross-section of the magnates of the first and second rank in the kingdom. The sheriffs were undoubtedly active in all the fields of which record survives. They held sheriff courts in both civil and criminal pleas, they presided over inquests or assizes, they assembled demesne revenues, fines and forfeitures and realised them for the king, and they called out and led the host; they were held accountable and accounted to him for them all with, so far as we know, regularity and thoroughness. Sometimes these things were done by another agent, but in the great majority of cases the sheriff himself was active in the king's business at all important levels. The level of responsibility of the constable was for the state of his castle, the thane or farmer for the demesne which was leased to him, the mair for arresting criminals and serving brieves, and all were responsible to the sheriff for these tasks. Only the provosts enjoyed the anomaly of both dependent and independent standing in relation to the king's other officers.

The financial responsibilities of the sheriff included the king's demesne. Thus the sheriff of Forfar in 1264 rendered two separate accounts: one was for the thanages of Forfar and Glamis, showing gross receipts for a year of 37 cows, 75 pigs, 1578 stones of cheese, 291 hens, 32 chalders of barley, 10 chalders of flour, 206 'clevins' of oats, and 800 eels; the other was for his bailiary and showed a gross money income of £485, including £60 for the ferme of Tannadice, a former thanage. Of this large money income a small fraction came from the profits of the sheriff's (£6) and the justiciar's (£31) courts, the rest from rents; £50 had been paid to the chamberlain, £204 was owed by the accountant, and the balance, some £230, had been spent, though we are told the details of only £70 of very miscellaneous expenses.[10] The same division into a produce and money account is found in 1264–6 in the sheriffdoms of Perth (£140 in money of which £20 was arrears), Kincardine, Elgin, Inverness (£133 in money rents only), Forres, Kinross, Dumbarton and in the south in Haddington, Edinburgh, Linlithgow, Roxburgh and Peebles. The sheriff of Ayr was commanded to provide henceforth each year 40 cows, 12 chalders of wheat, 40 of barley and 20 of oats for the king's needs (presumably by purchase) and the sheriff of Perth spent £62 on 360 salted beef carcases 'bought for the larder of the king'. After the king's death a change is noticeable—the produce rents were sold to the accountant except for small quantities consumed at the audit; this confirms the view that the king and his court had still consumed a large part of his income in kind.

It is striking that in a number of cases the produce rents come from estates close to the sheriff's castle: Forfar and Glamis to Forfar, Fettercairn to Kincardine, Kinclaven to its castle. More distant estates were either farmed for money or accounted directly at the exchequer and so might be recognised as small sheriffdoms—this seems to be the history of Kinross and Auchterarder. There was an obvious administrative convenience in leasing distant estates and retaining those close to the sheriff's castle. It is not clear how the king's rents were fixed, save that the chamberlain was responsible for doing so. The only region for which a rental of crown lands survives again shows a substantial money income, £430 from the sheriffdom of Aberdeen, £504 from that of Banff, though the latter includes £50 from burghs and a like sum which could be paid in kind. The verb *extenditur* in this rental implies valuation perhaps by an assize and it is even more interesting that the phrase 'old extent' (*antiquam extentam*), used of one thanage, suggests that already revaluation could not always be made effective in the king's interest against an older and lower valuation which had become customary.[11]

The sheriff, then, would handle money and produce, the latter to be consumed at court, the former disbursed by the sheriff, some in payment of regular fees or alms, some in special payments and expenses for which the warrant is almost never specified, and some handed over to the chamberlain. Thus the king's business might be

---

[10] It is possible that the accountant owed £280 and the balance spent would then be £155; *Exch. Rolls*, i, 8–9.

[11] *Aberdeen Registrum*, i, 55–8.

paid for from a different royal purse from year to year and the
chamberlain's receipts from the sheriffs in any one year were in many
respects a matter of chance. Thus, quite apart from uncertainty
about the period which it covers, the chamberlain's account of 1264
is of very limited value. It shows gross receipts of £2897 from the
'fermes of bailiaries', presumably from sheriffs and those holding
lands at ferme, £676 from the fermes of burghs, and £1808 from
'common receipts . . . with fines and reliefs'. Since it is clear that the
profits of justice were collected and accounted for by the sheriffs, the
word 'fine' here must have the sense of 'composition' or 'payment
in lieu of something due to the king'. It is noticeable that in the
accounts, admittedly incomplete, the sheriffs rarely answered for
reliefs, and it may be that these formed a substantial part of the
'common receipts'. It may be that the chamberlain was an early
'lord componitour', responsible for negotiating appropriate sums for
payment into the chamber. With arrears the total chamberlain's
receipts were £5413, but the auditors erred in the king's disfavour
by £100 in their summation. There is a total discharge of £6046,
of which £1038 was spent on paying knights and serjeants and for
horses and saddles (£720). This heavy military expenditure on the
warfare of 1263-5 was doubtless exceptional. But after 1286 a
number of gentry were paid fees (usually ten merks annually) as
knights retained by Alexander III, and at this rate the 270 merks
spent on knights' fees in 1264 represents twenty-seven knights; some
of these were doubtless retained also in peacetime. Almost £1700
was paid to merchants, nearly half of this for wine; this figure,
however, certainly covers two years. Messengers cost £150, the
king's presents £122 and his gambling £16. The remainder of the
expenditure was upon the queen's household, £796, and the king's
household, £2224, but of this latter amount the chamberlain had
not paid £600 which 'is owed to the countryside by the lord king'.
This must represent the king's right to prise and carriage, to com-
mandeer from his subjects goods and transport as needed by the
court but subject always to fair payment. Perhaps under the stress of
war, the king had first failed to pay his merchants' bills for 1263 and
had now left debts to the tune of £600 among his subjects for the
payment of which his chamberlain had no cash. There is no reason
to think that these debts went unpaid or that the king resorted to
disreputable means to pay them; after his death a Gascon merchant
presented a wine-bill for some £2000 but the amount was grossly

and unjustifiably inflated. On the other hand, in the inventories of lost records there is considerable evidence of loans by merchants to the king, loans which were repaid. These details leave us in no doubt that the chamberlain's duty (as *The King's Household* suggests) was to finance the royal household, for this is what all the expenditure amounts to. He must 'make purchases wholesale and regulate the king's dwelling' (that is, choose the king's dwelling place) with the king's assent, and regulate the state of the household for the seasons of the year so that it can live by purveyance (that is, payment) without ravaging the countryside (*pays*). The last word is echoed in the accounts by the *patria* to which the king owed £600.

*The King's Household* names four departments within the household, interdependent and doubtless subordinate to the chamberlain upon whom they relied for much of their receipts. This hierarchy is confirmed by the names of those gathered in the king's chamber at Edinburgh Castle in 1278.[12] The humblest was the clerk of the kitchen, responsible for keeping strict watch upon the use and consumption of provisions in kitchen and larder. An account of 'William the Cook, keeper of the door' (of the kitchen) in the 1260s shows him selling kitchen surplus for £162 over two years and paying the money over to the chamberlain. A much fuller account of 1330 shows this clerk receiving marts from the chamberlain (298), the sheriff of Ayr (16) and the clerk of liverance, who bought 8, and then a further 68½ carcases; he received 996 sheep from the chamberlain and 40 from the clerk of liverance, of which 60 were used at Robert I's funeral, 5 were lost in a storm, wolves and dogs got 37, and the rest were consumed in the household. And so his account proceeds through pigs, herring, dried fish, salmon, eels, peas, olive oil, salt, hides and skins, each item vouched for by a roll of household expenses when bought by the clerk of liverance, or by a roll of proof when expended by himself.

The treatise gives second place to the clerk of the wardrobe, responsible for all 'relics, jewels, vestments, robes, treasure and of all manner of clothes and furniture belonging to the hall, the chamber and the chapel of the king as well as spices, wax and other small items'. These he is to receive 'in gross' from the chamberlain, whose accounts do include purchases of these items, and, in 1329 and later, their delivery to the clerk of the wardrobe. The latter's accounts, however, were perfunctory statements of total receipts and disburse-

12 *Dunfermline Registrum*, no. 86.

ments which may be the significance of the phrase 'in gross'. That the treatise is otherwise accurate may be discovered from the paraphernalia of knives, cups, ecclesiastical vestments and relics deposited in the treasury at Edinburgh Castle in 1291 when there was no itinerating court to require them.

At the top of the hierarchy of clerks was he of the liverance, with two men under him, to 'deal with the king's provisions and make delivery in the hall and outside to each according to his due' and to be in charge of all in the household who handled victuals. The accounts of 1328 and later show that he kept the roll of household expenses, a list of cash purchases made by him for the other offices; but he was responsible not only for these cash purchases but also for receipts and disbursements of wheat, rye, bere, oats, bran, flour and wine. Now in 1278 the clerk of the provender (*prebenda*) came between the wardrobe and liverance in the hierarchy, and a similar place is given to him by *The King's Household*. His office, found under King William, is generally understood to be that of provisioning particularly with grain, in which sense *prebenda* was used in the twelfth century, and it seems that this clerk had responsibility for grain, ale and wine, the clerk of the kitchen a parallel responsibility for flesh in the late twelfth century and until at least 1278, while responsibility for money gave the clerk of liverance that increasing importance which is obvious in the reign of Alexander II. By 1292, however, liverance had taken over responsibility for grain as well as money and provender had changed his name and function to become clerk of the proof or audit,[18] who each night set up table at the door of the king's hall and with each of the other three clerks went over their daily account, allowing or disallowing items with the advice of the marshals and doorwards, before whose faces the produce had presumably passed, and drawing up his own roll of 'proof'. The rolls of expenses and proof were available at the exchequer as warrants for the claims of the clerks of the kitchen and liverance but, although frequently referred to in the fourteenth-century exchequer accounts, none has survived.

Was the 'proof' instituted before or after 1286? There can have been no household after 1286, and both clerkship and audit

---

[18] This is garbled in *The King's Household* as printed and presumably in the MS. Read: *Clerc de la Proueue* ... (i.e. preuve) *q'est appelle en auncien temps Clerc de la Prouendre*, Clerk of the Proof, who was called in olden times Clerk of the Provender.

must be assigned to the reign of Alexander III. Perhaps they were connected with the changes which took place in his household in the 1280s: the financing of his daughter's marriage and of separate households for the Lord Alexander and Queen Yolande. Beyond that we cannot go at present.[14]

We have dwelt upon the still significant royal income in produce and upon the size and source of the king's money income. Crown lands were probably the largest item, with the king's rights of lordship or superiority (for example wards and reliefs) running second. The profits of justice were comparatively unimportant. But one significant item scarcely figures in either the rolls or *The King's Household*, although we know a good deal about it in the fourteenth century—the king's income from his burghs. From the time of David I, when only the burghs yielded money income, the peculiar responsibility of the chamberlain for them was probably well-marked, since the chamber handled only money-income. From the institution of the exchequer by the late twelfth century, burgh officers probably rendered separate accounts,[15] and in the sheriff's accounts of the thirteenth century there are only two references to burgh fermes, one to Dumfries, where the sheriff was acting only as intermediary between burgh and chamberlain, the other to Auchterarder, where burgh and demesne lands were farmed together. It seems likely that the chamberlain had long—perhaps even in the twelfth century—been responsible for fixing for a year or period of years ahead the ferme payable by each burgh community to the king. The time taken for negotiation of the ferme would doubtless vary according to the size and importance of the burgh, but the pattern of an annual ayre by the chamberlain was doubtless already well established, though it must be admitted that *The King's Household* makes no mention of one.

It is even more difficult to find evidence of the granting and payment of taxation in the thirteenth century. An unusual document survives in a garbled text which, generously interpreted, tells us that at a council of earls and barons on 1 January, probably of 1218, a grant was made to Scone Abbey (for its fabric) of one penny annually for seven years from each house emitting smoke, on the

---

[14] See *A.P.S.*, i, 112; *Exch. Rolls*, i, 323–34 and generally indices to *Exch. Rolls*, i and ii, under Proof, Liverance, Wardrobe, Kitchen.

[15] For the provosts of Perth rendering account at the exchequer in 1267, *Kelso Liber*, no. 398.

king's demesnes both in burghs and elsewhere.[16] This is the closest
to tallage of the royal demesne that we can find in Scotland, but was
rather wider inasmuch as it was also granted from some baronial
demesnes. There may have been aids and tallages in thirteenth-
century Scotland (and we should remember that they were rare in
Henry III's England) but they have left few reliable traces.[17]

Among the records listed in 1292 were letters from eighteen
burghs quit-claiming (that is, presumably, cancelling) all the debts
owed to them by the king, the queen and their predecessors. Such
words suggest that the crown had yielded a considerable measure of
independence to the burgh communities and in return had received
loans, perhaps in the form of annual discharge higher than the
amount charged to the burgh—that is, consistent overspending on
the king's business. There is a further possibility in a curious tale of
Bower that, in order to prevent shipping losses, all exports of merchandise were forbidden by the king. A year later foreign ships
arrived laden with goods to exchange for those retained in Scotland
—and no one was to deal in such business, *burgesses only excepted*.
If the rest is garbled nonsense, the last phrase may represent a
further consolidation of the burgesses' monopoly in dealings with
foreign merchants, conceded in return for cancellation of royal
debts. An interesting feature of the list of eighteen burghs is that
while it includes most of the medium-sized towns, it does not include
Berwick, Edinburgh or Perth. These were the largest in Scotland
and correspondingly likely as a source of royal finance. It may be
that we should link this omission with the existence before 1272 of
a group of four burghs, Berwick, Roxburgh, Edinburgh and Stirling,
whose commissioners met to declare the law and custom of burghs
in Scotland. At a later date Haddington was the usual place of
meeting, the commissioners numbered sixteen, and the chamberlain
presided over the court, circumstances which probably applied in
the thirteenth century. At such a meeting the cancellation of royal
debt to the burghs could well have been first negotiated.

The introduction to Scotland of a duty upon the export of wool
and hides is less doubtful.[18] Known as the 'new' custom, this impost

---

[16] G. O. Sayles, 'A Reputed Royal Charter of 1218', *Sc. Hist. Rev.* xxxi
(1952), 138–9 where *nostrarum* must be supplied after *terrarum* in line 8 on
p. 139.

[17] See above pp. 388–9, 523.

[18] These two commodities certainly paid custom. Skins (known in England
as woolfells) must also have paid for they were both hide and wool.

must have been adopted from England, where it was introduced in 1275 at the rate of half a mark on the sack of wool and a mark on the last of hides, rates most probably also extended to Scotland.[19] The new custom is only known to have been payable at Berwick[20] which certainly handled a major part—perhaps more than half—of Scottish wool exports, but this is probably attributable to a quirk of accounting, and customs would surely be levied at other major ports such as Dundee.[21] The great custom was introduced to England with the agreement of merchants both native and foreign and became a major factor in manipulating credit facilities for the crown; it seems likely that in a modest way the same is true of Scotland. It is very noticeable that Berwick figured in the marriage settlement of the king's daughter, that Berwick was to provide a dower for his daughter-in-law if widowed, and that Berwick did provide the dower of his own widow. It seems not unlikely that some or most of the merchants from whom the king borrowed made their loans upon the security of Berwick's customs—one was certainly assigned repayment from them—and that the king's needs were enlarged by his marriage alliances. Unfortunately, there seems to be no evidence of the date at which the new custom was introduced; it cannot have been earlier than 1275 nor later than 1282.

The activities of the king's chancellor as keeper of the great seal had scarcely altered since the office was introduced in the twelfth century. The king's 'chapel' or chancery remained a remarkably small office and to judge from surviving examples there was little increase in the number of documents issued annually during the thirteenth century.[22] Charters and confirmations remained comparatively unchanging exercises in Latin brevity. Brieves that have survived are infinitely varying in their terminology and in the questions they ask. While there is reference to *breve de recto*, the

[19] These are the rates found in Scotland in the reign of Robert I.

[20] *A.P.S.*, i, 114 (at middle), 118.

[21] Each burgh accounted for its ferme etc., in detail; the customs account would be on the back of this. But Berwick had a single-payment feu-ferme and a separate customs account would be necessary. This appears in the inventories of lost records.

[22] Twice as many charters and letters have survived of Alexander II as of his son. Subtract letters to the English king and a group of brieves fortuitously preserved in England and the discrepancy is even more remarkable. It seems incontrovertible that fewer documents were issued to the church by Alexander III. But this is less true—if true at all—of the laity. And the majority of documents issued in any one year by either king was of brieves and similar ephemera. Here there seems to have been some increase in the later thirteenth century.

surviving evidence suggests that this was not 'the writ of right' but 'a writ to hear someone's claim (or right) to something' or in other words 'a pleadable brieve'. Such a brieve may have been a necessary preliminary to any contentious action using the now-general inquest, but the chancellor seems to have issued them freely upon any narrative. The non-pleadable brieve ordering enquiry into facts (such as 'name the true heir' or 'value property or lands') was usually returned to the chapel along with a record of the inquest's finding. It may have had a few stereotyped forms but there was nothing to confine the chancellor's clerks to the use of them. Warrants under the great seal to pay fees or allowances have survived in substantial number from 1286–92, only occasionally from before 1286; but this reflects the chance of survival not of issue, and they were probably issued in fair numbers each year.

The responsibilties of the chancellor were implicit in the discretion in using the king's name and seal which he enjoyed. He must be wise, discreet, know the law and be impartial to rich and poor for he is chief of the king's council. *The King's Household* also tells us that fees were charged for each document sealed and that the chancery could for a fee issue brieves 'of course' (that is, run-of-the-mill brieves) and pleadable brieves. There is no trace yet of a register of forms in the Scottish chancery and, in practice, the chancellor must have enjoyed considerable freedom over what he might seal. The same source tells us that for other documents he must have a warrant under the privy seal of the king (that is, kept by the king), but of the privy seal we can say only that Alexander III used it once in a letter to Edward I for lack of his great seal. No impression has been preserved and no identifiable example of its use as a warrant for the great seal is known. Since the Scottish chancery cannot have issued more than a small fraction of the letters found on the English chancery rolls—and these do not include writs for judicial actions, nor documents under the exchequer seal, all instruments calling for the great seal in Scotland—it is difficult to believe that pressure of business made a privy seal necessary. It is more likely that (as the surviving letter suggests) its use was a convenience, perhaps an infrequent convenience.

Within chancery the great seal was to be kept 'by one of the wisest and most discreet of the realm, for if this office be well governed it is the key and safety of the great seal and the prevention of all the errors which can arise in the court between the king and the baronage; and he shall have under him as many clerks as are required in reason'. Such an official, a clerk of the seal, has been discerned in the chancery of King William[23] and is likely to have been necessary under a chancellor who was bishop—and the office was held by a bishop from 1233 to *c.* 1247 as well as for other short periods. In 1257, when the Comyns seized the king at Kinross they took the seal from the dean of Dunkeld who carried it in place of his bishop, the chancellor.[24] His designation as 'vice-chancellor' was Fordun's and was not used officially; in general, thirteenth-century documents were reluctant to designate the functions of those under the chancellor or chamberlain, and we cannot be sure whether a carrier of the seal existed for most of the thirteenth century or whether *The King's Household* exaggerates his importance. It may have arisen from those associates of the chancellor appointed by Edward I in 1291 rather than from practice before 1286, in which case the attributes of keeper of the seal according to *The King's Household* should belong to the chancellor under Alexander III.[25] There is no trace of 'errors' arising between Alexander III and his barons though there were doubtless occasional strains after the difficulties of the minority. The jockeying during these difficulties to secure a chancellor complaisant to the party in power, and the curious history of the great seal itself between 1249 and *c.* 1260 fit neatly enough with the key position attributed to the chancellor as chief of the council and (by implication) of the *curia regis*.

This key position of the chancellor was probably connected intimately with the auditing of the king's accounts. We know all too little about the exchequer of the thirteenth century, but it is clear that it was not an office with staff but an *ad hoc* audit before which each burgh provost and sheriff, each bailie of lands who had escaped the sheriff's regulation, each justiciar and even the chamberlain himself had to compear either in person or occasionally by procurator, ideally each year, to state what he owed to the king and what allowances he claimed to set against that debt. The place

---

[23] *R.R.S.*, ii, 31.

[24] *Chron. Fordun*, i, 297; *Handbook of British Chronology* (2nd edn. 1961), ed. F. M. Powicke and E. B. Fryde, 174, for thirteenth-century chancellors.

[25] The printed text and translation are so punctuated as to relate this office to the privy seal, and I am quite sure that this is erroneous from 'for if this office . . .'. But in the text above I have gone further and related *lequel serra porte* to *lancien fee du seal*. I hope that this reinterpretation does not do violence to the easy-going ways of Anglo-Norman.

of audit varied: between 1261 and 1266 we know of audits at Arbroath, Scone, Newbattle, Linlithgow and Edinburgh, and in some years there were probably two sessions, although *The King's Household* suggests only one. The exchequer board for the chamberlain's account at Scone in 1264 consisted of two bishops (both former chancellors), five abbots, Sir Robert Menzies (a former chamberlain) and Sir John de Cambrun 'and the clerks of the chapel and of the court of the lord king'. In a later account of the sheriff of Berwick it was noted that he asked to be allowed 'twenty merks ... which were usually allowed by grace of the king each year, which in this account are not allowed *on account of the absence of the chancellor and chamberlain*'. These words signify not only that the chancellor and chamberlain knew of, perhaps even exercised, the king's discretion, but also that they were habitually on the auditorial board. In 1290 this consisted of three abbots, two knights, the chancellor 'and the remaining clerks of the royal dignity' and the chamberlain's depute, but the Guardians' instructions were sent to 'the chancellor and other auditors'.[26] *The King's Household* advises that the auditors be men of substance and discretion 'enjoined by commission with the chancellor and chamberlain' and, except for the exclusion of the chamberlain when his own account was audited, there seems little doubt that the 'business' element in the king's court, headed by chancellor and chamberlain, formed the auditorial board with the addition of a few prelates. The computing was probably done by the clerks of the chapel (that is, chancery) and of the court (that is, household—liverance, wardrobe, proof) while the prelates, chancellor, chamberlain and two knights close to the king and probably of the council judged the allowability of the accountants' claims. The exchequer, then, was a function to which chancery, household and council contributed, but in which the chancellor played a—and probably *the*—leading role.

A new office seems to have been created towards the end of Alexander III's reign and is further evidence of the overriding responsibility of the chancellor for the audit. The first clerk of the rolls (ancestor of the Lord Clerk Register) was William de Dumfries, appointed on the king's death in 1286; however, he probably exercised the functions of the office in 1282 when the archives in Edinburgh Castle were surveyed. Essentially he was keeper of the rolls of the chapel and of accounts, but he was more than an

[26] *Exch. Rolls*, i, 11, 22, 38–9, 45, 47–9.

archivist; according to *The King's Household* he had to ' "counter-roll" [that is, check] all the charters and documents issuing from the chancery and all the accounts of the exchequer, by his rolls which shall be called the royal rolls in chief'. A chancery official, his duties at the exchequer probably consisted in checking the accountants' figures against, for example, the records of pensions, fermes and arrears enrolled in chancery, by the chamberlain and at previous audits respectively, and now in his charge. In the chancery he presumably took charge of retours which may have been stitched together into a roll; less probable was the enrolment of outgoing charters other than in exceptional circumstances. Overall the inventories give an impression of lists of miscellanea among which only the foreign correspondence was regarded as permanently valuable.[27] But the failure of chancery to develop an adequate record of outgoing charters and letters—adequate, that is for the historian—is surely explained in part by its responsibility for and time spent on exchequer business.

Over all these instruments of government sat the council of the king. With a core of professional clerics and knights such as Sinclair, Fraser and Cambrun its members probably took an oath *de fideli consilio*.[28] The work of the council, the frequency of its meetings, its discretion in the absence of the king, these are matters upon which our sources are almost or wholly silent. Thus *The King's Household* simply assumes the council: the chancellor is 'head of the king's council' (twice); claims to offices of state should be adjudged 'in parliament and not by lesser council'. But the composition and functions of the 'lesser council' are not elaborated and probably for the very good reason that to govern 'according to the ancient custom and usage of the land' implied taking advice on each matter from the appropriate officer described in the tract—chancellor, chamberlain, justiciars, and so on. This was the king's responsibility. Advice is the essence of successful government, and on most counts Alexander III was a successful king: we may conclude that a council was continually involved in the administration of the realm in

[27] For consultation of a *rotulus capelle* in the audit see *Exch. Rolls*, i, 19. When in 1267 Alexander III ascertained from the *rotuli capelle nostre* that Tiron Abbey had enjoyed three merks annually from the burgh ferme of Perth, his clerks must, I think, have consulted previous account rolls and not charter rolls. *Kelso Liber*, no. 398.

[28] No oath, however, was mentioned for councillors in the records of the palace revolution of 1255.

matters both detailed and weighty. The rebuilding of the interior of Wigtown Castle was approved as a scheme of work 'by the council of the lord king'; the council ordered a survey and inventory of the letters in the treasury archives at Edinburgh Castle;[29] on the afternoon before the king's death the council sat in Edinburgh Castle debating a reply to a letter from Edward I. These are but glimpses of a continuous activity which was the governance of the kingdom.

In important matters the king took wider counsel. *The King's Household* speaks of his having 'common assembly and speech personally with all the prelates earls and barons' in which each side might assure the other of his or their goodwill and the magnates would advise the names of good ministers. This emphasis upon the rightful place of all the magnates is misleading; the king was responsible for summons and subject-matter, and doubtless also chose his own ministers. The tract must, however, reflect a very real sense of common discussion and common decision on important matters as a tradition in government. The events of 1249–58 may be seen as a period of apprenticeship for the magnates in which this tradition of government had to work without an effective king and with the threat of outside interference. The wonder is not that there were palace revolutions but that chaos was avoided. Already a common identity (or 'community') had been achieved and the meetings of these years suggest that 'common assembly' in the time of Alexander II and earlier had played a large part in this achievement. Henry III wrote of the *parleamentum* and *colloquium* of the Scottish king at which the Comyns were to be reconciled; in 1264 two *colloquia* were held at Edinburgh, doubtless to discuss peace with Norway and conquest of the Isles; the large quantities of food purveyed for these occasions are an indication of the attendance of many magnates. From the chronicles we learn that, in a 'great gathering' at Scone on 9 April 1285, the earldom of Menteith was claimed by William Comyn 'when the estates gatherit was' and that when certain Lombard bankers offered to found cities in return for privileges, the petition did not please 'certain of the estates of the kingdom' and was not effected.[30] In both cases the word 'estates' is an anachronistic term for an assembly, probably for parliament.

[29] I conclude this from the statement by Simon Fraser to the council that he had taken a certain document to Melrose Abbey. This statement was made on the eve of the survey.

[30] *Chron. Wyntoun*, ed. Amours, V, 138–9; *Chron. Bower*, ii, 130.

The name *colloquium* is first found for an assembly in 1235. The French equivalent, *parlement*, whence the latin *parliamentum*, was used in England and, although not found in Scotland till the 1290s, the continuity between *colloquium* and *parliamentum* is plain, so that we may translate both as 'parliament'.[31] The total of such assemblies recorded before 1286 is small but a number are attested in the first twenty years of the reign, and after 1286 they were held regularly by the guardians, surely in continuation of the practice of Alexander III's time. In a number of documents parliament seems to be a place where justice is done by the king, especially by bringing contending parties to amicable settlement. *The King's Household* proposed that all those claiming to hold office or fee heritably should have their title pronounced upon 'by the good assize of their peers and by good people who best know the matter . . . and let this be done *en plein parlement*' but the traces of judgements, whether of this kind or between private parties, are scanty. Among the Scottish records in 1292 was a sack with 307 pieces of parchment containing complaints, petitions and letters to the king, some of which must have been considered by the council in parliament; but of formal judgements in the king's court there were only 'two pleas in two schedules of which the judgements were given in the king's presence'—perhaps, but not necessarily, in parliament. The poverty of evidence may be explained by a statement by the bishops in 1250 that decisions in a recent council 'were scantily written down'[32] and the strongest argument in favour of the view that parliament was regularly or even frequently a judicial occasion is the clear evidence that it is true of the 1290s.[33]

Neither of the two most important gatherings of the reign is called a parliament in the document which each has left as our source but either may have been one. At the first, in December 1281, five bishops, six earls and five barons 'by common counsel of us all and by great deliberation which we have had together with the said king' affirmed the custom of the realm over the succession; at the

---

[31] It is noticeable that with Alexander III's letter in front of him, the English clerk wrote of 'the *colloquium* which you propose' and countered with 'the *parliamentum* which I propose'.

[32] '*Ea licet que in ultimo concilio apud Eddenburc celebrato vobis ac magnatibus uestris presentibus ordinata fuerant minime fuerint in scripturam redacta . . .' A.P.S.,* i, 425.

[33] A. A. M. Duncan, 'The Early Parliaments of Scotland', *Sc. Hist. Rev.,* xlv (1966), 36–47.

second, in February 1284, thirteen earls and twenty-four barons promised to accept Margaret, the Maid of Norway, as heir to the kingdom. Whereas on the second occasion only an unnamed selection of the participating magnates sealed the act, the first document names those who sealed as the participants and there were probably more than these sixteen present.

There was, however, a great difference in the circumstances which the documents sought to meet: the first was a reassurance of normality to the count of Flanders, the second a desperate solution to a pressing problem.

When 'the Scots chose Donald' as their king in 1093 they took advantage for the last time of the eligibility of all members of the royal race to succeed to the throne. From the accession of Edgar in 1097 until 1286 the rule of primogeniture among the descendants of Malcolm III and Margaret was followed and these seven kings undoubtedly established this rule as the custom of the realm. If at first there seems a marked contrast with the succession problems of contemporary England, upon closer examination the difference becomes much less. The three sons of Malcolm and Margaret succeeded with English backing; David I resorted to the Capetian practice of designating his successor in 1144 and 1152 and this discounts the view that primogeniture was established between 1097 and 1124. For twenty years after 1165 the heir presumptive was the king's brother, and when in 1195 the king sought to arrange the succession of his daughter and her proposed husband the magnates resisted, presumably in favour of Earl David. If at his birth the king's son Alexander displaced Earl David as heir, the king was sufficiently anxious to register the fact by having homage done to the boy when he was three years old (1201) and also, on his deathbed in 1214, by securing acceptance of his heir. Earl David had stood one step from the throne for thirty years and the lesson of King John's success in ousting his nephew Arthur in 1199 was, doubtless, too recent to be ignored. We may conclude that by the accession of Alexander II opinion had hardened decisively for succession by primogeniture, and that the element of choice survived only in the circumstance that Alexander II and Alexander III were young and required a positive decision by the magnates to proceed with the inauguration. None doubted that they should be enthroned.

The resolution of this problem raised another which caused civil war in England and foreign war in France—could a woman succeed as heir by primogeniture; and if not could she transmit to her husband or son the right to succeed? In Scotland the death of Earl John in 1237 left Alexander II as the only descendant of Malcolm III and Margaret in the male line. We have only a late and *ex parte* statement that Alexander II, passing over his three sisters and the three daughters of Earl John's eldest sister (and the husbands of all of them) recognised Robert Bruce, the son of Earl John's second sister, as heir presumptive.[34] Such recognition, although it was probably informal, fits well enough with the episode of 1195, and shows that the Scots ruled out female succession but not female transmission of the right to succeed. This must raise the difficulties posed by the chance—indeed the likelihood—that any one of the women standing between Bruce and the king might bear a son who would have a better claim than he (and on the same grounds) to succeed. This problem (which is really insoluble) was postponed by the birth of Alexander (III) in 1241.

Alexander III, too, had to wait for the birth of a son until the fifteenth year of his reign, but we have no evidence how the succession might have gone if he had died before that. In their assurance to the count of Flanders in 1281 the king and magnates stated that beyond memory it had been the custom of Scotland that if a king's son and heir predeceased the king leaving an heir of his body then the latter was heir to the kingdom.[35] But the working of this principle was further detailed: the heir male of the Lord Alexander and Margaret of Flanders would be heir to the kingdom even if Alexander III had other issue; if Margaret died leaving no heir male, if the Lord Alexander then remarried and had an heir male then this grandson would be heir after his father to the kingdom; but if this grandson died without heir of his body then the kingdom would come to the eldest female issue of Alexander and Margaret unless Alexander III had another son by a second marriage; and if this other son of the king had no heir of his body then the kingdom would come to the female heir of Alexander and Margaret. This elaborate tailzie fails to come plainly to grips with the problem of reconciling primogeniture with the admission of female heirs: if the Lord Alexander left only a daughter why should she yield the king-

---

[34] Admittedly the strict heir general was not an attractive proposition—the king's middle-aged oldest sister, mourning the loss of her only daughter and estranged from her broken husband, Hubert de Burgh, Earl of Kent.

[35] The precedent for this would be David I, Earl Henry and Malcolm IV.

dom to his younger half-brother; if the younger half-brother were to suceed and he then begot only a daughter, which woman should succeed? Looking to 1290–2 we may say that the tailzie explicitly demanded impartibility among daughters and came down unequivocally in favour of the eldest.[36] Indeed, its most striking feature is the admission that a woman might succeed to the kingdom; in these respects it anticipated the settlement of the English crown adopted by Edward I and the English royal family in 1290. The king was plainly optimistic, however, that he would remarry and have other issue, and the purpose of the document was chiefly to assure the count of Flanders that Alexander III's eldest son's sons would succeed to the throne before the king's own younger sons. Primogeniture was not unquestioned but something like a rule of succession had been agreed.

Only two years and three months later it seemed inadequate, for all the king's children had died, leaving the possibilities of a posthumous child born to Margaret of Flanders and of a child born to a new wife for the king and the certainty only of the king's grandchild in Norway. Accordingly, at Scone on 5 February 1284 the magnates put their seals upon a curious document, to which the king and bishops were parties only incidentally. It was their promise to the king and the heirs descended from his body who ought to be admitted to the succession[37] that failing issue, male or female, of the king and of the Lord Alexander then they would receive Margaret, the Maid of Norway, as their lady and as rightful heir of the king and would maintain her against all men. They further promised to the king and the executors of his testament that if upon his death any officers or debtors did not pay to the executors what they owed to the king, then the magnates would take poinds from them. For the discharge of all this the magnates subjected themselves to the jurisdiction of the bishops.

Both this document and that of 1281 contained a promise but there the resemblance ends, for the common counsel and deliberation, the declaration of custom and usage of 1281 are nowhere to be found three years later. The promise of 1284 would have been

---

[36] 'li roiaumes d'Escoche tout entirement revenroit et revenir deveroit a l'aisnet oir femelle.'

[37] This curious turn of phrase is perhaps puzzling. I think it means not 'those heirs of his body who ought to be admitted' but 'the heirs of his body, i.e. those who ought to be admitted.' Thus it stated the general ground upon which the Maid was rightful heir. For these settlements of the succession see above p. 592n.

unnecessary if it had covered a generally agreed and obvious course of action; it used firm and strict words of obligation; it was made for 'us all and each of us' but without any suggestion of consent and as its second part was aimed directly at those who did not accept the king's will, the first part was likewise aimed obliquely. The plainest evidence of baronial reluctance in this oath is to be found in the events after the king's death in 1286 when it was replaced by a new and very unspecific oath.

If, as we suggest, the magnates did not like the prospect of the succession of the Maid, the grounds for their reluctance are less certain; probably her sex, her youth and her Norwegian father all played their part. After 1286 there was occasional talk of 'the king [not "the queen"] who is to come' and it seems likely that the treaties of Salisbury and Birgham were negotiated so that the Scots could inaugurate a husband along with the Maid, whom even in 1284 they promised to accept as 'lady' and 'heir' but without mention of 'queen'. If Alexander III asked his barons to accept his granddaughter as their queen irrespective of whether she had a husband at her side or not, then he was repeating the demand of Henry I in England in 1127 and Margaret might have been the first queen regnant in feudal Europe. But his letter to Edward I in April 1284, calling the Maid 'our heir apparent' and indicating that her early marriage was called for shows that he had no such revolutionary notion. He saw her as bringing a kinsman of Edward I to the Scottish throne.

Although not presented in identical terms, the problem which was to trouble Scottish society for twenty years after 1286 had been present since 1284 and had, indeed, not only been prepared for by the king but also was expected by those others with a claim to the crown. It may seem unfortunate that Alexander III did not settle the crown upon John Balliol or Robert Bruce rather than his granddaughter but in truth no settlement could command overwhelming support and nothing less could have surmounted the crisis.

During the thirteenth century the kings of Scotland had created a political atmosphere whose essential quality was harmony, by distributing office in the state widely among the magnates so that they acquired insight into the methods and problems of government and became fit—that is, constructive—advisers of the king. The sources do not speak of the 'community of the realm' before 1286 but this 'abstract expression' acquired its meaning in Alexander

III's Scotland when the king sought common counsel of his barons. If unity of opinion was a fictitious 'consensus', it became real when opinion was accepted by the king and so transformed into the policy of government. Essential to the community as a source of political responsibility was the king whose authority provided the men of thirteenth century Scotland with their political ideas and vocabulary. Together they made a kingdom.

ROMAN SCOTLAND

- Roads
- Fort
- Marching camp
  (Marching camps at
  forts not shown)

Scone
Dornock
Innerpeffray
Broomhill
Dunning
Abernethy

*CALEDONII* Tribes mentioned
        by Ptolemy
*Maeatae* Other tribes

10    20    30 miles
10  20  30  40  50 km

?● Bellie

● Auchinhove

● Ythan Wells

● Kintore

*P i c t i*

● Normandykes

● Raedykes

*CALEDONII*

● Kair House

Stracathro
Keithock        Balmakewan
        Finavon   Marcus
Oathlaw                Kinnell
    Lunanhead
Cardean            Kirkbuddo
Gourdie        Eassie
Inchtuthil      Lintrose
                Gagie
        Bertha
Fendoch          Longforgan

Dalginross      2
                4    6   Carpow
Bochastle    *VERTUR-*  3
        *IONES*  Strageath
Menteith     *Maeatae*  Ardoch     Auchtermuchty    Bonnytown
            Dunblane

Camelon
            Cramond
        ANTONINE WALL         Inveresk
                            Pathhead
*NONII*
                                *VOTADINI*
Castledykes
Loudoun            Lyne
                            Newstead
        *SELGOVAE*

                Milton

Dalswinton    Birrens

*OVANTAE*            HADRIAN'S WALL
    Glenlochar
Gatehouse

# EARLY HISTORIC SCOTLAND

Birsay
Buckquoy

Underhoull

Papil
St.Ninian's
Isle
Jarlsho

Burghead
Rosemarkie
Forres
Turriff
Deer
Beauly
? F I D A C H
Mortlach
Applecross
Urquhart
? C E
Monymusk
Aberdeen
Dunottar
Brechin
Montrose
C I R C I N N
Dunkeld
Dunnichen
Lismore
Monifieth
Glendochart
F O R T R I U
Scone
Dunollie
Dundurn
Kilspindle
Iona
LORN
Moncrieffe
St Andrews
Muthill
Abernethy
Dunning
Norrie's Law
Kiloran
Loch Leven
Newburn
Bay
Colonsay
Aberfoyle
Dunblane
Markinch
Dunadd
Stirling
Dumyat
M A N A U
Dunbar
COWAL
Strathcarron
Abercorn
Din Eidyn
Traprain
Tarbert
Dumbarton
Law
Coldingham
Glasgow
Kingarth
Melrose
Bam
Islay
Kelso
KINTYRE
Dunaverty
R H E G E D
Dunragit
Mote of Mark
Kirkcudbright
Whithorn

0    10    20    30 miles
0  10  20  30  40  50km
▲  Fort
+  Ecclesiastical site
LORN  Provincial name

SECULAR LORDSHIP IN TWELFTH-THIRTEENTH CENTURY SCOTLAND

THE ISLES

CAITHNESS

Thurso
Halkirk

ROSS

SUTHERLAND

Cromarty
Duffus
Lochindorb

MORAY

BUCHAN

Huntly
Ellon
Garioch
Inverurie

Kildrummy

MAR

Aboyne
Lumphanan

Urquhart

Badenoch
Ruthven

Inverlochy
Lochaber

Tioram
Mingary
Aros
Cairnburgh
Ardtornish
Duart
Dunstaffnage
Argyll
Inchconnel
Dun Chonnuil
Duntroon

Blair
Moulin
Dunfallandy

ATHOLL

Brechin

ANGUS

Redcastle

GOWRIE

Invergowrie
Dundee

STRATHEARN

Kenmore

St.Andrews

Doune

Falkland

FIFE

MENTEITH

LENNOX
Catter
Balloch

Dirleton
Dunbar
Hailes
Yester

(Somerled's

Lordship)

Strathgryfe
Renfrew
Glasgow
Bothwell

Canongate

Roslin

Lauder
X

Home

Sween
Rothesay
Skipness

Cunningham
Ardrossan

Carnwath

Biggar

Lochranza
Brodick

Dundonald
Prestwick

Douglas

Ettrickdale
Hawick
Teviotdale
Eskdale

Kyle

Nithsdale

Annandale

Turnberry
Loch Doon

CARRICK

Lochmaben

Liddel

Galloway

Caerlaverock

Anwoth
Cruggleton

Buittle
Urr
Hestan

Annan

10  20  30 miles
10 20 30 40 50 km

Motte
Stone castle
Hall-house
Castle of unknown type
Burgh
Castle and burgh
FE  Earldom
le  Other province
– –  Boundary of Earl David's
       lordship c.1114-1124

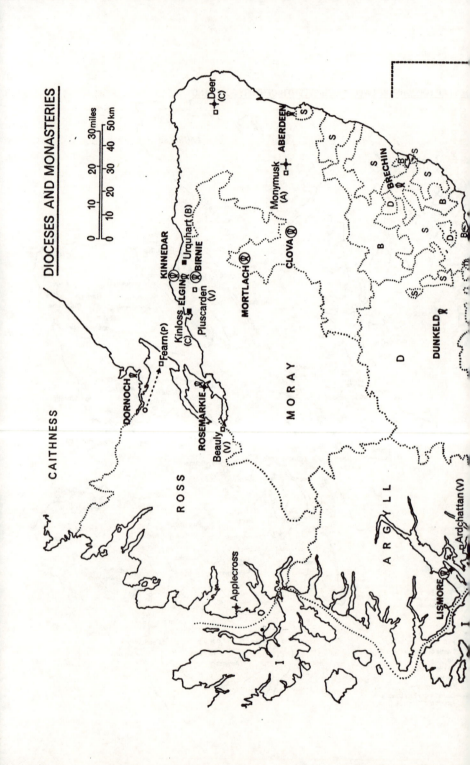

DIOCESES AND MONASTERIES

CAITHNESS

ROSS

MORAY

ARGYLL

DORNOCH ☩

Fearn(P)

ROSEMARKIE ☩

Beauly (V)

KINNEDAR ☩
ELGIN ☩
Kinloss (C)
Pluscarden (V)

Urquhart (B)
☩ BIRNIE

MORTLACH ☩

CLOVA ☩

Deer (C)

Monymusk (A)

ABERDEEN ☩

BRECHIN ☩

DUNKELD ☩

Applecross ☩

LISMORE ☩

Ardchattan (V)

0   10   20   30 miles
0   10   20   30   40   50 km

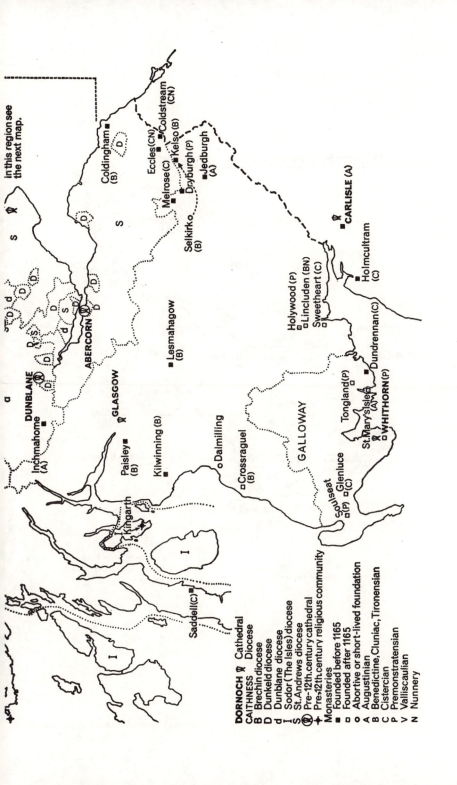

in this region see
the next map.

Inchmahome
(A)

DUNBLANE (D)

DORNOCH ⚲ Cathedral
CAITHNESS Diocese
B Brechin diocese
D Dunkeld diocese
d Dunblane diocese
I Sodor (The Isles) diocese
S St. Andrews diocese
⊗ Pre-12th.century cathedral
✝ Pre-12th.century religious community

Monasteries
■ Founded before 1165
□ Founded after 1165
○ Abortive or short-lived foundation
A Augustinian
B Benedictine, Cluniac, Tironensian
C Cistercian
P Premonstratensian
V Valliscaulian
N Nunnery

Coldingham
(B)

Coldstream (CN)
Eccles(CN)
Kelso (B)
Melrose(C)
Dryburgh(P)
Jedburgh
(A)

Selkirko
(B)

CARLISLE (A)

Holmcultram
(C)

Lesmahagow
(B)

Holywood (P)
Lincluden (BN)
Sweetheart (C)

Dundrennan(C)

GLASGOW ⚲

Paisley
(B)

Kilwinning (B)

ABERCORN ⊗✝

s

a

Dalmilling

Crossraguel
(B)

GALLOWAY

Tongland(P)

St. Mary's Isle
(A)

WHITHORN(P)

Soulseat
(P)

Glenluce
(C)

Kingarth✝

Saddell(C)

I

I

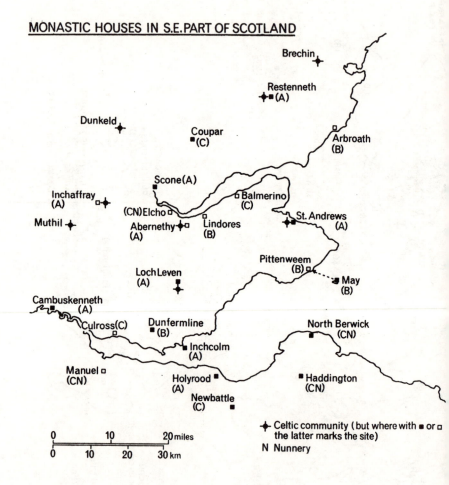

# MONASTIC HOUSES IN S.E. PART OF SCOTLAND

Brechin

Restenneth
(A)

Dunkeld

Coupar
(C)

Arbroath
(B)

Scone (A)

Balmerino
(C)

Inchaffray
(A)

St. Andrews
(A)

(CN) Elcho

Muthil

Abernethy
(A)

Lindores
(B)

Pittenweem
(B)

Loch Leven
(A)

May
(B)

Cambuskenneth
(A)

North Berwick
(CN)

Culross (C)

Dunfermline
(B)

Inchcolm
(A)

Manuel
(CN)

Holyrood
(A)

Haddington
(CN)

Newbattle
(C)

| 0 | | 10 | | 20 | miles |
| 0 | 10 | | 20 | | 30 km |

Celtic community (but where with ■ or □
the latter marks the site)

N Nunnery

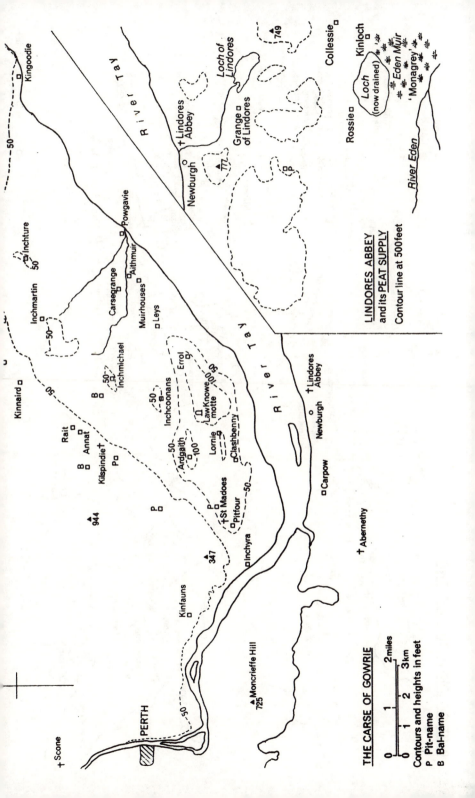

THE CARSE OF GOWRIE

0    1    2 miles
0   1   2   3 km

Contours and heights in feet
P   Pit-name
B   Bal-name

LINDORES ABBEY
and its PEAT SUPPLY
Contour line at 500 feet

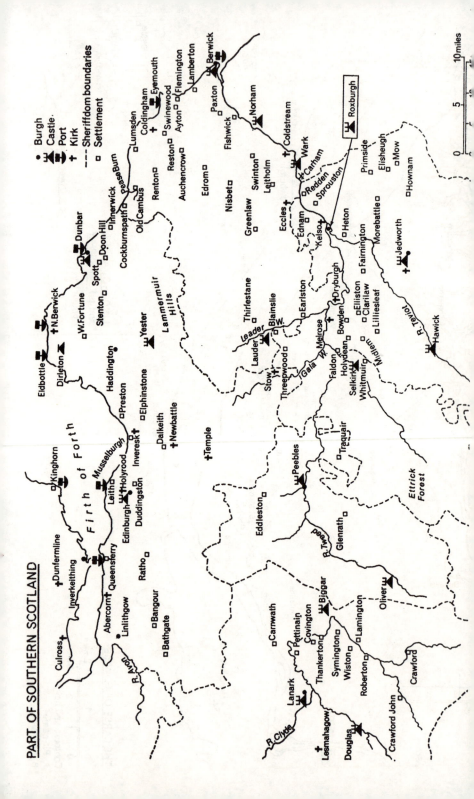

# PART OF SOUTHERN SCOTLAND

Burgh ●
Castle ◣
Port ⚓
Kirk ✝
Sheriffdom boundaries ---
Settlement □

Roxburgh

0 5 10 miles

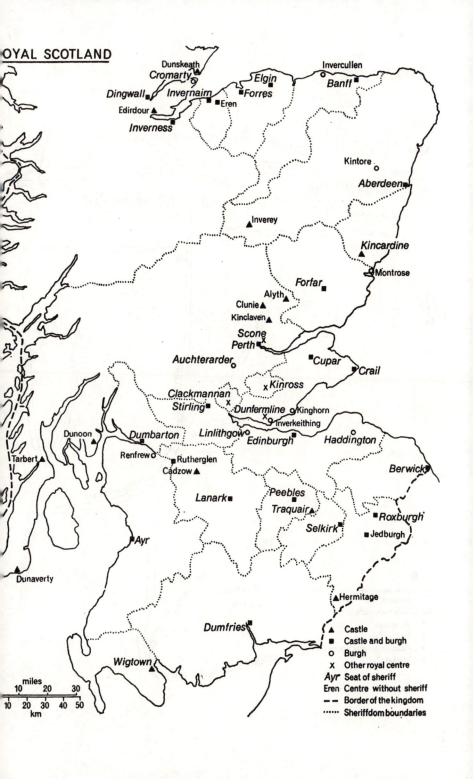

ROYAL SCOTLAND

Dunskeath
Cromarty
Invercullen
Elgin
Banff
Dingwall
Invernairn
Forres
Edirdour
Eren
Inverness

Kintore
Aberdeen

Inverey

Kincardine

Montrose
Forfar
Alyth
Clunie
Kinclaven
Scone
Perth
Cupar
Crail
Auchterarder
Kinross
Clackmannan
Stirling
Dunfermline
Kinghorn
Inverkeithing
Dumbarton
Linlithgow
Edinburgh
Haddington
Dunoon
Renfrew
Tarbert
Rutherglen
Cadzow
Berwick
Lanark
Peebles
Traquair
Roxburgh
Selkirk
Ayr
Jedburgh
Dunaverty
Hermitage
Dumfries
Wigtown

miles
10    20    30
10  20  30  40  50
km

▲ Castle
■ Castle and burgh
○ Burgh
✕ Other royal centre
*Ayr* Seat of sheriff
Eren Centre without sheriff
— — Border of the kingdom
· · · · · Sheriffdom boundaries

# EARLY EDINBURGH

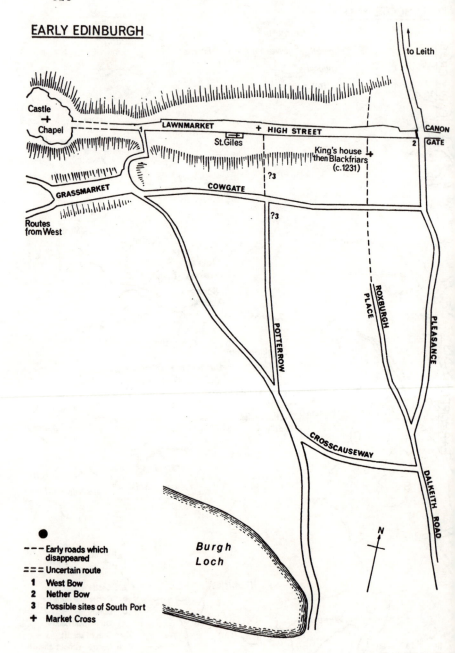

to Leith

Castle
+
Chapel

LAWNMARKET    + HIGH STREET

St.Giles

CANON

GATE

2

King's house
then Blackfriars
(c.1231)

?3

GRASSMARKET

COWGATE

?3

Routes
from West

POTTERROW

ROXBURGH

PLACE

PLEASANCE

CROSSCAUSEWAY

DALKEITH ROAD

N

● 
--- Early roads which
    disappeared
=== Uncertain route
1  West Bow
2  Nether Bow
3  Possible sites of South Port
+  Market Cross

*Burgh
Loch*

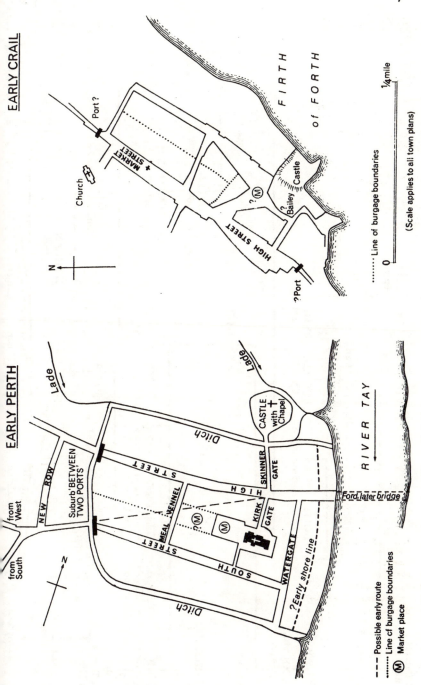

EARLY PERTH

EARLY CRAIL

Lade

Lade

Suburb 'BETWEEN TWO PORTS'

from West

from South

NEW ROW

MEAL VENNEL STREET

KIRK GATE

SKINNER GATE

HIGH STREET

SOUTH STREET

WAYGATE

CASTLE with Chapel

Ford, later bridge

?Early shore line

Ditch

Ditch

RIVER TAY

Church

MARKET STREET

Port?

HIGH STREET

?Port

Bailey Castle

FIRTH of FORTH

- - - Possible early route
...... Line of burgage boundaries
Ⓜ Market place

...... Line of burgage boundaries

0          ¼ mile

(Scale applies to all town plans)

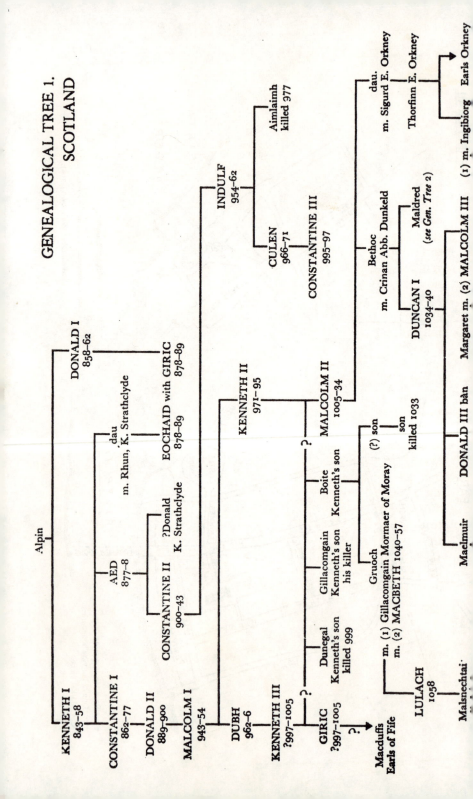

GENEALOGICAL TREE 1. SCOTLAND

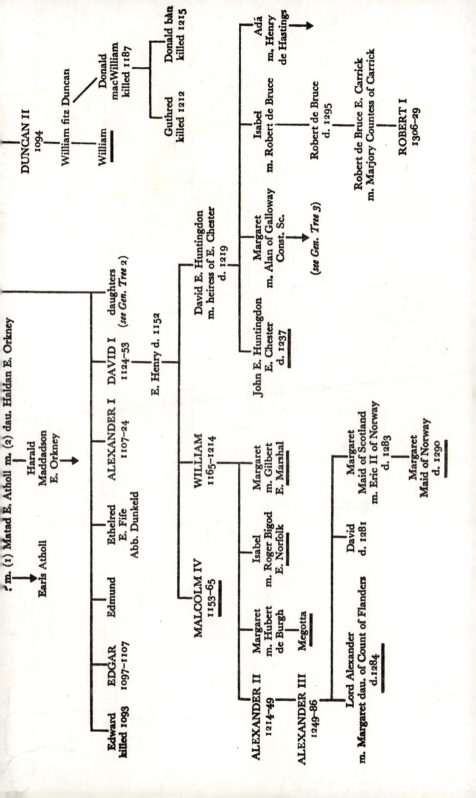

? m. (1) Matad E. Atholl m. (2) dau. Haldan E. Orkney

Earls Atholl

Harald Maddadson E. Orkney

Edward killed 1093

EDGAR 1097–1107

Edmund

Ethelred E. Fife Abb. Dunkeld

ALEXANDER I 1107–24

DAVID I 1124–53

daughters (see Gen. Tree 2)

E. Henry d. 1152

MALCOLM IV 1153–65

WILLIAM 1165–1214

David E. Huntingdon m. heiress of E. Chester d. 1219

DUNCAN II 1094

William fitz Duncan

William

Donald macWilliam killed 1187

Guthred killed 1212

Donald bàn killed 1215

ALEXANDER II 1214–49

Margaret m. Hubert de Burgh

Megotta

Isabel m. Roger Bigod E. Norfolk

Margaret m. Gilbert E. Marshal

John E. Huntingdon E. Chester d. 1237

Margaret m. Alan of Galloway Const. Sc.

(see Gen. Tree 3)

Isabel m. Robert de Bruce

Adà m. Henry de Hastings

ALEXANDER III 1249–86

Lord Alexander m. Margaret dau. of Count of Flanders d.1284

David d. 1281

Margaret Maid of Scotland m. Eric II of Norway d. 1283

Margaret Maid of Norway d. 1290

Robert de Bruce d. 1295

Robert de Bruce E. Carrick m. Marjory Countess of Carrick

ROBERT I 1306–29

GENEALOGICAL TREE 2.   ENGLAND

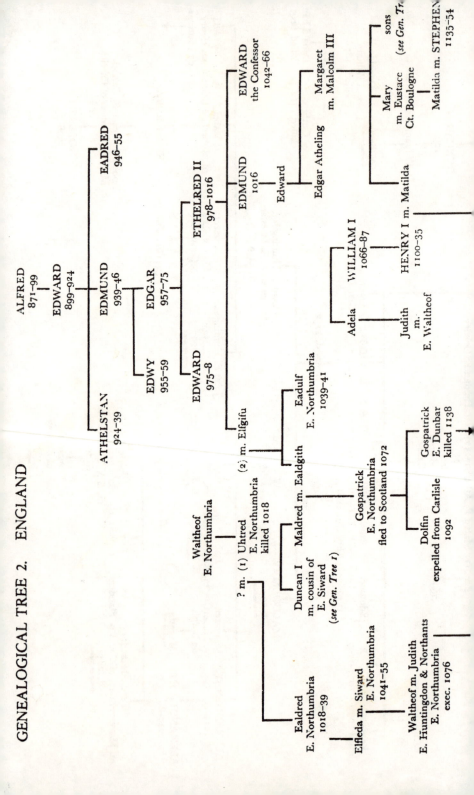

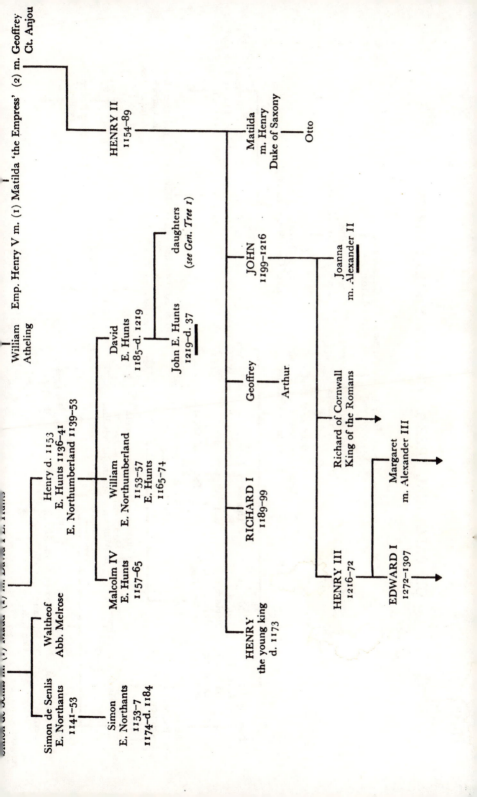

# GENEALOGICAL TREE 3.  GALLOWAY AND CARRICK

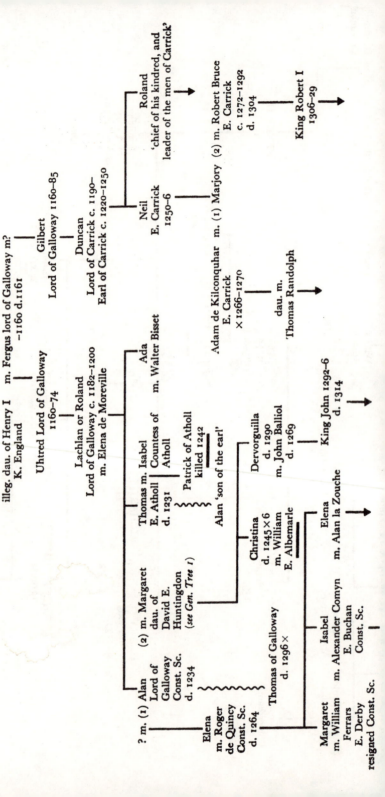

# GENEALOGICAL TREE 4. THE COMYNS

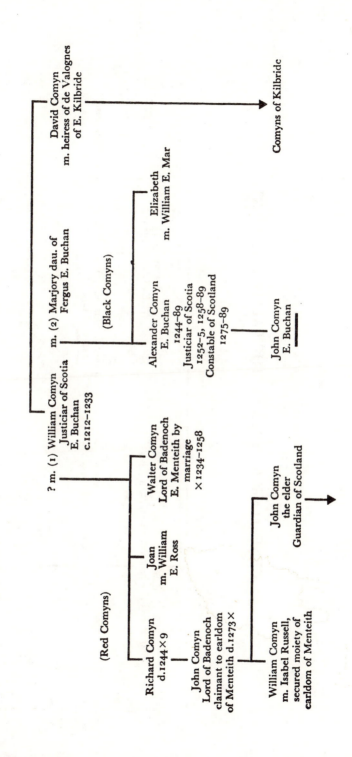

GENEALOGICAL TREE 5.  THE EARLDOM OF MENTEITH

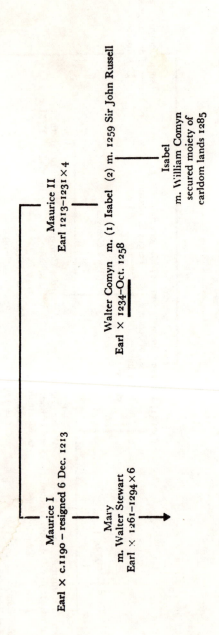

Maurice I
Earl × c.1190 – resigned 6 Dec. 1213

Maurice II
Earl 1213–1231 × 4

Walter Comyn  m. (1) Isabel  (2) m. 1259 Sir John Russell
Earl × 1234–Oct. 1258

Mary
m. Walter Stewart
Earl × 1261–1294 × 6

Isabel
m. William Comyn
secured moiety of
earldom lands 1285

# GENEALOGICAL TREE 6. THE EARLDOMS OF ATHOLL, FIFE, MAR, ORKNEY

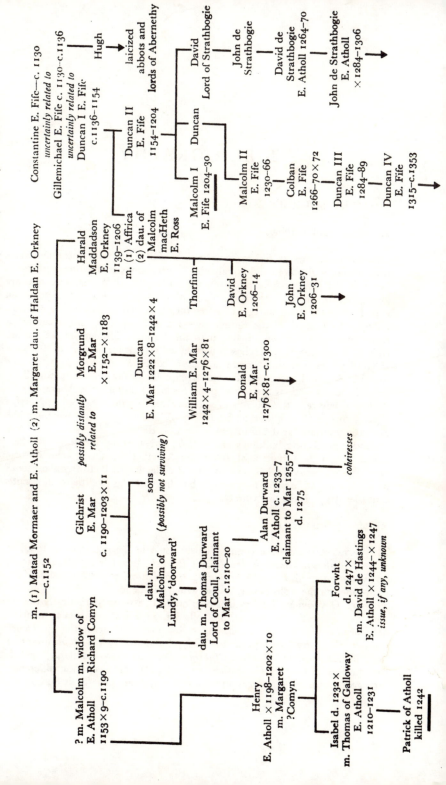

# BIBLIOGRAPHY

## PRIMARY SOURCES

### 1. Artefacts and buildings

Collections of prehistoric artefacts will be found in most local museums, usually poorly displayed and explained. The exceptions are the fine museums at Lerwick and Glasgow (Kelvingrove); the Kirkwall and Dundee museums are also good. In Scotland there is no law of treasure trove which anyone can explain, and the disadvantages of a free-for-all as well as the need to drive off pillagers from south of the Border have led to the policy, until recently, of either losing material or bringing it to the National Museum of Antiquities (this is in Edinburgh) which has important collections for all periods. Glasgow University's Hunterian Museum houses a collection of Roman sculptures found in Scotland, most with the repulsive quality of fourth-rate artistic effort, though the inscriptions may be of great historical importance. These may be studied at leisure in R. G. Collingwood and R. P. Wright, *The Roman Inscriptions of Britain* (Inscriptions on Stone) (1965). The coins in these two museums are also important for the history of Roman Scotland.

Some prehistoric buildings are well looked after by the state; the best groups are in the Orkneys, Shetland and Argyll. Few, if any, early historic buildings are preserved but there is a good collection of Pictish symbol stones in a museum at Meigle. For secular buildings of the twelfth to thirteenth centuries Argyll is the best county.

### 2. Guides to sources

The narrative sources are compendiously listed in the prefatory material to Alan O. Anderson's *Scottish Annals from English Chroniclers, 500–1286* (1908) and volume 1 of his *Early Sources of Scottish History, 500–1286* (1922). Many are printed in the Rolls Series, lists of which will be found in *British National Archives*, Government Publications Sectional List No. 24 (periodically revised editions), and in the volumes of the Rolls Series itself. Documentary materials have been printed by the publishing clubs, notably those of the nineteenth century; these are listed in C. S. Terry, *Catalogue of the Publications of Scottish Historical and Kindred Clubs and Societies 1780–1908* (1909) and its continuation to 1927 by C. Matheson (1928). The same volumes, differently arranged, are listed in *Sources and Literature of Scots Law* (Stair Soc. 1936).

especially chapter 22, and with a list of agreed abbreviations in 'List of Abbreviated Titles of the Printed Sources of Scottish History to 1560', a supplement to the *Scottish Historical Review*, October, 1963. Many are discussed below, pp. 639–43. Histories of 'noble' families contain many documents; there is a full guide in Margaret Stuart, *Scottish Family History* (1930) and a good one in J. P. S. Ferguson, *Scottish Family History* (1960). A guide to the important collections deposited in the Scottish Record Office is published by that Office as *Lists of Gifts and Deposits*, of which vol. i (1971) has appeared; G. R. C. Davis, *Medieval Cartularies of Great Britain* (1958) gives modern locations for most of the cartularies printed by the publishing clubs.

3. Narrative sources

There is an excellent edition of Tacitus, *Agricola* by R. M. Ogilvie and I. A. Richmond (1967) and later references to north Britain are collected in J. C. Mann, *The Northern Frontier in Britain from Hadrian to Honorius: Literary and Epigraphic Sources* (1969).

From the sub-Roman period up to 1286 the narrative sources are published in translation in A. O. Anderson, *Scottish Annals from English Chroniclers* (1908) and his *Early Sources of Scottish History, 500–1286* (2 vols., 1922). Bede's *Ecclesiastical History of the English People* is available in an excellent edition with translation by B. Colgrave and R. A. B. Mynors (1969). The *Anglo-Saxon Chronicle* may be studied in the translation by Dorothy Whitelock with David C. Douglas and Susie I. Tucker (1961), which makes plain the various readings of different versions. The Anglo-Saxon text is best studied in *Two of the Saxon Chronicles Parallel*, by Charles Plummer on the basis of J. Earle's edition (1892 in 1952 reprint), and, for the period after 1066 in C. Clark, *The Peterborough Chronicle, 1070–1154* (2nd edition, 1970).

As an introduction to the Irish annals K. Hughes, *Early Christian Ireland: Introduction to the Sources* (1972) is essential. The annals relating to Scotland are extracted and collected in *Chronicles of the Picts, Chronicles of the Scots and Other Early Memorials of Scottish History*, edited by W. F. Skene (1867); the most important set of annals is *The Annals of Ulster* edited by W. M. Hennessy (1887–1901). Recently in the *Proceedings of the Royal Irish Academy*, lxxii, c, (1972) 1–48, A. P. Smyth has advanced clear evidence that the earliest stratum in the Annals of Ulster was not a compendium of Irish and Iona annals, but one set of annals alone, kept at Iona from 563 until *c.* 740. This remarkable study throws a great deal of light upon the significance of Iona and of Adamnan; unfortunately, it came too late to be done full justice in my text.

The Gododdin of Aneirin has been made available by K. H. Jackson as *The Gododdin, The Oldest Scottish Poem* (1968) and the text is in I. Williams, *Canu Aneirin* (1938). The Senchus fer nAlban has been edited by J. Bannerman in *Celtica*, vii–ix (1966–71), in his *Studies in the History of Dalriada* (1974) and in Anderson, *Early Sources*, i, cl–cliii. The various king-lists were edited by W. F. Skene in *Chronicles of the Picts, Chronicles of the Scots . . .* (1867) but there is a new edition of the Duan Albanach by K. H. Jackson in *Scottish Historical Review*, xxxvi (1957). Again, these were translated by A. O. Anderson in *Early Sources*, i, but this field has been made very much her own by M. O. Anderson whose articles in *Sc. Hist. Rev.* xxxviii (1949), 31–42, 108–18, and *ibid*, xxix (1950) 13–22, are not wholly overtaken by her book *Kings and Kingship in Early Scotland* (1973), where she re-edits the king-lists.

Saints' lives must be treated with great caution as sources for historical events. There is clearly an historical stratum in *Adomnan's Life of Columba*, ed. A. O. and M. O. Anderson (1961) and in *Two Lives of St Cuthbert*, ed. B. Colgrave (1940). The eighth-century poem on Nynia is edited by W. MacQueen in *Transactions of the Dumfriesshire and Galloway Natural History and Antiquarian Society*, xxxviii (1959–60), 21–57. For St Patrick's letter the best edition is by L. Bieler, *Libri Epistolarum Sancti Patricii Episcopi* (1952). Later saints' lives are generally worthless but those of *St Ninian and St Kentigern* were edited by A. P. Forbes (1874). The life of St Waltheof, Abbot of Melrose, is in *Acta Sanctorum*, 3 August, vol. 1, and that of St Malachy in J. P. Migne, *Patrologia Latina*, clxxxii.

The native narrative tradition continues poor even in the twelfth and thirteenth centuries. There are two contemporary chronicles each available in an excellent modern edition: *A Scottish Chronicle known as the Chronicle of Holyrood*, edited by M. O. Anderson with some additional notes by A. O. Anderson (Scottish History Society 1938) and *The Chronicle of Melrose*, with an introduction by A. O. and M. O. Anderson and an index by W. Croft Dickinson (1936). There is also important material in the *Chronicle of John of Fordun*, ed. W. F. Skene (1871–2) and that of Walter Bower published as *Joannis de Fordun Scotichronicon cum Supplementis et Continuatione Walteri Boweri*, ed. Walter Goodall (1759). There is a good deal of Scottish matter in the *Chronicle of Man and the Sudreys*, ed. P. A. Munch and Rev Dr Goss (1874) (or ed. P. A. Munch, 1860).

Fortunately some English and French historians took a lively interest in Scotland, and most English chronicles have something to say on its history. The important collections of these chronicles are in the Rolls Series, notably *Annales Monastici*, ed. H. R. Luard (R.S. no. 36), *Chronicles of the Reigns of Stephen Henry II and Richard I*, ed. R. Howlett (R.S. no. 82) which includes the works of Ailred of Rievaulx and Robert de Torigni. Northern English historiography is represented by Symeon of Durham in *Symeonis Monachi Opera Omnia*, ed. T. Arnold (R.S. no. 75).

Two important works on the reign of David I should be used in editions by K. R. Potter: *Gesta Stephani* (1955) and *Historia Novella* (1955). For the second half of the twelfth century the two works by Roger Howden are indispensable: Benedict of Peterborough, *Gesta Regis Henrici Secundi*, ed. W. Stubbs (R.S. no. 49) and Roger Hoveden *Chronica* ed. W. Stubbs (R.S. no. 51). On their authorship and relationship see D. M. Stenton in *Eng. Hist. Rev.*, lxviii (1953), and F. Barlow in *Eng. Hist. Rev.*, lxv (1950).

Much less reliable than Howden are the chronicles of the St Albans school for the thirteenth century, the *Flores Historiarum* of Roger Wendover edited by H. G. Hewlett (R.S. no. 84) and the *Chronica Majora* of Matthew Paris ed. H. R. Luard (R.S. no. 57). For the later thirteenth century the *Chronicon de Lanercost*, ed. J. Stevenson (Maitland Club, 1839) is of value.

A useful collection of sources of all kinds for the period 1153–1214 was made by A. C. Lawrie in *Annals of the Reigns of Malcolm IV and William* (1910).

The campaigns of 1173–4 are described in detail in Jordan Fantosme, *Chronique de la Guerre entre les Anglois et les Ecossois*, ed. F. Michel (Surtees Soc. no. 11) and ed. R. Howlett in *Chronicles of ... Stephen* etc., (R.S. no. 82) vol. iii, both with translations. There is a less accessible but better modern edition by P. A. Becker in *Zeitschrift für Romanische Philologie*, lxiv (1944) and a discussion of Jordan in M. D. Legge, *Anglo-Norman Literature and its Background* (1963).

The Orkneyinga Saga and the saga of Haakon IV are edited with translations in *Icelandic Sagas*, ed. G. Vigfusson and G. W. Dasent (R.S. no. 88) and there are translations of the former by Joseph Anderson (1873) and A. B. Taylor (1938).

4. Documentary sources: public record

No public records of Scotland from before 1286 survived in Scotland until, in the present century, a few were recovered from London. Most of these had been printed in the first volume of *Acts of the Parliaments of Scotland*, which includes the particularly valuable inventories of records drawn up between 1282 and 1296. The early assizes or laws are also printed there but these may be used only with careful reference to the table of authorities, and with some thought as to the authenticity of each clause. A new edition is badly needed. Some financial records for 1263–6 and 1288–90 survived into the seventeenth century when partial transcripts were made; they are published in the first fifty pages of *Exchequer Rolls of Scotland*, i (1878), ed. J. Stuart. The English public records contain a great deal relating to Scotland, some of which was collected by Joseph Bain in his *Calendar of Documents relating to Scotland*, especially volumes i (1108–1272) and ii (1272–1307) (1881–4). It is often helpful to consult the printed *Rotuli Literarum Clausarum*, *Close Rolls*, *Calendar of Close Rolls*, *Rotuli Literarum Patentium*, and *Calendar of Patent Rolls* and the Record Commission edition of Rymer's *Foedera* for entries which also figure in Bain's *Cal. Docs. Scot.* Although strictly outside the period covered here there is much that looks back in *Rotuli Scotiae*, vol. i (1814), F. Palgrave, *Documents and Records Illustrating the History of Scotland* (1837) and J. Stevenson, *Documents Illustrative of the History of Scotland, 1286–1306* (2 vols, 1870). The extracts from English financial records up to 1216 in Bain's *Cal. Docs. Scot.* can be checked in the editions of the *Pipe Rolls*, published by the Pipe Roll Society. Most of the documents printed in the invaluable E. L. G. Stones, *Anglo-Scottish Relations, 1174–1328: Some Selected Documents* (1965), were drawn from the English records. The registers of papal letters are also prolific with Scottish entries, calendared by W. H. Bliss in *Calendar of Papal Registers, Letters*, i, (1893) and some printed in full in A. Theiner, *Vetera Monumenta Hibernorum et Scotorum Historiam Illustrantia* (1864).

## 5. Documentary sources: charters and other deeds

Early in this century A. C. Lawrie made a collection of all documents relating to Scotland and all documents of the Scottish kings relating to English lands up to 1153: *Early Scottish Charters* (1905) has done yeoman service even though its texts were normalised. Lawrie's comments as to authenticity are of little worth, but his notes are occasionally helpful. His omissions before 1153 were remedied in *Regesta Regum Scottorum, i, Acts of Malcolm IV*, ed. G. W. S. Barrow (1960), which is a fine diplomatic edition of all charters, letters and brieves of that king. *Regesta Regum Scottorum, ii, Acts of William I*, ed. G. W. S. Barrow with the collaboration of W. W. Scott (1971) is of even greater importance for the study of government. The continuation of this series into the thirteenth century will refresh our understanding of medieval administration; meantime *Handlist of the Acts of Alexander II*, by J. Scoular (1959) and *Handlist of the Acts of Alexander III, Guardians and John*, by G. G. Simpson (1960) are most useful tools.

Although not a record source, it will be most relevant to mention here the treatise on the king's administration written probably for King John, printed in *Scottish History Society Miscellany*, ii (1904), edited by M. Bateson under the misleading name The Scottish King's Household. A good introduction to these materials is a book whose subject is not so narrow as its title suggests: J. M. Thomson, *The Public Records of Scotland* (1922).

The documents in the *Regesta* and other collections have been culled from cartularies and collections of charters, mostly of religious houses, and many published in the nineteenth century. They are still the bedrock upon which any history of medieval Scotland must be founded and a word on their limitations is necessary. The cardinal principle of any edition, that whatever editorial practices may be followed they should be clearly stated, was not generally observed in the nineteenth century, nor did those editions indicate the source for each document or text printed. Thus, the *Liber Ecclesie de Scon* (Bann. and Maitland Clubs, 1843) contains numerous texts printed with representations of the contractions and taken from the original documents. Mingled among them are other texts taken from the two cartularies. The earlier cartulary, written about 1300, has no document earlier than Malcolm IV (1153–65) and includes his general confirmation stating that Scone Abbey had been devastated by a fire which reduced his predecessors' privileges to ashes so that he is now renewing them; it lists the gifts of Alexander I, David I, and Malcolm IV *seriatim* so that the abbey had evidently a surviving list of benefactions or copy of charters. Among the original documents still surviving is a notarial instrument of 1298 narrating the destruction by the English army of the chests containing the abbey's muniments and of the seals on its charters, charters granted by David I, Malcolm IV, William etc., but not apparently by Alexander I who is not named. Despite these misfortunes many original documents of 1153–1286 still survive; and many more were copied in the first and second cartularies. The latter is of the fifteenth century and begins with four charters of Alexander I, including a long general charter with a list of approving bishops and earls. The problem of the authenticity of these four is formidable. How does it come about that the cartulary of Nostel has a very differently worded version of the same substance as one of the four; how does it come about that this cartulary scribe had four charters of 1107–24 but none of 1124–53? If Scone Abbey kept a list of Alexander I's donations from which his general charter was concocted at a much later date, why are the gifts slightly different in his general charter from the version of them in Malcolm IV's confirmation? No certain answer can be given to these questions which raise doubts affecting the validity of the list of bishops and earls.

The titles of these volumes may conceal their very different characteristics. The largest single group of original charters, those of Coldingham Priory, is preserved by the Dean and Chapter of Durham, successors of the monks of Durham of whom Coldingham was a branch. These charters which came from a wide social range of benefactors were printed or summarised as an appendix to J. Raine, *The History and Antiquities of North Durham* (1852). They date from 1094 and the magnificent collection of seals attached to them, often yielding additional information, was catalogued by Canon W. Greenwell and C. Hunter Blair and printed in *Archaeologia Aeliana*[3], xii (1915), xiii (1916), xvi (1919). Coldingham was unusual in having no outlying possessions. Other major collections of original charters also relate to the environs of the monastery in question but in addition relate to more distant possessions and districts: Melrose Abbey, *Liber Sancte Marie de Melros* (Bann. Cl., 1837) documents of 1136× with Ayrshire (especially Carrick) documents; Holyrood abbey, *Liber Cartarum Sancte Crucis* (Bann. Cl., 1840) documents of *c.* 1140× with Galloway (including Iona Abbey) documents; Coupar Angus Abbey whose *Charters* (ed. D. E. Easson, S.H.S. 1947) date from *c.* 1160 and include some for Atholl; North Berwick Nunnery, *Carte Monialium de Northberwic* (Bann. Cl., 1847), a small collection with interesting Carrick writs. The *Charters . . . relating to the Abbey of Inchaffray* (S.H.S., 1908), however, begin in 1190 and scarcely look outside Strathearn, and those of Pluscarden Priory, founded in Moray in 1230 and printed in S. R. Macphail, *History of the Religious House of Pluscardyn* (1881) are also very local, and very valuable They show the see of Moray imitating the diplomatic of papal privileges in its charters. The paucity of such collections is obvious and must be explained by the secularisation of the monasteries in the sixteenth century, which also took place in England, and the disintegration of the ancient colleges at the cathedrals, which did not.

Thus, in some towns the property of the Friars passed after 1560 to other charitable uses, and their titles therefore went to a college or incorporation. This explains the survival of the *Charters of the Friars Preachers of Ayr* (1881), of those of *The Blackfriars of Perth* (ed. R. Milne, 1893) of Glasgow, *Munimenta Fratrum Predicatorum de Glasgu* (1846) and of Aberdeen, *Aberdeen Friars: Red, Black, White, Grey*, ed. P. J. Anderson (1909).

Of the Scottish cathedrals the only surviving muniments were some charters of Brechin which passed to the burgh there, *Registrum Episcopatus Brechinensis* (Bann. Cl., 1856), and the great collection of Glasgow Cathedral muniments, taken abroad at the reformation, lost during the French Revolution and hence known only from a medieval and several eighteenth-century cartularies, *Registrum Episcopatus Glasguensis* (Bann. and Maitland Clubs, 1843); it includes documents dating back to *c.* 1118. The parallel *Registrum Episco-patus Aberdonensis* (Spalding and Maitland Clubs, 1845) is derived from car-tularies, afflicted with forgeries, has nothing earlier than 1154 and is thin thereafter until the fifteenth century. The *Registrum Episcopatus Moraviensis* is also based on cartularies, and though its texts are entirely genuine, it has nothing earlier than 1165 and little earlier than the 1190s.

Our knowledge of cathedrals and episcopal possessions apart from these is derived from their involvement with others, especially with monastic houses.

There are fairly numerous monastic cartularies, again some dealing with districts not suggested by their titles. In general, the later the date of compo-sition the more unreliable the copyist, especially with proper names. The following account proceeds in general from south to north. The *Chartulary of the Cistercian Priory of Coldstream* (Grampian Club, 1879) compiled 1434, documents of *c.* 1150×, relates to the Tweed valley, but also to its founder and patrons, the earls of Dunbar. Some original charters, unprinted, are in the Scottish Record Office. Dryburgh Abbey was founded by the de Morevilles; *Liber Sancte Marie de Dryburgh* (Bann. Cl.) is a poor sixteenth-century copy of an earlier cartulary. Kelso Abbey (originally at Selkirk) has an especially valuable cartulary written *c.* 1330, *Liber S. Marie de Calchou* (Bann. Cl.), with many donors' charters of 1114–20×, but also including an invaluable register of late twelfth-century grants by the abbey especially on the lands of its Clydeside cell of Lesmahagow, and the 1300 extent of its demesnes dis-cussed above, chapters 12 and 13.

In the basin of the Forth, in addition to the Holyrood charters, there is much about Edinburgh in the topographically arranged *Registrum S. Marie de Neubotle* (Newbattle Abbey, Bann. Cl., 1849) written in the fourteenth century, texts of 1140×, and something in *Charters of the Abbey of Inchcolm*, ed. D. E. Easson and A. Macdonald (S.H.S., 1938) which is really a cartulary (of *c.* 1420) with documents of *c.* 1160×. The *Registrum Monasterii S. Marie de Cambuskenneth* (Grampian Club, 1872) is of unique diplomatic character. It is a copy of the abbey's charters made in 1535, each text authenticated by the Clerk Register of that date and the whole book 'confirmed' by the great seal of James V on a cord through the binding. After so much trouble the contents (charters of *c.* 1140×) are a little disappointing, especially when compared with the cartulary of Dunfermline Abbey, *Registrum de Dunfermelyn* (Bann. Cl., 1842) written mid-thirteenth century, arranged according to grantors (kings, popes, bishops, earls, etc.) from 1124 and with many later additions; there are many documents about Musselburgh and environs and some about Moray where the abbey had a cell at Urquhart. Two other houses in Fife had lands in and documents about Aberdeenshire: Lindores Abbey, *Chartulary of the Abbey of Lindores* (S.H.S., 1903) written in the mid-thirteenth century, texts of 1195×; and St Andrews Priory, *Liber Cartarum Prioratus Sancti Andree in Scotia* (Bann. Cl., 1841) written in the thirteenth century and later with notes of eleventh- and twelfth-century donations and charters of 1144×. Unpublished St Andrews Priory charters are in the National Library of Scotland. The cartulary of Balmerino Abbey, *Liber Sancte Marie de Balmori-nach* (Abbotsford Club, 1841), written in the fourteenth century, contains texts of *c.* 1220×, some untrustworthy, but with valuable materials about the towns of Perth and Dundee; it is poorly edited. Other Fife collections are *Records of the Priory of the Isle of May*, ed. J. Stuart, 1868, continued in *Proc. Soc. Antiq. Sc.*, xc (1956–7), documents of *c.* 1140× and for Culross Abbey, documents of 1219× in *Proc. Soc. Antiq. Sc.*, lx (1925–6).

The abbeys of Inchaffray, Scone and Coupar have already been mentioned. The only other important collection between Tay and Dee is the *Liber S. Thome de Aberbrothoc*, i (Bann. Cl., 1848) printing an early thirteenth-century cartulary and the *Registrum Vetus* (written *c.* 1330) of Arbroath Abbey, with a full record of the gifts to it ranging widely through Scotia from its foundation in 1178.

In the west there are only two monastic collections of significance to add to that of Glasgow Cathedral. Holm Cultram Abbey was a daughter of Melrose founded in 1150 and though situated in Cumberland its cartulary, *The Register and Records of Holm Cultram*, eds F. Grainger and W. G. Collingwood (1929) contains twelfth-century Dumfriesshire texts. Paisley Abbey, founded by the Stewarts *c.* 1163, has a valuable cartulary made in the sixteenth century. This *Registrum Monasterii de Passelet* (Maitland Club, 1832; New Club, 1877) also gives us much of our documentation of thirteenth-century Argyll.

The gaps in, or deficiencies of, these materials cannot be stressed too often. First, only a few collections of originals survive. Secondly, the cathedral kirks are poorly represented. Third, these are with only one exception—the Kelso cartulary—registers of gifts and charters received and they consequently tell us very little about the grants made by the religious, that is about their management of their possessions. Fourthly, the coverage in time is very uneven. Except for the six texts written in the margin of the gospel book of the community at Deer in the early twelfth century, edited by K. H. Jackson, *The Gaelic Notes in the Book of Deer* (1973), there is really no collection of documents relating to lands north of Tay dating to before 1153, and precious little earlier than 1178. In effect, southern Scotland plus Fife has a fifty-year lead in documentation over Scotia north of Tay. Fifthly and finally, there is a marked geographical gap in the surviving sources. Despite the nine religious houses established in the south-west (Holywood, Lincluden, Sweetheart, Dundrennan, Tongland, St Mary's Isle, Whithorn, Glenluce, Soulseat) not one cartulary or collection of charters from that region has survived; if there had been a survival we might be less tempted to see the lords of Galloway largely as they are depicted in English record sources.

Collections of family papers rarely contain material of date earlier than 1300. The most notable exception among the family histories produced by Sir William Fraser is *The Annandale Family Book of the Johnstones* (1894) with a few early Bruce and Annandale charters. Early Lennox charters are printed in Fraser's *Chiefs of Colquhoun and their Country* (1869) and in his *The Lennox* (1874), to be supplemented by one of the few rare secular cartularies, *Cartularium Comitatus de Levenax* (Maitland Club, 1837); the tangled sources for the history of an earldom are laid out in Fraser's *Red Book of Menteith* (1880). The charters of the Hays of Errol were printed in *Miscellany of the Spalding Club*, ii (1842). Occasional documents may be found in the *Reports* of the Royal Commission on Historical Manuscripts though it is always worth checking present location with the National Register of Archives (Scotland).

Burgh charters may be found in various places. Most of those before 1214 will be found in the *Regesta Regum Scottorum*. The following have charters before 1286: *Extracts from the Records of the Royal Burgh of Lanark*, ed. R. Renwick (1893); *Charters of the Royal Burgh of Ayr* (1883); *Charters and Other Writs Illustrating the History of the Royal Burgh of Aberdeen*, ed. P. J. Anderson (1890); *Charters and Other Documents relating to the City of Glasgow*, ed. J. D. Marwick (1897) but there is no good edition for other towns such as Dumbarton, whose important early charters survive in a seventeenth-century confirmation itself preserved in the Register of the Great Seal. Much the most useful source for all burghs is A. Ballard, *British Borough Charters 1066–1216* (1913) and A. Ballard and J. Tait, *British Borough Charters 1216–1307* (1923) which have the added advantage of presenting comparable material from England and Ireland, but which chop up the charters and print the sections of each under topic headings. The charters of Friars usually relate to burgh properties.

Burgh customs were edited in *Acts of the Parliaments of Scotland*, i, but there is also a handier edition with some commentary in *Ancient Laws and Customs of the Burghs of Scotland, 1124–1424*, ed. C. Innes (1868).

## 6. Documentary sources: ecclesiastical record

Scotland has no episcopal rolls or registers, but among the charters and cartularies are many episcopal *acta* and some texts of statutes made in the diocesan synods and provincial councils of the church. Particularly valuable for its long introduction, which ranges widely in the history of church and state and their institutions, is Joseph Robertson's *Concilia Scotiae: Ecclesiae Scoticanae Statuta* (1866); there is a good translation of the synodal decrees in *Statutes of the Scottish Church*, ed. D. Patrick (S.H.S., 1907). There is valuable material on David de Bernham in *Pontificale Ecclesiae S. Andreae*, ed. C. Wordsworth (1885).

## 7. Miscellaneous documentary sources

Some clubs and societies have produced collections of primary sources (both record and narrative) of miscellaneous provenance, as in the case of *Highland Papers* and *Wigtownshire Charters* (S.H.S.) and *Collections for a History of the Shires of Aberdeen and Banff* and *Illustrations of the Topography and Antiquities of the Shires of Aberdeen and Banff* (Spalding Club). There are also occasional *Miscellany* volumes with no unifying theme, notably those of the Bannatyne Club and S.H.S. Miscellaneous records figure in the *Calendar of the Laing Charters*, ed. J. Anderson (1899). Others are reproduced in facsimile (and transcription) in *Facsimiles of the National Manuscripts of Scotland* (1867–73). The student and general reader will find comprehensive and well-chosen collections from a variety of sources in the *Source Book of Scottish History*, ed. W. Croft Dickinson, Gordon Donaldson and Isabel A. Milne

(2nd edn, 3 vols, 1958, reprinted 1963), and in *Scottish Historical Documents*, ed. Gordon Donaldson (1970).

## 8. Biographical aids to study

The *Handbook of British Chronology* (Royal Hist. Soc., 2nd edn, 1961) has invaluable lists of kings, bishops, earls, chancellors and chamberlains. For kings A. H. Dunbar, *Scottish Kings* (2nd edn., 1906) is fuller though care must be taken in using his tables of regnal years since he believed that a king succeeded at his predecessor's last breath, which was probably not true until 1329. For the aristocracy the *Scots Peerage*, edited by J. Balfour Paul (9 vols, 1904–14), is an essential guide though it is weak on twelfth-century origins. Sometimes the *Complete Peerage*, by G.E.C. (2nd edn, 14 vols, 1910–59) is more accurate though with nothing on younger sons. Margaret Stuart, *Scottish Family History* (1930) and J. P. S. Ferguson, *Scottish Family Histories* (1906) lead one into the jungle of literature on this subject. Details of the episcopate are given in J. Dowden, *The Bishops of Scotland* (1912) and these, together with other dignitaries of the secular church, are conveniently listed in D. E. R. Watt, *Fasti Ecclesiae Scoticanae Medii Aevi* (1969).

## 9. Topographical aids to study

The most useful topographical guides to the country are F. H. Groome, *Ordnance Gazetteer of Scotland* (1882–5 and later editions) and Bartholomew's *Survey Gazetteer of the British Isles* (9th edn, 1966). Two of the great incomplete historical enterprises arranged topographically are G. Chalmers, *Caledonia* (1807–24, new edn, 1887–1902) and *Origines Parochiales Scotiae* (2 vols in 3, Bannatyne Club, 1851–4). The *Reports and Inventories* of the Royal Commission on the Ancient and Historical Monuments of Scotland are arranged by county, and until the *Inventory of Roxburgh* (1956) (inclusive) they are arranged by parish within the county. More recent volumes are arranged by date and class of monument. Each volume has been more thorough and inclusive than its predecessor; the country between the Tay and Ross-shire is still not surveyed.

Three important reference works are Ian B. Cowan, *Parishes of Medieval Scotland* (1967), G. S. Pryde, *The Burghs of Scotland* (1965), and D. E. Easson, *Medieval Religious Houses: Scotland* (1957), the last of which is under revision by I. B. Cowan.

H. R. G. Inglis, J. Matheson and C. B. B. Watson give a guide to *The Early Maps of Scotland* (3rd edn, 1973). The Ordnance Survey maps of *Iron Age, Roman, Dark Age* and *Monastic Britain* (and most recently *Britain before the Norman Conquest*) are indispensable; more specialised are the O.S. maps of *Hadrian's Wall* and the *Antonine Wall*.

## 10. Palaeographic and diplomatic aids to study

The history of critical scholarship of documents in Scotland begins with *Selectus Diplomatum et Numismatum Scotiae Thesaurus*, usually called

*Diplomata Scotiae*, ed. J. Anderson (1739). This includes engravings of documents some of which are now lost. The first volume of *Facsimiles of the National Manuscripts of Scotland* (1867) used a primitive photographic process to reproduce (with transcripts and translations) the *Book of Deer* pages with charter-notes, and numerous original twelfth- and thirteenth-century charters. An urbane introduction to the subject will be found in G. G. Simpson, *Scottish Handwriting, 1150–1650* (1973).

11. Linguistic aids to study

Any good Latin dictionary may be supplemented by the *Revised Medieval Latin Word-List from British and Irish Sources*, prepared by R. E. Latham (1965). For the vernacular, John Jamieson, *An Etymological Dictionary of the Scottish Language*, ed. John Longmuir (5 vols, 1879–87), will be superseded by W. A. Craigie, *A Dictionary of the Older Scottish Tongue* (1931–   ), of which the first four volumes have appeared.

12. Chronological aids to study

A. H. Dunbar, *Scottish Kings* (2nd edn, 1906) deals specifically with the chronology of Scottish history, but the *Handbook of Dates for Students of English History* (Royal Hist. Soc., 1945) has a relevance that extends north of the Tweed, and there are lists of Scottish officers of state, earls and bishops in *Handbook of British Chronology* (2nd edn), ed. F. M. Powicke and E. B. Fryde (1961).

13. Other aids to study (sigillography, heraldry and numismatics)

These fields are dealt with in the following works: H. Laing, *Descriptive Catalogue of Impressions of Ancient Scottish Seals* (Bannatyne Club) and *Supplemental Catalogue* (1866); J. H. Stevenson and M. Wood, *Scottish Heraldic Seals* (1940) (a rare work); A. Nisbet, *A System of Heraldry* (1816); R. W. Cochran-Patrick, *Records of the Coinage . . . to the Union* (2 vols, 1876); E. Burns, *The Coinage of Scotland* (3 vols, 1887); I. H. Stewart, *The Scottish Coinage* (2nd edn, 1967) and 'Scottish Mints' in *Mints, Dies, and Currency*, ed. R. A. G. Carson (1971), pp. 165–289, which is an essential guide to modern numismatics. J. D. A. Thompson, *Inventory of British Coin Hoards 600–1500* (1956) is marred by many inaccuracies but makes an adequate starting point for hoards.

## SECONDARY WORKS

1. General histories

The histories of J. H. Burton, P. Hume Brown and Andrew Lang have served for long enough, and only E. W. Robertson, *Scotland under her Early Kings* (1862), though very old, is still worth consulting for this period. None of the more recent general histories has an adequate treatment of the period before 1286 except W. Croft Dickinson, *Scotland from the earliest times to 1603* (New History of Scotland, 2nd edn, vol. i, 1965) which made insignificant changes to the period before 1286 from the 1st edition (1961). Specialists contributed to *Who are the Scots?*, ed. G. Menzies (1971) but the balance of chapters is disappointing. G. W. S. Barrow, *Feudal Britain* (1956) is a more convincing short account though including, of course, England, Ireland and Wales and covering the years 1066–1314.

The collections of essays by E. W. Robertson, *Historical Essays* (1871) and Cosmo Innes, *Scotland in the Middle Ages* (1860), *Lectures on Scotch Legal Antiquities* (1872) and *Sketches of Early Scotch History* (1861), though excellent in their way, are largely antiquarian, while R. W. Cochran-Patrick, *Mediaeval Scotland* (1892) is careless and misleading. The binding of Innes's books bears the impression of Alexander III's seal of minority (see above p. 556). Of first importance, however, are the collected papers of G. W. S. Barrow, *The Kingdom of the Scots* (1973), which range from the sixth century to the fourteenth.

Periodicals have made a large contribution to the advance of the study of the Middle Ages, notably the *Scottish Historical Review*, *Scottish Studies*, the *Innes Review* and, occasionally, *Proceedings of the Society of Antiquaries of Scotland* and *Records of the Scottish Church History Society*.

The shortage of illustrative maps, except in the study of place-names, will be remedied by the *Atlas of Medieval Scottish History* being edited by P. G. B. McNeill and R. G. Nicholson, which should appear in 1975.

### 2. General bibliographies

Most modern works have a select bibliography of relevant literature and a useful select bibliography will be found in the National Book League's *Reader's Guide to Scotland, a Bibliography*, which is periodically revised. The last edition was of 1968.

There are two relevant 'period' bibliographies: W. Bonser, *Romano-British Bibliography* (2 vols, 1964) and *Anglo-Saxon and Celtic Bibliography, 450–1087* (2 vols, 1957), and two important bibliographies on urban history (see below p. 652). Arranged topographically are A. Mitchell and C. G. Cash, *Contribution to the Bibliography of Scottish Topography* (S.H.S.) and its continuation, P. Hancock, *A Bibliography of works relating to Scotland, 1916–1950* (1960).

### 3. Prehistory

Archaeologists are no longer greatly interested in the history of prehistory, but are widely concerned about the validity of their techniques, on which see J. Coles, *Field Archaeology in Britain* (1972). It may be doubted whether a synthesis by a master hand, such as S. Piggott, *Ancient Europe* (1965), will have many successors. J. G. D. Clarke and S. Piggott, *Prehistoric Societies* (1965) is another stimulating introduction. There is still much of scholarly interest in the works of V. G. Childe who introduced Scottish archaeology to the twentieth century: compare his *Scotland before the Scots* (1946) with S. Piggott, *Scotland before History* (1958), both belonging to the era before absolute dating by C14 was widely practised. The best single-volume account of its subject is the symposium *The Prehistoric Peoples of Scotland*, ed. S. Piggott (1962), already outdated in several important respects. A. D. Lacaille, *The Stone Age in Scotland* (1954) and S. Piggott, *Neolithic Cultures of the British Isles* (1954) are classics of their decade and may be updated by the stimulating *Economy and Settlement in Neolithic and Early Bronze Age Britain and Europe*, ed. D. D. A. Simpson (1971). The two volumes of A. Henshall, *The Chambered Tombs of Scotland*, i (1963), ii (1971), are not only a fascinating inventory of one class of monument but also show how quickly archaeological interpretation must change. There is a good volume on *The Iron Age in Northern Britain*, ed. A. L. F. Rivet (1967), and, with a very different approach owing much to the Irish, Anne Ross, *Pagan Celtic Britain* (1967) or her more 'popular' book, *Everyday Life of the Pagan Celts* (1970). R. W. Feachem, *The North Britons* (1966) is disappointing. There are guide books to monuments in plenty: R. W. Feachem, *A Guide to Prehistoric Scotland* (1963) is difficult to use; the *Regional Archaeologies* of *South West Scotland* by J. G. Scott (1966) and of *South East Scotland* by G. and A. Ritchie (1972) are slighter but handier; another by E. MacKie is forthcoming. Of course, the *Inventories* of the Ancient Monuments Commission while indispensable, leave more and more to be desired the earlier they were published.

Papers on Scottish prehistory appear in most British archaeological journals but those with the greatest relevance are the venerable, occasionally hoary, *Proceedings of the Society of Antiquaries of Scotland* and the young, occasionally juvenile, *Scottish Archaeological Forum*.

## 4. Roman Scotland

The standard account of Roman Britain, with much on the Frontier, must be S. Frere, *Britannia* (1967) but this is a rapidly moving subject in which views advance markedly from year to year. Thus, a classic like Sir George Macdonald's *The Roman Wall in Scotland* (2nd edn, 1934) is now really of historiographical interest only. There is still a great deal of value in *Roman and Native in North Britain*, ed. I. A. Richmond (1958) which is also very readable. The fourth version of *The Antonine Wall* by A. S. Robertson (revised 1973) is a standard work by the acknowledged master brought well up-to-date. The stimulating work of O. G. S. Crawford, *The Topography of Roman Scotland North of the Antonine Wall* (1949) is worth reading for method if not for content, now largely outdated, as is S. N. Miller, *The Roman Occupation of South-West Scotland* (1952). J. Curle, *A Roman Frontier Post and its People* (1911) describes the fort at Newstead at the leisurely pace of an earlier generation; J. Clarke, *The Roman Fort at Cadder* (1933) is business-like, but a modern excavation report may be studied in A. S. Robertson, *The Roman Fort at Castledykes* (1964). For the study of the Roman frontier there are important articles in *Archaeologia Aeliana*, and periodical surveys of the state of knowledge in the *Journal of Roman Studies* and the new periodical *Britannia*. The native culture may be studied in F. T. Wainwright, *The Souterrains of Southern Pictland* (1963).

5. Early historic Scotland: the church

The best work on early Christianity is Charles Thomas, *Early Christian Archaeology of North Britain* (1971), but J. A. Duke, *The Columban Church* (1932) is still of great value, and J. Bulloch, *The Life of the Celtic Church* (1963) is a good unpretentious survey. What weight we should put upon the mission of Nynia is still a matter of doubt but few now accept W. Douglas Simpson, *The Historical St Columba* (1927 and later editions). The best scholarly work on this subject is discussed in J. MacQueen, *St Nynia: a Study of Literary and Linguistic evidence* (1961) and R. P. C. Hanson, *St Patrick: His Origins and Career* (1968). There are valuable essays in *Studies in the Early British Church*, ed. N. K. Chadwick (1958), especially one by K. H. Jackson on the sources for the life of St Kentigern, but *The Age of the Saints in the Early Celtic Church* by N. K. Chadwick (1961) is too hagiographic. There are, of course, works without number on the Christianity of that particularly Christian people, the Irish, but it is scarcely necessary to go beyond K. Hughes, *The Church in Early Irish Society* (1966), which is important, not only for the Columban period, but also for the Culdees. It is still worth looking at W. Reeves, *The Culdees of the British Islands* (1864) for the Scottish Culdee houses. Although superseded in some respects, the best general study of Bede was edited by A. H. Thompson, *Bede, His Life, Times and Writings* (1935).

6. Early historic Scotland: secular

The classic account by J. Romilly Allen and J. Anderson of *The Early Christian Monuments of Scotland* (1903) includes the Pictish symbol stones, so difficult of interpretation. Lacking the archaeological stimulus of a Sutton Hoo ship burial and the literary foundations of law-codes and chronicles, the discussions of Scotland in the age of the migrations and of emergent feudalism are necessarily episodic. The only systematic treatment, W. F. Skene, *Celtic Scotland* (3 vols, 1876–80, 2nd edn, 1886–90), though a great work in its day, was marred by inadequate knowledge of the Celtic languages and has been further eroded by archaeological advances. Nonetheless, remarkably little scholarly progress showed up in H. M. Chadwick, *Early Scotland* (1949) and it was not until the symposium edited by F. T. Wainwright, *The Problem of the Picts* (1955) that a new phase in the study of the fifth to tenth centuries began. Isabel Henderson, *The Picts* (1967) is a lively account with valuable insights into political and cultural history; also her contributions and those of others to *The Dark Ages in the Highlands* (Inverness Field Club, 1972). L. Alcock, *Arthur's Britain: History and Archaeology, 367–634* (1971) is the best recent book on England in the period with an account of the Picts and Scots. The only recent account of Gaelic history in the period is in M. Dillon and N. Chadwick, *The Celtic Realms* (1967) (N. Chadwick, *The Celts* (1970) differs little) which is particularly valuable on the heroic literature of the age of migrations; it has been criticised by scholars for its use of the Irish law texts on which K. Hughes, *Early Christian Ireland: Introduction to the Sources* (1972) is invaluable. M. O. Anderson, *Kings and Kingship in Early Scotland* (1973) is a very important new book of which, at the time of writing, no reviews from students of language have appeared. A summary of views on the period may be found in *Who Are the Scots?* ed. G. Menzies (1971), which is weak on the ninth to eleventh centuries. The *Inventory of Fife, Kinross and Clackmannan* (1933) was adequate for its time but, as elsewhere, has been put out of date by aerial photography and scientific dating. A modern survey, therefore, the *Inventory of Stirlingshire* (1963) should be exciting but disappoints. This strategic county seems poor in monuments of the period under discussion, as are Kintyre and Lorn—*Inventory of Argyll*, i (1971), ii (1974). There must be a suspicion that post-Roman and medieval sites are often ascribed to prehistory exclusively.

Some light is cast on the Gododdin by A. O. Curle, *The Treasure of Traprain* (1923) but other literature on this poorly excavated site is in journals, notably *Proc. Soc. Antiq. Sc.* There is always something to be learned on sub-Roman Britain from K. H. Jackson, *Language and History in Early Britain* (1953). For Strathclyde and Lothian, two symposia make tough but worth-while going: N. K. Chadwick (ed.) *Studies in Early British History* (1954) and N. K. Chadwick (ed.) *Celt and Saxon* (1963). P. Hunter Blair, *Roman Britain and Early England* (1963) and D. P. Kirby, *The Making of Early England* (1967) are contributions to English history by scholars with a particular interest in Northumbria and Cumbria, the partitioned lands. They supplement but do not supersede the insight of the great *Anglo-Saxon England* by F. M. Stenton; most references will be to the 2nd edition (1947) but I have also used the 3rd edition (1971) whose pagination differs somewhat. Also important are his collected papers, *Preparatory to Anglo Saxon England*, ed. D. M. Stenton (1970) with a long essay on Westmorland. The *Inventory of Roxburghshire* (1956) was up-to-date when produced, as were the rather less important inventories of *Selkirkshire* (1957) and *Peeblesshire* (2 vols, 1967). The older inventories of *East Lothian* (1924), *Midlothian and West Lothian* (1929), and *Dumfriesshire* (1920) are still interesting but those of *Kirkcudbright* (1914), *Wigtown* (1912) and *Berwickshire* (1915) are little more than very unreadable guidebooks.

There have been many particular studies of the period of Viking migrations in which Orkney and Shetland understandably figure large. Here F. T. Wainwright's chapters in the volume which he edited on *The Northern Isles* (1962) emphasise the loss sustained by scholarship through his untimely death. The bibliography to that volume under J. Anderson and G. Goudie gives the titles of the best early work on Viking Scotland. The volume contained only a note on the remarkable archaeological discovery described in A. Small, C. Thomas and D. M. Wilson, *St Ninian's Isle and its Treasure* (1973), which also throws some light on the shameful wrangle over the disposal of the hoard. Most of the archaeological literature is to be found in periodicals, and R. L. Bremner, *The Norsemen in Alban* (1923) and G. Henderson, *The Norse Influence on Celtic Scotland* (1910) are now of little value. A useful if dated conspectus of some archaeological materials (some collected twenty years before publication) is H. Shetelig, *Viking Antiquities in Great Britain and Ireland* (6 vols, 1940–54); J. R. C. Hamilton, *Excavations at Jarlshof* (1956) is a fine account of an important site. The *Inventory of Orkney and Shetland* (3 vols, 1946) and that of *The Outer Isles, Skye and the Small Isles* (1928) are disappointing not only in the quality of their comment but also in the illustrations. There are numerous books on the Vikings, the best general ones being: D. M. Wilson, *The Viking Achievement* (1970); G. Jones, *A History of the Vikings* (1968); P. H. Sawyer, *The Age of the Vikings* (1962, 2nd edn, 1971); H. Arbman, *The Vikings* (trans. A. Binns, 1961); J. Bronsted, *The Vikings* (1960). Of these Bronsted is the least, and Sawyer the most adventurous in discussion. No recent work attempts an account on any scale of the Viking impact on Scotland, in marked contrast with Ireland. See D. OCorráin, *Ireland before the Normans* (1972) as an example of detailed scholarship with important conclusions and R. H. M. Dolley, *Sylloge of Coins of the British Isles; The Hiberno-Norse Coins in the British Museum* (1966). There are discussions of aspects of the Viking movement in Scotland in *The Viking Congress*, ed. W. D. Simpson (1954); *Annen Viking Kongress*, ed. K. Falck (1955); *Fourth Viking Congress*, ed. A. Small (1965); *Fifth Viking Congress*, ed. A. Nicolaisen (1968). The *Saga Book of the Viking Society for Northern Research* is a periodical with occasional articles of importance.

7. Language and place names

The basic work which has stood the test of time to a remarkable degree is W. J. Watson, *Celtic Place Names of Scotland* (1926). A. MacBain, *Place Names, Highlands and Islands of Scotland* (1922) has notes and a preface by Watson. There are only two scholarly surveys of county place names for Scotland: W. M. Alexander, *Place Names of Aberdeenshire* (1952); A. Macdonald, *Place Names of West Lothian* (1941). And two for the Northern Isles: J. Jakobsen, *The Place Names of Shetland* (1936); H. Marwick, *Orkney Farm-names* (1952). Other work by H. Marwick is also scholarly: *The Place-names of Rousay* (1947) and *The Place-names of Birsay* (1970). His *The Orkney Norn* (1929) and J. Jakobsen *Etymological Dictionary of the Norn Language in Shetland* (2 vols, 1928–32) deal with the language once spoken in those islands. For the rest of the country, the contributions of M. Oftedal on Lewis place names are detailed and carefully argued and the papers of W. F. H. Nicolaisen in *Scottish Studies* and other journals are the more invaluable in that they are the only exposition by one pen on a range of the issues in place-name study since Watson wrote. The best introduction to this study is an essay by F. T. Wainwright, *Archaeology and Place Names and History* (1962). There is a helpful pamphlet published by the Ordnance Survey on non-Teutonic elements in *Place Names on Maps of Scotland and Wales* (no date, ?1969).

8. Political history from *c.* 1050

R. L. G. Ritchie, *The Normans in Scotland* (1954) is a lively piece of fine scholarship, though dealing only with the period 1057–1154. G. W. S. Barrow has made the twelfth and thirteenth centuries very much his own, and his work (*Feudal Britain, Regesta Regum Scottorum* i and ii, *The Kingdom of the Scots*) has already been mentioned. However, the first chapter of his *Robert the Bruce and the Community of the Realm of Scotland* (1965) is a sympathetic sketch of Alexander III's Scotland. C. T. Wyckoff, *Feudal Relations between the Kings of England and Scotland under the Early Plantagenets* (1897) is a useful account, neglected by historians of England and Scotland presumably because it ignored their inherited doctrines. I cannot see on my bookshelves any other monograph or biography in Scottish history which has any worthwhile contribution to make to the political history of the period. There is, however, a great deal in English history that is helpful. Two volumes of the *Oxford History of England*: F. M. Stenton, *Anglo-Saxon England* (3rd edn, 1971) and F. M. Powicke, *The Thirteenth Century* (1953) are beyond a cavil great works of scholarship, and Powicke has a valuable chapter on Scotland. His *King Henry III and the Lord Edward* (1947) is more detailed for Henry III; the appendices contribute to Scottish history. The twelfth century is less happily placed. There is no good account of Henry I; but there are two excellent books on his successor: R. H. C. Davis, *King Stephen* (1967) and H. A. Cronne, *The Reign of Stephen*, 1135–54 (1970). W. L. Warren, *Henry II* (1973) is weighty but there is no work of quality on Richard I and W. L. Warren's *King John* (1961) is disappointing. The best study of the reign taking account of the existence of Scotland is J. C. Holt, *The Northerners* (1961).

9. Secular institutions and the law

The institutions of Celtic Scotland are discussed in W. F. Skene's work of that name (1st edn, 1876, 2nd edn, 1886). There has been no systematic treatment in book form since then; J. Cameron, *Celtic Law* (1937) will leave the reader little wiser. The introductions by W. Croft Dickinson to *The Sheriff Court Book of Fife* (1928) and *The Court Book of the Barony of Carnwath* (1937) are indispensable, though they are stronger on the later Middle Ages than the period before 1300. Important also is Appendix D to *Fife Court Bk.*, on the origin of the sheriffdom. There is a useful survey in the *Introduction to Scottish Legal History* (Stair. Soc., 1958). Lord (T. M.) Cooper in his *Select Scottish Cases of the XIII Century* (1944) and his edition of the Scottish Glanville, *Regiam Majestatem* (Stair. Soc. 1947) sought to stimulate historical study of the law. Unfortunately, in the latter book his text is unscholarly and his conclusion as to the date of *Regiam Majestatem* (*c.* 1230) is at least ninety years too early. (See *Juridical Review*, NS. vi (1961) 199–217.) The best works on the law are G. Neilson, *Trial by Combat* (1890) and I. D. Willock, *Origins and Development of the Jury in Scotland* (Stair. Soc., 1966).

10. Town and country

Apart from work by G. W. S. Barrow in *The Kingdom of the Scots* there is little apart from articles worth reading on rural society in Scotland. M. M.

Postan, *Essays on Medieval Agriculture and General Problems of the Medieval Economy* (1973) reprints earlier papers. Standard works such as the *Cambridge Economic History* should be consulted, and it is likely that the *Agrarian History of England and Wales* will be useful (only vol. I, part ii, ed. H. P. R. Finberg (1972) on the Anglo-Saxon period has appeared for the periods before 1300). J. Titow, *English Rural Society 1200–1350* (1969) is helpful and there is usually a special relevance in studies of northern England such as I. Kershaw, *Bolton Priory, 1286–1325* (1973).

Apart from genealogical matters, the only works dealing with baronial society in Scotland are those by Barrow and Ritchie already mentioned.

C. Gross, *A Bibliography of British Municipal History* (1897) was reprinted with an introduction by G. H. Martin in 1966. It is supplemented by G. H. Martin and S. McIntyre, *A Bibliography of British and Irish Municipal History*, i (*General Works*) (1972).

There is a fairly extensive literature on towns, almost all (as the invariable use of 'burgh' shows) on institutional aspects. D. Murray, *Early Burgh Organization in Scotland* (2 vols, 1924–32), is long but has little worthwhile to say on the period. W. M. Mackenzie, *The Scottish Burghs* (1949) is helpful and even more so the introduction by W. Croft Dickinson to *Early Records of the Burgh of Aberdeen, 1317, 1398–1407* (S.H.S., 1957). C. Gross, *The Gild Merchant* (2 vols, 1890) is still valuable and deals with the gild in Scotland. G. S. Pryde, *The Burghs of Scotland* (1965) is a critical list only. The debate on European urban development from the fifth century to the twelfth is of marginal relevance but the student's crib, J. F. Benton, *Town Origins* (1968), includes a review of Yakov Levitsky's work on the development of Anglo-Saxon towns, work which is not otherwise available without a knowledge of Russian. Among many helpful works on English towns and trade after 1066 those by E. M. Carus-Wilson are pre-eminent: *Medieval Merchant Venturers* (1954) and her contribution to *Medieval England*, ed. A. L. Poole (1958). Fine studies which should not be ignored are G. A. Williams, *Medieval London, From Commune to Capital* (1963) and the papers in H. J. Dyos, *The Study of Urban History* (1968) by M. R. Conzen and G. H. Martin. The mass of comparative material in E. A. Gutkind, *International History of City Development* (8 vols, 1964–72) includes a volume (vi, 1971) which deals with Britain. The first part of *Historic Towns*, ed. M. D. Lobel (1969) includes a plan of Glasgow and each subsequent volume should include a Scottish town.

11. The church

The standard analysis is J. Dowden, *The Medieval Church in Scotland* (1910), and for narrative A. R. MacEwen, *A History of the Church in Scotland*, i (1913). Both are now somewhat antiquated and there are revisions of many points in journals. But the only modern treatments in book form of aspects of the Scottish church are F. Barlow, *Durham Jurisdictional Peculiars* (1950) and R. J. Brentano, *York Metropolitan Jurisdiction and Papal Judges Delegate, 1274–98* (1959). The student would be advised to approach the secular church through C. R. Cheney, *From Becket to Langton* (1956) in order to understand the aims of great popes like Alexander III and Innocent III.

G. V. Scammell, *Hugh du Puiset* (1956) is a life of a bishop of Durham whose dealings with Scotland were often unfriendly. The *Dictionnaire de Droit Canonique* is an invaluable work of reference. There is a chapter on Scotland in R. A. R. Hartridge, *A History of Vicarages in the Middle Ages* (1930), but this is now more fully dealt with in articles by I. B. Cowan. G. G. Coulton, *Scottish Abbeys and Social Life* (1933) is largely a waste of time; M. D. Knowles, *The Monastic Order in England* (1940) is the best introduction in English to twelfth-century monasticism, and J. C. Dickinson, *The Origin of the Austin Canons* (1950) and H. M. Colvin, *The White Canons in England* (1951) to two orders which had houses in Scotland on which their authors comment. An order with houses in Scotland but not found in England was the Valliscaulian, including Pluscarden, studied in S. R. Macphail, *History of the Religious House of Pluscardyn* (1881). For the friars the best introduction is M. D. Knowles, *The Religious Orders in Medieval England*, i (1948), followed by a vintage but excellent work on *The Scottish Greyfriars*, by W. Moir Bryce (2 vols, 1909).

## 12. Architecture

The standard works are D. MacGibbon and T. Ross, *Castellated and Domestic Architecture of Scotland* (5 vols, 1887–92) and their *Ecclesiastical Architecture of Scotland* (3 vols, 1896–7), to be brought up to date where possible by the *Inventories* of the Ancient Monuments Commission. Two good modern works are S. Cruden, *The Scottish Castle* (1960) and J. G. Dunbar, *The Historic Architecture of Scotland* (1966). W. M. Mackenzie, *The Mediaeval Castle in Scotland* (1927) is, so far as the pre-1286 period is concerned, a study in silly dogmatism, and J. S. Richardson, *The Medieval Stone Carver in Scotland* (1964) is spoiled by relying sometimes on the seventeenth-century forgeries of Fr. Brockie. W. Douglas Simpson, *The Ancient Stones of Scotland* (1965) should be treated with forbearance and charity: a bibliography of the author's very numerous and stimulating papers on Scottish medieval buildings would have served scholarship better.

## 13. Local history

Few local histories display a feeling for the period before 1286 or handle the sources acceptably. An exception may be W. D. Simpson, *The Province of Mar* (1943), and there is full documentation in C. Macdonald, *History of Argyll* (1950), which is curiously lacking in feeling for Argyll.

# INDEX

(Abbreviations: Mr = Master; unid. = unidentified)

Under personal names (e.g. Henry) the order of entries is generally that of social importance: King, King's son, Bishop, Abbot, Baron, lesser prelate. Cross references (e.g. under Athol, Earls of, or Papal legates) give the names in chronological order.